T0334288

Towards Gender Equity in Development

UNU World Institute for Development Economics Research (UNU-WIDER) was established by the United Nations University as its first research and training centre and started work in Helsinki, Finland, in 1985. The mandate of the institute is to undertake applied research and policy analysis on structural changes affecting developing and transitional economies, to provide a forum for the advocacy of policies leading to robust, equitable, and environmentally sustainable growth, and to promote capacity strengthening and training in the field of economic and social policymaking. Its work is carried out by staff researchers and visiting scholars in Helsinki and via networks of collaborating scholars and institutions around the world.

United Nations University World Institute for
Development Economics Research (UNU-WIDER)
Katajanokanlaituri 6B, 00160 Helsinki, Finland
www.wider.unu.edu

Towards Gender Equity in Development

Edited by
Siwan Anderson, Lori Beaman, and Jean-Philippe Platteau

A study prepared by the United Nations University World
Institute for Development Economics Research (UNU-WIDER)

OXFORD
UNIVERSITY PRESS

OXFORD
UNIVERSITY PRESS

Great Clarendon Street, Oxford, OX2 6DP,
United Kingdom

Oxford University Press is a department of the University of Oxford.
It furthers the University's objective of excellence in research, scholarship,
and education by publishing worldwide. Oxford is a registered trade mark of
Oxford University Press in the UK and in certain other countries

UNU-WIDER, Katajanokanlaituri, 6B, 00160 Helsinki, Finland

The moral rights of the authors have been asserted

First Edition published in 2018
Impression:2

Published in the United States of America by Oxford University Press
198 Madison Avenue, New York, NY 10016, United States of America

British Library Cataloguing in Publication Data
Data available

Library of Congress Control Number: 2018940940

ISBN 978–0–19–882959–1

Printed and bound by
CPI Group (UK) Ltd, Croydon, CR0 4YY

Foreword

In recent decades, empowering women in the developing world has become a primary policy goal. Quite apart from being a fundamental right on its own accord, increased female autonomy has been shown to generate other long-term benefits—such as reduced fertility, better educational and health outcomes for children, and a larger female political voice. Substantial progress toward gender equality has occurred but persistent key gaps, both in opportunity and capability between males and females across the globe, were the basis in 2016 for UNU-WIDER, in partnership with the University of Namur, launching the multidisciplinary research project, *Gender and Development*.

The project's focus is generating high-quality, high-impact economic research on a set of core issues in the gender and development field, with parallel efforts and activities ensuring that key results are exchanged with UNU-WIDER's key audiences—in particular, key policy makers in developing countries concerned with formulating and implementing effective policies targeted towards achieving gender equity in a meaningful manner.

This book is the crystallization of the entire research project drawn together, and I am most grateful to the editors, Siwan Anderson, Lori Beaman, and Jean-Philippe Platteau, for their analytical and editorial skills, and to the University of Namur for the scholarly collaboration. The book is a further advance in the field, providing essential reading analyses for economists, policy makers, and scholars of development.

UNU-WIDER gratefully acknowledges the support and financial contributions to its research programme by the governments of Finland, Sweden, and the United Kingdom. Without this vital funding our research and policy advisory work would be impossible.

Finn Tarp
Director, UNU-WIDER
May 2018

Acknowledgements

Special thanks are due to the members of the project's Scientific Committee— Martina Björkman-Nyqvist, Guilhem Cassan, Catherine Guirkinger, Jane Humphries, Agnes Quisumbing, Michele Tertilt, Christiane Timmermans, and Zaki Wahhaj. Their help in discussing and reviewing the different chapters is gratefully acknowledged.

Siwan Anderson, Lori Beaman, and Jean-Philippe Platteau
May 2018

Contents

Contents

Part III. Laws and Cultural Norms

List of Figures

List of Tables

List of Abbreviations

2SLS	two-stage least squares
CCT	conditional cash transfer
CDD	Community-driven development
CDR	community-driven reconstruction
CEDAW	Convention on the Elimination of all Forms of Discrimination Against Women
CHNS	China Health and Nutritional Survey
DHS	Demographic and Health Survey
EFM	excess female mortality
GDP	gross domestic product
GID-DB	OECD Gender, Institutions and Development Database
MFIs	microfinance institutions
MLSFH	Malawi Longitudinal Study of Families and Health
NGOs	non-governmental organizations
OLS	ordinary least squares
PSF	Poverty and Family Structure (by its French acronym)
RCT	randomized control trial
TDHS	Turkish Demographic and Health Survey
UCT	unconditional cash transfer

Notes on Contributors

Siwan Anderson is a Professor at the Vancouver School of Economics at the University of British Columbia, Canada. She is currently associate editor of the *Journal of Development Economics*, the *Review of Economics and Statistics*, and the *Journal of Globalization and Development*. She is a fellow of the Canadian Institute for Advanced Research (CIFAR).

Emmanuelle Auriol is a professor at Toulouse School of Economics. She is a fellow of the EEA, CEPR, EUDN, and CESifo and an editor of international academic journals. Over the years, she has received several grants and awards for her research, which is published in top international journals. She relies both on theory and empirical studies to derive policy recommendations in industrial organization, behavioural economics and development economics. Her research has also been featured in articles in journals as well as on television and radio.

Jean-Marie Baland is a Professor of Economics at the Department of Economics of the University of Namur. His research interests include the analysis of informal institutions in less developed economies, the determinants of deforestation and the consequences of poverty. Current research projects include the determinants of early mortality in South Asia and the definition of new poverty measures allowing for early mortality as a measure of serious deprivation.

Lori Beaman is an Associate Professor of Economics at Northwestern University. A development economist working on microeconomic issues, Lori's research interests are centred on two themes: social networks and gender. She is also an affiliate of the National Bureau of Economic Research (NBER), the Abdul Latif Jameel Poverty Action Lab (J-PAL).

Kjetil Bjorvatn is a Professor of Economics at NHH Norwegian School of Economics. His main research interests are in the fields of economic development and behavioural economics. He has published a number of articles in these areas, focusing on microfinance, entrepreneurship, and education.

John R. Bowen is Dunbar-Van Cleve Professor in Arts and Sciences at Washington University in St. Louis. He has been studying Islam and society in Indonesia since the late 1970s, and since 2001 has worked in Western Europe and North America on problems of pluralism, law, and religion, and in particular on contemporary efforts to rethink Islamic norms and civil law. Awarded a Guggenheim prize in 2012 and named a Carnegie Fellow in 2016, Professor Bowen has also served as a recurrent Visiting Professor at the London School of Economics.

Giulia Camilotti completed her PhD at the University of Namur. Her research interests include the economics of gender and the theoretical and empirical investigation of social norms.

Francisco Campos is a Senior Economist for the World Bank's Finance, Competitiveness and Innovation Global Practice. He's also Thematic Leader on Gender and Entrepreneurship for the World Bank's Africa Region Gender Innovation Lab. Francisco's main areas of expertise are linked to entrepreneurship, MSMEs, competitiveness, financial inclusion, and gender. He leads private sector development projects in fragile countries in Africa and various research studies on entrepreneurship. Prior to joining the World Bank, he held positions in a number of organizations on investment promotion and investment management.

Alba Evelyn Cortez is a Salvadoran lawyer, notary, university instructor, and human rights trainer. An expert in human rights, criminal law, and anti-discrimination law based on sex, she has authored thirteen publications on the rights of women to a life free from violence and discrimination. Currently, she is the academic coordinator of the training school of UDEMAS (the Union of Salvadoran Women Lawyers).

James D. Fearon is Geballe Professor in the School of Humanities and Sciences at Stanford University, Senior Fellow at Stanford's Freeman-Spogli Institute for International Studies, and a Program Member with the Canadian Institute for Advanced Research. His research focuses primarily on the causes and consequences of political violence.

Ina Ganguli is an Assistant Professor of Economics at the University of Massachusetts Amherst. Her primary research areas are labour economics and the economics of science and innovation. Her recent research has focused on the migration of high-skill workers, gender disparities in the labour market, and the formation of scientific collaborations. She is also an affiliated faculty at the Stockholm Institute of Transition Economics (SITE) at the Stockholm School of Economics, and a Fellow at the Institute for Quantitative Social Sciences at Harvard University. She holds a PhD from Harvard University.

Xavier Giné is a Lead Economist in the Finance and Private Sector Development Team of the Development Research Group at the World Bank. Since joining the World Bank, his research has focused on access to financial services and community driven development. Prior to joining the Bank, he was a postdoctoral fellow and lecturer at the Economic Growth Center at Yale University. He holds a BA in Economics from Universitat Pompeu Fabra in Spain, an MA and a PhD in Economics from the University of Chicago.

Markus Goldstein is a Lead Economist in the Office of the Chief Economist for Africa at the World Bank, where he heads the Africa Gender Innovation Lab. His research centres around issues of gender and land, firms, property rights, and youth employment.

José Santos Guardado Bautista is a Salvadoran lawyer, notary, researcher, and regular contributor to the Salvadoran law journal *Enfoque Jurídico*. His publications focus primarily on topics of human rights and gender. Currently, he works in the Crimes Against the Administration of Justice Unit in the Fiscalía General (Attorney General's Office) of El Salvador.

Selim Gulesci is an Assistant Professor at the Department of Economics, Bocconi University. He obtained his PhD from London School of Economics in 2011. His research is related to microeconomics of development with a focus on microenterprise growth; and the relationship between gender norms and human capital in developing countries.

Ricardo Hausmann is Director of Harvard University, Center for International Development and Professor of the Practice of Economic Development at the Harvard Kennedy School. Previously, he served as the first Chief Economist of the Inter-American Development Bank, where he created the Research Department. He served as Minister of Planning of Venezuela and as a member of the Board of the Central Bank of Venezuela. He holds a PhD from Cornell University.

Macartan Humphreys is a Professor at the Department of Political Science at Columbia University and director of the Institutions and Political Inequality unit at the WZB Berlin Social Science Center. His research focuses on the political economy of development, political accountability, and conflict processes.

Shareen Joshi is an Assistant Professor of International Development at Georgetown University. Her research focuses on gender, human capital, and political economy issues at the grassroots level. She has published in economics, demography, development studies, and South Asian studies.

Silvia Ivette Juarez Barrios is a Salvadoran lawyer, notary, and researcher with extensive experience drafting legislation that supports women's human rights and development. She currently coordinates the Program for a Life Without Violence for Women within the feminist organization ORMUSA.

Salma Khalid is an economist at the International Monetary Fund, Washington DC. Her research is in development microeconomics and behavioural and experimental economics, with a focus on factors influencing individual health seeking behaviours and health outcomes.

Nishtha Kochhar is a graduate student at the Department of Economics, Georgetown University. She has also worked as a research consultant with the Development Research Group at the World Bank. Her research interests include the microeconomics of gender, social networks, intra-household dynamics, and evolution of political institutions.

Hans-Peter Kohler is the Frederick J. Warren Professor of Demography in the Department of Sociology and a Research Associate in the Population Studies Center at the University of Pennsylvania. His primary research focuses on fertility and health in developing and developed countries. He has published widely on topics related to fertility, health, social and sexual networks, HIV/AIDS, biodemography, and well-being in leading scientific journals, and his work has had substantial influence on policy and media discussions related to demographic change.

Sylvie Lambert is a Professor at the Paris School of Economics and senior research fellow at INRA, Paris, France. Her research is centred on household and family economics in developing countries. Most of her work concerns the sub-Saharan African context, where she collected several household surveys. She holds a Master's in Economics and a PhD in Economics from Ecole des Hautes Etudes en Sciences Sociales, Paris, France. She teaches Development Economics in the PSE master programmes.

Sara Lowes is an Assistant Professor of Economics at Bocconi University. Her research interests are at the intersection of development economics, political economy, and economic history. Her research examines how understanding history and culture can inform development policy. Most recently, she has been working in the Democratic Republic of Congo.

Ghazala Mansuri is a Lead Economist in the Poverty and Equity Global Practice and the Development Research Group at the World Bank. She has published extensively in leading journals in economics and development, including the *American Economic Review*, the *Review of Economic Studies*, the *American Economic Journal: Applied*, and the *Journal of Development Economics*. She has also co-authored the book *Localizing Development: Does Participation Work?* Her research spans five broad areas: poverty, inequality and mobility, rural development, the economics of household behavior, the political economy of participatory development, and institutional and governance reforms for development. She holds a PhD in economics from Boston University.

Laura McGorman is a Public Policy Research Manager at Facebook, where she currently focuses on research related to Facebook's impact on the economy and the use of digital tools by small and medium enterprises. Prior to joining Facebook, Laura held positions at the US Department of Commerce, Opower, Harvard Business School, the World Bank, and USAID. She has a Bachelor's in Economics from Columbia University and a Master's in International Development from the Harvard Kennedy School of Government.

Amina Mohamed Maalim worked as a research assistant at The Choice Lab, NHH Norwegian School of Economics, and on the Girls' Empowerment project in Tanzania. Her Master thesis used qualitative data from the research project to study effects of business and health interventions on the development of business plans and empowerment.

Ana Maria Munoz Boudet is a Senior Social Scientist in the World Bank's Poverty and Equity Global Practice. She has worked on gender, poverty, and inequality issues in Latin America and the Caribbean, Europe and Central Asia, and Africa. She is a co-author of the *World Development Report 2012* on Gender Equality and Development. She holds a master's degree from the London School of Economics and doctorate studies from the University College of London.

Nathan Nunn is the Frederic E. Abbe Professor of Economics at Harvard University. He works within the fields of development economics, political economy, and economic history. He has undertaken extensive research on gender-related issues, both within Africa and globally. In addition, he has also researched a number of topics within the context of the Democractic Republic of the Congo.

Lars Ivar Oppedal Berge is an Associate Professor at NHH Norwegian School of Economics. Berge's research has focused on entrepreneurship, firm growth, and microfinance using various forms of experimental methods. His work has appeared in *Management Science* and in the *Journal of Economic Behavior and Organization*. Berge is also affiliated to the Chr. Michelsen Institute (CMI) and to the Choice Lab at NHH.

Obert Pimhidzai is a Senior Economist at the Poverty and Equity Global Practice of the World Bank, leading the Practice's work programme in Cambodia, Lao PDR, and Vietnam. Since joining the World Bank in 2009, Obert has worked in Kenya, Uganda, Mongolia, and Nigeria, focusing on poverty measurement and monitoring, poverty diagnostics, and undertaking service delivery assessments and resource tracking surveys. His current research focus is on ethnic minorities' poverty, distributional effects of fiscal policy, welfare impact of infrastructure investments, and mobility in the non-farm self-employment sector. He has a PhD in Economics from the University of Cape Town.

Jean-Philippe Platteau is author of several books and numerous academic articles. He has devoted his whole research career to studying the role of institutions in development and the processes of institutional change. The influence of non-economic factors and frontier issues at the interface between economics and sociology are a central focus of his work. Recently, he has been interested in the effects of family structures, customary norms, and religion. A central concern is how these can be possibly transformed, or perverted, through public action, political forces, and market development. Effects on women have received particular attention.

Nancy Qian is Professor of Managerial and Decision Sciences at Northwestern University's Kellogg School of Management. Her research uses empirical evidence to understand the role of demographic change, geography, and institutions in long-run economic development and growth.

Vijayendra Rao is a Lead Economist in the Development Economics Research Group at the World Bank. His research integrates his training in economics with theory and methods from anthropology and political science. He has published widely in the fields of development economics, development studies, and deliberative democracy.

Debraj Ray is Julius Silver Professor of the Faculty of Arts and Science and Professor of Economics at New York University. He is co-editor at the *American Economic Review* and a research associate of the National Bureau of Economic Research. He is a part-time Professor at the University of Warwick and research affiliate of the Instituto de Analisis Economico (CSIC) in Barcelona.

Vincent Somville is an Assistant Professor at NHH Norwegian School of Economics and an Associated Senior Researcher at Chr. Michelsen Institute. His is a development economist with two main overlapping research agendas, one in health and the other in finance and entrepreneurship. He is currently working in Tanzania on result-based financing of the health sector and on young women's health and entrepreneurship. He is also leading a project about banking and microfinance in India.

Rebecca L. Thornton is an Associate Professor in the Department of Economics at the University of Illinois at Urbana-Champaign. Her research focuses on health, education, and the status of women in developing countries. Across these topics, her work addresses core issues within Economics, including the role of subjective beliefs in decision-making and how social networks influence behaviour and beliefs.

Bertil Tungodden is a Professor at the Department of Economics, NHH Norwegian School of Economics, where he is the Director of the Research Center of Excellence—FAIR—and the founder of The Choice Lab. He is also an Associated Senior Researcher at Chr. Michelsen Institute. His research interests are experimental and behavioural economics, development economics, distributive justice, and social choice theory. He has published extensively in international academic journals in economics and philosophy.

Dominique van de Walle is a Lead Economist in the World Bank's Development Research Group. Her research interests are in the general area of poverty, vulnerability, gender and public policy, encompassing social protection, safety nets, and impact evaluation. Much of her recent research has been on Vietnam, South Asia, and sub-Saharan Africa. She holds a Master's in Economics from the London School of Economics and a PhD in Economics from the Australian National University, and began her career at the Bank as a member of the core team that produced the *1990 World Development Report on Poverty*.

Martina Viarengo is a Professor in the Department of Economics of the Graduate Institute of International and Development Studies of Geneva and a Faculty Associate at Harvard University, Center for International Development. Previously, she was an economist at the Centre for Economic Performance of the London School of Economics and a Postdoctoral Fellow at the Harvard University, John F. Kennedy School of Government. Her research areas include comparative public policy, international migration and the social dimensions of development. She holds a PhD from the London School of Economics.

Paola Villar is a Lead Economist in the World Bank's Development Research Group. Her research interests are in the general area of poverty, vulnerability, gender, and public policy, encompassing social protection, safety nets, and impact evaluation. Much of her recent past research has been on Vietnam, South Asia, and sub-Saharan Africa. She holds a Master's in Economics from the London School of Economics and a PhD in Economics from the Australian National University, and began her career at the Bank as a member of the core team that produced the *1990 World Development Report on Poverty*.

Jocelyn Viterna is Professor of Sociology at Harvard University. She has published widely in the fields of development, gender, and social mobilization. Her current project investigates the recent reversal of abortion rights in Central America, and its consequences for women's health and freedom.

Roberta Ziparo is an Assistant Professor at the Aix-Marseille School of Economics of the Aix-Marseille University since 2015. Her primary research interests include development, household, health economics, and microeconomic theory. Applying both theoretical and empirical tools, she studies the interaction of agents within groups and micro-institutions in general, with a special focus on the household and the family.

1

Introduction

Siwan Anderson, Lori Beaman, and Jean-Philippe Platteau

In recent decades, particularly since the 1979 international Convention on the Elimination of all Forms of Discrimination Against Women (CEDAW), empowering women in the developing world has become a primary policy goal. Quite apart from being a fundamental right on its own accord, increased female autonomy has been shown to incur other long-term benefits such as reduced fertility, better educational and health outcomes for children, and a stronger female political voice. The landmark United Nations Millennium Declaration committed member states to promote gender equality and the empowerment of women as effective ways to combat poverty, hunger, disease, and to stimulate sustainable development.

Indeed, many outcomes for women have improved—and at a pace that would have been inconceivable a few decades ago. Women have made unprecedented gains in rights, education and health, access to employment, and political positions. More countries than ever guarantee women and men equal rights under the law in such areas as property ownership, inheritance, and marriage. But, while significant progress towards gender equality and women's empowerment has been achieved, women and girls continue to suffer discrimination and violence in all parts of the developing world.

One of the starkest manifestations of gender discrimination is the notion of 'missing women', first coined by Amartya Sen, which captures the fact that the proportion of women in many developing countries is lower than would be expected if these girls and women had instead been born and died at the same rate, relative to boys and men, as they do in the developed world (Sen 1990). The resulting estimates suggest that more than 200 million women are demographically 'missing' worldwide. Inequality and neglect at all stages of women's lives lead to this alarming excess female mortality.

Table 1.1. Discriminatory social norms by U.N. sub-Region

Region	Genital Mutilation	Son Bias	Polygyny Accepted	Mobility Restricted
North Africa	0.36	0.26	0.50	0.50
East Africa	0.22	0.16	0.60	0.35
West Africa	0.48	0.17	0.82	0.39
Central Africa	0.08	0.08	0.92	0.58
Southern Africa	0	0.15	0.65	0.20
East Asia	0	0.29	0.36	0.25
South Asia	0	0.59	0.42	0.42
West Asia	0.03	0.40	0.65	0.82
Caribbean	0	0.01	0.10	0.10
Central America	0	0.12	0	0.17
South America	0	0.05	0	0.05

Data Source: Gender, Institutions and Development Database 2009, 2014 (GID-DB), OECD. Authors own computations which are based on unweighted averages across the countries in the U.N. sub-regions.

The rate at which girls die relative to boys is significantly higher in developing countries. Excess female mortality at birth or infancy account every year for an estimated 1.1 million missing girls (Anderson and Ray 2010). Economic growth has not made this problem disappear (Jayachandran 2015). The bulk of these missing female infants are in India and China, where the estimates have not significantly altered over the past two decades. These missing girls are most likely the result of overt discrimination in the household resulting from a strong preference for sons.

Column 3 in Table 1.1 reports on an index of son bias from the OECD Gender, Institutions and Development Database (GID-DB), which contains more than sixty data indicators of gender equality.[1] The son bias index combines measures of the incidence of missing women, a male-biased fertility preference, and son preference in education. The missing women component of the index captures the shortfall in the number of females in the sex ratio for ages 0–4, 5–9, 10–14, 15–64, and 65+, relative to the expected number if there were no sex-selective abortions, no female infanticide or similar levels of health care and nutrition regardless of the sex of the child. The son-biased fertility measure captures the share of males as the last child from women currently not desiring additional children or sterilized. The son preference in education is the percentage of people agreeing that university is more important for boys than for girls. This overall index of son bias is increasing in discrimination towards girls. From Table 1.1, we see that this index is highest in South Asia, followed by West Asia, then East Asia and North Africa.

---

[1] The GID-DB is the only database providing researchers and policy makers with key data on gender-based discrimination and social institutions. Covering 160 countries, the GID-DB contains comprehensive information on legal, cultural, and traditional practices that discriminate against women and girls. Refer to Jutting et al. (2008) for more details on this data.

Table 1.2. Discriminatory legal rights by U.N. sub-Region

Region	Widows Inherit	Daughters Inherit	Violence Laws	Rape Laws	Harassment Laws
North Africa	1.00	1.00	0.89	0.61	0.75
East Africa	0.57	0.61	0.45	0.43	0.37
West Africa	0.60	0.64	0.72	0.45	0.65
Central Africa	0.50	0.62	0.78	0.53	0.62
Southern Africa	0.50	0.40	0.45	0.35	0.55
East Asia	0.60	0.50	0.45	0.42	0.50
South Asia	0.67	0.67	0.54	0.58	0.25
West Asia	1.00	1.00	0.77	0.75	0.66
Caribbean	0.20	0.20	0.25	0.20	0.70
Central America	0.17	0.17	0.12	0.25	0.21
South America	0.28	0.28	0.17	0.28	0.08

Data Source: Gender, Institutions and Development Database 2014 (GID-DB), OECD. Authors own computations which are based on unweighted averages across the countries in the U.N. sub-regions.

This overt discrimination against daughters is widely acknowledged yet, legally across the developing world, girls still do not effectively have the same rights as boys. Column 3 in Table 1.2 provides a relative measure of daughters' ability to inherit. The index is equal to 0 if the law guarantees the same inheritance rights to both daughters and sons; it is 0.5 if the law guarantees equal rights but there are some customary, traditional, or religious practices that discriminate against daughters; and it is equal to 1 if the law does not guarantee the same inheritance rights to daughters and sons, or daughters have no inheritance rights at all. We see that across all developing countries, daughters effectively have fewer inheritance rights compared to sons. This unequal treatment is most severe in North Africa and West Asia.

Another gendered norm with extreme consequences for young girls is female genital mutilation. It is recognized internationally as a violation of the human rights of girls and women. It reflects deep-rooted inequality between the sexes, and constitutes an extreme form of discrimination against women. It is nearly always carried out on minors. At least 200 million girls and women alive today have been cut in thirty countries in Africa, the Middle East, and Asia.[2] Column 2 in Table 1.1 reports the percentage of women who have undergone any type of female genital mutilation across the developing regions. We see that this proportion is highest in West Africa at close to 50%.

Women in developing countries lack significant autonomy and typically depend crucially on their father in childhood, and their male partner in adulthood, for their livelihoods. As a result, marriage is typically one of the most important stages of a woman's life. In developing countries, marriage at a relatively young age is essentially universal. One of every four girls is married

---

[2] Refer to: https://data.unicef.org/topic/child-protection/female-genital-mutilation/#.

Table 1.3. Discriminatory marriage indicators by U.N. sub-Region

Region	Early Marriage	Initiate Divorce	Violence Attitudes	Violence Prevalence
North Africa	0.12	0.79	0.38	0.33
East Africa	0.22	0.08	0.53	0.46
West Africa	0.29	0.37	0.57	0.24
Central Africa	0.30	0.36	0.63	0.60
Southern Africa	0.07	0.30	0.30	0.24
East Asia	0.07	0.25	0.39	0.25
South Asia	0.24	0.67	0.36	0.39
West Asia	0.09	1.00	0.39	0.28
Caribbean	0.15	0	0.11	0.24
Central America	0.21	0	0.12	0.30
South America	0.14	0	0.16	0.39

Data Source: Gender, Institutions and Development Database 2014 (GID-DB), OECD. Authors own computations which are based on unweighted averages across the countries in the U.N. sub-regions.

before reaching the age of 18. Worldwide more than 700 million women were married as children.[3] Child marriage threatens girls' lives and health and limits their future prospects. Column 2 of Table 1.3 presents the prevalence of child marriage across the different developing regions, where we see this proportion is highest in parts of sub-Saharan Africa (30%) but also very significant in South Asia (24%) and Central America (21%).

Polygynous marriages can be prevalent. They are associated with an accelerated transmission of sexually transmitted diseases and age and power imbalances between spouses (Bove and Valeggia 2009). Column 4 of Table 1.1 presents an index of the acceptance or legality of polygamy across developing regions. It is an index between 0 and 1, where it is equal to 0 if it is illegal and then increases in its acceptance and legality. We see that this index is highest across Africa, but also significant in parts of Asia.

Within marriage, intimate partner violence is prevalent throughout the world. Almost one third of women who have been in a relationship report that they have experienced some form of physical or sexual violence by their partner in their lifetime.[4] Column 4 in Table 1.3 reports the percentage of women who agree that a husband is justified in beating his wife under certain circumstances. This is the case for well over a third of women across all regions in Africa and Asia and for the majority of women in East, West, and Central Africa. Column 5 of Table 1.3 reports the percentage of women who have experienced physical and/or sexual violence from an intimate partner at some time in their lives. This is the case for at least a third of women across all developing countries. In some parts of the world, this measure is

[3] Refer to: https://data.unicef.org/topic/child-protection/child-marriage/
[4] Refer to: http://www.who.int/mediacentre/factsheets/fs239/en/

astoundingly high: in Central Africa, 60% of women have experienced a form of domestic violence.

Still the laws are not in place to punish these violent acts. Columns 3 through 6 in Table 1.2 report whether the legal framework offers women legal protection from domestic violence (column 3), rape (column 4), and sexual harassment (column 5). For each of these variables, the index runs from 0 to 1 where: 0 implies there is specific legislation in place to address the crime, the law is adequate overall and there are no reported problems with implementation; 0.25 implies that the specific legislation is in place, the law is adequate, but there are repeated problems of implementation; 0.5 implies the specific legislation is in place but the law is inadequate; and for 1, there is no legislation in place to address the crime. We see that nowhere across the developing world are women perfectly protected by law from violence against them. Women receive the least legal protection in North Africa and West Asia.

Not only are women not lawfully protected against domestic violence, they can also face restrictions in their ability to leave an abusive household. Column 3 in Table 1.3 presents summary statistics on an index variable which is equal to zero if the law guarantees the same rights to initiate divorce to both men and women. The index increases as customary, traditional, or religious practices restrict this right for women, and is equal to one if the law does not guarantee the same rights to women as men or if women have no rights to initiate divorce at all. We see that only in the regions of Latin America and the Caribbean are women guaranteed identical rights to men in this regard.

The existence of restrictions on women's physical mobility is a major reflection of women's status in society. These restrictions arise from social, cultural, and religious norms (Guirkinger and Platteau 2017). Column 5 in Table 1.1 presents estimates of an index which decreases in line with women's freedom of movement and access to public spaces. These include restrictions on their ability to choose their place of residence, visits to their families and friends, or to apply for a passport. The index is equal to zero if the law guarantees the same rights to freely move to both men and women and then increases with the extent of customary, traditional, or religious practices that discriminate against women in this regard. At the extreme, the highest value of the index (equal to one), women have no freedom of movement. We see that, mobility restrictions are highest in West Asia, followed by Central and North Africa.

Unmarried adults in developing countries are typically widowed and the price of widowhood is particularly high for women. Increased vulnerability is not only the result of losing the main breadwinner of the household (the husband), but also property laws and employment norms which restrict the access of widows to economic resources (Anderson and Ray 2015). Patrilocal norms exacerbate the situation, where widows receive very little economic and social support from her late husband's family. Add to these a variety of customs such as rituals of seclusion and isolation. Column 2 in Table 1.2 provides a relative measure of widows' ability to inherit. The index is equal to 0 if the law guarantees the same inheritance rights to both widows and widowers; it is 0.5 if the law guarantees equal rights but there are some customary, traditional, or religious practices that discriminate against widows; and it is equal to 1 if the law does not guarantee the same inheritance rights to widows and widowers, or widows have no inheritance rights at all. We see that everywhere in Africa and Asia, widows have fewer inheritance rights than widowers. This inequality is most extreme in North Africa and West Asia.

Although women have entered the labour force in large numbers across much of the developing world in the past few decades, this has not translated into equal opportunities or earnings for men and women. Women systematically enter into lower-paying sectors than men (World Bank 2011). They are more likely to be engaged in unpaid family employment or work in the informal wage sector. When they do own land, they tend to operate smaller plots with less remunerative crops. We see from column 2 in Table 1.4 that their actual land ownership rates are extremely low. They are highest in the countries of Southern Africa where 28% of women own some land, and they are lowest in North Africa and West Asia, where only 4% of women own any land at all.

As entrepreneurs, women manage smaller firms in less-profitable and informal sectors. The gaps in productivity and growth between male and female-owned enterprises are extremely stark (Klapper and Parker 2011). In many developing countries, women entrepreneurs face systematic barriers to formal financial services. These can be in the form of explicit discrimination or differential treatment under the law where women are prohibited from obtaining requisite licences. In many parts of the Middle East and South

Table 1.4. Female economic and political indicators by U.N. sub-Region

Region	Land Ownership	Political Representation	Literacy
North Africa	0.04	0.20	0.58
East Africa	0.17	0.28	0.59
West Africa	0.07	0.14	0.31
Central Africa	—	0.16	0.60
Southern Africa	0.28	0.26	0.75
East Asia	0.15	0.17	0.87
South Asia	0.07	0.16	0.64
West Asia	0.04	0.10	0.86
Caribbean	0.15	0.23	0.81
Central America	0.18	0.24	0.87
South America	0.20	0.21	0.94

Data Source: Gender, Institutions and Development Database 2009, 2014 (GID-DB), OECD. Authors own computations which are based on unweighted averages across the countries in the U.N. sub-regions.

Asia, women are required to have a male family member co-sign a loan (Chamlou 2008). Relative to these economic inequalities across men and women, the political participation of women is by far the slowest to improve (Beaman et al. 2009). Column 3 in Table 1.4 reports the share of women in national parliaments. We see that this share is never greater than a quarter and is particularly low in the developing regions of Asia, as well as West and Central Africa.

Even without consideration of employment and political opportunities for women, educational opportunities for women remain a challenge. Over the last two decades there have been large-scale improvements in primary school enrolment in developing regions. Reports from the United Nations indicate that enrolment rates have reached 91% in 2015.[5] Nevertheless, we see from column 4 in Table 1.4, that literacy among women aged 15 and older is still very low. In West Africa, only a third of adult women are able to read and write.

As a result of this widespread mistreatment and overt discrimination in all dimensions of their lives, women lack significant autonomy. The central preoccupation of this book is to explore key sources of female empowerment and discuss the current challenges and opportunities for the future. Schematically, three main domains are distinguished. The first is marriage and women's relative bargaining position within the household. The second is the set of options available to women outside of marriage and in the context of her community, either in terms of economic opportunities or collective action. The third is overarching discriminatory laws and cultural norms.

1. Marriage

In developing countries, marriage is essentially universal and, typically, one of the most important stages of a woman's life. It is generally arranged by the parents, with women having little say in the choice of their partners. Due to women's significant lack of autonomy in all realms of their lives, they depend crucially on their husbands for their livelihoods and well-being. As result, marriage dissolution can have dire consequences for women.

Chapter 2 by Lambert, van de Walle, and Villar speaks directly to marital dissolution and the well-being of women in Senegal. They document how widowhood, compared to divorce, is correlated with lower levels of welfare, in both monetary and non-monetary measures. Poorer women are more likely to have suffered divorce and widowhood but are also more likely to be remarried. However, they continue to live in poorer households. Likewise, women

---

[5] Refer to: http://www.un.org/millenniumgoals/education.shtml

who are most likely to accept to be beaten by their husbands are remarried widows. This chapter demonstrates the complexity of consequences of different classifications of marital dissolution. On the optimistic side, highly educated women in Senegal seem to be able to use divorce to escape family authority and gain a relatively comfortable autonomy.

Chapter 3 by Thornton and Kohler examines how the HIV epidemic is affecting marriage dissolution in Malawi. Individuals typically lack perfect information about their spouse's HIV status and the risk they face from their spouse. As a result, individuals may leave a marriage fearing that their partner is HIV positive, even when they are not. This chapter examines how revealing the true information regarding the HIV status of couples can reduce this risk. In the study, some couples are offered an individual (private) HIV test, while others are offered a test together. Couples who were tested together were significantly less likely to get divorced. This suggests that revealing full information about HIV status reduced the concern over future HIV risk and thus decreased the risk of divorce. The chapter points to the importance of shared information across couples to prevent marital dissolution.

Aside from highlighting the importance of marriage for the well-being of women, there has been much debate in the women and development literature on how to empower women within their marriages. Female autonomy is typically defined as the ability of women to make choices and decisions within the household relative to their husbands. The whole question of autonomy does not, of course, arise if the household is viewed as a monolithic unit, with a single decision maker. However, there is now ample evidence contradicting this unitary model of the household. Accordingly, it is now accepted that, instead of being atomistic, the household in developing countries is better modeled as conflictual (Donni and Chiappori 2011). The main theoretical contribution of economists to the literature on female empowerment has been through bargaining theory. Bargaining models have demonstrated that women can be empowered by improving their threat options—which capture the level of well-being they could be assured of in the event that bargaining broke down with their spouses. Chapter 4 by Baland and Ziparo reviews this literature and points to important directions for future research. It highlights the role of uncertainty, information, commitment, and cooperation in household decision making and emphasizes which components are most relevant to poor countries. The chapter emphasizes how female autonomy is strongly restrained by a larger number of social norms that limit the scope of action of women inside and outside the household, and by the limited rights women have in the case of divorce. Moreover, the prevalence of juvenile and arranged marriage, as well as the complex structure of the household in most developing countries form serious limitations.

While marriage can be crucial for their livelihoods, women can be entirely dependent on their male partner for their wellbeing. As such, placing women in extremely vulnerable circumstances can significantly lower their autonomy and force them to accept behaviour that obviously runs against their interest. Chapter 5 by Gulesci demonstrates how conflict and forced migration can exacerbate domestic violence if women no longer feel they have a support network and if they have lost economic opportunities they had in their original community. This chapter finds that women who were displaced due to the Kurdish-Turkish conflict have experienced significantly more domestic violence and strikingly are more likely to say that it is acceptable for a husband to beat his wife. This chapter therefore highlights the possibility that a loss of economic opportunities caused by outside factors such as conflict can seriously worsen women's lives.

In much of the developing world, the institution of marriage is accompanied by mandated marriage payments. These payments can be substantial and have been shown to affect women's welfare and societies' distribution of wealth (Anderson 2007). In theory, bride prices encourage early marriage and high fertility rates. They have in turn been linked to domestic violence against women, owing to women's fear of returning to their natal home without being able to repay the payment. Chapter 6 by Lowes and Nunn revisits these issues in a careful examination of bride prices in the Democratic Republic of the Congo. However, they evidence the opposite of what theories would predict: larger bride prices are not associated with earlier marriage or with higher fertility. Instead, larger bride prices are correlated with better quality marriages, as measured by beliefs about the acceptability of domestic violence, the frequency of engaging in positive activities as a couple, and happiness as self-reported by the wives. This chapter highlights the need for further research before drawing conclusions regarding policies aimed at abolishing marriage payments.

2. Outside Options

Given the crucial importance of marriage for women in developing countries, and the corresponding household dynamics in determining female wellbeing, a crucial step towards empowerment is improving the options available to women outside the marital home. Outside economic opportunities are the most obvious among these options.

Early pregnancy among teenage girls is an important reason why girls in developing countries must frequently curtail their opportunities—both educational and career opportunities. Chapter 7 by Berge, Bjorvatn, Maalim, Somville, and Tungodden considers a number of different interventions which seek to reduce early pregnancy, with a focus on two types of programmes: those that affect the girls' mindset and those that directly affect girls' income-earning opportunities. Ultimately the most promising programmes seem to combine the two, motivating girls by changing their perspective and feeling of control over their lives, while also providing them with new opportunities where they can now apply their new outlook on life. The chapter indicates that training in both health (targeting the mindset) and entrepreneurship (targeting economic opportunities) have had an impact on the girls' locus of control. Moreover, the entrepreneurship programme was successful in stimulating new business plans, which can be seen as a first step towards economic empowerment.

Once in the labour market, occupational segregation is a major factor explaining the gender wage gap, in both rich and poor countries (ILO 2012). Many people in developing countries are self-employed so that understanding gender gaps in different sectors among the self-employed goes a long way toward explaining the overall gender gap phenomenon. Chapter 8 by Campos, Goldstein, McGorman, Boudet, and Pimhidzai looks at women entrepreneurs in Uganda. On average, these women are operating in sectors with lower returns. However, women who choose to enter male-dominated sectors end up earning as much as men and three times more than women who remain in traditionally female domains. Lack of information appears to be a key reason why women do not enter more profitable sectors, and direct exposure to individuals who are working in these sectors (typically male workers) can pave the way for women's entry.

One specific new economic opportunity for women comes from the expansion of microcredit, as microfinance institutions (MFIs) have become an increasingly important employer in developing countries. Chapter 9 by Ganguli, Hausmann, and Viarengo investigates gender gaps in career paths amongst employees in the largest MFI in Latin America. The question is interesting since many MFIs have a social mission and direct much of their lending to women. We might therefore expect that such organizations maintain pro-gender equity policies toward their employees as well. The chapter finds that in some parts of the organization, there is a gender gap favouring men but in other parts of the organization, women are outperforming them.

In addition to economic opportunities, women can also seek out each other as sources of empowerment. Women's expectations about their role in the community, and how they work together, can have an impact both on the women themselves and within their communities at large. In the context of Liberia, Chapter 10 by Fearon and Humphreys shows how women are more likely to contribute to public goods when they know that only other women are participating in the decision. That is, mixed-gender groups achieve a lower level of cooperation than all-women groups. This chapter further suggests that women sought to signal that women in their community have a powerful community spirit and a high sense of social solidarity. That is, social identity based on gender seems to exert a significant influence on the way women behave.

Policies can also help facilitate an increase in women's active role in the community. Chapter 11 by Giné, Khalid, and Mansuri looks at how a policy in Pakistan, which increased social mobilization by including women in a village-level decision-making institution, affected women's access to health care—a topic women expressed a deep concern about prior to the implementation of the policy. The decision-making institution was not given additional resources, but instead social mobilization allowed women to hold local health providers accountable for improving the quality of care they received.

3. Laws and Cultural Norms

Beyond outside opportunities for women within their communities, a crucial feature for female empowerment is obviously non-discriminatory laws and cultural norms. Chapter 12 by Viterna, Bautista, Barrios, and Cortez shows that not only has the Salvadorian state recently enacted regressive anti-abortion laws that are particularly severe but also, as is evident from an analysis of court materials, judges have interpreted the law in a strikingly strict manner. The overzealous attitude of the Salvadorian judges seems to be influenced by their fear of being accused of not duly applying the law. The problem is made even more serious by the fact that such fear percolates to law enforcers, including medical officers. Hospital doctors thus refer women brought to them for a miscarriage to the police for fear of being accused of failure to report a case of abortion. This is an example of a situation where the law is implemented with excessive force, leading to abuses and unfair treatment of women.

Fortunately, the opposite situation can also be encountered, as attested by the evidence in Chapter 13 by Bowen. This chapter is concerned with Islamic laws and practices regarding gender, particularly in the domain of family and personal status law (marriage, divorce, and inheritance). Although Islamic law is generally considered to be rather unfavourable to women, detailed studies of the practices of Islamic courts reveal that Muslim women fare better in matters of divorce than Catholic or Jewish women, for example. Overall, Islamic judges have a tendency to interpret the legal framework in ways that promote gender balance, especially in situations where they have a great deal of interpretive leeway. Thus, in Indonesia, even though both Islamic tradition and the letter of the current statutory law are gender-unequal, in practice the rule is that the person who has suffered the most should be compensated: and that is always the wife.

Some laws targeted at improving development outcomes can have perverse effects for women. A poignant example is the One-Child Policy (aimed at curbing overall fertility) in China which has been shown to be associated with widespread female infanticide (Banister 1987). Chapter 14 by Qian studies the effect of relaxing the One-Child Policy on gender-biased sex selection, family size, and the school enrolment of daughters. The chapter shows that there is a significant one-child disadvantage for the eldest child. For households with two or fewer children, an additional child significantly increases the school enrolment of the first child. These benefits of a second child are almost entirely driven by households where the two children are of the same sex. Moreover, the benefits are larger when the second child is a girl. The chapter also provides evidence that an additional child makes mothers more, not less, likely to enter the labour force and, as a result, the elder child enters school at a younger age. It thus seems that income demand caused by the additional child incites the mothers to work, which pushes the first child into school.

In much of the developing world, statutory laws coexist with informal rules or customs (Aldashev et al. 2012). Chapter 15 by Platteau, Camilotti, and Auriol shows how several theoretical frameworks can be used to explain the effectiveness of a statutory law when competing informal rules exist. This chapter thus explores the analytical conditions under which a social engineering approach that directly confronts a harmful custom with the objective of eradicating it (often in the name of human rights) can be effective or, alternatively, lead to dismal failure in the presence of customs. The authors argue that in many circumstances in which women have heterogeneous preferences, a social engineering approach ought to be complemented by a more indirect approach promoting outside economic opportunities for women and even by empowerment actions aimed at surmounting mobility-restricting norms. Female genital mutilation is one of the main examples used to illustrate the central argument developed in the chapter. The chapter develops a coherent conceptual framework containing the respective roles of statutory laws, on the one hand, and targeted economic and social development strategies, on the other hand, when the objective consists of improving the condition of women.

A set of gendered social norms that have assumed considerable importance in many parts of the developing world entail restrictions on women's physical mobility. As we have already seen, they are widespread throughout Africa and Asia. Chapter 16 by Joshi, Kochhar, and Rao shows that norms restraining the mobility of married women are more predominant among the upper castes of Indian society. In this context, women's seclusion is positively associated with social status or prestige. One might conjecture that variations in the incidence of mobility-restraining norms between castes make sense in the light of different work requirements. Simply put, while women from lower castes belong to poorer households and therefore need to work to sustain their family's livelihood, women from higher castes are free from this subsistence constraint and can therefore indulge in leisurely activities that reflect their high status. However, the evidence does not seem to support this benign view: high-caste women are reluctant to enter the labour force even when facing conditions of severe poverty that place them below the women from low and scheduled castes in terms of income. If they obey the seclusion norm in such instances, it is because they have internalized it or because violation would expose them to severe sanctions imposed by their community.

Finally, Chapter 17 by Anderson and Ray returns to a fundamental indicator of gender discrimination with the issue of excess mortality of women. The chapter shows that this problem is far from being confined to Asia, as previously thought, and is actually pervasive also in Africa. The chapter emphasizes that discriminatory laws against women in terms of marital and property rights as well as protection against domestic violence are positively related to young excess female mortality. Moreover, there may also be several cultural factors at play. In particular, patriarchal norms seem to determine a comparatively low status for women in Africa. In Muslim-dominated areas, this effect may have been strengthened by the influence of a religion that makes men the main agent responsible for guaranteeing the livelihood of the household. In some settings, boys and men traditionally eat first, and girls and women eat the leftovers. Finally, one cultural trait, the prevalence of female genital mutilation, appears to be positively correlated with young excess female mortality.

References

Aldashev, G., I. Chaara, J.-P. Platteau, and Z. Wahhaj (2012). 'Using the Law to Change the Custom'. *Journal of Development Economics*, 60(4), 795–828.

Anderson, Siwan (2007). 'The Economics of Dowry and Brideprice'. *Journal of Economic Perspectives*, 21(4), 151–74.

Anderson, Siwan and Debraj Ray (2010). 'Missing Women: Age and Disease'. *Review of Economic Studies*, 77, 1262–300.

Anderson, Siwan and Debraj Ray (2015). 'Missing Unmarried Women'. NBER Working Paper No. 21511.

Banister, J. (1987). *China's Changing Population*. Stanford University Press.

Beaman, L., R. Chattopadhyay, E. Duflo, R. Pande, and P. Topalova (2009). 'Powerful Women: Does Exposure Reduce Prejudice?' *Quarterly Journal of Economics*, 124(4), 1497–540.

Bove, Riley and Claudia Valeggia (2009). 'Polygyny and Women's Health in Sub-Saharan Africa'. *Social Science and Medicine*, 68(1), 21–9.

Chamlou, N. (2008). *The Environment for Women's Entrepreneurship in the Middle East and North Africa*, Washington DC, The World Bank.

Donni, O. and P.-A. Chiappori (2011). 'Nonunitary Models of Household Behavior: A Survey of the Literature'. In J.A. Molina (ed.) *Household Economic Behaviors*. New York, Springer.

Guirkinger, C. and J.P. Platteau (2017). 'The Dynamics of Family Systems: Lessons from Past and Present Times'. EDI Working Paper 16/03.1. https://edi.opml.co.uk/wpcms/wp-content/uploads/2017/06/EDI-PF-PAPER-03.2-Guirkinger-and-Platteau.pdf

ILO (2012). 'Global Employment Trends for Women'. Geneva, ILO.

Jayachandran, S. (2015). 'The Roots of Gender Inequality in Developing Countries'. *Annual Review of Economics*, 7, 63–88.

Jutting, J., C. Morrisson, J. Dayton-Johnson, and D. Drechsler (2008). 'Measuring Gender (In)Equality: The OECD Gender, Institutions, and Development Data Base'. *Journal of Human Development and Capabilities*, 9(1), 65–86.

Klapper, L. and S. Parker (2011). 'Gender and the Business Environment for New Firm Creation'. *World Bank Research Observer*, 26(7), 237–57.

OECD (2009). Gender, Institutions and Development Database 2014 (GID-DB) http://stats.oecd.org/Index.aspx?DatasetCode=GID2

OECD (2014). Gender, Institutions and Development Database 2014 (GID-DB) https://stats.oecd.org/Index.aspx?DataSetCode=GIDDB2014

Sen, Amartya (1990). 'More than 100 Million Women are Missing'. *The New York Review of Books*, 37(20).

World Bank (2011). *World Development Report 2012—Gender Equality and Development*, World Bank, Washington DC.

Part I
Marriage

2

Marital Trajectories, Women's Autonomy, and Women's Well-Being in Senegal

Sylvie Lambert, Dominique van de Walle, and Paola Villar[1]

1. Introduction

Marital trajectories in Senegal are often discontinuous. Divorce is frequent and widowhood is a common predicament for women, due in particular to the fact that women marry older men. In 2006/2007, spousal age gaps (male age minus female) averaged 11.2 in urban and 12.9 in rural areas. At the same date, around 18.5 per cent of ever-married adult women were currently widows or had remarried after widowhood and 13.2 per cent were currently divorced or remarried following a divorce.[2] Women confronted with divorce or widowhood most often remarry, and may well face one, or more, further marriage dissolutions during their lives. Remarriage appears to take place relatively rapidly: the median duration between widowhood and remarriage among those who remarry is one year. For those who are divorced it is two years.

Given how common these broken trajectories are, it is of interest to ask how they affect women's well-being. Work by economists on marital dissolution in low-income countries is relatively sparse and hardly exists for the African context, particularly with respect to divorce. There has been a bit more attention to widowhood, often indirectly through the study of female-headed

[1] Lambert and Villar are at the Paris School of Economics, Paris, France and van de Walle is with the World Bank in Washington, USA. The authors are grateful to Cait Brown for help with the DHS, to Ariel Gruver for excellent research assistance and to the World Bank's Knowledge for Change Trust Fund for its funding support. We thank two anonymous referees, Jean-Philippe Platteau and the participants at the University of Namur Gender and Development workshop in February 2017 for useful comments. These are the views of the authors and need not reflect those of the World Bank and its affiliated organizations. Corresponding author: Dominique van de Walle, 1818, H St. NW, Washington, DC, 20433; dpvandewalle@gmail.com
[2] The statistics given here are based on PSF1 data (described below).

households (Appleton 1996 (Uganda); Chapoto et al. 2011 (Zambia); Horrell and Krishnan 2007 (Zimbabwe); and van de Walle 2013 (Mali)). Other social sciences provide the core of our knowledge in this domain for Africa. As divorces are sometimes instigated by women, they are likely not to be universally detrimental to women's welfare. In fact, it has been suggested that early divorces may be a means for women both to escape family authority, and to climb the social ladder.[3] Indeed, first and usually early, marriages are often arranged with attending benefits to both families and may be experienced as a constraint from which one can be freed through divorce. Once divorced, given the lower stakes in terms of bride price for divorcees, women have more room for choosing their next partner (Dial 2008; Hertrich 1994; Locoh and Thiriat 1995; Yade 2007).[4] In contrast, widowhood, ensuing from adverse circumstances rather than choice, is universally seen as unfavourable to a woman's situation (Locoh and Thiriat 1995).

One may expect to find negative consequences associated with all types of dissolution that may or may not be tempered by remarriage. In unstructured, open-ended qualitative interviews conducted by two of the authors in Senegal in 2012, one of the dominant messages was that women who have the option not to remarry seized it eagerly.[5] Such women tend to talk about married life as an ordeal they are happy to be in a position to avoid. Echoed in the interviews were general preferences for non-co-residing husbands and/or mothers in law.

To date, there have been few studies of divorce or widowhood in Senegal. Antoine and Dial (2003) and Dial (2008) focus on a small selected sample of women with complex marital trajectories in Dakar only.[6] Another study using fertility surveys that estimated that 17 per cent of all unions dissolve within the first five years is likely to be out of date (Smith et al. 1984).[7] The 2015 World Marriage Data reveal that percentages of divorced (or separated) and non-remarried women in the population have been increasing slightly since the mid-1980s for all but those below age 30. Rates were between 2 and 3 per cent for ages 30 to 55 until the most recent period when they seem to have risen more for women over 40 than for younger ones. Current divorcees account for about 7 per cent of women in the 45–55 age range and only 4 per cent of those between ages 30 and 40 according to the 2014 Demographic and Health Survey (DHS) (Lambert et al. 2017, Table A1). Given that

---

[3] Recently, more economists are showing an interest in the links between divorce and social mobility (Cherchye et al. 2016).

[4] In our data, the average bride price paid for marrying a divorcee is about half that paid for a woman in her first marriage.

[5] Interviews transcribed in Lambert and van de Walle (2012).

[6] Findings in Antoine and Dial (2003) that one third of marriages end in divorce and that, for the youngest generation, 25 per cent of divorces occur within 7 years of marriage are likely to be highly specific to their sample.

[7] The survey used was part of the World Fertility Surveys.

the data do not record divorced and remarried women, this increase could be due to decreasing remarriage rates at older ages, either because age makes non-remarriage more socially acceptable nowadays or because it makes remarriage more difficult. For women aged 40–50 the percentage of non-remarried widows was higher than that for divorcees until the beginning of the 2000s. This has changed in recent years as the percentage of widows has remained fairly stable while that of divorced women has increased. The latest DHS indicates that the percentage of non-remarried widows is higher than that of divorcees only above age 50 when it reaches 12.5 per cent (Lambert et al. 2017, Tables A1 and A2).

To our knowledge, this study is the first to directly examine the relationship between marriage dissolution and women's well-being in Senegal. We focus on women because, as a result of large spousal age gaps, and the widespread practice of polygamy, ever-married men rarely, and then only temporarily, find themselves in a non-married state. In fact, although the share of ever-married men who are currently divorced is similar to that for women (2.5 per cent for men and close to 3 per cent for women), many fewer men than women are currently widowers (1.3 per cent of ever married-men versus 13.6 per cent of ever-married women).

The chapter uses recent nationally representative data from a new household survey and data from DHSs to document Senegalese women's marital trajectories. We describe a simple theoretical framework to help clarify the potential tradeoffs faced by women considering remarriage. This provides a schematic description of the channels through which marital dissolution and remarriage may affect women's well-being. We then turn to the data to examine selection into marital statuses, and how different marital trajectories correlate with current consumption levels and other individual dimensions of welfare.

The chapter finds that marital breakdowns and their aftermath are far from neutral in terms of women's well-being. Our empirical findings accord well with the schematic predictions from our theoretical framework and it is challenging to imagine an alternative explanation for the patterns revealed by the data. Poorer women are found to be more vulnerable to both dissolutions and remarriage, and hence to bear more of the costs while being nevertheless afforded a safety net in the form of a male protector following marriage dissolution.

Naturally, the form a woman's marital trajectory takes is the result of myriad influences including her family and individual characteristics, social norms and chance, as well as the legal and economic setting. Selection and endogeneity are rife in women's life courses. While the evidence is compatible with our model expectations, we acknowledge that the chapter does not establish beyond doubt a one-directional causality between marital status (and its trajectories) and welfare.

Using an individualized measure of consumption and the marital-status-specific parameters estimated from a consumption model, we simulate counterfactual consumption levels for women with different marital trajectories but otherwise identical characteristics. A subsequent decomposition analysis, which allows us to isolate the consumption impacts of remarriage, points to the persistent vulnerability of widows. In addition, the findings suggest that the safety net provided by remarriage is least effective in ensuring consumption levels for the most vulnerable widows who tend to remarry in levirate marriages. We suspect such widows were left no choice but to remarry given their need for economic support, and that, as suggested by the data, many were constrained to remain within their late husband's lineage due to the presence of young (male) children. For their part, divorcees suffer from smaller consumption losses relative to women in their first union, and do not fare differently by whether they remarry or not. Furthermore, individual characteristics that affect the quality of their marriages seem to matter in the same way for their second marriage.

The chapter begins in Section 2 with some background on the legal and institutional context for marriage in Senegal. Section 3 follows with a brief description of our data. Section 4 provides descriptive statistics on marital status and marriage trajectories before we expound on a simple theoretical framework to clarify the links between marital trajectories and women's welfare in Section 5. We examine selection issues in Section 6 and associations between marital status and women's welfare in Section 7. The final section concludes.

2. Marriage Dissolution in Senegal

Colonial legislators attempted to minimize social tensions by establishing a variety of coexisting legal statuses with respect to family law, and, more generally, the civil code (decree of November 10, 1903). The Senegalese people could either comply with the rules of a general statute (similar to French law), or elect to fall under the prescriptions of Islamic, Animist, or Christian statutes according to their beliefs (Brossier 2004; Yade 2007).[8] Nonetheless, a modern-day divorce law that gave women the right to secure a divorce was also introduced at the time. This was a major step forward for women who, until then, depended on their husband's agreement to be freed from matrimonial ties (Yade 2007). However, a wife seeking a divorce could be asked by the judge to reimburse what she and her family had received from the husband at marriage.

---

[8] Note that Islam was already the religion of the majority of the population at the end of the nineteenth century and that animism is perfectly compatible with both monotheist religions present in the country. The type of Islam practised in Senegal is in fact tinted by animist traditions.

In 1972, more than ten years after independence, a new set of family laws was approved. It aimed to unify the various statutes present under colonial rule. Two sources of differentiation remain, which are of primary interest for our purposes as they have consequences for divorcees and widows. In addition to providing dispositions for civil marriages, the law allows for Islamic and customary marriages performed in front of witnesses to be registered ex-post in the civil register. Furthermore, the Family Code contains two chapters dedicated to inheritance rights, one for the general case and one specific to the Muslim population, which constitute 95 per cent of Senegal's population.

Marriages recorded in the civil register can be ended by divorce. Divorce is a mandatory step for women who wish to remarry. The judge decides on the custody of children according to their best interests. In principle, the husband can be required to provide for the subsistence of his ex-wife.

Nevertheless, the majority of religious or customary marriages are never officially registered, and in such cases, customary practices apply in the case of repudiation or divorce, without any available legal recourse for either party.[9] Islamic law is not very favourable to women in general, but, as pointed out by Bowen (2017), what matters, and what differs vastly across countries, is its implementation. In Senegal, repudiation is officially prohibited but appears to remain fairly common de facto (Dial 2008). For divorce under customary law, the situation is very asymmetric between husband and wife. A man only needs two adult witnesses to repudiate his wife, while a woman can only ask for a separation with the final decision up to others. In such cases, the choice over child custody rests with the father. He can keep the children (once weaned) if he cares to. Interviews with divorced mothers of young children shows in a striking way the level of apprehension associated with the risk of losing their children at any moment, upon the father's decision.[10] Whether the husband contributes to child support when offspring remain with their mother is entirely at his discretion. In the case of an early divorce (approximately within two years of marriage) initiated by the wife, her family can be asked to reimburse the bride price. Nevertheless, we find no qualitative evidence of this actually taking place. At any rate, our data suggest that the existence of such a threat does not prevent rapid divorces (see Section 4). Rivière (1990) and Locoh and Thiriat (1995) argue that divorce in West Africa is mostly initiated by women.

In the case of widowhood, no official support systems exist other than when the late husband was a public servant (or possibly an employee of one of a few

---

[9] In our data, 20% of marriages are declared to be 'civil' or 'religious and civil'. The remaining 80% are declared to be 'religious' only. This is likely to overestimate the number of unregistered marriages, but is nevertheless indicative of a low level of formalization.

[10] See Lambert and van de Walle (2012).

large formal sector firms, such as the electricity provider). The civil service allocates a pension to widows equal to a third of the late husband's wage, to be shared among co-wives if the husband was polygamous. Nor can a widow systematically count on inheriting from her husband. Although the statutory Family Code states that wives must inherit a share equal to that of the children, inheritance practices under Islamic and customary patrilineal laws only allocate one eighth of the total bequest to the widow, to be shared among co-wives in the case of polygamy. In practice, and particularly in the many cases where inheritance is mainly illiquid (a house for example), wives are excluded from a bequest following their husband's death; the inheritance is shared among the husband's children, with sons inheriting more, and more frequently, than daughters (Lambert et al. 2014). A widow can remarry outside her late husband's lineage or in a levirate marriage, in which she marries one of his relatives, most often a brother. This arrangement allows her to stay with the children if the paternal lineage wants to keep them. Widowed women who have the option also frequently go to live with a son. Those who have sufficient means to support themselves, usually because they have independent access to housing, often choose not to remarry, an option aided by having grown sons (Lambert and Rossi 2016).

3. Data

The main data source is the first wave of the survey 'Poverty and Family Structure' (PSF, by its French acronym) conducted in Senegal in 2006–2007 and 2011 (De Vreyer et al. 2008).[11] The first wave (PSF1) provides a nationally representative sample of 1,800 households spread over 150 primary sampling units drawn randomly among census districts. About 1,750 records can be exploited. Households have unusually complex structures in Senegal (Bongaarts 2001; van de Walle and Gaye 2006). What we will refer to as a household is often a series of families related in some way and living together in a compound organized under one head and taking their meals together.

In addition to the usual information on individual characteristics, the PSF survey collected detailed information on marital trajectories. Age at first marriage and the number of previous unions are recorded for each individual. The circumstances (divorce or widowhood) of the last dissolution are known, as well as some characteristics of the previous spouse.

---

[11] Momar Sylla and Matar Gueye of the Agence Nationale de la Statistique et de la Démographie of Senegal (ANSD), and Philippe De Vreyer (University of Paris-Dauphine and IRD-DIAL), Sylvie Lambert (Paris School of Economics-INRA) and Abla Safir (now with the World Bank) designed the survey. The data collection was conducted by the ANSD.

A further aspect of the survey that is particularly important for our purposes is that it collected detail on the structure and budgetary arrangements of each household. To best reflect intra-household structure and resource allocation, households were divided into groups or 'cells' according to the following rules: the head of household and unaccompanied dependent members, such as his widowed parent, or his children, whose mothers do not live in the same household, are grouped together. Any unmarried brothers of the head would also be considered part of his cell. Each wife of the head and her children and any other dependents then form separate cells. Other women with children or other dependents, whose husbands are not present, are also considered cell heads. The same goes for any other family nucleus such as a married child of the household head with his/her spouse and children, or a sister of the head residing in the household with her children (typically post-divorce or while her husband looks for a job). This disaggregation emerged from field interviews as being the most relevant way to split the household into its component groups. This is in the same spirit as the procedure used for the Senegalese census of 1988 (van de Walle and Gaye 2006).

Consumption expenditures are recorded in several parts. First all common expenditures are collected (housing, electricity bills, food etc.). Food expenditures are compiled based on a detailed account of who shares which meal and how much money is specifically used to prepare the meal. Next, individual

Table 2.1. PSF1 sample of ever-married adult women, and mean log consumption by marital status

Marital status		Rural	Urban	TOTAL	Mean Log Consumption
First marriage	N	1,168	985	2,153	12.31
	%	71.35	64.89	68.24	
Remarried widow	N	95	60	155	12.22
	%	5.80	3.95	4.91	
Remarried divorcee	N	115	132	247	12.33
	%	7.03	8.70	7.83	
Widow	N	210	220	430	12.43**
	%	12.83	14.49	13.63	
Divorcee	N	49	121	170	12.55***
	%	2.99	7.97	5.39	
TOTAL		**1,637**	**1,518**	**3,155**	
Remarried widows in:					
a levirate marriage	N	51	20	71	12.06**
a non-levirate marriage	N	36	34	70	12.36
Unknown type of union	N	8	6	14	12.26

Note: Adults are defined as 15 and older. For 14 remarried widows, we have no information on whether the current husband is a relative of the deceased husband. Mean log consumption is the log of total cell consumption per capita (CFA francs per year). 1 dollar = 522.9 CFA francs in 2006. All significance tests are relative to once-married women, where *** $p < 0.01$, ** $p < 0.05$, * $p < 0.1$.

Source: Authors' calculations using PSF1.

consumption is collected at the cell level (e.g. expenditures on clothing, mobile phones, transportation, and food outside the home). Finally, expenditures that are shared between several cells but not the whole household are collected.

A measure of per capita consumption can then be constructed at the cell level allowing us to identify unequal consumption levels within households. The data allow us to construct a relatively individualized measure of consumption that we use to assess women's individual economic welfare.

The analysis presented in this chapter is mainly based on the sample of ever-married adult women (fifteen years of age and older), without age limit, from the 2006 PSF1 database. This sample is presented by marital status in Table 2.1.

A second source of data is the DHSs of 2005 and 2010 which we draw on for comparison purposes and to complement the analysis using PSF. Specifically, the DHSs assemble information on aspects of women's well-being, decision making and resource constraints that are not represented in PSF.

4. Marital Status in Senegal

Given the complexity of marital trajectories, computing divorce and widowhood rates from cross-sectional data is complicated, even when surveys contain recall of past marital history data. As noted in the Introduction, PSF1 identifies 18.5 per cent of ever-married women aged fifteen and older as ever-widowed. As can be seen in Table 2.1, the rates are similar in urban and rural areas. Regarding divorces, the overall average of 13.2 per cent hides a higher incidence in urban (16.7 per cent) than in rural areas (10 per cent). However, these numbers are a lower bound on the share of women who experience either widowhood or divorce. Nearly 7 per cent of ever-married women have had more than one dissolution. We have no information on how the union that preceded the last dissolution ended. If we assume that all women with more than one rupture and whose last breakup occurred because of a divorce had previously been widowed, this would give us an upper bound of 21.5 per cent of ever-married women who have experienced widowhood at least once. Conversely, if we assume that the previous dissolution of those identified as having been widowed was a divorce, the estimated upper bound to the proportion of women having suffered a divorce would be 17.3 per cent.

By comparison, the 2010 DHS for Senegal identifies 9.2 per cent of all women aged fifteen and older as widows (9.0 per cent in urban and 9.3 per cent in rural), and 1.1 per cent for those in the 15–49 age group. However, because of Senegal's high remarriage rates, these DHS statistics vastly underestimate the incidence of widowhood within a typical woman's lifespan. Looking instead at the 2005 DHS which collected more detailed information on marital history (albeit only for the 15–49 age group), 3.6 per cent and 4.6 per cent of women are ever-widowed in urban and rural areas respectively, reflecting rates of 2.1 per cent and 3.8 per cent remarried widows among women aged 15–49. There are far more ever-divorced women. The 2005 DHS identifies 13.1 per cent of all women aged 15–49 as married but previously divorced, while it finds that 5.4 per cent are currently divorced.[12] These numbers are in line with the PSF1 estimates, although PSF1 counts relatively more widows (6.7 per cent of widows or remarried widows in the 15–49 age group) and fewer divorcees whether remarried or not (14.1 per cent in total in that age group).

A notable fact is that most women who divorce eventually remarry, although fewer widows do so. Indeed, according to PSF1, 59 per cent of divorcees and 26 per cent of widowed women remarry. A majority remarry polygamous husbands (47 per cent and 72 per cent respectively compared to 36 per cent of first married women). Half of the remarried widows are remarried within a levirate union, among them 83 per cent in a polygamous union.

Using the latest DHSs for a number of countries for which details on marital histories were collected, Senegal's characteristically high remarriage rate following divorce appears to be shared with other West-African countries (see Lambert et al. 2017, Table 2, and Section 4).

There is naturally a strong positive age gradient to the likelihood of being widowed. The top panels of Figures 2.1 and 2.2 display the gradient by age and by marriage duration in PSF1, respectively. In Figure 2.1, we graph the proportion of all women of a given age (with no more than a single marital dissolution) who are ever-widowed. As expected, the share of widowed women steadily rises and at an increasing rate to reach close to 40 per cent of women aged 50–70 and almost 80 per cent of those aged 70 and older. In Figure 2.2, the y-axis gives the widowhood rate for a given marriage duration, among marriages that survived for at least that period of time.

The bottom panels of these figures show the equivalent computations for divorce rates. Here, the age patterns show a peak around the age of 40. However, divorce rates by marriage duration make it clear that those most at risk are recent marriages, since the rate of divorce is highest in the first five years of marriage.[13] This is driven by divorce in urban areas, where the divorce rate among recent marriages is more than twice as high as in rural areas, reaching an average of 1.4 per cent per annum during the first five years (against 0.6 per cent in rural areas). One-quarter of divorces happen within the first three years of marriage, while the median duration of marriages that ended with a divorce is 7.5 years. Divorces happen more rapidly for the younger generation, as the first quartile of the distribution of marriage

[12] Note that separated women are included in the same category as divorced.
[13] These results echo findings from the sparse literature (Antoine and Dial 2003; Locoh and Thiriat 1995; Smith et al. 1984).

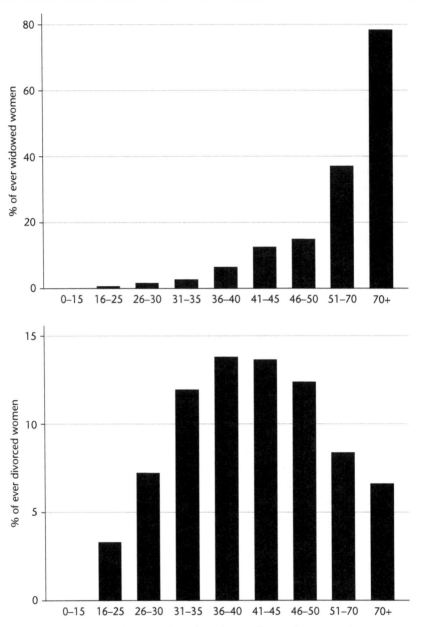

Figure 2.1. Percentage of ever-widowed and ever-divorced women by age groups, all areas

Note: Sample of all women with at most one marital dissolution.

Source: Authors' calculations using PSF1.

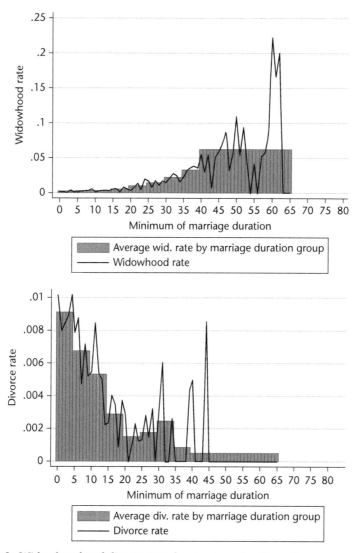

Figure 2.2. Widowhood and divorce rates by marriage duration, all areas

Note: upper panel = widowhood rate for a given marriage duration, among marriages that survived for at least that period of time. Lower panel = divorce rate for a given marriage duration, among marriages that survived for at least that period of time. Sample of women 15 and older with at most one marital dissolution.

Source: Authors' calculations using the PSF1.

duration is only two years for women under 40 against six years for women older than 40 (the corresponding medians are 5 and 14 years). These findings correspond well to the idea that some young women divorce to escape arranged marriages, while others, who may have impetuously engaged in a love marriage, tend to divorce quickly when disappointed with their husband,

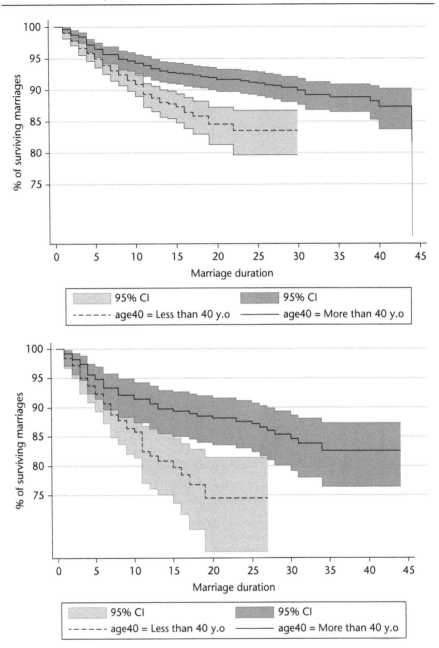

Figure 2.3. Incidence of divorce over time and space; upper panel, all areas; lower panel, Dakar

Note: Sample of women 15 and older with at most one marital dissolution.

Source: Authors' calculations using PSF1.

for example if he tries to limit their autonomy and prevent them from working or finishing their studies, as suggested by qualitative interviews.

After ten years of marriage, a high 8 per cent of unions have ended in divorce (see Lambert et al. 2017, Figure 3). Decomposing the sample into two cohorts (those aged below and above 40), as done in the first panel of Figure 2.3, reveals that the incidence of divorce has increased over time. In the second panel, it can be seen that this trend is even steeper in Dakar. In contrast, the rate of widowhood does not appear to have changed over time. The corresponding graphs (not shown) for two cohorts, whether split around the age of 40 or 60, are indistinguishable.

Finally, to give a sense of overall marriage instability, it is informative to look at union survival rates by women's ages. Among ever-married women, more than one-quarter have been through one marriage dissolution by age 45 (see Lambert et al. 2017, Figure 5).[14]

Ever-widowed and ever-divorced women tend to differ primarily in two dimensions: ever-divorced women are more often urban dwellers and they are three times more likely to have ever been to a French school. This is perhaps not surprising as these characteristics permit a greater autonomy and are likely to facilitate divorce. In addition, for demographic reasons and because divorcees remarry more often than widows, widows are older, have more living children and are more often heads of their households (Table 2.2).

Table 2.2. Differences in socio-economic characteristics between ever-widowed and ever-divorced women

	Ever-widowed	Ever-divorced
Rural area	0.52	0.39***
Age	58.68	40.21***
Age at first marriage	18.26	18.76
Ever been to a French school	0.13	0.37***
Total number of children (alive)	4.54	3.42***
Log of total household consumption per capita (CFA francs per year)	12.38	12.49*
Log of total cell consumption per capita (CFA francs per year)	12.38	12.42
Household size	10.73	10.09
Household head	0.32	0.17***
Cell head (incl. household head)	0.61	0.82***
N	585	417

Note: All characteristics are expressed as shares of the marital status group except for age, number of children, consumption aggregates and household size. Divorced includes separated women. All significance tests are relative to ever-widowed women, where *** $p < 0.01$, ** $p < 0.05$, * $p < 0.1$.

Source: Authors' calculations using PSF1.

[14] This number is comparable to the French case (29% of highly educated and 23% of less educated women have experienced one marital dissolution before age 45, 1999 data) (Lefèvre and Filhon 2005).

5. Marital Trajectories and Women's Welfare

In this section, we sketch a simple model of the tradeoffs faced by women upon marriage dissolution. Widowhood can be seen as a negative shock. By contrast, divorce, since it can be initiated either by the husband or the woman herself, may be anticipated, and hence, a positive or negative development for a woman.[15] Hence, we examine each situation in turn.

To represent the various dimensions of well-being described by women when discussing marriage, we describe women's utility as a function of three factors: the consumption level she commands (C), her autonomy (A), and the degree of social pressure to be married that she is subject to (SP).[16] Autonomy (or bargaining power) is simply given by a woman's position in the household: for example, a household head is more autonomous than the spouse of the head, who in turn may enjoy greater autonomy than the head's daughter-in-law. Wives of higher rank in a polygamous marriage may also be in a relatively weak position. Autonomy allows self-determination and therefore brings utility per se. The utility benefits of independence and of not having to take care of a husband were clearly expressed in most of the interviews we conducted, as was the preference for a monogamous rather than a polygamous union. On the other hand, one's position in the household also affects bargaining power and, therefore, the share of household resources one can benefit from. Thus, the level of consumption accruing to a woman depends on both the household's average level of consumption and the woman's bargaining power, as represented by her relationship with the household head. Finally, social pressure to remarry is mainly driven by two factors: age, and for widows, the gender of the progeny. Indeed, social norms make it largely unacceptable for a woman of childbearing age to remain unmarried. Young divorcees suffer from ill-repute and this social pressure imposes a utility cost on women that can be extremely high (as reflected in testimonials by interviewed remarried widows and divorcees of the difficulties of resisting family insistence on remarriage). Living with an adult son may alleviate some of this pressure. On the other hand, having a young son can render a levirate union unavoidable for a widow if the paternal lineage insists on keeping the child.

Utility can thus be expressed as:[17]

$$U(C(C_h, A), A, SP(x)), \tag{1}$$

---

[15] We interviewed both women who themselves chose divorce, and others claiming to have been surprised when their husband repudiated them. The latter were generally badly off (Lambert and van de Walle 2012).

[16] Note that this utility function ignores other dimensions of welfare often associated with widowhood and divorce, including bereavement, emotional loss, and changes in social status and identity.

[17] For generality, we allow A to enter on its own, but this does not change anything.

where C_h is household consumption and x is a vector of individual character-istics (such as the age and gender of children) that aggravate social pressure. C_h itself is classically a function of household characteristics that are not detailed here. A will belong to $[-1; 1]$, with the value 1 corresponding to a situation of greater autonomy, and -1 corresponding to a highly subordinate position. For illustrative purposes (and simplicity of exposition), let us assume in what follows that A can take only three values: -1, 0, and 1, describing a subsample of the possible situations. Examples of cases where A takes each specific value could be 1 for an un-remarried head of household; 0 for a woman in a monogamous first marriage, and -1 for a higher ranked wife in a polygamous levirate second union (a likely fate for many remarried widows).[18] SP varies between 0 and 1, taking the value 0 when the marital status of a woman doesn't give rise to any social disapproval and 1 when the risk of disrepute is at its maximum (young divorcee).

U_m is the utility level of a once-married woman.[19] This can be written as $U_m = U(C(C_{hm}, 0), 0, 0)$, where C_{hm} is the consumption level of the household of a woman in her first marriage.

When she becomes a widow, her utility changes to $U_{wy} = U(C(C_{hw}, 1), 1, 1)$ if she's young and to $U_{wo} = U(C(C_{hw}, 1), 1, 0)$ if she's old enough to avoid social pressure. C_{hw} is the consumption level in the household after the death of the husband. The gain in autonomy results in a positive boost in utility. On the consumption side, it is likely that $C_{hw} < C_{hm}$ since an income earner has passed away. For women with no education, no son to provide support, no pension, and living in rural areas, this drop may be very severe. Nevertheless, the increased access to household resources due to $A = 1$ may in some cases be such that $C(C_{hw}, 1) > C(C_{hm}, 0)$, so that being a widow doesn't necessarily entail a loss in individual consumption.

A widow then considers whether to remarry or not. Upon remarriage, her utility will reach $U_{wr} = U(C(C_{hwr}, -1), -1, 0)$. C_{hwr} is the consumption level of the household into which she can remarry. It may be relatively low, as a widow is not in a good position to choose a desirable match. Further, her position in this new marriage (in many cases as a higher-ranked wife in a polygamous union) may provide her with very low bargaining power.

---

[18] Clearly, these are only examples and for each woman, the exact level of A will depend not only on the general characteristics of the marriage (monogamous or not, levirate or not...) but also on the husband's characteristics and the quality of the match. Hence, a wife in a monogamous first union may well end up with a much lower level of A if she lives with her in-laws while a higher-ranked wife in a polygamous union may be given considerable freedom, the more so if she is no longer of childbearing age.

[19] In this chapter once-married refers to a currently married woman who has only ever been married a single time.

When a young widow chooses to remarry, it must be that $U_{wy} < U_{wr}$, and this can occur even though $C(C_{hw}, 1) > C(C_{hwr}, -1)$. This implies that this widow remarries despite a loss in consumption and a loss of autonomy, only because social pressure is unbearable.

We can therefore expect to see two types of widows remarrying: those for whom the social pressure is simply too costly (young ones), and those for whom the drop in consumption associated with the first husband's death is overly large. The consumption consequences of remarriage could be very different for the two widow-types. Those who remarry because of social pressure could well experience a considerable consumption cost, particularly if constrained to remarry in a given lineage and therefore deprived of the possibility of a more advantageous match. On the other hand, even if their situation worsens relative to their first marriage, impoverished widows may limit the consumption shock through remarriage.

When considering the trajectories of divorcees, the main difference is that remarriage possibilities may be anticipated, especially when the wife initiates the divorce. Upon divorce, a divorcee's utility level is given by $U_{dy} = U(C(C_{hd}, 1), 1, 1)$ if she is young and $U_{do} = U(C(C_{hd}, 1), 1, 0)$ if she is old. After remarriage, in a way similar to what was described above for widows, utility reaches $U_{dr} = U(C(C_{hdr}, 0), 0, 0)$. Here, autonomy is set at 0 (rather than -1) to take into account the fact that divorcees seem to have better remarriage prospects than widows, as, on average, they have more control on the timing of their search for a new partner.

It is likely that a woman would not initiate divorce if all these utility levels (figuring all the possible outcomes) were far below the utility level enjoyed in the first marriage. Hence, women who chose to divorce foresee either a sufficient income on their own and a bearable level of social pressure, or relatively good remarriage options. We can expect the most educated and urban women to more often remain on their own, and those without such assets to more often remarry. Marriage may be a good way to compensate for a lack of individual income generating capacity. Given self-selection, it is a priori unclear whether divorcees will on average be better off when remarried or not.

Repudiated wives, on the other hand, may suffer greater consumption losses and huge social pressure. They are likely to remarry but remarriage may not fully compensate in terms of living standards in this case.

6. Determinants of Current Marital Status

Following on from the simple theoretical framework outlined in the previous section, we now turn to the data to investigate potential selection not only into widowhood and divorce but also into remarriage, an issue not previously identified in the literature. We've argued that there is a strong presumption of differential selection into marital status. We try to dig deeper into the determinants of being in one status or another. Trajectories are decomposed into several successive steps. We first discuss the individual level correlates of widowhood and divorce, followed by those associated with remarriage, and finally those that correlate with various aspects of marriage quality.

6.1. *Selection into Widowhood and Divorce*

Tables 2.3 and 2.4 show how the probabilities of widowhood and divorce, and of remarriage, are correlated with women's individual characteristics. Older women understandably have a higher probability of widowhood (Table 2.3). Age is also significantly associated with divorce, although in a less pronounced way. Characteristics typically associated with higher standards of living are

Table 2.3. Probability of widowhood or divorce and women's characteristics: All areas

	Prob(widow)	Prob(divorce)
Rural area	−0.040***	−0.088***
	(0.014)	(0.018)
Ref: Husband working in the informal sector		
Husband: agricultural sector	0.015	0.042**
	(0.016)	(0.019)
Husband: private formal or public sector	−0.036**	−0.092***
	(0.017)	(0.019)
Husband: other sector	0.109***	0.093***
	(0.024)	(0.032)
Age at first marriage	−0.005***	−0.005***
	(0.001)	(0.002)
Ever been to a French school	−0.027+	0.064***
	(0.017)	(0.017)
Current age	0.010***	0.004***
	(0.000)	(0.001)
Ref: Wolof/Lebou		
Serere	0.021	0.014
	(0.019)	(0.023)
Poular	0.010	−0.007
	(0.015)	(0.018)
Other ethnicity	0.058***	0.012
	(0.016)	(0.020)
Mean of dep. Var	0.21	0.17
N	2593	2467
Pseudo R2	0.386	0.066

Note: Logit model, marginal effects shown. Sample of ever-married women. 'Husband' refers to the one prior to the widowhood or divorce.
*** $p < 0.01$, ** $p < 0.05$, * $p < 0.1$, + $p < 0.12$.
Source: Authors' estimations using PSF1.

Table 2.4. Probability of remarriage: All areas

	Probability of remarriage for widows	Probability of remarriage for divorcees	Probability of levirate remarriage for remarried widows
Ref: dissolution after age 40.			
Dissolution before age 25	0.470***	0.371***	−0.098
	(0.055)	(0.070)	(0.105)
Dissolution between ages 25–39	0.291***	0.261***	−0.113
	(0.030)	(0.072)	(0.087)
Last dissolution; rural resident	0.082**	0.109**	0.233***
	(0.035)	(0.054)	(0.075)
No children born from last union	−0.130*	0.065	
	(0.078)	(0.069)	
Had a son at time of dissolution	−0.023	−0.104**	0.249***
	(0.036)	(0.052)	(0.080)
Number of marital dissolutions	−0.016	−0.019	−0.128*
	(0.034)	(0.060)	(0.072)
Polygamous last marriage			−0.115
			(0.077)
Ever been to a French school	0.011	−0.121**	−0.274**
	(0.047)	(0.051)	(0.124)
Polygamous father	0.098***	0.071	0.054
	(0.037)	(0.049)	(0.094)
Fostered before age 15	0.123**	0.098	0.059
Ref: Wolof/Lebou	(0.048)	(0.068)	(0.107)
Serere	0.048	0.011	−0.009
	(0.054)	(0.070)	(0.102)
Poular	0.019	−0.054	−0.192**
	(0.043)	(0.059)	(0.092)
Other ethnicity	−0.043	−0.113	0.249***
	(0.045)	(0.076)	(0.080)
Mean of dep. var	0.27	0.59	0.49
N	488	353	140
Pseudo R2	0.258	0.146	0.189

Note: Logit models, marginal effects shown. Samples of ever-widowed women (Column 1) and ever-divorced women (Column 2).
*** $p < 0.01$, ** $p < 0.05$, * $p < 0.1$, + $p < 0.12$.
Source: Authors' estimations using PSF1.

negatively correlated with becoming a widow; this is true for both the socio-economic category of the deceased husband (men employed in the formal or public sector are more likely to survive) and for the wife's own level of education. This strongly suggests that widows are selected among poorer women, as has been found elsewhere.[20] In Senegal, this may reflect the negative correlation between income and life expectancy which has been well-documented worldwide (see, for example, Feinstein 1993), or the lower quality of the sanitary environment and access to health care of poor

[20] For example, on the basis of longitudinal data on health and retirement for the U.S., it has been shown that, allowing for the fact that poorer men are more likely than other men to die young, widows, and particularly young ones, are more likely to come from poorer households (Hurd and Wise 1989; Sevak et al. 2003).

households. Furthermore, we also observe a greater spousal age gap in poorer households, mechanically increasing the probability of widowhood for poorer women. Nevertheless, there is also a surprising negative correlation between rural residence at the time of dissolution and widowhood.

With respect to selection into divorce, the story is somewhat different. This is expected as, unlike with widowhood, divorce results from the choice of at least one spouse. A husband's positive characteristics are associated with a lower probability of divorce, while a wife's positive characteristics (education) are positively correlated with divorce. Furthermore, urban areas see more divorces. This suggests that women who have the means (social as well as economic) to exercise their independence are more likely to be divorced, probably often at their own initiative. That said, women appear to be less willing to divorce men with desirable economic situations.

6.2. *Selection into Remarriage*

Table 2.4 presents the correlates of remarriage following a dissolution (see Lambert et al. 2017, Table A6 for the rural urban decomposition of those estimates). Age at dissolution is the strongest correlate of remarriage for both divorcees and widows. Indeed, if the dissolution happens before the age of 25, the probability of remarriage is 1.8 times higher for widows and increases by more than 60 per cent for divorcees, relative to the situation in which the dissolution happens after age 40. Women with more traditional backgrounds are more likely to remarry (in particular after widowhood): this holds for rural dwellers, daughters of polygamous men, and women who were fostered in childhood. There may be different reasons for the latter two correlations, from a larger kin network to a better acceptance of polygamy. Irrespective of the age at dissolution, a polygamous husband awaits three-quarters of women who remarry following widowhood, and half of those who do so after divorce. Conversely, educated women, who are more likely to be divorced, are also more likely not to remarry following divorce (this is driven by urban divorcees). Finally, having a son from the previous union is correlated with lower remarriage for divorcees (a result driven by rural women).[21] Various channels may explain this correlation. On the one hand, for divorcees, having a grown-up son has a positive impact on consumption level (see Table 2.10), suggesting the possibility of material support that makes remarriage less necessary. On the other hand, it may be more difficult to retain custody of a son after remarriage. Finally, women who do not yet have a son, may feel the urge to remarry to maximize their chances of ever bearing one. Conversely, widows

---

[21] See Lambert et al. 2017, Table A6.

without children from the late husband are less likely to remarry, probably because levirate marriage is less of an option for them. As shown in the last column of Table 2.4, levirate unions are prevalent mainly in rural areas. Among widows who remarry, having a son from the previous union is strongly associated with remarrying into the deceased husband's family (levirate). Here again, women's education is associated with a somewhat lower probability of this traditional practice.

6.3. Remarriage Quality

Correlations observed in the DHS data between marital characteristics and women's autonomy (see Lambert et al. 2017, Table A8) suggest that a 'good' marriage is a monogamous one, without cohabitation with the husband, and a husband working in the formal sector. We therefore investigate the correlates of such 'good' quality remarriage for remarried women in Tables 2.5 and 2.6,

Table 2.5. Type of remarriage for widows by union and husband's characteristics

	Co-resides with husband	Polygamy	Husband works in the formal sector
Ref: dissolution after age 40.			
Dissolution before age 25	0.379***	−0.261***	0.035
	(0.090)	(0.101)	(0.101)
Dissolution between ages 25–39	0.283***	−0.134	−0.017
	(0.081)	(0.099)	(0.091)
Last dissolution; rural resident	0.009	0.128*	−0.097
	(0.077)	(0.074)	(0.075)
No children born in last union	0.309**	0.156	−0.294⁺
	(0.138)	(0.214)	(0.179)
Had a son at widowhood	−0.208***	−0.031	−0.000
	(0.072)	(0.086)	(0.080)
Number of marital dissolutions	0.128	0.021	0.029
	(0.093)	(0.085)	(0.078)
Ever been to a French school	−0.192⁺	−0.097	0.400***
	(0.117)	(0.088)	(0.083)
Polygamous father	−0.151*	−0.058	−0.146*
	(0.079)	(0.077)	(0.077)
Fostered before age 15	−0.129	−0.014	0.152⁺
Ref: Wolof/Lebou.	(0.087)	(0.083)	(0.095)
Serere	−0.399***	0.015	0.249**
	(0.127)	(0.124)	(0.118)
Poular	−0.155	−0.065	−0.015
	(0.100)	(0.107)	(0.104)
Other ethnicity	−0.161*	−0.139	0.019
	(0.098)	(0.092)	(0.103)
Mean of dep. var	0.51	0.74	0.33
N	133	132	123
Pseudo R2	0.265	0.106	0.223

Note: Logit model, marginal effects shown. Sample of ever-widowed women.
*** $p < 0.01$, ** $p < 0.05$, * $p < 0.1$, ⁺ $p < 0.12$.
Source: Authors' estimations using PSF1.

Table 2.6. Type of remarriage for divorcees by union and husband's characteristics

	Co-resides with husband	Polygamy	Husband works in the formal sector
Ref: dissolution after age 40.			
Dissolution before age 25	0.252**	−0.145	−0.227⁺
	(0.107)	(0.163)	(0.141)
Dissolution between ages 25–39	0.113	−0.055	−0.145
	(0.106)	(0.158)	(0.140)
Last dissolution; rural resident	0.014	0.016	−0.180***
	(0.071)	(0.076)	(0.070)
No children born last union	0.032	0.070	−0.138
	(0.080)	(0.085)	(0.089)
Had a son at time of divorce	−0.024	0.034	−0.090
	(0.079)	(0.082)	(0.078)
Number of marital dissolutions	−0.048	0.003	−0.038
	(0.059)	(0.072)	(0.075)
Ever been to a French school	−0.079	−0.153**	0.133**
	(0.071)	(0.075)	(0.068)
Polygamous father	−0.116*	0.144**	0.011
	(0.064)	(0.064)	(0.066)
Fostered before age 15	−0.093	−0.186**	0.069
Ref: Wolof/Lebou.	(0.075)	(0.085)	(0.083)
Serere	−0.129	−0.189*	−0.038
	(0.086)	(0.099)	(0.089)
Poular	−0.088	−0.167**	0.002
	(0.077)	(0.082)	(0.082)
Other ethnicity	−0.048	−0.102	−0.003
	(0.091)	(0.098)	(0.102)
Mean of dep. Var	0.73	0.48	0.34
N	207	207	198
Pseudo R2	0.084	0.087	0.105

Note: Logit model, marginal effects shown. Sample of ever-divorced women.
*** $p < 0.01$, ** $p < 0.05$, * $p < 0.1$, ⁺ $p < 0.12$.
Source: Authors' estimations using PSF1.

respectively for widows and divorcees, recalling that widows are more likely to remarry as higher-ranked wives in polygamous unions. In addition, a civil marriage (for the protection it provides), lack of cohabitation with the in-laws, and the possibility of living with one's children from the previous union seem to be other desirable characteristics. Correlations with the latter characteristics are presented in Table 2.7.

A late dissolution is associated with a lower probability of cohabitation, in particular, when the woman has passed childbearing age, and especially so for ex-widows (Tables 2.5 and 2.6). At the same time, it is related to a higher likelihood of remarriage in a polygamous union. Widows with children from a previous union are less likely to cohabit and even less so for those with a son at the time of dissolution.

Divorcees who have been to a French school and who were fostered before age 15 (two correlated characteristics) appear better able to avoid polygamy; yet having been brought up with a polygamous father increases the likelihood

Table 2.7. Type of remarriage by other union characteristics

	Has a civil contract	Lives with in-laws	Lives with children from previous union
Widows			
Dissolution before age 40	0.077	0.019	−0.114
	(0.066)	(0.044)	(0.083)
Last dissolution: rural resident	−0.179***	0.051	−0.034
	(0.056)	(0.044)	(0.073)
No children born in last union	0.005	0.027	.
	(0.093)	(0.065)	.
Had a son at widowhood	−0.080+	0.003	0.347***
	(0.051)	(0.035)	(0.051)
Number of marital dissolutions	−0.029	0.074***	−0.042
	(0.065)	(0.028)	(0.064)
Ever been to a French school	0.077	0.047	0.113
	(0.060)	(0.051)	(0.105)
Mean of dep. var	0.11	0.063	0.65
N	142	142	134
Pseudo R2	0.221	0.124	0.204
Divorcees			
Dissolution before age 40	0.025	0.156	0.215*
	(0.102)	(0.115)	(0.111)
Last dissolution: rural resident	−0.197***	0.138***	−0.282***
	(0.060)	(0.053)	(0.065)
No children born in last union	−0.072	0.103**	.
	(0.066)	(0.044)	.
Had a son at time of divorce	−0.105*	−0.045	0.203***
	(0.062)	(0.069)	(0.077)
Number of marital dissolutions	−0.094	−0.063	0.057
	(0.089)	(0.062)	(0.074)
Ever been to a French school	0.119**	0.021	−0.125
	(0.052)	(0.053)	(0.081)
Mean of dep. Var	0.18	0.13	0.55
N	227	227	177
Pseudo R2	0.171	0.129	0.119

Note: Logit model, marginal effects shown.
Sample of ever-widowed women for the upper part, and sample of ever-divorced women for the lower part.
*** $p < 0.01$, ** $p < 0.05$, * $p < 0.1$, + $p < 0.12$.
Source: Authors' estimations using PSF1.

of marrying into a polygamous union, maybe because it facilitates acceptance of this type of marriage.

Having been to a French school, having been fostered in childhood, and having had a monogamous father all correlate with marrying a husband with a formal sector job, and more so for widows than for divorcees. Finally, living in a rural area at the time of dissolution is unfavourable as it reduces access to husbands with formal jobs and increases the likelihood of polygamy.

Living in a rural area is associated with other negative outcomes (Table 2.7): divorcees in rural areas are less likely to have a civil contract for their marriages (this is true for widows as well); they are more likely to live with their in-laws, and are more at risk of not living with children from their previous union. Having a son from the previous union is positively correlated with the probability of living with children from the previous union after remarriage.

Interestingly, when we compare these results with the correlates of marriage quality in these various dimensions for women in their first marriage, it appears that a woman's education is associated with protection against polygamy and a higher probability of a civil marriage in the same way for them and for divorcees when they remarry. Conversely, it does not go hand-in-hand with such a protective role for widows upon remarriage (see Lambert et al. 2017 Table A7 for women in their first marriage).

7. Differences in Welfare Levels

To investigate associations between marital status and women's welfare, we first turn to some non-monetary individual welfare indicators as well as measures of decision making power and resource constraints available from the 2005 DHS. We then examine individualized measures of consumption using PSF1.

7.1. *Measures of Well-Being, Decision Making, and Constraints*

The focus of Tables 2.8 and 2.9 is all ever-married women aged 15–49. Table 2.8 begins with some descriptive statistics on key characteristics that arguably reflect aspects of a woman's living standards and well-being. It can be noted that close to one-quarter of this group have had a union dissolution.

Controlling for age (as women married only once are on average younger— Column 2), there doesn't seem to be any difference in body mass index (BMI) correlated with marital status (Column 5).

Differences appear in nearly every other dimension. Urban remarried widows live in significantly more asset-poor households than do once-married and widowed women, while urban divorcees are members of significantly richer households. In rural areas, ever-divorced women reside in less asset-poor households.

Current widows are about twice as likely as their remarried counterparts to have inherited most of their deceased husband's property suggesting a degree of autonomy and one reason why they have not remarried. Finally, the last two columns of Table 2.8 show the percentages of women who were born in rural areas but now live in urban areas, and vice versa. The first could reflect an escape from more stringent social norms, as suggested by the higher shares of widows and ever-divorced women who have followed this path. Alternatively, such women may have married into an urban family and simply remained there when the union ended. Likewise, being urban-born and ending up in

Table 2.8. Descriptive statistics on ever-married women by current marital status, Senegal 2005 DHS

| | % of ever-married women 15–49 | Age | H'hold head | BMI | % Under-weight (at mean age) | DHS asset index | | Received most of husband's property | Born rural, lives urban | Born urban, lives rural |
						Urban	Rural			
	(1)	(2)	(3)	(4)	(5)	(6)	(7)	(8)	(9)	(10)
Once-married	75.7	29.7	5.8	22.75	11.6	1.06	−0.54	—	8.3	4.8
Remarried widow	4.4	38.8	19.9	24.35***	8.5	0.67***	−0.57	16.0	6.1	5.6
Widow	1.5	38.5	32.2	25.35***	12.0	1.10	−0.41	30.9	14.1***	2.2**
Remarried divorcee	13.1	34.3	8.9	24.99***	10.3	0.93***	−0.43***	—	13.1***	6.0
Divorced	5.4	32.4	14.6	23.20*	10.3	1.35***	−0.30***	—	12.7***	3.1**

Note: All characteristics are expressed as percentages of the marital status group except for age (years), BMI, and the wealth index. All significance tests are relative to married-once women, where *** $p < 0.01$, ** $p < 0.05$, * $p < 0.1$. Underweight is defined as having BMI less than 18.5. Column (6) presents mean underweight conditional on age and aged squared and evaluated at mean age for the sample as a whole. Differences relative to once-married women are no longer statistically significant. Pregnant women are omitted from the BMI and underweight means. Divorced includes separated women. The Wealth index is generated by DHS using principal components analysis on assets; housing construction materials; and type of water access and sanitation facilities. The index places households on a continuous scale of relative wealth and refers to the household to which the woman belongs. Sample: ever-married women, aged 15–49

Source: Authors' calculations using Senegal's 2005 DHS.

Table 2.9. Measures of women's decision-making and access to resources by marital status, Senegal 2005 DHS (%)

	Has no say on:			Constraints on seeking health care:		Own earnings spent on household:		Beating justified:		Never watches TV
	Own health care	Large hh purchases	Visits to family	Permission	Cost	None	> half	If argue	Refuses sex	
Once-married	81.5	83.8	66.8	6.0	55.0	33.2	16.4	51.6	49.8	32.3
Remarried widow	66.7***	67.9***	50.3***	4.5**	70.7***	16.8***	34.0***	56.9	58.8***	43.1***
Widow	32.7***	44.4***	31.3***	2.1**	68.1***	33.8	44.3***	40.6	48.1	21.0**
Remarried divorcee	73.2***	76.7***	62.4***	4.8**	58.9***	31.1	20.7***	50.7**	46.9***	26.7***
Divorced	46.5***	70.3***	50.9***	4.9***	59.6***	38.1***	21.4*	38.3***	36.4***	15.5***

Note: The Table shows the % of women in each marital status answering positively to each question. 'Has no say' is defined as answering that each decision is taken by either the husband/partner alone or by someone else. Divorced includes separated women. Significance tests are relative to once-married women, where *** p < 0.01, ** p < 0.05, * p < 0.1. Sample: ever-married women, aged 15–49

Source: Authors' calculations using Senegal's 2005 DHS.

rural areas may be interpreted as a worsening of life conditions, and we see that current divorcees and widows are significantly less likely to have made this move. But, here too, an alternative story is selection into a rural marriage prior to the husband's loss.

Taken together, the statistics presented in Table 2.8 are consistent with a situation in which women who remarry are mostly those who cannot afford to remain husbandless, and despite remarriage, appear to be living in poorer households.

Women are asked various questions and their answers can be interpreted as indicative, or related to, their levels of voice within the household and the constraints they face. A number of suggestive patterns emerge when we examine how these vary with marital status (Table 2.9). Widows are the least likely to report having no say over decisions that affect them and their households, undoubtedly reflecting the fact that they are more often household heads. Women in their first union are the most likely ones to have no say in decision making, with remarried divorcees not far behind. Divorcees and ex-widows fall somewhere in-between, exchanging rankings depending on the activity.

In seeking health care for oneself, getting permission is a constraint faced by at most 5–6 per cent of Senegalese women, and appears not to be strongly associated with marital status. A much larger share of women point to a cost constraint, with the health care of remarried and current widows being the most liquidity constrained, at 71 per cent and 68 per cent respectively, and once-married women the least constrained at 55 per cent.

Incomes are not typically pooled across the members of a Senegalese household. Women contribute their labour to the household enterprise and its overall care, but their own earnings are in general for their own and their dependent's non-food needs. Women are asked what share of their earnings is spent on the household. The data suggest that on average around one-third of women contribute none of their own earnings to household needs. The one exception among marital statuses is for remarried widows, of which only a low 17 per cent surrender none of their earnings. Indeed, they are more likely to give up more than half of their personal earnings than other women (34 per cent versus 16 per cent for married and 21 per cent for ever-divorced women). The one exception is widows, who, since they more often head their households, are expected to do so. These statistics are consistent with the idea elaborated in Section 5 that widowed women without resources or a place to live often remarry poor men who can provide a degree of social insurance, but not much more than food and shelter.

Adult female DHS respondents were asked about whether a husband is justified in beating his wife if she goes out without telling him, neglects the children, argues with him, refuses sex, or burns the food. The responses follow the same patterns across women (only two are shown). Widows and divorcees are least likely, and remarried widows most likely to agree that a husband is justified in beating his wife. Here again, remarried widows stand out as in a particularly weak position.

Among women, a larger share of remarried widows never watch television (43 per cent) followed by women in their first marriage (32 per cent) and remarried divorcees (27 per cent). Current widows and divorcees are most likely to watch TV and access information and entertainment on a frequent basis. Such statistics could reflect economic constraints although alternative explanations are also possible (such as a lower burden in terms of household chores).

The above are simple correlations and one should of course be cautious about making causal interpretations. Note, however, that the associations between the descriptive statistics and potential indications of decision-making power and constraints faced are consistent with our simple theoretical framework and many of the relationships that emerge from PSF in what follows for women by marital status.

7.2. Differences in Consumption Levels

7.2.1. A CONSUMPTION MODEL

Using the PSF survey, we can document women's average consumption levels by marital status for each of the five groups considered (widow (W), remarried widow (MW), divorcee (D), remarried divorcee (MD), first marriage (M)). Simple descriptive statistics show that unconditionally, current divorcees and widows have the highest average cell per capita consumptions and, along with ex-divorcees, reside in higher per capita consumption households (Table 2.1).[22] Remarried widows fare the worst on average, particularly when they are in a levirate marriage with log average cell consumption of only 12.06 as opposed to 12.22 for all remarried widows. Widows remarried outside the lineage of their late husband enjoy a level of consumption more than 30 per cent higher than those in levirate unions. This may reflect the fact that remarried widows are different from other women in a few dimensions. As we saw in Section 6, they indeed cumulate a double negative selection: selection into widowhood, which suggests they were from relatively poor backgrounds to begin with, and selection into remarriage, with rural dwellers among them remarrying more often. Negative selection is even stronger for those remarrying one of their late husband's kin. Such disadvantage could also be due to remarriage itself, if entering into a second union after widowhood confines women to weak bargaining positions within their new households.

---

[22] Descriptive statistics on the five groups are given in Lambert et al. 2017, Tables A3–A5.

Table 2.10. Regressions of log cell consumption per capita

	Once married	Remarried widows	Remarried divorcees	Widows	Divorcees
Age	0.010	0.033+	0.020	−0.008	−0.007
	(0.010)	(0.021)	(0.019)	(0.015)	(0.020)
Age squared	−0.000	−0.0002	−0.000	0.0001	−0.00003
	(0.000)	(0.0002)	(0.000)	(0.0001)	(0.0002)
Age at first marriage	0.010**	0.002	0.008	−0.002	0.011
	(0.004)	(0.013)	(0.014)	(0.007)	(0.009)
ln household size	−0.315***	−0.035	−0.331***	−0.213**	−0.233**
	(0.059)	(0.147)	(0.094)	(0.087)	(0.111)
ln cell size	−0.193***	−0.096	−0.084	−0.049	−0.337**
	(0.053)	(0.136)	(0.172)	(0.085)	(0.138)
Share of children in cell	−0.442***	−0.658***	−0.749**	−0.461**	−0.757***
	(0.101)	(0.223)	(0.353)	(0.187)	(0.302)
Belongs to head's cell	0.088	0.020	−0.126	−0.010	0.194
	(0.085)	(0.170)	(0.165)	(0.10)	(0.153)
Cell head	−0.002	0.180	0.014	0.031	0.101
	(0.052)	(0.135)	(0.209)	(0.102)	(0.151)
French school	0.308***	0.475***	0.442***	0.460***	0.525***
	(0.055)	(0.149)	(0.128)	(0.111)	(0.132)
Koranic school	0.006	0.469***	0.222+	0.249***	0.071
	(0.066)	(0.177)	(0.136)	(0.089)	(0.191)
Fostered before age 15	0.030	0.176	−0.043	−0.045	−0.153
	(0.053)	(0.145)	(0.117)	(0.125)	(0.134)
Has son 18 or older	−0.044	−0.079	0.065	0.070	0.251**
	(0.038)	(0.112)	(0.113)	(0.092)	(0.126)
Husband informal	0.042	0.187*	0.269**	−0.079	−0.088
	(0.057)	(0.109)	(0.121)	(0.126)	(0.207)
Husband formal/public	0.209***	0.721***	0.355**	0.105	0.30
	(0.060)	(0.177)	(0.178)	(0.138)	(0.228)
Husband other	−0.071	0.399**	0.269	−0.002	0.022
	(0.102)	(0.192)	(0.228)	(0.143)	(0.280)
Polygamous marriage	−0.026	−0.090	−0.013	−0.123	0.110
	(0.049)	(0.146)	(0.140)	(0.082)	(0.115)
Urban residence	0.582***	0.358**	0.223+	0.628***	0.362**
	(0.074)	(0.148)	(0.141)	(0.129)	(0.152)
Constant	12.687***	10.831***	12.579***	12.635***	12.963***
	(0.229)	(0.148)	(0.535)	(0.468)	(0.474)
R-squared	0.37	0.46	0.35	0.28	0.48
Observations	2,082	146	241	394	160

Note: Robust standard errors are given in parentheses, clustered at the sampling unit level. 'Husband' is the current one for once-married women, and ex-husband for all other groups. Ditto for polygamous marriage. Husband in agriculture is the left out category. + $p < 0.12$, * $p < 0.1$, ** $p < 0.05$, *** $p < 0.01$
Source: Authors' estimations using PSF1.

To isolate the consumption implications of marital status itself from those of selection on the basis of observable characteristics, we conduct a decomposition analysis.

Table 2.10 presents regressions for women by marital status group of the log of cell consumption per person for the ith woman against a vector of attributes x_i. This set of regressions can be written as:

$$\ln C_i = \sum_{\forall j} (\alpha_j + \beta_j x_i + \varepsilon_{ij}) S_{ij} \quad (j = M, W, MW, D, MD) \tag{2}$$

Here, all parameters are marital-status specific, ε_{ij} is an error term, and $S_{ij} = 1$ if woman i is a member of group j and $S_{ij} = 0$ otherwise. Noting that $\sum_{\forall j} S_{ij} = 1$, we can re-write (1) such that the parameters for marital-status groups are evaluated as deviations from mean points for a given reference marital-status group k:

$$\ln C_i = \alpha_k + \beta_k x_i + \varepsilon_{ik} + \sum_{\forall j \neq k} [\alpha_j - \alpha_k + (\beta_j - \beta_k) x_i + \varepsilon_{ij} - \varepsilon_{ik}] S_{ij} \tag{3}$$

Estimating the model in this way also facilitates testing for the equality of the parameters. A special case is when only the intercepts differ, in which case the model is equivalent to running a regression with dummy variables for marital status.

We then use each group's own estimated parameters to predict consumption for a fixed reference group's mean covariates. For example, using the mean attributes of remarried widows ($\bar{x}^{MW}$) allows us to determine how much worse-off remarried widows are on average purely because they are remarried widows; this entails estimating for marital-status group j:

$$E_j[\ln C_i | MW_i = 0, x_i = \bar{x}^{MW}] - E_j[\ln C_i | MW_i = 1, x_i = \bar{x}^{MW}] \tag{4}$$

$$= \alpha_j + \beta_j \bar{x}^{MW} - \ln \bar{C}^{MW} \tag{5}$$

(Here $E_j[.]$ denotes the expectation formed over the parameters and error term distribution for group j, while $\ln \bar{C}^{MW}$ denotes the mean of log consumption for $j = MW$.)

7.2.2. CORRELATES OF CONSUMPTION

The regressions control for individual and household characteristics, which tend to be important in the Senegalese context and are common across all three groups of women. These include age, age squared, and age at first marriage; log household and cell size; the share of children in the cell; and a series of dummy variables for whether the woman was fostered as a child, attended a French or a Koranic school, has a son aged 18 or older, belongs to the household head's cell, is head of her own cell, (current or ex) husband's occupation (informal or formal sector or other, with agriculture the left out option), whether the current (or previous, for ever-widowed and ever-divorced women) marriage is (was) polygamous, and whether the woman lives in an urban or rural area.[23]

---

[23] Other variables—potentially relevant to living standards but not shared across the groups— were tested. For all currently married women, whether the husband co-resides and number of co-wives; for previously married women, the number of past dissolutions and ex-cowives; for remarried women, the duration of widowhood/divorce prior to remarriage. Only the number of

There are some notable differences in the models across marital-status groups. A higher age at marriage is associated with significantly higher consumption for once-married women, but not for women in other groups. Larger household size is associated with significantly lower consumption for all except remarried widows. However, not all the differences in coefficients are statistically significant. Taking once-married women as the reference, one can only reject the null that the coefficient on age at first marriage is different for widows, and the same is true for the coefficients on log household size but with respect to remarried widows. A higher cell size, and cell share of children are associated with lower consumption for all groups, although the first is only significantly associated with consumption for married and divorced women. But again, tests of the differences in coefficients relative to once-married women show that they are statistically indistinguishable from each other.

There are high returns associated with education. Having attended a French school has a substantial and highly significant (and statistically indistinguishable) return for all women. Koranic education is correlated with higher cell consumption for widows and women who have remarried. Indeed, controlling for age and other covariates, the effects of Koranic schooling on consumption are about the same as having attended a French school for ex-widows and half as much for ex-divorcees and widows. However, relative to once-married women, the difference is significant for ever-widowed women only. Having a son older than 18 appears to be a significant asset for divorcees.

The largest boost to the consumption of remarried women is having had a formal public or private sector employee as their (now deceased) husband. For ex-widows this effect ($\beta = 0.721$, t-stat = 4.07) far outweighs that of any other covariate. It likely captures the effect of receiving a pension and being able to keep it for oneself, as a source of personal income. For both groups, having had a husband in the informal and 'other' sectors is also associated with higher consumption, although tests reveal these not to be statistically different from that estimated for other women. Urban location significantly boosts consumption for all groups. The high coefficient for once-married women is only statistically different from that estimated for ex-divorcees.

7.2.3. DIFFERENCES IN PREDICTED CONSUMPTION BY MARITAL STATUS

The results in estimating Equation (5) are given in panel 1 of Table 2.11, where consumption is evaluated for the mean attributes of MW, and for 10-year age ranges with the first cutoff at age forty, and urban and rural areas separately.

---

dissolutions is ever statistically significant and this is for widows (with 1.3 the average number of dissolutions) at the 5 per cent level ($\beta_W = -0.13$, t = 2.10), and for divorcees (1.4), $\beta_D = -0.15$, t = 1.7). As other coefficients also change when these covariates are included, predicted effects on consumption (see Section 7.2.3) are altered only slightly. We restrict the model to the same covariates across groups.

Table 2.11. Estimated log cell consumption per capita differences, evaluated at mean attributes for reference woman at different ages

	Age groups:	15–40	41–50	51–60	61 +
Panel 1	*Urban:* Remarried widow	11.774	11.874	12.133	12.302
	Widow	0.549**	0.536***	0.405**	0.347+
	Once married	0.783***	0.578***	0.429***	0.343
	Divorcee	0.527*	0.492**	0.349	0.338
	Remarried divorcee	0.405+	0.315	0.105	−0.364
	Rural: Remarried widow	11.416	11.516	11.775	11.944
	Widow	0.280	0.266+	0.135	0.077
	Once married	0.559***	0.354***	0.205+	0.119
	Divorcee	0.524***	0.489**	0.345+	0.334
	Remarried divorcee	0.541***	0.450**	0.240	−0.229
Panel 2	*Urban:* Widow	12.443	12.632	12.681	12.638
	Remarried widow	−0.766***	−0.544*	−0.409	−0.532**
	Once married	−0.029	0.091	0.011	−0.077
	Divorcee	−0.163	−0.027	−0.117	−0.246
	Remarried divorcee	−0.283	−0.388	−0.523*	−0.820**
	Rural: Widow	11.816	12.005	12.054	12.011
	Remarried widow	−0.497**	−0.275	−0.140	−0.262
	Once married	0.017	0.137	0.057	−0.031
	Divorcee	0.103	0.239	0.149	0.020
	Remarried divorcee	0.122	0.016	−0.118	−0.415
Panel 3	*Urban:* Once married	12.451	12.430	12.478	12.556
	Widow	−0.098	0.062	0.011	0.080
	Remarried widow	−0.806***	−0.489***	−0.376***	−0.259
	Divorcee	−0.361+	−0.250	−0.095	−0.087
	Remarried divorcee	−0.400**	−0.273	−0.311*	−0.474**
	Rural: Once married	11.869	11.848	11.896	11.974
	Widow	−0.144	0.017	−0.035	0.035
	Remarried widow	−0.582***	−0.265+	−0.152	−0.035
	Divorcee	−0.140	−0.030	0.125	0.133
	Remarried divorcee	−0.041	0.086	0.048	−0.115

Note: Women 15 and older. *** $p < 0.01$, ** $p < 0.05$, * $p < 0.1$, + $p < 0.12$. Significance tests refer to differences relative to the reference marital status estimated consumption. Consumptions are predicted using own parameters and mean attributes of the reference marital status group for the indicated age range.

Source: Authors' estimations using PSF1.

This gives a first insight into the question of how much worse- or better-off remarried widows would be if their marital status changed. The table's second and third panels do the same for widows and once-married women, respectively using the mean attributes of widows and of once-married women in the various age groups.

Consumption differences are substantial when evaluated for the mean characteristics of ex-widows. In both urban and rural areas, and for most ages, ex-widows tend to have the lowest average per capita consumption. The differences are largest and most significant at young ages and dissipate as women age due to a positive age effect on consumption for remarried widows. Rural widows are an exception, with insignificant differences at all ages. Urban remarried widows would have been better off in any other marital status and, in particular, had they remained husbandless. There are two potential explanations for such a result. On the one hand, it could be that remarried widows differ in some unobserved characteristics (potential support from kin network or personal savings, for example) such that they are relatively poor and cannot support themselves without a husband. This would be consistent with the fact that the results are in large part explained by the very low constant term in the consumption equation for ex-widows relative to any other groups. On the other hand, it could also be, as posited earlier, that remarriage itself is not really a favourable outcome. Widows who remarry may be constrained to do so for social reasons (especially in the case of levirate marriages) and may end-up marrying into relatively poor households or with a weak position within the household due to their marital trajectory.

Panel 2 shows consumption differences when characteristics are fixed at the mean for W but parameters are allowed to vary by marital status. In urban areas, widows would be worse off as MW or MD throughout the age distribution. W also fare better than MW in rural areas, although the difference is statistically significantly different from zero only for the youngest group. Widows in rural areas do not seem to fare substantially worse than other marital-status groups. Differences favour these other groups but hardly ever significantly so. In total, widows who didn't remarry seem to have chosen the best option given their characteristics.

Finally, panel 3 fixes characteristics at the mean for M women. In urban areas, once-married women would be worse-off with their own characteristics but the parameters of the other groups. This is particularly true for MW and MD, for whom the predicted changes in consumption are statistically significant. Rural M women would generally have lower consumption levels in any other status and significantly so as MW under forty. Generally speaking, women in their first marriage seem to benefit from this unbroken marital trajectory.

The same exercise can be done using divorcees as the reference group. Results (not shown) indicate that divorcees would not have fared very differently had they stayed in their first union. Conversely, once-married women fare better than if they had ever been divorced, hinting at the positive selection of women into divorce.

Comparing widows and remarried widows for a given age at dissolution suggests that, in urban areas and given their characteristics, widows fare better as widows than they would do as remarried widows whatever their age at widowhood. Here again it is also the case that remarried widows would fare better if not remarried, irrespective of age at dissolution. In rural areas, the difference in the predicted consumption of these women according to whether they remarried or not is never significantly different from zero. The same results are found if we examine duration since widowhood. After a divorce, whatever the age at divorce or the duration since divorce, women have the same consumption level given their characteristics whether they remarried or not.[24]

7.2.4. DISCUSSION

Differences reflect both the consequences of a given marital trajectory and the selection processes that push or pull women into those pathways. One interpretation of these findings consistent with what we know is as follows. Women who become widows and remarry often do so out of necessity, encompassing the two non-mutually exclusive burdens underlined in the conceptual framework: a lack of resources and strong social pressure. Such women would appear to consist on the one hand, of a group of poorer women with little fallback position in the event of their husband's death, and on the other, of women who, due to social pressure, are compelled to remarry, often within their late husband's lineage. Their vulnerability is not captured by commonly considered observables such as education, age, place of residence, and the type of job held by the deceased husband, as otherwise we would expect to find them better-off when remarried rather than not (contrary to results presented in Panel 1 of Table 2.11). Clearly, the unobserved characteristics by which they differ from those who do not remarry explain part of the consumption gap. Comparing them with once-married women (less likely to be selected than widows), it appears that for them there is a large economic loss associated with widowhood at all ages. Remarriage does not, however, compensate them fully for such loss. Widows, on the other hand, do not seem to incur an economic cost from their marital status, pointing to a potential positive selection for those who do not (choose to) remarry.

8. Conclusions

Marital upheaval is frequent in Senegal. Using data from the 2006 Poverty and Family Structure household survey, we estimate that anywhere between 18.5 per cent and 21.5 per cent of ever-married Senegalese women have experienced widowhood, while somewhere between 13.2 per cent and 17.3 per cent have experienced a divorce. Many go on to remarry, and 7 per cent of ever-married women have more than one union rupture. For women, discontinuous marital trajectories are associated with different consequences according to whether they ensue from divorce or widowhood.

---

[24] See Lambert et al. 2017, Table 9.

In general, we find that poorer women, as identified by lower education and the deceased husband's inferior sectors of employment, are more likely to become widows than better off women. When it comes to divorce, it is urban and more educated women who exhibit a higher probability. Poorer women among both the widowed and divorced are more likely to remarry often joining a polygamous union, and for widows, a levirate one.

Confirming descriptions for sub-Saharan African countries by sociologists, and in accordance with the fact that divorce may be chosen, our analysis suggests that divorce is a means for some women to escape family authority and gain a relatively comfortable autonomy; while widowhood is correlated with more negative consequences in terms of welfare. In fact, current divorcees enjoy a higher level of consumption than any of the other groups of women we consider. This may be related to formal education which clearly plays an important role for divorcees. First and foremost, divorcees are more likely to be educated women. Upon divorce, higher education is correlated with a lower likelihood of remarriage, probably because these women have the economic and social opportunities to enjoy autonomy while maintaining an adequate standard of living. For those who do remarry, education is associated with better quality unions in various dimensions: more civil marriage contracts, husbands with formal sector jobs, and a lower likelihood of a polygamous husband.

Although education is associated with a lower probability of widowhood, more education is not related to increased social mobility for widows (although when they remarry it is less likely to be in a levirate marriage and more likely to be with a man holding a formal sector job). This may be linked to the fact that widows observed in the sample are on average older and therefore less educated than the average divorcee, as well as to differences in ages at dissolution. Although education opens marriage market options for relatively young women, it may not do so for women who are beyond child-bearing age. Over all, widowhood appears to be accompanied by negative consequences that are not mitigated by remarriage. This ensues from a double negative selection: first, poorer women are more likely to experience widowhood. Second, it seems that the most vulnerable among widows are those who are compelled to remarry (rural ones) and, for the uneducated ones and those who have a son with the deceased husband, to enter a levirate marriage. Levirate marriages are associated with the lowest consumption levels. There are two competing interpretations for this finding. Levirate marriage may be the only option for very poor widows, and happens mainly in very poor lineages. Alternatively, such marriages may act like a poverty trap for those women who cannot afford to refuse it, either because of a lack of independent means or because it is the only way to remain with their children. Those who can afford not to remarry do so, and maintain a level of consumption comparable to that of women in their first marriage, and thereby gain autonomy. However, differences in observed characteristics between widows and remarried widows do not suffice to explain the consumption gap. Thus, a worry remains that the causality runs the other way around, with remarried widows becoming vulnerable because of remarriage: as social pressure to remarry pushes them to enter a union with a status that may well be worse than that of other married women. Inquiry into the direction of causality is beyond the scope of this chapter but is clearly of importance. If social pressure makes remarriage unavoidable for some women, even at a cost in living standards, the implementation of social transfers to widows together with changes in child custody practices aimed at establishing the preeminence of the rights of parents over those of the paternal lineage, could contribute to alleviate this plight.

The correlations and analysis presented in this chapter underscore the relevance of marital status to women's welfare and suggest lower levels of well-being and autonomy for women and particularly widows, who have remarried following a dissolution.

References

Antoine, Philippe and Fatou Binetou Dial (2003). 'Mariage, divorce et remariage à Dakar et Lomé.' Actes du colloque de l'AUF: Familles du Nord, familles du Sud, Marseille 23–26 juin.

Appleton, Simon (1996). 'Women-Headed Households and Household Welfare: An Empirical Deconstruction for Uganda.' World Development 24(12): 1811–27.

Bongaarts, John (2001). 'Household Size and Composition in the Developing World in the 1990s.' Population Studies 55(3): 263–79.

Bowen, John (2017). 'Gender, Islam and Law.' WIDER Working Paper 2017–152. Helsinki: UNU-WIDER.

Brossier, Marie (2004). 'Les débats sur le droit de la famille au Sénégal: Une mise en question des fondements de l'autorité légitime?' Politique Africaine 96: 78–98 DOI: 10.3917/polaf.096.0078.

Chapoto, Antony, T. S. Jayne, and Nicole Mason (2011). 'Widows' Land Security in the Era of HIV/AIDS: Panel Survey Evidence from Zambia.' Economic Development and Cultural Change 59(3): 511–47.

Cherchye, Laurens, Bram De Rock, Frederic Vermeulen, and Selma Walther (2016). 'Should I Stay or Should I Go: Marriage and Divorce in Malawi' mimeo.

De Vreyer, Philippe, Sylvie Lambert, Abla Safir, and Momar B. Sylla (2008). 'Pauvreté et structure familiale, pourquoi une nouvelle enquête?' Stateco, 102: 261–75.

Dial, Fatou B. (2008). Mariage et divorce à Dakar. Itinéraires féminins, Col: Hommes et Sociétés, Khatalas-Crepos.

Feinstein, Jonathan (1993). 'The Relationship between Socioeconomic Status and Health: A Review of the Literature.' *The Milbank Quarterly* 71(2): 279–322.

Hertrich, Véronique (1994). *Dynamique démographique et changements familiaux en milieu rural africain. Une étude chez les Bwa au Mali*, thèse de doctorat, Université de Paris 1.

Horrell, Sara and Pramila Krishnan (2007). 'Poverty and Productivity in Female-Headed Households in Zimbabwe'. *Journal of Development Studies* 43(8): 1351–80.

Hurd, Michael and David Wise (1989). 'The Wealth and Poverty of Widows: Assets Before and After the Husband's Death.' In David Wise (ed.) *The Economics of Aging*, University of Chicago Press.

Lambert, Sylvie and Pauline Rossi (2016). 'Sons as Widowhood Insurance: Evidence from Senegal', *Journal of Development Economics*, 120: 113–27.

Lambert, Sylvie and Dominique van de Walle (2012). 'Transcription des entretiens menés avec des veuves et des divorcées au Sénégal'. World Bank.

Lambert, Sylvie, Martin Ravallion, and Dominique van de Walle (2014). 'Intergenerational Mobility and Interpersonal Inequality in an African Economy'. *Journal of Development Economics* 110: 327–44.

Lambert, Sylvie, Dominique van de Walle, and Paola Villar (2017). 'Marital Trajectories, Women's Autonomy and Women's Wellbeing in Senegal'. *WIDER Working Paper Series*, 2017–124. Helsinki: UNU-WIDER.

Lefèvre, Cécile and Alexandra Filhon (ed.) (2005). *Histoires de familles, histoires familiales. Les résultats de l'enquête Famille de 1999*, INED, Collection: Cahiers, n° 156, 2005.

Locoh, Thérèse and Marie-Paule Thiriat (1995). 'Divorce et remariage des femmes en Afrique de l'ouest. Le cas du Togo' *Population*, 50e année, 1: 61–93.

Rivière, C. (1990). *Union et procréation en Afrique*. L'Harmattan, Paris.

Sevak, Purvi, David Weir, and Robert Willis (2003). 'The Economic Consequences of a Husband's Death: Evidence from the HRS and AHEAD.' *Social Security Bulletin* 65(3).

Smith, D.P., E. Carrasco, and P. McDonald (1984). *Marriage Dissolution and Remarriage*, ISI, WFS, Comparative Studies n°34, Voorburg, London.

van de Walle, Dominique (2013). 'Lasting Welfare Effects of Widowhood in Mali'. *World Development* 51, 1–19.

van de Walle, Etienne and Aliou Gaye (2006). 'Household Structure, Polygyny and Ethnicity in Senegambia: A Comparison of Census Methodologies.' In Etienne van de Walle (ed.) *African Households: Censuses and Surveys*, New York, M. E. Sharpe Inc.

Yade, Awa (2007). 'Stratégies matrimoniales au Sénégal sous la colonisation.' *Cahiers d'études africaines*, 187–8: 623–42, http://etudesafricaines.revues.org/8342

3

Making Marriages Last

Trust is Good, But Credible Information Is Better

Rebecca L. Thornton and Hans-Peter Kohler[1]

1. Introduction

Since the seminal article by Lucas and Prescott (1971), economists have examined investments under uncertainty in a variety of contexts. Becker et al. (1977) applied the idea to marriage and divorce, suggesting that an increased likelihood of separation or divorce reduces the incentive for spouses to invest in marriage-specific assets. This theory has since been tested empirically by measuring changes in investments in marriage-specific capital, such as a spouse's education, children, household specialization, and home ownership, after the adoption of unilateral divorce laws (Stevenson 2007). Uncertainty about the quality or integrity of the marriage can also affect investments in the relationship. For example, with greater uncertainty about paternity, men are less willing to invest in their (alleged) offspring and more likely to divorce (Alexander 1974; Anderson and Greene 2005).

Perhaps nowhere more than in sub-Saharan Africa do individuals face such high levels of risk and uncertainty within marriage. In particular, with high

[1] We thank Susan Godlonton for collaboration on the conceptual framework, analyses, and earlier drafts. We are also grateful for comments from Taryn Dinkelman, Arland Thornton, and reviewers at UNU-WIDER. We gratefully acknowledge the generous support for the Malawi Longitudinal Study of Families and Health (MLSFH) by the Rockefeller Foundation, the National Institute of Child Health and Human Development (NICHD, grant numbers R03 HD05 8976, R21 HD050653, R01 HD044228, R01 HD053781), the National Institute on Aging (NIA, grant number P30 AG12836), the Boettner Center for Pensions and Retirement Security at the University of Pennsylvania, and the NICHD Population Research Infrastructure Program (grant number R24 HD-044964), all at the University of Pennsylvania. We are also grateful for pilot funding received through the Penn Center for AIDS Research (CFAR), supported by NIAID AI 045008, and the Penn Institute on Aging.

rates of HIV, the evidence is that marriage and other long-term relationships do not necessarily provide protection against HIV infection. For example, the Demographic and Health Survey (DHS) across Africa found that at least 25 per cent of married men and 11 per cent of married women reported having sex with a non-spousal, non-cohabiting partner in the previous 12 months (Curtis and Sutherland 2004). Evidence suggests that sexual relationships in Africa often include long-term concurrent sexual partnerships involving high rates of coital risk exposures among secondary partners (Harrison and O'Sullivan 2010; Morris et al. 2010). Indeed, research has found that a woman's risk of infection is greatest when married (Bongaarts 2007; Clark et al. 2009; Glynn et al. 2003). Because of these patterns, some advocates speak publicly about the potential dangers of marriage. Stephen Lewis, UN Special Envoy for HIV/AIDS, remarked, 'One of the most dangerous environments for a woman in Africa is to be married' (Lewis 2005).

Marriage may also make it more difficult to use condoms or abstain from having sex, even when individuals believe that condoms can protect against HIV infection. It has been shown that it may be more difficult to adopt or suggest preventative behaviours with a spouse or primary partner (Chimbiri 2007).

In addition to the increased HIV risk associated with marriage, there is also a great deal of uncertainty related to this type of risk. Individuals lack perfect information about their spouse's HIV status and the risk they face from their spouse (e.g. current and future fidelity), and there is evidence of widespread mistrust of partners. In a survey of men in committed partnerships in urban Malawi, they were asked about their level of trust in their partner: a full 70 per cent suspected their partner of having another partner.[2] Another survey in Malawi, conducted in rural villages, found that 22 per cent of women reported knowing their spouse had another partner and another 34 per cent reported they suspected or did not know.[3] In high HIV-prevalence areas, most people know others who are currently infected or have died of HIV, and many worry or believe there is a chance of future HIV infection.

Despite the challenges of adopting preventative behaviours within marriage, there is evidence that individuals within committed relationships do have some strategies that can help to reduce their risk. For example, individuals may increase communication within their marriage or partnership (Zulu and Chepngeno 2003), engage with others in the community to acquire information about or monitor fidelity (Hirsch et al. 2007), or end the relationship (Reniers 2008). In this chapter we focus on one of these strategies:

---

[2] Authors' own calculations using data collected among 1,448 uncircumcised men in Lilongwe in 2009. See Chikhumba et al. (2014).

[3] Authors' own calculations using 2004 Malawi Longitudinal Study of Families and Health (MLSFH) data from 1,530 adult women in rural Malawi (Kohler et al. 2015).

dissolution of a marriage in response to resolving one component of the uncertainty within marriage—a spouse's HIV status.

Previous research on divorce as a coping strategy has shown an association between the dissolution of marriage and increased suspicion about a partner's fidelity or that a partner has been found to be HIV positive (Grinstead et al. 2001; Porter et al. 2004). Reniers (2008), using panel data in rural Malawi, found that being worried about HIV and suspicious about a spouse's infidelity were significantly associated with an increase in the likelihood of divorcing in subsequent survey waves. Smith and Watkins (2005) also found in rural Malawi that marriage was significantly associated with worry about HIV risk; moreover, women who suspected their husbands of infidelity were more than twice as likely to become more worried over time, and becoming more suspicious increased the likelihood of becoming more worried by approximately 70 per cent.

While the association between HIV risk and divorce is suggestive of a behavioural response to risk and uncertainty, a causal interpretation may be biased by unobserved characteristics of individuals or the relationship that are omitted from the analysis. This chapter, on the other hand, examines the causal impact of learning a spouse's HIV status. To do so, we compare marital outcomes of HIV-negative couples, some of whom were randomly assigned to be counselled and tested, and to learn their HIV results together (rather than individually). Couples who tested together learned their spouse's HIV (negative) results along with their own, perfectly informing them of the current risk of infection they faced in the marriage.

Our results suggest large effects of couples' HIV testing on marriage. Two years after the HIV testing, we find a 3.8 to 4.8 percentage point reduction (from a base of 7.7 per cent among couples offered individual testing) in the likelihood of divorce or separation among couples who learned their HIV-negative results together.

In contrast to counselling alone, there are several mechanisms through which couples' counselling could impact marital outcomes. First, because each member of the couple learns the other's HIV test results, this provides credible evidence of a spouse's HIV status. This information could provide some information regarding a spouse's faithfulness or infidelity, either confirming or rejecting prior beliefs, which in turn could reduce worry or anxiety about future HIV risk. This may directly improve the marriage or could reduce the need to dissolve the marriage to protect oneself from HIV. A second feature of couples' counselling is that it could provide a forum for increased communication between spouses about sex or HIV. The importance of spousal communication is often emphasized in family planning programmes, and there have been numerous cross-sectional randomized studies that show positive correlations between spousal communication and contraceptive use. Increased spousal communication may also be effective in providing information useful for evaluating one's own risk of infection (Gregson et al. 1998; Schatz 2005; Zulu and Chepngeno 2003). While our data is too limited to fully identify the exact mechanisms, we show that those who participated in couples' counselling were significantly less likely to be worried about getting HIV and less worried about their last HIV test.

While this study is the first, to our knowledge, to examine the causal effect of couples' HIV testing on divorce, there have been several similar randomized and non-randomized studies. Angelucci and Bennett (2017) use panel data of adolescent girls to study the impact of repeat HIV testing and find that increased testing increases the likelihood of marriage over almost three years. Another study in the United States examines the impact of couple-based risk reduction interventions that were randomly allocated among 535 African American HIV serodiscordant couples. One year later, condom use was significantly higher and the number of unprotected sexual acts was significantly lower among those who were randomized into the couples' intervention, but there was no impact on concurrency or sexually transmitted diseases (El-Bassel et al. 2010). Lastly, a study in Tanzania randomized women attending antenatal clinics into receiving either individual or couples' HIV counselling and testing. In this study, however, the participation rates of women receiving the couples' counselling were significantly lower than the individual treatment because the couples counselling required that the women return for a subsequent visit; this differential compliance complicates statistical inference (Becker et al. 2010).

2. Research Design

2.1. *Data and Experiment*

To study the impact of couples' HIV testing, we use data from the Malawi Longitudinal Study of Families and Health (MLSFH) (Kohler et al. 2015) and the Malawi Incentive Project (Kohler and Thornton 2012). The MLSFH is a longitudinal study of men and women in three districts of rural Malawi. The original respondents included ever-married women and their husbands who were randomly selected from around 125 villages in 1998 and re-interviewed in 2001. In 2004, an additional sample of randomly selected adolescents/young men and women (aged 14–24) from the same villages was added to the original sample. Each respondent and respondent's spouse were eligible to be (re)interviewed in 2006, 2008, and 2010. Survey attrition has been documented in the MLSFH cohort profile, and while attrition has been selective, as is expected in contexts where migration and mortality are key factors resulting in attrition, there is no evidence that selective attrition biases the estimates of key relationships related to marriage or HIV-related behaviours (Kohler et al. 2015). During the surveys in 2004, 2006, 2008, and 2010, respondents were offered free home-based HIV testing (Kohler et al. 2015).

In 2006, a sub-sample of couples and individuals were randomly selected, based in part on their HIV and marital status in 2004, to be a part of the Malawi Incentives Project (Kohler and Thornton 2012). The study included both unmarried individuals and married couples, as well as HIV-positive and HIV-negative respondents, who had previously been recruited for the MLSFH. The aim of this project was to investigate whether financial incentives for remaining HIV negative would affect individuals' HIV risk-taking behaviour and HIV incidence. Our earlier analyses found no evidence supporting this hypothesis (Kohler and Thornton 2012).

In this chapter, we utilize a different design aspect of the Malawi Incentives Project study for investigating the role of how credible information about the spouse can affect marriage outcomes and behaviours within marriage. Specifically, in response to stipulation during the human subject research approval process, the design of the Malawi Incentives Project study adopted couples' testing and counselling for obtaining and communicating HIV test results to married participants. As a result, couples who were selected in 2006 for the Malawi Incentive Project were offered 'couples' counselling' in which they would test and learn HIV results together, rather than being offered an individual, private, HIV test.[4] Only a random sub-set of MLSFH respondents were selected for the Malawi Incentive Project, and only married couples who were selected for this project were offered couples' counselling. Married couples not selected for the Malawi Incentive Project were offered individual HIV testing and counselling, in the same fashion as was offered to unmarried MLSFH respondents.

Our analyses exploit the fact that, in essence, the design of the 2006 MLSFH study for the Malawi Incentive Project created a random assignment to couples' counselling. Couples' HIV testing involved spouses receiving counselling together and learning both spouses' HIV results together. Only individuals who were married and whose spouses were available were given the chance to have couples' counselling. Both spouses were required to individually agree to the couples' counselling and testing. If one member of the couple did not agree to couples' counselling, then both members of the couple would test for HIV as an individual.

---

[4] Respondents in the Malawi Incentives Project were surveyed and tested four times over the next 12–15 months. At the end of the third visit, respondents were offered another HIV test either as a couple—if initially assigned to a couples' test—or as an individual. Those who were offered couples' counselling were also part of the Malawi Incentives Project that offered monetary incentives to remain HIV negative for one year. Our analysis evaluates the impact of both couples' counselling and being part of the incentives study. Kohler and Thornton (2012) find no impact of being offered incentives on sexual behaviour or HIV status.

Surveys and HIV testing were again conducted in 2008 as part of the MLSFH. We have several sets of outcome variables measured in 2008. First, we examine the effect of couples' counselling on divorce or separation approximately two years after the 2006 HIV testing. A detailed retrospective marital history surveyed in 2008 allows us to measure marital dissolution. We also use questions asked in 2008 about how worried individuals were about getting HIV, getting HIV from their spouse, and about having their most recent HIV test. Respondents were asked: 'How worried are you that you might catch HIV/AIDS?'; 'Women can become infected with HIV/AIDS in a number of ways. Out of the following list, which one are you most worried about for yourself?'; and 'How worried were you about your last HIV test result?'. For all respondents, the last HIV test refers to the one conducted in early 2008 as part of the Malawi Incentives Project.

2.2. Sample

Figure 3.1 presents information on the sample and randomization. The sample includes women who were married and were interviewed in both 2004 and 2006. In addition, we restrict the sample to couples who were HIV negative in both 2004 and 2006. Individual women (who were married) are our unit of analysis. In total, 326 women were assigned to couples' counselling (treatment) and 283 were assigned to individual counselling (control).

To be counselled as a couple, both spouses had to have been available to meet with the survey team and were required to individually agree to couples' counselling. Approximately 33.4 per cent of those offered couples' counselling actually counselled with their spouse. The reasons why the remaining individuals did not take part in couples' counselling were that they were not found/interviewed, refused to take part, their spouse was not found, or they were tested as an individual.[5]

We use the variables collected in the survey conducted in 2006, before the HIV testing, as baseline data. Table 3.1 presents some of the baseline summary statistics and tests for balance across a number of characteristics as well as for differential attrition with respect to these baseline variables.

The average age in the control group was just over forty years with an average of approximately 4.3 years of education. Because the survey was conducted in three different regions, the sample was ethnically and religiously diverse, with 18.7 per cent being Yao, 30.1 per cent Chewa, and 39.9 per cent Tumbuka. The majority, 64.9 per cent, were Christian. An additional 16 per cent of the respondents were Muslim. Respondents had been married for an average

---

[5] Five respondents had no information on how they tested in 2006. These were dropped from the analysis.

Enrolment	Assessed for eligibility (n = 1,781) MLSFH sample, women contacted in 2004	
	Excluded (n = 500)	
	2004 characteristics:	Not married (n = 497) No HIV test (n = 224) HIV + or indeterminate (n = 69) HIV + spouse (n = 29)
	2006 characteristics:	No survey outcome in 2006 (n = 165) Not married in 2006 (n = 33) No HIV test in 2006 (n = 42) HIV + or indeterminate (n = 31) HIV + spouse (n = 1)
Allocation	Randomized (n = 690)	
	Control (n = 316)	Couples (n = 374)
Follow-up	No survey outcome in 2008 (n = 33)	No survey outcome in 2008 (n = 43)
Analysis	Analytical sample (n = 283)	Analytical sample (n = 326) Unknown couple testing in 2006 (n = 5)

Figure 3.1. Sample (CONSORT flow diagram)
Source: Authors' calculations.

of seventeen years, with 95 per cent of spouses living in the same village. Around 23 per cent of the individuals reported that their spouses had another partner when they met—further corroboration of the high levels of uncertainty related to a spouse's fidelity. The vast majority (9 out of 10), however, reported discussing HIV at the beginning of their relationship. Almost 10 per cent believed that their spouse was HIV positive when they met, increasing to 46 per cent at the time of the survey. Almost 40 per cent believed that their spouse might have another sexual partner, and 44 per cent said that they worried most about getting HIV from their spouse. Approximately 86 per cent believed that they had some future likelihood of HIV infection, whereas 47 per cent believed they had the infection at the time of the interview. Many were worried about getting HIV (45.3 per cent).

Column 2 presents the difference in average characteristics between those randomly offered to test as a couple and those offered to test individually.

Table 3.1. Baseline summary statistics

	Control mean		Testing randomization		Testing attrition	
	Mean	SD	Coefficient on treatment	SE	Coefficient on 'Treatment* Variable'	SE
	(1)		(2)		(3)	
Demographics:						
Age	40.756	(11.172)	−0.038	(0.753)	0.000	(0.002)
Years of schooling	4.268	(3.368)	−11.020	(66.530)	0.003	(0.007)
Yao	0.187	(0.390)	0.035	(0.188)	−0.057	(0.067)
Chewa	0.301	(0.459)	0.003	(0.019)	0.041	(0.056)
Tumbuka	0.399	(0.490)	−0.034	(0.020)	0.048	(0.056)
Other tribe	0.114	(0.318)	0.034**	(0.016)	−0.072	(0.069)
Christian	0.649	(0.478)	−0.003	(0.025)	−0.012	(0.043)
Muslim	0.158	(0.366)	−0.043	(0.033)	−0.061	(0.059)
Marriage-related:						
Years of marriage	17.073	(10.036)	−0.716	(0.784)	0.001	(0.002)
Spouse had partner when met	0.234	(0.424)	−0.014	(0.033)	0.057	(0.067)
Talked about HIV when met	0.900	(0.300)	−0.022	(0.034)	−0.029	(0.068)
Likelihood of spouse HIV when met	0.097	(0.390)	0.007	(0.030)	−0.088	(0.067)
Likelihood of spouse HIV now	0.456	(0.792)	−0.072	(0.064)	0.032	(0.035)
Spouse has another partner now	0.389	(0.488)	−0.004	(0.039)	0.096**	(0.044)
Biggest worry for contracting HIV is spouse	0.438	(0.497)	0.018	(0.038)	0.047	(0.054)
Spouse stays in the same village	0.952	(0.213)	0.006	(0.014)	0.152	(0.108)
HIV/sexual behaviour-related:						
Number of sexual partners (12 months)	1.412	(1.366)	0.130	(0.177)	0.027***	(0.010)
Likelihood of HIV infection now	0.470	(0.783)	−0.013	(0.064)	0.038	(0.036)
Likelihood of HIV infection future	0.859	(0.941)	0.020	(0.074)	0.006	(0.028)
Worried about catching HIV	0.453	(0.499)	−0.011	(0.040)	−0.041	(0.050)
Ever used a condom	0.206	(0.405)	0.039	(0.030)	0.126*	(0.071)
	N=316					

Note: The total sample includes 690 women. Column 1 presents the average and standard deviation of each variable among those who tested as an individual in 2006 (N=316). Each row in column 2 presents estimates from separate regression of the 2006 baseline variable on an indicator of being assigned to couples' testing in 2006 and region dummies. Each row in column 3 presents estimates from separate regressions of having attrited in 2008 on the baseline variable, an indicator of being assigned to couples' testing in 2006, the interaction of couples' testing and the baseline variable, and region dummies. Robust standard errors clustered by village. * significant at 10%; ** significant at 5%; *** significant at 1%.

Source: Authors' calculations.

Each number in column 2 is the coefficient of a single regression of the baseline variable on an indicator of being assigned into couples' counselling and region fixed effects. Standard errors are clustered by village. Almost all of the variables are balanced across treatment (couples) and control (individual testing).

Overall, 90 per cent of those in the sample were interviewed in 2008. There is no significant difference overall across individual vs couples' testing (coefficient 0.017, p-value=0.533). Column 3 presents tests of differential attrition. Each row in column 3 presents estimates from separate regressions of having attrited in 2008 on the baseline variable, an indicator of being assigned to couples' testing in 2006, the interaction of couples' testing and the baseline variable, and region dummies. Robust standard errors are clustered by village. There is some differential attrition across baseline variables—in other words, those assigned to couples' testing with certain baseline characteristics are more likely to attrit. Those who were assigned to couples' testing who believed their spouse had another partner, who had ever used a condom, or who reported more sexual partners, were more likely to attrit. The analytical sample—women with complete survey data—consists of 609 married women.

3. Results

3.1. Empirical Strategy

To empirically measure the impact of couples' counselling and testing on marital outcomes, we use the fact that couples' counselling was randomly offered and estimate the following intention to treat estimate (ITT):

$$Y_i = \alpha + \beta_1 Assigned\ Couple_i + X_i'\gamma + \varepsilon_i,$$

where *Assigned Couple* indicates that individual *i* was offered the opportunity to learn their HIV results as a couple rather than as an individual. In some specifications we include a vector of baseline controls that include age, age-squared, years of education, ethnicity, religion, ever having used a condom, and region fixed effects—each measured in 2006. We cluster standard errors by village and run linear ordinary least squares (OLS) regressions.

The main empirical strategy compares the marital behaviour in 2008 of couples who were offered individual HIV testing with couples who were randomly offered couples' counselling. We present results from this comparison (the intention to treat estimates) and the treatment on the treated estimates using an instrumental variables strategy:

$$Y_i = \alpha + \hat{\beta}_1 Tested\ as\ Couple_i + X_i'\gamma + \varepsilon_i$$

where *Tested as Couple* is estimated by:

$$Tested\ as\ Couple_i = \alpha + \beta_1 Assigned\ Couple_i + X_i'\gamma + \varepsilon_i.$$

3.2. Results

Table 3.2 presents the main results of the impact of couples' counselling on marital dissolution. First, the average rate of separation among those in the control group was 7.7 per cent. Couples' counselling reduced the likelihood of

Table 3.2. Effect of couples' counselling on divorce

Dependent variable:	Dissolved marriage in 2007 or 2008			
	OLS		IV	
	(1)	(2)	(3)	(4)
Assigned to couples' testing (ITT)	−0.038*	−0.048**		
	[0.0208]	[0.0231]		
Tested as couple (TOT)			−0.113*	−0.137**
			[0.0626]	[0.0651]
Additional controls?	No	Yes	No	Yes
Observations	609	609	609	609
R-squared	0.007	0.038	–	0.008
Mean of dependent variable in control	0.077			

Note: Columns 1 and 2 present the OLS estimate of having a dissolved marriage between 2006 and 2008 on an indicator of being assigned to couples' testing in 2006. Columns 3 and 4 present IV regressions where receiving couples' testing is instrumented with having been assigned to couples' testing. Controls in columns 2 and 4 include age, age-squared, years of education, ethnicity, religion, ever used a condom, and region fixed effects—each measured in 2006. Robust standard errors clustered by village. * significant at 10%; ** significant at 5%; *** significant at 1%.

Source: Authors' calculations.

divorce and is statistically significant in all specifications (with and without controls, OLS, and instrumental variables (IV)). The OLS estimates range from reducing the likelihood of divorce from 3.8 to 4.8 percentage points, while the IV estimates suggest a reduction of 11.3 to 13.7 percentage points. The IV estimates rescale the OLS estimates by the percentage in the treatment group who actually received couples' counselling (33 per cent). Because the IV estimate is considerably larger than the average rate of divorce in the control group, our preferred specification is the treatment effect on the treated (TOT) (i.e. OLS).

How did couples' counselling reduce divorce? One possible mechanism is the reduction in uncertainty about the risk of infection within the marriage. We present results consistent with this, finding that couples' counselling significantly reduced reported worry about present and future risk of infection (Table 3.3). Respondents who tested as a couple were less worried about getting HIV (by 8.2 to 5.6 percentage points with the OLS estimates and 24.3 to 15.7 percentage points with the IV estimates) and less worried about their last HIV test (by 4.7 to 4.1 percentage points and 14.1 to 11.5 percentage points with the OLS and IV, respectively). There is no significant effect of believing that the main cause of worry over HIV infection is due to infection from a spouse.

4. Conclusion

Throughout the world, marriage is one of the most significant events in a person's life, forming legal, economic, and social ties between spouses and

Table 3.3. Effects of couples' counselling on HIV worries

Dependent variable	Very worried about catching HIV				Worried most about spouse				Worried about last HIV test			
	OLS		IV		OLS		IV		OLS		IV	
	(1)	(2)	(3)	(4)	(5)	(6)	(7)	(8)	(9)	(10)	(11)	(12)
Assigned to couples' testing (ITT)	-0.082** [0.0368]	-0.0557 [0.0378]			0.0324 [0.0422]	0.00729 [0.0421]			-0.047* [0.0272]	-0.0405 [0.0288]		
Tested as couple (TOT)			-0.243** [0.112]	-0.157 [0.110]			0.0956 [0.125]	0.0206 [0.119]			-0.141* [0.0811]	-0.115 [0.0805]
Additional controls?	No	Yes	No	Yes	No	Yes	No	Yes	No	Yes	No	Yes
Observations	586	586	586	586	585	585	585	585	558	558	558	558
R-squared	0.008	0.121	0.007	0.122	0.001	0.051	–	0.051	0.006	0.054	0.015	0.061
Mean of dep variable in control	0.319				0.338				0.129			

Notes: Columns 1, 2, 5, 6, 9, 10, 11, and 12 present the OLS estimate of the dependent variable on an indicator of being assigned to couples testing in 2006. Columns 3, 4, 7, 8, 11, and 12 are IV regressions where receiving couples' testing is instrumented with having been assigned to couples' testing. Controls include age, age-squared, years of education, ethnicity, religion, ever used a condom, and region fixed effects—each measured in 2006. Robust standard errors clustered by village. * significant at 10%; ** significant at 5%; *** significant at 1%.

Source: Authors' calculations.

their extended families. While the benefits of marriage include specialization, the provision of insurance, risk sharing, and economies of scale, marriage can also be associated with risk and uncertainty. In high HIV-prevalent areas, interactions between husbands and wives are among the most important behaviours affecting HIV risks, long-term survival, and family well-being. Yet, contrary to common perception, marriage does not necessarily protect against infection. Infidelity and distrust are widespread, and protecting oneself may be even more difficult within a committed relationship.

In Malawi, where marriage is nearly universal, divorce is common, remarriage is frequent, and individuals are well aware of the connections between marriage and HIV risk (Anglewicz and Reniers 2014; Reniers 2008). The MLSFH analyses have shown that marriage is perceived as a risk for HIV infection, especially for women, and suspicion that one's spouse is unfaithful is correlated with a spouse's HIV status (Anglewicz and Kohler 2009; Smith and Watkins 2005). In this setting, most women overestimate the probability that their spouse is infected and the likelihood that he has another partner. Without credible evidence of the true risk faced in marriage, this distrust may result in the dissolution of perfectly safe and healthy relationships.

Individual-based HIV testing is informative for one's own current HIV status, and can motivate preventative behaviour. For example, HIV-positive individuals who learned their status in 2004 are more likely to purchase condoms in the short run (Thornton 2008). They also reported having fewer partners in 2006 and having used condoms more often during 2004–06 than those who did not learn their status (Fedor et al. 2015).[6] Yet individual counselling and testing is unable to provide credible information about a spouse's HIV status.

In our context, HIV is transmitted primarily through sexual intercourse, where a partner's HIV status is difficult to verify. And, to learn about a spouse's status—and thus one's own future risk of infection—men and women cannot rely on their spouse to truthfully disclose their HIV results. Qualitative evidence suggests potential dishonesty between spouses when disclosing HIV results. Gipson et al. (2010) heard from one woman in a focus group about what she would do if she were found to be HIV positive during individual testing: 'There would be lies. We won't tell each other the truth. After testing, I would tell my husband that I'm negative even if it's not true. I would smile when he is around and cry when he is absent. I wouldn't like to disappoint him'.

In couples' counselling on the other hand, each member of the couple learns the other's HIV test results, providing credible evidence of a spouse's

---

[6] Learning the HIV status in 2004 did not seem to affect the chances of divorce for either HIV-negative or HIV-positive MLSFH respondents after 2004; it did, however, reduce the number of sexual partners among HIV-positive respondents, reduce fertility, and increase condom use with spouses for both HIV-negative and HIV-positive respondents.

HIV status. Still, no prior study, to our knowledge, has addressed the inherent information asymmetry in HIV testing and counselling.

Our findings support other research that Malawians are not passive with respect to the risks they face, or believe they face, including through their spouses (Kohler et al. 2015). Importantly, credible information about their spouses' HIV status, rather than beliefs alone, would enable women to more optimally respond to risks, which might imply investing more in current marriages—rather than pursuing marital dissolution—if beliefs about HIV risks through the spouse are biased upward.

While our findings underscore the role of credible information for decision-making within marriage, it is unclear if specific interventions can affect spousal interactions and the stability of marriages. The key finding of our analyses is that when couples are counselled and test for HIV together, two years later they are significantly more likely to still be married and are significantly less likely to be worried about HIV infection. Couples' counselling may have directly improved the marriage or could have increased spousal communication. Learning of a spouse's HIV (negative) status may have provided some information about a spouse's faithfulness, or may have served as a signalling device. For example, spouses who refused couples' counselling when offered may have signalled an unwillingness to communicate their status to their partner and a belief that the likelihood of HIV infection was high (and conversely for those who accepted the couples' counselling). Thus, some information may have been revealed even before learning a spouse's HIV status.

The expansion of self-testing is starting to change this lack of access to credible information about partners' HIV status, but these innovations in testing are only now beginning to roll out and were not available during our study period. Hence, in making decisions about partner selection, condom use, marriage, and divorce, individuals are generally uncertain about the HIV status of their partners/spouses, and, mostly, individuals have limited options for obtaining credible information about their partners' HIV status.

Couples' testing and counselling is one primary approach to address this issue, providing couples with credible and verifiable information about each other's HIV status. Our study is the first to document the causal effect of HIV couples' counselling on marital stability and perceptions affecting marital behaviour. The key finding of our analyses is that uncertainty about a spouse's HIV status, often coupled with an overestimation of the probability of the spouse being HIV positive, seems to be an important driver of marital dissolution in contexts such as Malawi. Moreover, our analyses suggest that interventions such as HIV couples' testing and counselling—and in the future possibly rapid self-testing—that reduce this uncertainty and provide spouses with access to credible information about each other's HIV status, can have profound impacts on marital behaviours and marital stability.

More generally, our analyses suggest that uncertainty about partner characteristics and partner quality can be an important consideration for how couples behave within marriage and the extent to which they seek marital dissolution to avoid adverse marital outcomes. HIV is a prime example as HIV status is a key partner characteristic affecting health and long-term well-being, and a marital solution is one of the primary mechanisms for reducing the risks of HIV infection through a partner who is HIV positive. Yet, in the absence of credible information about a partner's HIV status, perceptions about that status can be misleading, resulting in possible inefficiently high levels of divorce and marital dissolution. Our analyses suggest that giving access to credible information about partner characteristics, in our case through couple-based HIV testing and counselling, can be an important avenue for increasing the stability of marriages and, because of the negative consequences of divorce on child outcomes (Chae 2016), also for increasing child human capital.

References

Alexander, R.D. (1974). 'The Evolution of Social Behavior'. *Annual Review of Ecology and Systematics*, 5(1): 325–83.

Anderson, E.R., and S.M. Greene (2005). 'Transitions in Parental Repartnering after Divorce'. *Journal of Divorce and Remarriage*, 43: 47–62.

Angelucci, M., and D. Bennett (2017). 'The Marriage Market for Lemons: HIV Testing and Marriage Market in Rural Malawi'. Working Paper. http://dornsife.usc.edu/assets/sites/1018/docs/marriage.pdf (accessed on 2 October 2017).

Anglewicz, P., and H.-P. Kohler (2009). 'Overestimating HIV Infection: The Construction and Accuracy of Subjective Probabilities of HIV Infection in Rural Malawi'. *Demographic Research*, 20(6): 65–96.

Anglewicz, P., and G. Reniers (2014). 'HIV Status, Gender, and Marriage Dynamics among Adults in Rural Malawi'. *Studies in Family Planning*, 45(4): 415–28.

Becker, G.S., E.M. Landes, and R.T. Michael (1977). 'An Economic Analysis of Marital Instability'. *Journal of Political Economy*, 85(6): 1141–87.

Becker, S., R. Mlay, H.M. Schwandt, and E. Lyamuya (2010). 'Comparing Couples' and Individual Voluntary Counseling and Testing for HIV at Antenatal Clinics in Tanzania: A Randomized Trial'. *AIDS and Behavior*, 14(3): 558–66.

Bongaarts, J. (2007). 'Late Marriage and the HIV Epidemic in Sub-Saharan Africa'. *Population Studies*, 61(1): 73–83.

Chae, S. (2016). 'Divorce, Remarriage, and Children's Outcomes in Rural Malawi'. *Demography*, 53: 1743–70.

Chikhumba, J., S. Godlonton, and R. Thornton (2014). 'Demand for Medical Male Circumcision'. *American Economic Journal: Applied Economics*, 6(2): 152–77.

Chimbiri, A. (2007). 'The Condom is an "Intruder" in Marriage: Evidence from Rural Malawi'. *Social Science and Medicine*, 64(5): 1102–15.

Clark S, M. Poulin, and H.-P. Kohler (2009). 'Marital Aspirations, Sexual Behaviors, and HIV/AIDS in Rural Malawi'. *Journal of Marriage and the Family*, 71(2): 396–416.

Curtis, S.L., and E.G. Sutherland (2004). 'Measuring Sexual Behaviour in the Era of HIV/AIDS: The Experience of Demographic and Health Surveys and Similar Enquiries'. *Sexually Transmitted Infections*, 80(2): ii22–ii27.

El-Bassel, N., L. Gilbert, S. Witte, E. Wu, T. Hunt, and R.H. Remien (2010). 'Couple-based HIV Prevention in the United States: Advantages, Gaps, and Future Directions'. *JAIDS Journal of Acquired Immune Deficiency Syndromes*, 55: S98–S101.

Fedor, T., H.-P. Kohler, and J. Behrman (2015). 'The Impact of Married Individuals Learning HIV Status in Malawi: Divorce, Number of Sexual Partners, and Condom Use with Spouses'. *Demography*, 52(1): 259–80.

Gipson, J.D, C.J. Muntifering, F.K. Chauwa, F. Taulo, A.O. Tsui, and M.J. Hindin (2010). 'Assessing the Importance of Gender Roles in Couples' Home-Based Sexual Health Services in Malawi'. *African Journal of Reproductive Health*, 14(4): 63.

Glynn, J.R., M. Caraël, A. Buvé, R.M. Musonda, and M. Kahindo (2003). 'HIV Risk in Relation to Marriage in Areas with High Prevalence of HIV Infection'. *Journal of Acquired Immune Deficiency Syndromes*, 33: 526–35.

Gregson, S., T. Zhuwau, R.M. Anderson, and S.K. Chandiwana (1998). 'Is There Evidence for Behaviour Change in Response to AIDS in Rural Zimbabwe?'. *Social Science & Medicine*, 46(3): 321–30.

Grinstead, O.A., S.E. Gregorich, K.H. Choi, and T. Coates (2001). 'Positive and Negative Life Events after Counselling and Testing: The Voluntary HIV-1 Counselling and Testing Efficacy Study'. *AIDS*, 15(8): 1045–52.

Harrison, Abigail and Lucia F. O'Sullivan (2010). 'In the Absence of Marriage: Long-term Concurrent Partnerships, Pregnancy, and HIV Risk Dynamics among South African Young Adults'. *AIDS and Behavior*. Oct, 14(5): doi: 10.1007/s10461-010-9687-y.

Hirsch, J.S., S. Meneses, B. Thompson, M. Negroni, B. Pelcastre, and C. Del Rio (2007). 'The Inevitability of Infidelity: Sexual Reputation, Social Geographies, and Marital HIV Risk in Rural Mexico'. *American Journal of Public Health*, 97(6): 986–96.

Kohler, H.-P., and R. Thornton (2012). 'Conditional Cash Transfers and HIV/AIDS Prevention: Unconditionally Promising?'. *World Bank Economic Review*, 26: 165–90.

Kohler, H.-P., S.C. Watkins, J.R. Behrman, P. Anglewicz, I.V. Kohler, R.L. Thornton, J. Mkandawire, H. Honde, A. Hawara, B. Chilima, C. Bandawe, V. Mwapasa, P. Fleming, and L. Kalilani-Phiri (2015). 'Cohort Profile: the Malawi Longitudinal Study of Families and Health (MLSFH)'. *International Journal of Epidemiology*, 44(2): 394–404.

Lewis, S. (2005). 'Commencement Speech at Harvard School of Public Health Graduation'. [Transcription] Available at: http://allafrica.com/stories/200506150664.html (accessed 2 October 2017).

Lucas, R.E., Jr, and E.C. Prescott (1971). 'Investment under Uncertainty'. *Econometrica*, 39: 659–81.

Morris, M., H. Epstein, and M. Wawer (2010). 'Timing is Everything: International Variations in Historical Sexual Partnership Concurrency and HIV Partnership Concurrency and HIV Prevalence'. *Plos One*, 5(11): 1–8.

Porter, L., L. Hao, D. Bishai, D. Serwadda, M.J. Wawer, T. Lutalo, R. Gray, and the Rakai Project Team (2004). 'HIV Status and Union Dissolution in Sub-Saharan Africa: The Case of Rakai, Uganda'. *Demography*, 41(3): 465–82.

Reniers, G. (2008). 'Marital Strategies for Regulating Exposure to HIV'. *Demography*, 45(2): 417–38.

Schatz, E. (2005). ' "Take Your Mat and Go!": Rural Malawian Women's Strategies in the HIV/AIDS Era'. *Culture, Health & Sexuality*, 7(5): 479–92.

Smith, K.P., and S.C. Watkins (2005). 'Perceptions of Risk and Strategies for Prevention: Responses to HIV/AIDS in Rural Malawi'. *Social Science & Medicine*, 60: 649–60.

Stevenson, B. (2007). 'The Impact of Divorce Laws on Marriage-Specific Capital'. *Journal of Labor Economics*, 25: 75–94.

Thornton, R. (2008). 'The Demand for, and Impact of, Learning HIV Status'. *American Economic Review*, 98(5): 1829–63.

Zulu, E.M., and G. Chepngeno (2003). 'Spousal Communication and Management of HIV/AIDS Risk in Rural Malawi'. *Demographic Research*, S1: 247–78.

4

Intra-Household Bargaining in Poor Countries

Jean-Marie Baland and Roberta Ziparo

1. Introduction

The present survey assesses the relevance of the collective model for the analysis of households in poor countries. As an economic unit, a household creates the possibility of mutual gains for spouses thanks to the possibility of joint consumption of public goods, risk sharing, and the exploitation of comparative advantages through specialization. The collective model, developed initially by Chiappori (1988), assumes that households behave efficiently, in the sense that there is no misallocation or waste of household resources, given the outside options of each spouse. These exogenous outside options determine the bargaining power of each spouse, and the resulting sharing of resources between spouses. The efficiency requirement is based on the idea that spouses interact repeatedly, know each other well, and care about each other.

In this survey, we describe the key features of the collective model and assess their relevance for developing economies. We first describe the collective model and its main implications in Section 2. In Section 3, we explore the role of uncertainty and risk. Welfare gains are made possible through the joint management of risks within the household. However, repeated shocks and uncertainty make it harder to satisfy the conditions of the collective model, as they lead to commitment problems. Section 4 focuses on the bargaining process itself, and describes how power imbalances, high adult mortality rates, and the prevalence of early or arranged marriages all undermine efficiency. In Section 5, we argue that outside options, which play a crucial role in the bargaining outcome, are themselves endogenous. They follow from decisions made by the parents or the future spouse in terms of health, education, or occupation and are subject to strategic manipulations before or during marriages. We then discuss the role of informational asymmetries and strategic behaviour between spouses in Section 6, particularly when it comes to income, savings, or fertility decisions.

Finally, the prevailing norms and institutions around inheritance, divorce, and occupation are essential determinants of the outside options. We argue in Section 7 that, in poor societies, they typically lead to imbalanced outcomes and conflictual situations. We also assess the relevance of the collective model for alternative family arrangements such as polygamous or multi-generational households. To conclude, we propose some promising research avenues.

2. Efficiency in the Household: The Collective Model

The canonical model of collective household decisions was developed by Chiappori (1988, 1992) and Bourguignon et al. (1993).[1] It is based on the central assumption that household decisions are Pareto-efficient, in the sense that no other feasible choice would have been preferred by all household members. It also requires that the participation constraint of each spouse is satisfied, which implies that the utility of each spouse is greater than under their outside option. If efficient, household decisions can be described as resulting from the maximization of a simple weighted sum of the utilities of the two spouses. In its simplest formulation, a household chooses the amounts of private goods consumed by each spouse, $C1$ and $C2$, and the amount of public good, Q. An allocation is efficient if and only if it maximizes $U1(C1,Q)+(z)U2(C2,Q)$, under the usual budget constraint.

The key feature of the model is the Pareto weight $\mu(z)$, which measures the relative weight of spouse 2 with respect to spouse 1, and is a (unique) function of z, a vector which includes prices, household income, and the 'distribution factors' that are all the variables in the economic environment that do not affect the preferences or the budget but that influence the decision process, such as the relative income of each spouse, the legal environment, or the gender ratio in the population. The weight is a direct measure of the bargaining power of each spouse and is determined by the relative importance of their outside options. These outside options represent what each spouse would get if he or she were to exit the co-operative decision process. They determine the participation constraint of each member in the household.

The concept of distribution factors is specific to the collective household model (see Browning et al. 2014 for more detailed discussions) as it allows household decisions to vary with changes in the relative position of each spouse. This is the key difference from the predictions of the unitary model,

---

[1] Chiappori and Mazocco (2017) provide an exhaustive survey of the collective model literature.

which have been rejected by various tests (see for instance Thomas 1994 and Lundberg et al. 1997, for the US and the UK).[2] This is particularly true for the large literature on developing economies that shows that, for a given household income, a change in the relative income of one spouse affects the pattern of household expenditures or other household decisions (see e.g. Duflo 2003; Haddad and Hoddinot 1995; Thomas 1994). In the context of the collective model, this change is directly interpreted as a change in the outside option of the spouse, which directly affects his/her bargaining power, and therefore his/her Pareto weight. While the decisions described in these studies have sometimes been misinterpreted as a sign of inefficiency in the household (see Haddad et al. 1997), they simply indicate that the unitary model, which assumes that the household behaves as a single decision unit and therefore does not allow the Pareto weights to vary with changes in the environment, should be rejected. Relatedly, the fact that the outcomes of these decision processes can be very inequitably distributed between the spouses may be the consequence of the low Pareto weight of one of the two spouses, but is again perfectly compatible with efficiency.

In the simplified model presented above, efficiency is relevant because of the presence of a public good, which affects the utility of both spouses. In its absence, there would be no gains in the collective decision, and each spouse would spend his/her individual income on private consumption goods. The efficiency requirement can generally be applied to all *dimensions that involve mutual gains in the household*, the other externalities in the household, which include risk sharing, task specialization, and various coordination problems. The underlying idea is that, since household members have repeated interactions and a good knowledge of each other's preferences and resources, and care about their partner, one can reasonably expect that no surplus is wasted in the household. It should, however, be noted that the model does not provide an explicit mechanism that describes how decisions are made, or how efficiency is achieved. We return to this question in Section 4.

An important contribution of the collective model is that, with enough detailed observations such as the presence of assignable goods in the expenditures, it allows the estimation of the resource share, and therefore of the Pareto weight, of each spouse. It also provides testable implications for collective rationality, which allow for the assessment of its empirical relevance. The most direct test of collective rationality relies on the assumption that the distribution factors affect intra-household sharing only through the Pareto weights. (It implies in particular that the marginal rate of substitution between any two goods with respect to a change in distribution factors does not depend

---

[2] Under transferable utility, the logic of the Rotten Kid theorem applies and both models yield identical predictions.

on the distribution factor considered. Another type of test relies on restrictions imposed on the Slutzky matrix, but requires household panel data with observable price changes.)[3] Empirically, however, it is critical that the distribution factors are exogenous to the household, such as the random participation in a welfare programme, aggregate gender ratios, changes in divorce laws, or market wages. It may thus seem reassuring that the collective model's restrictions are usually not rejected in the literature (see for instance Attanasio and Lechene 2014; Bobonis 2009; Chiappori et al. 2002).[4]

To our knowledge, these latter works directly assess necessary but not sufficient conditions for the validity of the collective model. This implies that other decision-making processes, with inefficient outcomes, may fail to be rejected by these tests. In particular, it is perfectly possible that a non-cooperative decision process generates various inefficient allocations that are compatible, given other preferences and sharing rules, with the collective model. The discriminatory power of the testable restrictions of the collective model is clearly an open issue for future research.

This question is all the more serious as there is now a large body of evidence that shows, using alternative testing procedures, that household decisions in developing economies are often inefficient. In his well-known paper, Udry (1996) documents large productive inefficiencies due to the misallocation of labour in family farms in Burkina Faso. Output losses due to inefficient allocations within the household were found to be of the order of 5 per cent. The big strength of this test is that it relies on production inefficiencies, which are easier to characterize and measure in a satisfactory way than less quantifiable contributions to household public goods, such as quality time with the children.

Several papers confirm the pervasiveness of household inefficiencies in developing economies. Apart from the misallocation of productive inputs, the literature highlights systematic under-contribution to public goods through the use of experimental games between spouses. For instance, Hoel (2015) runs a series of lab-in-the-field experiments in Kenya and finds that close to 100 per cent of households do not maximize their gains in a simple public good game, with an average loss of about 16 per cent. Other forms of inefficiency involve imperfect risk sharing (Dercon and Krishnan 2000), strategic appropriation of resources (Anderson and Baland 2002), lying and hiding (Ashraf 2009), or the strategic use of violence (Bloch and Rao 2002).

---

[3] Donni and Chiappori (2011) discuss identification and provide an overview of the empirical applications of the non-unitary models.
[4] A more recent approach developed by Cherchye, De Rock, Vermeulen, and various co-authors relies on the imposition of the revealed preference axiom on observed choices, and estimates intervals of the sharing rules that are compatible with these decisions (see, in particular, Cherchye et al. 2015b).

This set of evidence is troubling and calls into question the relevance of the collective model for actual decision making in developing economies. In the remainder of this chapter, we discuss the various dimensions along which the collective model has to be extended to reflect more closely the actual context of these decisions, and to what extent these can be problematic in the context of a developing economy.

3. The Collective Model and the Role of Time and Uncertainty

The collective model naturally extends to a dynamic environment (Chiappori and Mazzocco 2017). In this new setting, spouses are assumed to commit, at the time of marriage, to all future allocations of their resources. Efficiency is achieved by maximizing the weighted sum of the lifetime utility of each spouse, using all the future values of the relevant variables. Lifetime Pareto weights are determined, and depend on the distribution factors at the time of marriage as well as their future realizations. As a result, future changes in the outside options of spouses do not lead spouses to renegotiate their relative position in the household since all future events are correctly anticipated at the start. The resource share of each spouse is therefore given initially and remains constant throughout.

The collective model can be similarly generalized to accommodate risk and uncertainty. Collective rationality here implies that spouses fully share risks and pool their individual resources so as to smooth shocks among the household's members. Larger gains are generated when the correlation of income realizations between the spouses is low. As in the dynamic version of the collective model, the sharing rule is fixed ex ante and is independent of particular income realizations. Given a total level of income, the amount of resources assigned to each spouse remains the same and does not depend on their relative income (the *mutuality principle*). Moreover, in the absence of public goods and for constant prices, the ratio of the marginal utilities of income between the spouses remains constant across all states (Browning et al. 2014).

The mutuality principle provides a direct test of full efficiency, even though such a test requires additional assumptions in order to compare household decisions under different levels of total income (such as constant absolute risk aversion or CARA, utility functions, and equal risk aversion among spouses). Almost all the tests carried out in the context of developing economies reject efficiency, over time and for all possible states of the world (see in particular Dercon and Krishnan 2000; Dubois and Ligon 2011; Duflo and Udry 2004). Recent experimental evidence supports these negative results. For instance, Robinson (2012) randomly assigns income shocks in different households in

Kenya and observes consumption variations that cannot be reconciled with a model of full risk sharing.[5]

The limited commitment hypothesis and the resulting deviations from the first-best have been tested on US data in contexts where divorce laws have been changed. It has been shown that intra-household allocations do react to exogenous changes in the outside options (Mazzocco 2007; Voena 2015). These findings suggest that the full commitment hypothesis, whereby each spouse ties himself or herself to an agreement that specifies a given sharing rule for all possible periods and states of the world, does not hold.[6]

An alternative, developed in Mazzocco (2007) and Voena (2015), is to allow for a limited commitment set-up, in which spouses renegotiate the intra-household allocations whenever the outside option of one of them becomes relatively more attractive than the current arrangement. With limited commitment constraints:

> the allocation is renegotiated to make the spouse with a binding participation constraint indifferent between the outside option and staying in the household. This goal is achieved by increasing the weight assigned to the preferences of the spouse with a binding participation constraint or equivalently her decision power. The couple then consumes and saves according to the new allocation until one of the participation constraints binds again and the process is repeated. All this implies that consumption and saving decisions at each point in time depend on the individual decision power prevailing in that period and on all the variables having an effect on it.   (Mazzocco 2007)

This limited commitment set-up allows for partial risk sharing and can be reconciled with a second-best efficient collective model.[7]

This modified version of the collective model implies that the Pareto weights of the spouses can change over time according to the various shocks that affect them. The resulting decisions are not first-best efficient over the whole time horizon, but remain (interim-)efficient between the renegotiations. This extension of the collective model closely parallels the literature on risk sharing in developing economies. The latter highlights the importance of limited commitment constraints in risk arrangements, which requires that

---

[5] These tests are not definitive, however, as their significance hinges upon the relevance of the assumptions they are based upon. In principle, these negative results can be reconciled with ex ante efficiency if one assumes, for instance, different risk preferences across household members.

[6] Note also that if agents could perfectly anticipate and insure against all possible events, including changes in their outside options, on anonymous markets with enforceable contracts, the collective model would hold, with constant resource shares and no renegotiations. There are evidently a large number of practical reasons for which such markets with external enforcement do not exist, but the empirical evidence described above also indirectly indicates that they do not.

[7] Note that this discussion also applies to a dynamic decision model with certainty, as the incentive compatibility constraint reduces the feasibility of the optimal sharing rule for some future periods and leads to the adoption of a second-best sequence of sharing rules.

future gains under the arrangement exceed the current cost of the income transfer. As discussed by Coate and Ravallion (1993), inter-household insurance is subject to an 'implementability constraint' which limits the amounts to be transferred. This constraint places a limit on the more fortunate party's liability in order to prevent him/her from reneging on his/her obligation through defection (see also Genicot and Ray 2003). Such constraints are also at play between spouses.

Thanks to the predominance of farming, self-employment, and informal sector occupations, individual incomes in developing countries are highly volatile, unpredictable, and subject to various health, weather, and macroeconomic shocks.[8] These shocks should lead to frequent renegotiations between spouses—all the more so if the shock has long-lasting effects on future outside options. This occurs, for instance, when income shocks are positively correlated across time, as a particular positive income realization increases the chances of positive realizations in the future, which in turn increase one's future outside options. The presence of poverty traps also makes renegotiations more likely, if a particular income realization allows one member to exit poverty. As stressed above, uncertainty matters insofar as appropriate commitment devices are missing. This is an issue to which we shall return in the following section. Clearly, in the extreme case in which spouses cannot commit, Pareto weights are revised whenever a change in their outside option occurs, whether correctly anticipated or not. (This situation has not yet been discussed in the literature.)

As a result, a reasonable collective model approach to household behaviour in a developing economy is to assume that renegotiations between spouses are frequent. The collective model holds within states, for limited periods of time, but not across states over longer time periods. Its empirical relevance is therefore questionable: all the more so as most of the interesting variations for development policy involve changes in the outside options of the spouses. Full risk sharing should essentially be viewed as a theoretical benchmark against which observed decisions have to be compared.

4. Commitment and Household Negotiations

The previous discussion highlighted the central importance of commitment in the collective model. However, the latter is essentially silent about the way

---

[8] There is a large literature illustrating the various strategies used by households to reduce co-movements of income or increase risk-sharing opportunities, such as the diversification in occupations, exogamy, migration (see Molina 2015 for evidence on migration and household insurance), polygamy (Fenske 2012), and the co-residence of extended families.

commitment is implemented and co-operation is achieved. Two classes of mechanisms can conceivably underlie the ability of each spouse to commit to a long-term sharing rule, and thereby sustain a co-operative outcome in the household. The first is the standard repeated games argument; the other is based on love and other-regarding behaviour within the household.

4.1. Repeated Interactions and Outside Options

The conditions under which repeated interactions can sustain a co-operative agreement are well known.[9] The latter requires a non-finite horizon, since the standard backward induction argument otherwise applies. The discount factors cannot be too low, so that the current evaluation of future pay-offs from co-operation is sufficiently attractive (Abreu 1988). The mechanism relies on the ability of agents to punish 'deviating' behaviour: this ability should be sufficient to induce co-operation (for some discussion and experimental evidence, see Anderson and Putterman 2006; Fehr and Gächter 2000; Boyd et al. 2010).

The household comes out as a natural environment within which these assumptions hold. The largest rational (i.e. sub-game perfect) punishment that can be imposed on the other spouse is often associated with the outside option. Two alternatives are proposed in the literature to define the latter. The first is divorce, by which each spouse compares his/her pay-offs in the marriage to those if he/she were to live alone or find a new partner, taking into account the direct costs associated with the separation.

The other alternative is to consider that, absent an agreement, both partners behave non-co-operatively while remaining as a couple. For instance, in the simple collective model of household decisions with public goods, the non-co-operative provision appears the most natural definition of the outside option, whereby the equilibrium allocations correspond to a Nash equilibrium.[10] Public goods are then typically under-provided, as each contributor does not internalize the marginal value of the goods to his partner.[11]

---

[9] The Folk theorem points to the possibility that the efficient equilibrium can be reached but does not exclude other, less efficient equilibria.

[10] As Browning (2000) points out, if spouses do not consume any private good, the household equilibrium is efficient even when spouses behave in a non-co-operative way.

[11] As long as both partners contribute to the public good in equilibrium, the neutrality result of Bergstrom et al. (1986) indicates that the total equilibrium amount of public good provided does not depend on the distribution of income between spouses (see also Lechene and Preston 2011). Income pooling occurs and, as a consequence, income shocks to one spouse are essentially mutualized and transmitted to the other spouse, who adjusts his/her own voluntary contribution. In this setting, the number of public goods consumed in the household is not relevant. Browning et al. (2010) show that, irrespective of the total number of public goods in the household, spouses simultaneously contribute to at most one of these goods and specialize in the household tasks they prefer. When market wages differ between spouses, intra-household

In the context of developing economies, various norms and constraints limit the capacity of a spouse to punish his/her partner, either because they reduce the value of his/her outside option, or because they limit his/her right to exercise it. For instance, many societies do not give women the right to divorce, their only option in terms of punishment being to adopt passive non-co-operative behaviour within the marriage (see Section 7 for further discussion).

Second, the prevalence of long term hazards (disease, conflict, epidemics, etc.) and low life expectancy in developing countries directly affects the time horizon of a married couple, and therefore its ability to punish, and to sustain the 'co-operative outcome'. Lower discount factors render the repeated games argument less relevant. For instance, adult mortality rates (probability of dying between the ages of 15 and 60) in Benin in 2014 were equal to 270 per 1000 for men and 223 per 1000 for women. This implies that a randomly matched couple in Benin has a 57 per cent chance of surviving as a couple till the age of 60. For India, the mortality rates are respectively 217 and 145, for Guatemala 236 and 129, and for Cote d'Ivoire 388 and 424, so that the corresponding probabilities of a couple surviving to 60 are respectively 67 per cent, 66 per cent, and 35 per cent (World Bank 2016). This probability is particularly low in the southern part of Africa, due to high adult mortality. The survival probability of a couple is about 31 per cent in South Africa and 17 per cent in Lesotho. For low-income countries in general, it is equal to 55 per cent. These figures suggest that punishment threats can be much less effective in developing countries.[12]

4.2. Other-Regarding Behaviour

Love, or other-regarding behaviour, should play a role in facilitating co-operation in the household, typically by increasing the size of the collective surplus under the collective model. This may not always be the case, as altruism can, under some circumstances, reduce the punishment capacity of one spouse and thereby undermine co-operation in the household. A possible (non-co-operative) mechanism is the Samaritan dilemma (Coate 1995): the more one spouse cares about the other, the more he/she will devote resources to the well-being of the partner, irrespective of the other's behaviour. Hwang

specialization also naturally emerges, even if both spouses share identical preferences (Doepke and Tertilt 2014). In this setting, the spouse with a lower wage specializes in the provision of the time-intensive public good, such as household chores.

[12] While accurate information is harder to collect, divorce rates are not small either, even in African countries, for which the current estimated divorce rate (after more than fifteen years of marriage) is about 25 per cent on average, and above 40 per cent in countries such as Gabon, Central African Republic, or Liberia (see Clark and Brauner-Otto 2015).

and Bowles (2012) explore such interactions between altruism and reciprocal motives, whereby one player positively values the other's pay-offs. They show that, by weakening the punishment motive, a general increase in the level of unconditional altruism may reduce rather than increase contributions. The implication for the collective model is that love, when not fully reciprocal, may sometimes make the co-operative outcome less sustainable.

In Baland and Ziparo (2017), we develop a new behavioural rationale for altruism or love to run counter to efficiency: because of empathy, the physical presence of the partner changes the level of altruism that one normally experiences. This may lead him/her to take decisions, in particular income transfers or irreversible expenditures, which he/she regrets afterwards or would not agree upon ex ante, and which are therefore time-inconsistent. Anticipating this, he/she may want to undertake precautionary actions through long-term savings plans or excessive current expenditures that would not be necessary with a constant level of altruism.

In the non-co-operative literature, altruism usually increases resource sharing and contributions to public goods, and reduces opportunistic behaviour in 'prisoner's dilemma' situations (see in particular Foster and Rosenzweig 2001, and the survey by Durlauf and Fafchamps 2005).[13] Cherchye et al. (2015a) similarly show that an increase in caring between spouses brings allocations closer to efficiency. Moreover, love is associated with other feelings such as guiltiness and betrayal. Even when decisions are not repeated, the incentives to free-ride are reduced because each spouse may be afraid of losing the love of a partner if the latter were to observe their non-co-operative deviation. Similarly, using psychological games, Geanakoplos et al. (1989) assume that spouses' pay-offs depend on the expectation the partner has about their actions. Because of guilt, pay-offs are lower when the actions taken differ from these expectations. Free-riding in the game is systematically reduced.

Even though this is admittedly a controversial issue and convincing evidence is harder to provide, the traditions of early marriage, arranged marriages, or forced marriages in the case of unplanned pregnancy are pervasive in some developing countries. Such practices should reduce other-regarding behaviour in the resulting couples. For instance, according to the UNICEF global database (UNICEF 2016), early marriage is pervasive throughout the developing world. The proportion of women getting married before eighteen is equal to 41 per cent in the least developed countries, and exceeds 50 per cent in South Asia and Sahelian Africa. Child marriage (marrying before fifteen) affects on average 13 per cent of females in the least developed countries and more than 15 per cent in countries such as India (18 per cent), Chad

---

[13] Under perfect altruism, both the non-co-operative and the collective models become indistinguishable from the unitary approach.

(29 per cent), Niger (28 per cent), Somalia (45 per cent), Nigeria (17 per cent), and Bangladesh (18 per cent).[14] This, as well as related traditions, affects not only altruism in the household but also the relative position of women in marriages, as well as the future education and human capital of their children.

4.3. *Bargaining Frictions*

Finally, the collective model also assumes away frictions in the bargaining process. However, a large amount of evidence about household conflict, marital violence, and female suicide suggests that agreements are costly to reach and brutal force can be exercised in the negotiation process. According to the Demographic and Health surveys (DHS Program n.d.), and in spite of the inherent problems associated with this type of measure, it was estimated in 2005 that 33.5 per cent of married women in India and 22 per cent in Nepal had experienced some form of domestic violence during their lifetime. The proportion of women reporting spousal physical or sexual violence over the past twelve months can be as high as 44 per cent in Rwanda or 37 per cent in Colombia.

This issue also affects developed economies. According to a large-scale survey carried out by the EU Agency for Fundamental Rights (FRA 2014), 22 per cent of women in a stable relationship in Europe reported partner abuse in 2012. A 2012 United Nations' report (Manjoo 2012) labelled domestic abuse in Italy the 'most pervasive form of violence' in the country, affecting over 30 per cent of Italian women. According to the National Intimate Partner and Sexual Violence Survey of 2010 (Black et al. 2011), 35.6 per cent of women and 28.5 per cent of men in the US have been victims of their partner's violence during their lifetime. From this evidence, we can infer that inefficient bargaining within households does take place and, while falling outside the collective model approach, is worth a more systematic analysis. Furthermore, these 'frictions' are apparently more prevalent in developing countries: the proportion of adult women who find it justified for a husband or partner to beat his wife exceeds 75 per cent in countries such as Guinea, Mali, and Somalia.[15]

A limited number of papers investigate the role of domestic violence in the household bargaining process, particularly when preferences are not known and households may have to devote resources to reaching an agreement. For instance, Bloch and Rao (2002) propose a model of domestic violence in which, because spouses do not know with certainty the preference of the

---

[14] This proportion has been measured on the current cohort of women aged between 20 and 24. The proportion is evidently much higher for older cohorts.
[15] Of course, wife-beating can be interpreted as a punishment strategy, and could thus fall under the purview of the collective model. There is, however, clear evidence of physical oppression which falls outside a smooth, fair, and efficient negotiation process.

other spouse, household bargaining is more complex and leads to conflict. Along the same lines, Anderson and Genicot (2015) provide a bargaining framework in which both spouses have private information about the value of the union to themselves. A change in the value of the outside option value, brought about by some legal reform, leads to renegotiation and bargaining within the household. However, because of the presence of private information, this bargaining process is costly, and leads to distrust and violence within the couple.

> Conflict is an integral part of the bargaining process. When an offer (regarding the division of resources) is rejected, conflict ensues. Threatening separation does create an atmosphere of discord within the household that comes at a cost, and separation cannot be achieved instantaneously. At any point, though, individuals may instead choose the ultimate exit and commit suicide.
>
> (Anderson and Genicot 2015: 2)

An empirical application to property reforms in India showed that suicide rates and domestic violence increased as a consequence of a land property reform in favour of women.[16]

5. Endogenous Outside Options

We now examine more carefully the determinants of the outside options. First, as argued above, they depend partly on previous household decisions, essentially when the latter are irreversible, such as fertility, specialization, choice of residence, or labour market decisions. These decisions may also reinforce gender roles and specialization in the household. As discussed in Chiappori and Mazzocco (2017), the fact that some decisions affect the future outside options of the spouses should not undermine the relevance of the collective model. As long as those decisions are taken co-operatively after the marriage, they should be efficient.[17] According to the collective model, irreversible changes in the outside options of one spouse should be fully compensated by appropriate transfers or consumption choices by the other spouse.[18]

---

[16] See also Angelucci (2008); Bhattacharyya et al. (2011); Bobonis et al. (2013); Pollak (2004).

[17] Note that irreversibility as such can also promote efficiency in a non-co-operative setting. In a recent paper, Battaglini et al. (2014) show that, when goods are durable and accumulate irreversibly, the Pareto-dominating Markov equilibrium converges to the efficient steady state as the agents' discount factor converges to one. When 'the discount factor is high and depreciation is low, all equilibrium steady states are close to efficient.'

[18] For instance, the spouse withdrawing from the labour market could be compensated by a legal agreement granting him/her a larger share of the household property in case of divorce (see, for instance, Browning et al. 2014). In a limited commitment set-up, Bayot and Voena (2015) show that prenuptial agreements can be used to increase welfare when one of the spouses may have to

This argument relies on the ability of each spouse to commit to a well-defined pattern of future allocations. However, these irreversible decisions also affect the spouses' capacity to punish, particularly when they do not affect them in a symmetric way.[19] For instance, if a spouse decides irreversibly to exit the labour market, he/she cannot use the threat of not sharing his/her income to punish non-co-operative behaviour.[20] Lower punishment capacities may induce the partner to renege on her/his promises of future transfers and compensations. As a result, the collective agreement may fail to be self-enforcing, in the absence of legally binding constraints.

In developing countries, very little research is being done on the implications of strategic behaviour during marriage for large irreversible decisions, such as child education, land accumulation, migration, or residential choice. In the context of fertility choices, Ashraf et al. (2014) experimentally vary the observability of women's contraceptive use and show how use among Zambian women increases when the husband cannot detect it.

Interestingly, many irreversible decisions are taken before marriage, such as education or early career choices. These choices determine the future outside options of the spouse and can be strategically manipulated in order to strengthen one's own bargaining position, once married. For instance, later marriages should be observed in economies in which divorce restrictions are relaxed, as future brides strive to accumulate enough assets before entering into a stable relationship (see Ziparo 2017 for an analysis of the impact of French marital laws on women's education). In Chile, Kaufmann et al. (2013) find that young women entering an elite education programme tend to marry more successful spouses, with various implications in terms of income and fertility.[21] In Indonesia and Zambia, Ashraf et al. (2016) show how female education is used by parents as a strategy to increase the bride price on the marriage market. Higher levels of education should therefore be viewed as the result of a strategic decision to strengthen one's position on the marriage market and in future household decisions.

Marital payments are also dependent on highly strategic decisions. Gaspart and Platteau (2010)[22] argue that parents set the bride price at not-too-high

---

undertake an action that reduces his/her outside option afterwards. In particular, these agreements are Pareto-improving in households where divorce is a plausible threat and the wife decides not to enter the labour market.

[19] As shown by Basu (2006), the interaction between current choices and bargaining power leads in general to multiple equilibria, some of which are sub-optimal.

[20] Del Boca and Flinn (2012) provide an insightful model of labour household decisions with varying degrees of (second-best) efficiency depending on the household capacity to sustain co-operation.

[21] Chiappori et al. (2009) theoretically describe how marriage-market considerations may affect human capital investment.

[22] A similar argument is made by Bloch and Rao (2002).

levels (lower than the marriage market-clearing prices) so as to avoid future harassment of their daughters by their husbands. In a recent paper, Anderson and Bidner (2015) show how these payments are manipulated by parents in order to strengthen the intra-household bargaining weight of their own children.

These examples suggest that most pre-marital decisions are fundamentally non-co-operative, even when the collective model describes correctly the decisions taken after marriage. The strategic nature of irreversible pre-marital decisions has not yet been fully explored by the literature.

6. The Role of Asymmetric Information

In risky and volatile environments, the observation of the income realization of others, including the spouse, is not frictionless, which naturally gives rise to asymmetric information problems.[23] In an experimental setting in the Philippines, Ashraf (2009) provides evidence that individual consumption is substantially affected by changes in the information given to one spouse about the other's individual savings account. These asymmetries allow spouses to manipulate their savings or finance hidden consumption. For instance, Boozer et al. (2009) analyse spousal cross-reports of food expenditure in Ghana and find evidence of hidden consumption unknown to the other spouse. Ziparo (2016) reports findings in Cameroon from separate interviews of each spouse about the income and expenditures of the other spouse. She shows that spouses systematically under-estimate the income of their partner by about 30 per cent, and interprets this finding as evidence of hidden behaviour. Recent field experiments on transnational migrants shows that they tend to send smaller remittances to their spouses when they can better hide their incomes (Ambler 2013), and that they tend to save more when they can better control the use of their savings in their home country (Ashraf et al. 2015). However, as yet there has been no systematic analysis of the prevalence of misinformation among spouses in developing economies, and some more evidence on this issue would be welcome.

A number of careful case studies document the various costly strategies used by the spouses to conceal their income or their savings from one another, or to force household decisions to their advantage. Anderson and Baland (2002), for instance, provide evidence of strategic savings in Kenyan households, pointing out that women's participation in saving groups (Roscas) did help them to protect their saving from immediate consumption by their partner.

---

[23] Informational asymmetries also tend to weaken the sustainability of the co-operative agreement. Punishment requires the detection of non-co-operative behaviours, which are harder to detect and process under such information incompleteness.

Household members are willing to invest resources to hide their own income or to acquire information about their spouse. Baland et al. (2011) describe how, in Cameroon, individuals take out formal loans to appear in need and thereby hide their own accumulated savings from their spouse and their families. De Laat (2014) finds that individuals in split migrant couples in Kenya are willing to expend considerable resources to acquire information about one another.

A number of field experiments support these observations. For instance, Jakiela and Ozier (2016), in an experimental setting in Kenya, show that women were ready to incur significant losses for their gains in an investment game to retain private information. A similar finding is made by Boltz et al. (2015), who randomly varied the presence of the partner in an investment experiment in Senegal.[24] Castilla and Walker (2012, 2013) provide a direct test of the collective model by investigating the impact of income observability on income pooling within the household. They carried out a field experiment in Ghana where spouses in rural villages were randomly allocated prizes, either in cash or in kind, with half of them awarded in the presence of the other spouse and the other half in private. They show that the pattern of expenditures by each spouse varied substantially according to the information treatment.

Finally, it is worth noting that, for information problems to arise, the observed behaviour of the spouse should not indirectly reveal information on income. This implies in particular that consumption or savings also remain partly hidden. Drawing from a case study in Cameroon, Ziparo (2016) investigates how resource transfers between spouses can be manipulated by the donating spouse so as not to reveal information on his or her actual income.

Another strand of the literature documents the importance of moral hazard in productive labour within the family, when labour efforts are not easily observable. Jones (1983, 1986) claims that, in African societies, women systematically exert effort on their own fields, at the expense of their husband's crops. Fafchamps (2001) justifies the allocation of exclusive plots to different members of the household in African villages on the basis of limited commitment and ex post moral hazard. When the household head cannot commit to directly remunerating his wife for her effort on the collective plot, he may choose to grant her exclusive rights on a particular plot as a substitute for a direct payment. On the basis of field observations, Guirkinger and Platteau (2015) also underline the major role played by moral hazard on collective fields to explain the structure of family farms in Mali. While the extended

---

[24] Similar behaviour is also observed with respect to the extended family. For instance, Hadness et al. (2013) investigate how the effort exerted by a small sample of tailors in Burkina Faso varied depending on whether knowledge of a lucrative contract was made public to their extended family network or not. Observability implies a significant reduction in productivity (see also Beekman et al. 2015).

family is their primary focus, their argument easily extends to moral hazard within the household (see also Guirkinger and Platteau 2016 for a recent overview). The efficiency losses accompanying these various arrangements suggest that informational asymmetries are of critical importance for the productive efficiency of the household.

These findings suggest that unilateral deviations from optimal sharing of household resources are widespread, even if they involve some costs and are therefore inefficient from the household point of view. They follow from the fact that, unlike in more regulated developed economies, individual incomes, savings, and private expenditures are not easily observed. For instance, an ILO study shows that, in 2000, over 60 per cent of all employed persons in Europe had remained in their jobs for more than five years, and over 40 per cent for more than ten years (Auer and Cazes 2003). In the US in 1987, characterized by a much more mobile labour market, the corresponding numbers were 39 and 21 per cent. In contrast, in Columbia in 1988, only 24 per cent of the wage employees in the private sector had had their jobs for more than five years, and 12 per cent for more than ten years (Schaffner 2001). These high levels of labour mobility in developing economies allow for imperfect information sharing and strategic communication between spouses.

Information problems can also concern the partner's preferences (present and future).[25] The prevalence of arranged or juvenile marriages makes this issue even more salient in various developing countries (see above).[26] This allows spouses to use various strategies to hide their true preferences and turn the collective decisions in their favour. Additionally, arranged marriages may create initial distrust between the spouses, which makes truthful revelation of one's preferences even more problematic.

Co-operative models, even when asymmetries of information are included, cannot explain why hiding or lying may arise.[27] The collective model can in principle be extended to allow information revelation between spouses. Since Pareto efficiency is defined as the absence of resource wasting, whenever resource pooling increases household surplus Pareto efficiency requires information sharing. With incomplete information, the collective model needs to be reformulated by adding the appropriate incentive compatibility constraints to ensure that, in all possible states of the world, the spouses truthfully report the correct information. Adding these constraints modifies the Pareto weights

[25] Note also that knowledge about one's own future preferences is also needed, which, though convenient, does not a priori seem the most attractive assumption.
[26] Even more problematic for the collective model is the possibility that household members do not correctly anticipate their welfare or preferences under the outside option, which, by assumption, they never experience.
[27] One possible exception arises when one of the spouses suffers from inconsistent preferences, and might prefer his/her partner to hide his/her own income to avoid short-run temptations.

in the maximization problem of the household, and yields a second-best efficient outcome. In particular, if individual incomes are imperfectly observed by the spouses, incentive compatibility requires that the sharing rule assign more resources to private consumption than to public goods (relative to the public information case) and that private consumption be more sensitive than the public good to particular income realizations. Intuitively, this reduces the incentive for the spouses to hide part of their income for their private consumption (Doepke and Tertilt 2016).

The existence of allocations satisfying constraints of incentive compatibility, participation, and budget balance is not guaranteed, in particular when incomes are highly volatile. When such allocations do not exist, it is a priori not entirely clear which model is the most appropriate, even though a fully non-co-operative approach appears the most plausible alternative.[28]

7. The Role of Norms and Traditions

In their seminal paper, Lundberg and Pollak (1993) develop the idea of separate spheres in the marriage, whereby social norms determine separate sets of goods—that is, the 'spheres'—to which each partner contributes on his/her own.

> Gender casting, for instance, is common in many societies whereby certain tasks are reserved for women while others are reserved for men. Social roles may also be assigned to children, or to daughters-in-law, etc. By making men and women complementary in the tasks reserved to them, societies may seek not only to reduce haggling but also to make men and women necessary to each other and thus to reduce the risk of divorce. (Fafchamps and Quisumbing 2007)

Attributing separate spheres to spouses in the household creates complementarities between them that facilitate co-operation and reduce the scope for marriage dissolution.[29] In a similar spirit, restrictive practices in religious and social groups have been shown to support co-operation by making interaction with external parties less attractive (Iannaccone 1992; Potomos and Truyts 2016).

---

[28] Truthful revelation can be achieved by a revelation mechanism à la Groves-Clarke which requires full commitment and is not budget-balanced.

[29] As argued by Francois (1998), even if both spouses have identical characteristics ex ante and there is no ex ante discrimination, norms of gender roles can spontaneously emerge as a result of market forces. In a model where some effort must be spent in household tasks, he shows that gender can be used by employers as an indicator of the expected amount of effort a worker will devote to his/her workplace. By allocating more effort in the household at the expense of the workplace, a spouse of a particular gender gets lower return on the labour market, and the market adjusts by systematically offering higher wages to workers of the other gender. The equilibrium is characterized by ex post gender discrimination, based on employers' expectations, which themselves result from decentralized decisions taken by the workers.

In patriarchal societies, social norms or legal constraints allocate most of the decision power in the husband's favour.[30] In such situations, the household can be viewed as a single economic agent, whose decisions are efficient. The unitary model applies, and the resulting distribution of resources in the household is highly unequal. However, it is not clear that, by drastically reducing the within-marriage utility of the wife, such norms will necessarily lead to an efficient and non-conflictual outcome. By being close to her reservation utility, the wife may be tempted to engage in non-co-operative behaviour during marriage, since she has very little to lose anyway.[31]

These unbalanced outcomes could in principle lead to more frequent divorces or separations, the other 'non-co-operative' option. It is, however, evident that it is precisely in these societies that access to divorce, or remarriage, is hardly an attractive option for women because of the legal restrictions and the social stigma they involve. Thus, the institution of the bride price is often re-interpreted as a tool limiting the outside option of women, as families are expected to reimburse the price in the case of divorce.[32] In the terms of the collective model, these constraints simply reduce the outside options of the wife, thereby reducing her share in the collective surplus. In this way, the unequal distribution of resources within marriages is simply the result of an unequal social or legal determination of the outside options.

Besides divorce laws, the norms defining inheritance practices, occupations, or land rights are particularly relevant, as they typically vary by gender. While these variations are usually to women's disadvantage, several reforms in favour of women's rights have been implemented recently, particularly with respect to inheritance law (e.g. in India in 1994, Benin in 2002, Ghana in 1985, Congo in 1987, etc.). These recent changes can in principle be used to identify the causal impact of discriminatory norms, as done by La Ferrara and Milazzo (2017).[33]

---

[30] Patriarchal societies are still a dominant feature of most developing countries today, not only in Africa and the Middle East but also in Asia and Latin America. Moreover, they have been a hallmark too of developed countries such as those of Western Europe, in their past and even most recent histories. Patriarchal norms and attitudes persist even in supposedly 'non-gendered' societies, such as the US. They result in higher divorce rates for couples in which the woman is the main income earner. They also lead to worse marriage prospects among highly educated women (Bertrand et al. 2015, 2016).

[31] Note that, if the head of the household is altruistic enough, the fact that the other members may behave non-co-operatively does not necessarily create inefficiencies, as follows from the Rotten Kid theorem.

[32] This is the case, for instance, among the Fang ethnic group in Equatorial Guinea, in which a woman is expected to return the goods initially paid to her family, and can be put in prison if she fails to do so. In Uganda, a recent controversy arose nationwide about the obligation put on women to reimburse their bride price in the case of divorce.

[33] According to La Ferrara and Milazzo (2017), the matrilinear Akan group in Ghana did not traditionally allow male descendants to inherit land. They show that, by exploiting a legal change that introduced minimum quotas of land for each descendant, Akan males were typically compensated by being more educated, as compared to males of other ethnic groups.

Interestingly, it is not always clear that legal reforms apparently favourable to women necessarily increase women's welfare, at least in the short run. For instance, the aforementioned paper by Anderson and Genicot (2015) precisely looks at the negative consequences for women of reforms to inheritance law in their favour. Moreover, such reforms take place in ambiguous legal environments characterized by legal pluralism, where rules derive from multiple and possibly conflictual sources (Platteau and Wahhaj 2014). The uncertainty thus generated clearly creates costs in household negotiations, as disagreeing spouses refer to conflicting rules to assess their positions (see, e.g., Lagoutte et al. 2014 for a detailed analysis of the interaction between divorce laws, traditional rules, and religious leaders in Africa).

It is likely that poverty exacerbates the impact of gender-biased norms and further deteriorates women's position in families. For instance, poverty is associated with early marriages (see e.g. Corno and Voena 2016;[34] Hoogeveen et al. 2003), with lasting consequences for women's welfare such as early pregnancy or school drop-out. While these decisions lead to imbalanced outcomes, they can still be conceived of as individually efficient, but it is not clear that they are socially efficient. First, it is not clear that poor parents who decide to marry their daughter too early correctly internalize its impact on her future bargaining position or on the total surplus that can be generated in the household. Also, it is not clear that the newly-weds correctly internalize the long-run consequences of early pregnancy for their children in terms of health or cognitive abilities.

Following Boserup (1970), economists have recently explored the idea that gender-based norms are determined by the material conditions of the environment. As argued by Mikkola (2005: 18):

> Dowries were typical for the Eurasian monogamous marriage systems, while bride-prices are practiced in Africa, where polygyny is permitted and practiced. An explanation for the differing practices is given from the relative scarcity of land and labour. In Africa labour was traditionally the scarce resource, and consequently women were valued for both their productive and reproductive capabilities. This may have led to the practice of bride-price. In Eurasia, where land was in short supply, women were primarily valued for their reproductive ability and a dowry system was common.

Along the same lines, Alesina et al. (2013) argue that agricultural societies that traditionally rely on human strength (typically ploughing) tend to assign more rights to men. As argued in the anthropological literature, dowry payments are also more likely.

---

[34] This finding is true for societies in which bride price is prevalent. Otherwise, in the presence of dowry, Corno et al. (2016) show that bad weather shocks increase the age at marriage of girls.

Finally, the collective model has been developed with the nuclear household as the basic unit of analysis. It is not clear to what extent it applies to an extended household, which is the basic social unit in many developing economies, because of either polygamy or sibling and inter-generational co-residence. For instance, according to the World Family Map (2015), the percentage of children living in extended families exceeds 50 per cent in countries such as India, Nicaragua, Columbia, Congo, South Africa, and Turkey. Extended families imply multiple decision makers with various outside options. In her well-known paper, Duflo (2003) illustrates the role grandparents can play in education decisions in South Africa. With respect to the collective model, this multiplicity raises several issues.

First, coordination may be harder to achieve among all members in the family. Thus, in allowing various coalitions to emerge, there may not exist an obvious co-operative solution and the core may be empty.[35] Moreover, punishment strategies may be harder to implement or less effective, as they may also hurt other members of the family. Extended families also tend to exacerbate information and monitoring problems, while they probably provide a better risk-pooling institution (for a recent analysis of these trade-offs in the context of collective farms in Mali, see Delpierre et al. 2012). Finally, altruism is typically not symmetric under polygamy or co-living arrangements with in-laws. For instance, Pitt et al. (2006) show how, in multi-generational households in Pakistan, the welfare and health of young mothers is negatively affected by their co-residence with their mother-in-law.[36] Relatedly, Grogan (2007) measures the positive impact on educational achievements of being part of a nuclear household compared to being part of a three-generational household in Tajikistan, suggesting a causal mechanism between patri-locality and poverty.

Among polygamous households, there is also some evidence of non-co-operative behaviour among co-wives when it comes to savings or fertility, even if they may co-operate in other spheres such as land cultivation or child-raising. Rossi (2016) describes how, in Senegal, co-wives compete in taking fertility decisions to attract their husband's favours (see also Lambert and Rossi 2016 for remarried divorcees). Relatedly, Boltz and Chort (2015) show how married wives who are under the risk of polygamy tend to accumulate private savings to foster their outside option, but also to reduce their husband's ability to choose a new wife.

---

[35] As a matter of fact, the collective model naturally focuses on allocations that survive unilateral deviations.

[36] The mechanism in this situation is based on the asymmetric allocation of household tasks, which involves severe exposure to indoor air pollution.

While the collective model can in principle be extended to accommodate several members, the arguments above call into question its relevance for extended households. In societies in which nuclear families do not prevail, the application of the collective model requires the definition of the pertinent observation unit, which is not obvious and restricts the external validity of the exercise and its relevance for policies. For instance, applying the collective model to 'well-defined' nuclear households in South Africa would reduce the number of family units concerned to about one-third of its current number, leaving out the vast majority of extended families or single parents.

8. Conclusions

The collective model provides a significant benchmark, with important implications for poverty measurement and the analysis of the impact on individual welfare of various changes in the economic or institutional environment. However, the empirical literature on intra-household decision making documents a large number of clear departures from first-best efficiency in household decisions in developing countries.

A first set of papers, mentioned in Section 3, provides evidence of limited commitment and partial risk sharing in the household in both developed and developing countries. These behaviours can be viewed as second-best efficient: spouses share resources on the basis of their outside option and their participation constraint. The inefficiencies in consumption documented in the literature fall into this category.

A second set of papers directly shows the existence of behaviours that are incompatible with efficiency: sub-optimal allocation of resources in production,[37] hiding and lying, moral hazard, and domestic violence. Those behaviours are mostly documented in developing countries, suggesting that the conditions necessary to sustain efficiency are harder to satisfy in this context.

As previously discussed, two mechanisms are at play in order to sustain a co-operative outcome in the household: repeated interactions with a punishment threat and other-regarding behaviour within the household. We argue that the ability to punish may be strongly restrained by a larger number of social norms that limit the scope of action of women inside and outside the household and by the limited rights women have in the case of divorce. Moreover, the prevalence of juvenile and arranged marriage, as well as the complex structure of the household in most developing countries, limits the existence of symmetric other-regarding preference.

---

[37] Production inefficiency could also be interpreted as compatible with second-best efficiency in the presence of market incompleteness and lack of recursiveness of production decisions.

Most of the existing theoretical works developed in alternative to the collective model, typically based on non-co-operative behaviour, develop limited approaches that focus on specific situations. In this respect, they fail to propose a general framework. One possible research avenue, theoretically explored for instance by d'Aspremont and Dos Santos Ferreira (2014), allows for different levels of co-operation across households and across decisions (see also Cherchye et al. 2015a). One can hypothesize that co-operation problems could be more acute among very poor agents, which makes the issue even more interesting for development economists. Empirically, a framework characterizing varying 'degrees of co-operation' across different households would be particularly appropriate. Even more interesting would be to relate these degrees to environmental factors and policy changes. This approach has, however, not yet been explored. Alternatively, one could extend the approaches developed in the economics of organization to household negotiations and interactions, for instance by using models of hierarchies and delegations.

Our survey also indicates a number of interesting issues that require a non-co-operative approach and have been overlooked by the literature so far. First, we need to better understand the ways in which irreversible long-term decisions are taken and outside options are determined, both strategically but also through social norms and institutions. Moreover, the mechanisms relating the latter to bargaining processes and outcomes need to be better investigated. Second, we still know relatively little about information sharing in the household, and the relative importance of the different strategies followed to hide income and expenditures. Third, the economic analysis of spousal violence in developing countries, and of its social and economic determinants, is yet to be developed in a systematic way. Finally, too little research is being done on the variety of alternative living arrangements. Of central interest, there is the question of household formation and household splits, given their implications in terms of fertility, child welfare, pressure on natural resources, and risk management.

References

Abreu, D. (1988). 'On the Theory of Infinitely Repeated Games with Discounting'. *Econometrica*, 56(2): 383–96.

Alesina, A., P. Giuliano, and N. Nunn (2013). 'On the Origins of Gender Roles: Women and the Plough'. *Quarterly Journal of Economics*, 128(2): 469–530.

Ambler, Kate (2013). 'Don't Tell On Me: Experimental Evidence of Asymmetric Information in Transnational Households'. *IFPRI discussion papers* 1312. Washington, DC: International Food Policy Research Institute (IFPRI).

Anderson, C., and L. Putterman (2006). 'Do Non-Strategic Sanctions Obey the Law of Demand? The Demand for Punishment in the Voluntary Contribution Mechanism'. *Games and Economic Behavior*, 54: 1–24.

Anderson, S., and J.-M. Baland (2002). 'The Economics of Roscas and Intrahousehold Resource Allocation'. *Quarterly Journal of Economics*, 117(3): 963–95.

Anderson, S., and C. Bidner (2015). 'Property Rights over Marital Transfers'. *Quarterly Journal of Economics*, 130(3): 421–84.

Anderson, S., and G. Genicot (2015). 'Suicide and Property Rights in India'. *Journal of Development Economics*, 114: 64–78.

Angelucci, M. (2008). 'Love on the Rocks: Domestic Violence and Alcohol Abuse in Rural Mexico'. *The BE Journal of Economic Analysis & Policy*, 8(1): 43.

Ashraf, N. (2009). 'Spousal Control and Intra-Household Decision Making: An Experiment in the Philippines'. *American Economic Review*, 99(4): 1245–77.

Ashraf, N., E. Field, and J. Lee (2014). 'Household Bargaining and Excess Fertility: An Experimental Study in Zambia'. *American Economic Review*, 104(7): 2210–37.

Ashraf, N., D. Aycinena, C. Martinez, and D. Yang (2015). 'Savings in Transnational Households: A Field Experiment Among Migrants from El Salvador'. *Review of Economics and Statistics*, 97(2): 332–51.

Ashraf, N., N. Bau, N. Nunn, and A. Voena (2016). 'Bride Price and Female Education'. Unpublished mimeo.

Attanasio, O., and V. Lechene (2014). 'Efficient Responses to Targeted Cash Transfers'. *Journal of Political Economy*, 122(1): 178–222.

Auer, P., and S. Cazes (eds) (2003). 'Employment Stability in an Age of Flexibility. Evidence from Industrialized Countries'. Geneva: International Labor Organization.

Baland, J-M., and R. Ziparo (2017). 'Hyperbolic Altruism and Long Run Savings in the Family'. Unpublished mimeo.

Baland, J.-M., C. Guirkinger, and C. Mali (2011). 'Pretending to be Poor: Borrowing to Escape Forced Solidarity in Cameroon'. *Economic Development and Cultural Change*, 60(1): 1–16.

Basu, K. (2006). 'Gender and Say: A Model of Household Behaviour with Endogenously Determined Balance of Power'. *The Economic Journal*, 116(511): 558–80.

Battaglini, M., S. Nunnari, and T. Palfray (2014). 'Dynamic Free-Riding with Irreversible Investment'. *American Economic Review*, 104(9): 2858–71.

Bayot, D., and A. Voena (2015). 'Prenuptial Contracts, Labor Supply and Household Investments'. Working Paper. Chicago: University of Chicago.

Beekman G., M. Gatto, and E. Nillesen (2015). 'Family Networks and Income Hiding: Evidence from Lab-in-the-Field Experiments in Rural Liberia'. *Journal of African Economies*, 24(3): 453–69.

Bergstrom, T., L. Blume, and H. Varian (1986). 'On the Private Provision of Public Goods'. *Journal of Public Economics*, 29(1): 25–49.

Bertrand, M., E. Kamenica, and J. Pan (2015). 'Gender Identity and Relative Income within Households'. *Quarterly Journal of Economics*, 130(2): 571–614.

Bertrand, M., P. Cortés, C. Olivetti, and J. Pan (2016). 'Social Norms, Labor Market Opportunities, and the Marriage Gap for Skilled Women'. Mimeo. Chicago: University of Chicago.

Bhattacharyya, M., A.S. Bedi, and A. Chhachhi (2011). 'Marital Violence and Women's Employment and Property Status: Evidence from North Indian Villages'. *World Development*, 39(9): 1676–89.

Black, M.C., K.C. Basile, M.J. Breiding, S.G. Smith, M.L. Walters, M.T. Merrick, J. Chen, and M.R. Stevens (2011). 'The National Intimate Partner and Sexual Violence Survey (NISVS): 2010 Summary Report'. Atlanta, GA: National Centre for Injury Prevention and Control, Centres for Disease Control and Prevention.

Bloch, F., and V. Rao (2002). 'Terror as a Bargaining Instrument: A Case Study of Dowry Violence in Rural India'. *American Economic Review*, 92: 1029–43.

Bobonis, G.J. (2009). 'Is the Allocation of Resources within the Household Efficient? New Evidence from a Randomized Experiment'. *Journal of Political Economy*, 117(3): 453–503.

Bobonis, G.J., M. González-Brenes, and R. Castro (2013). 'Public Transfers and Domestic Violence: The Roles of Private Information and Spousal Control'. *American Economic Journal: Economic Policy*, 5(1): 179–205.

Boltz, M., and I. Chort (2015). 'The Risk of Polygamy and Wives' Saving Behavior'. PSE Working Papers 2015–23. Paris: Paris School of Economics.

Boltz, M., K. Marazyan, and P. Villar (2015). 'Income Hiding and Informal Redistribution: A Lab-in-the-Field Experiment in Senegal'. Unpublished mimeo.

Boozer, M.A., M. Goldstein, and T. Suri (2009). 'Household Information: Implications for Poverty Measurement and Dynamics'. Unpublished mimeo.

Boserup, E. (1970). *Woman's Role in Economic Development*. London: George Allen and Unwin Ltd.

Bourguignon, F., M. Browning, P.-A., Chiappori, and V. Lechene (1993). 'Intra-Household Allocation of Consumption: A Model and Some Evidence from French Data'. *Annales d'économie et de statistique*, 29: 137–56.

Boyd, R., H. Gintis, and S. Bowles (2010). 'Coordinated Punishment of Defectors Sustains Cooperation and Can Proliferate when Rare'. *Science*, 328: 617–20.

Browning, M. (2000). 'The Saving Behaviour of a Two-Person Household'. *The Scandinavian Journal of Economics*, 102(2): 235–51.

Browning, M., P.-A. Chiappori, and V. Lechene (2010). 'Distributional Effects in Household Models: Separate Spheres and Income Pooling'. *Economic Journal*, 120(545): 786–99.

Browning, M., P-A. Chiappori, and Y. Weiss (2014). *Economics of the Family*. Cambridge: Cambridge University Press.

Castilla, C., and T. Walker (2012). 'Gender Roles and Intra-Household Allocation: Identifying Differences in the Incentives to Hide Money across Spouses in Ghana'. 2012 Annual Meeting. Seattle: Agricultural and Applied Economics Association.

Castilla, C., and T. Walker (2013). 'Is Ignorance Bliss? The Effect of Asymmetric Information between Spouses on Intra-Household Allocations'. *The American Economic Review*, 103(3): 263–68.

Cherchye, L, S. Coseart, T. Demuynck, and B. De Rock (2015a). 'Noncooperative Household Consumption with Caring'. *KU Leuven working paper* DPS15.29. Leuven: Katholieke Universiteit Leuven.

Cherchye, L., B. De Rock, A. Lewbel, and F. Vermeulen (2015b). 'Sharing Rule Identification for a General Collective Consumption Model'. *Econometrica*, 83: 2001–41.

Chiappori, P.-A. (1988). 'Rational Household Labor Supply'. *Econometrica*, 56(1): 63–90.

Chiappori, P.-A. (1992). 'Collective Labor Supply and Welfare'. *Journal of Political Economy*, 100(3): 437–67.

Chiappori, P.-A., and M. Mazzocco (2017). 'Static and Intertemporal Household Decisions'. *Journal of Economic Literature*, 55(3): 985–1045.

Chiappori, P.-A., B. Fortin, and G. Lacroix (2002). 'Marriage Market, Divorce Legislation, and Household Labor Supply'. *Journal of Political Economy*, 110(1): 37–72.

Chiappori, P.-A., M. Iyigun, and Y. Weiss (2009). 'Investment in Schooling and the Marriage Market'. *The American Economic Review*, 99(5): 1689–713.

Clark, S., and S. Brauner-Otto (2015). 'Divorce in Sub-Saharan Africa: Are Unions Becoming Less Stable?' *Population and Development Review*, 41(4): 583–605.

Coate, S. (1995). 'Altruism, the Samaritan's Dilemma, and Government Transfer Policy'. *The American Economic Review*, 85(1): 46–57.

Coate, S., and M. Ravallion (1993). 'Reciprocity without Commitment: Characterization and Performance of Informal Insurance Arrangements'. *Journal of Development Economics*, 40(1): 1–24.

Corno, L., N. Hildebrandt, and A. Voena (2016). 'Weather Shocks, Age of Marriage and the Direction of Marriage Payments'. Unpublished mimeo.

Corno, L., and A. Voena (2016). 'Selling Daughters: Age of Marriage, Income Shocks and Bride Price Tradition'. Unpublished mimeo.

d'Aspremont, C., and R. Dos Santos Ferreira (2014). 'Household Behavior and Individual Autonomy: An Extended Lindahl Mechanism'. *Economic Theory*, 55(3): 643–64.

de Laat, J. (2014). 'Household Allocations and Endogenous Information'. *Journal of Development Economics*, 106: 108–17.

Del Boca, D., and C. Flinn (2012). 'Endogenous Household Interaction'. *Journal of Econometrics*, 166(1): 49–65.

Delpierre, M., C. Guirkinger, and J.-P. Platteau (2012). 'Risk as Impediment to Privatization? The Role of Collective Fields in Extended Agricultural Households'. Working Paper 1211. Namur: Department of Economics, University of Namur.

Dercon, S., and P. Krishnan (2000). 'In Sickness and in Health: Risk Sharing Within Households in Rural Ethiopia'. *Journal of Political Economy*, 108(4): 688–72

DHS Program (Demographic and Health Surveys) (n.d.). 'Domestic Violence Module Country Reports'. Available at: https://dhsprogram.com/ (accessed 24 April 2017).

Doepke, M., and M. Tertilt (2014). 'Does Female Empowerment Promote Economic Development?' NBER working paper 19888. Cambridge, MA: National Bureau of Economic Research.

Doepke, M., and M. Tertilt (2016). 'Asymmetric Information in Couples'. Unpublished mimeo.

Donni, O., and P.-A. Chiappori. (2011). 'Nonunitary Models of Household Behavior: A Survey of the Literature'. In J.A. Molina (ed.), *Household Economic Behaviors*. New York: Springer New York.

Dubois, P., and E. Ligon (2011). 'Incentives and Nutrition for Rotten Kids: Intrahousehold Food Allocation in the Philippines'. *CUDARE Working Paper* 1114. Berkeley: University of California.

Duflo, E. (2003). 'Grandmothers and Granddaughters: Old-Age Pensions and Intrahousehold Allocation in South Africa'. *World Bank Economic Review*, 17(1): 1–25.

Duflo, E., and C. Udry (2004). 'Intrahousehold Resource Allocation in Cote d'Ivoire: Social Norms, Separate Accounts and Consumption Choices'. *NBER Working Paper* 10498. Cambridge, MA: National Bureau of Economic Research.

Durlauf, S., and M. Fafchamps (2005). 'Social Capital'. In Philippe Aghion and Steven Durlauf (eds). *Handbook of Economic Growth*, Vol. 1. Amsterdam: Elsevier North-Holland.

Fafchamps, M. (2001). 'Intrahousehold Access to Land and Sources of Inefficiency: Theory and Concepts'. In A. de Janvry, G. Gordillo, J.P. Platteau, and E. Sadoulet (eds). *Access to Land, Rural Poverty and Public Action*. Oxford: Oxford University Press.

Fafchamps, M., and A.R. Quisumbing (2007). 'Household Formation and Marriage Markets in Rural Areas'. In T. Schultz and J. Strauss (eds). *Handbook of Development Economics*, Vol. 4. Amsterdam: Elsevier North-Holland.

Fehr, E., and S. Gächter (2000). 'Cooperation and Punishment in Public Goods Experiments'. *American Economic Review*, 90(4): 980–94.

Fenske, J. (2012). 'African Polygyny: Past and Present'. *CSAE Working Paper* WPS/2012-20. Oxford: Centre for the Study of African Economies.

Foster, A., and M.R. Rosenzweig (2001). 'Imperfect Commitment, Altruism, and the Family: Evidence from Transfer Behavior in Low-Income Rural Areas'. *The Review of Economics and Statistics*, 83(3): 389–40.

FRA (European Union Agency for Fundamental Rights) (2014). 'Violence against Women: An EU-Wide Survey. Main Results'. Vienna: FRA.

François, P. (1998). 'Gender Discrimination without Gender Difference: Theory and Policy Responses'. *Journal of Public Economics*, 68(1): 1–32.

Gaspart F., and J.-P. Platteau (2010). 'Strategic Behavior and Marriage Payments: Theory and Evidence from Senegal'. *Economic Development and Cultural Change*, 59(1): 149–85.

Geanakoplos, J., D. Pearce, and E. Stacchetti (1989). 'Psychological Games and Sequential Rationality'. *Games and Economic Behavior*, 1(1): 60–79.

Genicot, G., and D. Ray (2003). 'Group Formation in Risk-Sharing Arrangements'. *The Review of Economic Studies*, 70(1): 87–113.

Grogan, L. (2007). 'Patrilocality and Human Capital Accumulation: Evidence from Central Asia'. *Economics of Transition*, 15: 685–705.

Guirkinger, C., and J.P. Platteau (2015). 'Transformation of the Family under Rising Land Pressure: A Theoretical Essay'. *Journal of Comparative Economics*, 43(1): 112–37.

Guirkinger, C., and J.P. Platteau (2016). 'Family Dynamics, Resource Endowments, and Market Development'. Unpublished mimeo.

Haddad L., and J. Hoddinot (1995). 'Does Female Income Share Influence Household Expenditures? Evidence from Cote d'Ivoire'. *Oxford Bulletin of Economics and Statistics*, 57(1): 77–96.

Haddad L., J. Hoddinot, and H. Alderman (eds) (1997). *Intrahousehold Resource Allocation in Developing Countries: Models, Methods, and Policy*. Baltimore, MD, and London: Johns Hopkins University Press.

Hadness, M., B. Vollan, and M. Kosfeld (2013). 'The Dark Side of Solidarity'. Washington, DC: World Bank.

Hoel, J. (2015). 'Heterogeneous Households: A Within-Subject Test of Asymmetric Information between Spouses in Kenya'. *Journal of Economic Behavior & Organization*, 118: 123–35.

Hoogeveen, J., B. Van der Klaauw, and A.G.C. Van Lomwel (2003). 'On the Timing of Marriage, Cattle and Weather Shocks in Rural Zimbabwe'. World Bank Policy Research Working Paper 3112. Washington, DC: World Bank.

Hwang, S.-H., and S. Bowles (2012). 'Is Altruism Bad for Cooperation?' *Journal of Economic Behavior & Organization*, 83(3): 330–41.

Iannaccone, L. (1992). 'Sacrifice and Stigma: Reducing Free-Riding in Cults, Communes, and Other Collectives'. *Journal of Political Economy*, 100(2): 271–91.

Jakiela, P., and O. Ozier (2016). 'Does Africa Need a Rotten Kin Theorem? Experimental Evidence from Village Economies'. *The Review of Economic Studies*, 83(1): 231–68.

Jones, C. (1983). 'The Mobilization of Women's Labor for Cash Crop Production: A Game Theoretic Approach'. *American Journal of Agricultural Economics*, 65(5): 1049–54.

Jones, C., (1986). 'Intra-Household Bargaining in Response to the Introduction of New Crops'. In J.L. Moock (ed.). *Understanding Africa's Rural Households and Farming Systems*, Boulder, CO: Westview Press.

Kaufmann K., M. Messner, and A. Solis (2013). 'Returns to Elite Higher Education in the Marriage Market: Evidence from Chile'. Working Paper 489. Milan: IGIER (Innocenzo Gasparini Institute for Economic Research), Bocconi University.

La Ferrara, E., and A.M. Milazzo (2017). 'Customary Norms, Inheritance and Human Capital. Evidence from a Reform of the Matrilineal System in Ghana'. *American Economic Journal: Applied Economics*, 9(4): 166–85.

Lagoutte, S. (ed.), A. Bengaly, B. Youra, and P.T. Fall (2014). *Dissolution of Marriage, Legal Pluralism and Women's Rights in Francophone West Africa*. Copenhagen: Danish Institute for Human Rights.

Lambert, S., and P. Rossi (2016). 'Sons as Widowhood Insurance: Evidence from Senegal'. *Journal of Development Economics*, 120: 113–27.

Lechene, V., and I. Preston (2011). 'Noncooperative Household Demand'. *Journal of Economic Theory*, 146(2): 504–27.

Lundberg, S., and R. Pollak (1993). 'Separate Spheres Bargaining and the Marriage Market'. *Journal of Political Economy*, 101(6): 988–1010.

Lundberg S., R. Pollak, and T.J. Wales (1997). 'Do Husbands and Wives Pool Their Resources? Evidence from the United Kingdom Child Benefit'. *Journal of Human Resources*, 32(3): 463–80.

Manjoo, R. (2012). 'Report of the Special Rapporteur on Violence against Women, Its Causes and Consequences. Mission to Italy'. Geneva: Human Rights Council, United Nations General Assembly.

Mazzocco, M. (2007). 'Household Intertemporal Behaviour: A Collective Characterization and a Test of Commitment'. *Review of Economic Studies*, 74(3): 857–95.

Mikkola, A. (2005). 'Role of Gender Equality in Development—A Literature Review'. HEER Discussion Paper 84. Helsinki: Helsinki Center of Economic Research.

Molina, T. (2015). 'Regional Migration, Insurance and Economic Shocks: Evidence from Nicaragua'. IZA Discussion Paper 9494. Bonn: Institute of Labor Economics.

Pitt, M.M., M.R. Rosenzweig, and Md. N. Hassan (2006). 'Sharing the Burden of Disease: Gender, the Household Division of Labor and the Health Effects of Indoor Air Pollution in Bangladesh and India'. Unpublished mimeo.

Platteau, J.-P., and Z. Wahhaj (2014). 'Strategic Interactions between Modern Law and Custom'. In V.A. Ginsburgh and D. Throsby (eds), *Handbook of the Economics of Art and Culture*. Oxford: Elsevier North-Holland.

Pollak, R. (2004). 'An Intergenerational Model of Domestic Violence'. *Journal of Population Economics*, 17(2): 311–26.

Potomos T., and Truyts T. (2016). 'Symbols and Cooperation'. Unpublished mimeo.

Robinson, J. (2012). 'Limited Insurance within the Household: Evidence from a Field Experiment in Kenya'. *American Economic Journal: Applied Economics*, 4(4): 140–64.

Rossi, P. (2016). 'Strategic Choices in Polygamous Households: Theory and Evidence from Senegal'. PSE Working Papers 2016–14. Paris: Paris School of Economics.

Schaffner, J.A. (2001). 'Job Stability in Developing and Developed Countries: Evidence from Colombia and the United States'. *Economic Development and Cultural Change*, 49(3): 511–36.

Thomas, D. (1994). 'Like Father, Like Son; Like Mother, Like Daughter: Parental Resources and Child Height'. *Journal of Human Resources*, 29(4): 950–88.

Udry, C. (1996). 'Gender, Agricultural Production and the Theory of the Household'. *The Journal of Political Economy*, 104(5): 1010–46.

UNICEF (2016). 'UNICEF Data: Monitoring the Situation of Women and Children. Child Marriage. Current Status + Progress'. Available at: https://data.unicef.org/topic/child-protection/child-marriage/ (accessed 24 April 2017).

Voena, A. (2015). 'Yours, Mine and Ours: Do Divorce Laws Affect the Intertemporal Behavior of Married Couples?' *American Economic Review*, 105(8): 2295–332.

World Bank (2016). 'The World Bank, Indicators, Mortality Rate, Adult'. Available at: http://data.worldbank.org/indicator/SP.DYN.AMRT.MA (accessed 24 April 2017).

World Family Map (2015). 'Mapping Family Change and Child Well-Being Outcomes'. Washington, DC: Child Trends. Available at: https://www.childtrends.org/wp-content/uploads/2015/09/2015-39WorldFamilyMap2015.pdf (accessed 24 April 2017).

Ziparo, R. (2016). 'Why Do Spouses Communicate: Love or Interest? A Model and Some Evidence from Cameroon'. Unpublished mimeo.

Ziparo, R. (2017). 'The Impact of Matrimonial Regimes on Female Education and Labour Supply: Theory and Evidence from a Natural Experiment in France'. Unpublished mimeo.

5

Forced Migration and Attitudes Towards Domestic Violence

Evidence from Turkey

Selim Gulesci

1. Introduction

Civil conflicts and wars have many dire consequences, including forcing people to flee their homes. By the end of 2014, 59.5 million people had been displaced due to conflict, persecution, or human rights violations (UNHCR 2015). Among them, a large share (38.2 million) were internally displaced persons (IDPs) who had moved away from their homes but remained in their country of citizenship. Although forced migration affects millions of people, its effects are relatively understudied (Ruiz and Vargas-Silva 2013). In particular, we know little about the effects of conflict-induced displacement on gender norms and attitudes.

In this chapter, I explore the long-term consequences of internal forced migration for women's attitudes towards domestic violence in Turkey. According to official figures, between 1984 and 1999 around one million people[1] were internally displaced due to the conflict between the Turkish state and the Kurdistan Workers' Party (PKK) (HÜNEE 2005). Many of the migrants were Kurdish, lived in rural areas, and had to move to urban centres in the region or in the western parts of the country. As of 2009, fewer than 20 per cent of IDPs had returned to their original residence (IDMC 2013).

Theoretically, forced migration may affect women's attitudes to domestic violence through a number of mechanisms. Household bargaining models

---

[1] Some NGOs have claimed that this is gravely under-reported, and that the true number of displaced people is as high as three million (IDMC 2013).

predict that a change in women's access to economic opportunities may affect domestic violence. Forced migrants may lack necessary skills or networks to obtain employment at their destination. If such resources are rarer for women or it is more important for them to gain access to economic opportunities in the urban sector, it is likely that forced migration from rural to urban areas will reduce their bargaining power in the household. In Turkey, employment opportunities for low-skilled women are rarer in the urban sector than in the rural, while for men the difference is not as large (Aran et al. 2009; Tunali 2003). Therefore forced rural-to-urban migration may have led to a fall in women's intra-household bargaining power, which may have increased the incidence and acceptability of domestic violence. Alternatively, being forced to move from rural to urban areas may forcibly expose migrants to different cultural norms. Traditional gender roles may come into conflict with the cultural norms at the destination, causing conflict within the household. Moreover, the psychological and social consequences of being forced to migrate may increase the incidence of domestic violence and affect attitudes towards it. Ultimately, whether forced migration affects domestic violence, and if so through what mechanisms, are empirical questions.

To examine whether women who were forced to migrate during the conflict have different attitudes towards domestic violence, I use two different data sources. First, I use the 2008 and 2013 waves of the Turkish Demographic and Health Survey (TDHS). These surveys were targeted at a representative sample of women[2] and collected information on their health outcomes and basic socio-economic characteristics. In addition, information was recorded on their attitudes towards domestic violence and their migration histories. This enables me to test whether women who migrated due to the conflict have different attitudes towards domestic violence. In particular, I estimate a triple-difference model, exploiting differences in ethnicity (Turkish vs Kurdish women), region of birth/childhood (the conflict region vs the rest of the country), and timing of migration (whether they migrated during the conflict period (1984–99) or not). I find that Kurdish women who migrated from their homes during the conflict are more likely to believe that a husband is justified in beating his wife in at least one of the scenarios they were asked about. Controlling for observable characteristics such as age, family background, parental education, and birthplace, I find that women who were forced to migrate are 16 percentage points more inclined to believe domestic violence is acceptable. Examining the possible mechanisms behind this effect, I find some evidence consistent with the bargaining power hypothesis: forced migration increased the likelihood that the respondent's husband was working while

---

[2] In the 2008 TDHS, only women who had been married at least once were surveyed, while in 2013 all women (regardless of marital status) were surveyed.

she was not. Moreover, spouses of migrant women were more likely to have tried to control their wives by, for example, limiting their movements or social interactions. This may be in line with the idea that forced migration threatens the traditional male gender role more than the female role, and causes conflict in the household.

As another, suggestive, piece of evidence, I use a novel database that was compiled by one of the largest NGOs working to support women affected by domestic violence in eastern Turkey.[3] The data contains information on all women who applied to the NGO for help in dealing with domestic violence between October 2009 and December 2011. In the sample, there are more than 2,278 Kurdish applicants who were subjected to physical or sexual intrafamily violence. Among them, about 15 per cent reported that they had been forced to migrate due to security concerns, and there is a robust relationship between being a forced migrant and the duration as well as the extent of the domestic violence they experienced before seeking help from the NGO. In particular, women who were forced migrants were more likely to report that the abusive relationship had been going on for more than ten years and that the abuse had started at the beginning of the relationship. They were also less likely to have sought legal aid or alternative help, to have been forced to have sex against their will, and to have had a miscarriage due to domestic violence.[4] These findings suggest that women who had been forced to migrate had suffered domestic violence for longer and possibly of greater severity before deciding to seek help from the NGO (and were no more likely to have sought help elsewhere).

Taken together, the findings from the TDHS and the applicants' data imply that forced migration ensuing from the Kurdish-Turkish conflict changed women's attitudes towards domestic violence, making them more tolerant of it. Further research is needed to fully understand the mechanisms driving the effects of forced migration on attitudes towards and the incidence of domestic violence.

2. Background

The forced migration studied in this chapter was caused by the conflict between Turkey and Kurdish insurgent groups, mainly the PKK. The PKK was founded in 1978 under the leadership of Abdullah Öcalan, and transformed

---

[3] Due to the sensitive nature of the data, and in order to protect the anonymity of the respondents, the name of the NGO cannot be revealed.

[4] These findings are robust to controls for age, housing conditions, education, age at marriage, whether the applicant was forced into marriage, and whether she had an independent source of income.

into a paramilitary group in 1984. They started a guerrilla war, benefiting from the difficult terrain in the region for cover. In the ensuing fighting, Turkey both used its army and recruited local Kurdish villagers to create a paramilitary organization named 'village guards' (Ozar et al. 2013). Between 1984 and the late 1990s, an estimated 40,000 people lost their lives, and many villages were evacuated and/or destroyed in the largely Kurdish eastern and south-eastern parts of the country (Beriker-Atiyas 1997). The intensity of the fighting diminished with the capture of Öcalan in 1999, and in September 1999 a ceasefire was declared. The focus of this chapter will be on the forced migrations that took place in this period. The fighting resumed after 2004, and continued with lower intensity than in the 1990s until its re-escalation in 2015.

During the height of the conflict, a state of emergency was declared by the Turkish state in eleven provinces in the east and south-east of the country. These provinces were Bingöl, Diyarbakır, Elazığ, Hakkari, Mardin, Siirt, Tunceli, and Van, and the neighbouring provinces of Adıyaman, Bitlis, and Muş. The state of emergency came to be known as OHAL (from *olağanüstü hal* (extraordinary state) in Turkish), and the region came to be known as the OHAL region. Most of the forced migration took place within this area as inhabitants of many rural settlements were evicted.[5] While most of the displaced were from rural areas, there was also forced migration from some towns (e.g., Lice, Kulp, Cizre, and Şırnak) to other urban areas, and the majority of the displaced population was Kurdish (Kurban et al. 2007). A report by the Turkish Parliament Investigation Commission in 1998 highlighted three main reasons for the displacement: (1) the collapse of agriculture and animal husbandry due to the clashes; (2) the PKK's eviction of villagers who were cooperating with the state (i.e. becoming village guards); (3) the eviction by the security forces of villagers who refused to become village guards. Many of the migrants settled in urban centres in the region and some moved to western parts of the country. As of 2009, fewer than 20 per cent of IDPs had returned to their original residence (IDMC 2013).

For a long time the number of people forced to migrate during the conflict was disputed. Official government reports put this number at around 300,000, while many NGOs claimed it was as high as three million (IDMC 2013). In 2005 the Turkish government commissioned a comprehensive study to estimate the correct number. According to this report (HÜNEE 2005), between 925,000 and 1.2 million people were internally displaced due to the conflict. The same study showed that forced migrants on average had low socio-economic

---

[5] Although it was never officially declared an OHAL province, a lot of forced migration also took place in the neighbouring province of Ağrı (HÜNEE 2005). I include Ağrı province in the OHAL region for the empirical analysis, but the results are robust to its exclusion.

status and low schooling, and the majority (94 per cent) of them were either not employed or working in the informal sector (i.e. in jobs with no social security).

3. Conceptual Framework

The forced migration that was caused by the Turkish-Kurdish conflict may have affected migrants' attitudes towards domestic violence through a number of mechanisms.

In theoretical models of household bargaining, spousal violence can be a means to increase the abuser's bargaining power. An improvement in women's access to economic opportunities (such as employment or earnings) may decrease or increase the incidence of domestic violence, depending on the initial allocation of bargaining power within the couple and whether the reservation utility of the woman or her spouse is binding (Anderson and Genicot 2015; Bloch and Rao 2002; Eswaran and Malhotra 2011; Tauchen et al. 1991). This implies that a change in the economic opportunities of women relative to their spouses is likely to affect the incidence of domestic violence. Empirical literature testing these predictions has studied how women's employment or earning opportunities can influence the incidence of domestic violence across a variety of settings (e.g. Aizer 2010; Alesina et al. 2016; Amaral et al. 2015; Andenberg et al. 2016; Angelucci 2008; Bobonis et al. 2013; Chin 2012; Heath 2014; Heise and Kotsadam 2015; Hidrobo and Fernald 2013; van den Berg and Tertilt 2015). Broadly speaking, the evidence suggests that an increase in women's bargaining power reduces domestic violence in high-income settings, while it leads to an increase in domestic violence in low-income settings. If forced migration affects women's access to economic opportunities (relative to men's), it may change the likelihood of domestic violence and conflict within the family, which may in turn affect attitudes towards it.[6] In the context of the Turkish-Kurdish conflict, the forced migration occurred in the poorest parts of the country, among households that had limited income and education.[7] Moreover, in Turkey, women with low education typically have fewer employment opportunities in the urban sector relative to the rural sector, while for men the reverse is true on average (Aran et al. 2009; cf. evidence presented in Table A4). Thus forced migration

[6] There is little evidence about the interconnection between the incidence of domestic violence and women's attitudes towards it. García-Moreno et al. (2005) show that the two are positively correlated. Using micro data from a variety of settings, they show that women who experienced domestic violence are more likely to find it acceptable.

[7] The literature on the effects of forced migration on the employment and earnings of the migrants is largely limited to refugees in developed countries (Cortes 2004; Khan 1997).

in Turkey may have reduced the economic opportunities of women relative to men.

Another mechanism through which forced migration may affect attitudes is the migrants' exposure to different cultural norms. In the Turkish context, many forced migrants had to move from rural to urban areas, which on average have more progressive gender norms.[8] This may have brought traditional gender norms into conflict with more modern norms. Threats to the traditional male gender role may have led to an increase in the incidence of domestic violence (Atkinson et al. 2005). On the other hand, if migrants over time adopt the norms of their destinations, they may have lower tolerance of domestic violence compared with individuals from similar ex ante backgrounds who were not forced to migrate.[9]

Another alternative mechanism might be related to the long-run psychological consequences of being exposed to conflict. In psychology, social cognition theories propose that exposure to community violence may culminate in the normalization of the use of aggressive behaviours (e.g., Fowler et al. 2009). In economics, empirical studies have demonstrated a positive association between exposure to conflict and individuals' propensity to commit violent or criminal acts later on (Couttenier et al. 2016; Miguel et al. 2011; Rohlfs 2010), and the long-run psychological consequences have been highlighted as one of the potential mechanisms behind such effects.[10]

Last but not least, forced migration may result in the breaking apart of existing social ties and the loss of social capital. Without the support of their family and friends, women may have difficulty in leaving abusive relationships, which may increase the incidence and acceptability of violence.

---

[8] Domestic violence is widespread in Turkey. In a nationally representative survey, 42 per cent of women reported being subject to violence (TRPM 2008). While this figure is likely to be underreported, it is already high enough to place Turkey among the set of countries with the highest rates of domestic violence (Devries et al. 2013; WHO 2013). In terms of cultural tolerance towards domestic violence, the TDHS data used in this chapter shows that 20 per cent of female respondents said it was acceptable for a husband to beat his wife in at least one of the situations they were asked about. The rate was nearly double among respondents who lived in rural areas (31 per cent) compared with those from cities or towns (16 per cent).

[9] A burgeoning literature studies how migrating to another country may influence cultural norms, both at the destination and in the source country (see Barsbai et al. (2017) for a recent review), yet evidence on how migration affects the norms and attitudes of the migrants is rare. This is partly because estimates of the impact of migration on the migrants' attitudes are likely to suffer from selection bias, as people who choose to migrate are likely to have different attitudes from those who stay behind. In the case of forced migration, entire communities are typically uprooted, in a way that is exogenous to their pre-existing cultural norms or attitudes.

[10] A number of recent papers have studied the effects of war on domestic violence, and have found that exposure to conflict may increase its incidence (Justino et al. 2015; La Mattina 2017; Noe and Rieckmann 2013). Calderon et al. (2011) show that in Colombia forced migration due to conflict led to higher labour force participation and earnings for women, but also to higher rates of domestic violence.

4. Data

The data used in this study comes from two sources: (1) the TDHS; (2) data on applicants to one of the largest NGOs in Turkey providing support for women affected by domestic violence (henceforth referred to as 'applicant data').

4.1. TDHS Data

I use data from the 2008 and 2013 waves of the TDHS. In the 2008 wave, a representative sample of women aged 15–50 who had been married at least once was surveyed. In TDHS 2013, all women were sampled, regardless of their marriage history.[11] In addition to the respondents' basic demographic and socio-economic characteristics, the surveys collected information on their migration history and domestic violence attitudes. For migration, respondents were asked to report their birth province, the place where they had grown up (their main residence until age 12), and every location they had lived in for at least six months after the age of 12. If they had moved from one place to another, the timing of migration was recorded. On the basis of this information one can identify whether a respondent is from an OHAL province and if she migrated from there (or within the province from one location to another) during the conflict years (1984–99). Of the 16,216 women in the data, 2,860 were born and/or grew up in one of the OHAL provinces. Among them, 752 migrated from an OHAL province during the conflict period, and 2,108 did not. Respondents were asked to report whether they thought that a husband was justified in beating his wife if she (1) neglected their children's needs, (2) argued with her husband, (3) refused to have sex with him, (4) burned the food, (5) wasted money, (6) did not cook, or (7) neglected household chores.[12] On the basis of these, I define three summary indices: first, a dummy variable equal to one if the respondent thought it was acceptable for a husband to beat his wife in any one of these scenarios; second, the fraction of cases in which the respondent thought domestic violence was justified; and third, the first principal component of responses to the individual scenarios. On average, 20 per cent of respondents thought men were justified in beating their wives in at least one of the scenarios. For detailed descriptive statistics on these and background characteristics of the respondents, see Gulesci (2017: Table 1).

---

[11] In order to ensure that differences in sampling do not drive the estimates, I control for survey wave fixed effects throughout the empirical analysis.

[12] The last two scenarios were included in the 2008 TDHS but not in the 2013 TDHS. When constructing the aggregate indices, I use all available information within each survey wave. Restricting the analysis to the first five scenarios alone does not change the results qualitatively.

4.2. *Applicant Data*

The second data set was collected by one of the main NGOs offering support to women who are victims of violence in eastern and south-eastern Turkey—the provinces affected by the conflict. Depending on their needs, the NGO may offer the women legal, medical, psychological, or economic (e.g. in finding a job) assistance, as well as a chance to meet and forge bonds with other women who have been victims of violence.[13] The data contains information on all women who applied to the NGO for assistance between October 2009 and December 2011. Upon application (prior to receiving any support from the NGO) they were asked to complete a brief questionnaire about why they were applying, what type of abuse they had faced, and some information on their background (e.g., their age, education level, and work status). Importantly for the analysis, the survey contained questions on the applicant's migration status, which enables me to identify whether the applicant was forced to migrate due to the conflict.

I limit the sample to women who applied to the NGO seeking help because they were subject to physical or sexual domestic (intrahousehold) violence. This is clearly a selected sample. It only contains women who chose to report and seek help for any violence they experienced. I use this data to provide suggestive evidence about forced migrants' attitudes towards domestic violence relative to other applicants. In particular, I test whether forced migrants endured more domestic violence, in terms of duration or severity, before deciding to seek help. There are 3,582 cases in total of women who applied to the NGO to seek assistance in dealing with physical or sexual domestic violence. Of these, 2,278 were Kurdish and 349 had been forced to migrate.[14] The average woman in the sample is 37 years old, but there is a lot of age variation among them (the youngest applicant in the sample is 15, and the oldest 80 years old). I study the correlation between being a forced migrant and indicators of the duration and extent of the domestic violence experienced by the applicants, and any assistance they may have sought prior to their application to the NGO. For detailed descriptive statistics on this dataset, see Gulesci (2017: Table 2).

---

[13] The data was collected upon application, prior to any action taken by the NGO.

[14] The survey contained two questions on migration: whether it had taken place due to security concerns, and whether it had happened recently or more than ten years ago. Since the conflict in question took place between 1984 and 1999, and the data was collected between 2009 and 2011, I define anyone who reported having moved due to security concerns more than ten years before the interview as a forced migrant. While the label 'security concern' may seem general, discussions with the NGO workers who recorded the data suggest that this label was applied to identify forced migrants due to civil conflict as opposed to any other type of security concern.

5. Results

5.1. Identification

To identify the effects of forced migration on women's attitudes towards domestic violence in the TDHS, I estimate the following model:

$$y_{ipt} = a + \gamma K_i + \delta C_p + \vartheta M_{it} + \rho K_i C_p + \sigma K_i M_{it} + \tau C_p M_{it} + \lambda K_i C_p M_{it}$$
$$+ \beta' X_i + \theta_p + S_t + \varepsilon_{ipt} \tag{1}$$

where y_{ipt} is the domestic violence attitude of respondent i from province p whose migration status was revealed in period t; K_i and C_p are dummy variables for whether respondent i is Kurdish and from a conflict province respectively; M_{it} is a dummy variable if respondent i migrated during the conflict period (1984–99); X_i is a matrix of control variables;[15] θ_p and S_t are province of birth and survey wave fixed effects respectively. Standard errors are clustered by birth province to account for the fact that women born in the same province will have correlated outcomes. The parameter of interest is λ, which gives the triple difference between women from the conflict region (vs the rest of the country), who migrated during the conflict period (vs did not migrate in this period), who are Kurdish (vs Turkish). The key identifying assumption is that, conditional on the control variables, this triple difference should pick up the effect of being forced to migrate because of the conflict. On the basis of the discussion of the historical and political context in Section 2, it is reasonable to assume that Kurdish women who moved from the conflict provinces during this period were most likely forced to do so because of the conflict.

In the applicant data, I estimate:

$$y_{ip} = a + \sigma F_i + \beta' X_i + \theta_p + \varepsilon_{ipt} \tag{2}$$

where y_{ip} is the outcome of interest for applicant i from province p; F_i is a dummy variable equal to one if the respondent is a forced migrant; X_i is a vector of demographic and socio-economic controls;[16] and θ_p is the province of application fixed effects. Standard errors are clustered by province. The parameter of interest is σ, the difference between forced migrants and the rest of the applicants, controlling for other observable characteristics (including whether the respondent is a migrant in general).

---

[15] The control variables are the age of the respondent, age-squared, respondent's mother's and father's educational levels, and a dummy for whether the respondent's parents were related.

[16] In the baseline specification, the following control variables are included: age of the respondent, age-squared, and whether she is a migrant (forced or otherwise). In a second specification, I also control for whether the respondent has an independent source of income, the number of members living in the respondent's household, and dummy variables for whether the respondent is literate, lives in a *gecekondu* (a makeshift dwelling put up quickly without legal permission), was married younger than 15 or aged 16–17 (the reference category being that she married at 18 or older), and was forced to marry against her will.

5.2. Forced Migration and Women's Domestic Violence Attitudes in the TDHS

Table 5.1 presents the results of estimating the triple-difference specification in [1] on women's attitudes towards domestic violence in the TDHS data.[17] In Column (1), the dependent variable is an indicator for whether the respondent thought a man was justified in beating his wife in any of the scenarios she was asked about. The estimates imply that Kurdish women from the conflict region who migrated during the conflict are 16 percentage points more likely

Table 5.1. Forced migration and women's attitudes towards domestic violence

	Domestic violence is justified in any scenario	Fraction of scenarios in which domestic violence is justified	First principal component
	(1)	(2)	(3)
From conflict region x Migrated during conflict x Kurdish	0.163***	0.064***	0.504**
	(0.035)	(0.021)	(0.213)
Joint p-value	0.000		
Mean level of outcome (full sample)	0.203	0.080	−.008
Mean level of outcome (subsample)	0.321	0.145	0.622
Adjusted R-squared	0.088	0.097	0.077
Number of observations	16197	16197	15762

Each column provides the result of estimating specification [1] on respondents' attitudes towards domestic violence. For brevity, only the estimate for λ, the coefficient of the triple-interaction term, is reported. Estimates of other parameters of the model are reported in Gulesci (2017: Table B1). In 2008, respondents were asked to state if they thought domestic violence by a husband towards his wife was justified in seven different scenarios, while in the 2013 TDHS only five of these scenarios were used. In Column (1), the outcome variable is a dummy variable =1 if the respondent said she thought a husband was justified in beating his wife in any of the seven scenarios that were described to her. In Column (2) the outcome is the proportion of cases (out of the seven (five) scenarios read to her in the 2008 (2013) TDHS) in which the respondent said she thought a husband was justified in beating his wife. In Column (3) the dependent variable is the first principal component of seven (five) dummy variables each equal to 1 if the respondent stated she found domestic violence justified in the given scenario in the 2008 (2013) TDHS. 'From conflict region' is a dummy variable =1 if the respondent was born and/or grew up in one of the conflict provinces (Adiyaman, Agri, Batman, Bingol, Bitlis, Diyarbakir, Elazig, Hakkari, Mardin, Mus, Siirt, Sirnak, Tunceli, and Van). 'Migrated during conflict' is a dummy variable =1 if the respondent migrated at least once during the conflict years (1984–99). 'Kurdish' is a dummy variable =1 if the first language of either the mother or the father of the respondent was Kurdish. 'From conflict region x Migrated during conflict x Kurdish' is the triple-interaction term that identifies the effect of being forced to migrate due to the conflict. All regressions control for the following covariates: a dummy variable =1 if the respondent's mother ever went to school; a dummy variable =1 if the respondent's father completed primary school; a dummy variable =1 if the respondent's father graduated from secondary school or above; a dummy variable =1 if the respondent's parents were related by blood; province of birth and TDHS wave fixed effects. The reported 'joint p-value' is from a test for joint significance of estimates for 'From conflict region x Migrated during conflict x Kurdish' using seemingly unrelated regressions for Columns (1)–(3). The row 'mean level of outcome (subsample)' gives the mean of the outcome among Kurdish women from the conflict region who did not migrate during conflict. Robust standard errors are clustered by birth province. *** (**) (*) indicates significance at the 1% (5%) (10%) level.

Source: Author's calculations based on data from the 2008 and 2013 Turkish Demographic and Health Surveys.

[17] For brevity, the table only reports the coefficient of estimate for λ, the triple difference between women from the conflict region (vs the rest of the country), who migrated during the conflict period (vs did not migrate in this period), who are Kurdish (vs Turkish). The full set of results is reported in Appendix B.

to think that domestic violence is justified in at least one of these scenarios. This is a very large effect, both compared to the sample mean (20 per cent) and relative to the subsample of Kurdish women who did not migrate during the conflict (32 per cent). In Column (2), the dependent variable is the fraction of scenarios in which the respondent thought domestic violence was acceptable. The outcome is higher by 0.06 for Kurdish women who were forced to migrate during the conflict, which is a large effect relative to the sample mean (0.08) or compared to Kurdish women who did not migrate during the conflict (0.15). Finally, Column (3) shows the finding is robust to aggregating the responses using an alternative way—the first principal component of the individual questions on domestic violence. Overall, results in Table 5.3 imply that more than twenty years after the beginning and ten years after the end of the conflict in question, forced migrant women were more likely to find physical domestic violence justified.[18]

In order to assess the robustness of the estimates and the validity of the identification strategy, I explore two approaches. First, I conduct a placebo test where I estimate the triple-difference specification in [1] for women who migrated before the conflict period (i.e. prior to 1984). In other words, I substitute the dummy variable M_{it} with one that is equal to one if respondent i migrated before the conflict period. If the findings are driven by the forced migration ensuing from the conflict, then I should not find any significant differences in the domestic violence attitudes of Kurdish women who migrated before the conflict relative to those who did not and relative to Turkish women. The results are reported in Gulesci (2017: Table A1). The coefficient estimates for the triple-interaction term (λ) are negative and insignificant for all outcome variables, which builds confidence that the effects demonstrated before were driven by the forced migration and not by any other underlying differences across the comparison groups.

Second, as an alternative specification, I restrict the sample to Kurdish respondents and estimate the difference-in-difference between those who are from the OHAL provinces and those who migrated during the conflict period. Formally, I estimate:

$$y_{ipt} = \alpha + \delta C_p + \vartheta M_{it} + \tau C_p M_{ipt} + \beta' X_i + \theta_p + S_t + \varepsilon_{ipt} \qquad [3]$$

In this specification, the coefficient of interest is τ, the difference-in-difference between Kurdish women who were from the OHAL provinces versus the rest of the country, and those who migrated during the conflict relative to those who did not. The results are reported in Gulesci (2017: Tables A2 and A3). The

---

[18] Gulesci (2017: Table 2) presents the effects on individual scenarios that the respondents were asked about. The estimates for λ are positive for all and statistically significant for three out of the seven scenarios. Moreover, a test of joint significance of the coefficients is rejected at conventional levels.

estimated effects are qualitatively similar to the triple-difference approach in specification [1], but due to the smaller sample size some of the estimates lose precision. For example, in Table A2, the estimate for τ is not precise for the first principal component (Column (3)), but it is positive and significant for the other two indicators.

To return to the discussion in Section 3, a potential mechanism behind this change in women's attitudes might be that forced migration lowers the bargaining power of women relative to men and thus makes domestic violence more expected and acceptable in their households. To test this mechanism explicitly, I estimate specification [1] on the employment and schooling level of women and their husbands (thus limiting the sample to married women only). Results in Table 5.2 show that while forced migration did not have a significant effect on the employment probability of women in the long run

Table 5.2. Effects on employment and wealth

	Respondent is employed at the time of interview	Respondent's spouse is employed	Respondent is not employed but her spouse is	Above middle-wealth class
	(1)	(2)	(3)	(4)
From conflict region x Migrated during conflict x Kurdish	−0.014 (0.058)	0.078 (0.051)	0.112* (0.067)	−0.117** (0.054)
Mean level of outcome (full sample)	0.304	0.900	0.592	0.372
Mean level of outcome (subsample)	0.129	0.842	0.708	0.081
Adjusted R-squared	0.093	0.065	0.082	0.233
Number of observations	13721	13036	13733	13733

Each column provides the result of estimating specification [1]. For brevity, only the estimate for λ, the coefficient of the triple-interaction term, is reported. Estimates of other parameters of the model are reported in Gulesci (2017: Table B3). The sample is restricted to married women only. The dependent variable in Column (1) is a dummy variable =1 if the respondent is working at an income-generating activity at the time of the survey; in Column (2) it is a dummy variable =1 if the respondent's husband is working at an income-generating activity; in Column (3) it is a dummy variable =1 if the respondent's husband is working but the respondent is not working at an income-generating activity at the time of the survey. In Column (4) the outcome is a dummy variable =1 if the respondent's household is classified as in class 4 or 5 in the TDHS wealth index, which is based on their asset ownership and ranges from 1 (poorest) to 5 (richest). 'From conflict region' is a dummy variable =1 if the respondent was born and/or grew up in one of the conflict provinces (Adiyaman, Agri, Batman, Bingol, Bitlis, Diyarbakir, Elazig, Hakkari, Mardin, Mus, Siirt, Sirnak, Tunceli, and Van). 'Migrated during conflict' is a dummy variable =1 if the respondent migrated at least once during the conflict years (1984–99). 'Kurdish' is a dummy variable =1 if the first language of either the mother or the father of the respondent was Kurdish. 'From conflict region x Migrated during conflict x Kurdish' is the triple-interaction term that identifies the effect of being forced to migrate due to the conflict. All regressions control for the following covariates: a dummy variable =1 if the respondent's mother ever went to school; a dummy variable =1 if the respondent's father completed primary school; a dummy variable =1 if the respondent's father graduated from secondary school or above; a dummy variable =1 if the respondent's parents were related by blood; province of birth and TDHS wave fixed effects. The row 'mean level of outcome (subsample)' gives the mean of the outcome variable among Kurdish women from the conflict region who did not migrate during the conflict. Robust standard errors are clustered by birth province. *** (**) (*) indicates significance at the 1% (5%) (10%) level.

Source: Author's calculations based on data from the 2008 and 2013 Turkish Demographic and Health Surveys.

(Column (1)), it did widen the gap between them and their husbands in terms of employment probability. Column (3) shows that Kurdish women who migrated during the conflict are 11 percentage points more likely to be in a relationship where their spouse is working while they themselves are not. They are also 12 percentage points less likely to be classified as above middle-wealth class according to the wealth ranking provided by the TDHS. These effects are in line with forced migration leading to a change in intrahousehold bargaining power that favours the men in the family. In Turkey, on average, women's labour force participation is higher in the rural sector compared with the urban sector (Aran et al. 2009; Tunali 2003). Moreover, Tunali (2003) shows that women's unemployment rate is higher in the urban sector, which suggests that employment rates are even lower.[19] Given these patterns, forced migration in this context is likely to have widened the gap in employment opportunities of women relative to men, lowering their bargaining position. While this is in line with the bargaining power mechanism discussed in Section 3, it does not imply that this is the only mechanism that may be at work.

Finally, I explore whether forced migration increased the likelihood of the respondent's spouse behaving in a controlling manner. In the TDHS, every respondent who was (or had been) married was asked if her current or (if divorced or widowed) last partner had ever tried to prevent her from seeing her friends, limited her contact with her family, insisted on knowing where she was at all times, distrusted her with money, or accused her of being unfaithful. Table 5.3 shows the effect of forced migration on respondents' likelihood of having experienced such behaviours. Forced migration is associated with a 10 percentage point increase in the likelihood that respondents' husbands exhibited at least one of these behaviours (Column (6)). This effect is mainly driven by an increase in their partners' likelihood of insisting on knowing where she was at all times and preventing her from seeing her friends. This increase in men's attempts to control women's actions may be in line with a number of mechanisms that were discussed in Section 3. For example, forced migration may have brought traditional male gender roles into conflict with more modern roles, which may have induced men to become more controlling. Further research and more detailed data are needed to fully understand the key mechanisms driving the effect of forced migration on domestic violence attitudes.

---

[19] Gulesci (2017: Table A4) shows the pattern in the TDHS data. On average, 29 per cent of women living in urban areas are employed, while the corresponding rate is 39 per cent in rural areas. The gap is particularly high among women with low schooling. For men, the reverse is true: men in urban regions are more likely on average to have a job relative to those in rural areas.

Table 5.3. Effects on controlling behaviours of the spouse

	If respondent's current or last husband ever:					Aggregate indices	
	Prevented her from seeing her friends	Limited her contact with her family	Insisted on knowing where she was at all times	Distrusted her with money	Accused her of being unfaithful	Respondent experienced any of the situations in (1)–(5)	Principal component
	(1)	(2)	(3)	(4)	(5)	(6)	(7)
From conflict region × Migrated during conflict × Kurdish	0.089*** (0.030)	0.034 (0.025)	0.103* (0.056)	0.035 (0.041)	0.024 (0.028)	0.098** (0.049)	0.404** (0.154)
Joint p-value	0.000						
Mean level of outcome (full sample)	0.098	0.068	0.374	0.058	0.040	0.432	−0.003
Mean level of outcome (subsample)	0.124	0.095	0.437	0.059	0.030	0.506	0.115
Adjusted R-squared	0.012	0.006	0.032	0.002	0.004	0.032	0.014
Number of observations	14019	14017	14010	14008	14008	14025	13965

Each column provides the result of estimating specification [1]. For brevity, only the estimate for λ, the coefficient of the triple-interaction term, is reported. Estimates of other parameters of the model are reported in Gulesci (2017: Table B4). In Columns (1)–(5), the dependent variables are dummy variables =1 if the respondent's current or (if divorced or widowed) last husband sometimes or often behaved in the stated manner. They are defined on the basis of the question: 'Can you please tell me how often you experience(d) such situations in your relationship with your (last) husband? Often, sometimes, or never?' I combine the responses 'often' and 'sometimes', so the reference category is 'never'. The specific situations are: in Column (1), preventing her from seeing her female friends; in Column (2), limiting her contact with her family; in Column (3), insisting on knowing where she was at all times; in Column (4), distrusting her with money; in Column (5), accusing her of being unfaithful. In Column (6) the dependent variable is a dummy variable =1 if any of the dummy variables in Columns (1)–(5) is equal to 1. In Column (7) the dependent variable is the first principal component of the five dummy variables in Columns (1)–(5). 'From conflict region' is a dummy variable =1 if the respondent was born and/or grew up in one of the conflict provinces (Adıyaman, Ağrı, Batman, Bingöl, Bitlis, Diyarbakır, Elazığ, Hakkari, Mardin, Mus, Siirt, Sırnak, Tunceli, and Van). 'Migrated during conflict' is a dummy variable =1 if the respondent migrated at least once during the conflict years (1984–99). 'Kurdish' is a dummy variable =1 if the first language of either the mother or the father of the respondent was Kurdish. 'From conflict region × Migrated during conflict × Kurdish' is the triple-interaction term that identifies the effect of being forced to migrate due to the conflict. All regressions control for the following covariates: a dummy variable =1 if the respondent's mother ever went to school; a dummy variable =1 if the respondent's father completed primary school; a dummy variable =1 if the respondent's father graduated from secondary school or above; a dummy variable =1 if the respondent's parents were related by blood; province of birth and TDHS wave fixed effects. The reported 'joint p-value' is from a test for joint significance of estimates for 'From conflict region × Migrated during conflict × Kurdish' using seemingly unrelated regressions for Columns (1)–(7). The row 'mean level of outcome (subsample)' gives the mean of the outcome among Kurdish women from the conflict region who did not migrate during the conflict. Robust standard errors are clustered by birth province. *** (**) (*) indicates significance at the 1% (5%) (10%) level.

Source: Author's calculations based on data from the 2008 and 2013 Turkish Demographic and Health Surveys.

5.3. *Forced Migration and Domestic Violence Among Applicants to a Women's Shelter*

As an additional, suggestive piece of evidence, I explore the differences between forced migrant women and others who sought help from the shelter NGO in dealing with the consequences of domestic violence. Table 5.4 presents the results of estimating specification [2] on the duration of domestic violence experienced by each applicant and previous help sought prior to applying to the NGO. The estimates in Column (1) show that among Kurdish women who applied to the NGO for assistance, forced migrants—with controls for being a migrant in general—were seven percentage points more likely to have been in a relationship for over ten years and experienced domestic violence since the beginning of this relationship. This finding is robust to controlling for age at marriage, being forced into the marriage, housing conditions, and literacy level of the applicants (Column (2)). This suggests that forced migrant women suffered domestic violence for a longer period before deciding to seek assistance from the NGO. The rest of the table shows that forced migrants are also less likely to have sought any treatment or filed a legal complaint, and no more likely to have complained to other institutions or people, prior to seeking help from the shelter. This rules out the possibility that the reason why forced migrant women applied later was that they were receiving assistance from alternative institutions or people.

Table 5.5 shows the association between forced migration and some indicators of the extent of domestic violence experienced by the applicants. The first two columns show that forced migrants were five to six percentage points more likely to have been forced to have sex against their will—significant only when controls are added in Column (2). This corresponds to an increase of 12 per cent in the outcome relative to the sample mean. In Columns (3–4), the dependent variable is whether the applicant reported having had a miscarriage caused by the domestic violence she experienced. This likelihood is four percentage points higher among forced migrants, a large effect considering that in the entire sample only 8 per cent of women reported having had a miscarriage due to domestic violence. Taken together, the findings suggest that forced migrant women had endured domestic violence for longer and of greater severity before deciding to seek help from the NGO.

6. Conclusion

In this chapter, I studied the effects of forced migration caused by the Turkish-Kurdish conflict from the mid-1980s to the end of the 1990s on migrating women's attitudes towards domestic violence. Evidence from two separate data

Table 5.4. Duration of domestic violence and previous support sought

	Violence has been going on since the start of a 10+-year relationship		Received medical or psychological treatment		Filed a legal complaint		Complained to police, court, family, or friends	
	(1)	(2)	(3)	(4)	(5)	(6)	(7)	(8)
Forced migrant	0.069**	0.069**	−0.048**	−0.044**	−0.025*	−0.029**	−0.023	−0.027
	(0.029)	(0.029)	(0.019)	(0.019)	(0.013)	(0.014)	(0.030)	(0.030)
Basic controls	Yes	Yes	Yes	Yes	Yes	Yes	Yes	Yes
Additional controls	No	Yes	No	Yes	No	Yes	No	Yes
Mean level of outcome	0.304		0.129		0.060		0.597	
Adjusted R-squared	0.204	0.217	0.255	0.264	0.036	0.041	0.269	0.275
Number of observations	2278	2278	2272	2272	2276	2276	2278	2278

The table reports the results of estimating specification [2]. For brevity, only the estimate for α, the coefficient of 'forced migrant', is reported. Estimates of other parameters of the model are reported in Gulesci (2017: Table B5). The sample includes Kurdish women who applied to the women's shelter between October 2009 and December 2011 to seek assistance in relation to physical or sexual domestic (intrahousehold) violence. In Columns (1)–(2) the dependent variable is a dummy variable =1 if the relationship in which the applicant has experienced domestic violence started 10 or more years ago and she reports that the violence has been going on since the beginning of the relationship. In Columns (3)–(4) the dependent variable is a dummy variable =1 if the applicant reports having received medical, psychological, or other treatment due to the domestic violence she has experienced. In Columns (5)–(6) the dependent variable is a dummy variable =1 if the applicant has a legal document issued by the police or courts proving that she experienced domestic violence. In Columns (7)–(8) the dependent variable is a dummy variable =1 if the applicant says she complained about the domestic violence she experienced to anyone (e.g. friends, family, police, courts, etc.). 'Forced migrant' is a dummy variable =1 if the respondent reports that she was forced to migrate from her residence due to security concerns more than 10 years ago. 'Migrant' is a dummy variable =1 if the applicant ever migrated for any reason. 'Housing: *gecekondu*' is a dummy variable =1 if the applicant lives in a *gecekondu*, a makeshift dwelling put up quickly without legal permission, often by squatters. 'Household size' is the number of people living in the applicant's household. 'Literate' is a dummy variable =1 if the applicant reports that she is able to read and write. 'Age at marriage 15 or younger' is a dummy variable =1 if the applicant first married when she was younger than 16 years old. 'Age at marriage 16–17' is a dummy variable =1 if the applicant first married while she was 16 or 17. 'Forced to marry against her will' is a dummy variable =1 if the applicant reports that she was forced into the marriage she is currently in. 'Has independent source of income' is a dummy variable =1 if the applicant reports that she has an income source that is not dependent on her husband or other men in her family. All regressions control for province, month, and year of application fixed effects. Standard errors are clustered by province. *** (**) (*) indicates significance at the 1% (5%) (10%) level.

Source: Author's calculations based on applications to the shelter NGO.

Table 5.5. Extent of domestic violence

	Forced to have sex against her will		Had a miscarriage due to the violence	
	(1)	(2)	(3)	(4)
Forced migrant	0.048	0.060*	0.041**	0.035**
	(0.031)	(0.032)	(0.017)	(0.017)
Basic controls	Yes	Yes	Yes	Yes
Additional controls	No	Yes	No	Yes
Mean level of outcome	0.494		0.083	
Adjusted R-squared	0.261	0.267	0.199	0.205
Number of observations	2093	2093	2274	2274

The table reports results of estimating specification [2]. For brevity, only the estimate for α, the coefficient of 'forced migrant', is reported. Estimates of other parameters of the model are reported in Gulesci (2017: Table B6). The sample includes Kurdish women who applied to the women's shelter between October 2009 and December 2011 to seek assistance in relation to physical or sexual domestic (intrahousehold) violence. In Columns (1)–(2) the dependent variable is a dummy variable =1 if the applicant reports that she was forced to have sex unwillingly. In Columns (3)–(4) the dependent variable is a dummy variable =1 if the applicant reported having had a miscarriage caused mainly by the domestic violence she had experienced. 'Forced migrant' is a dummy variable =1 if the respondent reported that she was forced to migrate from her residence due to security concerns more than 10 years ago. 'Migrant' is a dummy variable =1 if the applicant ever migrated. 'Housing: *gecekondu*' is a dummy variable =1 if the applicant lives in a *gecekondu*, a makeshift dwelling put up quickly without legal permission, often by squatters. 'Household size' is the number of people living in the applicant's household. 'Literate' is a dummy variable =1 if the applicant reported that she was able to read and write. 'Age at marriage 15 or younger' is a dummy variable =1 if the applicant first married when she was younger than 16 years old. 'Age at marriage 16–17' is a dummy variable =1 if the applicant first married while she was 16 or 17. 'Forced to marry against her will' is a dummy variable =1 if the applicant reported that she was forced into the marriage she was currently in. 'Has independent source of income' is a dummy variable =1 if the applicant reported that she had an income source that was not dependent on her husband or other men in her family. All regressions control for province, month, and year of application fixed effects. Standard errors are clustered by province. *** (**) (*) indicates significance at the 1% (5%) (10%) level.

Source: Author's calculations based on applications to the shelter NGO.

sources (the TDHS and a database of applicants to a women's shelter NGO) suggests that women who were forced to leave their homes due to the conflict are more tolerant towards domestic violence. In the TDHS data, forced migrants were more likely to report that a husband was justified in beating his wife and to have experienced controlling behaviours by their husbands. Moreover, among the applicants to the shelter NGO, forced migrants had endured domestic violence for longer and of greater severity before deciding to seek assistance.

There may be multiple mechanisms that drive the impact of forced migration on attitudes towards domestic violence in this context. One possible mechanism is a fall in the bargaining position of women within the household, and a general worsening of their economic status. Moreover, forced migration increased the incidence of controlling behaviours by men, suggesting that it may have threatened traditional gender roles. Future research is needed on the extent to which other mechanisms—for example, the loss of social networks, or the psychological consequences of conflict exposure—may influence the way in which forced migration shapes migrants' attitudes towards domestic violence. Understanding the relative importance of these mechanisms across contexts is essential for designing effective policies to address the long-run consequences of forced migration for domestic violence.

References

Aizer, A. (2010). 'The Gender Wage Gap and Domestic Violence'. *American Economic Review*, 100: 1847–59.

Alesina, A., B. Brioschi, and E. La Ferrara (2016). 'Violence Against Women: A Cross-Cultural Analysis for Africa'. *NBER Working Paper* 21901. Cambridge, MA: NBER.

Amaral, S., S. Bandyopadhyay, and R. Sensarma (2015). 'Employment Programmes for the Poor and Female Empowerment: The Effect of NREGS on Gender-Based Violence in India'. *Journal of Interdisciplinary Economics*, 27(2): 199–218.

Andenberg, D., H. Rainer, J. Wadsworth, and T. Wilson (2016). 'Unemployment and Domestic Violence: Theory and Evidence'. *Economic Journal*, 126(597): 1947–79.

Anderson, S., and G. Genicot (2015). 'Suicide and Property Rights in India'. *Journal of Development Economics*, 114: 64–78.

Angelucci, M. (2008). 'Love on the Rocks: Domestic Violence and Alcohol Abuse in Rural Mexico'. *BE Journal of Economic Analysis & Policy*, 8(1): article 43.

Aran, M., S. Capar, M. Husamoglu, D. Sanalmis, and A. Uraz (2009). 'Recent Trends in Female Labor Force Participation in Turkey'. Ankara: World Bank and Turkey State Planning Organization.

Atkinson, M.P., T.N. Greenstein, and M.M. Lang (2005). 'For Women, Bread-winning Can Be Dangerous: Gendered Resource Theory and Wife Abuse'. *Journal of Marriage and Family*, 67(5): 1137–48.

Barsbai, T., H. Rapoport, A. Steinmayr, and C. Trebesch (2017). 'The Effect of Labor Migration on the Diffusion of Democracy: Evidence from a Former Soviet Republic'. *American Economic Journal: Applied Economics*, 9(3): 36–69.

Beriker-Atiyas, N. (1997). 'The Kurdish Conflict in Turkey: Issues, Parties and Prospects'. *Security Dialogue*, 28(4): 439–52.

Bloch, F., and V. Rao (2002). 'Terror as a Bargaining Instrument: A Case Study of Dowry Violence in Rural India'. *American Economic Review*, 92(4): 1029–43.

Bobonis, G.J., M. Gonzalez-Brenes, and R. Castro (2013). 'Public Transfers and Domestic Violence: The Roles of Private Information and Spousal Control'. *American Economic Journal: Economic Policy*, 5(1): 179–205.

Calderon, V., M. Gafaro, and A.M. Ibanez (2011). 'Forced Migration, Female Labour Force Participation, and Intra-Household Bargaining: Does Conflict Empower Women?' *Microcon Research Working Paper* 56. Bogota: University of the Andes, Faculty of Economics.

Chin, Y. (2012). 'Male Backlash, Bargaining, or Exposure Reduction? Women's Working Status and Physical Spousal Violence in India'. *Journal of Population Economics*, 25(1): 175–200.

Cortes, K.E. (2004). 'Are Refugees Different from Economic Immigrants? Some Empirical Evidence on the Heterogeneity of Immigrant Groups in the United States'. *Review of Economics and Statistics*, 86(2): 465–80.

Couttenier, M., V. Preotu, D. Rohner, and M. Thoenig (2016). 'The Violent Legacy of Victimization: Post-Conflict Evidence on Asylum Seekers, Crimes and Public Policy in Switzerland'. Discussion Paper 11079. London: CEPR.

Devries, K.M., J.Y.T. Mak, C. García-Moreno, M. Petzold, J.C. Child, G. Falder, and S. Lim (2013). 'The Global Prevalence of Intimate Partner Violence Against Women'. *Science*, 340(6140): 1527–8.

Eswaran, M., and Malhotra, N. (2011). 'Domestic Violence and Women's Autonomy in Developing Countries: Theory and Evidence'. *Canadian Journal of Economics*, 44: 1222–63.

Fowler, P.J., C.J. Tompsett, J.M. Braciszewski, A.J. Jaques-Tiuta, and B.B. Baltes (2009). 'Community Violence: A Meta-Analysis on the Effect of Exposure and Mental Health Outcomes of Children and Adolescents'. *Development and Psychopathology*, 21: 227–59.

García-Moreno, C., H.A. Jansen, M. Ellsberg, L. Heise, and C.H. Watts (2005). 'WHO Multi-Country Study on Women's Health and Domestic Violence Against Women: Initial Results on Prevalence, Health Outcomes and Women's Responses'. Geneva: WHO.

Gulesci, S. (2017). 'Forced Migration and Attitudes towards Domestic Violence: Evidence from Turkey'. WIDER Working Paper 2017/110. Helsinki: UNU-WIDER.

Heath, R. (2014). 'Women's Access to Labor Market Opportunities, Control of Household Resources, and Domestic Violence: Evidence from Bangladesh'. *World Development*, 57: 32–46.

Heise, L.L., and A. Kotsadam (2015). 'Cross-National and Multilevel Correlates of Partner Violence: An Analysis of Data from Population-Based Surveys'. *The Lancet Global Health*, 3(6): 332–40.

Hidrobo, M., and L. Fernald (2013). 'Cash Transfers and Domestic Violence'. *Journal of Health Economics*, 32(1): 304–19.

HÜNEE (2005). 'Türkiye Göç ve Yerinden Olmuş Nüfus Araştırması' [Research on Migration and Displaced Persons in Turkey]. Ankara: Ismat Publishing. Available at: http://www.hips.hacettepe.edu.tr/(accessed 23 April 2016).

IDMC (2013). 'Turkey: Internal Displacement in Brief'. Geneva: IDMC. Available at: www.internal-displacement.org/europe-the-caucasus-and-central-asia/turkey/summary (accessed 24 April 2016).

Justino, P., M. Leone, and P. Salardi (2015). 'Does War Empower Women? Evidence from Timor Leste'. IDS Evidence Report 121. Brighton: IDS.

Khan, A. (1997). 'Post-Migration Investment in Education by Immigrants in the United States'. *Quarterly Review of Economics and Finance*, 37: 285–313.

Kurban, D., D. Yukseker, A.B. Celik, T. Unalan, and A.T. Aker (2007). *Coming to Terms with Forced Migration: Post-Displacement Restitution of Citizenship Rights in Turkey*. Istanbul: TESEV Publications.

La Mattina, G. (2017). 'Civil Conflict, Domestic Violence and Intra-Household Bargaining in Post-Genocide Rwanda'. *Journal of Development Economics*, 124: 168–98.

Miguel, E., S.M. Saiegh, and S. Satyanath (2011). 'Civil War Exposure and Violence'. *Economics and Politics*, 23(1): 59–73.

Noe, D., and J. Rieckmann (2013). 'Violent Behaviour: The Effect of Civil Conflict on Domestic Violence in Colombia'. Discussion Paper 136. Göttingen: University of Göttingen, Courant Research Centre.

Ozar, S., N. Ucarlar, and O. Aytar (2013). *From Past to Present: A Paramilitary Organization in Turkey: Village Guard System*. Istanbul: DISA Publications/Berdan Publishing.

Rohlfs, C. (2010). 'Does Combat Exposure Make You a More Violent or Criminal Person? Evidence from the Vietnam Draft'. *Journal of Human Resources*, 45(2): 271–300.

Ruiz, I., and C. Vargas-Silva (2013). 'The Economics of Forced Migration'. *Journal of Development Studies*, 49(6): 772–84.

Tauchen, H.V., A.D. Witte, and S.K. Long (1991). 'Domestic Violence: A Non-Random Affair'. *International Economic Review*, 32: 491–511.

TRPM (2008). *Domestic Violence Against Women in Turkey*. Ankara: Elma Publishing.

Tunali, I. (2003). 'Background Study on Labour Market and Employment in Turkey'. Turin: European Training Foundation. Available at: www.etf.europa.eu/web.nsf/pages/Background_Study_on_Labour_Market_and_Employment_in_Turkey (accessed 14 November 2016).

UNHCR (2015). 'Mid-Year Trends'. Geneva: UNHCR. Available at: www.unhcr.org/56701b969.html (accessed 24 April 2016).

van den Berg, G., and M. Tertilt (2015). 'The Association Between Own Unemployment and Violence Victimization Among Female Youths'. *Journal of Economics and Statistics*, 235 (4–5): 499–513.

WHO (2013). 'Global and Regional Estimates of Violence Against Women: Prevalence and Health Effects of Intimate Partner Violence and Non-Partner Sexual Violence'. Geneva: WHO.

6

Bride Price and the Well-Being of Women

Sara Lowes and Nathan Nunn[1]

1. Introduction

The practice of paying a bride price—which is a payment from the groom or groom's family to the bride's family—at the time of marriage is a custom that is widespread throughout sub-Saharan Africa. Among the African societies represented in the Ethnographic Atlas, 83 per cent report having bride price practices. Historically and today, the magnitude of the bride price is often significant. It is not uncommon for bride price transfers to be in excess of a year's income and sometimes as large as seven or eight times annual income (Anderson 2007).

In recent years, this practice has come under criticism, particularly in Africa. A number of objections have been raised in both the media and in political discourse. Recent examples of articles from African newspapers criticizing the practice include Kelly (2006), IRIN News (2006), and Eryenyu (2014). The objections stem from the view that the practice is transactional in nature and, therefore, results in the commodification of women, which has adverse consequences. Husbands may feel they that because they have paid for their wives, they can mistreat them, leaving women in marriages prone to physical violence and conflict. The Ugandan women's rights group *Mifumi* has reported cases where men say 'I am beating my cows' when they hit their wives, where women are denied ownership of property, and where women may be expected to be sexually available to their husbands at any time and without protection (Eryenyu 2014). In response to these potentially negative

[1] Cammie Curtin provided excellent research assistance. Sara Lowes acknowledges generous financial support from the National Science Foundation Graduate Research Fellowship Program, Harvard IQSS, and the Harvard Center for African Studies.

effects of high bride price, Kenya's most recent round of marriage laws legislates that a token bride price must be counted as sufficient to meet the needs of the custom (Dudley 2014). The Zambian government has recently spoken out to discourage families from requesting exorbitant amounts for their daughters (Tembo 2014).

In many customs, the woman's parents are required to return the bride price if the woman leaves the marriage, particularly if she has not yet had any children. Thus, it is possible that the practice of bride price results in women being locked in the marriage because parents are unwilling or unable to repay the bride price. Due to this concern, Ugandan courts have outlawed the requirement for the bride price to be paid back upon divorce (Government of Uganda 2001; Mwesigwa 2015). The stated rationale for this legal change was that it 'would make it easier for women to leave abusive relationships' (Biryabarema 2015).

Another concern centres around the incentives that the bride price generates for parents. It has been argued that parents may have an incentive to 'sell' their daughters early to obtain the bride price payment, resulting in early marriage and higher rates of lifetime fertility. For example, Hague et al. (2011) report accounts from Uganda of parents taking children out of school so they can be married early in return for a bride price. In the words of one focus group participant, the 'selling [of] a human being because the family wants wealth, [and] selling your daughter at a tender age' are common. This is because 'people prefer to get wealth at the expense of their daughters' education' (p. 556). Consistent with this concern, Corno and Voena (2016) and Corno et al. (2016) find that adverse shocks to family income increase a woman's chance of early marriage among societies that practise bride price. Families appear to use early marriage, and with it the receipt of bride price, to smooth consumption. To combat early marriage due to bride price, the local government in Laikipia county, Kenya, has instituted a programme to give cows to parents whose daughters graduate from high school.

These views are not universal, however. While the view of the bride price as a purchase price of a wife is common in the (Western) media, this is very different from the general interpretation of the practice made by anthropologists. For example, Vroklage (1952) explicitly rejects the idea that a bride price is the price paid for the purchase of a woman. Interviewees told him, 'a bride is not a buffalo' and 'a bride is not an animal'. Vroklage (1952: 135) instead describes it as 'a compensation for the expense, the care and trouble spent on the bride's upbringing... It is compensation for the complete loss of a worker as a bride withdraws from her own kindred and henceforth belongs to her husband's.' Bride price is particularly common among groups that practise patrilineal descent, and is considered as a compensation payment for the bride's future children, who will no longer belong to her parents' family. In fact, in many groups, marriage is equated with the payment of bride price. In their work on the Kikuyu in Kenya, Adams and Mburugu (1994: 162) write that bridewealth (another term for bride price) is the primary indicator of marriage, with one respondent saying: 'There was no ceremony, but traditionally I am married because I paid the bridewealth.' With regard to the Sebei of Uganda, anthropologist Goldschmidt (1974: 312) notes that without the transfer of bride price there is no marriage and any children will not belong to the father's lineage.

In this chapter, we contribute to a better understanding of the effects of bride price by studying the relationship between the bride price amount and a range of outcomes. Motivated by the most common concerns that are associated with high bride price, we examine whether a higher bride price paid at marriage is associated with earlier marriage and higher fertility; a greater acceptance of violence within the home; decreased ability of the wife to leave her husband; lower-quality marriages; and lower levels of happiness for the wife. Our analysis also examines the closely related question of whether the custom of having to pay back the bride price upon divorce causes wives to be trapped in unhappy and low-quality marriages.

We contribute to answering these questions with survey data collected in Kananga, a provincial capital in the Democratic Republic of the Congo (DRC). We collect information from 317 marriages, for a total of 634 individuals. In this setting, the practice of the payment of bride price is widespread. Thus, our focus is on the value of the bride price payment and how this is related to different characteristics of the marriage. This can be contrasted to other studies that focus on the presence or absence of a bride price tradition (e.g. Bishai and Grossbard 2010 and Ashraf et al. 2016).

According to our estimates, there appears to be no evidence that a larger bride price payment is associated with earlier marriage or with higher fertility. We also find that larger bride price payments are associated with better-quality marriages as measured by beliefs about the acceptability of domestic violence, the frequency of engaging in positive activities as a couple, and the self-reported happiness of the wife. We also examine the correlates of the requirement for the bride price to be paid back upon divorce. Contrary to general concerns about this aspect of the custom, we find no evidence that this requirement is associated with women being less happy in their marriages. In fact, we find a positive association, although the coefficient is statistically insignificant. However, we do find that if the value of the bride price paid is very high (over US$1,000), then the requirement is, in fact, negatively associated with the happiness of the wife. Thus, the combination of a very high bride price and a requirement to pay back the bride price upon divorce is associated with wives being less happy.

Overall, our estimates do not provide overwhelming evidence in support of the concern that bride price has detrimental effects on the well-being of married women. In fact, the practice generally appears to be correlated with good outcomes. The one exception is that the combination of a very high bride price and the requirement for the bride price to be paid back upon divorce is negatively associated with the wife's happiness.

Although these estimates are conditional correlations and not causal estimates, and so should be treated with the necessary amount of caution, we do feel that they are informative. At the very least, these findings, combined with the dearth of other estimates of the correlates of bride price, suggest that much more research into the effects (or correlates) of bride price is needed, especially given the calls to amend or abolish the practice in many countries within Africa.

The rest of this chapter is structured as follows. The next section provides a description of the Congolese setting. Section 3 explains the data collection procedure, the sample, and our bride price measure. Section 4 reports our regression equations and our estimated relationships of interest, and Section 5 discusses the significance of these results and compares them to related evidence from other African samples. Section 6 concludes.

2. The Congolese Setting

In the DRC, bride price is referred to as *la dot* (the French word for dowry, though the payment is made from the groom's family to the bride's family) or *biuma* in Tshiluba, the language spoken in the south-central part of the DRC, where we collected our data. Although, historically, there was variation in marriage payment customs, today bride price is practised among all ethnic groups in this part of the DRC. Bride price also functions as legal proof of marriage, and a couple are not considered married until a bride price is paid in full. Therefore, bride price is also important for inheritance and determining the lineage of any children of the marriage since, if a husband dies, it allows a wife to prove that they were officially married. Chondoka (1988: 158) writes that traditionally 'marriages were all legalized on delivery of the "main" payments'.

The modern practice of bride price has its roots in pre-colonial customs. At that time, as in many other parts of Africa, the practice was widespread and common. The Ethnographic Atlas has data on sixty-four pre-colonial ethnic groups that are located within the DRC. Of these, approximately 90 per cent practised the payment of bride price and none had dowries. The remaining groups that did not practise payment of bride price tended to have token bride price (small symbolic payments) or bride service (where the husband performs

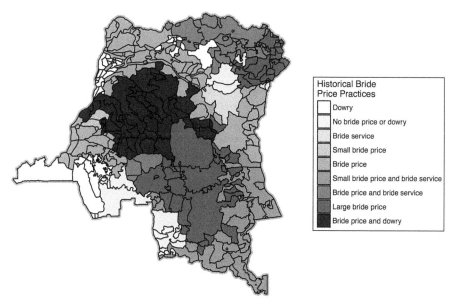

Figure 6.1. Spatial variation in historical bride price practices
Source: Authors.

work for the bride's family). Using more detailed data from Vansina (1966) on 300 ethnic groups within the DRC, we have coded historical bride price practices at a more disaggregated ethnicity level. These practices ranged from no payment of bride price, bride price payments of varying economic value, bride service, or payment of dowry. The spatial distribution of these practices is shown in Figure 6.1. The picture that emerges from the finer data from Vansina (1966) is broadly similar to that from the Ethnographic Atlas, although with a bit more variation and nuance. Of those groups represented in Vansina (1966), approximately 80 per cent practised some form of payment to the bride's family at the time of marriage. However, there has existed great heterogeneity in the size of these transfers, who is involved in the payments, and the terms under which bride price must be repaid.

Interviews and focus groups conducted by the authors with men and women in the DRC suggest that bride price is still very important for marriages. For both men and women, bride price payment signals honour and respect for the wife. As one Congolese woman explained, 'Bride price is important for all African women, but for Congolese women in particular ... The bride price is an official custom that expresses the love a husband has for his wife. For the parents of the wife, the bride price symbolizes a reward and an honour.' Without payment of the bride price, marriages are not recognized. In fact, some women believe it is better to live with a friend than to live with a man that does not want to pay the bride price. When asked about the role of bride price, a Congolese man noted: 'The bride price is how a man honours his wife.' However, he also says that the bride price serves as 'a guarantee that prevents the [woman's family] from taking her back when there is a dispute'. These interviews suggest that although the bride price is customarily associated with a man's commitment to his wife and is a signal of respect, it may also hinder the woman's options in the case of marital disputes.

3. Description of the Data and the Sources

3.1. *Sampling Procedure and Data Collection*

The surveys for the project were administered between June and October 2015 in Kananga, DRC.[2] Kananga is an ethnically diverse city of over one million people, and is the capital of Kasai Central province. The most populous ethnic group in the city is the Luluwa; however, there are dozens of other ethnic groups represented in the city. Figure 6.2 is a map of the DRC with the city of

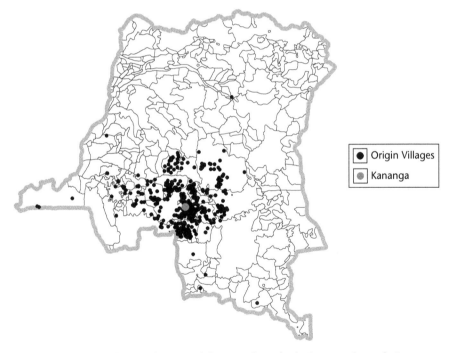

Figure 6.2. Villages of origin of the sample and ethnic group boundaries
Source: Authors.

---

[2] The data were collected for a project on matrilineal kinship systems and intra-household bargaining (Lowes 2017).

Kananga denoted by a large dot and the villages of origin of the individuals in the sample in smaller black dots.[3]

A screening survey was administered across the city to identify individuals in monogamous marriages. We selected 442 individuals by this means and asked them (and their spouses) to participate in the study. Ultimately, 320 of these 442 individuals agreed to participate in the study, yielding a sample of 640 individuals. Three men reported either not having paid bride price or not knowing the value of the bride price they paid. These couples were excluded from the analysis. The final sample consists of 634 individuals from twenty-eight different ethnic groups. Summary statistics for the sample are available in Lowes and Nunn (2017).

Couples were visited at their homes three different times by a team of one male enumerator and one female enumerator. The male enumerator met with the husband, while the female enumerator met with the wife. Thus, the husband and wife both undertook the surveys in private and away from their spouse. In the first visit, participants completed a long survey. This survey had questions on demographics, economic activities, land ownership, family history, and a child roster. During the second and third visits, individuals completed shorter surveys that asked questions about their views on gender norms and on characteristics about their marriage. The surveys were conducted in either French or Tshiluba, which are the languages spoken in this area of the DRC.

3.2. Bride Price and an Exploration of its Determinants

We first describe our primary variable of interest. In our surveys, both men and women were asked: 'At the time of your own marriage, what was the total value of the bride-price that was paid? Please include the cost of all of the goods and cash payments given as a part of the bride price.' The bride price can be paid in many forms, and usually involves some combination of goats, money, food, and other household items. Thus, our question explicitly asks the respondents to include the estimated value of all non-monetary items as well.

Although both the husband and wife were asked separately, we expect the men to have better information on the amount of the bride price paid because they were the person who made the payment and who was directly involved in the transfer of funds (sometimes with the help of their families). In our data, around 80 per cent of men report having contributed to the bride price payment. Additionally, 40 per cent of men report receiving help from their

---

[3] Village of origin is where an individual's family originates and is not necessarily the same as village of birth.

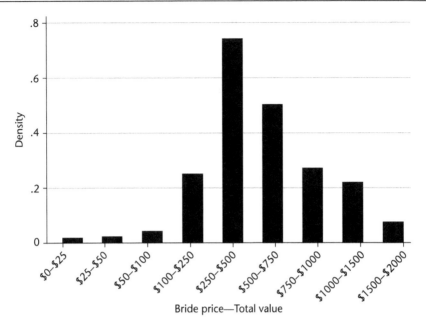

Figure 6.3. Distribution of bride price payments
Source: Authors.

fathers and 30 per cent report receiving help from their mothers. By contrast, because the payments are received by the wife's parents, she is not directly involved in the transfer of money and therefore is less likely to have detailed knowledge of the amount.[4]

Since the bride price is often paid in a variety of goods, it is difficult to assess an exact dollar value of the bride price. Therefore, we presented respondents with categories of the total value of all money and items paid as part of the bride price, and asked respondents to choose one of the categories. These categories, and the proportion of respondents with a bride price payment within each category, are reported in Figure 6.3. The modal bride price payment was between US$250 and US$500, a significant sum given that for a number of decades the average real per capita gross domestic product (GDP) of the DRC has been stagnant at around US$250 per person. Larger payments in excess of US$500 (two years of per capita GDP) are also common.

We begin by examining the correlates of bride price payments. The estimates are reported in Table 6.1. In Column 1, we examine the wife's education, age, and age squared as correlates. In Column 2, we add year of marriage,

---

[4] When wives are able to estimate the amount of bride price paid, the amounts of bride price paid reported by husbands and wives are highly correlated. However, women are more likely than men to report that they do not know the value of the bride price paid.

Table 6.1. Wife's characteristics and bride price

	Dep. var.: bride price amount		
	(1)	(2)	(3)
Wife's age	0.011	−0.016	−0.021
	(0.025)	(0.037)	(0.042)
Wife's age squared	−0.000112	0.000074	0.000168
	(0.000269)	(0.000337)	(0.000388)
Wife's years education	0.091***	0.096***	0.090***
	(0.026)	(0.027)	(0.027)
Year married		−0.011	−0.025
		(0.013)	(0.016)
Married in Kananga		−4.604	−3.637
		(25.625)	(25.792)
Year married*married in Kananga		0.002	0.002
		(0.013)	(0.013)
Husband's age			0.014
			(0.046)
Husband's age squared			−0.00032
			(0.00048)
Husband's years education			0.008
			(0.026)
Observations	317	317	317
Mean dep. var.	5.722	5.722	5.722

Notes: Robust standard errors in parentheses. *Years education* is the number of years of education. *Year married* is the year the couple were married as reported by the husband. *Married in Kananga* is an indicator variable equal to 1 if the couple lived in Kananga at the time of marriage. *Bride price amount* is a variable from 1 to 9 corresponding with various bride price values, where (1) is equal to US$0–25 and (9) is equal to US$1,500. $*p < 0.1$; $**p < 0.05$; $***p < 0.01$.
Source: Authors.

an indicator variable for whether the couple were married in Kananga (rather than in the village), and the interaction of these two variables (which allows the effect of year of marriage to be different inside and outside Kananga). In Column 3, we include the husband's education, age, and age squared.

Interestingly, we find that the wife's education is the only robust predictor of the bride price payment at the time of marriage. This finding is consistent with previous studies that have found that a wife's education is a strong predictor of the value of the bride price in Kenya (Borgerhoff Mulder 1995), Zambia, and Indonesia (Ashraf et al. 2016). In our sample, the mean value of the wife's education is 8.48 and the standard deviation is 3.65. Thus, a one-standard-deviation increase in the wife's education is associated with a $3.65 \times 0.09 = 0.33$ point increase in the bride price index. This is fairly sizeable given that the standard deviation of the index is 1.44 (the mean is 5.72).

Our estimates show that the amount of the bride price, conditional on education, is similar inside and outside the provincial capital of Kananga. Also, we find no evidence that the value of bride price payments has been systematically increasing over time. One concern in interpreting the coefficient on 'year married' is that it may be collinear with the wife's age and the husband's age. However, we obtain similar estimates regardless of whether these covariates are included in the estimating equation (estimates not shown here, but they are available upon request).

4. Estimating Equations and Empirical Results

4.1. Estimating Equations

For the analysis that follows, we estimate the following specification:

$$Y_{i,h,w} = a + \beta \, Bride \, Price \, Amount_{i,h,w} + \mathbf{X}_i \Omega + \mathbf{X}_h \Pi + \mathbf{X}_w \Gamma + \varepsilon_{i,h,w} \qquad (1)$$

where i indexes marriages that comprise a husband h and a wife w. $Y_{i,h,w}$ denotes our outcome of interest, which, depending on the specific measure, will measure a characteristic of the marriage, for the husband or for the wife. *Bride Price Amount*$_{i,h,w}$ is the amount of the bride price payment received by woman w's parents from husband h at the time of the marriage. Individuals recall the total value of the bride price and select the appropriate category among the options available (see Figures 6.3 and 6.4). We convert the categories into a scale that ranges from 1 to 9, increasing with the value of the bride price payment. $\mathbf{X}_h$ and $\mathbf{X}_w$ denote vectors of the following characteristics of the husband and wife, respectively: age, age squared, and educational attainment (measured in years). $\mathbf{X}_i$ denotes a vector of marriage characteristics, including the year of the marriage, an indicator that equals 1 if the marriage was in Kananga (the provincial capital where the surveys were conducted), and the interaction of the two.

4.2. Bride Price, Age at Marriage, and Fertility

We begin by estimating the relationship between the bride price payment and the wife's age at marriage. A potential concern with the tradition of bride price is that it induces parents to arrange for their daughters to be married at a younger age so that they can obtain the bride price payment. This might occur, for example, if the parents are credit constrained, and therefore need funds immediately, even if it comes at the cost of their daughter's future welfare. Therefore, we test for the presence of a relationship between the value of the bride price payment and the age at marriage by estimating equation (1) with the wife's age at the time of marriage (in years) as the dependent variable. The average age of marriage for women is nineteen years. By contrast, the average age of marriage for men is twenty-seven years.

The results are reported in Table 6.2. In this table, and all subsequent tables, the coefficients are not reported, but these tables are available in the related working paper (Lowes and Nunn 2017). Column 1 reports the estimates of

Table 6.2. Bride price, wife's age at marriage, and fertility

	Dep. var.: wife's age at marriage			Dep. var.: number of children		
	(1)	(2)	(3)	(4)	(5)	(6)
Bride price amount	−0.289	−0.177	−0.102	0.125*	0.095	0.065
	(0.213)	(0.155)	(0.141)	(0.075)	(0.067)	(0.061)
Wife-level controls, $\mathbf{X}_w$	Y	Y	Y	Y	Y	Y
Marriage-level controls, $\mathbf{X}_i$		Y	Y		Y	Y
Husband-level controls, $\mathbf{X}_h$			Y			Y
Observations	317	317	317	317	317	317
Mean dep. var.	19.37	19.37	19.37	4.208	4.208	4.208

Notes: Robust standard errors in parentheses. Wife's age at marriage is the age of the wife when the couple were married. Number of children is the number of living children a woman has. *$p < 0.1$; **$p < 0.05$; ***$p < 0.01$.

Source: Authors.

equation (1) with a more parsimonious set of covariates that only includes the wife-level covariates, $\mathbf{X}_w$. Column 2 adds the marriage-level measures, $\mathbf{X}_i$, and Column 3 adds the husband's characteristics, $\mathbf{X}_h$. In all specifications, we estimate a negative but statistically insignificant relationship between the bride price payment at marriage and the age at marriage. In addition to the coefficients being insignificant, their magnitudes are also small. For example, according to the estimate from Column 3, a one-standard-deviation increase in the bride price index (equal to 1.44) is associated with a decline in the age at marriage by $0.10 \times 1.44 = 0.14$ years. We also find that as we add more covariates to our estimating equation, the magnitude of the point estimate declines noticeably. This suggests that even the small estimated effects are potentially spurious. The point estimates appear to be converging towards zero with the inclusion of additional controls.

We next turn to fertility, which is an outcome that may be related to the age at marriage. If bride price leads to earlier marriage, then this may, in turn, cause higher fertility rates. Thus, we also examine the number of living children a woman has.[5] We estimate equation (1), with the number of children as the outcome of interest. The estimates are reported in Columns 4–6 of Table 6.2. The three columns report the same three specifications as in Columns 1–3. We estimate a positive relationship between bride price payments and fertility, although only the estimate in Column 1 is significant, and this only at the 10 per cent level. In addition, we find that as we add additional covariates the magnitude of the estimated effects converge towards zero. Lastly, the estimated magnitudes are also small. According to the point

[5] This does not take into account stillbirths or children that have died subsequently. Almost 25% of the women in the sample have had at least one child die during its first year of life.

127

estimates from Column 3, a one-standard-deviation increase in the bride price index is associated with the following increase in the number of children: $0.065 \times 1.44 = 0.09$.

Overall, we do not find evidence of an association between the value of the bride price and either a woman's age at marriage or the number of children that she has.

4.3. Bride Price and Attitudes About Domestic Violence

We now turn to an examination of whether bride price payments are associated with different attitudes about domestic violence on the part of husbands. In particular, a common concern is that the payment of a high bride price causes men to feel that because they have 'paid' dearly for their wife, they therefore have the right to mistreat her. We test for this possibility by estimating versions of equation (1) where the dependent variables are measures of men's self-reported views about the acceptability of domestic violence.

We measure the husband's attitudes about domestic violence using survey questions that we take from the DHS modules on domestic violence attitudes. Husbands are asked to report whether they believe that domestic violence is justified in five different situations. The situations are: (1) if the wife goes out without the husband's permission; (2) if she neglects the children; (3) if she argues with her husband; (4) if she refuses to have sex; (5) if she burns the food. For each scenario, the husbands chose an integer on a 1–5 scale, where 1 indicates that he 'Strongly Disagrees' (with domestic violence being justified in the situation) and 5 indicates that he 'Strongly Agrees' (with domestic violence being justified). We take the average of the answers in the five scenarios to obtain an index that ranges from 1 to 5 and that is increasing in the extent to which the husband believes that domestic violence is justified.

Estimates of equation (1), with the index of the husband's perceived acceptability of domestic violence as the outcome, are reported in Panel A of Table 6.3 in Columns 4–6. We estimate a positive effect in all three specifications. However, the estimates are generally not significant and are small in magnitude. According to the estimates of Column 6, a one-standard-deviation increase in the value of the bride price amount, results in an increase of $0.094 \times 1.44 = 0.14$ in the domestic violence index. This is equal to 6 per cent of the mean of the domestic violence acceptability index and 0.11 standard deviations. Although these effects are not completely trivial, they are fairly modest in addition to being imprecisely estimated.

We next examine the potential effects of bride price amounts on women's attitudes about domestic violence. The concern with high bride price payments is that wives may also believe that husbands can legitimately treat them badly if they have paid a high bride price. Thus, in Panel A of Table 6.3 in

Table 6.3. Bride price and domestic violence, marriage quality, and happiness

Panel A: Bride price and views about domestic violence

	Dep. var.: positive views of domestic violence index					
	Women			Men		
	(1)	(2)	(3)	(4)	(5)	(6)
Bride price amount	−0.153***	−0.163***	−0.172***	0.064	0.067	0.094*
	(0.035)	(0.036)	(0.036)	(0.050)	(0.050)	(0.050)
Wife-level controls, $\mathbf{X}_w$	Y	Y	Y	Y	Y	Y
Marriage-level controls, $\mathbf{X}_i$		Y	Y		Y	Y
Husband-level controls, $\mathbf{X}_h$			Y			Y
Observations	317	317	317	317	317	317
Mean dep. var.	2.470	2.470	2.470	2.322	2.322	2.322

Panel B: Bride price and marriage quality

	Dep. var.: frequency of activities index					
	Women			Men		
	(1)	(2)	(3)	(4)	(5)	(6)
Bride price amount	0.076**	0.076**	0.075**	0.119***	0.119***	0.114***
	(0.031)	(0.031)	(0.032)	(0.027)	(0.027)	(0.026)
Wife-level controls, $\mathbf{X}_w$	Y	Y	Y	Y	Y	Y
Marriage-level controls, $\mathbf{X}_i$		Y	Y		Y	Y
Husband-level controls, $\mathbf{X}_h$			Y			Y
Observations	315	315	315	315	315	315
Mean dep. var.	4.999	4.999	4.999	5.285	5.285	5.285

Panel C: Bride price and self-reported happiness

	Dep. var.: happiness					
	Women			Men		
	(1)	(2)	(3)	(4)	(5)	(6)
Bride price amount	0.188***	0.193***	0.192***	0.025	0.026	−0.005
	(0.037)	(0.038)	(0.038)	(0.033)	(0.033)	(0.035)
Wife-level controls, $\mathbf{X}_w$	Y	Y	Y	Y	Y	Y
Marriage-level controls, $\mathbf{X}_i$		Y	Y		Y	Y
Husband-level controls, $\mathbf{X}_h$			Y			Y
Observations	317	317	317	317	317	317
Mean dep. var.	2.681	2.681	2.681	2.700	2.700	2.700

Notes: Robust standard errors in parentheses. *Positive views of domestic violence index* takes the average response to the following questions: Domestic violence is justified if wife (1) goes out without husband's permission; (2) neglects children; (3) argues with husband; (4) refuses sex; (5) burns food; all questions answered with 1 = strongly disagree to 5 = strongly agree. The index sums the responses to each of the questions and divides by 5 to generate the average response. *Frequency of activities index* takes the average response to the following questions: How frequently do you and your spouse (1) laugh together; (2) work on a project together; (3) receive a gift; (4) walk together; (5) talk about your day; (6) discuss your feelings; all questions answered with 1 = never to 6 = more than once a day. The index sums the responses to each of the questions and divides by 6 to generate the average response. *Happiness* asks respondents to rate how happy they are on a scale of 1 = very unhappy to 5 = very happy. *Bride price amount* is a variable from 1 to 9 corresponding with various bride price values, where (1) is equal to US$0–25 and (9) is equal to US$1,500. *$p < 0.1$; **$p < 0.05$; ***$p < 0.01$.

Source: Authors.

Columns 1–3, we present the estimates with the wife's view on the acceptability of domestic violence in the household as the outcomes variable. We find evidence that a higher bride price paid at the time of marriage is associated with the wife being less accepting of domestic violence. All three coefficients of interest are negative and highly significant. According to the estimates of Column 3, a one-standard-deviation increase in the bride price payment index is associated with a decrease in the women's views of the acceptability of domestic violence that is equal to $0.172 \times 1.44 = 0.248$. This is a large effect that is equal to about 10 per cent of the mean of the domestic violence index and 0.43 standard deviations.

Overall, we find weak evidence that bride price amounts are associated with a greater reported acceptance of domestic violence for husbands, although these estimates are generally not significant and are small in magnitude. In contrast, the estimates show a significant and robust negative relationship between bride price amounts and the acceptability of violence for wives.

4.4. *Bride Price and Marriage Quality*

Another potential consequence of bride price is that it may affect the quality of the marriage. Therefore, we examine whether a higher bride price is correlated with marriage quality as measured by the frequency with which couples have positive interactions with each other. Husbands and wives were asked a series of questions about how often they did each of the following six activities with their spouse: laugh, work together on projects, receive gifts, walk together, talk about the day, and discuss their feelings. For each activity, the respondents chose from the following six response options: (1) never; (2) less than once a month; (3) once or twice a month; (4) once or twice a week; (5) once a day; and (6) more than once a day. We assign the reported numeric values to each response, and create an index equal to the average response value across each of the six activities. The final index ranges from 1 to 6 and increases with the frequency with which the couple engage in positive interactions. Most couples report engaging in positive activities fairly regularly, with the mean value being around 5.

Estimates of equation (1) with this outcome as the dependent variable are reported in Panel B of Table 6.3.[6] Columns 1–3 report estimates based on the woman's perception of the frequency of positive activities and Columns 4–6 report estimates based on the husband's perception. Across all specifications, we find that a higher bride price value is associated with a greater frequency of

---

[6] The sample size falls from 317 to 315 due to non-response.

positive interactions. According to the estimates from Column 6, a one-standard-deviation increase in the bride price index is associated with an increase of $0.114 \times 1.44 = 0.164$, which is equal to approximately $0.164/ 0.816 = 0.20$ standard deviations of the dependent variable. In addition, all estimates are highly significant, and the magnitude of the point estimates remain stable with the inclusion of additional covariates. Thus, the results suggest that a higher bride price is not associated with a lower-quality marriage, and in fact seems to be associated with better marriages, at least according to this particular measure of marriage quality.

4.5. *Bride Price and Self-Reported Happiness*

We now examine a related outcome, and one that directly measures women's well-being: self-reported happiness. We measure happiness using the following survey question: 'Taking all things together, would you say you are very unhappy, somewhat unhappy, neither happy nor unhappy, somewhat happy, or very happy? You can also look at these pictures to help you with your response.' The respondents were presented with emoticons of frowning and smiling faces to visualize the scale. Based on the respondents' answers, we create a variable that takes integer values between 1 and 5 and is increasing with their self-reported happiness.

We then estimate equation (1) with the wife's happiness as the outcome variable. Estimates are reported in Panel C of Table 6.3 in Columns 1–3. We find a robust positive relationship between the amount of bride price paid and the wife's self-reported happiness. The estimates are highly significant and stable across our three baseline specifications. The point estimate of 0.192 (from Column 3) suggests that a one-standard-deviation increase in the bride price index is associated with an increase of $0.192 \times 1.44 = 0.28$ points on the happiness scale. This is a sizeable effect given that the mean level of the happiness in the sample is 2.7 and that the standard deviation is 0.88.

The natural next question is what effect a higher bride price has on the husband's happiness. It is possible that a higher bride price is also associated with greater happiness on the part of the husband. However, it is also possible that the wife's happiness comes at the expense of the husband's happiness and so a higher bride price is associated with a less happy husband. We examine this by estimating equation (1) with the husband's happiness measure as the outcome of interest. Estimates are reported in Panel C of Table 6.3 in Columns 4–6. The estimated coefficients are very close to zero.

Overall, the estimates are consistent with a higher bride price resulting in greater happiness on the part of the wife, but having no effect on the happiness of the husband. These estimates are (perhaps) surprising given the general concern that a high bride price leads men to treat women poorly, leaving women in unhappy marriages where they are worse-off. Our estimates provide no evidence to support the validity of this concern. If anything, our findings appear to suggest that a higher bride price is associated with a better marriage, where the wife is happier.

4.6. Repayment Practices and Happiness

Another concern with the bride price is that it is often the case that if the marriage dissolves then the bride price must be paid back, in whole or in part, by the wife's family. The extent to which this convention is present, and is enforced, can vary depending on which party is perceived to be at fault, and whether or not the woman has had any children. The requirement of paying back bride price is believed to be a significant obstacle to women who would like to leave bad marriages, causing them to be stuck in these marriages.

In an attempt to provide evidence on this consequence of the bride price, we examine whether the presence of a requirement to pay back the bride price upon divorce is associated with less self-reported happiness by wives. If the practice of repayment causes women to be trapped in low-quality and unhappy marriages, then we would expect that married women who perceive there to be a requirement of repayment of the bride price upon divorce, on average, will be less happy.

To do this, we use information obtained from the following question: 'In the event of a divorce, how much of the bride price must be repaid?'. Respondents choose one of the following responses: all of it; most of it; some of it; a little bit of it; none of it; or don't know. Using their response, we then code a variable that equals 0 if none of it must be returned, 1 if some amount of it must be returned, and 2 if all of it must be returned. We add to our baseline estimating equation this measure, which is increasing in the extent to which the bride price must be repaid upon divorce.[7]

The estimates are reported in Columns 1–3 of Table 6.4. As shown, we find no evidence that the requirement to pay back the bride price upon divorce is associated with wives being less happy in their marriage. The coefficient on the repayment variable is not statistically different from zero. In addition, the coefficients are not negative, but positive. Though not significant, these estimates suggest that, if anything, a repayment requirement is positively associated with the wife's happiness.

---

[7] An alternative strategy is to create indicator variables for the categories of the index. All conclusions we report here remain if we do this.

Table 6.4. Bride price repayment customs and self-reported happiness

	Dep. Var.: wife's happiness					
	(1)	(2)	(3)	(4)	(5)	(6)
Bride price amount	0.186***	0.191***	0.190***	0.265***	0.276***	0.272***
	(0.038)	(0.038)	(0.038)	(0.041)	(0.041)	(0.041)
Amount pay back	0.069	0.078	0.065	0.926***	0.992***	0.933***
	(0.076)	(0.077)	(0.077)	(0.251)	(0.248)	(0.252)
Bride price amount*amount pay back				−0.146***	−0.156***	−0.148***
				(0.043)	(0.043)	(0.043)
Wife-level controls, $\mathbf{X}_w$	Y	Y	Y	Y	Y	Y
Marriage-level controls, $\mathbf{X}_i$		Y	Y		Y	Y
Husband-level controls, $\mathbf{X}_h$			Y			Y
Observations	317	317	317	317	317	317
Mean	2.681	2.681	2.681	2.681	2.681	2.681

Notes: Robust standard errors in parentheses. *Amount pay back* is a variable from 0 to 2, where (0) means none of the bride price has to be repaid upon divorce, (1) means some of the bride price must be repaid, and (2) means all of the bride price must be repaid. *Wife's Happiness* asks respondents to rate how happy they are on a scale of 1 = very unhappy to 5 = very happy. *$p < 0.1$; **$p < 0.05$; ***$p < 0.01$.

Source: Authors.

It is possible that the requirement to repay the bride price upon divorce is more detrimental when the value of the bride price paid is higher. We test for this possibility by including an interaction between the repayment variable and the value of the bride price measure. This allows the effect of the repayment requirement on the wife's happiness to vary depending on the value of the bride price that was paid at marriage.

The estimates are reported in Columns 4–6 of Table 6.4. Our estimates produce a coefficient for the interaction term that is negative and significant. According to the estimated magnitudes, the effect of the repayment index, which takes on the value of 0, 1, or 2 is given by: $0.926 - 0.146 \times$ *bride price amount*. Thus, the estimate relationship between the repayment index and the wife's happiness moves from being positive to negative when the value of the bride price index is greater than $0.926/0.146 = 6.34$. Therefore, when the value of the bride price index is 7, 8, or 9, then a requirement to repay the bride price is associated with lower happiness of the wife. The relationship is not significant for a bride price value of 7 ($p = 0.30$), but is significant for a value of 8 ($p = 0.05$) and a value of 9 ($p = 0.02$).

Overall, there is no evidence that the requirement to repay the bride price upon divorce is associated with wives being stuck in less happy marriages. However, this average effect does mask heterogeneity. When the value of the bride price that was paid at marriage is very high (above US$1,000), then there is a negative and significant relationship between the repayment requirement and the happiness of wives.

5. Taking Stock and Comparing Our Findings to Other Studies

To date, there is limited evidence about the correlates of bride price in the African context. One of the most robust findings, although about the causes of bride price and not its consequences, is that higher education is associated with higher bride price payments at marriage. The reason behind this association is explored in depth by Ashraf et al. (2016), who provide evidence that, within Zambia, the positive effect of the wife's education on her bride price is causal and widely known. In addition, they also show that this effect of education is taken into account when parents make the decision of whether to send their daughters to school. In our setting, we have also found a strong positive relationship between education and the value of the bride price.

A number of previous studies have examined the consequences of bride price values. In a recent working paper, Mbaye and Wagner (2013) examine over 2,000 respondents from eight regions in Senegal and find a significant negative relationship between higher bride price and fertility. This contrasts with our finding of no robust relationship between the value of the bride price and fertility. Although we estimated a positive relationship, the point estimates were generally not statistically different from zero. Along somewhat similar lines, the estimates from Mbaye and Wagner (2013) are only marginally significant and they are very small in magnitude. According to their estimates, if bride price increases by 100 per cent—a very large increase—fertility falls by only 0.04 children. Thus, taken together, our findings and the findings from Mbaye and Wagner (2013) seem to indicate that the value of the bride price appears to have no sizeable or robust relationship with fertility.

Although not the focus of their analysis, the study by Mbaye and Wagner (2013) also provides estimates of the relationship between bride price and a measure of appreciation of the wife by the husband. They find that a higher bride price is associated with less appreciation, although the coefficients are generally not statistically different from zero. This can be contrast to the spirit of our findings, which show a positive association between the value of the bride price and our different measures of the quality of the marriage.

The previous findings that are most directly comparable to the findings in this chapter are from qualitative studies. Comparing our findings to these studies, we find significant differences. For example, our findings that higher bride price is correlated with less acceptance of domestic violence, higher marriage quality, and greater happiness for women stand in stark contrast to the conclusions from casual observation or qualitative studies. A number of focus group and survey-based studies have shown that men and women tend to believe that the bride price results in less empowerment of women, worse marriages, and lower overall well-being. Results of this nature have been found in Uganda (Hague et al. 2011; Kaye et al. 2013) and Ghana

(Dery 2015; Horne et al. 2013). For example, in Hague et al. (2011), 84 per cent of 151 respondents reported that they believed that there was a strong connection between the value of the bride price and domestic violence.

There are many explanations for the differences in the findings. First, Africa is not a homogeneous unit. Thus, there could be significant heterogeneity across the large continent, which may result in differences in our relationships of interest. Thus, the effects of bride price may be different in the DRC than in Uganda, Kenya, or Ghana. A second possibility is that the actual effects of the bride price custom may be different from the perceived effects. Individuals observe the practice of the bride price, high levels of domestic violence, and low levels of female empowerment and may draw a link between them. Whether there is a general relationship in the data when looking across a large number of individuals is an empirical question. A third possibility stems from the fact that in qualitative studies participants' answers must be interpreted, and this is done through the lens of the researcher. Thus, there is concern that the researcher's prior assumptions affect the mapping that is made from statements in the focus groups to conclusions. Further, the presence of a researcher in the focus groups may affect the statements made by participants, and one worries, in particular, about 'demand effects', where participants are more likely to inadvertently (and without conscious realization) say what they feel the researcher wants to hear. This can be contrasted with surveys, which, though less rich in some dimensions, have the advantage that researchers are not present when the questions are answered. Instead, local enumerators ask the questions.

6. Conclusion

Bride price, which is payment from the groom and/or groom's family to the bride's family at the time of marriage, is an important cultural practice of many African societies. In recent years, there have been widespread concerns that the practice may have negative effects for women. One concern is that the monetary payment received by the bride's family at marriage may incentivize early marriage, leading to higher fertility. It is also believed that it may promote the view that husbands have 'purchased' their wives, resulting in worse treatment of wives. In many locations, the bride price must be paid back to the groom's family upon divorce. This may cause an obstacle to divorce and result in women being trapped in unhappy marriages. Thus, in general, there has been widespread concern that the practice is detrimental to the well-being of women.

In this chapter, we have used data related to these issues in an attempt to provide a better understanding of the potential effects of bride price. We did this by examining the empirical relationship between bride price payments and various outcomes of interest, using a sample of 317 married couples from Kananga, a city located in the DRC, a setting where almost everyone pays a bride price and marriages are not recognized as legitimate unless a bride price is paid.

We found no evidence that a larger bride price payment is associated with earlier marriage or with higher fertility. We also found that larger bride price payments are associated with better-quality marriages as measured by beliefs about the acceptability of domestic violence, the frequency of engaging in positive activities as a couple, and the self-reported happiness of the wife. We also examined the correlates of the requirement for the bride price to be paid back upon divorce. Contrary to general concerns about this aspect of the custom, we found no evidence that this requirement is associated with women being less happy in their marriages. In fact, we found a positive association, although the coefficient was statistically insignificant. However, we did find that if the value of the bride price paid was very high (over US$1,000), then the requirement is, in fact, negatively associated with the happiness of the wife.

Overall, we found that the evidence does not support the notion that the practice of bride price has detrimental effects on the well-being of married women. Perhaps surprisingly, in general, a higher bride price tends to be associated with good outcomes. The one exception is that the presence of a high bride price and the requirement for the bride price to be paid back upon divorce does appear to be associated with less happiness on the part of the wife.

We end by reminding the reader about an important caveat. Although informative and valuable, the relationships that we estimate cannot be taken as definitive evidence of the causal effect of high bride price and/or repayment requirements on women's well-being. Despite our attempts to control for potentially omitted factors, it is very possible that they still influence the estimates and impeded our ability to interpret them as causal. However, we do feel that the estimates we report here lead one to pause and recognize the need for greater research to understand the causal effects of the custom, particularly given the calls to abolish the practice in many countries within Africa.

References

Adams, B.N., and E. Mburugu (1994). 'Kikuyu Bridewealth and Polygyny Today'. *Journal of Comparative Family Studies*, 25(2): 159–66.

Anderson, S. (2007). 'The Economics of Dowry and Brideprice'. *Journal of Economic Perspectives*, 21(4): 151–74.

Ashraf, N., N. Bau, N. Nunn, and A. Voena (2016). 'Bride Price and Female Education'. Working Paper. Cambridge, MA: Harvard University.

Biryabarema, E. (2015). 'Uganda Court Says Divorced Husbands Cannot Demand "Bride Price" Refund'. Reuters Africa, 6 August.

Bishai, D., and S. Grossbard (2010). 'Far Above Rubies: Bride Price and Extramarital Sexual Relations in Uganda'. *Journal of Population Economics*, 23(4): 1177–87.

Borgerhoff Mulder, M. (1995). 'Bridewealth and Its Correlates: Quantifying Changes Over Time'. *Current Anthropology*, 36(4): 573–603.

Chondoka, Y.A. (1988). *Traditional Marriages in Zambia: A Study in Cultural History*. Cambridge: Cambridge University Press.

Corno, L., and A. Voena (2016). 'Selling Daughters: Age of Marriage, Income Shocks and the Bride Price Tradition'. Working Paper. Chicago, IL: University of Chicago.

Corno, L., N. Hildebrandt, and A. Voena (2016). 'Weather Shocks, Age of Marriage and the Direction of Marriage Payments'. Working Paper. Chicago, IL: University of Chicago.

Dery, I. (2015). 'Bride-Price and Domestic Violence: Empirical Perspectives from Nandom District in the North Western Region of Ghana'. *International Journal of Development Sustainability*, 4(3): 258–71.

Dudley, O. (2014). 'Highlights of the Marriage Act, 2014'. Available at: http://kenyalaw. org/kenyalawblog/highlights-of-the-marriage-act-2014/ (accessed 5 June 2017).

Eryenyu, J. (2014). 'Payment of Bride Price Turns Women into Commodities'. *Daily Monitor*. Available at: www.monitor.co.ug/OpEd/Letters/Payment-of-bride-price-turns-women-into-commodities/806314-2447104-n41iwj/index.html (accessed 5 June 2017).

Goldschmidt, W. (1974). 'The Economics of Brideprice Among the Sebei and in East Africa'. *Ethnology*, 13(4): 311–31.

Government of Uganda (2001). *A Compendium of Laws Relating to Domestic Relations in Uganda*. Kampala: LDC Publishers.

Hague, G., R.K. Thiara, and A. Turner (2011). 'Bride-price and its Links to Domestic Violence and Poverty in Uganda: A Participatory Action Research Study'. *Women's Studies International Forum*, 34: 550–61.

Horne, C., F.N.-A. Dodoo, and N.D. Dodoo (2013). 'The Shadow of Indebtedness: Bridewealth and Norms Constraining Female Reproductive Autonomy'. *American Sociological Review*, 78(3): 503–20.

IRIN News (2006). 'Study Links Payment of Bride Price to Abuse of Women'. Available at: www.irinnews.org/report/59032/tanzania-study-links-payment-bride-price-abuse-women (accessed 5 June 2017).

Kaye, D.K., F. Mirembe, A.M. Ekstrom, G.B. Kyomuhendo, and A. Johansson (2013). 'Implications of Bride Price on Domestic Violence and Reproductive Health in Wakiso District, Uganda'. *African Health Sciences*, 5(4): 300–3.

Kelly, A. (2006). 'Why Girls are Economically Challenged'. *The Guardian*. Available at: www.theguardian.com/katine/2009/aug/17/money-women (accessed 5 June 2017).

Lowes, S. (2017). 'Matrilineal Kinship and Spousal Cooperation: Evidence from the Matrilineal Belt'. Working Paper. Cambridge, MA: Harvard University.

Lowes, S. and N. Nunn (2017). 'Bride Price and the Wellbeing of Women'. *WIDER Working Paper* 2017/131. Helsinki: UNU-WIDER.

Mbaye, L.M., and N. Wagner (2013). 'Bride Price and Fertility Decisions: Evidence from Rural Senegal'. Discussion Paper 7770. Bonn: IZA.

Mwesigwa, A. (2015). 'Uganda Court Rules Against Refund of "Bride Price" After Divorce'. The *Guardian*, 17 August.

Tembo, S. (2014). 'Court Warns Against High Bride Prices'. *Times of Zambia*, 3 May. Available at: www.times.co.zm/?p=21383 (accessed 5 June 2017).

Vansina, J. (1966). *Introduction a l'Ethnographic du Congo*. Kinshasa: Centre de Recherche et d'Information Socio-Politiques.

Vroklage, B. (1952). 'Bride Price or Dower'. *Anthropos*, 47(1/2): 133–46.

Part II
Outside Options

7

Reducing Early Pregnancy in Low-Income Countries

A Literature Review and New Evidence

Lars Ivar Oppedal Berge, Kjetil Bjorvatn, Amina Mohamed Maalim, Vincent Somville, and Bertil Tungodden[1]

1. Background

> My first priority in life is to educate myself and, once I do, I will use my education to prevent cruel practices that other girls are being subjected to such as child marriage, circumcision and arranged marriages...Since I started Form one, it was very difficult for my parents to pay my fees or buy school uniform. I have many problems that bother me, for instance I am completing Form four and to date my parents have not paid the school fees. Sometimes when I go back home, I often cry. Therefore, I would like to say that I have many aspirations in life. However, I feel that I will not be successful due to the difficulties I am encountering...I do not have much more to say but I do have one worry. I would like you to give me advice. Once I finish school, what should I do in order to avoid the pressures of unwanted pregnancy and the expectation of early marriage?
>
> Adolescent girl, Morogoro region of Tanzania

[1] We would like to thank Femina Hip for excellent cooperation throughout the research project. In addition, we would like to thank Katanta Simwanza and Goodluck Charles for their assistance in developing the training material. We would also like to thank Tausi Kida and Linda Helgesson Sekei for their invaluable contributions in designing and implementing the research project. Special thanks for first-rate research assistance to Juda Lyamai. Finally, we would like to thank the editor, Jean-Philippe Platteau, Markus Goldstein, and participants in the UNU-WIDER Gender and Development Conference at Namur University for excellent comments and suggestions. We have received financial support from the Research Council of Norway, The Royal Norwegian Embassy in Tanzania, NHH Norwegian School of Economics, and the Chr. Michelsen Institute. The project has been administered by The Choice Lab.

This quote is from one of the participants in a research project on female empowerment that we conducted in Tanzania, and on which we will have more to say later in the chapter. It illustrates the challenges facing many adolescent girls in low-income countries, where early pregnancy and lifelong dependence upon family and partners threaten both their social and economic development.[2] In Tanzania, by the age of nineteen, more than 40 per cent of the girls have had their first child (data from the 2015–16 Tanzania District health survey).

Early pregnancies are generally associated with negative effects on women's health and education (Goldin & Katz 2002; Rasul 2008), as well as their economic achievement (Bailey 2006; Miller 2010). Early pregnancies are also associated with poor health outcomes for the child: children born to adolescent mothers generally have lower birth weight, and the risk of being still born or dying in the first weeks is 50 per cent higher when the mother is under 20 years old than when she is 20–29 years old (World Health Organization 2014).

It is therefore of great importance to understand which interventions are effective in delaying pregnancies among adolescent girls in developing countries, and the present chapter offers a review of the rich set of interventions that have been studied in the literature. In this review, we offer a novel approach to evaluating these types of interventions by distinguishing interventions that target girls' *mindset* (preferences and beliefs) from those that relieve constraints and expand girls' set of economic *opportunities*. The underlying idea is that early pregnancies may reflect both a certain mindset and a lack of alternatives. Changing the mindset, for instance by making girls more aware of the risks of early pregnancy or increasing their locus of control, can take place through education, as illustrated by the following statement by an adolescent girl in the Morogoro region of Tanzania, reflecting on a training programme on reproductive health:

> I have received training on fertility and health and been taught how to say no when a man asks you to have sex with him. You should have a firm stand in saying no and not fear him and start to bite your nails or dig your foot into the ground. You have to stare at him in the face and be serious. All the girls should receive education on how to say no.

On the other hand, girls may also delay pregnancies if they have greater economic opportunities, as a result of either cash transfers or vocational or entrepreneurship training programmes, as illustrated by the following statement by another adolescent participant in our research project:

---

[2] In the age group 15–19 years, the fertility rate is 108 per 1,000 women in sub-Saharan Africa compared with 25 per 1,000 women in the OECD (data.worldbank.org).

In August, I received training on entrepreneurship, which has enabled me to understand the opportunities available to me as a girl... After the training, I became more informed on how to start my own business, which will make me work hard for my future. In the next 5 years, I will have a huge business, which I know will bring in income. After completing my education, my life will be based in Morogoro. I do not expect to have children during this time until when I am employed or running my own business that will bring in income and independence from anyone else.

The quote reveals that the entrepreneurship training programme may not only expand girls' economic opportunities, but also changed their mindset, in the sense that they become more future orientation and independent. Hence, as will be illustrated throughout this chapter, there is not always a sharp distinction between field interventions that aim to change the mindset and field interventions that aim to improve the opportunities of adolescent girls; often they do both.

The most common approach to addressing early pregnancies has been to target the mindset dimension by providing adolescent girls with health and family planning information, sometimes combined with initiatives to improve access to contraceptives. But more recently, there has been a greater focus on expanding economic opportunities, in the form of both conditional cash grants and entrepreneurship training programmes. The increased focus on economic opportunities is also reflected in policy circles. For example, the WHO stresses the importance of improving economic opportunities and increasing the negotiation and life skills of adolescent girls to allow them to make safer sexual decisions and avoid unwanted sex.[3]

This chapter is divided into two parts. In the first part, we survey the literature on field interventions targeting early pregnancies and risky sexual behaviour. We limit ourselves to research on low-income countries from this century and to studies that include evidence on adolescents, which we define as people below eighteen years of age. We organize the survey in three sections: (i) interventions targeting mindset; (ii) interventions creating economic opportunities; (iii) interventions that target both dimensions. Recent reviews, which include evidence from high-income countries, consistently conclude that interventions that combine sexual education and improved access to contraceptives give better results than single interventions (Oringanje et al. 2016; The World Bank 2012). We argue in this chapter that even those combined interventions do not lead to clear and consistent results and that increasing economic opportunities, perhaps in tandem with health training, may be needed.

---

[3] See World Health Organization on Gender: http://www.searo.who.int/entity/gender/en/ (accessed 6 June 2017).

The second part of the chapter reports from a randomized control trial (RCT) that we are currently conducting in rural Tanzania with adolescent girls, and from which the above quotes are taken. We show how health training and entrepreneurship training have affected both the mindset, through an increase in the locus of control, and the economic opportunities of the girls, through making them more interested in starting their own business. In the analysis of this RCT, we move beyond studying responses to survey questions by conducting a text analysis of more than 3,000 essays written by adolescent girls about their hopes for the future. A weakness in the literature is the lack of evidence on the mechanisms through which the interventions work, and we believe that text analysis represents an innovative and promising tool for attaining a better understanding of how such interventions shape the mindset and behaviour of adolescent girls.

2. Literature

In this section, we review thirty papers that differ in several dimensions, such as context (countries and time), sample characteristics (gender, age), and research design (difference-in-difference, randomized control trials). Table 7.1 provides an overview of the papers, organized by the nature of the intervention (affecting mindset, economic opportunities, or both) and ordered by publication date. For each paper, the table provides the reference, a description of the interventions (type, country, year), the method, and the main impacts.

2.1. Changing the Mindset

The provision of health-related information, including family planning information, has traditionally been the most common method of reducing both early pregnancies and risky sexual behaviour. Some of these interventions focus on providing basic knowledge, assuming the targeted girls lack an understanding of both how to protect themselves against pregnancy and how STIs are transmitted.[4] Other studies address the social dimension, for instance by considering the impact of teaching abstinence until marriage.

We discuss the impact of the different interventions in three dimensions: knowledge and attitudes, sexual behaviour, and pregnancies. Overall, the

---

[4] Note the difference between 'STI' (sexual transmittable *infection*) and STD (sexual transmittable *disease*). Depending on the strain of the bacteria, virus, or protozoa, infections can (but may not always) cause a disease. Therefore, not all STIs cause STDs, but an STD is classified as an STI (https://www.medinstitute.org/2011/11/std-sti-sti-std-whats-the-difference/, accessed 31 March 2017).

Table 7.1. Literature overview

Paper	Intervention	Country (time)	Sample	Method	Main results
Mindset					
Eggleston et al. 2000	Health information in schools (promotion of both abstinence and safer sex)	Jamaica (1995–1997)	945 girls/boys Age: 11–14	DiD	After one year: - Almost no impact on reproductive health knowledge - No impact on attitudes towards sexual activity - No impact on contraceptive use
Kim et al. 2001	Multimedia campaign to promote sexual responsibility and increase reproductive health services by training providers	Zimbabwe (1997–1998)	1,400 women/men Age: 10–24	DiD (control site partly exposed to intervention)	- Little impact on general reproductive health knowledge - Positive impact on 'saying no to sex', abstinence, 'avoiding sugar daddies'
Magnani R.J. et al. 2001	School- and health-clinic-based adolescent reproductive health initiative: - Training courses for health workers in reproductive health services for adolescents - School sexual and reproductive health education curriculum	Brazil (1997–1999)	4,777 women/men Age: 11–19	DiD	- No impact on sexual or contraceptive-use behaviour - No impact on use of public clinics
Agha 2002	Subsidised condoms and promoting the use of condoms (peer educators, youth clubs, media campaigns)	Cameroon, Botswana, South Africa, Guinea (1994–1998)	Cameroon: 1,606 women/men Age: 12–22 South Africa: 221 women/men Age: 17–20 Botswana: 1,002 (increased to 2,396 at follow-up) women/men Age: 13–18 Guinea: 2016 women/men Age: 'young adults'	DiD	- Ambiguous effects on perceptions and beliefs, improving some but not others - Ambiguous effects on number of partners and condom use, with some significant impact on some of the indicators in some of the countries

(continued)

Table 7.1. Continued

Paper	Intervention	Country (time)	Sample	Method	Main results
Okonofua et al. 2003	Community participation, peer education, public lectures, health clubs in schools, and training of STD treatment providers. The treatment is compared to a control with no intervention	Nigeria (1997–1998)	1,896 women/men Age: 14–20	RCT in 12 schools (4 treated 8 control)	- Improvements in knowledge of STDs, condom use, awareness that the partner had an STD and STD treatment-seeking behaviour - Reduction in reported STD symptoms
Lou C.-H. et al. 2004	Build awareness and offer counselling and services related to sexuality and reproduction	China (2000–2001)	2,227 women/men Age: 15–24	DiD	- Increase in condom use
Tu et al. 2008	Follow-up to Lou et al. 2004.	China (2000–2001)			- No long-term impacts
Agha & Van Rossem 2004	Peer sexual health education intervention in secondary schools. The treatment is compared to a control with no intervention	Zambia (2000–2001)	416 women/men Age: 14–23	RCT (3 treated schools, 2 control)	- Positive changes in normative beliefs about abstinence - Reductions in multiple regular partnerships - No change in condom use
Cabezón et al. 2005	'TeenStar' abstinence-centred sex education programme. The treatment is compared to a control with no intervention	Chile (1996–1997)	1,259 girls Age: 15–16	RCT	- Reduced pregnancies
Magnani R. et al. 2005	Life skills education programme for all students in middle and secondary schools	South Africa (1999)	2,222 women/men Age: 14–24	Observational/IV	- Positive effects on sexual and reproductive health knowledge, perceived condom self-efficacy, and condom use at first and last sex - No consistent effects on age at sexual initiation, secondary abstinence, or partnering behaviours
Cartagena et al. 2006	Sexual health peer education	Mongolia (2004)	1,367 women/men Age: 15–19	Observational	- Increase in knowledge, reduction in traditional attitudes, and greater awareness of self-efficacy regarding HIV and sexual health - No increase in likelihood of practising safe sex

Study	Intervention	Country (Year)	Sample	Method	Results
Walker et al. 2006	The intervention had three arms: - HIV prevention course that promoted condom use - The same course with emergency contraception as back-up - The existing sex education course (control)	Mexico (2001)	10,954 students in 40 schools Age: 15–18	Cluster RCT	- No effect on condom use - Improved knowledge of HIV in both intervention groups - Improved knowledge of emergency contraception in corresponding group - Reported sexual behaviour similar in the intervention and control groups
Ross et al. 2007	The intervention had four components: - Community activities - Teacher-led, peer-assisted sexual health education in years 5–7 of primary school - Training and supervision of health workers to provide 'youth-friendly' sexual health services - Peer condom social marketing The treatment is compared to a control with no intervention	Tanzania (1998)	9,645 adolescents in 20 communities Age: 12–19 (a few above 19)	RCT	- Significant impact on knowledge, attitudes, and reported sexually transmitted infection symptoms - No consistent impact on biological outcomes
Doyle et al. 2010	Follow-up to Ross et al. 2007	Tanzania (1998)	13,814 women/men Age: 15–30	RCT	- Clear and consistent beneficial impact on sexual and reproductive health knowledge - Generally no significant impact on attitudes to sexual risk, pregnancies, or other reported sexual behaviours, except for some specific outcomes and sub-groups of subjects
Daniel et al. 2008	- Promoting delaying birth of first child until the mother is 21, and birth of second child until 36 months after first birth - Promoting contraception	India (2002–2004)	1,995 women Age: <25	DiD	- Increased contraceptive use
Dupas 2011	Four groups: - (a) Providing information on the relative risk of HIV infection by partner's age - (b) The government's official abstinence-only HIV curriculum - (a) and (b) combined - No intervention	Kenya (2003–2005)	2,422 girls/boys Age: 13–17	RCT	- Risk info: 28 per cent decrease in teen pregnancy - Official abstinence-only HIV curriculum: no impact on teen pregnancy

(continued)

Table 7.1. Continued

Paper	Intervention	Country (time)	Sample	Method	Main results
Dupas et al. 2017	Four groups: - Teacher training on the regular HIV prevention curriculum - 60-minute session on the regular HIV prevention curriculum delivered by an outside consultant - 60-minute session on the regular HIV prevention curriculum delivered by an outside consultant + 'Sugar Daddy Risk Awareness' information from Dupas (2011) - Control group without interventions	Cameroon (2010–2011)	3,154 girls from 318 schools Age: 15 on average	RCT	- Childbearing reduced by 25–48 per cent in all treatments
Opportunities					
Stecklov et al. 2007	CCT (conditional on children enrolling in and attending school and that family members obtain health care)	Honduras (2000–2002) Nicaragua (2000–2002) Mexico (1998–2003)	Honduras: 1,997 women Nicaragua: 2,000 women Mexico: 2,000 women Age: 12–47	DiD	- Honduras: CCT increased fertility (eligibility criteria incentivized childbearing) - No significant impacts in the other two countries
Feldman et al. 2009	Oportunidades Mexico Compared to no intervention	Mexico (1998–2003)	8,568 women Age: 15–49	RCT	- No effect on contraceptive use or birth spacing
Baird et al. 2010	CCT Zomba (conditional on school attendance) Compared to no transfers	Malawi (2007–2008)	3,805 women Age: 13–22	RCT	- Significant declines in early marriage, teenage pregnancy, and self-reported sexual activity
Alam et al. 2011	The Punjab Female School Stipend Programme: - Female CCT Compared to no stipend	Pakistan (2003–2009)	4,000 women Age: 12–19	RD DiD	- No effect on marriage delays or births

Study	Description	Country (year)	Sample	Method	Findings
Baird et al. 2011	Three arms: - UCT - CCT (conditional on school attendance) - No transfers	Malawi (2008–2010)	2,907 schoolgirls Age: 13–22	RCT	- Teenage pregnancy and marriage rates substantially lower in the UCT than the CCT group, entirely due to the impact of UCTs on these outcomes among girls who dropped out of school
de Walque et al. 2012	CCT (conditional on negative STD test) Two treatments: - Low-value transfer - High-value transfer The study also includes a control group without transfers	Tanzania (2010–2011)	10 villages, 2,399 of Age: 18–30	RCT	- High-value transfer reduced STD prevalence, directly measured using biological samples.
Jensen 2012	Three years of recruiting services to help young women in randomly selected rural Indian villages to get jobs in the business process outsourcing industry The treated villages are compared to control villages without recruiting services	India (2003–2006)	3,200 households, Age: 15–21	RCT at village level	- Women from treatment villages 5–6 percentage points less likely to get married or to have given birth over the three-year period of the intervention
Handa et al. 2014	UCT of US$20 per month. The treatment is compared to a control with no transfers	Kenya	1,433 women and men Age: 15–25	RCT	- Delay in age of sexual debut - No effect on HIV-risk-related behaviours such as condom use, number of partners and transactional sex
Heath & Mobarak 2015	Compare girls and boys living in villages that have gained, or have not gained, access to garment factories	Bangladesh (1980–2014)	30,180 women	DiD	- Women exposed to the garment sector delay marriage and childbirth
Mindset & Opportunities					
Bandiera et al. 2015	Vocational training and information on reproductive health in youth clubs The treatment is compared to a control with no intervention	Uganda (2008–2012)	5,000 girls Age: 14–20	RCT	- Increased likelihood of girls engaging in income-generating activities (driven by increased self-employment) - Increased private consumption - Decrease in teen pregnancy and early entry into marriage/cohabitation - Drop in share of girls reporting sex against their will

(continued)

Table 7.1. Continued

Paper	Intervention	Country (time)	Sample	Method	Main results
Buehren et al. 2015	Vocational training and information on reproductive health in youth clubs, combined with microfinance services	Tanzania (2009–2011)	150 villages	RCT	- No significant impact on childbearing, or other outcomes related to sexual behaviour
Duflo et al. 2015	The study has four components: - Education subsidies - Abstinence curriculum - Education subsidies and abstinence curriculum - Control group with no particular intervention	Kenya (2003–2010)	328 schools Age: average at baseline 13.5 years	RCT	Education subsidy programme: - Statistically significantly reduced teen pregnancy rate (from 16 to 13 per cent). - No impact on HSV-2 prevalence Abstinence curriculum alone: - No impact Combined treatment: - Reduction in both fertility and HSV-2 infection
Buchmann et al. 2016	The study has four components: - (a) Empowerment programme - (b) Financial incentive to delay marriage - (a) and (b) combined - Control group with no particular intervention	Bangladesh (2008–2013)	19,060 women in 446 communities Age: 10–19	RCT	Financial incentive: - Reduced the likelihood of teenage childbearing by 14 per cent. Empowerment programme and combined treatments: - No effect on childbearing

Note: CCT = conditional cash transfer, DiD = difference-in-difference, IV = instrumental variable, RCT = randomized controlled trial, RD = regression discontinuity design, UCT = unconditional cash transfer.

Source: The above-mentioned studies, as well as the authors' interpretation of these studies.

studies suggest that it is possible to influence knowledge and attitudes, but that inducing changes in sexual behaviour and reducing early pregnancies are much more difficult, in line with what is argued in an overview article by Gallant & Maticka-Tyndale (2004).

2.1.1. KNOWLEDGE AND ATTITUDES

Several studies report a positive impact on knowledge and attitudes. The HIV prevention programme in Mongolian secondary schools (Cartagena et al. 2006) made students more knowledgeable with regard to HIV and sexual health; the information campaign in Nigeria increased reported knowledge about STIs, condom use, and treatment-seeking behaviour (Okonofua et al. 2003); the health education project in Tanzania (Doyle et al. 2010; Ross et al. 2007) had a significant impact on the participants' health knowledge; a cluster RCT offering an HIV-prevention course in Mexico improved knowledge about HIV (Walker et al. 2006); and students in Zambia who followed a peer education programme in secondary schools were more positive regarding the use of condoms and abstinence shortly after the programme (Agha & Van Rossem 2004).

2.1.2. SEXUAL BEHAVIOUR

Media-based reproductive health campaigns have proven effective in increasing women's contraceptive use, as shown in Cameroon, Botswana, South Africa, and Guinea (Agha 2002). Similar results were found from a multimedia campaign in Zimbabwe, where young people in campaign areas were much more likely to report saying no to sex, to visit a health centre, and to use contraceptives (Kim et al. 2001). An information campaign in Nigeria also increased condom use, awareness that the partner had an STD, and STD treatment-seeking behaviour (Okonofua et al. 2003). In South Africa, R. Magnani et al. (2005) used an instrumental variables approach to estimate the impacts of a life skills education programme in middle and secondary schools. They report significant increases in condom use at first and last sex. The PRACHAR Project in Bihar (India) also increased the demand for and use of contraceptives through communication interventions (Daniel et al. 2008).

There are, however, several studies with less positive findings. In their evaluation of a sexual education programme in Jamaica, Eggleston et al. (2000) do not find significant impacts on contraceptive use after one year. In Brazil, a combination of school-based sexual education and youth-friendly health services did not affect reported sexual behaviours or contraceptive use (R. J. Magnani et al. 2001). A sexual education intervention in secondary schools in Zambia did not cause significant changes in condom use (Agha & Van Rossem 2004). Lou et al. (2004) base their report on an intervention that promotes contraception use among unmarried youths in Shanghai by building awareness and offering counselling and services related to sexuality and reproduction. They find a large, positive impact on contraception use shortly after the programme, but the effect vanishes three years later (Tu et al. 2008).

In Mongolia, Cartagena et al. (2006) evaluate the results of an HIV-prevention programme in secondary schools. Four years after the programme, they found no clear impact on (reported) safe sex practices. In Mexico, Walker et al. (2006) report from a cluster randomized trial with three groups, undergoing an HIV-prevention course with promotion of condom use, the same course including emergency contraception as a back-up, and the existing sexual education course. Reported condom use and sexual behaviour were similar in all groups. In another randomized trial, Ross et al. (2007) document the effects of a health education project in Tanzania with four components: community activities; teacher-led, peer-assisted sexual health education in primary schools; training and supervision of health workers to provide 'youth-friendly' sexual health services; and condom marketing. They observe a significant impact on reported STI symptoms, but not on biological outcomes. The follow-up study did not find significant impacts on reported sexual behaviours. Finally, in a randomized experiment involving 328 schools in Kenya, Dupas (2011) compares two groups: a control group in which the students received the standard national HIV curriculum; and a treatment group in which the students received information on the relative risk of HIV infection by partner's age and gender. Compared with the control group, the treatment group reported increased sexual activity (but reduced risky sex). The study further suggests that girls moved away from older partners and toward younger partners.

2.1.3. PREGNANCY

Cabezón et al. (2005) evaluate an abstinence-centred sex-education programme (TeenSTAR) in a Chilean high school in the mid-1990s. They randomized the programme within student cohorts, and followed the students for four years. They report a very large reduction in pregnancy rates: from 18.9 per cent to 3.3 per cent in the 1997 cohort and from 22.6 per cent to 4.4 per cent in the 1998 cohort.

Dupas (2011) found that the HIV risk treatment decreased the likelihood that girls started childbearing within a year by 28 per cent compared to the control group, while the abstinence programme had no impact. An additional important finding is that the treatment also increased reported sexual activity (but reduced risky sex). The study further suggests that girls moved away from older partners and toward younger partners.

Interestingly, Dupas et al. (2017) report from a similar experiment in Cameroon, where they compared a control group with groups (i) undergoing a one-hour HIV prevention session delivered by external consultants, (ii) undergoing the same one-hour session with additional information about the relative risk of HIV infection by partner's age, (iii) completing a one-hour self-administered HIV questionnaire, and (iv) following a classical HIV curriculum with their teacher. All treatments in this study reduced teen pregnancy by around 25 per cent.

In contrast to these positive findings, Doyle et al. (2010) report from a randomized intervention that provided sexual and reproductive health information, combined with 'youth-friendly' health services and subsidized condoms, in Tanzania. They do not find any impact on pregnancies or other sexual behaviours, despite strong improvements in knowledge. Similarly, Duflo et al. (2015), in Kenya, do not find any evidence of an impact on early pregnancy (or STIs) of an HIV curriculum stressing abstinence until marriage.

2.2. Expanding Economic Opportunities

During the last few decades, there has been a rise in interventions primarily aimed at changing economic opportunities in several development domains, including reproductive health. Interventions range from various cash-transfer schemes, conditioned, or not, on school enrolment and medical testing, to entrepreneurship or vocational training programmes.

There is limited evidence on the extent to which expanding economic opportunities also affects the mindset dimension, for instance in terms of locus of control. This may be important, since a change in the mindset has the potential to create a more durable effect from the intervention, going beyond the period of subsidies or training. We address this issue in the second part of this chapter, where we report from our ongoing study in Tanzania. Here, we limit ourselves to studying the impact on sexual behaviour and pregnancy. The overall impression is that the expansion of economic opportunities, particularly through financial incentives, can be effective, but that programme design matters.

2.2.1. SEXUAL BEHAVIOUR

Feldman et al. (2009) evaluate the effect of the conditional cash transfer (CCT) programme Oportunidades in Mexico, where the transfer was tied to regular health check-ups and school attendance, and report short-term, but no long-term, effects on contraceptive use. De Walque et al. (2012) study a randomized CCT programme where treated participants were eligible to receive a cash transfer if they tested negative for curable STIs. They compare high- and low-value transfers and find that that the high-value transfers reduced STI prevalence, measured by biomedical tests. Finally, Handa et al. (2014) report that a UCT of US$20 per month in Kenya lead to a significant postponement in the age of sexual debut.

2.2.2. PREGNANCY

Several studies find that interventions that change economic incentives affect early pregnancies. In Pakistan, Alam et al. (2011) studied female-targeted cash transfers in the form of school stipends, where the transfer was made conditional on a minimum school attendance of 80 per cent. They find increased school enrolment among eligible girls, which appears to have caused fewer teenage births and delayed marriage.

In their evaluation of the Zomba cash transfer programme for school attendance in Malawi, Baird et al. (2010) find large reductions in teenage pregnancy, early marriage, and self-reported sexual activity. In this study, school attendance was the only condition for the transfer, and the transfer as such was given in part to the student and in part to her guardian. In another experiment in Malawi, Baird et al. (2011) compare a CCT on school attendance with a UCT and a control group. Compared with the control group and the CCT, the UCT reduced the proportion of ever-pregnant women by 6.7 percentage points. They further show that the UCT effect comes from the girls who dropped out of school.

In India, another type of intervention had a large and significant impact on childbearing: it consisted of three years of recruiting services to help young women in randomly selected rural villages to get jobs in the business process outsourcing industry. Jensen (2012) finds that the intervention reduced the likelihood of getting married or giving birth over the three-year period by 5–6 percentage points. In the same vein, Heath & Mobarak (2015) report that the expansion of the garment industry in Bangladesh in the 1980s and 1990s pushed women to pursue further education and delayed marriage and childbearing.

Some studies do not find evidence that economic incentives reduce early pregnancies. Stecklov et al. (2007) evaluate the impact on fertility of the Oportunidades programme in Mexico as well as similar programmes in Nicaragua and Honduras, and do not find any impact on fertility of the programmes in Mexico or Nicaragua, and, surprisingly, an increase in fertility by 2 to 4 percentage points in Honduras. The authors argue that the increased fertility in Honduras could be due to the fact that eligibility for the programme required the household to include a pregnant woman or a child below three years old.

2.3. *Combined Treatments: Changing the Mindset and Expanding Economic Opportunities*

We have identified four studies that clearly target both mindset and economic opportunities. First, Duflo et al. (2015), in an RCT involving 328 schools in Kenya, compare the effects of (i) education subsidies (free uniforms), (ii) an HIV curriculum stressing abstinence, and (iii) both interventions combined. While the HIV curriculum had no impact, the education subsidy significantly reduced the teenage pregnancy rate, from 16 per cent to 13 per cent. Surprisingly, however, when the two programmes were implemented jointly, the pregnancy rate fell less than with the subsidy alone. The authors report that the HIV prevention curriculum, which focuses on an abstinence-until-marriage message, in fact increased early marriage. The effect of earlier marriage therefore probably counteracted the positive opportunity effect from the education subsidies on childbearing.

Second, Buchmann et al. (2016) set up an RCT clustered by communities in rural Bangladesh. They compare a control group with (i) an empowerment programme, (ii) a financial payment conditional on marriage delay, and (iii) the combination of the two. More than four years after treatment, they find that the girls in the conditional payment group are 14 per cent less likely to have given birth before the age of 20. On the other hand, the empowerment programme has no separate or additional effect.

Finally, Bandiera et al. (2015), in Uganda, and Buehren et al. (2015), in Tanzania, evaluate an out-of-school adolescent club organized by BRAC, which provided both health training (life skills) (affecting *mindset*), entrepreneurship training, including training of vocational skills (affecting economic *opportunities*), and a safe social space for the girls to gather and socialize. Bandiera et al. (2015) find a sharp increase in the participants' incomes and consumption after a two-year period, and correspondingly substantial reductions in rates of childbearing and marriage or cohabitation. The intervention also raised the likelihood of the girls engaging in income-generating activities by 72 per cent, while early pregnancy fell by 26 per cent. The study thus suggests that acting on both the *mindset* and *opportunities* fronts may be very effective. On the other hand, Buehren et al. (2015) do not find significant impacts in Tanzania, which they ascribe to challenges related to the implementation of the programme. These studies are, however, not able to disentangle the effects caused by the different parts of the programme. Our project in Tanzania, to which we shall shortly turn, is designed to address exactly that question.

2.4. *Overall Remarks on the Literature*

In evaluating the impact of interventions targeting early pregnancies and risky sexual behaviour, the literature has largely relied on self-reported measures of pregnancies, sexual behaviour, knowledge, and attitudes, with a few exceptions measuring biological outcomes. The overall picture is mixed, but, perhaps not surprisingly, it is easier to foster changes in knowledge and attitudes than in sexual behaviour and pregnancies. Still, the more recent trend focusing on the expansion of economic opportunities shows a lot of promise, with several evaluations documenting sustained improvements in behaviour and reductions in early pregnancies. This may indicate that lack of opportunities is a more binding constraint to healthy lives than lack of knowledge or other mindset variables.

3. New Evidence from Tanzania

To supplement the review of the literature, we provide a more detailed discussion of an ongoing research project in Tanzania that evaluates the impact of health training and entrepreneurship training for young females (Berge et al. 2016). The overall aim of this project is to study how different interventions, separately and in combination, may reduce early pregnancies by changing the girls' mindset and by providing them with economic opportunities. We do not yet have data on pregnancies, and thus our analysis will focus on the intermediate question of whether, in the short term, these interventions managed to empower the girls. In this respect, we focus on how the interventions affect the participants' *mindset*, in the form of *locus of control* and *sexual discourse*, and perceived future economic *opportunities*, in the form of business plans.

We focus on locus of control because it is commonly used as a measure of girls' control over their body and sexuality.[5] Individuals with an internal locus of control expect things in their lives to happen because of their own efforts, skills, and ability rather than through external factors such as luck or fate (Rotter 1966). It has also been argued that people with more locus of control are more likely to engage and succeed in entrepreneurial activities, as they have a more positive outlook towards life, they are more likely to take action, and are more persistent (Rauch and Frese 2007). Arguably, therefore, strengthening the locus of control can be important for improving both health and

---

[5] See, for instance, the ongoing research 'Negotiating a Better Future: The Impact of Teaching Negotiation Skills on Girls' Health and Educational Outcomes' led by Nava Ashraf, Corinne Low, and Kathleen McGinn, available at http://www.poverty-action.org/study/negotiating-better-future-impact-teaching-negotiation-skills-girls-health-and-educational (accessed 1 June 2017).

economic outcomes of adolescent girls, including delaying first pregnancy. At the same time, for an increase in locus of control to actually initiate changes in health and economic behaviour, the girls need knowledge about what represents risky sexual behaviour and economic opportunities that allow them to choose differently. Hence, targeting early pregnancies involves tackling an intricate set of relationships involving different mindset variables, including knowledge, and opportunities.

The following discussion aims to illustrate an alternative approach to evaluating this type of intervention, by showing how the use of the textual analysis of essays written by the girls can shed light on underlying mechanisms and supplement more traditional survey approaches.

3.1. *The Study Design*

We sampled eighty schools with at least twenty girls in the last year of secondary school (Form IV) in the regions of Tabora, Singida, Morogoro, and Dodoma in Tanzania, reaching almost 3,500 girls. The baseline data were collected in April–May 2013, and the follow-up with the essay writing in October–November 2013. The schools are all public (i.e. state) schools. They have on average sixty girls registered in Form IV, but only forty-three regularly attending. The girls mostly live in rural areas and were in the age range 16–18 at baseline, which is the age group for which we observe a sharp increase in fertility in rural Tanzania.

The average household of the girls consists of six members, and 20 per cent of households are headed by a woman. Half of the heads of households are farmers, the others either self-employed or public servants. At baseline, the majority declared that girls of their age typically have had their sexual debut. Eighty per cent also agreed with the statement '*Girls of my age sometimes receive money or gifts for having sex with older men*', and 60 per cent declared that the girls of their age are often sexually harassed. Most of them knew other girls who had dropped out of school because they were pregnant. Their knowledge of reproductive health was limited: one-third thought that it is not possible to get pregnant from a first sexual intercourse.

Among the schools in our study, we randomly allocated twenty schools to entrepreneurship training, twenty schools to health training, twenty schools to receive both entrepreneurship and health training, and twenty schools to control. Two teachers per school in the treatment groups attended an instructor session organized by our local partner, the non-governmental organization, Femina Hip. After these instructor sessions, in July–September 2013, the teachers implemented the training sessions with all the Form IV girls in their schools. Both the health training and the entrepreneurship training involved eight weekly training sessions of 1.5 to 2 hours, while those who got both types of training had two sessions per week over the eight weeks. The entrepreneurship programme trained the girls in customer care, marketing, record-keeping, pricing of products, and personal finance, and they were challenged to develop an entrepreneurial mindset and strengthen their self-confidence. The health programme provided information and guidance about contraception and the consequences of risky sexual behaviour, as well as gender equality.

3.2. *Text Analysis of Essays*

A few weeks after the completion of the training programmes, we asked the girls to write a short essay about where they envisioned themselves in five to ten years' time in terms of education, livelihood, marriage, and the challenges they expected to face.[6]

To shed light on how the intervention shaped the girls' ambitions and visions, we report from two types of text analysis, one in-depth and the other based on a word count. For the in-depth analysis, we translated 192 essays, written by girls from four schools in the Morogoro region, from Swahili to English. The remaining essays were digitized and used for the word-count analysis so as to reveal the occurrence of words relating to locus of control and business plans.

The strength of the in-depth analysis of the text, compared with the word count, is that it provides a more nuanced and reliable categorization of the essays. The strength of the word count is that it can be more easily implemented on a large scale. As we show below, the results are robust to the choice of method.

In the in-depth analysis, along the locus of control dimension, we assign a score of 1 to essays that reveal a strong sense of locus of control through the use of positive words such as '*I am confident*' and '*I am capable*'. In contrast, essays that have no positive words or have negative words such as '*I will not make it*' are assigned a score of 0 and are considered neutral.

For the word count text analysis, we first digitized the full sample of 3,128 hand-written essays, manually typing them into Microsoft Word documents. The documents were then converted and imported into Stata 14 for processing. All the analysis was done in the original language, Swahili, but we provide an English translation of the words used in this chapter.

---

[6] One may of course worry that the participants report what they believe the researchers want to hear. The risk of such reporting bias applies to all studies based on self-reported information. One could argue, however, that essays are less prone to this bias than specific survey questions, since it is less clear what exactly the surveyor would like the respondent to put in the essay.

The essays contained a total of 475,089 words. We removed all uninformative words (such as 'and', 'they', 'a'...) as well as punctuation (',', '.', '!'...). Finally, we removed all words that appeared fewer than thirty times in total. After this trimming, we were left with 112,648 words. These are the data that we use in the text analysis.

We scanned all the unique words and decided which ones should be included in each index:

- The general business index is equal to 1 if the essay contains the following words (and their variations): *business, entrepreneur, establish, self-employed, entrepreneurship.*

- The specific business index is equal to 1 if the essay contains the following words (and their variations): *funds, capital, sell, goods, shop, profit, gain, savings, customers, products, vegetable, sewing machine, poultry, fruit.*

- The locus of control index is equal to 1 if the essay contains the following words (and their variations): *I can, extrovert, confidence, independent, focus, toward the goal, I blossomed, opportunities, respect, self-respect.*

- The sexuality index is equal to 1 if the essay contains the following words (and their variations): *baby, maternity, love, sex.*

3.2.1. TEXT ANALYSIS: LOCUS OF CONTROL

In the in-depth analysis, we observe that the girls in the entrepreneurship training group appear to have the highest number of essays (49 per cent: an impact of 0.33, standard error = 0.1) with a score of one on the locus of control index, indicating a strong sense of control. The proportion is of 33 per cent in the health training group (impact = 0.17, standard error = 0.09) and of 35 per cent in the combined treatment (impact = 0.19, standard error = 0.09). The control group has the lowest proportion: 16 per cent of their essays show a strong locus of control. In the entrepreneurship training group, most of the girls appear to be confident in their essays and optimistic about the future with the use of words such as '*I am capable*' and '*I believe that I will succeed*'. In contrast, in the control group, most of the essays are neutral and there is no use of positive or affirming words.

By using the word counts on the full sample of essays, we gain a very consistent picture, with all treatment groups showing a greater sense of *locus of control*. Both the health and the combined interventions have the same impact on the locus of control index, which is equal to 0.06 (standard error = 0.03). The entrepreneurship training has an impact of 0.09 (standard error = 0.02).[7]

---

[7] The impact is measured by an ordinary least square estimation where we regress the indices on a dummy for each treatment group.

3.2.2. TEXT ANALYSIS: SEXUALITY

In terms of the sexuality index, we find that 42 per cent of the girls in the control group include words about sex in their essay, the proportion rises to 47 per cent in the health treatment group (impact = 0.05, standard error = 0.03), decreases to 38 per cent in the entrepreneurship training treatment group (impact of –0.04, standard error = 0.02), and it barely changes in the combined treatment group. This suggests that the health treated have integrated in their essays the sexual issues discussed in the training, while it appears that the entrepreneurship training made the girls less focused on sexuality issues. Interestingly, we observe that the two effects cancel each other out in the combined treatment.[8]

3.2.3. TEXT ANALYSIS: BUSINESS PLANS

We categorize, and distinguish between, essays mentioning business plans in general terms and those with more specific or detailed business plans. A business plan is regarded as general when there is mention of starting a business but no precision about the type of business. For instance, the statement *'In the future I would like to have my own business that will provide me with income'* was categorized as a general business plan. On the other hand, the statement *'I will start a business selling vegetables'* was regarded as a specific business plan. The rationale behind the distinction between general and specific business plans is to separate girls who have thought more carefully about setting up a business, for instance as a result of the entrepreneurship training, and those who have only vague ideas about their business future. Potentially, those with more developed business ideas are also more likely to set up a business once out of school.

Girls in control schools do mention business plans in their essays (11 per cent in the in-depth analysis and 32 per cent in the word count). Compared to them, the entrepreneurship training yielded more essays in which general business plans for the future are mentioned (in-depth analysis: impact = 0.67, standard error = 0.1; word count: impact = 0.34, standard error = 0.02). Interestingly, compared with the control group, the health group also has a much larger number of essays mentioning business plans, even though this group did not receive any form of entrepreneurship training (in-depth analysis: impact = 0.36, standard error = 0.09; word count: impact = 0.06, standard error = 0.02). This could be due to a general empowerment and mindset effect from the health training, as suggested by the increased sense of locus of control shown above. The combined training led to effects similar to those of the

---

[8] We do not have an in-depth analysis for the *sexuality* content.

entrepreneurship training (in-depth analysis: impact = 0.5, standard error = 0.09; word count: impact = 0.27, standard error = 0.02).

When we consider only specific business plans, we find that both the entrepreneurship and the combined training had similar effects. The effects of the health training however dissipate. In the in-depth analysis, we do not observe any control essay with specific plans. In the word count, 25 per cent of the control essays include some specific business plans. The treatment impact of the entrepreneurship training is equal to 0.35 (standard error = 0.08, in-depth analysis) and 0.16 (standard error = 0.02, word count). The combined training has an impact of 0.2 (standard error = 0.07, in-depth analysis) and 0.1 (standard error = 0.02, word count). The health training has an impact of 0.16 (standard error = 0.07) in the in-depth analysis, but no significant impact in the word count (impact = −0.02, standard error = 0.02).

3.3. Text Analysis: Overall Findings

We observe that the girls who have been in different treatment groups have very different hopes for the future. Compared with the control, the health group treated express a much higher sense of *locus of control* and are more likely to discuss *issues of sexuality*. On the other hand, only those who received the entrepreneurship training (the single treatment or together with health) mention clear, specific, *business plans*. Participants in the entrepreneurship training also demonstrate a greater sense of *locus of control*, but they mention *sexuality* issues to a lesser extent than people in the control group and in the health training.

If the delaying of pregnancies requires changes in both mindset (preferences and beliefs relating to sexual activity, pregnancy, and their consequences) and economic opportunities (economic alternatives to early marriage and mother-hood), our findings suggest that entrepreneurship training, alone or in combination with health training, is more effective than health training alone. The long-run follow-up data in this project, which will contain information on pregnancy, will establish whether this actually is the case.

4. Conclusion

Early pregnancies are associated with negative effects on young women's health outcomes, educational attainment, and future employment and economic opportunities. Interventions to reduce this problem typically target the young women's mindset, through educational programmes about reproductive health and family planning. In addition, interventions have targeted economic opportunities through cash transfers and, more recently, through entrepreneurship or vocational training.

The literature on interventions targeting the mindset dimension shows that success cannot be taken for granted. While such programmes typically manage to improve knowledge and change attitudes, the impact on pregnancies and sexual behaviour is rather mixed. One reason why changes in mindset do not necessarily result in changes in outcomes could be the lack of economic alternatives. If entering into a relationship with an older man is the only economically viable path to making a living, then changing the mindset is likely not to achieve much.

This is why interventions that seek to expand economic opportunities for adolescent girls are a promising policy agenda. Indeed, during the last few decades, there has been a surge in such interventions, ranging from conditional cash transfers to entrepreneurship training programmes. Again, the evidence on the effectiveness of such programmes to reduce early pregnancy and change sexual behaviour is rather mixed, and some of the positive impacts have proven to be short-lived. One possible reason why expanding economic opportunities does not necessarily lead to lasting changes in outcomes is that such changes may need to be combined with a change in girls' mindsets, including awareness of the risks involved in sexual activities. The opportunities must be there but the girls also need the mindset to seize them.

A few studies consider the impact of interventions that target both mindset and economic opportunities, and the results are encouraging. Given the complexity of such interventions, however, we do not know enough about the mechanisms of change. Do programmes such as youth clubs in Uganda, evaluated by Bandiera et al. (2015) and found to be highly successful in reducing early pregnancy, primarily work through a mindset change or through increasing economic opportunities? Or is there some other channel, such as providing girls with a safe space in which to socialize?

Our analysis of essays written by more than three thousand girls in rural Tanzania addresses the question of the mechanism of change. It indicates that training in both health (targeting the mindset) and entrepreneurship (targeting economic opportunities) has had an impact on the girls' sense of locus of control. Also, the entrepreneurship programme has been successful in stimulating new business plans, which can be seen as a first step towards economic empowerment. Our findings may thus contribute to explaining why economic interventions may be more successful than pure health interventions, since the entrepreneurship training appears to affect both the mindset and economic opportunities. This is an ongoing project, however, and we do not yet have evidence on how the intervention in the end affected pregnancy.

More work is needed in order to understand what types of intervention are more effective in reducing early pregnancies in developing countries, and how to understand the mechanism of change. We hope many researchers will join us in pursuing these promising and important avenues for future research in the coming years.

References

Agha, S. (2002). 'A Quasi-Experimental Study to Assess the Impact of Four Adolescent Sexual Health Interventions in Sub-Saharan Africa'. *International Family Planning Perspectives*, 28(2): 67. https://doi.org/10.2307/3088237

Agha, S., and Van Rossem, R. (2004). 'Impact of a School-based Peer Sexual Health Intervention on Normative Beliefs, Risk Perceptions, and Sexual Behavior of Zambian Adolescents'. *Journal of Adolescent Health*, 34: 441–52. https://doi.org/10.1016/j.jadohealth.2003.07.016

Alam, A., J. E. Baez, and X. V. Del Carpio (2011). 'Does Cash for School Influence Young Women's Behavior in the Longer Term? Evidence from Pakistan' (Policy Research Working Paper No. 5669). Retrieved from http://documents.worldbank.org/curated/en/996441468145471110/pdf/WPS5669.pdf

Bailey, M. J. (2006). 'More Power to the Pill: The Impact of Contraceptive Freedom on Women's Life Cycle Labor Supply'. *The Quarterly Journal of Economics*, 121(1): 289–320. https://doi.org/10.1093/qje/121.1.289

Baird, S., E. Chirwa, C. McIntosh, and B. Özler (2010). 'The Short-Term Impacts of a Schooling Conditional Cash Transfer Program on the Sexual Behavior of Young Women'. *Health Economics*, 19(S1): 55–68. https://doi.org/10.1002/hec.1569

Baird, S., C., McIntosh, and B. Özler (2011). 'Cash or Condition? Evidence from a Cash Transfer Experiment'. *The Quarterly Journal of Economics*, 126(4): 1709–53. https://doi.org/10.1093/qje/qjr032

Bandiera, O., N. Buehren, R. Burgess, M. Goldstein, S. Gulesci, I. Rasul, and M. Sulaiman (2015). 'Women's Empowerment in Action: Evidence from a Randomized Control Trial in Africa'. Retrieved from http://www.ucl.ac.uk/~uctpimr/research/ELA.pdf

Berge, L. I. O., K. Bjorvatn, F. Makene, L. Helgesson Sekei, V. Somville, and B. Tungodden (2018). 'Women's Economic Empowerment and Fertility: Long-Term Experimental Evidence from Tanzania' (unpublished).

Buchmann, N., E. Field, R. Glennerster, and S. Nazneen (2016). 'The Effect of Conditional Incentives and a Girls' Empowerment Curriculum on Adolescent Marriage, Childbearing and Education in Rural Bangladesh : A Community Clustered Randomized Controlled Trial' (unpublished), 1–37.

Buehren, N., M. Goldstein, S. Gulesci, M. Sulaiman, and V. Yam (2015). 'Evaluation of Layering Microfinance on an Adolescent Development Program for Girls in Tanzania' (unpublished).

Cabezón, C., P. Vigil, I. Rojas, M. E. Leiva, R. Riquelme, W. Aranda, et al. (2005). 'Adolescent Pregnancy Prevention: An Abstinence-Centered Randomized Controlled Intervention in a Chilean Public High School'. *The Journal of Adolescent Health: Official Publication of the Society for Adolescent Medicine*, 36(1): 64–9. https://doi.org/10.1016/j.jadohealth.2003.10.011

Cartagena, R. G., P. J. Veugelers, W. Kipp, K. Magigav, and L. M. Laing (2006). 'Effectiveness of an HIV Prevention Program for Secondary School Students in Mongolia'. *Journal of Adolescent Health*, 39(6): 925.e9–925.e16. https://doi.org/10.1016/j.jadohealth.2006.07.017

Daniel, E. E., R. Masilamani, and M. Rahman (2008). 'The Effect of Community-Based Reproductive Health Communication Interventions on Contraceptive Use Among Young Married Couples in Bihar, India'. *International Family Planning Perspectives*, 34(4): 189–97. https://doi.org/10.1363/ifpp.34.189.08

De Walque, D., W. H., Dow, R., Nathan, R., Abdul, F., Abilahi, E., Gong, and C. A. Medlin (2012). 'Incentivising Safe Sex: A Randomised Trial of Conditional Cash Transfers for HIV and Sexually Transmitted Infection Prevention in Rural Tanzania. *BMJ Open*, 2(1): e000747. https://doi.org/10.1136/bmjopen-2011-000747

Doyle, A. M., D. A. Ross, K. Maganja, K. Baisley, C. Masesa, A. Andreasen and MEMA kwa Vijana Trial Study Group (2010). 'Long-Term Biological and Behavioural Impact of an Adolescent Sexual Health Intervention in Tanzania: Follow-up Survey of the Community-Based MEMA kwa Vijana Trial'. *PLoS Medicine*, 7(6): e1000287. https://doi.org/10.1371/journal.pmed.1000287

Duflo, E., P. Dupas, and M. Kremer (2015). 'Education, HIV, and Early Fertility: Experimental Evidence from Kenya'. *American Economic Review*, 105(9): 2757–97. https://doi.org/10.1257/aer.20121607

Dupas, P. (2011). 'Do Teenagers Respond to HIV Risk Information? Evidence from a Field Experiment in Kenya'. *American Economic Journal: Applied Economics*, 3(1): 1–34. https://doi.org/10.1257/app.3.1.1

Dupas, P., E. Huillery, and J. Seban (2017). 'Risk Information, Risk Salience, and Adolescent Sexual Behavior: Experimental Evidence from Cameroon', *Journal of Economic Behavior & Organization* 145: 151–75. January 2018, https://www.sciencedirect.com/science/article/pii/S0167268117302810

Eggleston, E., J. Jackson, W. Rountree, and Z. Pan (2000). 'Evaluation of a Sexuality Education Program for Young Adolescents in Jamaica'. *Pan American Journal of Public Health*, 7(2): 102–12. Retrieved from http://www.ncbi.nlm.nih.gov/pubmed/10748661

Feldman, B. S., A. M. Zaslavsky, M. Ezzati, K. E. Peterson, and M. Mitchell (2009). 'Contraceptive Use, Birth Spacing, and Autonomy: An Analysis of the Oportunidades Program in Rural Mexico'. *Studies in Family Planning*, 40(1): 51–62. Retrieved from http://www.ncbi.nlm.nih.gov/pubmed/19397185

Gallant, M., and E. Maticka-Tyndale (2004). 'School-Based HIV Prevention Programmes for African Youth'. *Social Science & Medicine*, 58(7): 1337–51. https://doi.org/10.1016/S0277-9536(03)00331-9

Goldin, C., and L. F. Katz (2002). 'The Power of the Pill: Oral Contraceptives and Women's Career and Marriage Decisions'. *Journal of Political Economy*, 110(4): 730–70. Retrieved from http://ideas.repec.org/a/ucp/jpolec/v110y2002i4p730-770.html

Handa, S., C. T. Halpern, A. Pettifor, and H. Thirumurthy (2014). 'The Government of Kenya's Cash Transfer Program Reduces the Risk of Sexual Debut among Young People Age 15–25. *PLoS ONE*, 9(1): e85473. https://doi.org/10.1371/journal.pone.0085473

Heath, R., and A. M. Mobarak (2015). 'Manufacturing Growth and the Lives of Bangladeshi Women'. *Journal of Development Economics*, 115: 1–15. https://doi.org/10.1016/j.jdeveco.2015.01.006

Jensen, R. (2012). 'Do Labor Market Opportunities Affect Young Women's Work and Family Decisions? Experimental Evidence from India'. *The Quarterly Journal of Economics*, 127(2): 753–92. https://doi.org/10.1093/qje/qjs002

Kim, Y. M., A., Kols, R. Nyakauru, C. Marangwanda, and P. Chibatamoto (2001). 'Promoting Sexual Responsibility among Young People in Zimbabwe'. *International Family Planning Perspectives*, 27(1): 11. https://doi.org/10.2307/2673800

Lou, C.-H., B. Wang, Y. Shen, and E.-S. Gao (2004). 'Effects of a Community-Based Sex Education and Reproductive Health Service Program on Contraceptive Use of Unmarried Youths in Shanghai'. *Journal of Adolescent Health*, 34(5): 433–40. https://doi.org/10.1016/j.jadohealth.2003.07.020

Magnani, R. J., L. Gaffikin, E. M. de Aquino, E. E. Seiber, M. C. Almeida, and V. Lipovsek (2001). 'Impact of an Integrated Adolescent Reproductive Health Program in Brazil'. *Studies in Family Planning*, 32(3): 230–43. Retrieved from http://www.ncbi.nlm.nih.gov/pubmed/11686184

Magnani, R., K. MacIntyre, A. M. Karim, L. Brown, and P. Hutchinson (2005). 'The Impact of Life Skills Education on Adolescent Sexual Risk Behaviors in KwaZulu-Natal, South Africa'. *Journal of Adolescent Health*, 36: 289–304.

Miller, G. (2010). 'Contraception as Development? New Evidence from Family Planning in Colombia'. *Economic Journal*, 120 (545): 709–36.

Okonofua, F. E., P. Coplan, S. Collins, F. Oronsaye, D. Ogunsakin, J. T. Ogonor and K. Heggenhougen (2003). 'Impact of an Intervention to Improve Treatment-Seeking Behavior and Prevent Sexually Transmitted Diseases Among Nigerian Youths'. *International Journal of Infectious Diseases*, 7(1): 61–73. https://doi.org/10.1016/S1201-9712(03)90044-0

Oringanje, C., M. M. Meremikwu, H. Eko, E. Esu, A. Meremikwu, and J. E Ehiri (2016). 'Interventions for Preventing Unintended Pregnancies Among Adolescents'. In C. Oringanje (ed.) *Cochrane Database of Systematic Reviews*. Chichester, UK: John Wiley & Sons, Ltd. https://doi.org/10.1002/14651858.CD005215.pub3

Rasul, I. (2008). 'Household Bargaining Over Fertility: Theory and Evidence from Malaysia'. *Journal of Development Economics*, 86(2): 215–41. https://doi.org/10.1016/j.jdeveco.2007.02.005

Rauch, A., and M. Frese (2007). 'Let's Put the Person Back into Entrepreneurship Research: A Meta-Analysis on the Relationship Between Business Owners' Personality Traits, Business Creation and Success'. *European Journal of Work and Organizational Psychology* 16: 353–85.

Ross, D.A., J. Changalucha, A.I. Obasi et al. (2007). 'Biological and Behavioral Impact of an Adolescent Sexual Health Intervention in Tanzania: A Community-Randomized Trial'. *AIDS*, 21: 1943–55.

Rotter, J. B. (1966). 'Generalized Expectancies for Internal Versus External Control of Reinforcement'. *Psychological Monographs*, 80(1): 1–28. Retrieved from http://www.ncbi.nlm.nih.gov/pubmed/5340840.

Stecklov, G., P. Winters, J. Todd, and F. Regalia (2007). 'Unintended Effects of Poverty Programmes on Childbearing in Less Developed Countries: Experimental Evidence from Latin America'. *Population Studies*, 61(2): 125–40. https://doi.org/10.1080/00324720701300396.

Tu, X., C. Lou, E. Gao, and I. H. Shah (2008). 'Long-Term Effects of a Community-Based Program on Contraceptive Use Among Sexually Active Unmarried Youth in Shanghai, China'. *Journal of Adolescent Health*, 42(3): 249–58. https://doi.org/10.1016/j.jadohealth.2007.08.028.

Walker, D., J. P. Gutierrez, P. Torres, and S. M. Bertozzi (2006). 'HIV Prevention in Mexican Schools: Prospective Randomised Evaluation of Intervention'. *BMJ*, 332(7551): 1189–94. https://doi.org/10.1136/bmj.38796.457407.80.

The World Bank (2012). *World Development Report 2012—Gender Equality and Development*. https://doi.org/10.1080/13552070512331332273.

World Health Organization (2014). Adolescent Pregnancy. Retrieved 6 March 2017, from http://www.who.int/mediacentre/factsheets/fs364/en/#.WL0uYzXWtwY.email.

8

Breaking the Metal Ceiling

Female Entrepreneurs who Succeed in Male-Dominated Sectors

Francisco Campos, Markus Goldstein, Laura McGorman,
Ana Maria Munoz Boudet, and Obert Pimhidzai[1]

1. Introduction

Evidence from developed and developing countries indicates that there is significant gender segregation within the labour market, with women more likely to work in low-productivity sectors or less profitable businesses (Dolado et al. 2003; ILO 2012; World Bank 2011). In entrepreneurship, women-owned[2] businesses typically underperform compared to men's (see Klapper and Parker 2011, for an overview of this literature), tend to be smaller and grow less (Bruhn 2009: Bardasi et al. 2011: Kantis et al. 2005). While female participation in entrepreneurial activities varies by region, the gaps in productivity and growth between male- and female-owned enterprises are stark and remain large even in rich countries (Klapper and Parker 2011; World Bank

[1] This project benefited from the financial support of the UN Foundation, the World Bank's Bank-Netherlands Partnership Program Trust Fund, the Belgium Poverty Reduction Program, and the World Bank's Umbrella Facility for Gender Equality (UFGE). Elena Bardasi and Mayra Buvinic provided comments and guidance. Victoria Katende of Makerere University led the logistics and implementation of the qualitative assessments, and Nelson Matua supervised face-to-face interviews. The findings, interpretations, and conclusions expressed in this chapter are entirely those of the authors. They do not necessarily represent the views of the International Bank for Reconstruction and Development/World Bank and its affiliated organizations, or those of the Executive Directors of the World Bank or the governments they represent.
[2] See Aterido and Hallward-Driemeier (2011) for a discussion on the importance of the definition of female ownership between partial ownership and decision-making. In the setting of this study, 90 per cent of the enterprises have only one owner. For those in partnership, female ownership is defined in this study as the main business owner being a woman.

2011). Occupational segregation also comes with a growth cost. If we assume that skills are equally distributed among men and women at the start, the growth of an economy will be reduced by gender segregation of employment, as a given sector will not have access to the full set of skills that exist.[3]

In Africa, female participation in entrepreneurial activities is higher than in any other region, with women representing about half of non-farm business ownership. However, as in other regions, a range of studies show female-owned firms lag behind their male counterparts in a number of key measures of enterprise performance. They have sales that are lower than those of male-owned firms (Bardasi et al. 2011), they are less productive (Hallward-Driemeier 2013; Rijkers and Costa 2012), and are smaller than male-owned businesses. Women entrepreneurs in Africa tend to concentrate in some sectors such as hotels and restaurants, wholesale and retail trade, garments, textiles and leather goods, and other services (Bardasi et al. 2011). African men, on the other hand, have businesses distributed across a wider range of sectors, including construction and manufacturing.

Among the range of factors discussed in the literature to explain gender differences in entrepreneurial activity (Klapper and Parker 2011; World Bank 2011), the sector in which the firm operates is consistently found to be a major determinant of gender-related differences in performance and growth (e.g. Nichter and Goldmark 2009; Bardasi et al. 2011; Hallward-Driemeier 2013; Rijkers and Costa 2012). For example, Hundley (2001) estimates that women's concentration in the personal services sector explains as much as 14 per cent of the gender-based self-employment earnings differential. De Mel et al. (2009) find that female ownership loses statistical significance in explaining differences in performance once industry choice is controlled for. Results from Guatemala (Kevane and Wydick 2001) and India (Kantor 2005) suggest that constraints on female-owned firms and their sector concentration respond to factors such as the marginal value of time for home production, and constraints on location of business, among others.[4]

If industry concentration is important in determining future profitability and growth, understanding whether women's decision to enter these sectors is driven by constraints or preferences is key (see Bardasi et al. 2011, for an overview of this literature). Hasan et al. (2011) suggest that female entrepreneurs are often driven more by flexible work schedules or personal achievement than by a raw interest in profit or growth, contributing to preference-driven hypotheses. Similarly, Minniti (2010), among others, suggests that female entrepreneurs

---

[3] Cuberes and Teignier (2014) estimate this loss to be of 3.3 percent of GDP for sub-Saharan Africa due to gender gaps in entrepreneurship.

[4] Kantor (2005) shows that 36 per cent of female entrepreneurs operate home-based firms compared to 20 per cent of male entrepreneurs. Household firms are smaller and less likely to grow (Mead and Liedholm 1998).

exhibit less confidence than men in their skill sets and ability to take risks. Conversely, research in Africa (for instance Bardasi and Getahun 2008) and elsewhere (Brush 1992) has found that women are often constrained by factors such as limited access to finance and human capital development opportunities, which points more to a constraint-driven hypothesis.

In this chapter, we look at what factors help or hinder female entrepreneurs in moving out of traditionally female-concentrated economic sectors and into male-dominated trades. We do this in the context of Uganda, which shows the concentration pattern that the studies above refer to: only 6 per cent of women operate in male-dominated sectors[5] (i.e. where over 75 per cent of enterprises are male-owned[6]), while 34 per cent of men have businesses in those industries (UBOS 2006). And we consider three groups of possible factors. First, we look at whether the crossover entrepreneurs (women who own businesses in male-dominated industries) differ from other female entrepreneurs in their entrepreneurial skill or abilities. Second, we examine the possibility that their psychosocial[7] development explains their ability to overcome occupational segregation. Finally, as credit and human capital constraints are often cited as factors that hold back women's businesses no matter which sector they are in, we consider these factors too. We use a mixed-methods approach to examine these potential explanations.

The next section lays out the data we use and the methods by which they were collected. After exploring the characteristics of female-owned firms in our study sample, and comparing them with male-owned firms in terms of productivity and profits (Section 3), we move on to examine the relative roles of the three groups of factors mentioned above in determining which women cross over and which do not (Section 4). Challenges experienced once in business are detailed in Section 5. Section 6 draws on the findings to identify some areas for testing future policy interventions aiming to promote female participation in male-dominated sectors of the economy, as well as to support women who wish to cross over.

---

[5] In the literature, male-dominated sectors are often defined as those where more than 50 per cent of the firms are male-owned (over-representation) but, in this study, we focus on enterprises where male domination is over 75 per cent, because the over-representation in other data could just be a reflection of the specific sample, which is often not representative of the population, e.g., the World Bank/International Finance Corporation Enterprise Surveys are often not representative of the population of firms in a country (given the absence of a solid census of firms). While these classifications at the margin could potentially average out in a quantitative analysis, they matter considerably for a qualitative assessment, which is why we adopt the more conservative definition here.

[6] Of course, if more women were to operate in those sectors, they would cease to be male-dominated, but currently, and over time and across countries, the pattern is prevalent, and hence important to analyse.

[7] Here we use the definition of psychosocial as the interrelation between social and individual factors expressed in someone's behaviours and mind.

2. Data and Methods

This chapter draws on data collected in 2011 from a sample of entrepreneurs in urban Uganda from within and just outside Kampala, which are mostly part of the Katwe Small Scale Industry Association (KASSIDA). The data were collected as part of an evaluation of the impact of a skills and managerial training programme on business performance. The baseline survey included a total sample of 326 women and 409 men, of whom only 30 women owned businesses in male-dominated sectors. Table 8.1 shows the distribution of women and men across different industries and indicates the gender concentration in each sector. We use this data set (hereafter the KASSIDA data set), which has detailed information on assets, inputs, other costs, sales, and profits, to compare the performance of crossovers with both other women-owned businesses in traditional female sectors and male-owned businesses in the same sectors.

We also use the outcomes of a mixed-methods questionnaire collected uniquely for this chapter (hereafter the mixed-methods data set). This questionnaire was administered in July/August 2012 to 187 female entrepreneurs—67 working in male-dominated sectors such as those identified in the KASSIDA data set, and 120 working in traditionally female sectors. Table 8.1 shows the distribution of women in each sector in these datasets.

Table 8.1. Number of enterprises per sector in the KASSIDA and mixed methods data sets

Sector	Number of enterprises per sector in the KASSIDA dataset			Number of enterprises per sector in the mixed-methods dataset	
	Male-owned	Female-owned		Female-owned	
		Crossovers	Non-crossovers	Crossovers	Non-crossovers
Barbershop/hair salon	7	0	63	0	23
Carpentry	44	4	0	26	0
Catering	2	0	107	0	41
Electricals	11	1	0	1	0
Fitting and machinery	11	0	0	7	0
Foundry and forgery*	48	15	0	15	0
Metal fabrication	185	7	0	10	0
Shoe making and repair	33	3	0	8	0
Tailoring/knitting	68	0	126	0	55
Clay moulding	0	0	0	0	1
Total	409	30	296	67	120

Notes: * Forgery could be integrated into metal fabrication under a different definition of sectors. The definition used follows the list of sectors identified by KASSIDA to organize their work.

The sample size for the KASSIDA dataset is larger than in the analysis that follows as we do not observe all variables for all firms listed here.

Source: Authors' own construction.

As the study was designed to include both formal and informal businesses, it is not representative of all enterprises in the Kampala area.[8] Instead, for the mixed-methods data set, an initial sample of crossover respondents was drawn from the KASSIDA data set (21 in all) and complemented by additional crossover participants identified through snowball sampling. For non-crossovers, 60 respondents were identified through a random sample of the KASSIDA data set,[9] and an additional 60 were matched to the crossover sample on a small list of pre-business characteristics.[10] The objective of the matched subset was to enable a sufficient sample of individuals with characteristics relatively similar to crossovers before the inception of their business, with the main difference being that they took different paths due to a set of factors to be explained in the analysis.

The mixed-methods dataset is based on semi-structured interviews to capture a wide range of information about female entrepreneurs, including their background, family history, education, entrepreneurial capacity/tendency (risk aversion,[11] personality profile, IQ), access to networks, presence of role models, and a host of other factors. In addition to these quantitative measures, there were open-ended questions that allowed participants to supply answers in their own words and elaborate on the path that led them to be in a specific business sector.[12]

To complement the information obtained in individual interviews, we conducted seventeen focus group discussions with crossovers, non-crossovers, clients, suppliers, and (male) employees, with approximately six participants per group. Focus groups of entrepreneurs included cases where only one sector was represented, as well as others that included a mix of both crossovers and non-crossovers. Additionally, we interviewed a set of community leaders and credit providers to gauge the structural constraints facing both female entrepreneurs in male-dominated sectors, and those in female-dominated sectors. Including various actors in the business and community environments allows us to better measure community-wide perceptions on female participation in entrepreneurial activities, enabling a better understanding of why so few female entrepreneurs decide to cross over.

---

[8] The inclusion of informal businesses results in the lack of an accessible sample frame from which to draw.

[9] Respondents from the KASSIDA data set included members of both the treatment and the control groups, the former of which had received technical and managerial training, the latter of which had not.

[10] These characteristics included nearest neighbour on age, age squared, and completion of primary education.

[11] The games on risk aversion were not considered for this analysis because, half-way through implementation, survey audits indicated problems in administering this part of the survey.

[12] Interviews were recorded and there was space in the questionnaire for additional writing of questions and answers.

3. The Profitability and Productivity of Male- and Female-Owned Firms

In this section, we investigate the differences in size and firm-level perform-ance between firms owned by women crossovers and non-crossovers, as well as between crossover firms and those owned by men operating in the same sectors. We use the KASSIDA data set (discussed above) to document these differences and examine to what extent the differences are explained by production inputs and the scale of the operation.

We start by looking at the profits of different firms. Looking within female-owned firms, we find that many of the women who cross over make higher profits than women who do not (Figure 8.1), in line with the literature on the importance of sectors in explaining gender gaps (Bardasi et al. 2011; Klapper and Parker 2011). We also find that the relative profits of female crossover firms versus male-owned firms in the same sectors are more similar than those of female-owned firms in different sectors (Figure 8.2), indicating that busi-nesses owned by women that cross over to male-dominated sectors perform similarly to male-owned businesses in those sectors.

Crossover firms are different from those of women who stay in female-dominated sectors. Table 8.2 shows these differences to be, first, in the average

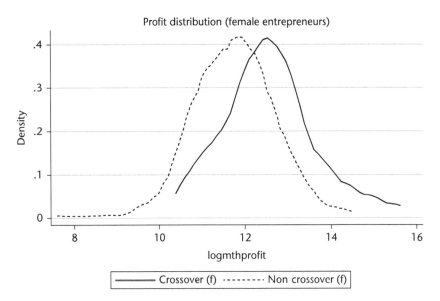

Kernel = epanechnikov, bandwidth = 0.4290

Figure 8.1. Distribution of (log) monthly profits for women crossovers and non-crossovers—KASSIDA data set

Source: Authors' own construction.

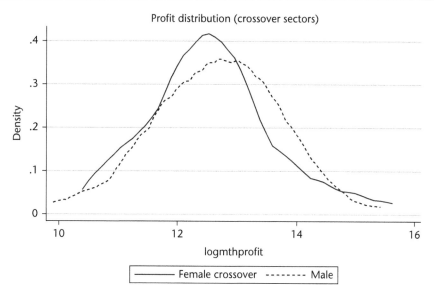

Kernel = epanechnikov, bandwidth = 0.4290

Figure 8.2. Distribution of (log) monthly profits for women crossovers and men in same sectors—KASSIDA data set
Source: Authors' own construction.

revenue of a crossover firm, which is about three times that of a non-crossover firm; similarly, profit is more than double. The crossover firms operate at a larger scale, with significantly higher levels of labour and capital. Crossover firms are also older, and more likely to have received support in the form of business or technical training. There also appear to be some differences in terms of finance—crossovers are more likely to belong to a savings and credit co-operative organization (SACCO) and to have received business development services such as assistance on business planning, developing promotional materials, and expanding market access. In terms of business practices, crossovers are significantly less likely to be running a business that they themselves started. In terms of personal characteristics, crossovers show some differences from non-crossovers: they are older, have a somewhat different education profile, and are more likely to be widowed.

When comparing male- and female-led firms within the male-dominated sectors we find no differences in core business indicators such as profit, revenue, and capital across male- and female-owned firms in the crossover sectors.[13] However, there is a significant difference in the number of workers,

[13] See working paper version of this chapter for table with complete results, WIDER Working Paper 2017/166.

Table 8.2. Summary statistics for female-owned enterprises—KASSIDA data set

	Total	StDev	Crossover	Non-crossover	Difference
Financials					
Revenues past month (UGX '000)	1,058	2,246	2,697	914	1,783***
Profits past month (UGX '000)	229	392	494	205	289***
Investment					
Net capital invested (UGX '000)	2,056	5,880	5,312	1,769	3,543***
Number of workers	2.6	2.0	3.9	2.4	1.5***
Inputs consumed past month (UGX '000)	377	783	968	325	643***
Personal characteristics					
Age	37	9	42	36	6***
Married	53	50	40	54	−14
Widow	13	34	32	11	21***
Less than primary education	12	32	30	10	20***
Primary school is max. education	52	50	26	54	−28***
Secondary school is max. education	24	43	30	24	7
Completed more than secondary	13	33	13	13	0
Previously worker in sector	13	33	12	13	−1
Received business or technical training in past	43	50	72	40	32***
Financial literacy index (0–1)	0.5	0.1	0.5	0.4	0.1***
Technical literacy index (0–1)	0.4	0.2	0.4	0.4	0.0
Owns more than one business	15	36	24	14	10
Household and business activities simultaneously	30	46	44	29	15
Business characteristics					
Business owner started this firm	93	26	84	93	−9*
Saw market opportunity when starting business	56	50	48	57	−9
Has business partners	3	16	0	3	−3
Business is registered	46	50	44	46	−2
Age of business	9	7	14	9	5***
Size of business network (log)	3.2	1.1	3.4	3.1	0.2
Access to finance					
Has bank account	51	50	60	50	10
Has received business support	14	18	19	13	6*
Belongs to SACCO	18	39	32	17	15*
Has received loan	32	47	44	31	13
Harassment (past 12 months)					
Has been sexually harassed	16	37	8	17	−9
Other type of harassment[+]	42	49	40	42	−2
N	309		25	284	

Notes: *** $p < 0.01$, ** $p < 0.05$, * $p < 0.1$. At the time of the survey, 1 US$ = UGX 2,250.

[+] other type of harassment includes: threats to shut down business; shouting, scolding, making a nuisance in or near enterprise premises; vandalism of premises or merchandise; confiscation of property or merchandise; pushing or shoving; and beating.

Source: Authors' own construction.

with female-owned firms averaging 1.7 fewer workers than their male-owned counterparts. This could be related to a different allocation of capital and labour, but could also just be due to different sub-sector composition. Most differences are in terms of business practices. Women, not surprisingly, are much more likely to mix household and financial resources than men, but are significantly less likely to have a business partner (indeed none of the cross-overs does) and less likely to be registered. Female entrepreneurs in these sectors are more likely to belong to a SACCO than male entrepreneurs; and the characteristics of the entrepreneurs are also different. Women are older than their male counterparts, have a slightly different educational profile (although the years of education, not shown here, are not significantly different), are less likely to be married and more likely to be widowed, and score lower on our measure of technical skills.[14]

The preceding discussion suggests that women crossovers and non-crossovers operate at different scales but also have a range of different business practices and personal attributes. In order to disentangle the relative impact of scale, we turn to production function estimates. We use a Cobb-Douglas production function of the form $Y_{ij} = AK_{ij}^{\alpha}L_{ij}^{\beta}M_{ij}^{\gamma}$ where Y_{ij} is output of firm i in sector j and modelled as a function of capital, K_{ij}, labour, L_{ij}, intermediate material inputs, M_{ij}, and total factor productivity (TFP), A. This approach investigates if these factors account for the potential gaps in productivity between crossovers and other groups. Moreover, we assess if the observed differences are associated with a suboptimal scale of operations for a specific group.

We acknowledge the limitations of this analytical approach, namely the potential problems of endogeneity, including omitted variable bias, simultaneity, and self-selection issues. Nevertheless, such an analysis is helpful in identifying the initial factors that might be relevant in explaining the unconditional differences in performance.

Table 8.3 shows the estimates of production functions for female-owned firms, with and without controls for capital, labour, and material inputs.

We see that crossovers have higher sales than non-crossovers, even after accounting for the capital, labour, and material inputs invested in the business, as the crossover variable remains significant in the second set of estimates. A second conclusion is that scale does not appear to be driving the enterprise outcome differences (here measured in terms of sales) between crossover and non-crossover female entrepreneurs. The coefficients on log capital, labour, and inputs are significant and smaller than 1, indicating decreasing returns to scale. The interaction terms with being a crossover firm (the last three rows) are not significant, indicating that they too experience decreasing returns to scale. Thus, differences in economies of scale do not appear to be driving the levels of sales across these two types of enterprises, suggesting that other potential factors are at play.

---

[14] This is a set of questions designed to carefully measure skills within a given sector (e.g. 'how far in inches from the scalp would you apply a chemical relaxer?' for hair salon or 'what is the minimum size of wire used for making an industrial welding machine?' for electrical).

Table 8.3. Production function estimates for female-owned enterprises

Dependent variable: log Sales, restricted sample of women-only (KASSIDA data set)

	est1		est2	
	B	se	B	Se
Crossover	1.027***	0.193	2.817*	1.552
log Capital			0.086**	0.038
log Labour			0.558***	0.073
Log Material Inputs			0.103***	0.035
cross*lnK			−0.121	0.140
cross*lnL			0.481	0.329
cross*lnM			−0.091	0.159
_cons	13.089***	0.072	10.388***	0.559
N	309		309	
r2	0.065		0.256	
Non-crossovers CRS (p-value of F-test)			0.0014***	
Crossovers CRS (p-value of F-test)			0.9519	
Crossovers RS = Non-crossovers RS (p-value of F-test)			0.3266	

Notes: *** $p < 0.01$, ** $p < 0.05$, * $p < 0.1$. CRS = constant returns to scale; RS = returns to scale.

Source: Authors' own construction.

4. Who Crosses Over?

We know that women who break into male-dominated industries are different from women in traditional female-dominated sectors, but there is no clear theory to explain why they do what they do or what factors are associated with women who successfully cross over.[15]

To examine this question, we explore three potential sets of reasons as to how a small subset of women end up with businesses in male-dominated industries. First, we look at whether these women are 'superwomen' with superior skills and abilities. That is, they are above-average entrepreneurs, whose inherent intelligence and personality characteristics predispose them to success, and they can thus spot, and capitalize on, the opportunities presented by male-dominated sectors. Second, we explore whether it is not ability, but their psychosocial development which has helped these women to circumvent or overcome the norms that identify certain economic activities as 'male'. Here we will look at a range of psychosocial characteristics—the interrelation between social and individual factors expressed in someone's

---

[15] Among some of the studies that have looked at this issue, Bruni et al. (2004) and Anna et al. (2000) focus on women's choices for traditional female sectors, suggesting that these choices are driven by an assessment of which industry presents the lowest barriers to entry—from capital to skills, but not on the specific factors that drive women into non-traditional sectors.

behaviours and thoughts—including family background and role models, and we draw on an in-depth analysis of the entrepreneur's own account of how she ended up in her current profession. Third, we consider whether these are just the 'lucky' few women who somehow managed to overcome structural inequalities in education or human capital more generally, and access to finance, and thus move into these higher-return sectors.

It may well be that these three explanations overlap, and that their combination makes a successful crossover. One non-crossover woman noted the role of both norms and ability when she said: 'Such women are "superwomen". They have the characteristics of men.' But it might also be, as a crossover foundry owner indicates, that the differences are less: 'No, we are not different. It just takes a mindset and the necessary information to do this business.'

For this analysis, we use the mixed-methods data set, which has a larger sample of crossovers and was designed for this study. Hence, the depth of the information collected is much greater on this topic than the KASSIDA data set, which was originally designed to achieve other objectives.

4.1. *Information*

Before we take an in-depth look at the groups of factors, there is one potential market failure that could explain why some women do not cross over: information.

As shown in Figure 8.1, women who cross over have significantly higher profits than those who do not. Hence, it is possible that women who remain in female-dominated sectors simply do not know that they are making less. In our mixed-methods interviews, we asked about this.[16]

What we find is that most of the women who do not cross over believe that they make the same as or more than those in the crossover sectors.[17] Some of them are right and some are wrong—the distributions of profits across crossover and non-crossover sectors overlap. Hence, to examine the potential information barrier, we divide the non-crossovers into those whose profits are below the mean in the crossover sectors and those whose profits are above the mean. Figure 8.3 shows the results.

---

[16] The questions used in the survey were the following: '[If crossover] Do you think you are making more, the same, or less money than you would if you were in a sector where women typically operate?'; '[If non-crossover] Do you think you are making more, the same, or less money than you would if you were in a sector where men typically operate?'. In both cases, the respondent had three options: 1—Making more money; 2—Making the same money; and 3—Making less money.

[17] It is also true that most of the crossovers think that they make more than the non-crossovers, even those crossovers that make less. However, this is only a major issue for non-crossovers, as they are the ones in general not taking advantage of the opportunities in the male-dominated sectors.

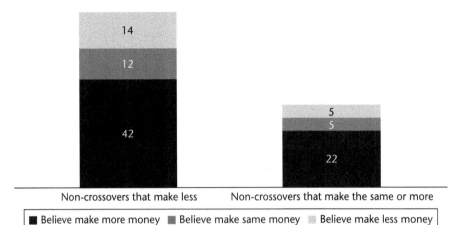

Figure 8.3. Non-crossovers' beliefs on profitability (percentage)—Mixed-methods data set

Source: Authors' own construction.

The difference in the size of the bars confirms that most of the non-crossovers have lower profits than the mean for crossovers. Moreover, this figure shows that non-crossovers are unaware of the potential profitability of crossing over. Looking at the bar on the left for non-crossovers with lower profits than the mean for crossovers, almost 80 per cent of non-crossovers that make less than crossovers think they make the same or more.

4.2. Other Factors

While information is clearly one barrier to crossing over for some women, we now take a deeper look at the characteristics of the entrepreneurs themselves for other explanations. To examine these characteristics, we run a series of regressions using the mixed-methods data set. The results are in Table 8.4. In what follows, we discuss two sets of OLS regression results.[18] Recall that the mixed-methods data set has two sets of non-crossover women: those who were matched to the crossovers on a small set of pre-business characteristics, and a group of randomly selected women. Given these two groups, we discuss results for both of them combined (columns A–C) and for the matched sample (columns D–F).[19]

---

[18] We have also run probit models, obtaining similar results, although the results in these models are more extreme given the small sample size and the rare outcome. These are available from the authors upon request.

[19] Summary statistics for the variables used in the regressions can be found in the working paper version of this chapter, WIDER Working Paper 2017/166.

4.2.1. SKILLS AND ABILITIES

We first analyse how innate skills and abilities are correlated with the decision to cross over to male-dominated sectors.

We used two cognitive tests, a digit-span recall exercise (measuring working memory) and a Raven's test (which captures fluid intelligence—the ability to understand complex problems and problem solving—as per Yuan et al. 2006) to determine if innate ability and/or intelligence predict the likelihood of being a crossover. The digit-span exercise involves respondents being shown a card with a four-digit number on it, with the card then being taken away. Ten seconds later, respondents are asked to repeat the number that was written on the card. If respondents recall the number correctly, enumerators then show them a five-digit number, with the process continuing up to eleven digits. In the Raven's progressive non-verbal reasoning test, enumerators provide twelve printed pages to each respondent, each of which contains a four-by-four pattern with one quadrant missing. Below the pattern are six figures, one of which fits the pattern, with the patterns becoming progressively more difficult. Respondents were given five minutes to complete as many of the patterns as possible.

In Table 8.4, we can see that the digit-span test is not a significant predictor of crossing over. On the other hand, the results on the Raven's test suggest that women with *less* fluid intelligence are more likely to cross over. While statistically significant, these effects are fairly small: getting one more matrix correct is associated with about a 3-percentage-point decrease in the likelihood of crossing over.

In addition to cognitive measures, the team considered a variety of non-cognitive tests to gauge respondents' levels of innate entrepreneurial spirit (see Khwaja and Klinger, ongoing; and Rauch and Frese 2007). This class of measures may be useful in predicting the success of entrepreneurs over time (see, for example, de Mel et al. 2010). We asked respondents to rate a level of agreement with questions that evaluated their personal levels of self-efficacy, locus of control, agreeableness, conscientiousness, and emotional stability on a scale from strong disagreement to strong agreement. As with the cognitive measures, the results in Table 8.4 do not show that the crossovers score unambiguously as more entrepreneurial than non-crossovers. Three of our measures (locus of control, agreeableness, and conscientiousness) show no correlation with the likelihood of being a crossover. However, women who score lower on emotional stability (this includes getting irritated more often and stressed about things) are more likely to be crossovers. On the other hand, women who score higher on self-efficacy (the ability to complete tasks and reach goals) are significantly (at the 10 per cent level) more likely to be crossovers in a subset of these specifications.

Table 8.4. Correlates of 'being a crossover'

	OLS combined			OLS matched		
	A	B	C	D	E	F
1. Personal characteristics						
Age	−0.003	−0.001	−0.003	−0.004	−0.001	−0.003
Father owned or managed family enterprise	−0.113	−0.093	−0.155	−0.200*	−0.206*	−0.227*
Mother owned or managed family enterprise	−0.224**	−0.165**	−0.190**	−0.203**	−0.125	−0.178*
Proportion of male siblings	0.030	0.047	0.032	0.097	0.119	0.072
Boy ratio, father owned enterprise interaction	−0.037	−0.038	−0.028	−0.059	−0.087	−0.052
Marital status: reference—married/living with a partner						
Divorced	−0.128	−0.176*	−0.086	−0.163	−0.198*	−0.117
Widowed	−0.140	−0.138	−0.112	−0.208*	−0.215*	−0.193
Never married	0.253*	0.196	0.291**	0.453**	0.451**	0.382*
Religion: reference—Catholic						
Protestant	−0.162	−0.188*	−0.158	−0.131	−0.221*	−0.083
Muslim	−0.088	−0.077	−0.074	−0.078	−0.069	−0.024
Pentacostal	−0.060	−0.099	−0.029	−0.014	−0.085	0.071
Region of birth: reference—Kampala						
Eastern	0.04	0.063	0.068	0.024	0.095	0.061
Central	−0.004	0.051	−0.013	0.011	0.076	0.026
Western	0.009	0.064	0.051	0.062	0.087	0.118
Northern	0.152	0.248	0.302	0.019	0.187	0.180
Foreign country	−0.092	−0.024	−0.106			
2. Skills and abilities						
Raven's test score	−0.034**	−0.032**	−0.034**	−0.035**	−0.033**	−0.028*
Digit test score	0.030	0.039	0.052	0.037	0.026	0.046
Locus of control aggregate score	0.009	−0.069	−0.250	−0.130	−0.143	−0.598
Agreeability score	−0.129	−0.050	−0.118	−0.274	−0.106	−0.450
Emotional stability score	−1.371**	−0.976**	−1.384**	−0.77	−0.471	−0.797*
Conscientious	0.531	0.268	0.622	0.32	0.555	−0.325
Self-efficacy	0.984*	1.106*	0.898	0.333	0.548	0.533
3. Psychosocial factors						
Male role model	0.220**	0.214**	0.188*	0.204*	0.124	0.167
First job was in non-male dominated sector	−0.461***	−0.434***	−0.398***	−0.619***	−0.644***	−0.532***
Exposure origination: Reference—self idea						
Someone's suggestion		0.216**			0.232*	
Was offered job in sector by family or friend		0.315**			0.21	
Observed others in sector		0.149			0.104	
Worked for a wage in sector— qualitative recode		0.028			−0.025	
Exposure enabling factor: Reference—self idea						
Suggested to me			0.334*			0.241
Offered job by a family member or friend			0.175			0.158
Observed others			0.104			0.118
Worked for stranger			−0.158			−0.169
Was trained			0.057			0.115

4. Capital

Years of education	−0.005	0.008	−0.008	−0.012	0.039	−0.022
Years of education squared	0.000	−0.001	0.000	0.000	−0.004	0.001
Owned an enterprise in another sector	0.151*	0.148*	0.141*	0.193**	0.173*	0.175*
Choose sector for low capital requirements	0.050	0.019	0.005	0.118	0.054	0.032
Delayed starting enterprise saving for capital	0.148*	0.123	0.136	0.107	0.142	0.051
Years of experience in previous jobs	−0.009	−0.011	−0.009	−0.002	0.001	−0.002
Previous years of experience squared	0.000	0.000	0.000	0.000	0.000	0.000
Trained while waiting to start business		0.017			0.180	
Constant	1.033	0.520	1.004	1.689**	0.660	2.176**
N	133	133	133	91	91	91
Adjusted R-Squared	0.370	0.407	0.432	0.566	0.588	0.592

Notes: * $p < 0.1$, ** $p < 0.05$, *** $p < 0.001$.

Source: Authors' own construction, mixed-methods data set.

In a meta-analysis of a wide range of studies on the relationship between personality traits and business creation and success, Rauch and Frese (2007) find that self-efficacy is positively correlated with business success, but not with business creation. This would suggest that the crossovers have personality traits in common with successful entrepreneurs. On the other hand, Rauch and Frese also find that locus of control is significantly related to success, while Zhao and Seibert (2006) find differences between entrepreneurs and managers on agreeableness. And the lack of a significant difference on these dimensions suggests that the crossovers are not markedly different to the non-crossovers in key non-cognitive entrepreneurship traits.

In sum, these results, combined with the cognitive tests, show that while the women who cross over may be different in some dimensions of personality, they are not more likely to score uniformly higher in skills that would aid them in becoming successful entrepreneurs.

4.2.2. PSYCHOSOCIAL FACTORS

Individual characteristics interact with one's environment in a range of ways that might impact the choice to cross over into male-dominated sectors. To make this set of factors tractable, we break them down into different sub-groups.

We start with an examination of the family background of the entrepreneurs. As shown in Table 8.4, women whose mothers are entrepreneurs are less likely to cross over, suggesting a continuation of professions within the family. Nonetheless, while we might expect the father's entrepreneurial background or the sex composition of one's siblings to matter as an influence in crossing over to 'male' activities, the results indicate that they do not.

We know that women who cross over are less likely to have started their own business and are more likely to be widowed. This would suggest that a path to crossing over is to inherit a business, perhaps from a husband. However, our analysis in Table 8.4 indicates that when we control for a range of factors, this does not appear to be the pathway to becoming a crossover. Relative to married women, divorced and widowed women are, if anything, less likely to be crossovers. Women who have never been married or have never lived with someone are significantly more likely than married women to be crossovers.

A critical path to crossing over seems to be having had a male role model in youth. In seeking to understand the importance of different psychosocial factors, we identify the women's reported role model in youth. Table 8.4 shows that women with a male role model are 12–22 percentage points more likely to be crossovers. This provides an indication of how men are involved in the transition of women to higher-profit sectors. We asked the respondents who these role models were, and the results are presented in Table 8.5. We see that, within the male relative category, fathers are a more common role model for crossovers relative to non-crossovers. However, as

Table 8.5. Identity of role models and individuals who introduced entrepreneurs to their sectors (%)

5.a. Identity of role model in youth (%)

	Crossover	Non-crossover	Difference
Male	32.6	18.1	14.5*
Female	67.4	81.9	−14.5*
	100	100	
Male relative	21.3	14.0	7.3
Female relative	40.4	55.8	−15.4*
Non-related male	10.6	5.8	4.8
Non-related female	27.7	24.4	3.2
Total	100	100	
N	47	86	133

5.b. Identity of individuals introducing entrepreneurs to their sectors (%)

	Crossover	Non-crossover	Difference
Mother	1.8	10.6	−8.8**
Father	7.3	1.9	5.4*
Other male family member	20.0	5.8	14.2***
Other female family member	10.9	16.4	−5.4
Female friend/community member	29.1	26.0	3.1
Male friend/community member	12.7	3.9	8.9**
Teacher	1.8	26.9	−25.1***
Other	16.4	8.7	7.7**
Total	100	100	
N	55	104	159

Notes: *** p < 0.01, ** p < 0.05, * p < 0.1.

Source: Authors' own construction.

shown in the results on family background in Table 8.4, the channels of influence are not as direct as if crossovers became entrepreneurs in a sector because it was where their fathers used to work, since there is no significant relationship with the variable 'Father owned enterprise'.[20]

Nevertheless, the importance of certain kinds of men is again evident when we ask who first exposed the entrepreneurs to their sector. Table 8.5b shows the distribution of the responses of crossovers versus non-crossovers. Crossovers are more likely to be introduced to their sector relative to non-crossovers by fathers, male friends/community members, and other male family members. Two of our respondents summarize the role of these male mentors: 'Through his encouragements [and] help, I kept my savings until I got what was enough to start up. He mentored me after I finished my diploma.'; 'My spouse was in carpentry when we married. His friend taught me the skill because my spouse wanted me only to manage and do sales for him.'

On the other hand, non-crossovers are more likely to be introduced to their sectors by mothers and teachers. Indeed, teachers are one of the main sources of exposure to the non-crossover sectors, particularly in the case of tailors who learn how to sew at school or attend special training provided by other institutions (church, charities, and non-governmental organizations). This suggests that the education system, as it now stands, is one of the reinforcing factors in maintaining the gender segregation of sectoral choice.

Returning to Table 8.4, we also look at variables that may be critical in terms of initial exposure. Specifically, having a first job in a non-male-dominated sector is negatively associated with being a crossover. This suggests strong path dependence in these women's careers—with an initial job in a non-crossover sector, they are much less likely to switch.

To better understand the pathways to becoming a crossover, we also undertook a coding exercise of women's stories of how they ended up in their current sector of employment, drawing on both quantitative and qualitative data. We coded two separate sets of variables from these data. The first is what we label the exposure origination, which is meant to capture where the original idea/impetus for choosing a sector came from. As individuals cited many factors in their stories about the decision to start/join a business in a specific industry, we ordered these factors through time. The first identified factor was coded as the exposure origination and is used under the assumption that what matters is where the original idea comes from. As per Table 8.4, the options for coding the exposure to sector include self-idea, someone's suggestion, offered job in sector by family or friend, observed others, or worked for a wage in the sector.

---

[20] We tested for, and did not find, collinearity between 'Father owned enterprise' and 'Male role model'.

Alternatively, we use the last identified factor to define the sector participation enabling factor, which would imply that the last step is explanatory of the final decision taken. For example, one of the crossovers in metal fabrication described her process of getting into the business as follows: 'I lost my capital in charcoal selling and I was unemployed, then a friend invited me to join a workshop of metal fabrication where I was taught the skills. She first taught me how to produce, and then I started my own business.' Her origination factor is 'someone suggested' while her enabling factor is 'training'. Both the sector participation origination and the sector participation enabling factor are included in the analysis in Table 8.4. However, since they are obviously overlapping, we run them separately in columns B and C and E and F.

When we focus on what started the process, we can see that, relative to the idea coming from the entrepreneur herself, the role of others appears to be significantly more important. Someone's suggestion and being offered a job in the sector by a friend or family member are significant and positive in predicting the likelihood of crossing over, relative to own idea. These results seem to confirm the importance of active engagement from others in enabling women to move into male-dominated sectors. Our participation enabling factors suggest that, relative to self-initiation, 'suggested to me' is positively correlated with being a crossover, but only in the combined sample, and significant only at the 10 per cent level.

The qualitative work confirms active exposure to the sector as a relevant intermediate step in the trajectory to becoming a crossover, either by engaging in actively learning the trade or through being taken to the firm by an active intermediary or enabler—friend, family member—who not only suggests starting in the trade but also brings the person to either their own business or someone else's.

4.2.3. CAPITAL

Capital and skills are factors typically associated with gender gaps in entrepreneurship. We start our examination of capital with human capital. Table 8.4 shows that education, the most common measure of human capital, does not significantly affect the probability that a woman is a crossover. This is also true for years of experience in the previous job, and age, which will capture all accumulated experience. But one area where experience matters is whether the entrepreneur owned an enterprise in another sector. This is positively correlated with being a crossover (at the 10 per cent level).

It is difficult to capture the importance of credit constraints at the time that a woman decided to enter these sectors. To get at the influence of financial capital, we asked two questions: (1) did the woman choose this sector because of the low capital requirements; and (2) did the entrepreneur choose to delay setting up her business, and was this because she was saving to accumulate capital? The results in Table 8.4 indicate that these entrepreneurs do not choose their sector—crossover or non-crossover—based on the capital require- ments. The one exception to this is when we use the combined sample and do not control for the pathway to becoming a crossover. In this case, delaying the enterprise start-up to accumulate capital is positively correlated with being a crossover, but only at 10 per cent.

In sum, human and financial capital do not appear to play a role in being a crossover. In terms of skills and abilities, crossover entrepreneurs do not seem to have more innate intelligence than non-crossovers. Their personalities are somewhat different, but not in ways that uniformly predict business success. What seem to be critically important for the crossover decision, however, are psychosocial factors. Key among these is the importance of male role models, and the active role of 'gate openers' these role models, or other individuals, play in the female entrepreneur's access to the crossover sector and in break- ing traditional norms.

But the challenge is not only to successfully break into a new sector, but also to stay in the sector.

5. Sustaining a Crossover Business

The issues that crossover entrepreneurs face in developing their businesses start with the establishment of the enterprise. Of the many business-related challenges faced by crossovers and non-crossovers when establishing their enterprise, crossovers are more likely to experience some of the problems we might expect women who are pioneers in a sector to face. The most common constraint that crossovers mention is low technical skills. Here, the mixed- methods data lines up with our earlier discussion of the KASSIDA data. A smaller fraction of crossovers also mentions the difficulty of finding suppliers and delivering their products to clients. Notably, when we ask them directly if their suppliers charge them more because of their gender, 13 per cent of crossovers say yes, compared to 4 per cent of non-crossovers.

While finding customers in the first place is not a challenge faced by the crossovers, this is far and away the major problem cited by non-crossovers (over 44 per cent). From the focus group discussions with clients of metal fabrication and carpentry, it emerges that crossovers are perceived as being better at tracking their orders and as providers of better customer care than male business owners. This strategy might work to keep clients for crossovers. Clients and suppliers acknowledge that female business owners have lower technical skills, which, for example, limits the range of products the cross- overs can offer. According to these clients and suppliers, the crossovers 'depend too much on their male employees to carry out hard tasks such as firing, lifting, and delivering'. Furthermore, when asked 'If you had a big contract, who would you give it to: a male or female business owner?', the qualitative responses pointed to male-owned firms when it came to metal fabrication and carpentry because of the skill levels required to deliver on time.[21]

Given that crossovers are defying gender norms, we might expect crossover entrepreneurs to be more isolated. When asked if they have difficulty establishing networks, 40 per cent of crossover entrepreneurs say yes compared to only 14 per cent of non-crossovers. Crossovers know roughly the same number of people in their sector as non-crossovers do, although fewer of these people (but not statistically significantly fewer) are women. 54 per cent of them interact with other business owners at least once a month to discuss business issues, while this is true for only 39 per cent of non-crossovers.[22] And crossovers are as likely as non-crossovers to interact with other women to discuss business issues.

Another potential dimension in which issues may arise for crossover entrepreneurs is in the harassment they receive as they operate their business. When looking at reported sources of harassment for crossover and non-crossover female entrepreneurs,[23] the major form of harassment that both crossovers and non-crossovers face is a threat to shut down the business (most commonly by the police), but this threat is significantly more frequent for crossovers. In addition, crossovers experience more frequent vandalism of their premises. These could be because crossovers stand out within their sectors. However, they could also be features of the sectors within which crossovers operate. For example, compare a metal fabricator and a caterer. A caterer can pack up most of her capital and move her business quite easily, while a metal fabricator is more likely to have larger machinery that makes her business less mobile.[24]

The third significant difference in harassment unambiguously indicates the vulnerability of women who choose to cross over—they are almost twice as likely to experience unwanted sexual proposals than those who do not cross over,[25]

---

[21] If this is the case, it would suggest crossovers would engage in a higher number of smaller activities than men. Information on type of products sold suggests this is the case for women doing metal work. One woman noted that her difficulties in finding male employees to help with the physically demanding work had influenced her decision about the type of products she was offering.

[22] This difference is significant at 10 per cent.

[23] See table with details in the working paper version of this chapter, WIDER Working Paper 2017/166.

[24] The KASSIDA data set provides some support for this fact, as there are no significant differences between men and women in the crossover sectors across the forms of harassment. However, this is not a primary focus in the KASSIDA data collection and some numbers appear less reliable.

[25] These findings on sexual harassment are not confirmed in the KASSIDA data set, where reporting of sexual harassment is lower in general and for crossovers. This is likely partly related to methodological differences. As Ellsberg et al. (2001) and Ellsberg and Heise (2002) show,

although they are equally likely to report sexual harassment to be among the three most prominent problems faced by businesswomen in Uganda interested in entering their sector (23 per cent of crossovers and 21 per cent of non-crossovers). Harassment also appears prominently as part of the disadvantages faced by crossovers as seen by clients and community leaders.

When we asked entrepreneurs about the issues they currently face in their business, the most common answer (at around 35 per cent) for both crossovers and non-crossovers was credit. In the twelve months prior to the survey, the most common source of credit for crossovers and non-crossovers was a microfinance institution (29 and 30 per cent respectively), but crossovers are more likely to access a formal bank as a second option—18 per cent of crossovers used this source, compared with only 7 per cent of non-crossovers. By contrast, non-crossovers borrow from a female friend/community member (16 per cent of non-crossovers and 6 per cent of crossovers), perhaps because crossovers cannot rely on other women who work in their sectors. Only 10 per cent of crossovers borrowed from their spouse, and 3 per cent of non-crossovers did so.

When asked if their spouse knew about their business, 94 per cent of non-crossovers answered yes, compared to 78 per cent of crossovers. Reported spousal knowledge of earnings was much lower—34 per cent for crossovers and 21 per cent for non-crossovers (this difference is not statistically significant). However, most entrepreneurs contributed to their household expenses from what they earned in their businesses, mostly used for food or cooking fuel. Crossovers are more likely to contribute to covering the often large and lumpy expenditure on school fees (26 per cent vs 14 per cent).

In addition to the monetary contributions, it is possible that the household demands on women's time may constrain their ability to provide the supervision that larger crossover enterprises require. But when we compare crossover women to non-crossover women using the mixed-methods data set, we find that crossover women spend significantly fewer hours per week (62 hours versus 67) working in the business. And they spend about the same amount of time taking care of children and/or the elderly (14 hours versus 16—not statistically different). These results show us is that if childcare duties are indeed a constraint, they matter through limits on the growth of the firm, but not through the sectoral choice.

---

reported experiences of violence are very sensitive to methodological factors such as type and structure of the survey, interview setting and privacy levels, sex of the interviewer, and whether the instrument is quantitative or qualitative. The mixed-methods survey design and implementation—including a more personal approach to individuals' own experience in the form of a dialogue—was better suited to learning about these issues. United Nations (2014) and Ellsberg and Heise (2005) also note that under-reporting of violent experiences in questions related to violence inserted in surveys about other unrelated issues is of frequent occurrence.

6. Designing Policies to Support Women Who Want to Cross Over

This chapter explores an area heretofore unexplored in the literature on enterprises and occupational segregation. As such, there is not a literature on potential policies for us to draw on. In what follows, we provide a set of policy recommendations based on what is suggested by the analysis above. However, the lack of tested interventions in this area and the limitations of descriptive analysis mean that experimentation and rigorous impact evaluations[26] of these policies—using different combinations of interventions and in different contexts—are critical. It is also important to note that we limit our recommendations to those factors identified above that are malleable or can be changed by a direct policy intervention.

The first ingredient in a policy to support women who wish to cross over is information. A significant majority of the women who have not entered male-dominated sectors think that they make the same as or more than enterprise owners in these sectors when, in fact, they do not. They recognize that information is a factor and it needs to come early in life. Information will enable women to make better-informed choices about their business sector. Findings from an evaluation of the Kenya national vocational training programme suggest that this approach may be enough to change minds (Hicks et al. 2011). In the Kenya programme, before training enrolment decisions and course selections, some women received information on the difference between expected earnings for graduates of male-dominated trades versus female-dominated trades, as well as a video presentation about successful Kenyan female car mechanics. Women who received the intervention were 9 percentage points more likely to express preference for a male-dominated course, and 5 percentage points more likely to enrol in one.

However, information alone is not likely to be enough. A second element of a potential programme is to provide supportive engagement with those who can help guide women as they seek to enter and then operate businesses in male-dominated sectors. A mentor from the entrepreneur's existing network of family and friends, or sympathetic (or empathetic) outsiders. In our qualitative work, both crossovers and non-crossovers agreed that they would allow their daughters to cross over if someone reliable was to introduce them to the sector.

Third, and related to information, our analysis suggests that early exposure to the sector can help, and one way to achieve this is to work or undertake apprenticeships, ideally in businesses owned by people within the networks of

---

[26] Given that these policies will involve directly confronting well-entrenched norms, it is critical to integrate qualitative work in these rigorous impact evaluations.

trust. The qualitative work suggests a distinction between active and passive observation. Passive participation characterizes women in female-dominated sectors. Active participation, which is key for crossovers, consists of being close to the business, working in a business doing sales or managing the storefront, providing services and inputs for crossover business, and/or being invited to learn. Apprenticeships or other experiences working in a crossover business may be a critical way not only to impart basic skills to potential crossovers but also to engage in active participation.

Other considerations that may help with the success of this type of intervention include early targeting—crossovers are much more likely to have their first job in a crossover sector—such as younger women who are just entering the labour market—longer support—crossovers needed more time to acquire experience and capital—and awareness of context. This last point is key. Responses from our key informant interviews show both the potential for opposition as well as support by local leaders. One Muslim leader stated: 'I would not recommend anyone to sensitize to our women about male-dominated sectors. It is "Haramuh"—not accepted by religion. The way they dress is not allowed because they put on tight trousers. They cannot pray five times a day, they have no time'. On the other hand, a Local Chairman said: 'It is a very good idea. I also wanted my daughters to join such jobs because these jobs pay well ... [Crossing over] is a very good thing and that is where the world is heading. If there was an opportunity, I would join the team to sensitize the people in my zone.' Normative restrictions and social sanctions can be important obstacles that can be lessened with adequate work at the community level. Otherwise social perceptions will not only impact sector choice, but might also prevent women from accessing credit or financial support or building lasting networks.

Finally, once women start to cross over, it is critical to support them as their businesses grow (e.g. with support for networks or crossover-specific business organizations). As the data and the words of our respondents indicate, the process of crossing over is a continuous one, with different issues arising at different stages in the process.

References

Anna, A.L., G.N. Chandler, E. Jansen, and N.P. Mero (2000). 'Women Business Owners in Traditional and Non-Traditional Industries'. *Journal of Business Venturing*, 15(3): 279–303.

Aterido, R., and M. Hallward-Driemeier (2011). 'Whose Business Is It Anyway? Closing the Gender Gap in Entrepreneurship in Sub-Saharan Africa'. *Small Business Economics*, 37(3): 443–64.

Bardasi, E., and A. Getahun (2008). 'Unlocking the Power of Women'. Chapter prepared for the Ethiopia Investment Climate Assessment (ICA). In World Bank, *Toward the Competitive Frontier: Strategies for Improving Ethiopia's Investment Climate*. Washington, DC: World Bank.

Bardasi, E., S. Sabarwal, and K. Terrell (2011). 'How Do Female Entrepreneurs Perform? Evidence from Three Developing Regions'. *Small Business Economics*, 37: 417–41.

Bruhn, M. (2009). 'Female-Owned Firms in Latin America: Characteristics, Performance, and Obstacles to Growth'. *Policy Research Working Paper* 5122. Washington, DC: World Bank.

Bruni, A., S. Gherardi, and B. Poggio (2004). 'Entrepreneur-Mentality, Gender and the Study of Women Entrepreneurs'. *Journal of Organizational Change Management*, 17(3): 256–68.

Brush, C.G. (1992). 'Research on Women Business Owners. Past Trends: A New Perspective and Future Directions'. *Entrepreneurship, Theory & Practice*, Summer: 5–30.

Cuberes, D., and Teignier, M. (2014). 'Aggregate Costs of Gender Gaps in the Labor Market: A Quantitative Estimate'. *UB Economics–Working Papers*, 2014, E14/308.

De Mel, S., D. McKenzie, and C. Woodruff (2009). 'Are Women More Credit Constrained? Experimental Evidence on Gender and Microenterprise Returns'. *American Economic Journal: Applied Economics*, 1(3): 1–32.

De Mel, S., D. McKenzie, and C. Woodruff (2010). 'Who Are the Microenterprise Owners? Evidence from Sri Lanka on Tokman versus De Soto'. In J. Lerner and A. Schoar (eds), *International Differences in Entrepreneurship*. Chicago: University of Chicago Press for the NBER.

Dolado, J., F. Felgueroso, and J. Jimeno (2003). 'Discrimination et inégalités/Discrimination and Unequal Outcome'. *Annals of Economics and Statistics/Annales d'Économie et de Statistique*, 71/72: 293–315.

Ellsberg, M., and L. Heise (2002). 'Bearing Witness: Ethics in Domestic Violence Research'. *The Lancet*, 359(9317): 1599–604.

Ellsberg, M., and L. Heise (2005). 'Researching Violence against Women. A Practical Guide for Researchers and Activists'. Washington, DC: World Health Organization.

Ellsberg, M., L. Heise, R. Pena, S. Agurto, and A. Winkvist (2001). 'Researching Domestic Violence against Women: Methodological and Ethical Considerations'. *Studies in Family Planning*, 32(1): 1–16.

Hallward-Driemeier, M. (2013). 'Enterprising Women: Expanding Economic Opportunities in Africa'. Washington, DC: World Bank and Agence Française de Développement (AFD).

Hasan, R., R. Afzal, and S. Parveen (2011). 'Motivational Orientation and Perceived Social Support among Pakistani Female Entrepreneurs in Attock District'. *Journal of Gender and Social Issues*, 10: 37–55.

Hicks, J.H., M. Kremer, I. Mbiti, and E. Miguel (2011). 'Vocational Education Voucher Delivery and Labor Market Returns: A Randomized Evaluation among Kenyan Youth'. Report for Spanish Impact Evaluation Fund, Phase II. Washington, DC: World Bank.

Hundley, G. (2001). 'Why Women Earn Less Than Men in Self-Employment'. *Journal of Labor Research*, 22(4): 817–29.

ILO (2012). 'Global Employment Trends for Women'. Geneva: ILO.

Kantis, H., P. Angelelli, and V.P. Koenig (2005). 'Developing Entrepreneurship: Experience in Latin America and Worldwide'. Washington, DC: Inter-American Development Bank/Fundes International.

Kantor, P. (2005). 'Determinants of Women's Microenterprise Success in Ahmedabad, India: Empowerment and Economics'. *Feminist Economics*, 11(3): 63–83.

Kevane, M., and B. Wydick (2001). 'Microenterprise Lending to Female Entrepreneurs: Sacrificing Economic Growth for Poverty Alleviation?'. *World Development*, 29(7): 1225–36.

Klapper, L., and S. Parker (2011). 'Gender and the Business Environment for New Firm Creation'. *World Bank Research Observer*, 26(2): 237–57.

Mead, D.C., and C. Liedholm (1998). 'The Dynamics of Micro and Small Enterprises in Developing Countries'. *World Development*, 26(1): 61–74.

Minniti M. (2010). 'Female Entrepreneurship and Economic Activity'. *European Journal of Development Research*, 22(3): 294–312.

Nichter, S., and L. Goldmark (2009). 'Small Firm Growth in Developing Countries'. *World Development*, 37(9): 1453–64.

Rauch, A., and M. Frese (2007). 'Let's Put the Person Back into Entrepreneurship Research: A Meta-Analysis on the Relationship between Business Owners' Personality Traits, Business Creation, and Success'. *European Journal of Work and Organizational Psychology*, 16(4): 353–85.

Rijkers, B., and R. Costa (2012). 'Gender and Rural Non-Farm Entrepreneurship'. *World Development*, 40(12): 2411–26.

UBOS (2006). 'Uganda National Household Survey 2005/06'. Kampala: Uganda Bureau of Statistics.

United Nations (2014). 'Guidelines for Producing Statistics on Violence against Women'. New York: UN Department of Economic and Social Affairs, Statistics Division.

World Bank (2011). *World Development Report 2012: Gender Equality and Development*. Washington, DC: World Bank.

Yuan, K., J. Steedle, R. Shavelson, A. Alonzo, and M. Oppezzo (2006). 'Working Memory, Fluid Intelligence, and Science Learning'. *Educational Research Review*, 1: 83–98.

Zhao, H., and S.E. Seibert (2006). 'The Big Five Personality Dimensions and Entrepreneurial Status: A Meta-Analytical Review'. *Journal of Applied Psychology*, 91(2): 259–71.

9

Career Dynamics and Gender Gaps Among Employees in the Microfinance Sector

Ina Ganguli, Ricardo Hausmann, and Martina Viarengo[1]

1. Introduction

Microfinance institutions (MFIs) are commonly identified as empowering women and making them key actors in generating social change and economic development. Yet little is known about the gender parity among employees within the lending institutions themselves and how this can impact development. In this project, we use rich data covering all employees working in the largest MFI in Latin America from 2004 to 2012 to document and understand gender differences in the career paths of MFI employees. Are there gender gaps in promotion and earnings? How large are they? Are there differences in the main career paths within the microfinance institution (in sales vs. administration)? We also link data on the gender and loan information of clients to data on the employees working with them to understand whether gender differences are related to the types and outcomes of the clients themselves, providing broader insights into the ways in which the gender of employees can impact the performance of MFIs and the development process.

While MFIs are an increasingly important employer of individuals in the developing world, and many of the commercially successful microfinance institutions employ thousands of individuals[2] (e.g., Roodman and Qureshi

[1] We would like to thank the editors Siwan Anderson, Lori Beaman, and Jean-Philippe Platteau; the Scientific Committee of the UNU-WIDER 'Gender and Development' project as well as an anonymous referee; and Iris Bohnet, Richard B. Freeman, and Lant Pritchett, for helpful discussions and comments on an earlier draft of this chapter. We thank Catalina Martinez for research assistance. We would like to thank the MFI for sharing the data for the analysis.
[2] For example, the Grameen Bank employs 22,924 individuals in 2,422 branches in Bangladesh (www.grameen-info.org/grameen-bank-at-a-glance/, accessed 17 April 2017) whereas Bancosol

2006: 39), there is very little evidence on the state of gender differences in employment and career dynamics in the MFI sector. In fact, while 'breaking the glass ceiling' has become an important corporate objective in many economic sectors, there appears to exist an opposite trend in the MFI sector, where female leadership has diminished in recent years (Iskenderian 2011).

The case for gender equality in the context of new business models that pursue both social impact and financial returns, which characterize MFIs, is based on two main explanations. First, women tend to have a comparative advantage in the specific skills of the non-profit sector (Lansford et al. 2010), so they help to maintain the balance between the business and the development objectives of new business models. Second, generating deep social change and gender empowerment requires women to be seen as leaders and active drivers of development (WWB 2010). Moreover, as microfinance expands in Latin America and other emerging economies, it is rapidly becoming part of the mainstream financial landscape. A fundamental and neglected question, which our study will shed light on, is whether gender gaps in career dynamics in MFIs operate in a similar way to those in the financial sector.

In the case of MFIs, we might expect them to be more gender-friendly employers, given their documented important role in increasing financial access for women in particular, which has been shown to play a powerful role in development. It has been shown that income and assets in the hands of women are associated with larger improvements in child health, and with larger expenditure shares of household nutrients, health, and housing (Thomas 1990, 1994, and Duflo 2003, 2012, among others). Female employees may understand better how to pursue these goals if women understand the female market segment better and clients tend to feel more comfortable with female staff (WWB 2012).

Some of the most compelling relevant analysis to date comes from Strøm et al. (2014), who used a global panel of 329 microfinance institutions in 73 countries covering the years 1998–2008, and found a relationship between female leadership and the performance of MFIs, which is mainly driven by the female market orientation of MFIs and not by better governance. However, to date, there is very little evidence in the existing literature that has examined the micro-foundations of gender gaps in the microfinance sector.

In this regard, our chapter takes a micro-level approach by using rich information on all employees in one MFI to look at the dynamics within a firm that operates in many different regions of the same country. Specifically, we document the nature of gender gaps in career dynamics in the microfinance sector, focusing on differences in the administrative career path and the

employs 2,740 staff members in 313 offices in Bolivia (<https://reports.themix.org/> accessed 17 April 2017).

193

sales career path within the firm. We document differences in these career paths between male and female employees in terms of promotion, exit, and wages. We then examine how the characteristics of employees in the sales career path of the firm are related to the characteristics and outcomes of clients, including patterns of assortative matching, and the number and terms of loans clients receive.

Our main results are as follows. First, we show in the raw data that in both the administrative and the sales career paths there is close to gender parity at the entry level, but gender gaps emerge at the higher ranks, particularly for the administrative career path. However, when we look at the hierarchy within the lowest rank of the sales division—the loan officers—who make up the lion's share of the employees working within the MFI, a different pattern emerges. Here, the gender gap essentially reverses, so that women become the greater share of the loan officers at the higher ranks.

Second, we investigate these differences further in a regression framework. We show that in the administrative career path, the overall differences by gender in the probability of promotion disappear after controlling for area of practice and rank, as well as individual characteristics. However, at the intermediate level of 'Líder',[3] a significant gap in the probability of promotion favouring men persists.

By contrast, within the sales division, we find that the gender gap in promotion is small (around 2 per cent) but significant even after including controls. The gap is highest at the most highly ranked position ('Gerente'[4] to 'Gerente Regional'[5]). There is also some evidence that family factors play a role in the sales division regarding promotion, with women who are married being more likely to be promoted compared to unmarried women.

When we focus on the loan officers ('Promotor' and 'Asesor'[6]), we find that, as the raw data suggest, women are more likely to advance through the ranks within these levels. Even after controlling for individual and other covariates, the probability of promotion is higher for women than for men. We also find some evidence that if a woman's immediate supervisor is also a woman, she is even more likely to be promoted than if the supervisor is a man.

In terms of exit, we show that within the administrative division there does not appear to be differential exit by gender, while, in the sales division, women are about 4 per cent less likely to exit after controlling for covariates. Turning to wages, we show a striking result: while there are not significant gender differences in promotion overall in the administrative path, there is a

---

[3] This corresponds to the position of 'head'.
[4] This corresponds to the position of 'manager'.
[5] This corresponds to the position of 'regional manager'.
[6] Both of these job titles correspond to the position of 'loan officer'. The difference between a 'Promotor' and an 'Asesor' is outlined in Section 3.

significant gender wage gap, even after controlling for covariates, and this gap appears to be largest at the highest ranks. Meanwhile, in sales, where there are significant differences in promotion by gender, the wage differences disappear after including controls. In contrast, among loan officers the wage gap reverses, so that women earn higher wages on average than men.

Third, we turn to an analysis of client data matched to loan officers. We find that female Promotores are no more likely to work with female clients than with male clients (for non-female-only loan products) after controlling for covariates, which suggests that assortative matching by gender is not occurring. However, we do find that female Asesores are 1.8 per cent more likely than male Asesores to work with female clients. We also find some evidence of differences in the types of clients that male and female officers work with, such as female Promotores appearing to work with clients who receive better terms (lower interest rates) and who have had previous loans with the MFI, compared to those with whom male Promotores work (for female-only products).

Overall, this analysis shows that the dynamics of gender gaps are complex and vary within the largest MFI in Latin America. The empirical findings also suggest that different factors have an impact on the dynamics of gender gaps at different stages of the career path. There is heterogeneity across the different divisions. Gender gaps in the administrative division seem to be more similar to the dynamics in career paths observed in the financial sector, whereas in the division that is core to the microfinance sector, a reversal of the gender gap is observed. In terms of the loan officer matching process, we document that female employees tend to be associated with those loans that have better conditions and consequently a higher expected probability of repayment.

Our study makes three main contributions. First, this is the first study that examines gender gaps in wages and career trajectories in the microfinance sector. While the existing research has highlighted the fact that gender gaps are larger at the higher ranks of microfinance institutions, our analysis provides evidence on the micro-foundations of gender gaps in career dynamics within the microfinance sector by relying on a unique panel data set that allows us to examine how gender gaps emerge and evolve.

Second, our study shows the complexity of the dynamics of gender gaps within MFIs. We document to what extent gender gaps differ along the career trajectories of the administrative and the sales divisions. Specifically, our analysis shows that gender gaps increase with seniority in the administrative division, whereas there is a reversed gender gap in the lower ranks of the sales of microcredit products division, which is the division that characterizes the microfinance sector. This is an important result because it shows the extent to which, in the administrative division—the 'back office' of the organization, where employees do not have interaction with the clients of the MFI—the dynamics of gender gaps are similar to those observed for professionals in the traditional financial and corporate sectors. On the other hand, in the sales division, the 'front office' of the organization, where employees are in contact with the core clients of the microfinance sector (i.e. women), the gender gap is reversed, although only at the lower ranks of the division.

Third, our study also provides some evidence on how the gender of employees can impact the outcomes of clients. It documents that women employees tend to have clients with better terms and clients who have previously received loans. This finding is consistent with the existing evidence which suggests that employees may be better positioned to work with clients of the same gender (Beck et al. 2014).

Finally, our study also contributes to defining the agenda for future research in this area. Specifically, more research is needed in order to understand how organizations in the microfinance sector change with development. A reversal of the gender gap was observed at the lower ranks of the division that operates in close contact with the microfinance clients—that is, women. Will this shift gradually affect the higher ranks of the sales division and then the 'back office' of the organization? How long will this take? Or will the reversal be limited within those positions where women have a comparative advantage in interacting with female clients? Answers to these questions have important implications for the evolution of the sector, and at the micro level for understanding how women's empowerment on the employer side of the microfinance sector is shaped.

The rest of the chapter is structured as follows. Section 2 presents the relevant literature on gender gaps in professional sectors, and specifically in the financial and microfinance sectors, and possible explanations for these gender gaps. Existing studies on loan officer–client gender matching and the relationship between gender and client outcomes are also briefly reviewed. Section 3 describes the institutional background, Section 4 presents data, empirical strategy, and descriptive statistics. Section 5 presents the main findings. Section 6 provides concluding remarks.

2. Literature Review

2.1. *Gender Gaps in Career Dynamics Among Professionals*

Women's underperformance in the corporate and financial sectors has been widely documented in the existing literature (e.g. Babcock and Laschever 2003; Bertrand et al. 2010). Most of the existing studies have examined gender differences in compensation, while only a few more recent ones have examined career trajectories (e.g. Ganguli et al., 2016). However, there is no study at present that has documented gender gaps among employees in the microfinance sector. The rapid expansion of the microfinance industry in recent decades, the fact that the size of the microfinance organizations themselves often increases at a very fast pace (World Bank 2000), and the fact that in several countries women represent a significant share of both clients and the workforce of MFIs,[7] all call for an understanding as to whether men and women in the microfinance sector follow similar career paths.

In this context, the theoretical framework that seems to best characterize the pattern of compensations and promotions in the MFI institution examined is the one related to 'tournament theory', pioneered by Lazear and Rosen (1981). They first observed that the remuneration received by employees depends on their rank within the organization, and their relative performance with respect to their peers. This framework has been found to have significant empirical support in several professional occupations, ranging from modern corporate law firms (Gilson and Mnookin 1989) to academia (Lazear and Shaw 2007). Among the factors that contribute to explaining gender gaps in labour market outcomes, existing studies have identified both supply-side (e.g., work experience, preferences, aspirations) and demand-side (e.g., system of selection, implicit barriers) factors.

2.2. Assortative Matching: Client and Loan Officer

The economic literature related to the process of assortative matching goes back to Becker (1973). In his pioneering analysis, Becker examined the pattern of sorting along individual-level traits and characteristics between spouses in the marriage market. In the context of our study, gender can be regarded as a characteristic that defines a group identity (e.g. Akerlof and Kranton 2000) which has an impact on the matching process between clients and officers, and ultimately on credit outcomes given the role played by loan officers in credit distribution (Brau and Woller 2004). In the existing literature the gender aspect has mainly been examined in terms of female participation at the aggregate level (e.g. Boehe and Cruz 2013; D'Espallier et al. 2011; Hartaska et al. 2014). The assortative matching pattern at the micro level has only been examined in a few recent studies. For example, Beck et al. (2013) and Beck et al. (2014) rely on a data set provided by a commercial lender serving microenterprises and small–medium-sized enterprises in Albania and examine the pattern of gender matching between loan officers and clients.

2.3. Client–Loan Officer Matching

Existing studies that have examined the impact of individual-level gender matching between client and loan officer have found mixed results that vary

[7] See MIX Market: http://www.themix.org/mixmarket (accessed 17 April 2017).

according to the credit outcome examined. On the one hand, Beck at al. (2013), examining the matching pattern within a large Albanian commercial firm, find that loans managed by female officers are less likely to become problematic loans, but female officers experience an advantage over their male counterparts only with experience. On the other hand, Beck et al. (2014) find that borrowers matched to loan officers of the opposite gender experience less advantageous loan conditions. Agier and Szafarz (2013) examine a large sample of loan applications from a Brazilian microfinance institution and find a significant gender gap among clients in terms of loan size, which is not related to the loan officer's gender.

3. Institutional Background

The microfinance sector is expanding at a very fast pace in developing countries. According to Microfinance Information Exchange (MIX) estimates, there were approximately 100 million borrowers from MFIs in 2011 (Di Benedetta et al. 2015). The largest MFIs are located in different regions of the world, and they vary in terms of governance structure. Examples include Bandhan in India, Bank Rakyat in Indonesia, BancoSol in Bolivia, Grameen Bank in Bangladesh, and Compartamos Banco in Mexico.

In this context, we focus on the largest microfinance institution in Latin America. We position this leading Latin American institution within the MFI sector by relying on the MIX Market database, the largest database on the global microfinance industry, which provides background and balance sheet information for over 1,800 microfinance institutions worldwide. The MFI examined is among the top ten worldwide in terms of personnel employed and number of active borrowers, with an average of 201 borrowers per staff member. It also ranks in the top ten with respect to the number of women borrowers. It is included in about the top 5 per cent in terms of yield on gross portfolio (nominal).[8]

The microfinance institution we study shares many characteristics with big players in the financial world. It can be compared to other world-leading MFIs along several dimensions. First, many of them have experienced the transition from socially oriented non-profit microfinance to for-profit microfinance (Cull et al. 2009). Second, they are regulated deposit-taking institutions. Third, they target low-income women with both individual and solidarity-group lending methods and have a low share of non-performing loans.

---

[8] This information was extracted from the MIX Market database and refers to the most recent data available (www.mixmarket.org, accessed 17 April 2017). A more precise URL cannot be provided without disclosing the name of the MFI we are studying, but more information is available from the authors upon request.

The MFI is divided into two main divisions: administrative (headquarters and non-headquarters) and sales. In 2012, the sales division employed 79 per cent of all employees, while 21 per cent were employed in administration (headquarters).

In the empirical analysis, we pool the headquarters and non-headquarters administrative division employees. There are twenty-eight areas of practice in the most recent year for which the data are available. The administrative division includes areas of practice such as accounting, internal audit, marketing, control management, corporate strategy, external relations, finance, legal, operations management, risk management, innovation, and human resources.

There is a well-defined hierarchy within each area of practice in the administrative division. The lowest-ranked positions are 'Auxiliar' and 'Analista', followed by an intermediate position ('Coordinador'), two middle-management positions ('Líder', and 'Gerente'), and the two top ranks of the division ('Subdirector', and 'Director'). Associated with each position is a job description which provides a list of tasks and activities that employees are expected to carry out, and objectives they should meet.

The sales division follows a different hierarchy, and therefore will be considered separately in the empirical analysis. Entry-level positions ('Promotor', and 'Asesor de Crédito') are followed by three middle-management positions ('Coordinador de Unidad', 'Coordinador de Crédito', and 'Subgerente de Oficina'), and two upper-management positions ('Gerente de Oficina de Servicios Regional' followed by 'Gerente Regional').

The loan officer, as in the majority of MFIs, plays a key role in terms of providing clients with assistance in their loan application, defining conditions of the loan, and monitoring its repayment. Also, this is reinforced by the nature of the MFI's operations, wherein the majority of transactions are decentralized and loan officers go to meet potential clients in the field (Roodman and Qureshi 2006).

There are two positions equivalent to 'loan officer' in the MFI: 'Promotor', and 'Asesor de Crédito'. Loan officers in each category are expected to perform specific tasks. 'Promotores' are expected to identify possible clients among individuals with a productive activity, to supervise the creation of lending groups according to the guidelines of the MFI, and to develop the other products of the MFI. Meanwhile, 'Asesores de Crédito' are expected to deliver the financial resources related to the loan to individuals and groups and to collect repayment in instalments according to the guidelines and method approved by the MFI. There are four different ranks that relate to the level of seniority of the loan officer: 'Nuevo', 'Junior', 'Senior', and 'Maestro'. Figures depicting the career trajectories in the administrative and sales divisions, and further details about the selection process are available in Ganguli et al. (2017: Section 3).

4. Data and Empirical Approach

4.1. *Data*

We have compiled a rich individual-year-level panel data set based on human resource records of the firm that includes all employees working in the MFI from 2004 to 2012. This unique data set allows us to address research questions related to the micro-foundations of gender gaps in career dynamics in the MFI that have not been addressed before. Our analytical sample includes annual data on demographics, earnings, and job characteristics for almost 30,000 employees working in the MFI from 2004 to 2012. We have linked these employees in 2012 to 336,000 clients and 341,000 loans. The client data includes demographics for the client and measures such as loan characteristics and prior credit products received.

Much of our analysis examines differences for the main career paths in the firm (administrative and sales) as well as for loan officers (within the sales division) separately. Table 9.1 shows some descriptive statistics for the main employee data sample for each of these groups (administrative, sales, and loan officers) by gender for the first and last year in our sample (2004 and 2012). As Table 9.1 shows, most of the employees working for the MFI are in fact loan officers, and thus they make up the largest share of our sample. Table 9.2 shows some descriptive statistics for the client sample, which we matched to employee data for 2012.

First, we note the dramatic growth in the MFI over this period, during which the number of employees increased close to tenfold. Second, the share of employees with education above college level increased dramatically in both divisions. In terms of differences in characteristics by gender, we see that in the administrative path women tend to be slightly younger than men, while in sales women are older on average. Women are less likely to be married in both divisions. For the subsample for which information is available about children, we see that in the administrative path women tend to have fewer children than men, while in sales women have more children than men. The loan officers have more children on average than the employees in the sales or administrative paths as a whole.

Figure 9.1 shows the share of women by career path at each rank. In the administrative career path (Figure 9.1a), the gender gap favours women at the 'Analista' and 'Coordinador' levels but then begins to favour men at the higher ranks, beginning at the 'Líder' level. In the sales division (Figure 9.1b), 'Promotores' and 'Coordinadores' are close to gender equality, while for 'Asesores' and the highest ranks there are shares of women similar to those in the higher ranks of the administrative path. In Figure 9.1c, we look at the ranks within the loan officer positions, and we see that here the gender gap is reversed—that women make up a greater share of the loan officers at the

Table 9.1. Employee summary statistics by career path and gender, 2004 and 2012

Administrative

	2004		2012	
	Men	Women	Men	Women
Age (years)	28.91	27.10	32.14	29.15
Tenure (years)	1.88	1.31	2.15	2.25
Bachelor (%)	0.79	0.67	0.83	0.76
Above bachelor* (%)	0.19	0.13	0.63	0.58
Evaluation (ave. score)	N/A	N/A	94.31	95.30
Married (%)	0.38	0.23	0.40	0.21
Children* (ave. no.)	N/A	N/A	0.14	0.07
N	118	216	1,069	2,049

Sales

	2004		2012	
	Men	Women	Men	Women
Age (years)	27.16	27.67	28.30	29.24
Tenure (years)	0.97	1.25	1.10	1.43
Bachelor (%)	0.67	0.55	0.50	0.44
Above bachelor* (%)	0.07	0.06	0.31	0.27
Urban (%)	0.19	0.24	0.34	0.39
Married (%)	0.43	0.29	0.43	0.30
Children* (ave. no.)	N/A	N/A	0.70	0.87
N	595	656	6,430	5,525

Sales—Promotor/Asesor levels

	2004		2012	
	Men	Women	Men	Women
Age (years)	25.90	27.06	27.64	28.64
Tenure (years)	0.55	0.85	0.66	0.90
Bachelor (%)	0.57	0.47	0.46	0.41
Above bachelor* (%)	0.06	0.05	0.27	0.24
Urban (%)	0.18	0.24	0.34	0.40
Married (%)	0.40	0.28	0.41	0.28
Children* (ave. no.)	N/A	N/A	1.31	1.42
N	416	513	4,996	4,367

Note: * Information on average number of children and educational level attained is only available for a subset of employees.
Source: Authors' calculations based on data described in Section 4.

Table 9.2. Client summary statistics, 2012

Client/loan characteristics	Gender of employee assigned to client	
	Female employee	Male employee
Female clients (%)	0.954	0.941
Female-only product (%)	0.855	0.822
Age of clients	39.013	39.090
Number of previous loans	8.056	7.838
Amount of loan (Mexican peso)	9120.82	8850.52
Payment amount (Mexican peso)	804.88	796.72
Loan length (weeks)	20.48	20.83
Urban (%)	0.407	0.341
N	163,232	178,004

Source: Authors' calculations based on data described in Section 4.

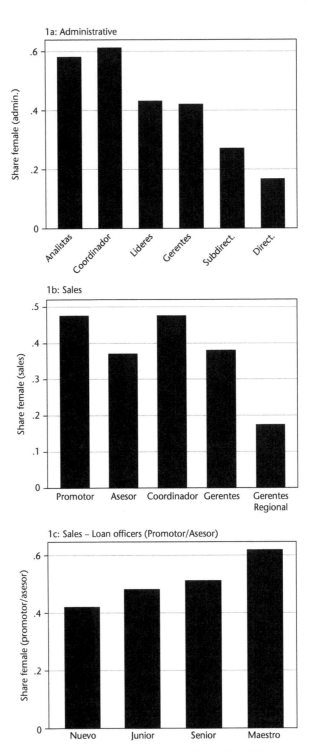

Figure 9.1. Share of women by rank, 2012

higher ranks, with 60 per cent of the 'Maestro' rank women. Figures showing that there have not been notable changes over the period of 2004–12 in the share of women by rank for each division are available in Ganguli et al. (2017: Section 4).

4.2. Empirical Approach

4.2.1. GENDER GAPS IN EMPLOYEE PROMOTION, EXIT, AND WAGES

Given the panel nature of our data, which provides us with annual observations for the same employees for every year they are working in the firm, we follow other studies examining promotion and exit probabilities and estimate probit models, where we define promotion as a binary variable equal to 1 if an employee moved to a higher rank (position) the next year and 0 otherwise (e.g. Blau and DeVaro, 2007). Exit is defined as a binary variable equal to 1 if an employee was no longer in the firm the next year and 0 otherwise.

We estimate the models separately for each career path (administrative or sales) and also for loan officers separately to account for the differences in the nature of the gender gap documented in the previous sections. For promotion, we first run the model on a female dummy only, to estimate the raw gender differential in promotion probability. We then include rank, area of practice, and year dummies, and additional variables for worker and job characteristics (age, tenure in the firm) to estimate whether the differential remains after accounting for these observable characteristics. The full specification of the probit model is as follows for individual i in year t:

$$\Pr(Promoted_{it+1}) = \Phi(\beta_0 + \beta_1 Female_i + \beta_2 Age_{it} + \beta_3 Age_{it}^2 + \beta_4 Tenure_{it} + \beta_5 Tenure_{it}^2 + \beta_7 X_i + \gamma_t)$$

where for employee i working in year t, *Female* is a dummy for a female employee, *Age* is measured in years (precise, from human resources records), and *Tenure* is defined as years in the firm. X indicates a vector of other variables we include in different specifications, including highest degree obtained and the gender of the employee's supervisor. We have two measures of the gender of the employee's supervisor: 'immediate supervisor', which is the direct supervisor of the employee, and 'superior supervisor', which is the supervisor of the entire division in which the employee works.

We are primarily interested in the coefficient on the female dummy, which will be a measure of the differential likelihood of promotion for women compared to men. All models for the sales sample include an urban dummy. All models include a full set of time dummies using the year of the observation to account for time trends in terms of promotion probabilities within the firm, and dummies for which area within the institution the employee works in ('Dirección'). We also use robust standard errors clustered at the employee level. All probit results presented are the marginal effects at the means of continuous variables, while for binary independent variables they reflect predicted probabilities when the variable increases from 0 to 1.

We run the same regressions to predict exit. For wage gaps, we run an ordinary least squares (OLS) regression, where now our dependent variable is log of wages, and we are again interested in the coefficient on the female dummy:

$$ln(wage)_{it} = \beta_0 + \beta_1 Female_i + \beta_2 Age_{it} + \beta_3 Age_{it}^2 + \beta_4 Tenure_{it} + \beta_5 Tenure_{it}^2 + \beta_7 X_i + \gamma_t$$

For these regressions, we include the same control variables as in the promotion and exit regressions, as indicated in Tables 9.3–9.6.

4.2.2. ANALYSIS OF CLIENTS AND EMPLOYEES

In the next part of the analysis, we examine the patterns of matching between clients and loan officers by gender. We then examine whether the gender of the loan officer appears to impact credit outcomes. For these specifications, we closely follow the approach in Beck et al. (2013).

First, we examine whether clients are more likely to be matched with female loan officers after controlling for observable covariates. We run the following regression for loan officer ('Promotor' or 'Asesor') i and client j:

$$Female\ officer_i = \beta_0 + \beta_1 Female\ client_j + \beta_2 X_{ij} + \partial_{ij}$$

where X is a vector of covariates including sales level ('Nuevo', 'Junior', 'Senior', 'Maestro'), state dummies, an urban dummy, and product dummies.

As Beck et al. (2013) describe, the coefficient on *Female client* shows whether client gender is related to loan officer gender conditional on covariates. If we can reject the null hypothesis that this coefficient is 0, then this would suggest that there is effectively random matching of loan officers to clients. If we cannot reject the null, then this suggests assortative matching with regard to gender. Note the lion's share of the MFI's loan products are for women only; for this specification, as we want to compare matching of female vs. male clients to officers, we restrict the sample to only clients with non-female-only products.

In the next part of the analysis with the client data, we estimate whether the gender of the loan officer appears to impact credit outcomes, including loan terms. We run the following regression for loan officer i and client j:

$$Loan\ outcome_{ij} = \beta_0 + \beta_1 Female\ officer_i * Female\ client_j + \beta_2 Female\ officer_i * Male\ client_j + \beta_3 Male\ officer_i * Male\ client_j + \beta_4 X_{ij} + \partial_{ij}$$

where *Loan outcome* includes a proxy for the interest rate (calculated as the difference between the payback amount and loan amount divided by the loan amount) and how many previous loans the client has received. X is a vector of covariates including sales level ('Nuevo', 'Junior', 'Senior', 'Maestro'), state dummies, an urban dummy, and product dummies. The key coefficients of interest are the gender pairs between loan officers and clients, with the omitted category being *Male officer–Female client*. We run the analysis separately for 'Promotor' and 'Asesor' positions and also for female-only products (only relevant for 'Promotor') and non-female-only products.

5. Results

We next present results from our regression analysis to examine the determinants of the probability of promotion and exit by gender. First, we estimate probit models for the probability of promotion and of exit separately by career path (administrative or sales) and for loan officers. In these specifications, we are interested first in estimating the magnitude of the difference in the probability of promotion for men and women by looking at the female coefficient. Then we add controls to see how the coefficient changes, to see whether the differences in promotion can be explained by these variables.

In Table 9.3 we present the promotion probability results for the administrative career path, and in Table 9.4 we present the results for the sales career path. In Table 9.3, Column 1, we see that the raw gap (no controls) favours women, with women being 1.7 per cent more likely to be promoted. However, the overall differences by gender in the probability of promotion disappear after controlling for individual characteristics, area of practice, rank, and time trends. Yet, a significant gap in the probability of promotion favouring men persists at the intermediate level of 'Líder'.

In contrast, within the sales division (Table 9.4), we find that a gender gap in promotion favouring men persists even after including controls. Column 3, with all controls, shows that the gap is small (around 2 per cent) but significant. In Column 4 we see that the gap is highest at the most highly ranked position ('Gerente' to 'Gerente Regional'). In the last column we include an interaction of the female dummy with a married dummy. The estimates provide some evidence that family factors play a role in the sales division regarding promotion, with women who are married being more likely to be promoted compared to unmarried women. We find some evidence of interaction effects of the female dummy and tenure within the firm (not presented here) in the sales division, but not in the administrative division.

Turning to the separate promotion regressions for loan officers ('Promotor' and 'Asesor') in Table 9.5, we find that, as the raw data suggests, women are more likely to advance through the ranks within these levels. Even after controlling for individual and other covariates, women are approximately

Table 9.3. Promotion regressions, administrative division

	(1)	(2)	(3)	(4)	(5)	(6)	(7)
Dep. Var.: Promote							
Female	0.0177*	−0.0107	−0.0125	0.0558**	−0.0197	−0.0162	−0.0229
	(0.00906)	(0.0134)	(0.0131)	(0.0279)	(0.0192)	(0.0226)	(0.0155)
Age			−0.0109	0.0151	−0.0141	−0.0170	−0.0111
			(0.0107)	(0.00951)	(0.0114)	(0.0167)	(0.0107)
Age2			0.000151	−0.000150	0.000198	0.000278	0.000155
			(0.000159)	(0.000136)	(0.000168)	(0.000244)	(0.000158)
Tenure			0.0202***	−0.0172***	0.0180**	0.0300**	0.0199***
			(0.00741)	(0.00504)	(0.00780)	(0.0131)	(0.00746)
Tenure2			−0.00103	0.000871*	−0.000774	−0.00220	−0.000986
			(0.000863)	(0.000464)	(0.000902)	(0.00175)	(0.000870)
Headquarters			0.135***	−0.0769***	0.121***	0.212	0.134***
			(0.0391)	(0.0271)	(0.0414)	(0.144)	(0.0391)
Female x Coordinador				−0.0503			
				(0.0348)			
Female x Líder				−0.111***			
				(0.0389)			
Female x Gerente				−0.0583			
				(0.0382)			
Female x Subdirector				−0.0452			
				(0.0560)			
Female immediate supervisor					−0.0122		
					(0.0231)		
Female x female immediate supervisor					0.0323		
					(0.0305)		
Female superior supervisor					0.0128		
					(0.0280)		
Female x female superior supervisor					−0.0361		
					(0.0348)		
Number of children						−0.0268	
						(0.0202)	
Female x no. children						−0.00968	
						(0.0512)	
Married							−0.0172
							(0.0205)
Female x married							0.0344
							(0.0281)
Rank dummies	Yes	Yes	Yes	Yes	Yes	Yes	Yes
Direction (area) dummies	Yes	Yes	Yes	Yes	Yes	Yes	Yes
Year dummies	Yes	Yes	Yes	Yes	Yes	Yes	Yes
Observations	3,950	2,751	2,735	2,745	2,470	1,176	2,735

Notes: *** p < 0.01, ** p < 0.05, * p < 0.1. Robust standard errors clustered by individual are in parentheses. Estimation is by probit. Dependent variable is promotion, which is defined as a binary variable equal to 1 if an employee moved to a higher rank the next year and 0 otherwise. Marginal effects presented at the means of continuous variables. For binary independent variables, marginal effects reflect predicted probabilities when the variable increases from 0 to 1. For more information and a more detailed description of the variables, see Section 4.2.

Source: Authors' own analysis as described in Section 4.

Dep. Var.: Promote

	(1)	(2)	(3)	(4)	(5)	(7)	(8)
Female	-0.00966***	-0.0188***	-0.0237***	-0.0220***	-0.0247***	-0.0238***	-0.0298***
	(0.00222)	(0.00307)	(0.00317)	(0.00368)	(0.00432)	(0.00500)	(0.00409)
Urban		0.0114***	0.0149***	0.0148***	0.0141***	0.0150***	0.0146***
		(0.00396)	(0.00400)	(0.00400)	(0.00519)	(0.00427)	(0.00401)
Age			0.0229***	0.0229***	0.0218***	0.0247***	0.0236***
			(0.00279)	(0.00280)	(0.00380)	(0.00313)	(0.00282)
Age2			-0.000357***	-0.000358***	-0.000344***	-0.000383***	-0.000365***
			(4.62e-05)	(4.64e-05)	(6.29e-05)	(5.19e-05)	(4.65e-05)
Tenure			0.0453***	0.0452***	0.0611***	0.0487***	0.0452***
			(0.00419)	(0.00414)	(0.00455)	(0.00453)	(0.00420)
Tenure2			-0.00539***	-0.00532***	-0.00728***	-0.00561***	-0.00540***
			(0.000905)	(0.000895)	(0.00110)	(0.000992)	(0.000908)
Female x Asesor				0.00493			
				(0.0105)			
Female x Coordinador				-0.00326			
				(0.0112)			
Female x Gerente				-0.0585***			
				(0.0182)			
Female immediate supervisor						-0.0107**	
						(0.00477)	
Female x female immediate supervisor						0.000459	
						(0.00679)	
Female superior supervisor						0.000146	
						(0.00520)	
Female x female superior supervisor						0.00465	
						(0.00739)	
Married							-0.0111**
							(0.00446)
Female x married							0.0139**
							(0.00641)
Highest degree dummies	No	No	No	No	Yes	No	No
Rank dummies	No	Yes	Yes	Yes	Yes	Yes	Yes
Direction dummies	No	Yes	Yes	Yes	Yes	Yes	Yes
Yr dummies	No	Yes	Yes	Yes	Yes	Yes	Yes
Observations	49,001	37,048	37,048	37,048	20,963	32,941	37,028

Notes: *** $p < 0.01$, ** $p < 0.05$, * $p < 0.1$. Robust standard errors clustered by individual are in parentheses. Estimation is by probit. Dependent variable is promotion, which is defined as a binary variable equal to 1 if an employee moved to a higher rank the next year and 0 otherwise. Marginal effects presented at the means of continuous variables. For binary independent variables, marginal effects reflect predicted probabilities when the variable increases from 0 to 1. For more information and a more detailed description of the variables, see Section 4.2.
Source: Authors' own analysis as described in Section 4.

Table 9.5. Promotion regressions, Promotor/Asesor

	(1)	(2)	(3)	(4)	(5)	(6)
Dep. Var.: Promote						
Female	0.0362***	0.0307***	0.0443***	0.0467***	0.0279***	0.0448***
	(0.00384)	(0.00506)	(0.00534)	(0.00702)	(0.00880)	(0.00682)
Urban		-0.000710	-0.0143**	-0.00492	-0.0120	-0.0140**
		(0.00670)	(0.00703)	(0.00893)	(0.00741)	(0.00704)
Age			-0.000911	-0.00553	-3.22e-05	-0.000897
			(0.00407)	(0.00544)	(0.00425)	(0.00409)
Age2			1.30e-05	7.57e-05	-5.53e-06	1.33e-05
			(6.72e-05)	(8.97e-05)	(7.01e-05)	(6.73e-05)
Tenure			-0.0562***	-0.0482***	-0.0578***	-0.0564***
			(0.0112)	(0.0183)	(0.0125)	(0.0112)
Tenure2			-0.0119***	-0.0202**	-0.0121**	-0.0119***
			(0.00437)	(0.00894)	(0.00496)	(0.00436)
Female immediate supervisor					-0.00749	
					(0.00817)	
Female x female immediate supervisor					0.0327***	
					(0.0114)	
Female superior supervisor					0.00661	
					(0.00878)	
Female x female superior supervisor					-0.00691	
					(0.0122)	
Married						4.91e-05
						(0.00793)
Female x married						-0.00102
						(0.0110)
Highest degree dummies	No	No	No	Yes	No	No
Rank dummies	No	Yes	Yes	Yes	Yes	Yes
Direction (area) dummies	No	Yes	Yes	Yes	Yes	Yes
Year dummies	No	Yes	Yes	Yes	Yes	Yes
Observations	39,009	29,638	29,638	17,614	26,714	29,622

Notes: *** $p < 0.01$, ** $p < 0.05$, * $p < 0.1$. Robust standard errors clustered by individual are in parentheses. Estimation is by probit. Dependent variable is promotion, which is defined as a binary variable equal to 1 if an employee moved to a higher rank the next year and 0 otherwise. Marginal effects presented at the means of continuous variables. For binary independent variables, marginal effects reflect predicted probabilities when the variable increases from 0 to 1. For more information and a more detailed description of the variables, see Section 4.2.

Source: Authors' own analysis as described in Section 4.

4–5 per cent more likely to be promoted than men (Columns 3 and 4). In Column 5, we find some evidence that if a woman's immediate supervisor is also a woman, she is even more likely to be promoted than if the supervisor is a man.

In Ganguli et al. (2017: Table 6) we estimate exit regressions that show that within the administrative division there does not appear to be differential exit by gender, while in the sales division women are about 4 per cent less likely to exit, after controlling for covariates. There is a similar estimate for loan officers alone.

In Table 9.6, we estimate the gender wage gap for each career division. Here, we see a striking result across the career path types. While there were no significant gender differences in promotion in the administrative path after including controls, we see in Column 2 that women earn about 3 per cent lower wages after controlling for covariates. While this estimate is small in magnitude, Column 3 shows that the gap is much larger and mainly coming from the highest ranks. Meanwhile, in sales, where there were significant differences in promotion by gender, the wage differences disappear after including controls (Column 5). However, at the intermediate ranks ('Coordinador' and 'Gerente'), there are wage gaps. In Column 8, we see a different result for loan officers. Here, the wage gap reverses, with women earning about 0.5 per cent more than men on average, even after including controls.

Finally, we turn to the analysis of client data matched to loan officers. We examine matching among loan offers and clients by gender in Table 9.7. Here, Column 1 shows that female 'Promotores' are more likely to work with female clients, but, similar to Beck et al. (2013), after controlling for covariates, we show in Column 2 that women 'Promotores' are no more likely to work with female clients than male clients (for non-female-only loan products). This suggests that assortative matching by gender is not occurring. In Column 4, however, we do find that female 'Asesores' are 1.8 per cent more likely to work with female clients.

In Table 9.8, we examine whether there are differences in the loan terms and in whether the client is a return borrower depending on the officer–client match by gender. In Columns 1 and 2, we restrict the sample to 'Promotores' working with female clients who borrowed through female-only products. The results show that female 'Promotores' appear to work with clients who receive slightly better terms (lower interest rates) and have had previous loans with the MFI, compared to male 'Promotores'. Meanwhile, for the mixed gender products, male 'Promotores' appear to work with male clients receiving lower interest rates than those working with female clients. Male clients working with either male or female 'Promotores' have had fewer previous loans than female clients (Column 4). The last two columns show the results for 'Asesores' (who do not work with female-only product clients in

Table 9.6. Wage regressions

ln(wage)	Administrative			Sales			Promotor/Asesor		
	(1)	(2)	(3)	(4)	(5)	(6)	(7)	(8)	(9)
Female	-0.405***	-0.0280***	-0.0153	-0.0609***	-0.00203	0.00827***	0.00628*	0.00432***	0.00457***
	(0.0322)	(0.00745)	(0.0123)	(0.00736)	(0.00184)	(0.00157)	(0.00321)	(0.00158)	(0.00154)
Headquarters		0.111***	0.111***						
		(0.0172)	(0.0171)						
Age		0.0132**	0.0127**		0.0105***	0.0106***		0.00749***	0.00750***
		(0.00612)	(0.00577)		(0.00131)	(0.00130)		(0.00113)	(0.00113)
Age2		-8.37e-05	-7.52e-05		-0.000126***	-0.000127***		-9.17e-05***	-9.19e-05***
		(8.97e-05)	(8.41e-05)		(2.18e-05)	(2.16e-05)		(1.90e-05)	(1.90e-05)
Tenure		0.00994**	0.0108**		0.105***	0.105***		0.137***	0.137***
		(0.00438)	(0.00436)		(0.00335)	(0.00324)		(0.00405)	(0.00405)
Tenure2		7.53e-05	2.89e-05		-0.00776***	-0.00765***		-0.0113***	-0.0113***
		(0.000473)	(0.000472)		(0.000620)	(0.000604)		(0.00104)	(0.00104)
Female x Coordinador			-0.0127						
			(0.0179)						
Female x Lider			-0.00335						
			(0.0177)						
Female x Gerente			0.00361						
			(0.0232)						
Female x Subdirector			-0.111***						
			(0.0375)						
Female x Director			-0.277***						
			(0.0684)						
Urban					0.151***	0.151***		0.162***	0.162***
					(0.00225)	(0.00225)		(0.00201)	(0.00202)

	(1)	(2)	(3)	(4)	(5)	(6)	(7)	(8)	(9)
Female x Asesor						-0.00265			-0.00232
						(0.00694)			(0.00694)
Female x Coordinador						-0.0546***			
						(0.00772)			
Female x Gerente						-0.0462***			
						(0.0124)			
Female x Gerente Reg.						-0.0277			
						(0.0329)			
Constant	7.327***	6.547***	6.518***	6.462***	5.404***	5.422***	6.262***	5.720***	5.720***
	(0.0303)	(0.109)	(0.106)	(0.00574)	(0.0203)	(0.0212)	(0.00227)	(0.0300)	(0.0300)
Rank dummies	No	Yes	Yes	No	Yes	Yes	No	Yes	Yes
Direction (area) dummies	No	Yes	Yes	No	Yes	Yes	No	Yes	Yes
Year dummies	No	Yes	Yes	No	Yes	Yes	No	Yes	Yes
Observations	12,833	3,950	3,950	49,707	49,001	49,001	39,009	39,009	39,009

Notes: *** p<0.01, ** p<0.05, * p<0.1. Robust standard errors clustered by individual are in parentheses. Estimation is by OLS. Dependent variable is log wages. For more information and a more detailed description of the variables, see Section 4.2.

Source: Authors' own analysis as described in Section 4.

Table 9.7. Matching of loan officers and clients

	Promotor		Asesor	
Female officer	(1)	(2)	(3)	(4)
Female client	0.0149***	0.00471	0.0218**	0.0179*
	(0.00727)	(0.00664)	(0.00885)	(0.0101)
Urban		−0.0184		0.0611
		(0.0413)		(0.0613)
Constant	0.432***	0.753***	0.366***	1.018***
	(0.0144)	(0.134)	(0.00695)	(0.249)
Sales-level dummies	No	Yes	No	Yes
State dummies	No	Yes	No	Yes
Product dummies	No	Yes	No	Yes
Observations	43,926	43,926	12,745	11,071

Notes: *** $p<0.01$, ** $p<0.05$, * $p<0.1$. Robust standard errors clustered by loan officer are in parentheses. Estimation is by OLS. Dependent variable is a dummy for whether a loan officer is female. For more information and a more detailed description of the variables, see Section 4.2.

Source: Authors' own analysis as described in Section 4.

Table 9.8. Loan officer–client gender and loans

	Promotor				Asesor	
	Female-only products		Mixed-gender products		Mixed-gender products	
	(1)	(2)	(3)	(4)	(5)	(6)
	Interest (inferred)	Previous loans	Interest (inferred)	Previous loans	Interest (inferred)	Previous loans
Female officer	−0.00761***	0.220***				
(male officer)	(0.00295)	(0.0591)				
Female officer–female client			−0.000518	0.109	−0.0797	0.0388
(Male officer–female client)			(0.00131)	(0.0666)	(0.0824)	(0.170)
Female officer–male client			−0.000513	−2.036***	0.00208	−2.831***
			(0.00139)	(0.0580)	(0.0799)	(0.126)
Male officer–male client			−0.00185***	−2.096***	0.126***	−2.855***
			(0.000702)	(0.0557)	(0.0355)	(0.120)
Urban	0.00372	−1.130***	0.00258	0.109*	0.0188	−0.315*
	(0.00448)	(0.0920)	(0.00165)	(0.0649)	(0.143)	(0.161)
Constant	0.0514***	11.27***	1.442***	3.208***	1.940***	3.649***
	(0.0133)	(0.236)	(0.00292)	(0.185)	(0.168)	(0.539)
Sales-level dummies	Yes	Yes	Yes	Yes	Yes	Yes
State dummies	Yes	Yes	Yes	Yes	Yes	Yes
Product dummies	Yes	Yes	Yes	Yes	Yes	Yes
Observations	284,561	284,561	43,926	43,926	11,071	11,071

Notes: *** $p<0.01$, ** $p<0.05$, * $p<0.1$. Robust standard errors clustered by loan officer are in parentheses. Estimation is by OLS. Dependent variable is interest rate (inferred) or number of previous loans. For more information and a more detailed description of the variables, see Section 4.2.

Source: Authors' own analysis as described in Section 4.

our sample). Here, again, male clients working with either male or female 'Asesores' have had fewer previous loans. In terms of interest rates, female 'Asesores' work with women with lower rates, while male 'Asesores' work with men with higher rates, compared to male 'Asesores' working with female clients.

6. Discussion and Concluding Remarks

In this chapter, we have used rich data from the largest MFI in Latin America to document and understand gender differences in the career paths of MFI employees. While MFIs are increasingly important as employers of individuals in the developing world, there is very little evidence on the state of gender differences in employment and career dynamics in the MFI sector. Our analysis contributes to developing an understanding of gender gaps in career dynamics in this key sector in the development process.

We document important differences within the MFI by career path in the nature of gender gaps and their dynamics. First, we show in the raw data that the MFI exhibits a similar pattern to that found in other professional sectors, where there is close to gender parity at the entry level but gender gaps favouring men emerge at the higher ranks, and this is particularly true in the administrative career path. However, within the lowest ranks of the sales division—the loan officers, who work directly with clients and make up the largest share of the institution's employees—there is a strikingly different pattern. At this level the gender gap is reversed, so that women are represented more than men at the higher ranks within these positions.

Our regression analysis highlights the clear differences in gender gaps by career path. While there are no significant gender differences in promotion in the administrative path, there is a significant gender wage gap, even after controlling for covariates, and this gap appears to be largest at the highest ranks. Meanwhile, in sales, there are significant differences in promotion by gender, but wage differences disappear after including controls. However, among loan officers the wage gap reverses, so that women earn higher wages on average than men. Our analysis of the loan officer and client data indicates that matching of clients and loan officers in terms of gender may be influencing loan terms and outcomes, with female loan officers more likely to be working with clients who have had previous loans, and better terms.

Our analysis points to the important role that the gender dynamics within MFIs can potentially play in the development process. Our results suggest that the MFI is a gender-friendly employer when it comes to the loan officers— those at the front line of the MFI—as promotion and wage gaps here actually favour women. However, within the rest of the organization, the gender gaps are of a similar nature to those in other professional sectors, where women earn lower wages and are less likely to reach the highest ranks.

Our study makes several contributions and points to several important areas of future research. As the first study to document gender gaps in wages and career trajectories in the microfinance sector, it shows that the dynamics of gender gaps within MFIs are complex. We show that gender gaps increase with seniority in the administrative division while a reversed gender gap is found at the lower ranks in the division that characterizes the microfinance sector—those responsible for the sale of microcredit products. This is important, as it shows the extent to which, in the 'back office' of the organization where employees do not interact directly with the clients of the MFI, the dynamics of gender gaps are similar to those observed for professionals in the traditional financial and corporate sectors. On the other hand, in the 'front office' of the organization, where employees are client-facing and deal primarily with female clients, the gender gap is reversed, although only at the lower ranks of the division.

This study suggests that more research is needed in order to understand how organizations in the microfinance sector change with development. A reversal of the gender gap was observed at the lower ranks of the division that operates in close contact with the primarily female microfinance clients. This leads to several questions defining the agenda for future research, such as: Will this shift gradually affect the higher ranks of the sales division and then the 'back office' of the organization? How long will this take? Or will the reversal be limited within those positions where women have a comparative advantage in interacting with female clients? Answers to these questions have important implications for the evolution of the sector, and at the micro level for understanding how women's empowerment on the employer side of the microfinance sector is shaped.

References

Agier, I., and A. Szafarz (2013). 'Microfinance and Gender: Is There a Glass Ceiling on Loan Size?' *World Development*, 42: 165–81.

Akerlof, G.A., and R.E. Kranton (2000). 'Economics and Identity'. *Quarterly Journal of Economics*, 115: 715–53.

Babcock L., and S. Laschever (2003). *Women Don't Ask: Negotiation and the Gender Divide*. Princeton, NJ: Princeton University Press.

Beck, T., P. Behr, and A. Guettler (2013). 'Gender and Banking: Are Women Better Loan Officers?' *Review of Finance*, 17: 1279–321.

Beck, T., P. Behr, and A. Madestam (2014). 'Sex and Credit: Is There a Gender Bias in Lending?' Working Paper 29. London: Faculty of Finance, Cass Business School.

Becker, G.S. (1973). 'A Theory of Marriage: Part I'. *Journal of Political Economy*, 81(4): 813–46.

Bertrand M., C. Goldin, and L. Katz (2010). 'Dynamics of the Gender Gap for Young Professionals in the Financial and Corporate Sectors'. *American Economic Journal: Applied Economics*, 2: 228–55.

Blau, F.D., and J. DeVaro, 2007. 'New Evidence on Gender Differences in Promotion Rates: An Empirical Analysis of a Sample of New Hires'. *Industrial Relations: A Journal of Economy and Society*, 46(3): 511–50.

Boehe, D.M., and L.B. Cruz (2013). 'Gender and Microfinance Performance: Why Does the Institutional Context Matter?' *World Development*, 47: 121–35.

Brau, J., and G. Woller (2004). 'Microfinance: A Comprehensive Review of the Existing Literature'. *Journal of Entrepreneurial Finance*, 9(1): 1–27.

Cull, R., A. Demirgüç-Kunt, and J. Morduch (2009). 'Microfinance Meets the Market'. *Journal of Economic Perspectives*, 23(1): 167–92.

D'Espallier, B., I. Guérin, and R. Mersland (2011). 'Women and Repayment in Microfinance: A Global Analysis'. *World Development*, 39(5): 758–72.

Di Benedetta, P., I.W. Lieberman, and L. Ard (2015). 'Corporate Governance in Microfinance Institutions'. Washington, DC: World Bank. Available at: https://openknowledge.worldbank.org/handle/10986/22059 (accessed 17 April 2017).

Duflo, E. (2003). 'Grandmothers and Granddaughters: Old-Age Pensions and Intrahousehold Allocation in South Africa'. *World Bank Economic Review*, 17(1): 1–25.

Duflo, E. (2012). 'Women's Empowerment and Economic Development'. *Journal of Economic Literature*, 50(4): 1051–79.

Ganguli, I., R. Hausmann, and M. Viarengo (2016). 'Gender Differences in Professional Career Dynamics: New Evidence from a Global Law Firm'. Mimeo. Cambridge, MA: Harvard University.

Ganguli, I., R. Hausmann, and M. Viarengo (2017). 'Career Dynamics and Gender Gaps Among Employees in the Microfinance Sector'. WIDER Working Paper 2017/117.

Gilson, R.J., and R.H. Mnookin (1989). 'Coming of Age in a Corporate Law Firm: The Economics of Associate Career Patterns'. *Stanford Law Review*, 41(3): 567–95.

Hartarska, V., D. Nadolnyak, and R. Mersland (2014). 'Are Women Better Bankers to the Poor? Evidence from Rural Microfinance Institutions'. *American Journal of Agricultural Economics*, 96(5): 1291–306.

Iskenderian, M.E. (2011). 'Women as Microfinance Leaders, Not Just Clients'. *Harvard Business Review Blog*, 16 March, available at https://hbr.org/2011/03/women-as-microfinance-leaders.

Lansford, M., V. Clements, T. Falzon, D. Aish, and R. Rogers (2010). 'Essential Leadership Traits of Female Executives in the Non-Profit Sector'. *Journal of Human Resource and Adult Learning*, 6(1): 51–62.

Lazear, E., and S. Rosen (1981). 'Rank-Order Tournaments as Optimum Labor Contracts'. *Journal of Political Economy*, 89(5): 841–64.

Lazear E., and K. Shaw (2007). 'Personnel Economics: The Economist's View of Human Resources'. *Journal of Economic Perspectives*, 21(4): 91–114.

Roodman, D., and U. Qureshi (2006). *Microfinance as Business*. Washington, DC: Center for Global Development.

Strøm, R.Ø., B. D'Espallier, and R. Mersland (2014). 'Female Leadership, Performance, and Governance in Microfinance Institutions'. *Journal of Banking and Finance*, 42: 60–75.

Thomas, D. (1990). 'Intra-Household Resource Allocation: An Inferential Approach'. *Journal of Human Resources*, 25: 635–64.

Thomas, D. (1994). 'Like Father, Like Son: Like Mother, Like Daughter. Parental Resources and Child Height'. *Journal of Human Resources*, 24: 950–88.

WWB (2009). *Where Did All the Women Go?* New York: Women's World Banking.

WWB (2010). *Transforming the Landscape of Leadership in Microfinance: Maintaining the Focus on Women*. New York: Women's World Banking.

WWB (2012). *Annual Report*. New York: Women's World Banking.

World Bank (2000). *Microfinance Handbook: An Institutional and Financial Perspective*. Washington, DC: World Bank.

10

Why Do Women Co-Operate More in Women's Groups?

James D. Fearon and Macartan Humphreys[1]

1. Introduction

A substantial amount of development programming assumes that women have preferences or aptitudes that are more conducive to economic development. And indeed development funding is often channelled through women's groups rather than through all-male or mixed-gender traditional and modern authorities. For example, conditional cash transfer programmes commonly deliver funding to female household heads, and many microcredit schemes focus on women's savings groups. Programmes and reforms to increase women's empowerment in low-income countries are advocated on the grounds that, in addition to simple fairness, women in political office will spend more on public goods or on more-needed public goods, and empowered women in families will lead to more investment in agricultural productivity and children's health and education. Duflo (2012) reviews a growing literature assessing these and related hypotheses. Many studies find evidence that directing resources or political power towards women and women's groups increases

[1] This chapter uses data from an experiment implemented jointly with Jeremy Weinstein, to whom we are deeply indebted. We thank also Nicholai Lidow and Gwendolyn Taylor for leading the game and follow-up survey data collection teams in the field, and Andrea Abel, Jessica Gottlieb, and Amanda Robinson for their fieldwork on the public goods games. We thank the National Ex-Combatant Peace-Building Initiative for its research support in Liberia, in particular K. Johnson Borh and Morlee Zawoo, and Brian Coyne. We thank Lily Medina for excellent research support for the analysis of this chapter. AUSAID, through a grant to the Center for Global Development, provided the resources to implement the behavioural measures described in this chapter; the Center for Democracy, Development, and the Rule of Law provided funding for fieldwork expenses, and the International Growth Center provided support for final data compilation and analysis.

children's well-being and public investments in clean water and (perhaps) other public goods.[2]

In this regard, the views of the development community (Gates 2014; World Bank 2012) often reflect those of the rural poor in many low-income countries. For example, it is often held that extra cash is more likely to be spent on alcohol and grilled meat by men, versus household needs or productive investment by women. Women may also be seen as more community-minded on average—indeed our own survey data, described below, reflects such views.

What is not clear from these accounts, however, is whether these beliefs reflect views about the attitudes and behaviour of women versus men, or rather some features of women's groups in particular. Also not clear is the reason for any such differences in behaviour across genders or gender groups.

We examine these questions by analysing play in a public goods game in northern Liberia in which the gender composition of groups making collective decisions over public goods was randomly assigned.[3] We find that women did contribute substantially more than men, *though only when they knew that they were playing with other women*. In public goods problems involving equal numbers of men and women, men and women contributed similar amounts, and markedly less on average than in the groups with only women players.

This main finding partially supports the arguments of development practitioners who seek to engage communities through women-only groups. It does not provide clear evidence in favour of the assumption that women are per se more community-minded when asked to make decisions between private and social goods (though of course this could be the case for particular public goods in particular settings).

It is one thing to find that in a particular context all-female groups generate more collective action, and another to explain why. In the second part of the chapter we use Bayesian methods, data from surveys of game players, and knowledge of a multiplier on contributions that was randomly varied across players, to estimate a simple structural model of individual decisions about how much to contribute. The goal is to gain insight into how the motivations of the women acting in the all-women groups differed from those of men and women in the mixed groups.

---

[2] Duflo cautions, however, that for economic development, women's empowerment 'is not the magic bullet it is sometimes made out to be' (2012: 76), stressing that women face so many constraints that any multiplier effects of alleviating any one may be limited or absent, and that women's empowerment can yield improvement in some dimensions at the expense of others.

[3] The data (Fearon et al. 2014) can be accessed at https://dataverse.harvard.edu/dataset.xhtml? persistentId=doi:10.7910/DVN/28006.

The model and data allow us to estimate the weight that people in our sample put on four different underlying motivations, or preferences, that could factor into different contribution decisions:

1. the value the individual places on the expected use of the total amount of money raised;

2. the individual's fear of discovery of their own contribution and thus possible sanctioning;

3. the individual's concern with matching what others do; and

4. the intrinsic value (or cost) the individual has for contributing, including both opportunity costs for the money donated and any positive value for signalling 'community spirit' by contributing.

The results suggest that women in the all-women groups had stronger intrinsic motivation to contribute than both women and men in the mixed groups. That is, they would have contributed a substantial share of their endowment irrespective of beliefs about what it would be spent on, fear of discovery, or desire to match others' contribution levels.

These patterns are consistent with field observations suggesting that women in the all-women communities may have contributed more in order to signal that the women of their community have powerful community spirit. Thus a sense of group solidarity and implicit competition—a social-identity effect—may have favoured collective action. If this is correct, it would suggest a mechanism that might favour channelling development aid through women-only groups in some contexts, but not necessarily others.

In Section 2 we describe the context of our study and provide a description of the experiment. In Section 3 we provide the basic results, showing differences in behaviour between gender groups and the effects of group composition. Section 4 compares our results with the most closely related results in the literature, found in Greig and Bohnet (2009). Section 5 explores mechanisms more thoroughly, using a simple structural model to assess the role of intrinsic incentives and three types of instrumental incentives, relating to conformity concerns and concerns over sanctioning. While all three of these appear to play a role, the differences in intrinsic incentives between conditions appear most salient. In the concluding Section 6 we speculate, based on the results presented and additional field observations, about possible reasons for the main finding. We suggest that the evidence for strong intrinsic motivation to contribute is consistent with the hypothesis that many game players thought they were signalling community quality to potential donors. Women in the all-women groups may have been more strongly motivated in this way due to a social-identity effect—a sense that they were playing for, or representing, 'team women' of the village.

2. A Public Goods Game in Post-Conflict Liberia

We examine differences in the effects of the gender composition of groups by analysing play in a public goods game implemented in 2008 following an international development intervention in Liberia.

As described in Fearon et al. (2015), we used a public goods game to assess the effects of a community-driven reconstruction (CDR) program implemented between 2006 and 2008 in 83 communities in two districts in northern Liberia, Voinjama and Zorzor. Funded by the UK's Department for International Development and implemented by the International Rescue Committee, the programme sought to foster reconciliation and improve local-level governance in the wake of a long civil war that ended in 2003, and that was particularly intense in these districts. Secondarily, the implementers and funders hoped that the funds provided would have positive economic effects. The primary goal of the intervention, however, was institution building to improve the collective action capacities of post-conflict communities.

Based on the popular model of 'community-driven development' (Mansuri and Rao 2012), CDR works by giving communities power in selecting how the offered aid will be used, and also in governing the implementation and management of projects that result. The 'catch' is that communities are required to construct and use donor-specified institutions for choosing and managing the projects. In particular, under aid agency guidance, the communities elect community development committees (CDCs) in open elections that (at least in this case) exclude the main traditional leaders (chiefs). The CDCs then deliberate and hold town meetings to decide on how the development funds provided will be spent, subject to some parameters given by the aid agency.[4]

The public goods games, implemented in 2008 after the CDR interventions were (almost entirely) completed, were our primary measurement strategy for estimating whether the CDR programme had a causal impact on treated communities' ability to generate collective action after a devastating civil war. The games presented both treated and control communities with a small-scale challenge of organizing to raise funds that we would match at an average rate of 250 per cent, for a project chosen entirely by the community in

---

[4] In our case, projects had to be for community-wide rather than private or narrowly targeted benefit, and purchase of capital equipment for income-generating projects (such as a rice mill) was not allowed. The projects chosen tended to involve construction of community facilities, such as community meeting houses and guest houses (approximately 35 per cent), latrines (30 per cent), and hand-dug wells (15 per cent). A few projects (less than 5 per cent) focused on school or health clinic construction; almost none were in agriculture, skills training and small business development, and other income-generating activities. The median value of total grants was about US$13,000 for a community, the specific amount depending on the community's size and their proposals.

whatever manner they decided. Described to the communities as a 'small-scale development project' in which they could obtain matching funds depending on how much they raised from contributions made during the game, the measurement strategy was intended to approximate the kind of real-world collective-action problem communities had faced in the CDR programme (which also required matching contributions), or indeed any community collective problem.

The basic protocol was as follows: we held a community meeting in each of the eighty-three villages, announcing that a public goods game would be played the following week to determine how much financing would be provided to a community for use in any way the community desired. Attendees of the meeting were told that twenty-four households would be randomly selected and then a randomly chosen adult from each of those households would receive a sum of money (300 Liberian dollars, LD, or about US$5). The game player could then decide, in private, how much of this to keep and how much to contribute towards a public good. It was explained that after the game had been played, we would hold another public meeting to open the private contributions and then add our 'matching' contributions on top, according to a multiplier known in advance to each game player and identified on the envelope. The total amount raised would then be given to three 'community representatives' who could be selected by the village in any manner they wished in the week between the first community meeting and game day.

Notice that communities knew that in the week between the initial meeting and game day, they (or their leaders, or whoever) had time to decide how the funding would be used and could engage in mobilization activities around participation in the game. They did not know which individuals would be picked to play and so could not lobby or pressure specific people.[5]

When we implemented the public goods game we included two variations that would allow us to assess differences in play between men and women, as well as the effects of group composition. The first variation, similar to that employed by Greig and Bohnet (2009), was that in half the communities we sampled 24 women to play the game and in half we sampled 12 men and 12 women. As a result, we have data on the individual contributions of 504 men and 504 women in 42 communities, who played knowing that other game players were 11 of the same gender and 12 of the other gender, and of 971 women in 41 communities who played knowing that all 23 other game players were women.

---

[5] For greater detail on the development intervention and the public goods game, see Fearon et al. (2015).

The second variation is in the multiplier applied to contributions. Within each village/gender block half the players had their contributions increased by a factor of two and the other half had theirs increased by a factor of five. Below, we use this variation to seek to assess the role of other-regarding preferences in contribution decisions.

In addition to the games data we also gathered data from a survey implemented immediately after a player made their private contribution choice. From this survey we constructed a set of measures used in the analysis that follows.

Our focus in this chapter is on the main effect of the gender composition treatment, the difference between contribution levels in the 42 'mixed' communities where 12 men and 12 women played the game, and the 41 'all-women' communities where 24 women were selected to play. This gender composition treatment was assigned by us at random, independently from the CDR treatment assignments. We should note that due to low power, we were not able to have a treatment arm of villages in which only *men* were selected to play the game, which limits our ability to draw some inferences, as discussed below.

3. Basic Results

The basic results are in evidence in the raw game data. Women in the mixed condition give about the same as men—indeed slightly less (220 compared to 225 on average). But they give considerably more in the women-only condition (246). This latter effect can be interpreted causally as the effect of gender composition on women's contributions.

Table 10.1 shows these results with estimation of treatment effects implemented at the village level, taking account of randomization blocks, including status with respect to the CDR intervention (see Fearon et al. 2015 for details on the randomization), together with Neyman standard errors and p values generated via randomization inference for the full sample of women (Column 1) as well as for the urban and non-urban sub-populations. We see a large and strongly statistically significant treatment effect: 30 LD is approximately 28 per cent of

Table 10.1. Effects of gender composition

	All	In quarters	Outside quarters
Mixed villages (12/12 male/female)	218.55	182.15	240.86
Homogeneous villages (24 female)	248.62	232.91	252.61
Difference (average treatment effect)	30.06	50.75	11.75
N	82	28	54
p (ri)	0.00	0.00	0.15
s.e. (Neyman)	9.43	13.59	11.73

Source: Authors' own construction.

one standard deviation of the average individual contributions in the mixed communities, and it is almost twice the size of the average effect of getting the 400 per cent interest rate versus the 100 per cent rate.

In the second and third columns of Table 10.1, we report evidence of an interesting and puzzling heterogeneity for which we have no confident explanation. Of the 83 communities studied, 28 (12 assigned to all-women and 16 to mixed) were 'quarters' of a larger town, and thus slightly more urbanized than the remaining 55 villages, which were rural. Average contributions in the public goods game were much lower in the quarters, reflecting, perhaps, lower levels of organization and mobilization capacity (Fearon et al., 2015). But we see that the gender composition effect is much larger in the quarters: mixed communities in quarters generated very low contributions, whereas the quarters where only women played did much better. In line with our argument and interpretation of the evidence on the CDR treatment effect in Fearon et al. (2015), this difference could result from women's traditional organizations functioning better for mobilization in the quarters than the official chief and sub-chief system, which seemed less well established than in the rural communities. But this is speculation.

Our goal in what follows will be to make sense of the basic pattern of substantially greater collective action produced in the communities where women knew that only other women were making contribution decisions, versus communities where both men and women played the game.

4. Comparison with Greig and Bohnet (2009)

Greig and Bohnet (2009) implemented a study closely related to ours which allows for the possibility of assessing the consistency of findings in two locations on the continent.

Though our game was similar in many ways to the game studied in Kenya by Greig and Bohnet (2009), a number of important differences are worth highlighting. In the Kenya study all participants came from a single community whereas in our study communities were the unit of randomization. In Kenya, participants played in groups of four in a type of lab established at the community centre; we worked with much larger groups of twenty-four subjects that were randomly sampled from villages, with these subjects playing in their own homes. The endowments in the Kenya game were smaller—approx. US$0.64 rather than approx. US$5; the multiplier was 2 whereas ours was either 2 or 5.[6] Because of the different sizes of the groups, however, the

---

[6] In Greig and Bohnet, for every x contributed, all four members received $x/2$.

private returns to the public investment were much smaller in our study. In the Kenya experiment, the players were the only beneficiaries of the contribution—which could lead to a total value of less than US$3—whereas in Liberia the entire village (median population of about 500) could in principle benefit from a project worth up to US$400. Also critical is the fact that the Kenya experiment did not allow for pre-play communication whereas the Liberia experiment did. In total, Greig and Bohnet (2009) studied 270 subjects in 68 groups of 4 whereas we studied 1979 subjects in 83 groups of 24 (with limited attrition).

A key feature of the Kenya analysis is the use of data on player expectations about the play of others, generated by asking subjects about how much on average they expected other game players to play. We have similar data for Liberia, reported in Table 10.3, including a measure of the number of others that players expected to contribute nothing; the number of others they expected to contribute the full amount; an estimate of the expected average contribution using these numbers; and a measure of whether they expected men or women to contribute more, or about the same (recorded here as 0 for men give more, 0.5 for the same, and 1 for women give more).

We see from Table 10.2 that expectations broadly tracked the compositional condition. Women did not have higher expectations about the contributions of others than men did in the mixed condition, but did have higher expectations in the women-only condition. Nevertheless, women in both conditions reported believing that women would contribute more than men in the mixed condition, while men on average said they expected equal contributions by gender. These facts could on their own give rise to a belief in overall higher levels of contribution by others in the women-only condition—a feature we return to below.

Table 10.3 uses essentially the same specification as in Greig and Bohnet (2009, table 1); there is no interaction term in our model because we do not have an all-male group, and we cluster standard errors at the group level (the level of randomization). For ease of interpretation, we use women in mixed groups as the base condition and then look at the differences for men, and for

Table 10.2. Expectations given different treatments

	Women-homog.	Women-mixed	Men-mixed
Expected share giving 0	0.11	0.13	0.14
Expected share giving 300	0.85	0.80	0.81
Expected average amount given by others	273.45	258.66	254.52
Actual average given by others	245.93	223.03	222.81
Predict women give strictly more	0.83	0.73	0.48

Source: Authors' own construction.

Table 10.3. (External) replication of Table 1 (cols 1 and 2) in Greig and Bohnet (2009)

	1	2	3	4
Constant	220.44	106.97	109.92	86.71
	(8.39)**	(20.51)**	(20.49)**	(32.74)**
Homogeneous	25.50	19.54	15.46	80.63
	(9.65)**	(10.54)	(8.68)	(40.24)**
Male	4.96	10.99	6.30	10.84
	(6.92)	(9.33)	(6.88)	(35.21)
Expectations		0.38	0.39	0.47
		(0.07)**	(0.07)**	(0.12)**
Homog. x Expectations				−0.24
				(0.15)
Male x Expectations				−0.017
				(0.13)
N	1979	1093	1979	1979

Note: ** indicates $p < .01$. Errors are clustered at the group level.
Source: Authors' own construction; Greig and Bohnet 2009.

women in all-female games ('homogeneous'). The results in Column 2 use list-wise deletion for the often-missing expectations variable; in Column 3 we impute average community values for missing expectations, while controlling for missingness and allowing for different effects for units with missing data. We note that in this specification, and later specifications that employ expectations, the model includes a post-treatment variable (expectations), and the other coefficients can only be interpreted as direct effects conditional on strong assumptions outlined in Baron and Kenny (1986).

We see some features here that are consistent with Greig and Bohnet and some differences. First, our constant is considerably larger (as a share of endowments) than those found in Kenya and more in line with, if not greater than, those found elsewhere: even the group that contributed the least, women in the mixed condition, gave about 220/300 = 73 per cent of their endowment. Thus the evidence of weak social capital from the Kenya study is not replicated here. This could be related to the facts that our participants were on average members of relatively small rural communities rather than a large urban slum, and that the communities also had a week to inform community members about the game and the projects. On the other hand, as noted above, personal returns from contributing were arguably much smaller in our setting (because diffused over the broader community).

Second, as in the Kenya study, we find that women give considerably less in the mixed condition than in the women-only condition. In Greig and Bohnet (2009) the marginal effect for women in the mixed condition was a drop equal to about 10 per cent of the endowment (it is not clear whether this effect is significant or not). We see a drop of 26 Liberian dollars (or 30 from the non-parametric estimation in Table 10.1), which is also close to 10 per cent of the endowment. In addition we see a strong relationship between expectations and contributions, though our estimated coefficient is considerably lower, at close to one third compared to one half in Kenya.

An important point of difference between the results, however, is that we do not see strong evidence that women contribute less than men in the mixed condition. (We are unable to assess whether the effects of the mixed condition are different for men and for women.) And so the explanation provided in Greig and Bohnet for the effect of homogeneous groups on women does not find clear support here. Greig and Bohnet argue that women have overly pessimistic expectations in the mixed conditions while men have overly optimistic expectations. In contrast (see Table 10.2), women and men have similar expectations in mixed groups—they are both overly optimistic—and although women expect contributions to be about 14 LD higher in homogeneous communities, this is nowhere near large enough to account for differences in play, if the effects of expectations in Table 10.3 are to be believed.[7] Perhaps as importantly, as seen in the final column, the estimated effects of expectations appear to be weaker for women (by about 50 per cent) in homogeneous groups.

5. Model and Implications for Interpreting the Evidence

If (inaccurate) differences in expectations cannot account for the effect of composition, what can?

In Fearon et al. (2015) we found evidence that contributions were related to greater levels of mobilization activity in the week before the game in CDR-treated communities, although only in communities where both men and women could be selected to play. Mobilization does not, however, appear to explain why women contributed more in the women-only villages.

In the survey, we asked if the respondent had been contacted by anyone about how to play the game, about the community project, or about staying home on game day, and also about whether they knew of other community meetings to discuss the game and whether they knew the community representatives' names. Table 10.4 shows that the average of yes or no responses (yes equals 1) for these five questions is slightly greater for women in the homogeneous groups versus women in the mixed groups, although this difference is not statistically significant. The rates are about the same for

---

[7] In contrast, the differences in beliefs are close to large enough in Greig and Bohnet to account for the differences in play, at least using their model estimates. There, the homogeneous condition was associated with a 13.5-percentage-point increase in expectations, which translates into a $0.57 \times 13.5 = 7.7$-point difference in behaviour, not very different to the observed 9.5-point difference.

Table 10.4. Reports of mobilization activity by condition and CDR treatment status, 0–1 scale

	Women in all-women	Women in mixed	Men in mixed
All	0.46	0.41	0.47
No-CDR	0.47	0.33	0.42
CDR	0.45	0.48	0.51

Source: Authors' own construction.

women in the women-only condition as for men in mixed. Dividing the sample by whether the community received the CDR programme (which does appear to have affected mobilization activity in the mixed communities), we see that in the no-CDR, mixed-group villages, women were markedly less mobilized than women in the no-CDR, all-women villages. However, in the CDR-treated villages, if anything, there is more mobilization of both genders in the mixed groups. So overall this factor does not seem likely to explain why contributions were higher in the women-only communities.

Experiments are excellent for drawing inferences about what causes what, but, by itself, finding that X causes Y does not explain why this is. An explanation is arguably more important in social science settings than in, say, drug testing, since causal effects are more likely to differ across contexts. This puts a greater premium on learning about mechanisms (which is arguably where the 'science' is in biomedical research as well).

In what follows we develop a simple structural model of the decision to contribute that has parameters of interest corresponding to four different possible motivations for contributing. We then use a Bayesian hierarchical model to estimate these structural parameters, and finally compare the estimates and implications for women in the women-only villages to men and women in the mixed villages. The idea is to use the structural model to help with the problem of drawing inferences about mechanisms from a diverse set of survey responses and the results of several experimental manipulations that are themselves implemented at different levels.

We highlight that our analysis in this section is exploratory; although we set out to measure effects of composition on contributions we only focused on parameter estimation after seeing the core results.

5.1. *Model of Decision Making*

We assume that when deciding what contribution $x_i \in \{0, 1, 2, 3\}$ to make, players seek to maximize:

$$u_i(x_i) = a_i x_i - \gamma_i(x_i - p_i \hat{x}_i)^2 + r_i x_i + \phi_i q_i x_i$$

where $\hat{x}_i$ is i's expectation regarding the average contribution of others in the same village, r_i is i's multiplier, and q_i is the i's perceived probability of having his or her action discovered by others.[8] For simplicity we ignore the expected benefits from contributions by others (these drop out under the assumption of linear gains in the public good).

Note that we assume quasilinear utility and treat the valuation of the public goods as the numeraire. This is captured by the absence of a coefficient on $r_i x_i$. Recall that r_i is either 2 or 5 and was randomly assigned to i by us; q_i and $\hat{x}_i$ are empirical measures derived from the survey data. Our structural parameters of interest are α_i, γ_i, ρ_i, and ϕ_i.

- Parameter α_i reflects the intrinsic value of contributing to the public good. This is often assumed to be negative, reflecting the opportunity cost of not having the money for own spending, although we allow for the possibility that it is positive on net. For example, it can be positive if individuals feel sufficiently good about doing what they see as the right thing, or they see making a contribution as a signal to the community, to the foreign donors running the project, or even to themselves that they are 'good types' who are community-spirited.[9]

- $\gamma_i \geq 0$ and $\rho_i \geq 0$ reflect conformity concerns: with $\rho_i = 1$ a player values contributions equal to those of others contributing; with $\rho_i < 1$ a player seeks to contribute less than others; and with $\rho_i > 1$ she seeks to contribute more than others. Parameter γ_i measures the weight that i puts on matching what he or she believes others are doing (or, more precisely, ρ_i times this).

- Parameter ϕ_i reflects i's valuation of incentives arising from social rewards or punishments from contributions. Note that we assume that players can be concerned about sanctioning from the village for less-than-complete contributions and do not assume that sanctioning relates only to deviations from equilibrium play.

Individuals choose between options $x_i \in \{0,1,2,3\}$ (in hundreds of Liberian dollars). For purposes of estimation, we will assume that the most consequential variation across individuals in a community is in α_i, their marginal value for contributing independent of use of the funds, or desire to match or avoid punishment, relative to the other motivations. Fixing the other parameters, the optimal choice for individual i is increasing in α_i and can be characterized by three cut-points in α_i of the form $c_i^j = (2j - 1)\gamma_i - (2\gamma_i \rho_i \hat{x}_i + r_i + \phi_i q_i)$ for $j = 1, 2, 3$.

---

[8] Contributions and expected contributions by others were rescaled for the Bayesian analysis; see replication code. In addition, q was rescaled to lie in [0.01,0.99].

[9] Individual contributions were anonymous—not seen by the community—although game players were told that their individual contributions could be observed by the researchers at a later date.

If $a_i < c_i^1$ then i optimally would choose $x_i = 0$. If $a_i \in (c_i^1, c_i^2)$ then $x_i = 1$ is preferred; $a_i \in (c_i^2, c_i^3)$ implies $x_i = 2$, and $x_i = 3$ if $a_i > c_i^3$.

In particular, suppose that in a village the a_i are distributed by the cdf F, whereas the other parameters (γ, ρ, ϕ) depend only on gender and village-level features, including whether the group composition in the village is mixed or homogeneous. Then for each i we have probabilities for choices of $x_i \in \{0,1,2,3\}, w_i^x$, where

$$w_i^0 = F(c_i^1)$$

$$w_i^1 = F(c_i^2) - F(c_i^1)$$

$$w_i^2 = F(c_i^3) - F(c_i^2)$$

$$w_i^3 = 1 - F(c_i^3).$$

It follows that if we specify a distribution F for the a_i—say, normal with mean a and standard deviation σ—then we can compute the likelihood of the observed choices of x_i for the twenty-four game players in a particular community. The five unknown parameters entering the likelihood function—and characterizing motivations to contribute—are $\Theta = \{a, \sigma, \gamma, \rho, \phi\}$.

For ease of reference Table 10.5 summarizes the meaning of each motivation or preference parameter, along with some estimation assumptions discussed in the next section.

5.2. Empirical Model

We use a multilevel Bayesian model to estimate the key parameters, letting these be a function of respondent gender and treatment condition. Our model estimates the parameters in the first equation in Section 5.1, as a function of treatment condition, taking q and $\hat{x}$ as given.[10]

Let $\theta[i]$ denote the value of the parameter $\theta \in \Theta$ that we use to calculate the likelihood that person i chose the observed x_i.

Under the assumption that a_i is not observed, the likelihood is calculated using the probability that an individual takes action $x_i \in \{0,1,2,3\}$, given by the categorical distribution with event probabilities w as defined above.

$$L(x_i) = f_{categorical}(x_i | w(r_i, q_i, \hat{x}_i, a[i], \phi[i], \gamma[i], \rho[i], \sigma[i])$$

These individual-level parameters are generated from condition- and group-level parameters as follows. Let W_i, M_i, and H_i denote indicator variables for

---

[10] Thus in the model presented here we do not model $\hat{x}$ as a function of treatment, though this can in principle be added as an additional component of the likelihood function. We note that since $\hat{x}$ is post-treatment, treating it as fixed, as done here and also in Greig and Bohnet (2009), could in principle introduce post-treatment bias.

Table 10.5. Parameter estimates

Parameter	Motivation/preference	Estimation assumptions	Men (mixed)	Women (mixed)	Women-only	Composition effect	Pr > 0
α_i	i's marginal value for contributing independent of use of funds, matching, and sanctioning concerns	i's marginal value for contributing independent of use of funds, matching, and sanctioning concerns	–	–	–	–	–
α	Mean of the distribution from which α_i is drawn	Varies by community and potential condition for each gender	0.76	–0.2	5.13	5.33	0.92
σ	Standard deviation of the distribution from which α_i is drawn	Varies by potential condition	12.41	12.41	11.95	–0.47	0.41
ϕ	Weight on contributing to avoid sanctioning/discomfort if revealed to have given less than 300 LD	Weight on contributing to avoid sanctioning/discomfort if revealed to have given less than 300 LD	1.68	0.38	3.09	2.72	0.75
γ	Weight put on matching target contribution $\rho\hat{x}_i$	Varies by potential condition for each gender	3.07	2.95	2.07	–0.88	0.04
ρ	Share of reported expectation $\hat{x}_i$ that i would ideally match if no other motivations	Varies by potential condition for each gender	0.94	0.99	0.81	–0.17	0.28

Notes: The composition treatment conditions are women-only and mixed. By 'varies by potential condition' we mean that there are distinct parameters for women for each of these two conditions. σ is constrained to be the same for men and women in the mixed condition; the final column shows the posterior probability that the difference between women-only and mixed conditions (for women) is positive.

Source: Authors' own construction.

being a woman player in a mixed village, male in a mixed village, or female in a homogeneous village, respectively, and let $\theta_j, j \in \{H, W, M\}$ denote condition-level parameters, described below.[11]

We let a and ϕ vary by condition and village as combinations of village-level and condition-level features.

$$a[i] = M_i a_M + W_i a_W + H_i a_H + v^a_{v[i]}$$

$$\phi[i] = M_i \phi_M + W_i \phi_W + H_i \phi_H + v^\phi_{v[i]}$$

where $v[i]$ denotes the village to which i belongs. We assume the village-level random effects have distributions given by: $v^a_v \sim N(\mu_a, \sigma_a)$ and $v^\phi_v \sim N\left(\mu_\phi, \sigma_\phi\right)$.

Other parameters we let vary by condition only; thus for $\theta \in \{\gamma, \rho, \sigma\}$:

$$\theta[i] = M_i \theta_M + W_i \theta_W + H_i \theta_H$$

Each of these last three is constrained to be positive. In addition we constrain $\sigma_M = \sigma_W$. We employ diffuse priors on all parameters and hyperparameters, given by normal (or half normal) distributions with mean 0 and standard deviation of 5.

Thus we estimate different parameters for men and for women for each treatment condition. That is, we use the model not simply to measure parameters but also to infer the counterfactual parameters that would arise were women in different treatment conditions. We thus seek to assess whether gains due to composition may be attributed to differences in instrumental motivations deriving from expectations about the actions of others, concerns around sanctioning, or differences in valuations of the public good or in terms of intrinsic motivations. In addition we allow for considerable village-level heterogeneity, at least for parameters a and ϕ.

5.3. Effects on Structural Parameters

Estimated posterior means for our five structural parameters in three conditions (women-only, women in mixed communities, and men in mixed communities) are shown in Table 10.5. There are two sorts of comparisons of interest. First—and most relevant to our question of why higher contributions were made by women in the women-only groups—is the treatment effect of the group's gender composition on women players. For parameter θ this is given by $\theta_H - \theta_W$ in the fifth column. Second, within each condition we can compare the relevant weight the average respondent is estimated to have put on different motivations. Recall that these numbers are relative to the value

---

[11] We note a slight abuse of notation here since we let a_i denote person i's value for a as defined above, and a_M, a_F, a_H denote condition-level parameters.

put on money raised from the game for the community, which has been normalized to 1.

Consider the treatment effects on women players first. The most striking positive effect we see here is the difference in a for women between conditions. From these estimates, a—the village-/condition-level mean of the distribution of a_i—is five points higher for women in the homogeneous community, and is, on average, positive. This means that for the typical woman in these groups, every 100 LD invested gives the equivalent of an intrinsic 500 LD direct positive return in units of the value of the total funds raised, independent of what anyone else does. With σ around 12, approximately one third face marginal costs of contributing and two thirds marginal benefits (more generally, these shares depend on the village-level intercept also). By contrast, in the mixed group, the mean for women is negative and close to 0, meaning that the typical woman gains no intrinsic benefits from contributing, and half face costs.

In the typical case we observe little responsiveness to fears of sanctioning and see little difference across conditions.

We see relatively large *negative* effects on γ, however, meaning that in the gender-homogeneous groups women put *less* weight on matching what they expected others to contribute than they did when they knew they were playing with men. Note that in most cases ρ is close to 1, though possibly lower in the homogeneous group condition; thus if there were no other considerations, both men and women in the mixed groups would have wanted to match what they thought others were doing, whereas women in the homogeneous condition would have wanted to undercut others a bit (though the difference between these is not tightly estimated). Overall, the matching incentives pulled offers upwards whenever players were optimistic about the contributions of others.[12] The result of this is that women in homogeneous groups had a substantially *weaker* motivation to contribute in order to match what others were expected to do, but this negative effect was more than offset by the increase deriving from the greater intrinsic motivation to contribute that worked through a.[13]

The estimates also provide a sense of the relative importance of different motivations in game players' contribution decisions. For instance, in the mixed groups, on average, both men and women have γ values around 3, which means they put about three times the weight on the discomfort of deviating from the expected contribution of others by 100 LD as they did on

---

[12] In particular, we can see from the utility function that the marginal gains in contributions are increasing in γ (that is, $\frac{\delta^2 u}{\delta x_i \delta \gamma} > 0$) when $-2(x_i - \rho\hat{x}) > 0$ or $x_i < \rho\hat{x}$. Note that here we consider best responses, treating expectations as exogenous.

[13] The negative effect arising from the drop in γ is partially compounded by the drop in ρ, which lowers women's targets for matching.

increasing the total contributed by 100 LD. Women in the homogeneous condition similarly put more weight on conformity, though not as much as in the mixed groups. The sanctioning concern seems to matter hardly at all relative to the other motivations in any condition. As noted, the big difference is in the weight put on contributing, independent of the total raised or the conformity concerns. The suggestion is that especially for many women in the homogeneous condition, but also to a smaller degree for men in the mixed groups, contributing was typically not seen as a net cost that they would not want to pay unless they thought that what the money raised would be spent on would compensate them. Rather, the results suggest that for many game players, the game did not have the structure either of a classical public good problem, or of a simple coordination game in which contributing is costly but one might do it for conformity reasons. Instead, for quite a few players, contributing appears to have been a dominant strategy, independent of hopes for what the money raised would be spent on.

6. Conclusion

Employing a public goods game in 83 villages in northern Liberia, we use random assignment of gender composition of the groups of individuals making contribution decisions to estimate the causal effect of playing with a mixed-gender group versus a group comprising only women. We find that the all-women groups contributed substantially more to a community project than did either men or women in the communities where both genders played. This is therefore a group composition effect rather than a 'women are unconditionally more community-minded' effect. Women contributed more when they knew they were playing with other women, but not more than men in the mixed groups.

Our main result thus supports the logic of practitioners who seek to engage communities through women-only groups. It does not provide clear evidence in favour of arguments or the assumption that women are per se more community-minded when asked to make decisions between private and social goods, although this might be the case for particular public goods in particular settings.

The basic finding is similar to that of Greig and Bohnet's (2009) lab experiment conducted in a Nairobi slum, where groups of four played a public goods game in different gender compositions. They also found that women contributed more in all-women groups than in mixed sets. The similarity is interesting given the many differences in the set-up and context.

Our account of why women contribute more in women-only groups differs from the explanation given in the Kenya experiment. In Kenya, differences appeared to result from women holding overly pessimistic views about the behaviour of players in mixed groups (whereas men held overly optimistic views). In contrast, in Liberia differences in the beliefs of men and women were slight and differences in expectations across conditions did not appear large enough to account for differences in contributions, at least when our estimated model was employed.

Rather, our model and the data suggest that women placed great intrinsic value on contributing to the production of public goods when they knew that they were working collectively with other women. We cannot assess systematically whether this is because mobilization undertaken by women in advance of play was more effective at clarifying appropriate norms of behaviour, or extracting promises around behaviour, or whether the intrinsic motivations stemmed from greater solidarity within the gender groups.

We close, however, with some speculation motivated by the model results and field observations. In the initial community meetings to introduce the project and game, our local collaborators[14] explained that we had two main purposes: to provide some funds for a small development project that the community could choose, and also to conduct research to understand better the people and their lives in these communities. The second reason was given as a way of explaining why we were employing the unusual game procedure, which was referred to both as a process of raising matching funds (an idea that many communities were familiar with), and as a 'game'. (Using a local analogy, participants and enumerators sometimes spoke of a 'lucky ticket', meaning that getting picked to play was like winning a lottery.)

Attendees at the initial meetings where the game was explained immediately and audibly grasped the conflict between private and social good posed by the decision of how much of the endowment to keep and how much to put in the envelope. On one occasion (at least), an attendee was heard to say 'They are testing us', meaning that his interpretation was that we wanted to learn how community-spirited people in their village were. Our introductory scripts emphasized that the decision to keep some or all of the endowment was private and that it could be justifiable to do so—we avoided any language clearly identifying contribution as the right choice. Nonetheless, a possible inference by community members would have been that if the community contributed a lot, they would be more likely to receive more development assistance in the future.

If so, then game players may have had a rationale for contributing largely independent of interest rates, expectations about others' contributions, or value for the community project. The act of contributing the whole endowment may have been understood by some or many participants as a signal of

---

[14] The Liberian non-governmental organization NEPI (Network for Empowerment and Progressive Initiative).

community spirit to outsiders thought to have access to more resources. It was evident that residents of these impoverished communities were desperate for 'development', a term they frequently used. This rationale could explain some part of our estimates of powerful intrinsic motivations to contribute.[15]

But how, if at all, might such a rationale explain the greater contributions of women when they knew they were playing only with other women? This is speculative, but a possibility suggested by some field observations is that the motivation to signal was greater the more a player identified with the defined set of other game players. Understanding yourself as a representative of 'the women' of the community rather than as a random community member may increase the desire to signal—to the outsiders, to the rest of the community, and to yourself—that you and your group are made of the right material. On hearing that only women could be chosen to play the game, the women in the audience sometimes seemed to feel pleased and important, perhaps as if proud or excited to be chosen as representatives of their community. (By contrast, occasionally one or two men would lose interest and walk away when it was announced that only women could be chosen.)

If correct, this interpretation also sheds light on the effects of the CDR programme itself. We note that these effects of the composition treatment are quite different from the effects on parameter values we estimate for the CDR treatment, using an analogous model. In models that include parameters for CDR effects (not reported here) we see that although both CDR and gender homogeneity are associated with greater contributions, parameter estimates suggest that CDR is associated with a *drop* in α which is offset by changes in γ and ρ. This is consistent with an interpretation in which group homogeneity induces identity concerns, whereas CDR facilitates collective action through enhanced coordination. Though CDR is sometimes promoted as a way of fostering greater group identity, these results, consistent with our analysis in Fearon et al. (2015), suggest that it was organization and not identity that mattered.

The speculation above is in line with a large literature and tradition, not much known or drawn on in the design of development interventions, of motivating collective action by appeals to subgroup solidarity or even between-group competition.[16] It is understandable that development practitioners, who put a high premium on inclusion and avoidance of conflict, would not consider trying to generate collective action by these means. But perhaps creative thinking might

---

[15] We note that this motivation might also bias our expectations measure upwards, contributing to the apparent 'over-optimism' we observe. That is, when asked how much they thought others in the community would contribute in the game, some respondents may have been saying, in effect, 'A lot, because this is a good community you should bring development to'.

[16] It is unfortunate that with only 83 communities under study we did not have the power to include a third treatment of villages where only men could play the game. This might have shed light on whether we observed an 'all-women' effect or a single-gender group effect.

be able to harness the power of group identification and competition in order to generate collective action in support of development projects, without, or with minimal, downside risks.

References

Baron, Reuben M., and David A. Kenny (1986). 'The Moderator–Mediator Variable Distinction in Social Psychological Research: Conceptual, Strategic, and Statistical Considerations'. *Journal of Personality and Social Psychology*, 51(6): 1173–82.

Duflo, Esther (2012). 'Women's Empowerment and Economic Development'. *Journal of Economic Literature*, 50(4): 1051–79.

Fearon, James, Macartan Humphreys, and Jeremy Weinstein (2014). 'Replication Data for: How Does Development Assistance Affect Collective Action Capacity? Results from a Field Experiment in Post-Conflict Liberia'. Dataverse. Available at: https://dataverse.harvard.edu/dataset.xhtml?persistentId=doi:10.7910/DVN/28006 (accessed 8 May 2017).

Fearon, James D., Macartan Humphreys, and Jeremy M. Weinstein (2015). 'How Does Development Assistance Affect Collective Action Capacity? Results from a Field Experiment in Post-Conflict Liberia'. *American Political Science Review*, 109(3): 450–69.

Gates, Melinda French (2014). 'Putting Women and Girls at the Center of Development'. *Science*, 345: 1273–75.

Greig, Fiona, and Iris Bohnet (2009). 'Exploring Gendered Behavior in the Field with Experiments: Why Public Goods Are Provided by Women in a Nairobi Slum'. *Journal of Economic Behavior & Organization*, 70(1): 1–9.

Mansuri, Ghazala, and Vijayendra Rao (2012). *Localizing Development: Does Participation Work?* Washington, DC: The World Bank.

World Bank (2012). *World Development Report: Gender Equality and Development*. Washington, DC: World Bank.

11

The Impact of Social Mobilization on Health Service Delivery and Health Outcomes

Evidence from Rural Pakistan

Xavier Giné, Salma Khalid, and Ghazala Mansuri

1. Introduction

Community-driven development (CDD) is viewed as an important vehicle for improving public sector accountability and the quality of public service delivery by both governments and donors. Despite this, evidence on the effectiveness of CDD programmes remains mixed. This is due, in part, to the inherent difficulty of evaluating interventions that aim to change the nature of the interaction between citizens and the state. Such interventions usually have complex and unpredictable trajectories of change (Mansuri and Rao 2013). However, it is also due to a fundamental characteristic of the CDD approach. Communities are offered a bundle of distinct interventions, usually simultaneously, making it difficult to identify what aspects of a programme worked or did not work in a specific context.

A case in point, and one which is of some policy interest, is the investment that CDD programmes make in the social mobilization of poor and disenfranchised groups. Virtually all CDD programmes invest considerable resources in supporting community organizations. These organizations are meant to provide a platform for disadvantaged groups to engage in collective action around development priorities and interact with and influence institutions of the state, at the local level. Assessing the impact of these investments is difficult, however, since social mobilization is invariably combined with resource injections for community infrastructure, asset transfers for the poor, skills training or microcredit, all of which can have an impact on the demand for improved public services or influence over the policy process through other channels.

In this chapter, we provide evidence on the impact of social mobilization on the quality of public service delivery in a context where other simultaneous inputs are absent. The Social Mobilization for Empowerment (MORE) programme was implemented as a large-scale randomized intervention in rural Pakistan in 2010. It is a typical CDD programme in design, however, in the first three years of the programme, treatment villages were only provided support for social mobilization. By assessing programme impact at this three-year mark, in mid-2013, we can decouple the impact of social mobilization from the injection of resources or other inputs.

The social mobilization effort focused on encouraging self-help and collective action within the community as well as better linkages with government. In treatment villages, citizens were organized into grassroots organizations which appointed representatives to a village-level institution that had the authority to decide on village development priorities and to eventually allocate resources from a village development fund (VDF), which was assessed and provided after the midline of the programme was done in mid-2013.

The social mobilization effort had a strong focus on increasing the participation of women in the village-level decision-making bodies. Since women identified access to primary health care as critical to their own needs and those of their children, at baseline, we look at the impact of mobilizing women on public health provision. It is important to note that the social mobilization effort did not focus on health-related issues and no information was provided to community members on the performance of local public health providers.

The context we study is characterized by relatively high levels of maternal and child mortality, and malnutrition among infants and young children. Women have low decision-making power within the household and social mores restrict female mobility and autonomy. Education levels among adult women also remain extremely low, limiting their ability to access information or engage effectively with service providers. This context allows us to examine whether social mobilization targeted at women can lead to an improvement in the performance of public health providers even in a context of low female literacy and mobility.

Rural villages in Pakistan have access to two types of health care providers. The first is a female community health provider known as the Lady Health Worker (LHW). LHWs deliver a range of services related to maternal and child health including pre- and post-natal care, well-baby visits, child growth monitoring, childhood immunization, family planning, and health education. Because LHWs are field workers who make home visits, particularly targeting households with young children or women of childbearing age, they are the first line of direct access to public health care. In addition, the house of each LHW is declared as a Health House where residents can go in case of emergency to receive basic treatment or advice. Due to this, LHWs are typically selected from and reside within the villages that they serve. While each village is entitled to an LHW, their presence was not universal at project start in 2010. In fact, only 62 per cent of villages reported having a LHW assigned to them.

The second type of health care provider is the Basic Health Unit (BHU), a primary care health facility that typically serves multiple villages within a catchment area. LHWs are responsible for making referrals of all pregnant women to the BHU which delivers additional pre- and post-natal care services and deals with minor illness of all types. While all villages in the study had a BHU within their catchment area, BHUs varied substantially in both quality and the availability of trained medical staff. Since exposure to the MORE programme was randomized at the village-level, and the catchment area of a BHU typically includes both mobilized and non-mobilized villages, we expect community mobilization to be less effective at influencing BHU-level outcomes, as compared to effects on village-based LHWs.

We examine the effects of community mobilization on two sets of health-related outcomes. The first focuses on women's interactions with service providers (health care utilization, access to and quality of care from LHWs), the second looks at improvements in health outcomes for women and young children such as the incidence of illness, ante- and post-natal care, well-baby checkups, and child immunization.

We find no significant improvements overall in the utilization of BHUs. However, there is a substantial reduction in reported wait-times at these facilities and an improvement in the odds of a woman's pregnancy being registered at the BHU as well as in the odds of receiving post-natal care. Since LHWs connect women to BHUs and are the first providers of post-natal care, we cannot disentangle whether the improvements in registration or post-natal care are due to improvements in service delivery at the LHW or BHU level. However, women are significantly more likely to report having been visited by an LHW. They also report significant improvements in ante-natal and post-natal care provided by the LHW, as well as significantly higher LHW well-baby visits, including a visit to check child height.

By contrast, outcomes that are not driven by the type or quality of care provided by LHWs, such as the incidence of diarrhoea or stunting, which depends far more on community level factors such as water quality and sanitation conditions and household health behaviours, such as the use of soap or barefoot walking among children and adults, registered no improvement.

These findings suggest that community collective action can improve the performance of service providers only if the provider is accessible and can be held accountable by the village. This chain of accountability is most effective if the purview of the service provider is at the level of the mobilized community, as is the case with LHWs, and less effective, as in the case of

BHUs, for providers who are located at the supra-community level and are therefore accountable to multiple stakeholders.

The rest of the chapter is organized as follows. The next section describes the literature on social mobilization and health. Section 3 describes the data we use for the analysis, Sections 4 and 5 provide the econometric framework and results, and Section 6 concludes.

2. Community-Driven Development and Health

The existing literature on community-based health service interventions suggests potentially positive impacts of CDD activities on health outcomes, particularly in the domain of maternal and child health. However, since these interventions bundle several activities together, one cannot isolate the impact of community mobilization alone. Community-based health service programmes encompass a range of activities that focus on maternal and child care and household health behaviours. These interventions can be roughly divided into two categories: (1) projects where communities are encouraged to take an active role in resource allocation, and (2) interventions where community volunteers or community-based health workers are mobilized to deliver health services or information.

For example, Chase and Sherburne-Benz (2001) examine the impact of community organization and resource allocation via the Zambia Social Fund on health and education outcomes. They find that communities using social investment funds to construct a health facility see higher utilization of primary care services and lower utilization of hospital services compared to control communities, but they find no overall difference in total health care utilization between treated and control communities.

Other community-based health projects mobilize communities to improve health through direct engagement with formal service providers. Binka et al. (2007) implement a randomized intervention in Ghana to compare the efficacy of providing trained nurses to communities versus community volunteers. While in this study, volunteers on their own do not improve child survival significantly, the combination of volunteers working together with trained nurses outperforms nurses working on their own. This suggests a strong role for community organization in improving health outcomes when used as a supplement to formal provision. Björkman and Svensson (2009) evaluate the impact of citizen report cards on quality of health care delivery. They find that improvements in outcomes and service provision vectors can be best explained through the degree of community engagement with the programme as opposed to supply driven factors such as the engagement of the staff.

Interventions in India (Tripathy et al. 2010) and Nepal (Manandhar et al. 2004) use community facilitators to organize women's groups that tackle, among other subjects, health behaviours and health entitlements. Both randomized trials find improvements along a range of outcomes, with large reductions in neonatal mortality.

On balance, the literature on CDD and health suggests that communities can play a significant role in improving community health through various mechanisms including resource allocation, health service delivery, dissemination of information, and monitoring of service providers. However, the literature to date, while suggestive of a positive role for social mobilization alone, has not identified it cleanly.

3. The MORE Programme

The goal of the MORE programme is to foster social mobilization and strengthen community development through the creation of community- and village-level organizations and the provision of village-level development funds. The programme was implemented in partnership with the Pakistan Poverty Alleviation Fund (PPAF). Social mobilization activities in the study areas were supported by a key partner of the PPAF, the National Rural Support Program (NRSP). NRSP is the largest community based development NGO in Pakistan in terms of outreach and coverage, and currently operates in fifty-one districts spread across all four provinces of Pakistan. NRSP identified 158 villages drawn from five districts where it currently has presence. The identified villages had no prior history of social mobilization by either NRSP or any other organization. A total of 108 study villages were randomly assigned to treatment status with the remaining being held as controls.

In treatment villages, representatives from NRSP helped organize villagers into grassroots organizations of fifteen to twenty members called Community Organizations (COs). The aim of the COs is to provide a platform for collective efforts and allow members to pool their resources for common development goals. COs hold regular meetings where members can discuss local issues, prioritize community needs, and resolve any conflicts at the local level.

The procedure followed by NRSP for social mobilization was standardized in all the villages and districts to allow comparability. In the treatment villages, a social mobilization team (SMT) approached a few people in the village to help organize a meeting of the community with the Social Organizer (SO). In that meeting, the SO introduced the concept of Community Organization (CO) and how villagers can pool their resources to create a platform for collective efforts. The SO shared examples of other areas where people formed COs and were able to achieve significant improvement in their lives through this platform.

241

The SO also informed the community that the basis on which they would get funds for developmental activities is the 'number of households organized in a village', where a household is considered organized if at least one member (male or female) is an active member of a CO and has attended more than one CO meeting. A minimum of 40 per cent of the village population needed to be organized in order to be eligible for the village development grant, with the size of the grant increasing with the number of households organized past the 40 per cent cut-off, thus providing a strong incentive for broad mobilization. In addition, the inclusion of women and poor households in the mobilization and CO formation process was actively encouraged.

Once 40 per cent of village households had at least one CO member, the village formed a Village Support Organization (VSO). This village institution comprises two elected members from each CO in the village. One of the main tasks of the VSO was the design and implementation of the Village Development Plan (VDP), a document that prioritized village development projects to be funded by the grant. The grant could be used for any productive purpose for the general benefit of the entire community including physical infrastructure, health, education, training, asset transfers, and other livelihood activities. The amount of the grant varied from village to village depending on the total number of households and percentage of households that were organized in that village. On average, villages received a grant totalling 2,897,883 Pakistan rupees (PKR), or 10,482 PKR per household in the village. The VSO was also charged with the management of the grant and the active involvement of community members in monitoring and promoting transparency.

The MORE intervention was successful at encouraging broad participation from the community. On average, 59 per cent of households in treatment villages were organized. Women were well-represented in the community mobilization activities, comprising 51 per cent of CO members and 41 per cent of VSO members per village, on average.

The timing of the intervention and data collection allows us to isolate the impact of community mobilization from the direct impacts of the village-level grants. In each treatment and control village, households were surveyed at baseline, after the formation of the first COs in treatment villages. Households were surveyed again 3 years later at midline. In treatment villages, the midline survey occurred after approval of the VDP but before the disbursement of grant funds. This study focuses on impacts at midline between treatment and control villages, which isolates the impact of community mobilization.

3.1. *Data*

The baseline and midline surveys were administered to a random sample of forty households drawn from each of the treatment and control villages and included detailed modules on health facility utilization, health outcomes and household health behaviours.

All adult women in the household were separately surveyed for specific sub-modules related to maternal health, ante-natal and post-natal care, and child birth and health outcomes. Respondents were asked about their most recent pregnancy in the past three years to cover relevant health care utilization for pregnancies occurring between the baseline and midline data collection. Finally, all women in the household were asked about their interaction with the LHW assigned to their village. As discussed above, the quality of service provided by the LHW should be responsive to changes in local accountability, given that the LHW is recruited from within the community that she serves.

3.2. Sample Characteristics

Table 11.1 presents the mean of village level characteristics and checks for balance between treatment and control villages. Villages have about 279 households living in seven to eight settlements on average. Villages are relatively poor, with about 52 per cent of households below the poverty line and landless households comprising about 67 per cent of all households. Households have between six and seven members on average. Most household heads (63 per cent) do not have formal education.

Table 11.1. Descriptive statistics

	All	Treatment	Control	P-Value (T=C)
Number of Villages	158	108	50	
Number of Households (HHs)	5828	3990	1838	
Ever Married Women 15–40 years	6109	4169	1940	
Women w/pregnancies in past 3 yrs	2762	1907	855	
Children <= 3 years of age at midline	4509	3060	1449	
Village Population (No. of HHs)	278.98	267.32	284.38	0.499
		(18.5)	(14.9)	
No. of Settlements	7.50	7.82	7.35	0.720
		(1.1)	(0.7)	
No. of villages in Union Council	10.93	10.74	11.03	0.685
		(0.6)	(0.4)	
Proportion of Landless HHs in Village	0.67	0.67	0.66	0.820
		(0.030)	(0.020)	
Proportion of Poor HHs in Village	0.52	0.52	0.53	0.690
		(0.006)	(0.005)	
Number of HH members	6.34	6.33	6.34	0.968
		(0.163)	(0.127)	
HH heads with primary education	0.15	0.15	0.14	0.587
		(0.012)	(0.006)	
HH heads with middle education	0.18	0.17	0.19	0.365
		(0.017)	(0.013)	

Source: Authors' compilation.

When we compare treatment and control villages we find no relationship between treatment assignment and any of these variables, giving us confidence in the success of our randomization. In fact, when we run a regression of treatment status as the dependent variable against all of these variables, the p-value for the F-test that all the variables are jointly significant is 0.98.

Table 11.2 provides a description of the variables used in the analysis that follows. Our outcomes of interest are broadly classified as incidence of illness, utilization of health services, quality of care provided by the BHU, maternal

Table 11.2. Description of variables

Variable Name	Description
Illness Characteristics	
Incidence of Illness	Fell ill in past month (1=Yes)
N. of Consultations	(If sick) Number of health care providers consulted
Govt. Provider Consulted	(If sick) Govt. health care provider was consulted (1=Yes)
BHU Utilization	
Wait Time	(If used BHU) Wait time at BHU
Consult Fee	(If used BHU) Amount of consultation fee paid at BHU
Convey Concerns	(If used BHU) Able to convey concerns to service provider (1=Yes)
Treated Well	(If used BHU) Treated well by the service provider (1=Yes)
BHU Index	Index combining Wait Time, Consult Fee, Convey Concerns, Treated Well
Pregnancy	
Pregnancy	Pregnant in the past 3 years (1=Yes)
Pregnancy Registered	(If pregnant) Registered with the BHU (1=Yes)
Antenatal Care	(If pregnant) Received ante-natal care during this pregnancy (1=Yes)
Pre-Preg Index	Index combining Pregnancy Registered and Ante-natal Care
Post-natal Care	Received post-natal care following delivery (1=Yes)
Birth Registered	Child was registered at BHU after delivery (1=Yes)
Weight Recorded	Child was weighed at birth (1=Yes)
Post-Preg Index	Index combining Post-natal Care, Birth Registered, Weight Recorded
Lady Health Worker Performance and Satisfaction	
Visit	LHW visited during last pregnancy (1=Yes)
Ante-natal Care	Ante-natal care received from the LHW (1=Yes)
Post-natal Care	Post-natal care received from the LHW (1=Yes)
Height Visit	Received well-baby visits for checking height/weight of baby (1=Yes)
Vaccination Visit	Received well-baby visits for vaccination/immunization help (1=Yes)
LHW Index	Index of LHW Visit, Ante-natal Care, Post-natal Care, Height Visit
Assigned to Village	HH reported that an LHW is assigned to their village (1=Yes)
Frequency of Visits	(If LHW assigned) Freq. of visits in a month (Recall period: Last 3 months)
Satisfaction	(If LHW assigned) Satisfied with services/advice provided by LHW (1=Yes)
Immunization and Health Outcomes for Children (0–3 years)	
Incomplete Immunization	Child not fully immunized against Polio, BCG, Measles, or DPT (1=Yes)
Immunization Card	Child has an immunization card (1=Yes)
Diarrhoea Incidence	Child had diarrhoea in the last 6 months (1=Yes)
Stunting Incidence	Height of the child indicates stunted linear growth (1=Yes)
WASH Outcomes	
Use Soap	Self-report of whether soap is used for washing hands (1=Yes)
Saw Soap	Enumerator could verify presence of soap in household (1=Yes)
Adults Barefoot	Adults in HH walk barefoot in the settlement (1=Yes)
Children Barefoot	Children in the HH walk barefoot in the settlement (1=Yes)

Source: Authors' compilation.

health and child health outcomes, and perceptions regarding the quality of care provided by the LHW.

4. Econometric Framework

Given random assignment to treatment and control villages, we can compare midline outcomes between experimental groups in order to establish the causal impact of the treatment on the variables of interest. We estimate the following specification:

$$Y_{ivb} = a + \beta T_{vb} + \gamma_b + \varepsilon_{ivb} \qquad (1)$$

where Y_{ivb} is the outcome of interest for household i in village v mapped to SMT branch b. T_{vb} is an indicator for whether village v was assigned to the treatment group, and γ_b are SMT fixed effects. The coefficient β measures the impact of social mobilization by capturing the difference in the outcome between treatment and control villages. We cluster standard errors at the village level since treatment is assigned at the village level. To allay concerns related to multiple hypothesis, we also create composite indices of related variables (see Kling et al., 2007) and assess treatment effects relative to these indices in addition to their individual components.

5. Results

The first set of outcomes in Table 11.3 relate to the overall incidence of illness in the past month and health services sought for these episodes of illness. Column 1 indicates that at midline, self-reported incidence of illness is significantly lower among households in treatment villages relative to those in

Table 11.3. Illness incidence

	(1)	(2)	(3)
	Incidence of Illness	No. of Consultations	Govt. Provider Consulted
Treated village	−0.043***	0.053**	0.026
	(0.016)	(0.023)	(0.023)
N	44,265	12,505	11,494
R-squared	0.038	0.030	0.015
Mean of Dep. Var. in Control Villages	0.316	1.040	0.199

Note: The symbols *, **, and *** represent significance at the 10, 5, and 1 per cent level respectively. Standard errors are reported in parentheses below the coefficient and are clustered at the village level. All specifications include social mobilization team effects. Variables are defined in Table 11.2.

Source: Authors' compilation.

Table 11.4. Utilization of Basic Health Unit (BHU)

	(1)	(2)	(3)	(4)	(5)
	Wait Time	Consultation Fee	Convey Concerns	Treated Well	BHU Index
Treated village	−5.821***	9.407	0.007	−0.010	0.060
	(1.756)	(20.395)	(0.022)	(0.025)	(0.051)
N	1003	1003	1003	1003	1003
R-squared	0.175	0.075	0.026	0.092	0.129
Mean of Dep. Var. in Control Villages	20.7	37.9	0.960	0.934	

Note: The symbols *, **, and *** represent significance at the 10, 5, and 1 per cent level respectively. Standard errors are reported in parentheses below the coefficient and are clustered at the village level. All specifications include social mobilization team effects. Variables are defined in Table 11.2.

Source: Authors' compilation.

control villages where no mobilization had occurred. Households in treatment villages also appear to consult a larger number of providers when a household member is ill, as shown in Column 2. While over 90 per cent of households report seeking some form of consultation during episodes of illness, only 20 per cent of households seek health services from government providers. Column 3 reports no increase in the likelihood of utilizing government health service providers following social mobilization.

Table 11.4 analyses whether assignment to treatment results in an improvement in the experiences of households using the BHU. Column 1 reports a statistically significant reduction of roughly six minutes in wait times reported at the BHU among households in treated villages. However, no other indicator shows significant improvement. Consequently, our BHU index which combines all measures of BHU performance has a positive but insignificant coefficient. Note that the sample is smaller because only households that visited the BHU facility provided information on their performance.

Tables 11.5 and 11.6 look at maternal outcomes pre- and post-delivery, as well as child outcomes immediately following birth. Since LHWs are the first point of contact for pregnant women and BHUs provide the secondary level of care, this set of outcomes could plausibly have been influenced by better performance of BHUs or LHWs. Table 11.5 reports pre-delivery outcomes while Table 11.6 focuses on post-delivery mother and child outcomes. Since these data cover pre-delivery outcomes for completed pregnancies, and there was only a three-year period between the start of social mobilization and midline data collection, we expect weaker effects on pre-natal outcomes due to the lower exposure to treatment.

Column 1 of Table 11.5 shows that at midline there had been no increase in the odds of pregnancy from the base of 44 per cent at baseline. There is a statistically significant 20 per cent increase in the odds of a pregnancy being

Table 11.5. Maternal health—pre-delivery

	(1)	(2)	(3)	(4)
	Pregnancy	Registered	Ante-natal Care	Pre-Preg Index
Treated village	0.013	0.052*	0.013	0.072
	(0.015)	(0.030)	(0.023)	(0.048)
N	6109	2762	2762	2762
R-squared	0.009	0.225	0.270	0.329
Mean of Dep. Var. in Control Villages	0.441	0.256	0.553	

Note: The symbols *, **, and *** represent significance at the 10, 5, and 1 per cent level respectively. Standard errors are reported in parentheses below the coefficient and are clustered at the village level. All specifications include social mobilization team effects. Variables are defined in Table 11.2.

Source: Authors' compilation.

Table 11.6. Maternal health—post-delivery

	(1)	(2)	(3)	(4)	(5)
	Post-natal Care	Child Died at Birth	Birth Registered	Weight Recorded	Post-Preg Index
Treated village	0.065**	0.008	0.011	0.021	0.097**
	(0.027)	(0.007)	(0.019)	(0.014)	(0.043)
N	2762	2762	2626	2626	2626
R-squared	0.194	0.006	0.575	0.008	0.282
Mean of Dep. Var. in Control Villages	0.269	0.021	0.421	0.038	

Note: The symbols *, **, and *** represent significance at the 10, 5, and 1 per cent level respectively. Standard errors are reported in parentheses below the coefficient and are clustered at the village level. All specifications include social mobilization team effects. Variables are defined in Table 11.2.

Source: Authors' compilation.

registered at the BHU, over a base of 26 per cent, but no significant change in the odds of receiving ante-natal care. Overall, the effect of social mobilization on improvements on pre-pregnancy maternal health, captured in Column 4 of Table 11.5, is not significant.

Examining the post-delivery outcomes (Table 11.6), we find a significant and sizeable increase in utilization of post-natal care in treatment villages. The likelihood of seeking post-natal care increased by 26 per cent in treatment villages, relative to a base of 27 per cent. In contrast, there is no change in the odds of child mortality at birth, birth registration, or the recording of weight at birth. Overall, the coefficient for the post-pregnancy index is significant at conventional levels, driven in large part by the substantial increase in post-natal care.

Tables 11.7 and 11.8 focus on the performance of LHWs. Table 11.7 looks at the incidence of specific services provided by the LHW while Table 11.8 looks at household perceptions of satisfaction with the LHW service provision. Column 1 of Table 11.7 indicates that the likelihood of the LHW visiting pregnant

Table 11.7. Lady health worker (LHW) health service provision

	(1)	(2)	(3)	(4)	(5)
	Visit	Antenatal Care	Postnatal Care	Height Visit	LHW Index
Treated village	0.068*	0.053***	0.028**	0.046***	0.139***
	(0.038)	(0.020)	(0.012)	(0.014)	(0.042)
N	2762	2762	2762	2626	2626
R-squared	0.355	0.204	0.099	0.012	0.286
Mean of Dep. Var. in Control Villages	0.353	0.142	0.034	0.041	

Note: The symbols *, **, and *** represent significance at the 10, 5, and 1 per cent level respectively. Standard errors are reported in parentheses below the coefficient and are clustered at the village level. All specifications include social mobilization team effects. Variables are defined in Table 11.2.

Source: Authors' compilation.

Table 11.8. LHW performance and satisfaction

	(1)	(2)	(3)	(4)	(5)	(6)
		All Women			Pregnant in Past 3 Years	
	Assigned	Freq.	Satisfaction	Assigned	Freq.	Satisfaction
Treated village	0.133**	−0.029	0.017	0.150**	0.059	0.029
	(0.055)	(0.037)	(0.033)	(0.064)	(0.059)	(0.043)
N	5828	4160	4220	1466	1034	1041
R-squared	0.142	0.012	0.065	0.173	0.017	0.083
Mean of Dep. Var. in Control Villages	0.621	1.050	0.686	0.603	1.07	0.692

Note: The symbols *, **, and *** represent significance at the 10, 5, and 1 per cent level respectively. Standard errors are reported in parentheses below the coefficient and are clustered at the village level. All specifications include social mobilization team effects. Variables are defined in Table 11.2.

Source: Authors' compilation.

women in treatment villages rose by 19 per cent from a base of 35 per cent in control villages. Treatment villages also report a 37 per cent higher probability that pregnant women received ante-natal care from LHWs, from a base of 14 per cent and a near doubling of LHW provided post-natal care, though from a very low base of 3 per cent (Columns 2 and 3). Given that there was an insignificant increase in the level of ante-natal care in treatment villages overall, the increase in care provided by the LHW implies a substitution away from other providers to the LHW.

Turning to child outcomes, we again see a significant and large increase in the probability of receiving a well-baby visit by the LHW to check infant height and weight. The odds of the LHW making a well-baby visit more than doubled in the treatment sample, though again the probability in control villages was only 4 per cent (Column 4). The impact of social mobilization on our LHW index, which combines standardized measures from Columns 1–4, is positive and statistically significant at the 1 per cent level.

Table 11.8 captures household perceptions of LHW performance in two samples. Columns 1–3 include all women of reproductive age while Columns 4–6 restrict the sample to women who had a completed pregnancy in the past three years. In both samples we see a large and significant increase in the odds of households reporting that an LHW was assigned to their village. The size of the effect ranges from 20 to 25 per cent, depending on the sample, from a base of 60 per cent in control villages. This result may be explained by a greater presence of an already assigned LHW in the community or the assignment of new LHWs to a previously unserved village. Interestingly, conditional on being in a village with an assigned LHW, treated households do not report an increase in the frequency of LHW visits or a higher satisfaction with LHW visits relative to households in control villages.

Tables 11.9 and 11.10 turn to health outcomes for infants and young children up to three years of age. For this sample of children, Column 2 of Table 11.9 reports that the odds of having an immunization card are substantially higher in treatment communities (39 per cent increase from a base of 11 per cent in control communities). However, there is no statistically significant

Table 11.9. Immunization outcomes (children 3 years and under)

	(1)	(2)
	Incomplete Immunization	Immunization Card
Treated village	−0.038	0.041*
	(0.030)	(0.019)
N	4372	4372
R-squared	0.195	0.096
Mean of Dep. Var. in Control Villages	0.354	0.106

Note: The symbols *, **, and *** represent significance at the 10, 5, and 1 per cent level respectively. Standard errors are reported in parentheses below the coefficient and are clustered at the village level. All specifications include social mobilization team effects. Variables are defined in Table 11.2.
Source: Authors' compilation.

Table 11.10. Incidence diarrhoea and nutritional outcomes

	(1)	(2)
	Diarrhoea	Stunting
Treated village	−0.015	0.001
	(0.026)	(0.026)
N	4372	1915
R-squared	0.035	0.005
Mean of Dep. Var. in Control Villages	0.370	0.535

Note: The symbols *, **, and *** represent significance at the 10, 5, and 1 per cent level respectively. Standard errors are reported in parentheses below the coefficient and are clustered at the village level. All specifications include social mobilization team effects. Variables are defined in Table 11.2.
Source: Authors' compilation.

Table 11.11. Wash outcomes

	(1)	(2)	(3)	(4)
	Soap		Barefoot Walking	
	Use	Saw	Adults	Children
Treated village	0.009	0.033	−0.042	−0.039
	(0.014)	(0.025)	(0.026)	(0.030)
N	5823	5823	5823	4764
R-squared	0.041	0.111	0.091	0.054
Mean of Dep. Var. in Control Villages	0.926	0.637	0.385	0.624

Note: The symbols *, **, and *** represent significance at the 10, 5, and 1 per cent level respectively. Standard errors are reported in parentheses below the coefficient and are clustered at the village level. All specifications include social mobilization team effects. Variables are defined in Table 11.2.

Source: Authors' compilation.

impact on the completeness of the immunization record in Column 1. It is worth noting that conditional on having an immunization record available, completeness rates for immunization were at 65 per cent among controls. This complements the results on LHW service provision in Table 11.7, since LHWs typically identify children eligible for immunization and work together with field workers to provide them. Table 11.10 finds no significant impact of social mobilization on the incidence of diarrhoea (Column 1) or child stunting (Column 2) in children aged three and under.[1]

Finally, Table 11.11 shows no change in the use of soap or the incidence of walking barefoot in the home or around the village. Overall, this suggests weak evidence for improvement in water and sanitation outcomes or other household health behaviours. Again, this may not be surprising as no particular investments aimed at either water and sanitation or preventative health information were made by the time the midline data were collected.

6. Conclusion

In this chapter, we assess whether social mobilization aimed at strengthening women's participation in collective action can improve the performance of public health providers even in the absence of ancillary health inputs or financing. We find little overall improvement in the quality of services

---

[1] Column 2 has fewer observations because the measure for stunting requires the age in months that was only collected at endline. There was some attrition in the sample, including an entire district (Nowshera) which could not be surveyed due to security concerns. As a check, we examine immunization outcomes and incidence of diarrhoea for this restricted sample and find similar results compared to the full sample.

provided by supra-village public providers like Basic Health Units (BHU). In contrast, we see a substantial increase in the quality of service provision by village-based skilled female health workers under the Lady Health Worker programme. BHUs cater to multiple villages in a catchment area, not all of which were organized, limiting the capacity of any one village to influence BHU level performance through any collective action measures. In comparison, the LHW's catchment area is limited to the village in which she typically resides, allowing for a more effective exercise of collective action on the part of the community in ensuring her presence and monitoring her performance.

Specifically, we find that a range of health services which fall under the purview of the LHW show a significant improvement in villages that were mobilized. This includes access to ante-natal care, post-natal care, and well-baby visits. Households in mobilized villages are also far more likely to report receiving visits from LHWs during pregnancy or reporting that they have an LHW assigned to their village. The improvement occurs in a context where there was no treatment effect on the odds of pregnant women receiving any ante-natal care, suggesting a substitution away from other public and private providers towards LHWs. This is not the case for post-natal care, where we find a sizeable increase in access to care among women in mobilized villages. Given that LHW provision of post-natal care is low at baseline, even the doubling of care by LHWs that we observe in treated villages cannot explain the overall increase in access to post-natal care. This implies a greater use of private facilities by women in mobilized villages given that there is no increase of BHU utilization.

Our results suggest that while community collective action is not a panacea for improving all levels of public service delivery, it can be quite effective in improving aspects of service delivery where community members have enforcement and monitoring capacity. The results also show that the active engagement of women in efforts to improve community collective action can have important payoffs in improved service provision targeted towards to the needs of women and young children.

References

Binka, Fred N., et al. (2007). 'Rapid Achievement of the Child Survival Millennium Development Goal: Evidence from the Navrongo Experiment in Northern Ghana.' *Tropical Medicine & International Health*, 12.5: 578–93.

Björkman, Martina, and Jakob Svensson. (2009). 'Power to the People: Evidence from a Randomized Field Experiment on Community-Based Monitoring in Uganda.' *The Quarterly Journal of Economics*, 124.2: 735–69.

Chase, Robert S., and Lynn Sherburne Benz. (2001). 'Household Effects of Community Education and Health Initiatives: Evaluating the Impact of the Zambia Social Fund.' World Bank, Washington, DC Processed.

Kling, Jeffrey R., Jeffrey B. Liebman, and Lawrence F. Katz. (2007). 'Experimental Analysis of Neighborhood Effects.' *Econometrica*, 75.1: 83–119.

Manandhar, Dharma S., et al. (2004). 'Effect of a Participatory Intervention with Women's Groups on Birth Outcomes in Nepal: Cluster-Randomised Controlled Trial.' *The Lancet*, 364.9438: 970–9.

Mansuri, Ghazala, and Vijayendra Rao. (2013). *Localizing Development: Does Participation Work?* Washington, DC: World Bank Publications.

Tripathy, Prasanta, et al. (2010). 'Effect of a Participatory Intervention with Women's Groups on Birth Outcomes and Maternal Depression in Jharkhand and Orissa, India: A Cluster-Randomised Controlled Trial.' *The Lancet*, 375.9721: 1182–92.

Part III
Laws and Cultural Norms

12

Governance and the Reversal of Women's Rights

The Case of Abortion in El Salvador

Jocelyn Viterna, José Santos Guardado Bautista,
Silvia Ivette Juarez Barrios, and Alba Evelyn Cortez[1]

1. Introduction: Analysing Rights Reversals

Regardless of whether development is defined as economic growth or as the achievement of individual capabilities, scholars overwhelmingly concur that state governance plays an important role in its promotion (Cohn 2016; see also Viterna and Robertson 2015). Nowhere is this importance more salient than in the analysis of gender and development (Fallon and Viterna 2016). In the past, state governments regularly denied women the right to vote, own property, and be educated. Still today, many states continue to use the categories of 'men' and 'women' to legislate inequalities in terms of who can marry whom, who can exercise control over their own sexual and reproductive behaviour, who can be drafted into military service, who can inherit family wealth, who can testify in court, who can wear what kinds of clothing, who can legally beat their spouse, who can receive parental leave from work, who can initiate a divorce, who can choose their marriage partner, and who can leave their home at will.

State governments also powerfully regulate gender in more indirect ways (Brush 2003). For example, states' decisions about social welfare provision define families, affect men's and women's relative power within marriages, and contribute to the formation and mobilization of gender identities (Orloff

[1] The authors thank Greg Davis, Chris Curry, Jean-Philippe Platteau, Siwan Anderson, Lori Beaman, and the participants in the UNU-WIDER Workshop on Gender and Development for their helpful comments in the development of this paper.

1993). State tax systems place differential value on paid and unpaid labour. State labour laws shape expectations and opportunities for mothers and fathers. And state health systems assign different values to different bodies when determining access to various kinds of treatment. Because of the power encapsulated in state institutions, development scholars often see states as critical arenas through which to work for improved gender equality.

Interestingly, scholars studying the relationship between states and gender equity typically imagine this relationship as unidirectional. They ask, 'How can existing institutions of governance...be reformed or redesigned to incorporate gender justice and promote gender equality and women's human rights?' (Mackay and Waylen 2014: 489), and they suggest that institutional reforms are the best way to achieve these goals. Scholars then typically measure progress by asking first whether or not institutional reforms have been implemented (e.g. Has state X adopted formal gender quotas in legislative elections, or not? Has state Y created a new institution to monitor gender mainstreaming, or not?), and second, whether or not implemented institutional reforms have achieved their desired effects (e.g. Has women's parliamentary participation increased in state X, or not? Has state Y passed more equitable legislation, or not?).

Yet inherent in these dichotomous classifications is a dichotomous assumption: states are either progressing toward gender equity, or stagnating. Social change is implicitly imagined as unidirectional; states move forward, or they do not.

But what if states' governance of gender is *not* unidirectional? What if, in addition to stagnation or progress, states also sometimes *reverse* the rights they have already granted to women? What might development scholars and practitioners miss if they study only progress and fail to examine the conditions leading to a reversal of previously granted rights?

El Salvador provides a powerful example of how states can reverse rights already granted to women. Prior to 1997, El Salvador legally allowed abortion in only three circumstances: when the pregnancy endangered the life of the mother; when the foetus had deformities incompatible with life outside the womb; and when the pregnancy was the result of sexual assault. Illegal abortions were readily available and seldom prosecuted. This situation changed dramatically in 1997, when the Legislative Assembly in El Salvador revised its criminal code to ban abortion in every circumstance, even when the pregnancy threatens a woman's life. Furthermore, in 1999, the Salvadoran Legislative Assembly passed a constitutional amendment requiring the government to protect human life from 'the moment of conception'—an amendment that makes it difficult to re-introduce even limited abortion rights in the future.

El Salvador's revised legal restrictions on abortion have profoundly and negatively affected poor women's lives. Most directly, poor women whose bodies are endangered by pregnancy are now unable to acquire the medical treatment they need—an abortion—and instead are left to die in public hospitals (Viterna and Reifenberg 2017: 8). The revised law has also had indirect consequences. After the new restrictions on abortion were passed, several institutions within the Salvadoran government became invested in prosecuting abortion 'crimes'. Today, girls who want an abortion but cannot access it are increasingly likely to commit suicide (MINSAL 2014; Moloney 2014). And remarkably, poor women who suffer miscarriages or stillbirths in El Salvador are now sometimes first charged with abortion, and then convicted of 'manslaughter' or 'aggravated homicide', and sentenced to up to forty years in prison (Agrupación 2013; Viterna and Guardado Bautista 2014, 2017; Viterna 2017).

The case of abortion in El Salvador illustrates clearly that gender rights do not simply stagnate or progress; they also reverse, and sometimes suddenly. Moreover, El Salvador is not the only country to pass new abortion restrictions in recent decades. Poland, for example, went from a country where abortion was broadly legal to a country where abortion was broadly restricted in 1993 (Kulczycki 1995). And like El Salvador, the Dominican Republic, Nicaragua, Malta, Philippines, the Vatican, and a number of sub-state regions in Mexico now ban all abortions—even those necessary to save a woman's life (United Nations 2011).[2] El Salvador is not even the only country to jail women for failing to bring a pregnancy to term: women in nations as distinct as Mexico, Rwanda, and the United States have been incarcerated for similar crimes.[3] Yet El Salvador, to our knowledge, is the only nation that regularly sentences women to thirty or forty years in prison for 'murdering' their stillborn children. As such, it provides an extreme case that is especially well suited to hypothesis generation (Gerring 2007).

Using the extreme case of El Salvador, this chapter asks: How might identifying and investigating reversals in gender rights improve our understanding of gender, development, and state governance? We have theories about how states progress toward more equitable governance of gender, but these theories tend to contrast progression with non-progression, and hence confound stagnations and reversals. We do not at present have theoretical tools to

---

[2] Chile was included in this list prior to 19 July 2017, when the state legislature voted to permit abortion in very limited circumstances (the courts ruled that the law was constitutional on 21 August 2017). Note, too, that the criminal code in Honduras does not allow abortion under any circumstances, although the Code of Medical Ethics allows abortion when pregnancy endangers a woman's life. In Haiti, laws do not expressly allow an abortion to save the life of the mother, but the principles of the law have been interpreted to allow therapeutic abortion. See www.un.org/esa/population/publications/2011abortion/2011wallchart.pdf for details.

[3] On the USA, see Paltrow 2013, Paltrow and Flavin 2013; on Mexico, see Pain et al. 2014, Gaestel and Shelley 2014; on Chile, see Casas-Becerra 1997; on Nepal, see Ramaseshan 1997; on Rwanda, see Filipovic 2015.

understand why reversals happen, or how consequential they might be. Nor do we understand whether the factors leading to reversals in one area of governance might challenge progress in other areas, or conversely, actually co-exist with, or even support, progress in other realms. Looking at reversals thus not only opens our analytical lens to the full range of possible transformations in state governance (reversals, stagnations, and progress), but also requires scholars to better operationalize the multifaceted nature of state governance. In investigating a single case study, this chapter does not provide generalizable results, but rather it develops an argument for why gender rights reversals should be studied by development scholars, and it generates hypotheses to be tested in future studies.

In the pages that follow, we first investigate the historical socio-political context that gave rise to the abortion rights reversal in El Salvador. We then examine the law's effects in the lives of four women, paying particular attention to how the multifaceted failures of state governance in El Salvador exacerbated the negative consequences of the legislative regression. We conclude by outlining how studying *rights reversals* as distinct phenomena from *rights stagnations* may improve our scholarly understanding of the relationship between gender and development more broadly.

2. Data

Studying the historical development of El Salvador's total abortion ban, and its consequences, is complicated by a lack of data. There are no history books that document why this particular legislation was passed at this particular moment in Salvadoran history, or why it has been enforced with such vigour. Nor can we simply look at statistics on maternal mortality to understand the magnitude of the health problem because, according to the Salvadoran doctors interviewed, the state's maternal mortality numbers hide the true nature of the abortion problem by failing to document when a pregnancy exacerbated the illness that was the cause of a woman's death. For example, if a pregnant woman was diagnosed with cancer and doctors withheld chemotherapy from that woman for fear of damaging the foetus in her womb, when the woman died the documented cause of death would be cancer. The fact that her treatment was withheld because of an absolute ban on abortion, which leaves doctors fearful of doing anything that might 'kill' a foetus, has, doctors believe, previously not been captured in statistics.[4] And likewise, although it is relatively easy to document the number of women imprisoned

---

[4] Recent changes in how the World Health Organization recommends 'counting' maternal mortality may make statistics more reliable in the near future.

for the 'aggravated homicide' or 'unintentional aggravated homicide' of their newborns, it is much more difficult to access the hundreds of pages of court documents for each case to analyse whether the state's evidence actually supports such a conviction (that is, whether a woman really did murder her newborn), or whether the woman appears to have suffered a naturally occurring miscarriage or stillbirth. It is even more difficult to gain access to the affected women for interviews, as the Salvadoran state severely limits visiting rights to individuals that have been imprisoned.

As a result, our analysis triangulates information from multiple data sources, including an analysis of twenty-five years of newspaper articles from the major daily in El Salvador, *El Diario de Hoy*; a local NGO's count of cases where women were tried and imprisoned for the murder of a 'newborn'; in-depth analysis of court cases from twenty individuals (including consultation with specialists in forensic pathology, obstetrics, and gynaecology and with legal scholars to ensure accurate interpretation of the data); and interviews with thirteen Salvadoran doctors, three officials in the Salvadoran Ministry of Health, activists from four women's organizations, eight deputies in the Legislative assembly, and fourteen women currently or formerly incarcerated for aggravated homicide or attempted aggravated homicide of their newborns.[5]

3. The Historical Path to Rights Reversals in El Salvador

What are the likely causes of rights reversals for women? Although we anticipate that there are several possible paths that countries may follow, we believe that El Salvador's reversal stemmed from a moral panic generated by the Salvadoran economic elite and strengthened by transnational events, and from the resulting incentivization of local institutions to prosecute marginalized women.

South African sociologist, Stanley Cohen, introduced the idea of 'moral panic' to describe a kind of collective hysteria that can erupt, especially when societies undergo a period of upheaval that threatens to transform traditional power relations (Cohen 1972). Moral panics work to re-impose a traditional social order by targeting as 'villains' or 'folk devils' the very marginalized group that appears to be gaining power in the transitional moment.[6]

---

[5] This number includes an interview with one formerly incarcerated woman's parents, since the woman herself died in prison.

[6] Labelling something a 'moral panic' does not mean that the thing has never happened but, rather, that the extent and significance of the thing has been wildly exaggerated. For example, one could suggest that some areas of the United States are currently experiencing a moral panic about (white) women being raped by immigrants. To label this a 'panic' does not suggest that no women have ever been raped by an immigrant, but rather that both the perception of and the response to the problem are wildly out of proportion to its actual extent.

According to Cohen, states often respond to moral panics by proposing highly punitive laws and stricter enforcement.

We argue that a moral panic about 'killer mothers' erupted in El Salvador in the mid-1990s, just as the nation was experiencing a powerful transitional moment. El Salvador has a long history of extreme inequality, with a relatively few individuals historically controlling the vast majority of the nation's land, wealth, and power (Dunkerley 1982). In 1980, a socialist-inspired guerrilla army, the FMLN (Frente Farabundo Martí para la Liberación Nacional), declared war against the elite-controlled, and USA-backed, Salvadoran state to challenge both the extreme economic inequalities in the nation and the violent military actions that the state was using to maintain those inequalities. The FMLN never overthrew the ruling government but, after twelve years of fighting, it won significant concessions through a United Nations-brokered Peace Accord. Specifically, the 1992 Accord conferred formal status on the FMLN as a political party, initiated a land redistribution programme, reduced the size and political power of the military, encouraged a revision of the existing legal code, and scheduled competitive elections for 1994.

Prior to 1992, abortion did not seem to be on the public agenda. From 1989 to the end of 1992, there was not a single reference to local-level abortion issues or activism in *El Diario de Hoy*.[7] Anti-abortion editorials only began to appear in the newspapers in 1992 but, even then, political parties seemed to give the issue limited attention.

However, in 1994, the situation changed dramatically. This was the year of the first post-Peace Accord election in El Salvador, and the first time the traditional political and economic elite of the country had been required to share the Legislative Assembly with the very leftist insurgents they had been battling. This was also the year that the United Nations held its Population Conference in Cairo, a conference that Pope John Paul II claimed was the First World's attempt to force abortion on poor countries in order to control their populations. As the anti-abortion groups in El Salvador increasingly adopted the Pope's rhetoric as their own, and as the local Catholic Church increasingly lent its voice to the anti-abortion agenda, right-wing political groups also began to engage with the topic. Indeed, as the right-wing parties realized how effectively the anti-abortion rhetoric allowed them to demonize the new FMLN party, it became a central campaign issue. The FMLN had not only promoted gender-equitable policies during its twelve years as a guerrilla movement, but it had also encouraged (and even required) women's

---

[7] Abortion was only mentioned as a sidebar during these years. Specifically, *El Diario* regularly reported on Pope John Paul II's anti-abortion speeches during his tours of other parts of the world, but these reports mentioned abortion only in passing as the topic of the Pope's speech, not as a topic of interest in itself. More typically, these articles focused on providing human interest information about the city in which the Pope was speaking.

participation in such gender-bending activities as guerrilla warfare (Viterna 2013). Arguing against abortion rights allowed the Right to frame itself as the defender of traditional social norms—the protectors of unborn babies, women's chastity, and the sanctity of families against anti-free market, anti-family, anti-religion, pro-violence, pro-feminist Communists—without having to seriously engage the Left's proposals for transforming the nation's rampant poverty.

The importance of abortion for El Salvador's national identity was intensified by two UN conferences: the 1994 World Population Conference in Cairo, and the 1995 World Conference on Women in Beijing. While both of these are heralded by scholars and practitioners as watershed moments for promoting women's rights around the world, in El Salvador these conferences largely served to solidify the power of the Christian Right. Specifically, El Salvador chose as its representative its new first lady, Elizabeth Calderon del Sol. A member of the economic elite, a representative of the right-wing party ARENA, and an outspoken opponent of abortion, Calderon del Sol was celebrated in *El Diario* for vocally 'defending El Salvador's sovereignty' at these conferences, and ensuring that no transnational legislation was passed that would 'force' legal abortion on El Salvador. The newspaper noted with pride that Calderon del Sol was the only Latin American representative assigned to the committee that drafted the final conference declaration in 1994. Pope John Paul II even made statements praising Calderon del Sol's leadership role in countering what he saw as 'pro-abortion' initiatives at the United Nations. The Pope's praise was highlighted with pride by Salvadoran news outlets, likely reinforcing many Salvadorans' understanding of their nation as a recognized and esteemed international leader in the anti-abortion movement.

By 1997, the year of the second post-Peace Accord election, the anti-abortion movement in El Salvador had been largely institutionalized in the Foundation Yes to Life (Fundación Sí a la Vida), an organization that was regularly spotlighted in the media for its anti-abortion activism. It was in this year that the Foundation presented a formal request to the legislative assembly that its revised criminal code not allow any exceptions to abortion—even for the life or health of the pregnant woman. The Foundation then launched a powerful media campaign to educate Salvadoran society on the 'horrors of abortion'. The Catholic Church was a powerful ally; it mobilized thousands of schoolchildren from parochial schools and bussed them to the Legislative Assembly to rally in favour of the total abortion ban (Mejía 1997), while the Archbishop of San Salvador, Fernando Sáenz Lacalle, publicly compared abortion to the 'Nazi death camps' (Garcia 1997). Other high-status individuals also joined the cause: professional organizations like doctors' unions issued statements in favour of the total ban (Galdamez and Joma 1996), and the new (right-wing) minister of health claimed that, regardless of what law was eventually passed, he and his doctors would refuse to practise abortions for any reason in public hospitals in El Salvador (*El Diario de Hoy* 1997).

The FMLN initially presented a united position in favour of maintaining legal abortion in limited circumstances, but it did not have enough party votes to prevent the absolute abortion ban from becoming law. Immediately after the absolute ban was passed, Archbishop Lacalle sent a letter to the legislative assembly saying that it was not enough to reform the criminal code; the country also needed to amend the constitution to define life as beginning at conception (Duarte 1997). The right-wing party ARENA responded by immediately proposing a foetal personhood amendment and using its legislative majority to pass the first of the two votes needed to approve the amendment. The FMLN again voted en bloc against the amendment, even though it again did not have enough votes to prevent its passage.

Despite their professed concern to protect unborn life, ARENA deputies nevertheless waited two years before putting the second constitutional amendment vote on the agenda. Their strategy was clear: they introduced the issue immediately prior to the 1999 presidential election, so that the FMLN would again be forced to defend abortion rights publicly at a critical campaign moment. This tendency of the Right to launch major pro-life campaigns only in election years lends credence to the argument that, in the face of a social transformation that made it difficult for the Right to use its earlier methods of maintaining power, right-wing politicians and activists were fomenting a moral panic about abortion to gain political power through elections. Legislative elections in El Salvador occur every three years, and presidential elections every five. The abortion issue had erupted in 1994, during the first post-war presidential and legislative elections, and again in 1997, during the second post-war legislative election. As a result, the FMLN had a difficult choice to make in 1999. FMLN deputies were certain that the abortion issue had damaged their outcomes in the previous elections and a show in favour of abortion at this moment would lessen not only their opportunity to win the executive office in 1999, but also their chance to increase their legislative representation in the 2000 election. Consequently, the FMLN decided to drop its party-wide support of limited abortion rights, and allow individual deputies to 'vote their conscience'. As a result, the personhood amendment was passed in 1999, the large majority of FMLN members voting in its favour.

By the turn of the century, we argue, a generation of right-wing state personnel had come to power in large part by stoking a moral panic about abortion, and defining themselves as defenders of the unborn. The Chief of Police, the Attorney General, the Minister of Health, the Ombudsman for Human Rights, and many deputies and mayors had now adopted strong, public, anti-abortion stances. However, when the usual target of their anti-abortion attacks—the FMLN—agreed to their legislative demands in 1999, these political leaders did not declare 'mission accomplished' and cease their activism. Rather, they appear to have looked for a new target that would allow them to maintain their politically lucrative anti-abortion agenda. The new target they identified, it appears, was the 'evil' mothers who would 'murder' their own children through abortion and infanticide.

The adoption of this new target is illustrated in *El Diario* articles. Whereas anti-abortion articles in the 1990s focused on attacking the UN, the FMLN, and feminists, the articles from 2000 onward began to adopt a new villain: the evil mother. To illustrate, one 2001 article, titled 'Crimes without Punishment', begins:

> The numbers of newborns being thrown into latrines, trash receptacles, or vacant lots by their own mothers is alarming. Very few children are able to survive this misfortune. The authorities need to capture these women red-handed to process them for aggravated homicide, but to the contrary, these crimes never come to light and are given complete immunity. (Garcia 2001a)

Another 2001 article, 'Stories of Hearts of Stone', states: 'They are human beings who only lived the nine months that they were in their mothers' wombs. Upon birth, they await the sweet hands of a mother, but what they find instead are the talons of soulless women' (Garcia 2001b). It was also at this time that prominent state officials began speaking publicly about their work to prosecute mothers who would 'murder' their own babies through abortion or infanticide. Of note, these two terms—abortion and murder—began to be used interchangeably in the statements made by these public officials (Viterna and Guardado Bautista 2017).

The media's new assault on 'evil mothers' paralleled a similar transformation in state institutions. According to our respondents, shortly after the 1999 constitutional amendment, the Attorney General's office began advising public hospitals of their legal obligation to report to the authorities any woman suspected of inducing an abortion. Medical staff we talked to had been uniformly taught that anyone who did not report a woman with signs of a provoked abortion would themselves be in danger of arrest as an 'accomplice' to abortion. One respondent even noted that, in about 1999, all hospitals were instructed to post the phone numbers of the Attorney General's office and the national police by their telephones to incentivize the reporting of suspected abortions, and that they received a pamphlet that outlined their responsibility to denounce such women.

The increased pressure on medical staff to report abortions dovetailed with another, less intentional, institutional change. Specifically, rates of criminal violence in El Salvador have escalated dramatically since the end of the civil war. Prosecutors working in the homicide division of the Attorney General's office often have around 500 cases on their desks at any given time, and they are often asked to pursue cases against violent gang members, who, it is rumoured, routinely threaten prosecutors or their families with violence if their case is pursued. Prosecutors are also sometimes asked to prosecute defendants with financial resources: individuals who can engage skilled defence attorneys from the private sector, as well as pay for expert witnesses and even forensic examinations, which makes prosecution especially difficult for the poorly resourced state prosecutors. Given the institutional pressure put on these state officers to process cases and to meet monthly quotas, it is perhaps not surprising that women like those described below are processed much more quickly than are others awaiting trial (Viterna and Guardado Bautista 2014). The women themselves are already vilified in the media as baby-killers; they have no economic or criminal power, and so cannot threaten the prosecutor, much less carry out such threats; they are obliged to use state-provided defence attorneys, who do little to prepare for their cases; and the 'evidence' against these women—the body of the dead infant—is typically easy to find as 'proof' of their guilt, in contrast to the many people who are 'disappeared' by gang violence. For these reasons, prosecutors likely find the cases of marginalized women highly attractive from a prosecutorial standpoint. The conditions of the country may therefore intersect powerfully with the political campaign against abortion to incentivize Salvadoran state institutions to prosecute—quickly and harshly—impoverished women.

In the above history, we examined the socio-political processes behind the adoption of the total abortion ban in El Salvador. Specifically, we argued that in a moment of extreme political uncertainty, the political elite in El Salvador utilized narratives about 'abortion as murder' to generate a moral panic and secure their positions as political leaders of the nation. This is demonstrated by the success of this narrative in maintaining the Right's political popularity in the years following the transition, and by the regular timing of the Right's anti-abortion campaigns to coincide with national elections. We have further argued that the Pope's public recognition of El Salvador as an anti-abortion leader at UN conferences may have solidified 'protectors of the unborn' as a key component of Salvadoran national identity. And finally, we have noted that the institutions tasked with enforcing the new abortion law were incentivized to do so both directly (through pressure from political leaders and the media to prosecute 'evil mothers') and indirectly (because impoverished women who have suffered obstetrical emergencies are easier to prosecute than violent gang members or people with resources). Next, we look at the consequences of these legal and institutional transitions in four women's lives.

4. Four Women's Stories

4.1. *Estela (2017)*

Estela,[8] a Salvadoran mother of three, was pregnant with her fourth child when she began having chest pains and extreme shortness of breath. Her local doctors diagnosed a chronic cardiovascular problem and referred her to the National Women's Hospital in El Salvador—the facility best equipped to treat pregnancy complications. When women become pregnant, the volume of blood in their bodies increases by 50 per cent, requiring their hearts to work harder. As a result, it is not unusual for pregnant women to become aware of chronic heart problems that had not been evident before. Indeed, Estela had delivered three children vaginally, without complications, prior to this pregnancy. Nevertheless, by the time Estela arrived at the national hospital with her fourth pregnancy, her 'maternal cardiovascular risk' was what the World Health Organization's guidelines classify as level IV, which indicates an 'extremely high risk of maternal mortality or severe morbidity'. The recommended treatment is pregnancy termination (European Society of Gynecology 2011: 3158). Estela was twenty weeks pregnant. The doctors at the National Hospital for Women explained the situation to Estela, and she and her family all expressed a clear desire to interrupt the pregnancy, even though the foetus could not survive such a premature birth. Nevertheless, the hospital leadership decided that the recommended procedure would put the doctors in danger of incarceration for performing an illegal abortion. They thus decided to transfer Estela to a different hospital better equipped to monitor her cardiac condition. At twenty-six weeks, Estela went into labour, and was returned to the Women's Hospital. She delivered a 700 g baby via caesarean. Both Estela and the baby died shortly after delivery, leaving Estela's three children without their mother.

4.2. *Manuela (2008)*

Manuela,[9] a single mother of two living in extreme poverty, had been abandoned by her *compañero* seven years earlier. In 2008, Manuela walked the 3 km distance to her local health clinic three times to discuss how ill she was feeling. In addition to experiencing extreme tiredness and nausea, she was concerned about several masses growing on the side of her neck. The local health clinic

---

[8] Estela is a pseudonym. This case was reported to the first author by two separate doctors, in two separate, anonymized, interviews.

[9] Manuela is a pseudonym. The data for this case are a 2017 report by the Inter-American Commission on Human Rights (IACHR), copies of Manuela's court documents, communication with a doctor who researched the case for IACHR, and an interview by the first author with Manuela's parents.

did not have a qualified doctor on its staff at the time, and the medical practitioners who saw Manuela not only failed to diagnose the serious disease behind her symptoms—lymphoma—but also failed to realize that she was pregnant. Instead, during the first two visits, they told Manuela that she was suffering from gastritis, and both times they prescribed the same wholly inadequate treatment: 500 mg of amoxicillin every eight hours, and 500 mg of acetaminophen every six hours. It is unclear whether Manuela herself knew she was pregnant. Later, when Manuela was approximately seven months pregnant, she began to experience powerful abdominal cramps. Perhaps thinking she was having another attack of 'gastritis', she went to the pit toilet located down a steep hill behind her home. There, she experienced a precipitate and premature birth of what forensic evidence indicates was a stillborn baby. Manuela passed out from the loss of blood. When she regained consciousness, she pulled herself back up the steep terrain to her humble, dirt-floor home. Her mother found her there a short while later, lying in a pool of blood and fading in and out of consciousness. Her mother convinced a neighbour with a truck to take Manuela to the same clinic that had missed her pregnancy and misdiagnosed her lymphoma on earlier occasions. Upon realizing that she had given birth, the clinic called the police. The police originally arrested Manuela for abortion, but by the time her case went to trial, the charge had become aggravated homicide. She was sentenced to thirty years in prison.

Manuela's legal rights were systematically violated throughout the course of her treatment and trial. The practitioner who treated Manuela at the clinic at the time of her medical emergency wrote on her medical chart that the pregnancy was from an 'infidelity', given that Manuela's *compañero* had abandoned her seven years earlier. The police interrogated Manuela in the hospital without first reading Manuela her rights, and without allowing her legal representation. Manuela's illiterate parents were also interrogated. The police threatened Manuela's mother that she, too, could go to jail as an accomplice if Manuela did not admit to the crime. Her father was asked to sign a paper that he was told would help his daughter, but which was actually a statement condemning her. He signed with a thumbprint, because he had never learned to write his name. The doctor who had performed the autopsy claimed that the infant had been born alive and had been suffocated in the latrine, but used a discredited examination to claim that there had been a live birth and offered no evidence of suffocation. Indeed, the doctor's own report notes that the oesophagus and the lungs of the dead foetus were free of debris, casting significant doubt on his own conclusions. The Office of Legal Medicine insisted that the grandparents take on additional debt by travelling to the local municipality and paying to register both the birth and the death of the foetus—actions not required for stillborn babies. Manuela refused to sign any of the documents the police gave her—not her supposed confession, nor her acceptance of the state-assigned lawyer—yet she was imprisoned anyway, as the court documents argued that she was caught *'en flagrancia'* of aggravated homicide. It was not until a year after her arrest that Manuela was finally diagnosed with lymphoma. She was given a treatment schedule by her doctor, but the prison regularly missed taking her to hospital for treatment. In January 2010, when she was gravely ill, she was finally admitted to hospital, where she died in April 2010. She had not seen her children since she had been arrested, more than two years before.

4.3. *Carmen (2007)*

Originally from a rural zone, eighteen-year-old Carmen[10] was working as a domestic employee in an urban area of El Salvador in October 2007. The oldest of nine children, she had been working full time since she was twelve years old to help her mother cover household expenses, given that her father had abandoned them. She had never had a boyfriend, and she had never before been pregnant. She earned $80 per month.[11]

Nine months earlier, Carmen had been raped by a neighbour of her employer. She had left that job to avoid continuing to see her rapist, and soon afterwards, while working in her new job, realized she was pregnant. When she began to have labour pains, she asked her new employer, a woman who was currently separated from the father of her child, for the salary she was due so that she could travel to her family and get help with the birth. Her employer said no, presumably because she did not have the money to pay Carmen. That night, in the bed in her small room, Carmen self-birthed her son. She reports that he whimpered a few times and died in her arms. Carmen passed out, bleeding profusely. According to Carmen, when her employer opened the door the next morning and saw her lying in blood, with a dead infant at her side, she simply closed the door and walked away in horror. She nevertheless asked Carmen to care for her (the employer's) own child while she was at work. At about one o'clock in the afternoon, the employer returned and, according to Carmen, said she was going to take Carmen to the hospital to avoid having 'two deaths' in the household. By the time they arrived at the hospital, the employer's own testimony notes that Carmen was fading in and out of consciousness. The employer told the doctors that she did not know what was wrong with Carmen, and that Carmen had only told her she was experiencing a 'heavy menstruation'. When the doctors told the employer

---

[10] The data for this case are Carmen's court documents, and an interview between Carmen and the first and second author.

[11] For comparison, in 2015, the minimum wage in an El Salvador textile factory was $250 per month.

that Carmen had just given birth, the employer denied knowing that Carmen was even pregnant. The hospital reported Carmen to the authorities.

What happened next is difficult to determine because the court documents are filled with contradictions. Although Carmen states that the infant's cadaver was left lying on her bed in plain sight, and that she herself told the doctor at the hospital where to find it (a story corroborated by one version of the court documents), and although all the court documents concur that Carmen's room was no larger than a small closet, the police nevertheless report requiring much time, and several searches, to find the cadaver. Some documents say that it was the employer herself who found the body; other documents say that it was the employer's ex-partner, and father of her child; still others say that the police accompanied the ex-partner to the house, where they found the body together. Indeed, the court documents could not even agree on whether the plastic bag in which the baby was supposedly found, 'hidden' under the bed, came from the 'Despensa de Don Juan' store or the 'Super Selectos' store. Nor is there any explanation of why so many searches by so many people were required to find a cadaver that in the end was reportedly found directly under the bed in the tiny room where the birth occurred. Only upon interviewing Carmen years later, and learning that the employer's ex-partner was also a police officer, do we begin to make sense of the conflicting reports. It appears that the police provided contradictory information because they were not telling the truth, but rather inventing stories to try to corroborate the employer's false story. By making it appear that Carmen was trying to hide the dead infant, they would help to exonerate their fellow officer's ex-partner, and mother of his child, from responsibility for the baby's death.

Despite the extensive contamination of the scene from multiple people 'looking' for the baby, the autopsy reported 'no external or internal evidence of trauma' on the foetus. The forensic doctor listed the cause of foetal death as 'undetermined', and concluded: 'with the available studies completed, it is not possible to determine the cause of death.'

The autopsy also included several inconsistencies that the forensic doctor never attempted to explain. First, the baby's measurements were given as 52 cm tall, 2,500 g in weight, with a plantar foot length of 5 cm. Generally speaking, these measures correspond to the height of a foetus in its ninth month of gestation, the weight of a foetus in its seventh or eighth month of gestation, and the foot length of a foetus in only its fifth month of gestation; such discordant measurements suggest that the foetus was not getting the nutrients it needed to develop properly while in the womb. Second, the foetal autopsy lists in the Histopathology Report indicate that the infant's heart suffered from 'vascular congestion'. Third, the autopsy notes that the umbilical cord did not have the correct number of arteries connecting the mother to the baby, a condition associated with stillbirths. And finally, despite the fact that the autopsy clearly states that the cause of death was 'undetermined' and that there were 'no signs of trauma to the baby's body', either externally or internally, the autopsy nevertheless classified the 'type of death' as 'violent'. Legal Medicine never provided any reasoning for this classification at any point in the trial.

In the end, the sentencing judge provided only one rationale for Carmen's guilty verdict: he argued that Carmen must have been guilty of homicide because she hid the pregnancy and lied about the birth to her employer. In other words, the judge clearly accepted the employer's testimony as truth, despite the employer's clear incentive to misrepresent the situation. In an earlier statement, a different judge had also attributed guilt to Carmen because she did not seek medical help during the child's birth. Taken together, these judges justified their guilty verdicts solely on their contention that Carmen did not act appropriately at the moment of the birth.

Remarkably, at the moment in the statement where the judge is expected to discuss the 'action' for which Carmen is condemned, he simply writes the word 'action', making it clear that the judge himself has no idea what Carmen supposedly did to warrant a homicide verdict:

> ACTION: In accordance with the evidence obtained in the present case it is determined that the defendant, CARMEN, performed *an action* that affected a legally protected life, given that the defendant actively produced the death of a NEWBORN, who was her son, thereby causing irreparable harm [our emphasis]

Carmen was sentenced to thirty years in prison for allegedly committing an unspecified, unknown, and unmotivated action that somehow resulted in the 'violent' death of her newborn child, all without leaving any marks on its tiny body. During the course of the trial, any evidence that would have supported Carmen's version of the events—the unexplained abnormalities in the foetal body, the likely effects of severe haemorrhaging on her mental state, the fact that she was prevented from getting help by her employer, the intimate relationship between her employer and the police officer who examined the scene of the crime—were simply never presented.

4.4. *Maria Teresa (2011)*

In November 2011, twenty-eight-year-old Maria Teresa[12] lived with her six-year-old son and his paternal grandparents in a corrugated metal shack located in a poor, urban barrio. Her son's father had abandoned them years before, but she continued to live with and care for his elderly parents. Maria Teresa

---

[12] Maria Teresa's story is compiled from her court documents, from observing one trial proceedings, and from interviews with two of Maria Teresa's neighbours, her mother-in-law, and Maria Teresa herself. Her story was also reported by the authors in the *Health and Human Rights Journal* (see Viterna and Guardado Bautista 2017).

worked in a factory during the day, ironing labels onto clothes with a heavy press. On evenings and weekends, she supplemented her factory income by picking up small jobs cleaning houses and washing clothes. Maria Teresa did not realize she was pregnant from a brief relationship that had ended months earlier; she was still experiencing regular vaginal bleeding, which she had interpreted as her monthly period, and her stomach never grew. Nor was she the only one who missed the pregnancy. Neither her neighbours nor her family members had noticed a growing belly. Extraordinarily, Maria Teresa had also visited the doctor multiple times in the previous months because she was experiencing sharp pains in her back, and not even the doctors recognized that she was pregnant. At one point, the doctors diagnosed Maria Teresa with a bladder infection, a condition known to cause pregnancy complications. Later, when the back pains became so severe that Maria Teresa could barely walk or stand and had to miss several days of work at the factory, the doctors prescribed injections three times a day with what Maria Teresa believes was Diclofenac, a drug that is not recommended for pregnant women. Maria Teresa asked a neighbour to inject her while she was at home, and a nurse at the factory clinic injected her at midday when she returned to her strenuous job there.

After more than a month of three-times-daily injections, Maria Teresa woke one night with a strong thirst. She left her small shack to get a drink from their only source of water—an outdoor spigot—but was interrupted by a strong urge to defecate. She quickly entered the pit latrine outside their home where, to her horror, she felt a 'little ball' fall out of her body. She cried out for help, and then passed out in a pool of blood. Maria Teresa's mother-in-law heard the fall and called an ambulance. When Maria Teresa arrived at the hospital, she was in hypovolemic shock. Realizing she had given birth, the doctors reported Maria Teresa to the police for suspected abortion. The state's attorney upgraded the charge to aggravated homicide. Although the autopsy data indicated that the foetus likely died in utero and was then expelled, the judge nevertheless found Maria Teresa guilty and sentenced her to forty years in prison. In his statement, the judge reasoned that Maria Teresa had been pregnant before, so she must have known she was pregnant this time. She therefore must have been hiding her pregnancy, waiting to 'carry out her criminal plan within the area of her household, looking for a moment during which there weren't any other persons around to carry out this homicide'.

4.5. *Putting the Cases in Context*

The four cases outlined above are not isolated events. Given the paucity of statistics, it is unclear how many women, like Estela, have died from their inability to access a therapeutic abortion, although the doctors we interviewed stated that they are never allowed to interrupt a pregnancy when the foetus still has a heartbeat—not even when women are in grave danger of death. Data on women's incarceration are somewhat easier to discover. Specifically, a local women's organization has found and documented thirty-five cases to date where women who appear to have suffered an obstetrical emergency of some sort have been convicted of attempted aggravated homicide or aggravated homicide of their newborns. Many, like Maria Teresa, Carmen, and Manuela, were initially charged with abortion, and only had the charges upgraded to 'homicide' during the course of the trial. At the time of writing, such convictions continue at an average rate of one or two per year; the most recent was in July 2017, when nineteen-year-old Evelyn was sentenced to thirty years for birthing what appears to have been a stillborn baby into the pit toilet behind her house (Viterna 2017). We have reviewed court documentation from twenty of these thirty-five cases, and we have spoken directly with thirteen of the women who received convictions, plus the family of Manuela. Although we do not have space to review the cases here, we note that in every case, the total abortion ban's effects were exacerbated by failures of the state in other areas of women's lives:

- **Protection from abject poverty:** In all but one of the cases we reviewed, the prosecuted women were living in poverty, a poverty often exacerbated because either their fathers or their partners had abandoned them, leaving them or their mothers with many children to feed, and no state support for child care or education, which would facilitate employment. Poverty is highly correlated with premature delivery, foetal birth defects, and poor foetal growth, likely because women without economic resources are more likely to suffer from malnutrition, more likely to be exposed to environmental toxins through their workplace or neighbourhoods, and less likely to be enrolled in pre-natal care or to have the resources they require to access health care when needed.

- **Protection from child labour:** Many women, like Carmen, were sent to work outside the home from as young as twelve years old. These youngsters were often sent to work in isolating situations, such as living and working inside an employer's home, or picking coffee in remote areas of plantations, which left them vulnerable to abuse.

- **Protection from abusive labour conditions:** Many incarcerated women, like Carmen, worked as domestic labourers, where they were paid paltry amounts, worked constantly from the moment they woke up until the moment they went to sleep, failed to receive pay, and often were extremely limited in their ability to physically leave the household without their employer's permission.

- **Protection from violence:** At least eight of the twenty women whose cases we reviewed became pregnant because of a rape; at least two suffered from routine and brutal violence by their male partners.

271

- **Guarantee of education:** Most of the women incarcerated for abortion-related 'crimes' had little or no educational attainment. This lack of education in some cases restricted the women's ability to recognize that they had become pregnant. It also lessened their capacity to defend themselves in court, as they often were unable to read their own trial documents; nor had they been educated as to their right to due process.

- **Guarantee of health care:** Many of the women were held responsible for not realizing they were pregnant, when the very state-provided medical staff from whom they sought help also did not realize they were pregnant and may even have prescribed treatments that exacerbated the conditions leading to stillbirths. At the moment of medical emergency, the staff that treated the women failed to note even the most basic of information that would help the courts determine whether a medical emergency had occurred (information like blood pressure, body temperature, and the condition of the placenta), and sometimes even inscribed a woman's guilt onto her medical chart. As noted above, Manuela's doctor wrote in her file that she was pregnant 'from an infidelity'; in another case, someone wrote in a chart that a woman 'apparently threw away her baby'. In none of these cases was doctor–patient confidentiality respected.

- **Guarantee of due process:** As noted above, these women were convicted despite a lack of evidence that any crime had been committed. The pressure that the anti-abortion movement had put on public institutions to prosecute women who 'murdered' their own babies through abortion, the prosecuting attorneys' quotas that incentivized pursuing the most socially marginalized individuals, and the willingness of police and investigating attorneys to believe the statements of relatively wealthy employers rather than those of their impoverished domestic employees, all exacerbated a system that already lacked the expertise and resources to provide due process to individuals charged with a crime.

It is important to note that, according to our interviews, women with financial means can still access abortions, therapeutic or otherwise, by attending private clinics. It is only women who are already marginalized by the state in these other ways who must also risk their lives by going to a public hospital when they suffer complicated pregnancies or births.

5. Discussion

We began this chapter by asking whether the reversal of women's rights is a different social and political phenomenon from the stagnation of women's rights. We investigated this question first by documenting the historical process by which abortion rights were reversed in El Salvador, and then by examining the consequences of that reversal for women's lives. We are now in a position to draw conclusions.

First, rights reversals are indeed different from rights stagnations and, as such, merit analysis by scholars of gender and development. Newly restrictive laws differ from restrictive laws that have been on the books for decades, because new reversals are often put in place through a powerful mobilization of political will and public opinion. This mobilization likely ensures that new laws are in the public eye and emphatically enforced in a way that long-existing laws are not. Moreover, once political parties and their leaders have gained power by tying their political careers to the pursuit of a rights reversal, then those same political players will have a vested interest in maintaining the reversal, and thus their political careers, in the future. These processes suggest that rights reversals are harder to change than rights stagnations.

Second, scholars have already pointed to the 'gap' that exists between laws on the books and laws in practice (Gould and Barclay 2012). Even when progressive laws are written, these scholars argue, whether and how they are actually enforced depends largely on decisions made by 'street-level bureau-crats' who incorporate their personal ideas and beliefs into their work activ-ities (Lipsky 2010). For example, new laws against gender-based violence may not make an actual difference in women's lives because the specific police officers tasked with enforcing the laws may choose to ignore women's claims of spousal abuse, or because judges who believe that all men have the right to punish their wives may choose not to prosecute such crimes. Intriguingly, the case of abortion in El Salvador demonstrates that this same gap between laws and enforcement can affect regressive, not just progressive, legislation. However, when regressive laws are passed, street-level bureaucrats exercise their discretion toward *harsher* prosecution than what is legislated, rather than the reverse. As the cases above demonstrate, when women are thought to be 'baby-killers', Salvadoran state officials are willing to 'manufacture' guilt even when no evidence of guilt exists, and to extend initial charges of abor-tion to homicide, with its higher penalties. Importantly, it is only a certain kind of woman who is targeted by the hyper-application of the abortion ban: poor, poorly educated, exposed to violence, reliant on public health care, and isolated from networks of social support. Critically, the fact that the hyper-prosecution of these laws in El Salvador continued even after the FMLN came to power suggests that the norms and practices of hyper-prosecution are now firmly institutionalized in the practices of state personnel. Such institutional-ization is evident in the medical schools in El Salvador, which no longer train doctors to perform abortions, even though in certain cases this is the indicated treatment to save a woman's life; in the hospitals, where doctors are advised from their intern year onward of the requirement to report suspected abortions;

in police forces, which now have protocols for examining the 'crime scene' of a woman's uterus; in the Office of Forensic Medicine, where specialists have been trained to use faulty tests to 'prove' the live birth of an infant, and to suggest that proving live birth is somehow sufficient to also prove homicide; and among judges, who have now established numerous precedents for finding women guilty of murder only because they supposedly did not do enough to ensure that their foetus was born healthy. The institutionalization of such over-enforcement practices demonstrates for us the most worrisome consequence of rights reversals. It is quite likely that, at some point in the future, limited abortion rights will be re-legalized in El Salvador. However, even when the law is changed, it is difficult to imagine that the accompanying institutional practices—practices that have been consistently employed by state employees over the last twenty years and that closely align with the moral panic about homicidal mothers in El Salvador—will be transformed.

Third, state failures in other areas of women's lives compound the potential negative consequences of rights reversals. The great majority of women prosecuted for the 'murder' of their newborns were already in precarious positions due to their lack of economic well-being, lack of formal education, lack of power in the workplace, lack of protection from violence, and lack of quality medical care. If the Salvadoran government had provided better protection for women in any one of these other areas of state provision, the likelihood of suffering hyper-prosecution from this particular rights reversal would have been lower. We therefore suggest that the greater a state's failure in other areas of women's lives, the greater the likelihood that regressive laws will harm those women. It is probably because of these multiple and overlapping state failures that progressive institutional change is considered to be a very slow process, but regressive institutional change appears to occur rapidly.

Fourth, scholars of gender and development must investigate not only when and how reversals occur, but also how they coexist with, and perhaps even stem from, gender progressions. The idea of a moral panic stems from situations where a formerly marginalized group is gaining power at moments of social transition. Moral panics serve to put these individuals 'back into place' by demonizing them, typically by suggesting that they are harming innocent victims (Cohen 1972). The case of El Salvador suggests that transnational pressures to promote gender equity may in some contexts contribute to a backlash against women's rights. It is particularly interesting that the UN Population Conference of 1994 and the UN Women's Conference of 1995 are both held up as watershed moments for women's equality among scholars and practitioners of gender and development, but that these same two conventions actually contributed to a rights reversal in El Salvador. We suggest that, at times of social upheaval, political actors often seek to reinforce traditional gender norms as an effective means of countering the perceived radical nature of the times (see also Viterna 2012). Consequently, by including 'rights reversals' in their analyses, scholars of gender and development can begin to investigate whether gender progress in some areas of governance can coexist with, or even contribute to, rights reversals in others.

References

Agrupación Ciudadana por las Despenalización del Aborto Terapeutico, Ético, y Eugenésico, El Salvador (2013). 'From Hospital to Jail: The Impact on Women of El Salvador's Total Criminalization of Abortion'. *Reproductive Health Matters*, 22(44): 52–60.

Brush, L.D. (2003). *Gender and Governance*. Walnut Creek: Altamira Press.

Casas-Becerra, L. (1997). 'Women Prosecuted and Imprisoned for Abortion in Chile'. *Reproductive Health Matters*, 5(9): 29–36.

Cohen, S. (2011 [1972]). *Folk Devils and Moral Panics*, 3rd Edition. Abingdon: Routledge Classics.

Cohn, S. (2016). 'The State and Development'. In G. Hooks (ed.), *The Sociology of Development Handbook*. Oakland: University of California Press.

Duarte, C. (1997). 'Dice el Arzobispo: Todavía no concluye la lucha anti-aborto'. *El Diario del Hoy*. 28 April: 75.

Dunkerley, J. (1982). *The Long War: Dictatorship and Revolution in El Salvador*. London: Verso.

El Diario de Hoy (1997). 'Rechazan despeanlizar aborto'. 24 April: 7.

European Society of Gynecology (2011). 'ESC Guidelines on the Management of Cardiovascular Diseases During Pregnancy'. *European Heart Journal*, 32: 3147–97.

Fallon, K.M., and J. Viterna (2016). 'Women, Democracy, and the State'. In G. Hooks (ed.), *The Sociology of Development Handbook*. Oakland: University of California Press.

Filipovic, J. (2015). 'Women in Rwanda are Being Jailed and Shamed for Having Abortions'. *Cosmopolitan*, 9 October. Available at: www.cosmopolitan.com/politics/a47478/rwanda-abortion/ (accessed 24 October 2017).

Gaestel, A., and A. Shelley (2014). 'Mexican Women Pay High Price for Country's Rigid Abortion Laws'. *The Guardian*, 1 October. Available at: www.theguardian.com/global-development/2014/oct/01/mexican-women-high-price-abortion-laws (accessed 24 October 2017).

Galdamez, E., and S. Joma (1996). 'Médicos se pronuncian contra el aborto'. *El Diario de Hoy*. 28 December: 7.

Garcia, J. (1997). 'Arzobispo pide detener el aborto'. *El Diario de Hoy*. 13 January: 61.

Garcia, J. (2001a). 'Crímenes sin castigo'. *El Diario de Hoy*. 8 January: 6.

Garcia, J. (2001b). 'Historias de corazones de piedras'. *El Diario de Hoy*. 8 January: 6.

Gerring, J. (2007). *Case Study Research: Principles and Practices*. New York: Cambridge University Press.

Gould, J.B., and S. Barclay (2012). 'Mind the Gap: The Place of Gap Studies in Sociolegal Scholarship'. *American Review of Law and Social Science*, 8: 323–35.

Kulczycki, A. (1995). 'Abortion Policy in Postcommunist Europe: The Conflict in Poland'. *Population and Development Review*, 21(3): 471–505.

Lipsky, M. (2010 [1980]). *Street-level Bureaucracy: Dilemmas of the Individual in Public Services*. New York: Russel Sage Foundation.

Mackay, F., and G. Waylen (2014). 'Gendering "New" Institutions'. *Politics and Gender*, 10(4): 489–94.

Mejía, F. (1997). 'Jóvenes dicen "Sí a la Vida!"' *El Diario de Hoy*, 25 April: 2.

MINSAL (2014). As cited in Amnestia Internacional. *Al Borde de la Muerte: Violencia Contra Las Mujeres y Prohibición del Aborto en El Salvador*. London: Amnesty International. Available at: https://www.amnesty.org/es/documents/AMR29/003/2014/es/ (accessed 24 October 2017).

Moloney, A. (2014). 'Rape, Abortion Ban Drives Pregnant Teens to Suicide in El Salvador' [sic]. *Reuters*, 12 November. Available at: www.reuters.com/article/us-el-salvador-suicide-teens/rape-abortion-ban-drives-pregnant-teens-to-suicide-in-el-salvador-idUSKCN0IW1YI20141112 (accessed 24 October 2017).

Orloff, A. (1993). 'Gender and the Social Rights of Citizenship: The Comparative Analysis of Gender Relations and Welfare States'. *American Sociological Review*, 58: 303–28.

Pain, J., R. Tamés Noriega, and A.L. Beltran y Puga (2014). 'Using Litigation to Defend Women Prosecuted for Abortion in Mexico: Challenging State Laws and the Implications of Recent Court Judgments'. *Reproductive Health Matters*, 22(44): 61–69.

Paltrow, L.M. (2013). '*Roe v Wade* and the New Jim Crow: Reproductive Rights in the Age of Mass Incarceration'. *American Journal of Public Health*, 103(1): 17–21.

Paltrow, L.M., and J. Flavin (2013). 'Arrests of and Forced Interventions on Pregnant Women in the United States, 1973–2005: Implications for Women's Legal Status and Public Health'. *Journal of Health Politics, Policy and Law*, 38(2): 299–343.

Ramaseshan, G. (1997). 'Women Imprisoned for Abortion in Nepal: Report of a Forum Asia Fact-finding Mission'. *Reproductive Health Matters*, 5(10): 133–8.

United Nations (2011). *World Abortion Policies*. Available at: www.un.org/esa/population/publications/2011abortion/2011wallchart.pdf (accessed 24 October 2017).

Viterna, J. (2012). 'The Left and "Life": The Politics of Abortion in El Salvador'. *Politics and Gender*, 8(2): 248–54.

Viterna, J. (2013). *Women in War: The Micro-processes of Mobilization in El Salvador*. Oxford: Oxford University Press.

Viterna, J. (2017). 'The Real Reason El Salvador Jails Women for Stillbirths? It's Called Moral Panic'. *Los Angeles Times*, 30 July. Available at: www.latimes.com/opinion/op-ed/la-oe-viterna-el-salvador-abortion-crime-moral-panic-20170730-story.html (accessed 24 October 2017).

Viterna, J., and J.S. Guardado Bautista (2014). 'Independent Analysis of Systematic Gender Discrimination in the El Salvador Judicial Process'. [White Paper].

Viterna, J., and J.S. Guardado Bautista (2017). 'Pregnancy and the 40-year Prison Sentence: How "Abortion is Murder" Became Institutionalized in the Salvadoran Judicial System'. *The Health and Human Rights Journal*, 19(1): 81–93.

Viterna, J., and N. Reifenberg (2017). *La política es complicada; la ciencia es concluyente: El aborto terapéutico salva la vida de las mujeres*. David Rockefeller Center for Latin American Studies. Available at: https://scholar.harvard.edu/files/viterna/files/libro_jocelyn_final.pdf (accessed 9 November 2017).

Viterna, J., and C. Robertson (2015). 'New Directions in the Sociology of Development'. *Annual Review of Sociology*, 41: 1–27.

13

Gender, Islam, and Law

John R. Bowen

1. Introduction

This chapter considers both the broad issue of Islam and women's welfare, and, at greater length, the specific issue of how legal systems with Islamic elements treat women.[1] The empirical focus will be on that domain of Islamic law found most widely, namely, marriage and divorce. Given the chapter's brevity, the main goal is to set out questions and variables, not to review all the literature.[2]

It is rather easy to make an a priori case that Islam is bad for women, and that Islamic law is particularly bad. Reports of forced marriage or so-called 'honour killings' confirm the suspicions held by many in the West (and not only there) that Islam motivates the mistreatment of Muslim women.

Indeed, these reports combine the two tropes that haunt even scholarly accounts of Islam: violence and gender. Often, commentators relate them, usually through the poignant story of a Muslim woman mistreated by her family or by a religious authority. Both tropes invoke the notion of Islamic law as well, portrayed as a patriarchal code that has not managed to escape medieval times. And certainly one can point to *prima facie* legal inequalities, in inheritance shares, the value of witnesses, and divorce procedures.

But are Islam and Islamic law intrinsically bad for women? Or, how would we subject the claim, and the trope about gender, to empirical evaluation? For example, how can we disentangle the effects of patriarchal regional cultures from the effects of Islamic law? How can we compare the gendered effects of Islamic court practices to the most probable alternatives? In short, how can

---

[1] I would like to acknowledge the excellent comments made on an earlier draft of this paper by Jean-Philippe Platteau and Jane Humphries, and by colleagues attending the book workshop held at Namur in February 2017, as well as discussions with Lawrence Rosen.
[2] In particular, penal law is not considered here; see Abubakar (2012) for Pakistan and Nigeria.

we—or can we?—isolate 'Islam' and 'Islamic law' from other dimensions of a gendered social world?

In this short chapter, we begin with broad-scale efforts to answer this question and gradually narrow the focus over the succeeding sections, focusing on women's and men's relationships to Islamic law in a narrow sense—that is, as a set of institutions that draw on the authority of a state to resolve disputes and to give state-legal force to certain social practices. The main intent of this contribution is not to claim definitive conclusions, but to try to better specify the questions and some of the ways we can better understand the issues.

2. Islam and Women's Welfare

At the most general level, what can we say about the relationship of Islam to women's welfare? Is there a way to detect an 'Islamic effect' on women's roles and rights in the broader world of everyday social life?

2.1. *Macro*

The broadest starting point might be the Gender Inequality Index of the United Nations Development Programme (UNDP 2015), which aggregates several distinct variables: maternal mortality, adolescent birth rate, shares of seats in parliament, secondary education, and labour force participation. Countries are given an overall index (higher numbers indicate greater levels of gender inequality) as well as indices for each variable. As one would expect, highly industrialized countries do best, especially northern European welfare states. As one moves down the list, one finds heterogeneous groupings of Muslim and non-Muslim countries. Between 0.200 and 0.300 are (in order of increasing inequality): Malaysia, Hungary, the UAE, Tunisia, and (nearly tied) the United States and Saudi Arabia. Much further down the list are (following the same ordering): Brazil, Indonesia, Senegal, Guatemala, Pakistan, and India. Countries in sub-Saharan Africa are most likely to have the highest inequality scores. The general picture given by the entire aggregate index is that gender equality is not neatly associated with one or another religion, social development plays an important role in reducing gender inequality, and disentangling causal factors requires a more sophisticated analysis.

Other broad comparisons on one variable similarly show that women do not simply do worse or better depending on whether they live in a country with a majority Muslim population, or with Islamic elements in the legal system. For example, if we consider the percentage of members of the lower house of the national parliament (or the single house in cases of unicameral systems) in 2015, we find that Tunisia (31 per cent), Afghanistan (28 per cent), and France (26 per cent) have similar percentages, just ahead of Britain (23 per cent), Pakistan (21 per cent), Saudi Arabia (20 per cent), and the United States (19 per cent) (IPU 2016). Or, if we consider women's share of enrolment at university-level schools, we find Saudi Arabia and Tunisia in the top ten, near Sweden and Norway, but Yemen and Bangladesh close to the bottom, near South Korea and Nepal (McDaniel 2014). These rather superficial metrics suggest that there is no simple correlation between Islam and women's welfare. The Saudi Arabia data also indicate that women can succeed, on some measures, in a country following the relatively conservative Hanabali legal school—even if on others (especially those regarding the obligatory presence of a male guardian) they face strongly patriarchal rules.

The closest to a spatial 'laboratory' that we can find to help analyse the effects of Islam on women's welfare is the co-presence of large Muslim and Hindu populations in South Asia, and the contrast of Muslim populations in South and Southeast Asia. In 1990, Amartya Sen argued that, as he put it, 'More than 100 Million Women Are Missing', if one compares the ratio of women to men to a background or expected ratio (Sen 1990). Slightly more boys are born than girls (about 105 boys to 100 girls), but women live longer than men if they are given equal care. The result is that there are slightly more women than men in areas where care is roughly equal, such as in Europe, the United States, and Japan. Elsewhere things vary, and much of the debate ever since the publication of Sen's argument has been on how and why things do vary. For example, there are more women than men in sub-Saharan Africa and Southeast Asia, but fewer women than men in North Africa and South Asia. These regions are multi-religious. The demographic contrasts thus suggest important differences in the ways people value women and men from one cultural region to another. They also contribute to refuting the idea that Muslim women are everywhere demographically disadvantaged because they are Muslims. For example, Indonesia, with the world's largest Muslim population, has a demographic ratio of 1.00, approximately the same as for Iceland, Israel, and Kenya. India and Pakistan have roughly the same ratios (1.08 and 1.06, respectively), despite their difference in religious composition. There are also sub-regional contrasts that point to political and economic differences, such as between the Punjab (fewer women) and Kerala (more women) within India.[3]

We will not consider here all the diverse accounts of what factors produce these differences. Proximally, differences in medical care and feeding clearly are among the mechanisms that produce the differences in survival between

---

[3] The numbers indicate total sex ratios, male/female, 2015 estimates; see CIA (n.d.).

men and women, but what drives the variation in those mechanisms is less clear. Sen (1990) suggested that women's employment outside the household and property ownership might account for these regional contrasts, in that women would be viewed as more valuable, but the labour differences themselves needed explaining. Sen did not discuss religion, but others (Bhalotra et al. 2009) have pointed to a 'Muslim advantage' in India: that, although in general, Indian Muslim children fare less well economically than do Indian Hindu children, Muslim women are less disadvantaged relative to Muslim men than is the case for Hindus. Whatever the reasons for this, it runs counter to stereotypes concerning women and Islam.[4]

2.2. Meso

Very useful in further identifying the causal relationships have been longitudinal studies. For example, Kabeer et al. (2014) examine distribution and change in sex ratios, pointing to increased female employment in Bangladesh as a probable explanation for narrowing sex ratios (and declining women's economic activity rates in India as explaining a rising son preference in that country). Furthermore, sex ratios are much higher in Pakistan than in Bangladesh (both with largely Muslim populations), leading the authors to urge greater attention to such community-specific factors as marriage and divorce norms, and degree of familiarity between spouses prior to marriage, rather than religion per se.

The broad band of Middle Eastern and South Asian countries have large Muslim populations and are also generally characterized as having relatively patriarchal societies. Can we disentangle patriarchy from any particular religion? A regression analysis (Braunstein 2014) was used to assess the relative explanatory power of direct measures of patriarchy versus religion in shaping economic growth. The study concludes that the most powerful explanatory variables are those that directly measure 'patriarchal rent-seeking'—that is, 'socially wasteful efforts to establish and claim the economic rents associated with male privilege' (Braunstein 2014: 60). The author explicitly criticizes economists' use of a 'Muslim' dummy variable in studies of economic growth, usually and too vaguely defined as whether over half of a country's population is Muslim. Similar conclusions were reached by Ross (2008), who argues that for Middle Eastern countries it is oil rents (protecting patriarchal norms from pressure to expand women's labour force participation) and not Islam that best explains variation (over time and in cross-sectional analyses) in women's labour force participation and representation in parliaments.

---

[4] For more on the quickly changing gender dimensions of Islamic law reform in South Asia see Abbasi (2017), and regarding criminal law, not discussed here, see Abubakar (2012).

The demographic ratio data indicate regional effects; the other figures suggest that we must look for other mechanisms. And as we narrow our focus to law, it will lead us to study interpretations of Islamic law and practices in deciding legal cases.

3. Women and Islamic Law

What is 'law'? There is no exact match of an Islamic term with the European-language terms referring to 'law' or 'right'. The relevant Islamic terms—*shari`a, fiqh, haqq, hukm*—refer both to the widest sphere of normativity—all that God commands—and to specific practices. If *fiqh* is close to the Anglo-American sense of case law or jurisprudence, it depends on the ultimately unknowable pathway for humans in all their affairs, or shari`a. Other religions also include references to such broad and ultimately unknowable divine plans, as when Baptists refer to 'God's plan' or as found in the Calvinist idea of unknowable, particular election. We should consider the category of *shari`a* as a repertoire of normative statements to which Muslims turn for guidance or for sacred support for their particular ideas, directives, and actions (Bowen 2013).

What is meant by 'Islamic law' here is something much more concrete than *shari`a*—namely, those aspects of state-law systems that explicitly draw from Islamic texts and traditions. These legal systems consist of statutes, court decisions, executive orders, and legal practices of various sorts that could be enforced by the state. The rest of this chapter concerns a narrow question: is Islamic law prejudicial towards women? That is, do the practices of making judgments with reference to Islam systematically work against the interests of women? Does the reference to Islam itself introduce a prejudicial element with respect to daughters, wives, or women more generally? Here the main issues have to do with the material effects of judgments, with issues of fairness, certainty, and welfare more generally. They also require disaggregating cultural from Islamic sources of discrimination, a task that is conceptually fraught as well as empirically challenging, as was adumbrated above.[5]

Pursuing this task requires us to distinguish between legal categories and explicit rules, on the one hand, and the interpretations and practices of everyday life, on the other. The latter give us a better idea of the way that Islam makes a difference regarding gender. We may find that Islamic legal

---

[5] A second, related question *not* taken on here has to do with the broader sense of normativity expressed by the term *shari`a*. Does following *shari`a* diminish the capacities or the 'agency' of women? Here the main issues have to do with the everyday relations of women and men, and with the vexed notions of agency and autonomy, notions that, again, pose both conceptual and empirical challenges. For detailed ethnographic accounts of these issues see, for example, Jouili (2015) and Mahmood (2005); economists' observations are included in Ebru et al. (2014).

categories indicate an inequality of status, but that practices are guided by ideas of equality. It may be generally the case that in religious legal systems progress towards substantive equality involves preserving formal inequalities and bringing about practical convergences of legal practices with goals of achieving greater gender equality.[6] Secular legal systems may be more likely to exhibit the opposite tendency—namely, to proclaim formally equal rights and then to subvert those claims in practice.[7]

Two methodological conclusions follow. First, studies of everyday life—in cities and villages, in courtrooms and domestic foyers, in workplaces and schools—must provide the basic evidence. Little is to be learned from reading scripture without understanding contexts of interpretation and applications. Second, the questions should be approached in a spirit of the counterfactual. The question is not to compare the real world to an ideal one—one that is without prejudice or discrimination—but to explore the mechanisms that have to do with Islam. Even when we have limited evidence to explore a counterfactual hypothesis, that way of thinking should guide our weighing of the evidence.

3.1. *Micro*

With these issues in mind, what do we find from research about the gendered nature of Islamic legal practices? The most useful evidence derives from studies of Islamic courts. How do women fare in courts that draw on Islam, and with respect to what issues? Ideally we would then compare these outcomes with those using alternative mechanisms for resolving disputes, or processes for allocating resources and performing social standing (e.g. marriage and divorce). This comparison could be used to pose the counterfactual question: does doing legal business with reference to Islamic law harm women or benefit them (or make no difference) when contrasted with the most proximate alternative ways of doing the same business? This question is (at least in theory) subject to study in contexts where there are actually existing alternatives, where, for example, an inheritance dispute could be heard in an Islamic court or in a state court not relying on Islam, or settled in a village-level forum. Alternatively, longitudinal studies can examine the results of changes in the laws applied. Although little evidence along these lines is yet available, asking the question in a counterfactual way should guide future research.

In what follows the article draws from the domain of family law, or personal status law, mainly concerning marriage, divorce, and inheritance. Across much of Muslim Asia, Africa, and the Middle East, colonial rulers applied versions of their particular Western laws for criminal or commercial disputes.

---

[6] I make this argument in Bowen (2016).
[7] US examples would be voting rights for African Americans and pay equity for women.

To some extent, they sought to codify local customary law regarding petty disputes, but even where they codified Islamic family law, notably in the case of Anglo-Muhammadan law, it retained Islamic references. There was less incentive to radically reshape family law than was the case in other domains. The nineteenth-century Ottoman legal reforms also drew from Western codes and courts. In the twentieth century, newly independent states began with holdover colonial law and gradually wrote their own legal codes, and in most cases these codes preserved or augmented the 'Islamic element'.

Looking back across the long history from pre-colonial to post-colonial experiences, we find among the major transformations in Islamic family law the creation of multi-judge tribunals and the drafting of law codes. If in a fifteenth-century qadi court, a single judge drew on his knowledge of scripture, jurisprudence, and the local lay of the land—consulting a mufti for a fatwa on matters of Islamic law when required—his twentieth- and twenty-first-century descendants are likely to be a court with several judges, all state officials, who apply written law, including codified versions of Islamic law.

4. Marriage and Divorce

In Islam, marriage (*nikah*) is a contract, requiring both parties' consent, whose primary effect is to render legitimate sexual relations between a man and a woman. Most Muslims take very seriously the idea that proper religious marriage is required to avoid sin. When a marriage has broken down, ways must be sought to allow the woman and the man to remarry. This imperative explains the possibility of divorce. The Qur'an and the *hadith* make clear three things concerning divorce. First, divorce should be avoided and mediation sought to help a marriage to continue. Second, if a marriage cannot continue, then it should be ended. Third, men have the right to divorce their wives. They should 'retain them honorably or set them free honorably' (Q. 2:231).[8] The ambiguity concerns precisely how a woman can initiate a divorce. And this ambiguity has given rise to loud debates and contested legislation throughout the Islamic world. The variation and change in the outcomes give us a window into the mechanisms promoting or reducing gender equality.

An asymmetry is built into the categories of divorce as set out by classical scholars across the different legal schools. A man can pronounce a *talaq*, or unilateral divorce, and normally the divorce would become final at the close of

---

[8] For the following discussion of classical and Ottoman opinions and rulings, I draw from Tucker (2008: 84–132). A succinct analysis of family law on marriage and divorce can be found in Hallaq (2009: 271–86). On the debates in Egypt around family law reform, see Fawzy (2004), and an extensive study of family laws across Arab states is in Welchman (2007); see also Esposito (1982). I examine the Indonesian debates and changes in Bowen (2003).

the ʿidda (the mandatory waiting period, normally three menstrual cycles). The wife also may take steps to end a marriage, but not unilaterally. The oldest possibility arises in the case where the husband had given the power to divorce to his wife, to be used if and only if he were to take a second wife. He could take an oath to the effect that, were he to remarry, this *talaq* would automatically occur. Later on, this 'delegated talaq' (*talāq tafwīz*) was to appear on some marriage contracts.

A wife could also approach a judge and ask that an annulment (*tafrīq* or *faskh*) be pronounced. The conditions for annulment were quite narrow in classical writings. Impotence was clearly a valid reason, on grounds that the purpose of marriage was to produce a lineage. Insanity and some other physical defects were accepted by some, as was the husband's disappearance, on which the Maliki legal school was the most lenient, requiring an absence of only four years before annulling the marriage. A woman whose marriage was annulled had the same rights as a wife divorced by *talaq*, including the full payment of her *mahr*, the 'marriage gift' from the husband to the wife (often not paid in full at the time of marriage), and maintenance during the period of ʿidda.

A third category of divorce has provided the basis for much modern-era legal reform. In a *khulʿ* divorce, a woman who wishes to have a divorce proposes to her husband that he divorce her in exchange for a payment of some amount, often the amount of the marriage gift, the *mahr*. In a well-accepted hadith, a wife approached the Prophet and said that, although she found no fault with her husband, she feared she might stray beyond the bounds of marriage were she to stay with him. The Prophet said she should return the garden that her husband had given her, and then told the husband to divorce her.[9]

There are other divorce categories, for example the *mubārʾa*, or divorce by mutual agreement, to be used if both the husband and the wife wish to end the marriage, but much of the debate in Islamic circles has concerned the *khulʿ*. Often it has been the judge who proclaims the marriage to have ended, but most classical jurists agreed that a judge could not do it alone, that the husband's consent was required for a *khulʿ* to take effect, thus limiting the role of the judge to ensuring that the procedures had been followed. Does that make the *khulʿ* a kind of *talaq*, because the husband utters the divorce formula? Or is it a kind of annulment in those contexts where a judge is involved? These debates are consequential in that financial consequences follow from a category decision. In a *talaq* or annulment, the husband must pay any remaining *mahr*; in a *khulʿ*, the wife often either gets no *mahr* or must repay *mahr* she has already received.

---

[9] The *hadith* is found in the collection by al-Bukhari: book 68, hadith 22 by one numbering scheme, and vol. 7, book 63, hadith 197 by another. There are many online collections, among them Sunnah.com, http://sunnah.com/bukhari/68/22 (accessed 30 June 2017).

Such are the categories. What does their use mean for women seeking to divorce? Ottoman Empire records from the eighteenth century give us insight into how judges interpreted the categories at that time. Ottoman judges, who followed the Hanafi legal school, broadened the legitimate grounds for annulment to include abuse, lack of support, and desertion. They did so in part by recognizing doctrine from other legal schools when doing so would permit the end of a disastrous marriage, and, in part, by 'bundling' abuse with blasphemy—an older ground for annulment—and arguing that a true Muslim would not beat his wife, therefore a man who did so was not a Muslim.

From these records, we also know that *khul`* had become prevalent through-out Ottoman lands, and that it exhibited what have since become standard features in Islamic courts. If reasons for ending the marriage are given in an Ottoman court, they are usually of the 'our marriage is over' sort. The wife usually forgives all debts and payments due her by her husband and returns any *mahr* already paid. The appearance in court is to register the divorce; the husband has performed it elsewhere. His consent is, therefore, presumed to be part of the *khul`* process. Practices at this time indicate that *khul`* was not a way for a woman to obtain a divorce against her husband's wishes.

If we focus on the fact that, categorically, men have the right to effect a divorce unilaterally while women require an act by a judge, then we can say that the procedures have maintained a basic gender inequality. But if we take a broader, comparative view, and consider the history of Muslim women's divorce rights vis-à-vis, say, Catholic or Jewish women's rights, then the picture shifts. We noted the prophetic *hadith* that supports a woman's right to initiate a divorce. Historical records show that women have exercised those rights over centuries. Post-colonial statutes have affirmed those rights in many countries that draw on Islamic law. By contrast, Catholic women cannot divorce and retain rights to take communion; they lose their full religious status. Orthodox Jewish women do not have the option to ask a judge to dissolve their marriage; the husband must deliver the divorce certificate. In secular terms as well, divorce is recent in Western law, and no-fault divorce, the Western secular-law equivalent to 'divorce by discord', was only available in all fifty states in the United States in 2010—New York State was the final hold-out.

5. Contemporary Practice

5.1. *Outcomes*

Most close observers of divorce proceedings in Islamic courts (and in non-state Islamic tribunals) agree on three things. First, women bring more cases to courts than do men. Second, at least within the court itself, women win more often than they lose. Third, although far more difficult to quantify, women are more strategic in their use of Islamic courts.

Why would these differences be found? First, often the alternative venues are less favourable to women than are Islamic courts. Informal rural or urban mechanisms for transmitting property more often favour men than women. Second, for some purposes women may feel more compelled to appeal to a court than do men (or indeed are more compelled legally than are men to do so). Such is the only way they can effect a divorce, for example. Third, because of these first two factors, women become more adept at using the courts, and perhaps the formal legal system more generally. Beyond these general findings it is difficult to say more, because of a 'coding' difficulty: what counts as winning a case? If the couple reconciles, we would need to know the real intentions of each party to be able to say who got what she or he wished. In many Islamic courts, divorce is usually granted; given that, do we construct metrics of monetary awards to determine who got the better of the situation? This brief review of the issues makes it clear that only detailed ethnographic or, just possibly, historical work can provide even tentative answers to the broader questions.

First, the general findings. When Lawrence Rosen analysed historical and contemporary data regarding Islamic courts, he concluded that 'Women commonly "win" their law suits in the family courts of the Muslim world roughly 65–95 per cent of the time' (Rosen 2017). Rosen points out some of the difficulties in compiling the necessary evidence, and the fact that we often do not know if other 'side bargains' are being struck. (In his own work in the court of the Moroccan city of Sefrou, Rosen (2017) found that in 1965, the court ruled in favour of women almost two-thirds of the time, across a range of types of cases.)

If we focus in on cases where a wife asks the court to dissolve her marriage, the available evidence indicates that women usually win their divorce if they pursue the case. In some countries, a major reason for this outcome is the gradual acceptance of marital discord as grounds for dissolution. In Morocco, legal reforms passed in 2004 led to a sharp rise in divorce suits, most brought by, and won by, women, and almost all women who brought suit on grounds of discord, notably easy to prove, won. Women's suits based on the husband's absence or failure to adequately support his wife were also granted most of the time: in a Cairo sample from 1972–82, women won 95.5 per cent of their cases on these grounds or on other grounds involving the husband's failure to adequately fulfil his role. In 2000, new laws were passed in Egypt explicitly allowing *khul*` divorces, and a Cairo study done in the early 2000s found that 67 of 69 women bringing *khul*` divorce suits obtained their divorces (Rosen 2017).

We need to look in greater depth at the financial implications of different forms of divorce cases. In general, a judge may determine fault and harm if the right type of suit is brought. In addition, if the husband initiates the divorce, or if a judge finds him at fault, then he must pay any of the marriage payment (*mahr*) that is outstanding. But if the wife brings suit to divorce according to the rules of *khul`*, then she forgoes her rights to full payment of *mahr*, and indeed may be ordered to return payments already made; she also becomes ineligible for certain other court-ordered payments. Thus, there can be a good or a bad 'win' in terms of the financial consequences.

But, in some cases, reforms in divorce law have also changed the idea of the gendered power balance in negotiating marriage and divorce. Sonneveld (2010, 2012) points out that in the Egyptian case, the legislative reform transformed the idea of *khul`* divorce, from a transaction requiring the husband's consent to an empowering of women to take unilateral action. *Khul`* reform in Middle Eastern and North African countries spans a long time period, at least since the early 1990s, and takes various forms. Furthermore, sometimes *khul`* reform has taken place as part of a package that also increased women's rights to work (making it more difficult to isolate the *khul`* effect). Hassani-Nezhad and Sjögren (2014) conclude that in Middle Eastern countries, making divorce easier for women to initiate has increased women's labour force participation, especially for younger women. This case strengthens our overall argument that it is to particular institutions and interpretations within Islam that we should turn to account for variation in women's status or welfare, and not to identification as Muslim.[10] And we must keep in mind that family law reforms do not win universal approval from Muslim women or men. In a study in Morocco, Chaara (2012) finds indeed that urban, highly educated women are more likely to oppose the 2003 reform, and to argue for maintaining the traditional, patriarchal family.

Beyond the question of statutory change, ethnographic studies show that, overall, judges have tended to interpret the legal framework in such a way as to favour women when possible, for example by using wide definitions of 'harm' (*darar*) done to a woman and narrow definitions of her 'disobedience' (*nushûz*), which is the basis of counter-claims sometimes made by husbands (for example: Bowen 2003; Hirsch 1998; Lemons 2010; Peletz 2002; Solanki 2011; Stiles 2009; Vincent-Grosso 2012; Voorhoeve 2014).

5.2. Mechanisms

Let us take a more micro-level look at the mechanisms that seem to be at work in shaping outcomes. In most of the cases already referred to, statutes or codes are supposed to guide judges' work. But judges also respond to

---

[10] See, more generally, Duflo (2012) on the importance of divorce reform for women's welfare.

extra-legal forces, which can include views on Islamic law that diverge from those contained in such codes. In addition, litigants may use courts as arenas for bargaining about family dynamics and resources. Studies in diverse countries shed light on one or more of these mechanisms.

First, Tunisia gives us an example of a very 'progressive' family law code, and it raises the question of whether judges enforce the terms of the code or rely on older, and more conservative, Maliki jurisprudence. In 1956, within a few months of Tunisia's independence, President Bourguiba had appointed a commission to propose a new Personal Status Code, the commission had done its work, and the President had submitted the new Code to the ruler (the Bey, an office to be abolished the following year) for his signature (Voorhoeve 2014). The Code gave women more autonomy, for example by not requiring the consent of a male guardian (*wali*), and by prohibiting polygamy. Both measures challenged previous, and still predominant, local understandings of Islamic legal practices. The Code also redefined Islamic marriage and divorce as state matters: failure to register a religious marriage with the state became a crime, and divorce was only recognized if it had occurred in court. The Code provides for divorce with or without fault, and for divorce suits to be brought by either party.

So, in a top-down fashion, the Tunisian state quickly legislated radical changes in the form of a gender-balanced code that gave the courts a greater role than before, and also broke with dominant local understandings. What has happened in practice? One conjecture was that Islamic judges would look for ways to appeal to older, conservative tenets of *shari`a*—in the Tunisian case the Maliki legal school. But, at least in Tunis, such does not appear to be the case. Rather, in those realms of legal judgment where judges have a great deal of interpretive leeway, they have developed norms of gender balance, thereby preserving the general direction of change set down by the Code. For example, the legal category of *nushûz*, generally predicated only of wives with respect to their husbands, allows for a wide range of interpretations and procedural decisions. The Tunis family court (where almost all judges are women) has generally accepted the norm that to abandon the marital home without good cause would indeed count as *nushûz*, and in a divorce case could lead a judge to award the husband damages. But they also hold that if a wife claimed that she did so for good reason, she should be believed unless the husband can prove otherwise. Furthermore, even when the court found that a wife had committed *nushûz*, they refrained from awarding damages (Voorhoeve 2014: 166–72).

The anthropologist Maaike Voorhoeve (2014: 233–35) finds that even when judges invoke terms drawn from the broader worlds of *shari`a* texts, i.e. go beyond the legislation, they justify doing so as a way to give greater cogency to vague terms contained in the law. In the above example, judges invoke *nushûz* as a matrix for interpreting the Code's term 'harm'. But they do not justify a decision by referring to *shari`a* over and against the Code. In the family courts, at least in Tunis, the Tunisian state seems to have succeeded in 'positivizing' *shari`a*—that is, replacing the broader world of texts with the Code. Why this is so (and whether it is true for other parts of the country) is unclear: the Tunisian state keeps a tight rein on the judiciary, so fear could play a role, but so could the legal socialization of judges through their training.

Second, Indonesia differs from Tunisia in two ways that are useful for our discussion. First, the official commentaries on the Indonesian Compilation of Islamic Law state that this document is entirely derived from widely accepted principles of Islamic jurisprudence (*fiqh*)—even when it makes innovations in the interests of equality and fairness. It also preserves conservative or gender-asymmetric clauses, e.g., regarding the wife's 'disobedience'. Second, in the domain of inheritance, Indonesia allows most Muslims the option of seeking the resolution of a conflict in an Islamic or in a civil court.

The Compilation (KHI 82–84) states that *nushûz* occurs when a wife fails to do her duty of 'serving her husband' and (149–52) that a judgment of *nushûz* blocks her from receiving personal divorce payments (although child support obligations are not affected). And yet in a 2012 observation of cases across three Indonesian courts and discussions with other research teams, I and my research team never saw these provisions invoked in formal decisions.[11]

Instead, judges set payment amounts based on their overall judgments of the moral conduct of each party. Judges think about *nushûz*, but they avoid explicitly finding *nushûz* to have occurred, even when all the conditions are there for such a finding. In recent Indonesian-based fieldwork, a number of judges and scholars explained that they found the legal category too difficult to apply. As one scholar, a former head of the ulama council in Aceh province, put it: 'Maybe she left the house without telling him [her husband], but maybe he did not support her and she had to go out and find food. And if both work of course she leaves the house. There really is no formula on nushûz that the judges could use.' In court after court, the mainly male judges told us that they never found the wife to have committed *nushûz*. A woman judge on the Islamic trial court in Banda Aceh, Hurriyah Abubakar, explained the silences of the judges: 'The husbands also commit nushûz but it's never called that. However, if the judge finds male disobedience, then the amount of muta'a and nafkah idda awarded to the wife will be raised. The basis is that the person who has suffered the most should be compensated, and that is always the wife.' In this case, even though both Islamic tradition and the letter of the current law are gender-unequal, practice seems to be more complicated.

---

[11] This and the following materials come from interviews carried out in Aceh and South Sulawesi in 2011–12.

What about inheritance? In Islamic inheritance law, daughters and sons have different claims on an estate. Roughly speaking, daughters receive one-half the share given to sons, and a widely accepted rule, one with Qur'anic support, prevents one or more daughters from inheriting the entire estate. The rationale for the disparity is that Islam also requires husbands to completely cover household expenses, and women's assets and income can be spent as they alone see fit. Of course reality is not like this, and most households across the world have some sort of pooling arrangement.

These considerations apply to other Muslim contexts as well. In much of the Middle East, for example, although urban property and buildings are owned outright and may be divided in Islamic fashion, farmland is divided according to other legal provisions, and often remains in the hands of sons/brothers. Annelies Moors showed that inheriting property is not necessarily indicative of women's status. When a woman inherits property, this inheritance could be a mark of her social status—that she is of a wealthy, high-status family—or it could happen because she is in a weak situation and must try to claim property to survive—even then, she is likely to find herself subsequently deprived of the property by more powerful brothers or cousins. Not taking a share may provide her with more assistance from her brothers' households than would be gained by making a claim (Moors 1995: 48–76).

Studies in Indonesia also point to the relative efficacy of Islamic courts in awarding inheritance shares to daughters, when contrasted with village-level forums or, in many cases, with civil courts that apply customary law. Many customary law rules of division favour men, and, whether or not civil courts are involved, brothers and uncles tend to delay divisions for many years, or even across a generation. Therefore, even when the formal rules for inheritance seem to be less favourable for women in an Islamic court (where daughters receive less than sons) than in a civil court or by following village rules (where residence in the village or membership in the lineage often determines who receives use rights on collective land), in practice women may find that they benefit by seeking a rapid property distribution with full property rights through an Islamic court (Bowen 2003).

Third, for Iran a series of studies show us the role of judges in tipping the balance between the parties. A conservative set of laws and judicial establishment coexist with practical wrangling through the courts by women and men. A high level of promised marriage payment (*mahr*) comes due if a husband divorces his wife using the *talaq* procedure. The anthropologist Ziba Mir-Hosseini (1993, 1999) documents ways in which a sympathetic judge allows a divorce proceeding to stretch out, giving time to the wife to bargain with her husband for his consent. Even though the husband's right to unilaterally divorce his wife is clear, a judge can schedule a series of reconciliation sessions involving diverse relatives in order to push the husband towards a settlement. Wives may hold out for custody of children or favourable monetary settlements in exchange for agreeing to the divorce. In these cases, despite the husband's divorce rights, the judge's mandate to attempt reconciliation can tip the bargaining scale in favour of the wife.

In this context, women learn ways to work around the law. The jurist Arzoo Osanloo (2009) shows how Iranian women's claims to be rights-bearers are nourished in Qur'anic study groups but also by the codification of Iranian civil law that makes explicit individual rights; the framing is thus in terms of multiple pathways for asserting rights, rather than the strategic manipulation of references in the courtrooms. Osanloo (2009: 129–34) argues that women become rights-bearing subjects, adept at formulating their cases in legal terms, precisely because they have to go through the courts to obtain a divorce, whereas men, because they are assured that they have the right of unilateral divorce, remain relatively ill-equipped to speak the language of the law. Women become more conversant in civil law and in a liberal subjectivity than do men. In other countries as well, ethnographic accounts of Islamic family courts show that women are actively manipulating the system to further their interests. Sometimes this means obtaining a divorce; sometimes it means bringing suit for divorce as a move in a long-term bargaining game with the husband. On the other hand, courts are supposed to try to reconcile the couple, and they may pressure the wife to give up a rights-based claim. The result for women is a mixed picture.

Across a large number of country cases, women or men may have more than one legal option, usually a civil court or a family court. Ido Shahar shows how women assess the relative advantages of each in deciding where to press a suit for maintenance. Palestinian feminist pressure for Muslim and Christian women's access to family courts in maintenance suits, where they could receive higher awards, led the *shari`a* court to issue a circular that allowed its judges to determine maintenance amounts, and to very quickly raise the amount of the awards (Shahar 2015: 99–106).

What leads judges to act in ways that seem to ally with women? Courts may favour women to the extent that they see them as the weaker party. The favouring may be by way of placing the burden of proof on the husband. Such is often the case with regard to husbands' claims of *nushûz*, for example, or, in a related move, by stipulating, either explicitly or implicitly, that the very fact that the wife brought a divorce suit is *prima facie* evidence of marital discord and thus grounds for divorce. Tunisian judges take a wife's suit for maintenance as evidence of the husband's failing; it is then up to him to prove that he does indeed pay maintenance. They also require the husband to prove claims of disobedience and to prove that there was no justification for the wife's disobedience—for example, that leaving the home was not done in order to work, visit relatives, etc. (Vincent-Grosso 2012: 185–90).

National laws also may do this: Indonesian and Malaysian laws both require husbands wishing to take a second wife to prove they are capable of financing two households and treating both women equally. That such equality of treatment is both broad and difficult opens the door to discretionary denials of polygamy requests. It also is important that the judges making these decisions increasingly include women. For example, in 2005, 28 per cent of all Tunisian judges were women, but in the Tunis city child and family court, 88 per cent of judges were women (Voorhoeve 2014: 13).

Finally, non-state tribunals show how Islamic scholars reason in similar cases and articulate their practices with state courts. In India, *shari`a* councils (*dar al-qaza*) operate today as non-state tribunals and are concentrated in the three states of Bihar, West Bengal, and Orissa. A study of a *dar ul-qaza* in Patna (Bihar) found that most often women brought requests for dissolution of their marriages, or *faskh*, in which the judge may award maintenance or compel the husband to pay the *mahr* that he had promised but not yet paid. Much less frequently, they requested that the court oversee the *khul`* process. Women who requested *faskh* were better educated and more aware of their legal rights (Hussain 2007: 86–91). By contrast, a Mumbai *dar ul-qaza* can award judgments of *khul`*, but if it finds the wife was not at fault, she keeps the *mahr* (Solanki 2011: 278–81). But the *dar ul-qazas* have no enforcement powers, and judges are unable to compel husbands to comply with an award of *mahr* or maintenance. Only by taking a case to a state court (which can adjudicate matters according to the religious code applicable to the parties) can a husband be forced to comply (Redding 2010; Lemons 2010).

These tribunals inspired efforts to set up *shari`a* councils in Britain. Since the early 1980s, several such councils have heard women's requests for dissolution of their marriages, and generally grant those requests (Bowen 2016). These dissolutions concern only the religious dimension of the marriage and have no civil-law effects. Unlike in India, the two legal realms of civil law and Islamic law are distinct in Britain, and a party cannot appeal a *shari`a* council decision to a civil court. However, the councils do take into account a completed civil divorce, often hastening their own procedure on grounds that the marriage is effectively over. (For Canada see Macfarlane 2012).

6. Conclusions

The Islamic legal tradition features both a broadly shared set of texts and traditions and a wide array of interpretations and practices. From the very beginning of Islam, rulers and judges developed new ways of applying the traditions to changing situations. Many of these new applications involved ways to grant women greater autonomy, for example in divorce proceedings, without departing from the broader scriptural framework, usually by adding a legal requirement that marriage or divorce (or other events) be carried out under the aegis of the court. We can thus speak of a 'positivization' of Islamic law. In developing those modifications, some states have inflected Islamic law in the direction of greater gender equality. This direction of change has accelerated in the years following the Second World War, in particular as newly independent nations sought to balance claims to build a culturally distinct nation with aspirations to develop a modern version of that cultural tradition. These aspirations are not universally shared, however, in particular in the Gulf states, where additional grounded research on legal practices is needed. Debates about the possibilities or the horizons of gender equality remain central to tensions across regions and legal systems. What we note here is that in a large number of Muslim-majority countries, legal practices have been consistent with a broadly progressive agenda.

References

Abbasi, Z. (2017). 'Women's Right to Divorce under Islamic Law in Pakistan and India'. *ShariaSource*, blog post. Available at: https://shariasource.blog/2017/01/27/womens-right-to-divorce-under-islamic-law-in-pakistan-and-india/ (accessed 30 June 2017).

Abubakar, M.U. (2012). 'Gender Justice and Islamic Laws of Homicide and Bodily Hurt of Pakistan and Nigeria: A Critical Examination'. PhD thesis. Warwick: University of Warwick.

Bhalotra, S., C. Valente, and A. van Soeast (2009). 'The Puzzle of Muslim Advantage in Child Survival in India'. Discussion Paper 4009. Bonn: Institute for the Study of Labor.

Bowen, J.R. (2003). *Islam, Law and Equality in Indonesia: An Anthropology of Public Reasoning*. Cambridge: Cambridge University Press.

Bowen, J.R. (2013). 'Contours of Sharia in Indonesia'. In M. Künkler and A. Stepan (eds), *Democracy and Islam in Indonesia*. New York: Columbia University Press, 149–67.

Bowen, J.R. (2016). *On British Islam: Religion, Law, and Everyday Practice in Shari`a Councils*. Princeton: Princeton University Press.

Braunstein, E. (2014). 'Patriarchy versus Islam: Gender and Religion in Economic Growth'. *Feminist Economics*, 20(4): 58–86.

Chaara, I. (2012). 'Pro-Women Legal Reform in Morocco: Is Religion an Obstacle?' Working Paper 685. Giza: Economic Research Forum.

CIA (Central Intelligence Agency) (n.d.). *The World Factbook*. Washington, D: Central Intelligence Agency. Available at https://www.cia.gov/library/publications/the-world-factbook/fields/2018.html (accessed 30 March 2016).

Duflo, E. (2012). 'Women's Empowerment and Economic Development'. *Journal of Economic Literature*, 50(4): 1051–79.

Ebru, K., J.C. Olmsted, and E. Shehabuddin (2014). 'Gender and Economics in Muslim Communities: A Critical Feminist and Postcolonial Analysis'. *Feminist Economics*, 20(4): 1–32.

Esposito, J.L. (1982). *Women in Muslim Family Law*. Syracuse, NY: Syracuse University Press.

Fawzy, E. (2004). 'Muslim Personal Status Law in Egypt: The Current Situation and Possibilities of Reform through Internal Initiatives'. In L. Welchman (ed.), *Women's Rights and Islamic Family Law*. London: Zed Books, 15–91.

Hallaq, Wael B. (2009). *Shari'a: Theory, Practice, Transformations*. Cambridge: Cambridge University Press.

Hassani-Nezhad, L., and A. Sjögren (2014). 'Unilateral Divorce for Women and Labor Supply in the Middle East and North Africa: The Effect of Khul Reform'. *Feminist Economics*, 20(4): 113–37.

Hirsch, S.F. (1998). *Pronouncing and Persevering: Gender and the Discourses of Disputing in an African Islamic Court*. Chicago: University of Chicago Press.

Hussain, S. (2007). 'Shariat Courts and Question of Women's Rights in India'. *Pakistan Journal of Women's Studies: Alam-e-Niswan*, 14(2): 73–102.

IPU (2016). 'Women in National Parliaments'. Inter-Parliamentary Union, online report. Available at: http://www.ipu.org/wmn-e/classif.htm (accessed 4 July 2017).

Jouili, J.S. (2015). *Pious Practice and Secular Constraints: Women in the Islamic Revival in Europe*. Stanford, CA: Stanford University Press.

Kabeer, N., L. Huq, and S. Mahmud (2014). 'Diverging Stories of "Missing Women" in South Asia: Is Son Preference Weakening in Bangladesh?' *Feminist Economics*, 20(4): 138–63.

Lemons, K. (2010). 'At the Margins of Law: Adjudicating Muslim Families in Contemporary Delhi'. Doctoral thesis. Berkeley: University of California. Available at: http://escholarship.org/uc/item/6f66n4dn#page-1 (accessed 30 March 2016).

Macfarlane, J. (2012). *Islamic Divorce in North America: A Shari`a Path in a Secular Society*. Oxford: Oxford University Press.

Mahmood, S. (2005). *Politics of Piety: The Islamic Revival and the Feminist Subject*. Princeton, NJ: Princeton University Press.

McDaniel, A. (2014). 'Women's Rising Share of Tertiary Enrollment: A Cross-National Analysis'. *FIRE: Forum for International Research in Education*, 1(2): 1–21.

Mir-Hosseini, Z. (1993). *Marriage on Trial: A Study of Islamic Family Law*. Revised edition. London: I.B. Tauris.

Mir-Hosseini, Z. (1999). *Islam and Gender: The Religious Debate in Contemporary Iran*. Princeton, NJ: Princeton University Press.

Moors, A. (1995). *Women, Property and Islam: Palestinian Experiences, 1920–1990*. Cambridge: Cambridge University Press.

Osanloo, A. (2009). *The Politics of Women's Rights in Iran*. Princeton, NJ: Princeton University Press.

Peletz, M.G. (2002). *Islamic Modern: Religious Courts and Cultural Politics in Malaysia*. Princeton, NJ: Princeton University Press.

Redding, J.A. (2010). 'Institutional v. Liberal Contexts for Contemporary Non-State, Muslim Civil Dispute Resolution Systems'. *Journal of Islamic State Practices in International Law*, 6(1); Saint Louis University Legal Studies Research Paper 2010–21. Available at: http://ssrn.com/abstract=1648945 (accessed 30 March 2016).

Rosen, L. (2017). *Islam and the Rule of Justice*. Chicago: University of Chicago Press.

Ross, M.L. (2008). 'Oil, Islam, and Women'. *American Political Science Review*, 102(1): 107–23.

Sen, A. (1990). 'More than 100 Million Women Are Missing'. *New York Review of Books*, 29 December 1990. Available at: http://www.nybooks.com/articles/1990/12/20/more-than-100–million-women-are-missing/ (accessed 30 March 2016).

Shahar, I. (2015). *Legal Pluralism in the Holy City: Competing Courts, Forum Shopping, and Institutional Dynamics in Jerusalem*. Farnham: Ashgate.

Solanki, G. (2011). *Adjudication in Religious Family Laws: Cultural Accommodation, Legal Pluralism, and Gender Equality in India*. Cambridge: Cambridge University Press.

Sonneveld, N. (2010). 'Khul` Divorce in Egypt: How Family Courts Are Providing a "Dialogue" between Husband and Wife'. *Anthropology of the Middle East*, 5(2): 100–20.

Sonneveld, N. (2012). *Khul Divorce in Egypt*. Cairo: American University in Cairo Press.

Stiles, E. (2009). *An Islamic Court in Context: An Ethnographic Study of Judicial Reasoning*. New York: Palgrave Macmillan.

Tucker, J.E. (2008). *Women, Family, and Gender in Islamic Law*. Cambridge: Cambridge University Press.

UNDP (2015). *Gender Development Index*. United Nations Development Programme Human Development Reports, online. Available at: http://hdr.undp.org/en/content/gender-development-index-gdi (accessed 30 June 2017).

Vincent-Grosso, S. (2012). 'Maktub: An Ethnography of Evidence in a Tunisian Divorce Court'. In M. Voorhoeve (ed.), *Family Law in Islam*. London: I.B. Tauris, 171–98.

Voorhoeve, M. (2014). *Gender and Divorce Law in North Africa*. London: I.B. Tauris.

Welchman, L. (2007). *Women and Muslim Family Laws in Arab States: A Comparative Overview of Textual Development and Advocacy*. Amsterdam: Amsterdam University Press.

14

The Effect of China's One Child Policy on Sex Selection, Family Size, and the School Enrolment of Daughters

Nancy Qian

1. Introduction

The effect of family size on child 'quality' is a question of longstanding interest to economists. The effect is a priori ambiguous.[1] On the one hand, a large literature in economics provides evidence that parents trade off the quantity of children with the quality of children, which implies that the quality of children declines as family size increases (e.g. Becker and Lewis 1973; Becker and Tomes 1976).[2] On the other hand, child psychologists such as Iacovou (2001) and Zajonc and Markus (1975) emphasize social interaction and learning-by-doing. They argue that increases in the number of children can increase the quality of children because it provides children opportunities to teach and learn from each other.[3] Alternatively, there may simply be economies of scale in the costs of childcare for items such as clothes

---

[1] In the labour and household economics literature that we discuss later, quality typically refers to education or health, among other attributes.

[2] The textbook quantity–quality tradeoff argues that as women's wages rise, the cost of having children increases, and hence, parents will have fewer children. These models assume that parents equalize investment across children. Thus, reducing the number of children will naturally increase the *average* quality of children. The classic quality–quality model does not allow for differences across children.

[3] Iacovou (2001), a child psychologist, argues that the disadvantage could be because children benefit from social interactions with other children. Using detailed data on time-use of children in the UK, she finds that the one-child disadvantage decreases with the amount of time a child spends playing with other children after school. In the learning-by-doing discussed by Zajonc and Markus (1975), older children are predicted to benefit more from having additional siblings than the youngest child because it is assumed that children teach younger children and benefit especially from teaching.

and textbooks such that an additional child lowers the marginal cost of quality for all children. In the rural Chinese context, this can be seen in Table 1A in Qian (2017), which shows that average per child expenditures on household chores and childcare for rural Chinese households decrease significantly with the number of children.

For policy makers in developing countries today, understanding this relationship is especially relevant as many governments have attempted to curb population growth as a way of increasing average human capital investment. Both China and India, the world's two most populous countries, have experimented with different family planning policies to limit family size. This study addresses the effect of family size by examining the impact of increasing the number of children from one to two on school enrolment in rural China. To establish causality, I exploit region and birth year variation in relaxations of the One Child Policy (OCP).

There are two main difficulties. First, there is the possibility of parental heterogeneity. For example, if parents who value education more also prefer to have fewer children, then the correlation between quantity and quality will overestimate potentially negative effects of family size. Endogeneity may also arise from the quality of the first child. For example, if parents are more likely to have a second child when the first child is of high quality, the correlational evidence will under-estimate the potentially negative effects of family size. To address these issues, past studies have carefully constructed strategies that exploit the exogenous variation in family size caused by multiple births or the sex composition of the first two children (Angrist et al. 2010; Black et al. 2006; Conley 2004; Lee 2004; Rosenzweig and Wolpin 1980; Rosenzweig and Zhang 2009).[4] While previous works provide important evidence, the strategies they employ cannot be applied to all contexts. Specifically, the estimates from using the sibling sex composition instrument is most suitable for studying the effect of increasing the number of children from two to three, and cannot be an excludable instrument if parents practise sex selection. Estimates from using the twins instrument can lack external validity to non-twin children.

The principal contribution of this chapter is to address these problems and estimate the effect of increasing the number of children from one to two. I exploit regional and time variation in the relaxations of China's OCP.

---

[4] The sibling sex composition methodology argues that parents prefer children of mixed sex. Therefore, they are more likely to have a third child if the first two are of the same sex. The twins methodology argues that the occurrence of twins (before the introduction of fertility treatments) is uncorrelated to individual characteristics. Hence, twinning is a plausibly exogenous source of variation for family size. Both methodologies examine the effect of an additional sibling for families with at least two children. Angrist et al. (2006) used both techniques and found that the results are similar.

I use the relaxation that allowed families to have a second child if the first child is a girl to instrument for the family size of first-parity children born before the relaxation was announced. Three facts are exploited: first, an individual is only affected by the relaxation if she is born in a relaxed area; second, among first-born children born in relaxed areas, only girls are affected; and third, a girl is more likely to gain a sibling due to the relaxation if she is younger at the time of the policy announcement. The instrument for family size is the triple interaction term of an individual's sex, date of birth, and region of birth. The interaction between whether a girl was born in a relaxed area and her birth year estimates the effect of the relaxation on family size. The additional comparison with boys controls for region-specific changes in school provision (and other cohort changes) that affected boys and girls similarly. This strategy differs from previous methods in that it essentially compares one-child households with two-child households. Interpreting the two-stage least squares (2SLS) estimates as causal assumes that absent the introduction of the relaxation, the *difference* between households with first-born daughters and those with sons would have moved along parallel trends for villages that received the relaxation and villages that did not. This is the standard parallel trends assumption applied to a triple-difference setting. I do not take this assumption as given and will carefully consider and provide evidence against potential caveats in the robustness section.

The ordinary least squares (OLS) estimates show that for households with three or fewer children, the number of siblings is negatively correlated with school enrolment. However, for households with two or fewer children, having a younger sibling is positively correlated with the school enrolment of the eldest child. This is consistent with the descriptive evidence that shows that only children are, on average, less likely to be enrolled in school relative to children from two-child families, who are, on average, more likely to be enrolled in school relative to children from three-child families.

The 2SLS results show that for households with two or fewer children, an additional child significantly increases the school enrolment of first children by up to 16 percentage points. The fact that the 2SLS estimate is larger in magnitude than the OLS estimate is consistent with the existence of parental heterogeneity in preferences for education and quality.

The main results show that there is a significant one-child disadvantage for the eldest child, which is consistent with the belief that children benefit from teaching younger siblings, and also with the possibility that there may be economies of scale in raising children. They do not unambiguously reject the Beckerian quantity–quality tradeoff model since that model makes predictions about the average outcomes of children, and I can only examine the outcomes for the eldest child. However, for quantity to have no average effect on quality given my findings for the eldest child, there would have to be inequality across children, which would also be inconsistent with a simple Beckerian case.

In addition to the main results, we attempt to investigate the mechanisms underlying them. First, I investigate the hypothesis that the positive effect of an additional child is driven by economies of scale in childrearing costs. Under the assumption that there are larger economies of scale regarding school for children of the same sex (e.g. children can more easily share clothes if they are the same sex), I explore this hypothesis by examining whether the benefit of the second child is larger when the two children are the same sex. The results show that the benefits of a second child are almost entirely seen by households where the two children are of the same sex. This is consistent with the presence of economies of scale.

Second, I examine the hypothesis that the benefit of an additional child is driven by an increase in permanent income. For example, if adult children provide parents with income, then an additional child will increase the permanent income of the household. If parents can borrow against their children's future income, this could increase investment in schooling. Under the assumption that parents expect sons to earn more than daughters, I test this hypothesis by investigating if the benefits of a second child are larger when the second child is a boy. The results show the opposite pattern: the benefits are larger when the second child is a girl. Therefore, our results do not seem to be driven by increases in permanent income, which is perhaps not surprising since households in rural China are generally believed to be credit constrained. Note that because the sex of the second child is not random due to sex selection, these results should be interpreted very cautiously as only suggestive evidence.

Finally, I investigate the possibility that the main results occur due to binding income constraints. If the financial costs imposed by an additional child outweigh schooling costs, then parents may increase their labour supply in the labour market and substitute public schools for self-provided childcare. The data limit the extent to which I can investigate this hypothesis. I examine the effect of an additional child on the mother's labour supply and school delay. The results are suggestive, but imprecisely estimated. They suggest that an additional child causes mothers to be *more* likely to enter the labour force and causes the elder child to enter school at a younger age. These results are consistent with the hypothesis that income demand caused by the additional child causes mothers to work and the first child to begin school. Interestingly, they suggest the possibility that public schools are being used as a form of low-cost childcare. This is important because it implies that classic frameworks for understanding the relationship between family size and children's schooling may be inadequate for contexts where schooling costs are low and can be used as a form of subsidized childcare by parents.

This study makes several contributions. First, it adds to the existing literature on the effects of family size. The results from this literature have been
mixed.[5] Most of these studies have focused on the effect of additional children
conditional on there already being two children. I add to these studies by
being the first to provide evidence for the one-child disadvantage (at least for
the eldest child), which suggests that the effect of family size may be non-
monotonic across family size. The finding that additional children benefit the
schooling outcomes of the eldest child is similar to Angrist et al.'s (2010)
finding for Israel. The implication that the effects of family size may differ
across birth orders supports the findings of Black et al. (2006) for Norway.

Second, this study provides an evaluation of the effects of the OCP, one of
the most restrictive and large-scale family planning policies ever undertaken.
While demographers and sociologists have conducted many descriptive studies of the policy's impact on fertility and sex ratios, the lack of local enforcement data has heretofore prevented an examination of the causal effect of the
OCP on child outcomes. The findings indicate that the OCP decreased female
survival by up to ten percentage points, and the relaxation was successful in
reducing the sex selection to pre-OCP levels. Interestingly, the results also
show that the previous rule on four-year birth spacing was well enforced, a fact
that has received little attention in policy debates or academic studies. In
rigorously evaluating the effects of the OCP, the first stage of this chapter is
closely related to a recent study by Ebenstein (2010), which uses Chinese
Census data to show that regional sex ratios are closely linked to the level of
fines for violating the OCP. More generally, this study adds to the large
literature on the effects of family-planning-policy-induced fertility. Recent
examples from the Chinese context include Dasgupta et al. (2011), who
study the effect of reduced fertility on the marriage market. Similarly, Banerjee
et al. (2014) examine the effect of reduced fertility on savings in urban China.
Since family-planning policies both reduced fertility and exacerbated the boy-
biased sex imbalance in China, my work is also related to a recent study on
savings by Wei and Zhang (2011).

Finally, the suggestive results on mothers' labour supply add to studies on
the relationship between subsidized childcare and mothers' labour supply. For
a recent example, see Baker et al.'s (2008) study of Quebec, where they find

---

[5] On the one hand, studies have found family size to have no effect or even a positive effect on
child outcomes in Israel (Angrist et al. 2006), Korea (Lee 2004), the United States (Kessler 1991),
China (Guo and VanWey 1999), and Africa (Gomes 1984). On the other hand, the effect of family
size on education has been found to be negative in India (Rosenzweig and Wolpin 1980), France
(Goux and Maurin 2003), the United States (Berhman et. al. 1989; Conley 2004; Stafford 1987),
and China (Rosenzweig and Zhang 2009). The studies described here all focus on cross-sectional
evidence. Alternatively, Bleakely and Lange (2005) examine time-series evidence in the American
South. They find that increased schooling causes a decrease in fertility. See Schultz (2005) for a
detailed critique of the empirical literature.

that universal childcare significantly increases maternal labour supply. In a developing context, a recent study by Schlosser (2011) finds that subsidized pre-school increases the labour supply of Arab mothers in Israel.[6]

The chapter is organized as follows. Section 2 discusses family-planning policies and education in rural China. Section 3 describes the data. Section 4 presents the empirical strategy. Section 5 presents the empirical results. Section 6 offers concluding remarks.

2. Background

2.1. *Family Planning Policies*

In the 1970s, after two decades of explicitly encouraging population growth, policy makers in China enacted a series of measures to curb population growth. The policies applied to individuals of Han ethnicity, who make up 92 per cent of China's population. Beginning around 1972, the policy 'Later [age], longer [the spacing of births], fewer [number of children]' offered economic incentives to parents who spaced the birth of their children at least four years apart. The OCP was formally announced in 1979. Actual implementation began in certain regions as early as 1978, and enforcement gradually tightened across the country until it was firmly in place in 1980 (Banister 1987; Croll et al. 1985).[7] Second births became forbidden except under extenuating circumstances. Local cadres were given economic incentives to suppress fertility rates. In the early 1980s, parts of the country were swept by campaigns of forced abortion and sterilization and reports of female infanticide became widespread (Banister 1987; Greenlaugh 1986).

Local governments began issuing permits for a second child as early as 1982. However, permits for a second child were not widespread until the Central Party Committee issued 'Document No. 7' on 13 April 1984. The two main purposes of the document were to: (1) curb female infanticide, forced abortion, and forced sterilization; and (2) devolve responsibility from the central government to the local and provincial government so that local conditions could be better addressed. In other words, it allowed for regional variation in family-planning policies. The document allowed for second births for rural couples with 'practical' difficulties, and strictly prohibited coercive methods.[8] The main relaxation following Document No. 7 is called the '1-son-2-child'

---

[6] Blau and Currie (2006) provides an overview of this literature.

[7] Past studies generally consider the OCP to have only affected the family size of cohorts born after 1979–80. However, this chapter will show that because of the previous four-year birth spacing rule, the OCP affected cohorts born in 1976 and after.

[8] Practical difficulties included households where a parent or first-born child was handicapped, or if a parent was engaged in a dangerous industry (e.g. mining).

rule. It allowed rural couples to have a second child if the first child was a girl (Greenlaugh 1986). The explicit purpose of this relaxation was to decrease female infanticide of the first-born child.

White (1992) found that 5 per cent of rural households were allotted second child permits in 1982. These permits were generally granted to regions with extremely high levels of infanticide. After Document No. 7, the permits expanded to 10 per cent of the rural population in 1984, 20 per cent in 1985, and 50 per cent by 1986.

Document No. 7 made provincial governments responsible for both maintaining low fertility rates and reducing infanticide. While the exact process of granting permits is unclear, I use county-level data on family-planning policy to show in the next section that the probability of a county obtaining the 1-son-2-child relaxation is positively correlated with the rate of pre-relaxation sex selection, and both are positively correlated with distance from the provincial capital. These facts most likely reflect that in order to maintain low aggregate fertility rates and reduce excess female mortality (EFM), provincial governments granted relaxations to regions that were distant from the administrative capital and where EFM was more prevalent. The higher prevalence of sex selection in rural areas can be due to both more boy-preference in distant rural areas and the fact that geographic distance increases the provincial government's logistical difficulty in preventing EFM.[9] Issues of identification that arise from the correlation of obtaining a relaxation and sex selection will be addressed explicitly in the section on robustness.

2.2. *Rural Education*

Rural primary schools are exclusively provided by the state in the period of this study. Relative to other developing countries, the cost of schools was very low. Nevertheless, during the time period of this study, there was much inequality in provision across regions—both across provinces and across counties within a province. This was a result of fiscal reforms that occurred during the early 1980s. The fiscal system reduced subsidies from rich regions to poor regions. The system of 'eating from separate pots' (*fen zao chi fan*) devolved expenditure responsibilities from the central and provincial governments onto local governments in order to give the latter stronger incentives to generate revenue. The ratio of the per capita schooling expenditure in the highest-spending province to the lowest-spending province doubled in one decade. Many rural schools were closed; rural enrolment rates dropped

---

[9] Levels of income between counties with some relaxation and counties with no relaxation are comparable in the CHNS data. This is consistent with the findings of Qian's (2008) study of rural China, which found that total household income had no effect on sex selection.

dramatically and did not recover until the mid-to-late 1990s (Hannum and Park 2002). Using spending data from Gansu Province, they found that per capita school expenditure was positively correlated with income and that significant variation in school quality existed across counties. They found little variation within counties, suggesting that studies examining education outcomes should focus on variation at the county level. Hannum (2002) showed that the difference in school provision between rich and poor areas was much greater for middle schools and high schools than for primary schools. This is consistent with the China Health and Nutritional Survey (CHNS) data used in this study, where primary school enrolment remained stable while middle school and high school dropout rates increased for poor areas (Hannum and Park 2002).

The CHNS data show that counties with some relaxation and counties with no relaxation had similar geographic access to schooling in 1989. However, the data do not reveal the quality of schooling or the changes in school availability during the early 1980s. Because relaxed areas tend to be more rural, it is likely that the quality of schools declined in relaxed areas during the same time that the 1-son-2-child relaxation took effect. To control for this, I will compare outcomes for girls to boys within counties. The strategy is robust as long as the changes in school quality and the economic conditions that determine school quality in relaxed areas have the same impact on boys and girls.

3. Data

This chapter matches the 1 per cent sample of the 1990 Population Census with the 1989 CHNS at the county level. The 1990 Population Census contains fifty-two variables, including birth year, region of residence, whether an individual currently lives in his/her region of birth, sex, and relationship to the head of the household. The data allow children to be linked to parents. Thus, family size and birth order of children within a household can be calculated. Because the identification is partially derived from the region of birth, the sample is restricted to individuals who reported living in their birth place in 1990. The CHNS uses a random cluster process to draw a sample of approximately 3,800 households with a total of 16,000 individuals in eight provinces that vary substantially in geography, economic development, public resources, and health indicators. Most importantly, the survey provides detailed village- and township-level information on family-planning policy enforcement. Since ethnic minorities were exempt from all family-planning policies, I restrict the analysis to four provinces that are mostly composed of individuals of Han ethnicity. The matched dataset contains twenty-one counties in four provinces.[10] These provinces are in the middle and upper ranges of gross domestic product (GDP) and GDP growth during this period. The CHNS data are aggregated to the county level in order to be matched to the 1990 Census. Since the policy data are at the village and township levels, the aggregated dataset reports the percentage of the population in each county that is exposed to the relaxation.

For the analysis of family size and education, the sample is restricted to first-born children in cohorts born during 1962–81. The reference group in the regression analysis is comprised of individuals born during 1962–72. Those born after 1981 are excluded because, after the relaxation, parents who preferred larger families may have chosen to keep girls in order to have a second child. Consequently, the 2SLS estimate, if it does not exclude those born after 1981, will be biased by parental preferences and will show that girls with larger family sizes are better-off.

Table 1a in Qian (2017) shows the time and money allocated for household chores according to the number of children in the household. It shows that as family size increases, parents allocate less time to household chores and less money to food. Interestingly, even time allocated to childcare declines with the number of children. This is important for understanding our results later. Panels A and B in Table 1b in Qian (2017) show that among first-born children, girls, on average, have more siblings, more educated parents, and higher school enrolment. Panels C and D show that only-children are more likely to be male, have more educated parents, and are more likely to be enrolled in school. This is consistent with the identified concern that parents with more education may prefer to have fewer children and value education more.

To use individuals in counties without relaxations as a control group for individuals in counties with relaxations, I would like the two groups to have similar characteristics in every respect other than the relaxation. Table 1c in Qian (2017) compares first-born children born in counties with no relaxation and first-born children born in counties with some relaxation. It shows that the two types of counties have similar demographic characteristics. Each has approximately 55 per cent males among the first-born children. Family size and sex composition of siblings are similar. Children born in relaxed areas have slightly more educated parents. School enrolment in both counties with and counties without relaxations are approximately 50 per cent. Panel B shows that in counties with some relaxations, 38 per cent of first-born children are born in villages or townships with the relaxation. Counties with relaxations are further away from urban municipalities.

---

[10] Liaoning, Jiangsu, Shandong, and Henan.

The treatment group comprises children who are 9–14 years old in 1990. In principle, they should be enrolled in primary school or junior high school. The control group comprises children who, in principle, should be in high school. The descriptive statistics show that children in counties with the relaxation must, on average, travel further to attend primary school. This biases against my finding a positive effect of the relaxation on school enrolment. The distances to middle schools and high schools are very similar between counties with and without the relaxation.

One potential concern with Chinese data on children is the fear that parents will misreport the number of children in order to evade the OCP. Past studies have compared hospital birth records and Population Census data to show that misreporting is typically a problem for children under two years old and the data for older children are typically accurate (Zeng et al. 1993). Since I use data from 1990 to study children born close before and after 1976 (who were around 14 years old by the time the data were collected), misreporting should not affect my study.

4. Empirical Strategy

Figure 14.1 plots the total number of children against the birth year of the first-born child. It shows that children born in more recent years have smaller family sizes. This reflects both the fact that parents of young children may not have finished having children and a decrease in family size over time. To reveal the commonly seen OLS evidence for the quantity–quality tradeoff, I regress a dummy variable for school enrolment on dummy variables for the number of children in a household. Children from one-child households are the reference group. Figure 14.2a plots the coefficients. It shows that family size is negatively correlated with school enrolment regardless of whether county-fixed effects are controlled for. However, this confounds the family size effect with several factors: (1) younger children are more likely to be in school; (2) younger children will have fewer siblings because their parents may not have finished having children; and (3) quantity and quality may be jointly determined by parental preferences. Controlling for birth years addresses the first two problems and causes the relationship between family size and school enrolment to become non-monotonic. Figure 14.2b plots the coefficients for family size when controlling for birth year fixed effects.[11] Relative to the reference group of children from one-child families, children from two-child

---

[11] Estimates for the coefficients plotted in Figures 14a and 14b are shown in Table B1 in Qian (2017) (see Appendix B).

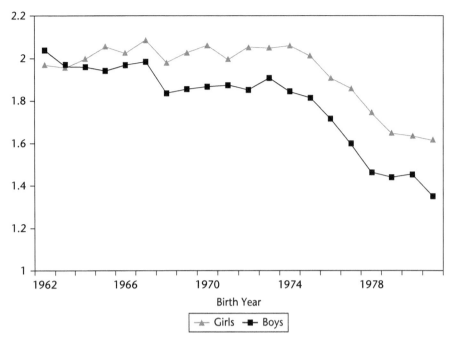

Figure 14.1. The number of children in household by birth year for households with three or fewer children

Source: Author.

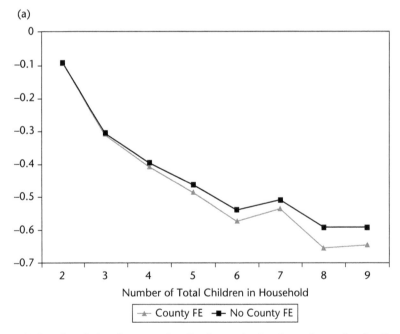

Figure 14.2a. Correlation between family size and school enrolment by family size with no birth year controls (coefficient for the number of total children in the household)

Source: Author.

(b)

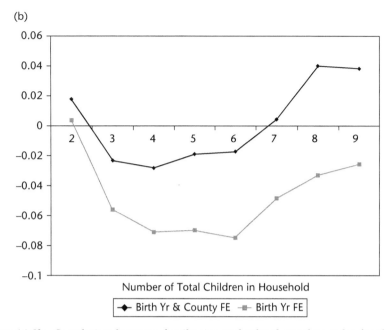

Figure 14.2b. Correlation between family size and school enrolment by family size with birth year controls (coefficient for the number of total children in the household)
Source: Author.

families have higher school enrolment. However, the correlation between enrolment and family size is negative for households with 2–5 children.

The main second-stage equation will control for birth county and birth year fixed effects. It can be written as:

$$enrol_{itc} = sibs_{itc}b + X'_{ict}\kappa + \sum_{l=1973}^{1981}(urban_c \times d_{il})\delta_l + a + \gamma_t + \psi_c + \varepsilon_{itc} \qquad (1)$$

School enrolment for individual i, born in county c, birth year t, is a function of $sibs_{itc}$, the number of siblings he or she has; X_{ict}, individual characteristics; the interaction term between $urban_c$, distance to urban area, and d_l, a variable indicating whether an individual was born in year l; γ_t, birth year fixed effects; and ψ_c, county fixed effects.

This faces the problem that the number of children and investment in these children are jointly determined by parents. Hence, if parents who value education also prefer smaller households, then OLS will overestimate the negative effect of an additional sibling on schooling. I address this by exploiting plausibly exogenous variation in family size caused by relaxations in the OCP. Sex, date, and region of birth jointly determine an individual's exposure to the 1-son-2-child relaxation. The relaxation allowed parents to have a second child only if the first-born child was a girl. Therefore, family size should be positively correlated with being a girl. Since parents are more likely to have a second child if the first girl was younger when the relaxation was announced, family size should be negatively correlated with the age of the first girl. The interaction between whether a girl was born in a relaxed area and her age estimates the effect of the relaxation on family size. The additional comparison with boys controls for changes in policies such as education provision that affected both boys and girls similarly. The instrument for family size is therefore the triple interaction of an individual's sex, year of birth, and region of birth. Only the combination of the three is exogenous. The exclusion restriction for the instrument is that it must be correlated with family size and only affect school enrolment via the family size channel.

To understand the identification strategy, I first estimate the effect of the policy on family size for boys and girls separately. If the policy were fully enforced, it should increase the number of siblings for first-born girls who the OCP prevented from having younger siblings. The relaxation should have no effect on the family size of boys. I estimate the following equation separately for samples of first-born boys and girls born during 1962–81:

$$sibs_{itc} = \sum_{l=1973}^{1981} (relax_c \times d_{il})\beta_l + \gamma_t + a + \psi_c + v_{itc} \tag{2}$$

The number of siblings for individual i, born in county c, birth year t, is a function of: the interaction term of $relax_c$, the extent of relaxation in county c and d_{il}, a dummy indicating whether the individual was born in year l; γ_t, birth year fixed effects and ψ_c, county-fixed effects. The reference group comprises individuals born during 1962–72. It and all of its interaction terms are dropped. For all regressions, standard errors are clustered at the county level.

Then, to assess the statistical difference of the effect on boys and girls, I pool the data to estimate the first-stage equation with the triple interaction terms on the right-hand side (RHS):

$$\begin{aligned} sibs_{itc} = &\sum_{l=1973}^{1981} (relax_c \times girl_{itc} \times d_{il})\beta_l + \sum_{l=1973}^{1981} (relax_c \times d_{il})\delta_l \\ &+ \sum_{l=1973}^{1981} (girl_{itc} \times d_{il})\zeta_l + (relax_c \times girl_{itc})\lambda + girl_{itc}\kappa \\ &+ a + \gamma_t + \psi_c + v_{itc} \end{aligned} \tag{3}$$

The number of siblings for individual i, born in county c, birth year t, is a function of: the triple interaction term of $relax_c$, the extent of relaxation in county c, $girl_{itc}$, a variable indicating whether a child is a girl and d_{il}, a dummy variable indicating whether the individual was born in year l; the interaction term of $relax_c$ and d_{il}; the interaction term between $girl_{itc}$, and d_{il}; the interaction term between $relax_c$ and $girl_{itc}$; $girl_{itc}$; γ_t, birth year fixed effects; and ψ_c, county-fixed effects. As before, the reference group of cohorts born in 1962–72 and all its interactions are dropped. β_l is the difference in the effect of being born in a relaxed area on family size between girls and boys born in year l. The estimates should be zero for earlier cohorts who were not affected by the OCP and relaxation and positive for later affected cohorts. β_l is the effect of being born in a relaxed county on family size for an individual born in year l.

Like simple differences-in-differences estimators, cohort-invariant differences across regions are differenced out by the comparison across cohorts. Changes across cohorts which affect different regions similarly are differenced out by the comparison across regions. The triple difference adds the advantage that cohort-varying differences that affect boys and girls similarly across regions are also differenced out by the comparison between girls and boys within each cohort and region. The exclusion restriction is only violated if a change with differential impacts on areas with and without the relaxation *and* on boys and girls occurs at the same time the relaxation took effect. In other words, the 2SLS estimate will be biased only if there is a sex-specific change at the time of the relaxation in relaxed regions. For example, if local governments of relaxed regions implemented a programme encouraging girls to attend school when the relaxation was enacted, then the 2SLS will confound the effects of this programme with the effects of family size. There is little reason to think that such a change occurred. The main concern with this strategy arises from the fact that the relaxations were introduced to curb sex selection. If the relaxation is strongly correlated with the extent of sex selection for OCP cohorts, two potential problems will arise. First, unobserved factors correlated with sex selection may affect education investment differentially for boys and girls. This will bias the estimates if the factors driving sex selection are time varying.[12] Second, there might be selection bias regarding the parents who choose to keep girls in relaxed regions. The main concern is that parents of girls in relaxed regions could have different unobservable characteristics from parents of girls in regions without the relaxation in such a way that would bias the 2SLS estimates upwards. For example, parents of girls in relaxed regions may, on average, have a higher consumption value for all things related to children, such as education relative to parents of girls in non-relaxed regions. Then, the 2SLS estimate will overestimate the true effect of family size on school enrolment. I investigate this by first examining the

---

[12] For example, Qian (2008) finds that increasing relative adult male wages increases sex selection and that increasing relative adult male wages decreases girls' schooling relative to that of boys. This would cause a downward bias in the 2SLS estimates.

The CHNS does not have accurate data on individual income within the household since much rural production is conducted at the household level and income cannot be accurately assigned to individual members. Consequently, I cannot directly examine the role of relative earnings in this study.

effect of the relaxation on the fraction of males by birth year using the following equation:

$$male_{itc} = \sum_{l=1969}^{1989}(relax_c \times d_{il})\beta_l + \gamma_t + a + \psi_c + v_{itc} \qquad (4)$$

The probability of being male for individual i, born in county c, birth year t is a function of: the interaction terms between $relax_c$, and birth year dummy variables, d_{il}; birth county fixed effects, ψ_c; and birth year fixed effects, γ_t. β_l is the correlation between being born in a relaxed county and the sex ratios of your cohort for each birth year l.

Then, to estimate the magnitude of the effect of the relaxation on sex ratios, I estimate the following equation using the sample of first-born children:

$$male_{itc} = \sum_{l=2}^{3}(relax_c \times post_{il})\delta_l + a + \gamma_t + \psi_c + \varepsilon_{itc} \qquad (5)$$

The probability of being male for individual i, born in county c, birth year t is a function of: the interaction term between $relax_c$ and $post_{il}$, a variable indicating the individual's cohort group; ψ_c, county-fixed effects and γ_t, cohort-group-fixed effect. In the section on robustness, I will use the estimate of δ_l to compute bounds for the main results. The children are divided into three groups according to birth cohort.

The reference group comprises individuals not affected by the OCP and the relaxation (born before 1978). The second group comprises children born after the OCP but before the relaxation (1978–81). The third group comprises children born after the relaxation (1982–89). $\hat{\delta}_l$ is the effect of the OCP on sex selection in relaxed areas relative to areas without the relaxation. For robustness, I use it to calculate the extent to which the main results can be driven by selection under certain assumptions.

5. Empirical Results

5.1. The Correlation Between Family Size and Schooling

Panels A and B of Table 2 in Qian (2017) show the estimates from equation (1). All regressions control for the full set of double interaction terms from equation (3).[13] Panel A shows that among households with three or fewer children, an additional sibling is negatively correlated with the school enrolment of the first child by 1.1 percentage points. However, since the 2SLS will reveal the effect of increasing the number of children from one to two, the

---

[13] he double interactions include the interaction term of $relax_c$ and d_{il}; the interaction term of $girl_{itc}$ and d_{il}; the interaction term of $relax_c$ and $girl_i$; and $girl_{itc}$. The reference group comprises cohorts born during 1962–72. The dummy variable for the reference cohort and all its interactions are dropped.

relevant OLS comparison should be on a sample of individuals with one or no sibling. Panel B shows that in this restricted sample, an additional sibling is *positively* correlated with the school enrolment of the eldest child by approximately 1.5 percentage points. Estimates in both cases are statistically significant at the 1 per cent significance level and robust to controls.

Note that the number of observations change slightly across the different estimates of the analysis because the control variables are not always available for the full sample. In this chapter, I present results using the largest possible sample. All of the results are nearly identical when the estimates are repeated on a restricted sample where all controls are available for all observations. These results are not reported for brevity and are available upon request.

5.2. *The Effect of the 1-Son-2-Child Relaxation on Family Size*

I first estimate equation (2) on separate samples for boys and girls. The estimates are shown in Table 3, columns (1) and (2), in Qian (2017). The estimates for girls are statistically significant at the 1 per cent level for individuals born in 1976 and later. This is consistent with the fact that before the OCP was introduced in 1979–80, there was a four-year birth spacing law. Hence, the OCP was binding for cohorts born four years before its introduction. The estimates for boys are statistically insignificant. The coefficients are plotted in Figure 14.3a. It shows that family size for boys and girls were similar for cohorts born 1973 and 1976, after which the family size for girls increased and the family size for boys remained the same.

The estimated coefficients for the triple interaction terms from equation (3) are shown in Table 3, column (5), in Qian (2017). They are statistically significant at the 5 per cent level for the individuals born 1977–81. Figure 14.3b plots the coefficients for the triple interaction term. It shows that the boy–girl difference in the effect of being born in a relaxed area on family size is zero for unaffected cohorts and positive for the affected cohorts. On average, the relaxation increased family size of first-born girls by approximately 0.25 children. The discrete change in the effect of the triple interaction term between individuals born before 1976 and those born afterwards is consistent with the claim that the OCP was binding for cohorts born four years prior to its enactment. This is evidence for the effective enforcement of the previous four-year birth spacing.

5.3. *The Effect of the 1-Son-2-Child Relaxation on Enrolment*

I first estimate the effect of the relaxation on enrolment separately for boys and girls using an equation identical to equation (2), but replacing the dependent variable with enrolment, the outcome of interest. The reference

(a)

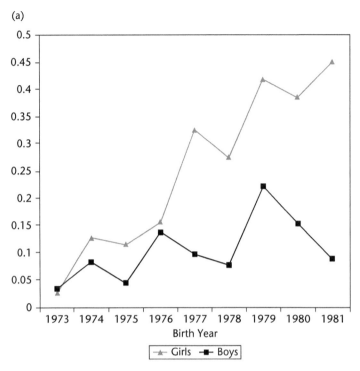

Figure 14.3a. The effect of relaxation on family size (coefficients of the Interactions between born in a relaxed area × birth regions)
Source: Author.

group comprises individuals born during 1962–72. The coefficients for girls and boys are shown in Table 3, columns (3) and (4), in Qian (2017). The estimates are statistically significant for girls. Figure 14.4a plots the estimates for boys and girls. The plot of the reduced form shows that girls affected by the relaxation (born 1976 and after) had higher education enrolment than boys, whereas girls unaffected by the relaxation (born before 1976) had lower school enrolment rates than boys.

The estimates in Figure 14.4a show that, relative to areas without the relaxation, enrolment for both boys and girls decreased after primary school. This is consistent with the hypothesis that school provision and quality in relaxed regions relative to regions without the relaxation declined during this period. I control for this by comparing the effect of the relaxation on enrolment for boys with the effect of the relaxation on enrolment for girls. I estimate an equation similar to equation (3), with school enrolment as the dependent variable. The reference group comprises individuals born during 1962–72. The coefficients are shown in Table 3, column (6), in Qian (2017). The estimates show that for older cohorts not affected by the relaxation, individuals born in

(b)

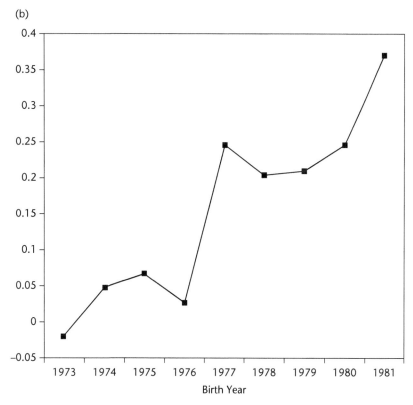

Figure 14.3b. The effect of relaxation on family size (coefficients of the interactions between dummy for girl × born in a relaxed region × birth year)
Source: Author.

relaxed areas had on average 1–17 per cent less school enrolment than areas without the relaxation. However, for cohorts affected by the relaxation, individuals born in relaxed areas were on average enrolled in school 5 per cent more than individuals born in areas without the relaxation. The estimates are statistically significant at the 1 per cent level. Figure 14.4b plots the triple difference reduced form estimates. It shows that school enrolment in relaxed areas was higher for girls of the affected cohort than for boys. Note that the year-by-year first stage and reduced form estimates use the full sample. Estimates for a sample restricted to households with three or fewer children are presented in Table B2 in Qian (2017) (see Appendix 2).

5.4. *The Effect of Family Size on Enrolment*

Table 2 panel C in Qian (2017) shows the 2SLS estimates for households with three or fewer children. It shows that for a sample where 49 per cent of

(a)

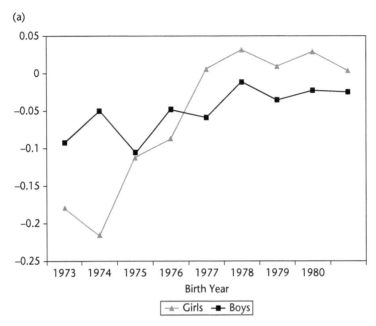

Figure 14.4a. The effect of relaxation on school enrolment (coefficients of interactions between born in relaxed region × birth year)

Source: Author.

(b)

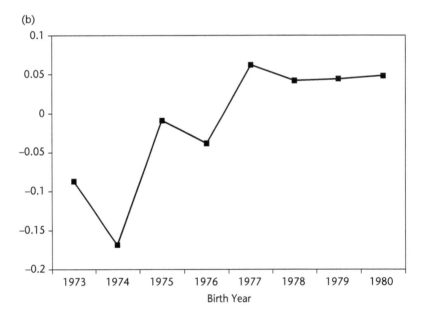

Figure 14.4b. The effect of relaxation on school enrolment (coefficients of interactions between dummy for girl × born in relaxed region × birth year)

Source: Author.

individuals were enrolled in school, an additional sibling increased enrolment of first children by approximately 14–16 percentage points. The estimates are statistically significant at the 1 per cent level. Panel D restricts the sample to households with two or fewer children. The estimates show that for a sample where 54 per cent of individuals were enrolled in school, an additional sibling increased enrolment of first children by approximately 12 percentage points. The estimates are mostly statistically significant at the 10 per cent level.

5.5. Robustness

The main results show that eldest children with younger siblings are more likely to be enrolled in school than those without younger siblings. I consider and provide evidence against the concern that the instrument affects the school enrolment of the first child through channels other than family size (i.e. the exclusion restriction is violated). They are not presented here because of space constraints. Please see in Qian (2017).

5.6. Mechanisms

A second child can increase school enrolment of first children for several reasons. I consider some of the most obvious hypotheses. First, there could be economies of scale in schooling costs. These could include costs related to textbooks, school fees, clothes, or food for school. Unfortunately, the data do not allow me to examine these costs directly. Second, I explore the hypothesis that a second child increases school enrolment of the first through permanent income channels. I provide suggestive evidence against these alternatives. Because of space constraints, please see Qian (2017).

Finally, I explore the possibility that having a second child increases the enrolment of first children by increasing the demand on cash income. I find evidence consistent with the hypothesis that parents view schools as an alternative source of childcare for the first child and send her to school while the mother enters the labour force. Please see Qian (2017).

6. Conclusion

This chapter estimates the effect of family size on school enrolment of first-born children. It resolves the problem of joint determination by exploiting the plausibly exogenous variation in family size caused by relaxations in the OCP. The results show that both the OCP and the previous four-year birth spacing policy were well enforced, and that the 1-son-2-child relaxation increased family size for girls born in relaxed areas. Then, it uses the variation in family size caused by this relaxation to show evidence that a second child increased school enrolment of the first child. The empirical results provide empirical evidence for a novel insight about first-born children, who have thus far been the focus of most existing empirical studies of quantity/quality. They show clearly that first-born children benefit from having a younger sibling.

It is beyond the scope of this chapter to provide conclusive evidence on the mechanisms driving the main effects. The empirical findings suggest that economies of scale in schooling and increased income demand from an additional child could play important roles. Interpreting these results outside of the context of rural China requires caution. This is especially true if parents in these other contexts do not have access to inexpensive public schooling or good labour market opportunities.

References

Angrist, J.D., V. Lavy, and A. Schlepper (2006). 'Multiple Experiments for the Causal Link Between the Quantity and Quality of Children'. Working Paper. Cambridge, MA: MIT.

Angrist, J.D., V. Lavy, and A. Schlosser (2010). 'Multiple Experiments for the Causal Link between the Quantity and Quality of Children'. *Journal of Labor Economics*, 28(4): 773–824.

Baker, M., J. Gruber, and K. Milligan (2008). 'Universal Child Care, Maternal Labor Supply and Family Well-Being', *Journal of Political Economy*, 116(4): 709–45.

Banerjee A., X. Meng, T. Porzio, and N. Qian (2014). 'Aggregate Fertility and Household Savings: A General Equilibrium Analysis Using Micro Data'. Working Paper 20050. Cambridge, MA: NBER.

Banister, J. (1987). *China's Changing Population*. Stanford, CA: Stanford University Press.

Becker, G.S., and H.G. Lewis (1973). 'On the Interaction Between the Quantity and Quality of Children'. *The Journal of Political Economy*, 81(2) Part 2: S279–S288.

Becker, G.S., and N. Tomes (1976). 'Child Endowments and the Quantity and Quality of Children'. *The Journal of Political Economy*, 84(4) Part 2: S143–S162.

Berhman, J., R. Pollak, and R.A.P. Taubman (1989). 'Family Resources, Family Size and Access to Financing for Education'. *The Journal of Political Economy*, 97(2): 389–419.

Black, S.E., P.J. Devereux, and K.G. Salvanes (2006). 'The More the Merrier? The Effect of Family Composition on Children's Education'. *The Quarterly Journal of Economics*.

Blau, D.M., and J. Currie (2006). 'Who's Minding the Kids? Preschool, Day Care, and After School Care.' In F. Welch and E. Hanushek (eds), *The Handbook of Economics of Education*, Vol. 2. New York: North Holland.

Bleakely, H., and F. Lange (2005). 'Chronic Disease Burden and the Interaction of Education, Fertility and Growth'. Working Paper. New Haven, CT: Yale University.

Conley, D. (2004). 'What is the "True" Effect of Sibship Size and Birth Order on Education? Instrumental Variable Estimates from Exogenous Variation in Fertility'. Working Paper. New York: New York University.

Croll, E., D. Davin, and P. Kane (eds) (1985). *China's One Child Family Policy*. London: Macmillan.

Dasgupta, M., A. Ebenstein, and E. Sharygin (2011). 'China's Marriage Market and Upcoming Challenges for Elderly Men'. Policy Research Working Paper. Washington, DC: World Bank.

Ebenstein, A. (2010). 'The "Missing Girls" of China and the Unintended Consequences of the One Child Policy', *Journal of Human Resources*, 45(1): 87–115.

Gomes, M. (1984). 'Family Size and Education Attainment in China'. *Population and Development Review*, 10(4): 647–60.

Goux, D., and Maurin, E. (2003). 'The Effects of Overcrowded Housing on Children's Performance at School'. CEPR Discussion Paper 3818. Washington, DC: CEPR.

Greenlaugh, S. (1986). 'Shifts in China's Population Policy, 1984–1986: Views from the Central, Provincial, and Local Levels'. *Population and Development Review*, 12(3): 493–515.

Guo, G., and L.K. VanWey (1999). 'Sibship Size and Intellectual Development: Is the Relationship Causal?' *American Sociological Review*, 64(2): 169–87.

Hannum, E. (2002). 'Education Stratification by Ethnicity in China: Enrolment and Attainment in the Early Reform Years'. *Demography*, 39(1): 95–117.

Hannum, E. and Park, A. (2002). 'Educating China's Rural Children in the 21st Century'. Mimeo.

Iacovou, M. (2001). 'Family Composition and Children's Educational Outcomes'. Working Paper. Colchester: Institute for Social and Economic Research.

Kessler, D. (1991). 'Birth Order, Family Size and Achievement: Family Structure and Wage Determination'. *Journal of Labor Economics*, 9(4): 413–26.

Lee, J. (2004). 'Sibling Size and Investment in Children's Education: An Asian Instrument'. Working Paper. Fayetteville, AR: University of Arkansas at Fayetteville.

Qian, N. (2008). 'Missing Women and the Price of Tea in China: The Effect of Income on Sex Imbalance'. *Quarterly Journal of Economics*, 123(3): 1251–85.

Qian, N. (2017). 'The Effect of China's One Child Policy on Sex Selection, Family Size, and the School Enrolment of Daughters'. UNU-WIDER Working Paper 2017/159.

Rosenzweig, M.R., and K.I. Wolpin (1980). 'Testing the Quantity–Quality Fertility Model: The Use of Twins as a Natural Experiment'. *Econometrica*, 48(1): 227–40.

Rosenzweig, M.R., and J. Zhang (2009). 'Do Population Control Policies Induce More Human Capital Investment? Twins, Birthweight, and China's "One Child" Policy'. *Review of Economic Studies*, 76(3): 1149–74.

Schlosser, A. (2011). 'Public Preschool and the Labor Supply of Arab Mothers: Evidence from a Natural Experiment'. Working Paper. Tel Aviv: Tel Aviv University.

Schultz, T.P. (2005). 'Effects of Fertility Decline on Family Well-Being: Evaluation of Population Programs'. Draft for MacArthur Foundation Consultation Meeting.

Stafford, F.P. (1987). 'Women's Work, Sibling Competition and Children's School Performance'. *The American Economic Review*, 77(5): 972–80.

Wei, S.-J., and Zhang, X. (2011). 'The Competitive Saving Motive: Evidence from Rising Sex Ratios and Savings Rates in China'. *Journal of Political Economy*, 119(3): 511–64.

White, T. (1992). 'Birth Planning Between Plan and Market: The Impact of Reform on China's One-Child Policy'. In Joint Economic Committee (ed.), *China's Economic Dilemmas in the 1990s: The Problems of Reforms, Modernization, and Interdependence.* Armonk, NY: M.E. Sharpe.

Zajonc, R.B., and G.B. Markus (1975). 'Birth Order and Intellectual Development'. *Psychological Review*, 82(1): 74–83.

Zeng, Y., T. Ping, G. Baochang, X. Yi, L. Bohua, and L. Yongpiing (1993). 'Causes and Implications of the Recent Increase in the Reported Sex Ratio at Birth in China'. *Population and Development Review*, 19(2): 283–302.

15

Eradicating Women-Hurting Customs

What Role for Social Engineering?

Jean-Philippe Platteau*, Giulia Camilotti* and Emmanuelle Auriol**

1. Introduction

Since the birth of modern development economics in the period immediately following the Second World War, attention has been mostly directed to the determinants of long-term economic growth performance and, in a subsequent stage, to issues of income distribution and poverty reduction. The implicit assumption was that the material level of living is the critical component of individual welfare and that non-economic factors, social norms and practices, in particular, change gradually in response to the enlargement of opportunities that accompanies economic growth (see Lewis 1955; Bauer and Yamey 1957; Meier and Baldwin 1957; Hirschman 1958). Recent thinking has called into question this 'organic approach' to development in two ways. First, personal welfare or human happiness is crucially influenced by non-economic factors, such as autonomy, participation in communal life, freedom to develop own talents and pursue own ends, dignity, and self-esteem. The presence or absence of these conditions determines whether or not destitution is added to poverty (Dasgupta 1993). Second, even if non-economic determinants of welfare are overlooked, the ability to seize upon economic opportunities, which affects economic progress, may be constrained by social norms and informal rules

* Centre for Research in the Economics of Development (CRED)
** Toulouse School of Economics March 19, 2018

The authors are especially grateful to Vijayendra Rao for detailed and constructive comments on a previous version of the paper. They also wish to thank Siwan Anderson, Charles Becker, Larry Blume, Steven Durlauf, and Catherine Guirkinger for helpful suggestions.

that do not automatically vanish as growth proceeds (Platteau 2000; Platteau and Peccoud 2010).

Reflecting the above questioning is the growing tendency to promote deliberate changes in customs, particularly those which hurt the interests of one or several population groups and may therefore be regarded as harmful in the present circumstances. This active attitude toward harmful customs is characteristic of what may be called 'social engineering'. The human rights approach, which has gained increasing currency since the 1980s, is an important component of social engineering. In matters of gender equality, for example, the first visible step in that direction is the Convention to Eliminate all forms of Discrimination Against Women (CEDAW), adopted by the United Nations in 1979. For the first time, it was stated explicitly that member states 'should engage to modify the social and cultural patterns of conduct of men and women, with a view to achieving the elimination of prejudices and customary and all other practices which are based on the idea of the inferiority or the superiority of either of the sexes or on stereotyped roles for men and women'. This document opened the way for actions combining legal interventions in the name of universal human rights, and the effective mobilization of victims so that they can perceive themselves as right-holders. In short, legal and preference changes are advocated. Non-Governmental Organizations (NGOs) and international agencies, UNICEF in particular, have run many initiatives that both refer to legal or quasi-legal principles and attempt to drive preference change.

To find more precision about the objectives of the human rights approach, one may refer to the UN fact sheet on Harmful Traditional Practices Affecting the Health of Women and Children published in 1995 (OHCHR, 1995). This document identifies five main harmful practices, namely, female genital cutting, early marriage and dowry, son preference, female infanticide, and early pregnancy and practices related to child delivery, which are clearly identified as human rights violations.

An essential feature of the social engineering approach is thus that it directly confronts the harmful custom with a view to eradicating it, often in the name of human rights. An alternative, more indirect approach, consists of encouraging changes in the technological, economic, or social environment in order to modify the costs and benefits of norm abidance. The difference between this indirect approach and the 'organic' approach advocated by many development economists of the 1950s (see above) lies in the fact that endogenous growth processes do not necessarily lead to the cost/benefit changes that cause harmful customs to disappear: specific policies may be required to generate the economic incentives susceptible of modifying them.

In this chapter, we want to explore the analytical conditions under which social engineering is more likely to succeed or fail when it comes to suppressing gender-biased customs. A dominant theory that has guided many efforts on the ground is a coordination game in which a bad Nash equilibrium has been selected because of pessimistic expectations of agents. There are other possible situations, however, and they need to be represented by other types of games. What we set out to do is to discuss the main possible interaction frameworks that can produce anti-women (Nash) equilibria, and to derive policy implications from the corresponding games. This will necessitate that we differentiate between games involving agents with homogenous preferences and those involving heterogeneous agents (here, great attention will be paid to different possible shapes of the distribution of preferences and their differentiated effects), between coordination games and bargaining games, and between coordination games and the rival claimants' game. Also, the influence of group membership on individual beliefs, preferences, and opportunities, or the role of social influences will have to be recognized.

Only then will we be able to determine which approach is more appropriate for fighting against harmful customs in varying contexts and what is the appropriate time frame within which it is realistic to expect results. In particular, we aim to understand the various roles that the statutory law can play and at highlighting the conditions under which legal interventions can be expected to be effective and whether and when they need to be supplemented, or replaced, by other strategies or policies.

To probe into this issue, we start by looking at the possible impact of the law on harmful customs in different situations depicted as games. We first look at situations in which the law has an expressive effect, starting with the most well-known model which assumes that all agents have identical anti-custom preferences (Section 2). We then remove the assumption of preference homogeneity to consider the more general case in which agents with different preferences interact in a purely decentralized manner (Section 3). In a third step, we review attempts to model the impact of the law assuming that it has a deterrent effect. Deterrence can be activated by the people themselves, by the state or by the informal authority (Section 4). After understanding the conditions under which the law can be effective, we turn to the possibility of changing preferences, which will be done in a heterogeneous agents' framework (Section 5). In the next step (Section 6), attention is shifted to situations where harmful customs are modified as a result of changes in the cost-benefit environment. Finally, we discuss the role of culture and the way strong feelings of identity can make eradication of harmful practices more difficult (Section 7). In the conclusion (Section 8), we derive the main lessons from our analysis.

Since this chapter follows a theoretical approach, its content is necessarily technical and difficult to grasp for readers with no training in microeconomics. However, the theoretical arguments exposed in its successive parts will be illustrated by examples drawn from available empirical works. Besides providing a theoretical scaffolding suited for our purpose, we therefore propose a reasoned survey of the relevant literature. This is done in separate sections so that the interested reader with no background in economics can directly go to them and obtain a basic understanding of our contribution.

2. The Expressive Effect of the Law: Homogeneous Agents

2.1. Theory

A first mechanism through which the law can affect a custom is the so-called 'expressive' effect of the law (Cooter 2000; McAdams 2000; Kahan 1997; Galbiati and Vertova 2014), which corresponds, in economics, to the idea of the law acting as a focal point in a coordination game (for a critical discussion of this approach, see Basu 2015). By definition, when the law has no enforceable sanction, the only way it can influence behaviour is through its expressive function. Coordination games are used to model customs that are considered social norms. The starting point of the social norm literature, pioneered by Schelling (1960) and Akerlof (1980), is that individual choice depends on how many people in the reference group will adopt a given behaviour.[1] A direct implication is that it is difficult to move away from the equilibrium outcome when agents' expectations have converged on that outcome.

Let us start from the simplest case in which all agents have identical preferences and therefore agree on the ranking of the various possible equilibrium outcomes. If a socially inferior outcome prevails, such as is the case when a harmful custom is established, it can only be because agents have (converging) pessimistic expectations. In other words, everybody dislikes the norm but nobody wants to deviate from the habit of following it given the expected behaviour of the others (see Akerlof 1976; Kuran 1987, 1988, 1997). In this framework, the custom is a focal point and, to remove it, one only needs a mechanism able to make agents change their expectations in a coordinated manner so that they can establish their preferred outcome. One such mechanism is a statutory law that would act as a new focal point.

For the sake of illustration, consider the following female genital cutting (FGC) game. There are two players representing parental couples belonging to two different households in the community. They have to decide whether to circumcise their daughter (strategy C) or not (strategy R). The payoff matrix displayed in Table 15.1 is based on the common view that FGC can be analysed as a coordination game (see Mackie 1996; Mackie and LeJeune 2009): parents wish to adopt the same behaviour because of the need to find a good match for their daughters on the marriage market. We label μ the benefit of

---

[1] We do not define the nature of the reference group, even when it is labelled the 'community'. A 'community', indeed, need not correspond to the whole village society, for example.

Table 15.1. A game of female genital cutting

		Parents of household 2	
		Cut daughter (C)	Reject the practice (R)
Parents of household 1	Cut daughter (C)	$\mu - \theta V, \mu - \theta V$	$-\theta V, 0$
	Reject the practice (R)	$0, -\theta V$	$\underline{\mu, \mu}$

coordination, whether it is derived from coordinating on cutting or from coordinating on not cutting. When coordination is on cutting, however, parents also incur a cost, denoted as θV, where θ can be thought of as reflecting the health risk to which girls are exposed when cut while V is an amplifying factor created by the external environment (say, the anti-cutting pressure exerted by the government, donor countries, or non-governmental organizations). The payoffs obtained in case of mismatch are therefore $-\theta V$ for the parents who cut their daughter, and zero for those who have refrained from doing so.

In such a game, assuming that $\mu - \theta V > 0$, there are three Nash equilibria (NE).[2] There are two NE in pure strategies: the two parental couples cut their daughter, the (C, C) outcome, or both of them refuse to do so, the (R, R) outcome (see the underlined joint payoffs). There also exists a Nash equilibrium in mixed strategy in which each parental couple plays 'cutting' (C) with probability $\frac{\mu + \theta V}{2\mu}$ and 'not cutting' (R) with probability $\frac{\mu - \theta V}{2\mu}$. Limiting our attention to NE in pure strategies, we see that only one of the two equilibria, (R, R) is socially efficient, yet expectations may lead the players to select the inefficient outcome, (C, C). Once trapped in this nasty equilibrium, players do not want to deviate from their strategy: everybody agrees that the practice is harmful and should be abandoned but 'no one dares to be the first to abandon it' (Abdalla 1982: pp. 94–5, cited from Mackie 1996: 1014). The inefficient equilibrium is then a focal point. Yet, in this game, it could be abandoned if the right kind of intervention, a legal ban of FGC, for example, makes the outcome (R, R) a new focal point by driving the agents' expectations to converge on it.

The above game is important precisely because the story that it underpins has been so influential among non-governmental and international organizations working to improve women's and children's well-being in a human rights framework.[3] In other words, many officers in charge of designing interventions intended to fight against harmful practices have found the social norm approach and its emphasis on coordination incentives quite appealing on the conceptual level.

---

[2] Note that, when the cost entailed by cutting is so large that $\mu - \theta V < 0$, there is a unique equilibrium (R, R).

[3] Female genital cutting is considered as a violation of human rights, in particular, of the right to be free from all forms of discrimination against women; the right to health, to body integrity and to freedom from violence. All these rights are protected by international treaties such as the CEDAW.

A striking illustration are the anti-FGC interventions promoted by UN agencies, such as UNICEF and UNFPA (the specialized agencies for Children and for Population, respectively), as well as by a number of non-governmental organizations (NGOs). Consider the experience of Tostan, an NGO focused on the task of eliminating FGC (and early marriage) throughout the West Africa region. Enacted in 1999, a law banned this practice in Senegal, the country where Tostan has its headquarters. In its work with rural communities, Tostan framed FGC as a human rights violation and, as part of a broader programme to empower women, it made explicit reference to existing laws and conventions designed to protect women's and children's rights. Its strategy was clearly based on the social norm approach since its ultimate step was to achieve declarations whereby people from different village communities publicly announce the abandonment of the harmful practice. Public declarations were thus intended to serve as both a coordination and a commitment device, expected to become the new focal point for these communities.

An important remark about equilibrium selection in games with multiple equilibria serves as a natural transition to the presentation of the available empirical evidence in the next subsection. The concept of risk dominant equilibrium elaborated by Harsanyi and Selten (1988) offers a valid alternative to the concept of a focal point to sort out the selection problem that arises in multiple-equilibria games. In a 2×2 game, an NE is considered risk dominant if it is less risky (i.e. it has the largest basin of attraction) and the more uncertainty players have about the actions of the other players, the more likely they will choose the risk dominant strategy in preference to the payoff dominant strategy, which correponds to the Pareto-superior or socially efficient strategy. This has been shown in the context of large populations with the help of evolutionary theory: agents who are not perfectly rational (they have some myopia) tend to select the risk dominant equilibrium over a sufficiently large number of successive periods.[4] In the well-known stag hunt game, the risk dominant equilibrium is socially inefficient. This dilemma, however, does not arise with the FGC game depicted in Table 15.1: the risk dominant equilibrium, (R, R), is also the payoff dominant equilibrium.[5] That (R, R) is risk dominant is evident from a simple glance at Table 15.1. Not only is the payoff

---

[4] Two separate evolutionary models support the idea that the risk dominant equilibrium is more likely to occur. In both models, the agents play multiple two-player games and are matched randomly with opponents. The first model, based on replicator dynamics, predicts that a population is more likely to adopt the risk dominant equilibrium than the payoff dominant equilibrium. The second model, based on best response strategy revision and mutation, predicts that the risk dominant state is the only stochastically stable equilibrium (see Kandori et al. 1993; Young 1993; Fudenberg and Levine 1998).

[5] The condition for the (R, R) equilibrium to risk dominate the (C, C) equilibrium is that the product of deviation losses when both players play (R, R) exceeds the product of deviation losses when they both play (C, C).This condition, which requires that $\theta V > 0$, is always satisfied for the game depicted in Table 15.1.

received when coordinating on R higher than the payoff received when coordinating on C, but it is also the case that the loss incurred if the other player deviates from (R, R) is not larger than the loss incurred if deviation is from (C, C).[6] We are therefore in the presence of a game where, although players are uncertain about the other players' actions, they will evolutionarily select the Pareto-superior equilibrium. In more concrete terms, the theory of risk dominance predicts that the practice of FGC should not be observed.

2.2. Empirical Evidence

While theoretically appealing, the definition of female genital cutting as a social norm which gives rise to a coordination problem has not been empirically established. Bellemare et al. (2015) in a cross-country analysis of the custom in West Africa find that, on average, 87 per cent of the variation in FGC persistence (measured as the individual's support for the practice) is explained by individual level and household characteristics. They additionally find that the more widespread the practice is in a country, the more individual factors explain its persistence. Both findings are at odds with the coordination game used to explain FGC, since, in this game, the persistence of the custom is explained by how many people practise it rather than by household and individual characteristics. These results also suggest that strategies other than public declarations and pledging, such as targeting individuals, might be more effective in countries where FGC is pervasive.

For Sudan, Efferson et al. (2015) have tested the validity of the coordination model of FGC which has inspired development agencies and NGOs. If FGC is a social norm at the community level, then communities should have either a zero or 100 per cent FGC incidence and an important discontinuity in FGC rate between the two types of communities should be observed. Using a sample of girls from forty-five communities, they find neither extreme rates of FGC nor discontinuity in the distribution of FGC incidence across communities. These findings point to the absence of a common cutting norm at that level. It is still possible that coordination takes place at another level than the community, in particular if the community does not completely overlap with the marriage pool (under the assumption that coordination takes place within the marriage network). However, the authors find a high level of endogamy within communities. Moreover, in each community a substantial number of households declared that they could marry with families not practising FGC.

---

[6] Because the game is symmetric, the condition for (R, R) to risk dominate (C, C) is reduced to requiring that the sum of the payoffs received by agent 1 when the combination of plays is (R, R) and when the combination is (R, C) is greater than the sum of payoffs obtained from (C, C) and (C, R).

Finally, an implicit association test has been run[7] within each community to check the presence of any discontinuity in normative attitude towards FGC. If, within the same community, two separate norms, cutting and not cutting, coexist, a bimodal distribution of the individual scores from the test should be observed: individuals should either show a positive attitude towards FGC or a negative one. However, the authors do not find any implicit association between being cut and positive or negative values: the distribution of test scores is unimodal and centred on zero. The authors conclude that their findings are not compatible with a model of coordination (with homogenous preferences) either within the communities or the marriage pool.

In a companion study (Vogt et al. 2016) the authors show how heterogeneity within communities and families can be exploited to change attitudes towards FGC. They run an experiment where movies dramatizing diverging opinions on FGC within an extended family are used as treatment in some villages of South Sudan. The treatment outcome is obtained through an implicit association test, and what comes out is an improvement in the perception of uncut girls in the treated group. This result is therefore achieved in the absence of any trigger of beneficient coordination, just by working on the level of individual perceptions.

In a study conducted in the Senegalese region of Kolda, Camilotti (2015, 2016) has explicitly studied the impact of Tostan's intervention, the potential role of the public declaration mechanism, and the possible effects of the legal ban on FGC. Tostan actually used two methods to achieve the termination of cutting. First is the aforementioned expressive law effect to be achieved through a public commitment destined to assure everyone that all community members are ready to abandon the practice of cutting. Second, is a training programme emphasizing the health cost of cutting. While the former component assumes that everybody dislikes the FGC practice, the latter assumes that people follow it because they underestimate its cost for the girls who are cut. The main findings of Camilotti can be summarized as follows. First, the impact of the intervention that can be ascribed to Tostan's programme as such exists but appears to be quite limited: in the targeted villages, the cutting practice has largely persisted. Second, there is evidence that the new anti-FGC environment, which includes the new law, generates perverse effects in the form of a lowering of the age at cutting, with potentially noxious consequences on the level of health. Third, there is no evidence that public declarations have worked as a coordination and commitment device.

---

[7] The implicit association test is a way to test the strength of the connection people make between two concepts without explicitly asking their opinion. In the present context, individuals were shown on a screen two drawings of girls, one cut and one uncut, and a set of either positive or negative words that they had to associate to one of the girls.

Fourth, there is nevertheless some evidence suggesting that coordination might take place at the level of the extended family network. Taken together, Camilotti's first three findings suggest that the expressive law effect did not materialize because the game's payoff structure is not that of a coordination game. Moreover, it is evident from the first two findings that Tostan's intervention did not succeed in raising θ so much as to make $\mu - \theta V$ negative. If it were the case, indeed, everybody would have stopped cutting girls.

Lastly, using a dataset of 24,000 women born between 1949 and 1995 in Burkina Faso, Novak (2016) again shows that households within a community have heterogeneous preferences for FGC. A key determinant of the willingness to abandon FGC is formal education: women who have received any formal education are more ready to abandon FGC than uneducated women.

Overall, the results of the four above studies indicate that the conceptualization of FGC as a coordination game in which agents have homogeneous anti-FGC preferences is misleading. A legal ban of FGC or any other device that should work as a new focal point will perform poorly if expectations regarding other people's behaviour are not the leading determinant of behaviour. Scepticism about the empirical relevance of the game depicted in Table 15.1 confirms the doubts raised by the discussion of risk dominance at the end of the previous subsection: in a dynamic context, agents should select the socially efficient equilibrium since it coincides with the risk dominant equilibrium. Since empirical evidence attests that FGC is a widespread practice in some societies, we are led to call the above game into question.

Evidence also suggests that individual preferences are not identical so that a coordination game with symmetric payoffs does not apppropriately reflect reality. In the following, we therefore develop an alternative framework that is explicitly based on the assumption of heterogeneous preferences yet still belongs to the social norm approach. As a matter of fact, observations that there is no massive abandonment of the FGC practice but that a minority of people respond to a change in the (legal) environment do not, in and of themselves, form a sufficiently strong basis to dismiss the social norm/coordination analytical approach.

Such a choice does not imply that we want to rule out another possible explanation, which could simultaneously account for persisting coordination on the socially inefficient equilibrium and unequal prevalence of the FGC practice both across and within communities. These phenomena could be observed if people have homogeneous anti-custom preferences but coordination takes place at other levels than the village or the inter-village network. For example, as suggested by Munshi and Myaux (2006) with regard to the use of contraception in rural Bangladesh, there exist strong sub-village networks (in this instance, religious groups) through which people coordinate their actions related to social activities. However, because evidence points to the importance of individual- or household-level determinants of behaviour vis-à-vis FGC, and because considerations of spouse matching on the marriage market do not seem as paramount as some literature suggests, we believe that we are on rather firm grounds when we emphasize the role of heterogeneous preferences and try to understand their implications for coordination equilibria.

3. The Expressive Effect of the Law: Heterogeneous Agents

In order to keep our canonical model of heterogeneous preferences as simple and as general as possible, we abstract from certain features specific to particular social norms, for example, the future value at marriage of women who are cut (see Chesnokova and Vaithianathan (2010) for an example of modelling FGC in the marriage market).[8]

In conformity with the social norm approach (see Granovetter 1978; Schelling 1960), we assume that the positive component of the agent's utility function varies positively with the proportion of the population that follows the custom.[9] The negative component, however, is idiosyncratic and reflects the agent's aversion to the custom or the cost incurred by following it. Adapting from a model recently proposed by Auriol and Platteau (2016), the net utility obtained by an agent from following the (harmful) custom is written:

$$U_i = u(P) - \theta_i V(E)$$

where P stands for the proportion of the population that abides by the custom, θ_i is the coefficient of aversion to the custom of individual i, E represents the (legal) environment bearing upon the custom, and $V(E)$ represents the way this environment translates into a cost of following the custom. The positive component of utility, $u(P)$, is assumed to be linear: $u(P) = \mu P$. It therefore has the following properties: $u'(P) > 0$, $u''(P) = 0$, $u(0) = 0$, $u(1) = \mu$. Moreover, each member of the population is characterized by a parameter $\theta_i \in [0, 1]$, which is distributed according to the continuous density $f(\theta)$ and cumulative

---

[8] In a marriage market, heterogeneity could be present only on the men's side: some men prefer to have a wife who has been cut while others do not. If they ignore whom they are going to attract, potential brides (more precisely, their parents) might opt for FGC even though they dislike that custom. Equilibrium will then depend on the degree of heterogeneity in the husbands' preferences for FGC, assuming that no bride wants it. This could be entirely consistent with situations of partial prevalence of the FGC norm and with its determination by individual preferences. Empirical evidence, however, suggests that heterogeneity of preferences characterizes women as well as men. This is an additional reason why we stick to a general model of norm abidance in which preferences are not differentiated on the basis of gender.

[9] A different way to model social norms is by assuming that non-conformity leads to a decrease in utility due to sanctions or loss of reputation. The utility loss is then proportional to the number of people following the norm (see Akerlof 1980; Ambec 2008).

distribution $F(\theta)$ functions. For a given environment E, agents therefore incur different costs depending upon their degree of aversion towards the custom (the greater this aversion, the higher θ_i). The first derivative, $V'(E)$, is assumed to be positive, implying that an environment that has become more hostile to the custom, reflected in an increase of E, causes higher costs for those who continue to follow it. Note that the cost expression is multiplicative, implying that the hostility of the environment entails higher costs for the agents who are more averse to the custom.

At equilibrium, if we consider the case of the indifferent agent whose aversion coefficient is defined as $\theta_i = \theta^*$ such that the agent's net utility from the custom is equal to zero, we observe that $P = \int_0^{\theta^*} f(\theta)d\theta = F(\theta^*)$. This means that the proportion of the population which has a lower or equal aversion toward the custom than the indifferent agent is equivalent to the proportion of the population that abides by the custom (having a positive or null net utility from the custom).

The utility of the indifferent agent then is:

$$\mu F(\theta^*) - V(E)\theta^* = 0, \text{ implying } \frac{\mu F(\theta^*)}{V(E)} = \theta^* \tag{1}$$

where $F(\theta^*) = P$, the proportion of people who abide by the custom. Equation (1) requires that an interior solution exists.

Since there are obviously multiple Nash equilibria in such a static coordination game (in particular, the Nash equilibrium where nobody follows the custom, $\theta^* = F(\theta^*) = 0$, always exists), it is convenient to restrict the number of equilibria by introducing some dynamics in the game. We thus assume that at each point of time there is a probability that a new agent is added to the pool of existing members. This new agent is drawn at random from the set $[0, 1]$ according to the density function $f(\theta)$. He (she) enters the pool of members with a given θ^a, and will have to decide whether to follow the custom or not. He (she) chooses to abide by it if $\mu F(\theta^*) > \theta^a V(E)$, where $F(\theta^*)$ is the equilibrium point before the entry of the new agent. This assumption helps us to solve the selection issue: an equilibrium can be selected only if it is stable. Formally, following Auriol and Benaim (2000), the stability condition is written: $\mu f(\theta^*) - V(E) < 0$.[10]

It is evident that the characteristics of the equilibria critically depend on the shape of the distribution function over θ_i, for a given level of $V(E)$.

---

[10] For Auriol and Benaim (2000), indeed, if we let $dx/dt = g(x)$ be an autonomous differential equation, and $x(t) = x^*$ is an equilibrium so that $g(x^*) = 0$, the following result is obtained: if $g'(x^*) < 0$, the equilibrium $x(t) = x^*$ is stable, and if $g'(x^*) > 0$, the equilibrium is unstable. Applied to our problem, we have: $d\theta^*/dt = \mu F(\theta^*) - \theta V(E)$. The condition $g'(x^*) < 0$ therefore implies $\mu f(\theta^*) - V(E) < 0$.

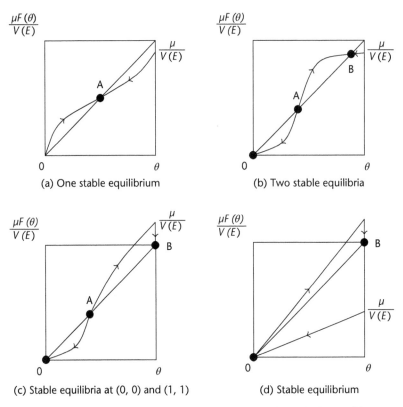

Figure 15.1. Examples of coordination games with multiple equilibria

Source: Authors

Figure 15.1 shows some possible situations. The horizontal axis represents the type of agents, θ_i, and the curve shows the agent's utility from conforming to the custom divided by the common component of the individual cost, $\frac{\mu F(\theta)}{V(E)}$. Given equation (1), an equilibrium is when the 45° line, corresponding to the identity function $\theta = \theta$, crosses the curve. It is a stable equilibrium if, increasing θ_i, the curve reaches the intersection point from above the 45° line.

We can now examine important possible equilibrium configurations. To begin with, Figure 15.1a depicts the case where the density function $f(\theta)$ is U-shaped (i.e. convex), representing a distribution of people which puts more weight at the extremes. In this bimodal distribution, there are thus two masses of individuals with very high or very low aversion to the custom. With such a polarized population, the interior equilibrium, when it exists (that is, when the two curves have an intersection point, such as they have at point A), is stable: any random perturbation around the equilibrium point will bring the system back to that point. Indeed, the curve $\frac{\mu F(\theta)}{V(E)}$ lies above the identity function beneath the intersection point and below the identity function beyond that point. We can therefore conclude that, with a U-shaped density function, a fraction of the people follows the custom while the remainder does not, provided that the curve crosses the identity line. This (stable) interior equilibrium is unique.[11]

Figure 15.1b describes a quite different situation in which most of the people tend to be concentrated around the middle of the distribution of θ values: the density function $f(\theta)$ is unimodal and its peak lies around the middle of the [0, 1] range. This means that the majority of people have a moderate (medium) aversion to the custom. In this figure, the first intersection point (denoted by A) is unstable while the second one (denoted by B) is stable. In such an instance, there are two possible stable equilibria: either nobody follows the custom or a rather large proportion of the population does. It is easy to check from Figure 15.1c that, if the curve $\frac{\mu F(\theta)}{V(E)}$ crosses the 45° degree line only once (at point A) inside the [0, 1] range, the second intersection point would lie on the vertical axis so that $\frac{\mu F(\theta)}{V(E)}$ exceeds θ at $\theta = 1$ (implying that $\mu > V(E)$). The solution $\theta^* = F(\theta^*) = 1$ is therefore a possible (stable) equilibrium and we have a case where either nobody or everybody follows the custom.

Let us now turn to extreme situations in which the overwhelming majority of the people have either very low or very large values of θ_i. It is then easy to see that a unique stable equilibrium will prevail. If almost all the people are clustered around a value of θ_i close to zero, and $\mu/V(E)$ is high enough, the $\frac{\mu F(\theta)}{V(E)}$ curve will have a strongly concave shape which entirely lies above the 45° line and crosses the vertical axis above the point $\frac{\mu F(\theta)}{V(E)} = 1$. The only (stable) equilibrium is then $\theta^* = 1$: everybody sticks to the custom. Conversely, if almost all the people are clustered around a value of θ_i close to one, and μ/V is small enough, the $\frac{\mu F(\theta)}{V(E)}$ curve will have a strongly convex shape which entirely lies below the 45° line: nobody follows the custom.

A last case to consider is that of a uniform density function that translates into a linear cumulative distribution function. As Figure 15.1d shows, two main possibilities arise: either the $\frac{\mu F(\theta)}{V(E)}$ curve lies entirely below, or entirely above the 45° line. In the former case, which corresponds to a situation where $\mu/V < 1$, the unique stable equilibrium is $\theta^* = 0$: nobody abides by the custom, which is according to intuition since the utility obtained when everybody follows the custom, μ, is smaller than the cost $V(E)$. In the latter case, which

---

[11] If the cost element of the utility function is additive so that a hostile environment creates a fixed cost, there would then be a minimum positive value of $\theta, \theta min$, below which nobody would follow the custom. This is because even these agents require that a positive fraction of the community abides by the custom for themselves to agree to do so. The curve $\frac{\mu F(\theta)}{V(E)}$ would start to rise from this point, θmin, that is, necessarily below the 45° degree line, and there would be an additional intersection point, which would nevertheless correspond to an unstable equilibrium.

corresponds to a situation where $\mu/V > 1$, the unique stable equilibrium is $\theta^* = 1$: everybody abides by the custom since even the most averse person draws a net benefit from custom abidance.

We have earlier discussed the expressive role of the law in a coordination game when multiple stable equilibria exist, highlighting the way it can theoretically help to change the focal point and move from one equilibrium to another. Allowing for preference heterogeneity, we now understand that the final equilibrium the law can lead to fundamentally depends on the underlying distribution of preferences (or aversion) to the custom. Thus, when many people have a moderate aversion toward the custom so as to be clustered around the average value of θ (see Figures 15.1b and 15.11c), the law can possibly act as a new focal point entailing the disappearance of the harmful custom (the shift from large or total adoption to zero adoption). But if the distribution of preferences is such that no equilibrium exists at (0,0), when the density function is U-shaped, for example (see Figure 15.1a), the total disappearance of the harmful custom cannot be achieved by changing people's expectations. This point has been stressed by Cooter (2000).

That the distribution of preferences plays a critical role has now become clear: it determines the type of effect that we should expect from any coordination device aiming at changing people's expectations. In particular, coordination might not be enough to eradicate harmful social norms, as has been empirically shown in the aforementioned study of Camilotti (2015, 2016). As a consequence, interventions designed for modifying the payoffs or the preferences of individuals are most likely needed. From the model depicted above, it is actually evident that the law can activate another mechanism rather than the expressive one: a stricter law can thus increase the cost of following the custom, $V(E)$, which amounts to changing the payoff matrix. Equilibrium outcomes can consequently be modified. The increase in the cost is reflected in the fact that being caught breaking the law now leads to punishment by the formal authority. This is what in the legal literature is called 'the deterrent effect of the law'. We explore this dimension in the following section.

Before embarking upon that task, however, a remark deserves to be made. We have assumed above that agents take their decision to follow the harmful custom or not in a simultaneous manner. It is well known that in coordination games sequential playing instead of simultaneous playing yields the efficient equilibrium. For example, in the simple 2×2 game of excision depicted in Table 15.1, if one of the parental couples could make the decision in a first move while the other couple decides thereafter, the first-mover would always choose to abstain from cutting the daughter. This is because, having done so, the first-mover knows that it will be in the interest of the second-mover to follow suit. This outcome obeys the logic of a coordination game and obviously causes the socially inefficient (0,0) equilibrium to vanish.

Things are more complicated when preferences are heterogeneous. Indeed, the outcome then depends upon the preference of the first-mover. If the first-mover rather likes the custom, he (she) will follow it and the second-mover may choose to make the same decision although being rather averse to the custom. But the converse outcome could also happen: if the first-mover rather dislikes the custom, he (she) will shun it and the second-mover may choose to also renounce the custom although being less averse to it. This nicer result is obtained by Mackie (1996, 2000) in the context of an n-person game. Considering again the case of female genital cutting, he shows that the disappearence of the custom can start from a group of individuals with a high aversion to the custom: the group of custom-breakers grows in size until a critical mass is reached and the utility from non-cutting becomes higher for everybody. Note that the underlying assumption behind this cascade model of the type proposed by Kuran (1988, 1997) is a distribution of preferences similar to the one assumed in Figures 15.1b and 15.1c. An important question is therefore whether the position of first-mover(s) is randomly decided, or whether those individuals with highest aversion to the harmful custom are ready and able to take up the leadership position. It is obvious that the second possibility is more conducive to the demise of the harmful custom than the first one.

4. The Deterrent Effect of the Law

4.1. *Theory Based on the Social Norm Approach*

We are now ready to examine the impact of the law when its function includes punishing deviant behaviour when detected: the expected cost of punishment is the ultimate threat that leads people to re-negotiate the custom. This is a standard element of the law and economics approach, where prominence is given to the legal tool and to a positive probability of being caught. The law therefore changes the payoffs of the game, increasing the cost of following the custom and modifying the agents' cost-benefit configuration.[12]

In the model used in Section 3, the government creates an environment, labeled E, which is either more or less hostile to the harmful custom. A larger value of E means that the environment is more hostile, thereby inflicting greater cost on custom-followers. A direct effect of a larger E is to cause a fall

---

[12] Such an approach, it may be noted, is based on a conception of the law as a change-driver and it stands in striking contrast to the alternative view of the law as formalization of dominant values prevailing in the society. Thus, for Benabou and Tirole (2011), the law 'is not merely a price system for bad and good behaviour, it also plays an important role in expressing and shaping the values of societies'. Laws (and policies) thus reflect the knowledge that legislators (and decision makers) have about societal preferences, and 'these same community standards are also what shapes social norms (conferring esteem or stigma) and moral sentiments (pride and shame)' (pp. 1–2).

in $\frac{\mu}{V(E)}$, and therefore a downward shift of the $\frac{\mu F(\theta)}{V(E)}$ curve. In Figure 15.1a, the effect of that downward shift is to lower the equilibrium value of θ, and therefore also that of $F(\theta)$. The proportion of custom-followers therefore decreases.

Formally, we specify the objective function of the government by simply assuming that the positive component of its utility increases as the proportion of custom-followers decreases while the negative component is a cost function linear in the number of E units. That is, we write:

$$MaxU^p = v(1 - F(\theta)) - cE$$
$$E, \theta \qquad (2)$$
$$s.t. \ \mu F(\theta) = \theta V(E)$$

where $v'(.) > 0$, $v''(.) \leq 0$, and c measures the (constant) unit cost. The government, acting as a principal, maximizes U^p with respect to E and θ subject to the citizens' participation constraint. We assume that a stable solution exists for θ^*. Replacing E in the principal's objective function by its value in the participation constraint, the maximization problem can be simplified thus:

$$\underset{\theta}{Max} \ v(1 - F(\theta)) - cV^{-1}\left[\frac{\mu F(\theta)}{\theta}\right]$$

where V^{-1} is the inverse function of $V(E)$.

The first-order condition, with respect to θ, comes out as:

$$v'(1 - F(\theta))f(\theta) = -c(V^{-1})'\frac{\theta\mu f(\theta) - \mu F(\theta)}{\theta^2}$$

The interpretation of this condition is straightforward: at equilibrium, the marginal benefit for the government of a one unit decrease in the number of agents following the custom is equal to the marginal cost. The marginal cost is itself measured by the unit cost of hostility of the environment times the number of additional environmental hostility units needed to deter one more agent from following the custom. The LHS of this equilibrium condition is obviously positive. As for the RHS, it is positive if $\theta f(\theta) < F(\theta)$. This condition is automatically satisfied if the stability condition for θ is itself satisfied.[13] Under the same condition, the comparative-static effect of a more hostile environment on the fraction of people following the harmful norm is unambiguously negative: $d\theta/dE < 0$ and, therefore, $d(F(\theta))/dE < 0$.[14]

If we allow for corner solutions, the existence of which depend on the shape of $f(\theta)$, other outcomes become possible. In particular, it may happen that the

---

[13] The condition for stability that we derived earlier is: $\mu f(\theta) - V(E) < 0$. Substituting the value of $V(E)$ as given in equation (1), it is straightforward that the condition can also be written thus: $\mu\left[f(\theta) - \frac{F(\theta)}{\theta}\right] < 0$. This implies that $\theta f(\theta) < F(\theta)$.

[14] From the participation constraint $\mu F(\theta) - \theta V(E) = 0$, we get that $\frac{d\theta}{dE} = \frac{\theta V'(E)}{\mu f(\theta) - V(E)}$. Therefore, $d\theta/dE$ is negative if $\mu f(\theta) < V(E)$, or $\theta f(\theta) < F(\theta)$.

government's increased effort to make the custom more costly to follow leads to its complete abandonment, as dreamed up by the proponents of the social engineering approach. This will happen if, in Figure 15.1a for example, the downward shift of the curve $\frac{\mu F(\theta)}{V(E)}$ is such that it now lies entirely below the identity function: in this instance, from a positive value in the $[0, 1]$ range, θ^* falls to zero. Another possibility, however, is that the government's intervention produces no impact at all. Consider the case in which the function $\frac{\mu F(\theta)}{V(E)}$ is strongly concave and lies entirely above the identity function, reflecting a situation in which the reward for custom abidance is quite large. The equilibrium is the corner solution $\theta^* = 1$. It is quite possible in this instance that an increase in E, which causes a decrease in $\mu/V(E)$, will not be large enough to lower the value of θ^* below unity.

Before moving to another analytical setting, it is natural to ask whether, given a U-shaped density function for example, the government will optimally choose θ in the range $[0, 1]$ (such as depicted in Fig. 15.1a), or $\theta = 1$ (if the whole curve is shifted upwards in such a way that it lies entirely above the 45° line). The answer to that question hinges upon a comparison between the sensitivity of the people to the hostile pressure against the custom (as measured by E), that is, on the shape of $V(E)$, on the one hand, and the weight attached by the government to the objective of removing that custom, that is, the form of $v(1 - F(\theta))$, on the other hand. As it turns out, it is when the former is large in relation to the latter that the government will choose the undesirable corner solution while, in the opposite case, it will choose the interior solution where fewer people (less than the complete population) abide by the custom.[15]

4.2. Theory Based on Antagonistic Preferences

To analyse the deterrent effect of the law, there is an alternative to the social norm (and coordination) framework used so far. It consists of positing antagonistic preferences between alleged beneficiaries and victims of the custom: the game is played between rival claimants and what payoff one party gets is lost by the other party. A first example of this setting is a bargaining model in which two agents have diverging interests and the resulting conflicts can be settled by appealing to the court. In this framework, the cost of legal proceedings for the parties involved in the litigation represents the threat point, so that a law more favourable to one of the parties will increase his (her) bargaining power and lead to a Nash bargaining position closer to her preferred choice.

Following Platteau and Wahhaj (2014), let us assume that the custom is favourable to agent 1 and harmful for agent 2. We call α the degree to which

---

[15] The proof of that result is not straightforward and actually requires the use of explicit functions. The interested reader can find a proof by analogy in Auriol and Platteau (2017).

the customary rule is applied (with $a \in [0, 1]$). Since agent 1, who earns a, derives maximum benefit from the full implementation of the custom, her preferred choice is $a = 1$. Agent 2 is in the opposite situation and her preferred choice is $a = 0$, implying that the custom is not applied at all. If the conflict of interests is not settled informally, it is referred to the court which always chooses the degree of implementation f. Since the court is, by assumption, more favourable to the interests of agent 2, the party victimized by the custom, we have that $f < a$. If the stake involved is set to 1, a and f are also the amounts accrued to agent 1 under the custom and the law, respectively. Likewise, $(1-a)$ and $(1-f)$ denote the amounts accrued to agent 2. For example, the stake is the amount of parental wealth and the custom is the rule governing its distribution between a son and a daughter upon inheritance. Or the stake is the wealth of a deceased husband and the custom is the rule governing its distribution between the widow and the in-laws. Functions V_1 and V_2 measure the utilities obtained by each party from the wealth inherited. Finally, C_1 and C_2 represent costs, respectively for agents 1 and 2, of accessing the formal court, including not only the legal fees and the time spent in litigation procedures, but also the psychological and other costs that claimants incur when they use the statutory law system. Because the latter cost component is likely to hit the claimant harder than the defenders, it is reasonable to assume that $C_2 > C_1$. If the difference between C_1 and C_2 is not too large, we expect that a change in the formal law which gives the weaker party (the daughter or the widow) a greater share of the wealth would improve her utility from the threat point and lower that of the stronger party. In a large number of cases, this would also improve his (her) welfare from bargaining at the other party's expense. Too see this, write the Nash bargaining solution to the problem as:

$$a^* = \underset{0 \leq a \leq 1}{argmax} \ [V_1(a) - (V_1(f) - C_1)][V_2(1-a) - (V_2(1-f) - C_2)]$$

Assuming $V_i'(.) > 0$ and $V_i''(.) \leq 0$, with $i = 1, 2$, the first-order condition is given by:

$$V_1'(a)[V_2(1-a) - V_2(1-f) + C_2] - V_2'(1-a)[V_1(a) - V_1(f) + C_1] = 0 \quad (3)$$

The derivative of (3) with respect to f gives the following expression:

$$\frac{da}{df} = -\frac{V_1'(a)[V_2'(1-f)] - V_2'(1-a)[-V_1'(f)]}{SOC}$$

Since the numerator of the above expression is positive and since the denominator corresponds to the second-order condition, which is negative in the solution to the bargaining problem, we have that $da/df > 0$. Bearing in mind that a legal reform in favour of agent 2 is reflected by a fall of f, this is seen to cause a decrease in the share of agent 1, measured by a.

Note that, if we refer to the marriage market framework mentioned at the beginning of Section 3 in connection with FGC, it is possible that the impact of the law on the situation of the vulnerable party will be undermined by the prevailing marriage market equilibrium. This is because, if women seek good husbands, the social norm can arise despite antagonistic preferences. When this is the case, a social engineering approach will have to produce an effect large enough to affect not just individual preferences but marriage market equilibria. Legislation against dowry and domestic violence in India seems to have run up against such a difficulty.[16]

4.3. *Empirical Evidence on the Effect of Women's Empowerment*

In Guirkinger and Platteau (2016), we review recent studies that test the impact of the law on anti-women customs. Evidence from these studies is broadly compatible with the predictions of bargaining theory, yet not in an unambiguous and complete manner. In particular, there is a possibility that laws intended to enhance women's status yield perverse effects. Such a possibility has been illustrated by Anderson and Genicot (2015) who show that a more gender-equal inheritance law in India has increased suicide rates for both men and women. To explain their results, the authors argue that increased access to inheritance raises a woman's bargaining power with the consequence of engendering more conflicts over household resources. In the same vein, Ali et al. (2014) have shown that in Rwanda a legal reform aimed at improving land access for legally married women has had a positive impact on plans to bequeath land to girls, yet only for male-headed households. In female-headed households, the opposite effect has been observed. The proposed explanation is that, in a virilocal exogamous society, 'transferring land to females would imply putting one's old age support at risk and that doing so would be particularly challenging for female heads who may lack other support mechanisms' (2014: 273)

A central lesson to learn from the (limited) available literature is the following: any law aimed at modifying personal status and position within such a vital fabric as the family is bound to generate complex and indirect effects that a simple bargaining approach fails to capture entirely. This is patent when the bargaining power acquired through a new law improves or worsens the condition of women in dimensions not targeted by the legislator.

In the remainder of Section 4, we want to draw attention to an alternative approach to the use of the law to combat harmful customs. It departs from the standard social norm approach in two important ways. First, instead of playing a coordination game, individuals play a rival claimant's game, implying that they

---

[16] We are thankful to Vijayendra Rao for having drawn our attention to this point.

have antagonistic preferences. Second, an informal authority structure coexists with the formal legal order, thus creating a situation of legal dualism.

4.4. An Alternative Theory with Formal-Informal Interactions

In the model developed by Aldashev et al. (2012a, 2012b), instead of being given, the custom is chosen by a traditional authority. This authority is intrinsically conservative, implying that it is in favour of customs that protect the interests of traditional elite or dominant groups at the expense of other people, for example, men at the expense of women. The game that depicts the social interactions between the elite and the non-elite is a rival claimant's game of the kind assumed in Section 4.2 (antagonistic preferences). The customary authority, however, may consider the possibility of reducing the retrograde character of the custom because it is also sensitive to its social influence and local power, which itself depends on the size of its jurisdictional domain. In turn, the size of its jurisdiction is determined by the number of local residents who seek and abide by its judgment when a conflict arises. This is where the statutory law performs its role. By assumption, it is more progressive than the custom and, therefore, people disadvantaged by the custom may be induced to appeal to the modern court which strictly applies the law. Yet, they will actually do it only if the value of the more favourable judgment obtained in the court exceeds the cost of circumventing the customary authority (or ignoring its judgment), which includes not only the cost of going to the court but also the cost of calling that traditional authority into question.

A central result of the above theory is what the authors have called the 'magnet effect of the law': a more progressive law may induce the traditional authority to change the custom in the same direction. Although the custom will not move as far as the law, it is transformed to the benefit of the disadvantaged sections of the population. In this way, even the victims who choose to stay within the traditional jurisdiction will benefit from the legal reform, albeit indirectly. The underlying mechanism is the following: by improving the exit opportunity available to these groups, the law enhances their bargaining strength. Their members can now threaten to appeal to the modern court and the customary authority, which, acting strategically, changes the custom to prevent the threat from being carried out.

Another result, which cannot be obtained by the bargaining theory sketched in Section 3, is that too radical a law may defeat its purpose in the sense that the interests of the intended beneficiaries (say, the women) may be eventually harmed rather than promoted by the legal intervention. A plausible mechanism becomes evident once the model is refined by allowing modern judges to behave in a way similar to the customary authority. More precisely, the modern judges now have their own intrinsic and idiosyncratic preferences about the law and, in deciding the actual settlement of a case, they balance the cost of departing from their preferred outcome if they were to implement the law strictly against the benefit of doing what they are supposed to do, that is, to apply the law (they obtain a positive utility from law abidance). There exists a threshold value of the statutory law above which a judge will stop passing judgments prescribed by it and start to follow his (her) own preferred judgment. Since there are as many such thresholds as there are values of the preferred judgment among the modern judges, a radical law might deter a significant proportion of the judges from applying it strictly so that these judges will now choose to provide judgments according to their own, more conservative preferences. The overall effect may be to reduce the expected value of the judicial outcome for the disadvantaged people whom the law seeks to protect (Aldashev et al. 2012b).

The same argument can be actually applied to modern law enforcers, as suggested by Kahan (2000). Legal enforcers have a preference for enforcing the legal verdict, which is their formal duty, but suffer a loss of utility increasing in the distance between this verdict and their preferred outcome. If the distance becomes too large, they stop enforcing the law (Platteau and Wahhaj 2014: 659).

In their works, the authors of the 'magnet effect' theory have provided a number of illustrations in support of their approach. Interestingly, most of these examples deal with issues of gender, with a particular focus on inheritance practices in poor countries of Asia and sub-Saharan Africa. It is worth noting that in all empirical studies concluding that legal reforms affect customary practices, the presence of a 'magnet effect' cannot be ruled out. In fact, it may well be part of the bargaining argument invoked. This is particularly evident in the case of the study of Roy (2015) where the impact of the Hindu Succession Act is shown to be partial and gradual, operating through compensations rather than through changes in the inheritance practices themselves.

5. Changing Preferences

5.1. *Preliminary Considerations*

A limitation of the models discussed in Sections 3 and 4 is that they rely on two restrictive assumptions: to change expectations, agents must not only be reasonably well informed about the content of the law, but they must also believe that other agents will also expect the law to be effective. The latter requirement means that payoffs will not be changed unless the threat of punishment for law-breaking is credible. It is nonetheless a known fact that laws that criminalize customary practices and protect human rights often remain dead letters. This is especially true for developing countries where the legal system is weak, and it is also true whenever laws are introduced under severe international pressure but without a true commitment by the government to implement them. To cite just one example among many, when in Senegal the law to ban FGC was voted, the MP who introduced the bill in the parliament was quoted claiming that the government will not seriously apply the law (Shell-Duncan et al. 2013: 817).

The analytical framework used in Section 4 can throw light on the government's credibility issue. Thus, a low commitment of the government or the ruler can be represented by a small value of the weight attached to policies aimed at removing harmful customs. In such conditions, it is easily shown that the government will choose a low value for E and many people will continue to follow the custom.[17]

Besides obvious problems of transparency and credibility, legal interventions present the additional difficulty that they may not succeed in changing the perceptions that right-holders have of themselves. The process through which victims of unfair customs can change the perception they have of themselves is therefore a crucial element in achieving change through a social engineering approach. They must first realize that they are the victims of a discriminatory treatment and, in a second step, that they have the right to be in a better situation (Merry 2009; Nussbaum 2000: 140). The problem is that individuals tend to internalize and appropriate the system of values they are immersed in. With regard to domestic violence, for example, 29 per cent of women in countries with available data considered in 2012 that wife beating is justified when the wife is arguing against the husband, 25 per cent when she refuses sex, and 21 per cent when she burns food. In Ethiopia, 81 per cent of women justified wife beating for at least one of these reasons (World Bank, 2012: 84).

5.2. The Effect of Preference Heterogeneity

For social change to happen, a process of awareness-building must clearly take place so that women, or other victimized groups, develop their capacity to aspire and exert voice (Appadurai 2004). The social norm setting described in Section 3 provides us with a first approach to explore the role of preference changes (see Figure 15.2).

In order to facilitate the discussion of the effect of the shape of distribution $f(\theta)$, we start by considering an initial situation in which $f(\theta)$ is U-shaped. With respect to the utility function $U_i = \mu F(\theta) - \theta_i V(E)$, we assume that E is set

---

[17] Assume that the positive component of government's utility, $v(1 - F(\theta))$, has the following specific form: $v = W(1 - F(\theta^*))^\beta$, where W is a constant and $0 < \beta < 1$. A government with a low (high) credibility is then represented by a low (high) value of W.

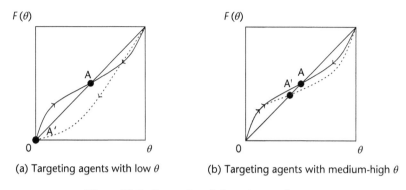

(a) Targeting agents with low θ (b) Targeting agents with medium-high θ

Figure 15.2. Examples of changing preferences
Source: Authors.

in such a way that $V(E) = \mu$. Since we want E to be fixed, it is immaterial how we set its value. We then have that the $\frac{\mu F(\theta)}{V(E)}$ function is transformed into the cumulative distribution function $F(\theta)$. In Figure 15.2a, the intersection point between the transformed function and the identity function may therefore be interpreted as an equilibrium (in this instance, as it should be, the function is equal to zero when $\theta = 0$ and to one when $\theta = 1$). We know that this equilibrium is stable. To suppress the custom entirely, what is required is a shift from that interior equilibrium to the corner equilibrium $(0, 0)$. Since the latter is not a stable equilibrium accessible with the initial distribution $f(\theta)$, the shape of that distribution has to be altered. If the transformation results in a cumulative distribution function that has the shape depicted by the dotted curve in Figure 15.2a, the desired shift occurs and the harmful custom disappears. Concretely and in full accordance with intuition, this means that a bunch of people who initially had a relatively low aversion to the custom must become more averse so that they move rightwards on the CDF. The move must be important enough to ensure that the $F(\theta)$ curve no longer lies above the 45° degree line even in the range close to $\theta = 0$.

More realistically, as many NGOs have experienced, effort should first focus on agents with a moderate aversion to the harmful custom. As is evident from Figure 15.2b, changing the attitudes of people located to the immediate left neighbourhood of A will cause a shift of equilibrium from A to A'. This more modest effect may be the only feasible outcome in the short or medium term.

A different initial distribution of preferences would lead to different predictions in terms of identification of the people whose preferences should be moved. Consider the case of a logistic or a normal distribution with two possible equilibria, one where everybody follows the custom and the other where nobody does (see Figure 15.1c). To transform such a game in a way that only the $(0, 0)$ equilibrium is accessible, people to the centre-right of the distribution, that is people with medium-high aversion to the custom, should be targeted for preference change. In this case, moving people with low aversion to the custom would not radically affect the equilibrium outcome.

5.3. The Role of Opinion Leaders

There is an alternative way in which we can interpret the variable P used in our basic model. We can indeed conceive that there is a continuum of individuals of equal mass but some individuals carry more weight than others. In this case, $f(\theta)$ measures the influence that individual θ wields over the rest of the population. The cumulative function $F(\theta)$ is re-interpreted accordingly. It follows that a move from the continuous line to the dashed line in Figure 15.2a can be obtained by targeting effort to change preferences on the influential individual who was initially rather tolerant toward the custom. The mass of followers will then automatically modify their opinions in the same direction. More sophisticated approaches to the role of leaders in changing public opinion have been proposed such as the ones proposed by Bidner and Francois (2013) and by Acemoglu and Jackson (2015).

The role of 'opinion leaders' in facilitating change has been studied in different domains such as technological adoption, health, and education. The challenge is to identify those opinion leaders and target them, which can be seen as trying to define the network structure that matters for a specific innovation.[18] Thus, in a study concerned with FGC, Diabate and Mesple-Somps (2014) found that Malian migrants to non-FGC countries play an important role in influencing decisions about FGC when they come back to their village (after controlling for selection into migration and return migration). Having observed attitudes in a non-FGC country, they come home with changed opinions on the custom and they eventually become important vectors of change. This finding confirms the conclusion reached in well-identified studies that show the positive effect on existing norms and practices of the exposure of leaders to 'progressive' external contexts.

As a final remark, we want to stress that, to the extent that the social norm framework is an appropriate way to address the issue of harmful customs, it still provides us with only a stylized approach to preference change. We need a better understanding of how individual preferences can be changed practically. Economists have paid a lot of attention to the impact of better information on the situation of disadvantaged groups, including women. For example, Jensen and Oster (2009) have shown that the introduction of cable television

---

[18] Interesting insights can be derived from the theory of social networks (Goyal 2012; Easley and Kleinberg 2010; Jackson 2008). In particular, is an agent influential in terms of the number of direct links that he (she) possesses (degree centrality), in terms of the total number of agents to whom he (she) is linked, either directly or indirectly (Katz centrality), or in terms of the importance of the agents to whom he (she) is linked (Eigenvector centrality)?

is associated with an improvement of women's status in rural India. This improvement is reflected in perceptible decreases in the reported acceptability of domestic violence towards women and son preference (as well as increases in women's autonomy and decreases in fertility). Other studies, however, conclude otherwise. If it is relatively easy to design interventions that improve people's knowledge, it is much harder to get that improved knowledge translated into changed behaviour, especially when it is the only existing intervention (see the survey of Berge et al., Chapter 7 in this book, which deals with early pregnancy specifically).

A major interpretative problem with many such studies, however, is that they cannot determine whether the women's improved outcomes are the consequence of changed preferences or of empowerment understood as enhanced bargaining strength that results in greater determination to assert one's rights and to defend one's interests. It is quite likely that, in many cases, the two processes take place simultaneously, as suggested by Sanyal et al. (2015). From their careful study of a women's empowerment intervention in Bihar (India), they conclude that seven years of continuous efforts succeeded in dramatically transforming women's preferences and dispositions. Long-standing normative restrictions that were constitutive of the symbolic boundary of gender gradually broke down as a result of multi-faceted actions focused on increasing women's physical mobility, recalibrating symbolic and social boundaries, and facilitating access to new networks of persons and systems of knowledge.

6. Macro-Level Changes

6.1. Theory

In the previous sections, we presented two different social engineering approaches to harmful customs and their underlying theoretical foundations: legal interventions and activities aimed at changing the victims' and the perpetrators' preferences.

The social engineering approach, and the human rights discourse in particular, risk associating harmful customs with a given 'culture' or 'identity', often wrongly seen as fixed over time (Merry 2003). Harmful customs are the result of specific socio-economic contexts: they have been established as social equilibria of games defined by particular preferences and constraints. Even if they tend to be sticky and survive to mutated conditions in the macro-environment, we cannot rule out the possibility that they will vanish in response to sufficiently large and sustained changes in the technological, economic, or social environment.

The effects of a changing environment are easily elucidated with the help of theoretical approaches that have already been discussed. Thus, in the social norm framework, a change in the environment favourable to the demise of a harmful custom can be represented as an increase in the cost of following it (an exogenous increase in E) as a result of greater determination by the government to fight against inefficient customs. In a simple bargaining framework, an improvement in the victims' exit opportunities and the associated increase in their bargaining strength are the factors responsible for the decline of harmful norms. The same interpretation also applies to the 'magnet effect' theory: the effect on the custom of expanded outside economic opportunities for the victims is formally analogous to the effect of a more progressive legislation. This is not surprising since the operating mechanism is the same whether the triggering factor is a change in the statutory law or in the scope of outside opportunities, i.e. the conferring of increased bargaining power upon the weaker party.

Change need not happen, however. In the social norm framework, assuming heterogeneous preferences, an increase in E may not be large enough to cause a shift from the initial equilibrium: this is evident if we are initially at the corner solution $\theta = 1$ and the shift of the $\frac{\mu}{V(E)}$ curve is not important enough to move from the corner solution to an interior solution. It is also possible to write games with homogeneous agents in which a norm that was initially efficient persists although it has become inefficient after a change in the macro-environment. This is the case if it risk-dominates a new (Nash) equilibrium that is efficient given the new payoffs.

6.2. Empirical Evidence

In this section, we present evidence of the role of economic, technological, and demographic factors in changing harmful social norms. Far from being exhaustive, our review is limited to a few examples that are particularly suggestive.

6.2.1. FOOTBINDING AND FEMALE GENITAL MUTILATION

The recent emphasis on female cutting as a social norm—and therefore on coordination—has at least partially originated from the parallel between this custom and footbinding in China. As pointed out in Mackie (1996), footbinding can be interpreted as a social convention: the act of binding the feet of a girl signals her good qualities, such as modesty. Not doing it in a context where everybody follows the practice would leave the girl unmarried. The custom appeared in the Sung dynasty (960–1279) and 'spread by imitation until people were ashamed not to practice it'. It became normal practice by the Ming dynasty (1368–1644) and lasted for no less than 1,000 years (Mackie 1996: 1001). It suddenly ended during the years culminating in the 1911–12 revolution. Mackie argues that the central factor behind the rapid disappearance of footbinding was the campaigning efforts of the natural-foot movement, identified with liberal modernizers and women's rights advocates. By analogy, FGC could be fought in the same way (1996: 1013–14).

Another explanation of the demise of footbinding nevertheless exists in the anthropological literature, and it emphasizes the critical role of the economic environment. Thus, Gates and others (Gates 2001; Bossen et al. 2011; Brown et al. 2012) highlight the importance of quickly changing economic conditions during the twentieth century as the most powerful engine behind the collapse of footbinding. They view the custom as part of an economic system that depended on women's intensive labour, in particular in the textile sector: binding feet forced girls to become sedentary and start domestic activities at an early age, such as spinning and weaving and other handwork for whose products there was a high demand. More importantly, they argue that footbinding declined when industrial textile production—more efficient and cheaper—developed on a large scale, which undermined the competitiveness of women's artisanal, home-based production. Using quantitative and qualitative data collected in different rural areas of China, they find suggestive evidence that the presence of footbinding coincided with the presence of sedentary economic activities for women.[19] Furthermore, the timing of its demise corresponds to the emergence of industrially produced textile goods on the local markets.

In the same vein, Fan and Wu (2016), build a marriage-market model to explain the rise and demise of footbinding: assuming a preference for footbinding, the authors define the custom as a costly pre-marriage investment which becomes relevant when there is growing variation in the quality of male partners. Footbinding arises first among upper-class women, where the opportunity cost of footbinding is lower. While benefits from marrying-up increase, footbinding spreads among working-class women. However, for them the loss of physical ability due to footbinding decreases their value on the marriage market. The decision to practise the custom will therefore depend upon the women's role in the labour market. In this setup, an increase in the opportunity cost of footbinding due to technological change can affect the equilibrium outcome.

According to the authors, and in line with the work of Gates and coauthors, the demise of foot-binding was caused by the decline of household-based

---

[19] In Fujian, in the south-eastern part of China, different counties presented heterogeneity both in the incidence of footbinding and the type of activities available for women. In Tong'an, where weaving and spinning persisted over time and there was little agricultural land, 32 per cent of living informants have been bound during their life (92 per cent of their mothers). In Hua'an county, where textile activities have been replaced by portage, only 17 per cent of living informants have been bound (against 91 per cent of their mothers). In the interviewed villages in Nanjing, 9 per cent of the informants and 56 per cent of their mothers experienced footbinding: this was a poor area, with little spinning and weaving and where women were employed in agricultural activities (Gates 2001).

textile work and increased labour opportunities in factories, which require women to be mobile. Finally, they empirically establish that, at the county-level, higher suitability of rice relative to wheat (women have a comparative advantage in rice production) is associated with less footbinding among working-class women. On the other hand, a comparatively high suitability of household handicraft work is correlated with a larger incidence of footbinding.

6.2.2. EARLY MARRIAGE AND MARRIAGE RESTRICTIONS

Limited evidence is available that points to the influence of economic factors on the girls' age at marriage. Thus, in Zimbabwe, Hoogeveen et al. (2003) find that negative idiosyncratic shocks to livestock reduces age at marriage for unmarried daughters. The family of the groom traditionally pays a bride price in cattle, which is an important agricultural asset. A decrease in livestock can then push families to marry daughters from an insurance motive. In India, in rice-growing areas, a positive rainfall shock delays marriage for girls, whose labour productivity increases (Mbiti 2008): this suggests that increasing women's productivity could have a positive impact on age at marriage. A recent paper by Corno et al. (2016) reasonably argues that the effect of economic shocks on age at marriage for girls is conditional on the underlying marriage payment system. Comparing sub-Saharan Africa, where the bride price payment prevails, with India where the dowry system dominates, they find that a negative shock (droughts) on household income drives parents to marry their daughters earlier than usual in Africa but later in India. A simple equilibrium model of the marriage market is proposed to account for this intuitive result: income shocks affect the timing of marriage because the transfers that occur at the time of marriage are a source of consumption smoothing.

European history also suggests that economic circumstances matter for the shift from early to late marriage pattern. Voigtländer and Voth (2013) thus trace back the origin of late marriage in Europe to the Black Plague period. After the Plague, indeed, female employment opportunities improved as animal husbandry developed in response to greater land availability. As a condition of employment in husbandry, all farm servants had to remain celibate with pregnancy and marriage resulting in termination of employment. Marriage ages therefore increased after 1350 (2013: 2228). Conditions were nevertheless different in Mediterranean and Eastern Europe. In the former region, large herds could not be sustained throughout the whole year without resorting to trans-humance; in the latter, husbandry remained uncompetitive vis-à-vis grain production (see also Hartman 2004).

Customary rules governing marriage are also liable to change under the pressure of evolving economic or demographic conditions. A striking illustration of this possibility rests on anecdotal yet insightful evidence (*Economist* April 2015). It concerns inter-caste marriage restrictions, ranging from prohibitions of all unions between people of different castes to restrictions of marriage between people of the same village. In northwestern India, these rules are laid down by informal local councils known as *khaps*, and they are strictly enforced by them, if necessary by resorting to honour killings. While these customs have been in force for five centuries, even when they were declared illegal by the Supreme Court of India, they have recently been called into question. Thus, in April 2014, the *Satrol khap*, the largest in Haryana, relaxed its ban on inter-caste marriage and made it easier for villagers to marry among their neighbours. The cause behind this rather surprising decision was the declining male-female sex ratio in the state (114 males of all ages for every 100 females in Haryana), which made marriage increasingly difficult for men. In the eyes of the customary authorities, a conflict thus arose between two aspects of their traditions: inter-caste and other marriage prohibitions and the associated value of purity, on the one hand, and marriage as a source of identity and manhood, on the other hand. In choosing to relax the former, the *khaps* aim at keeping the latter tradition alive.

6.3. *Final Remarks*

Two final remarks need to be made before moving to the last stage of our analysis. First, as our above example from Haryana shows, different customs may have to be considered simultaneously rather than separately. This is because customs may be interlinked, giving rise to the possibility that customs which were compatible with each other cease to be so as a consequence of changes in the environment. The consistency of the traditional system of rules is then disrupted and the transformation or disapperance of one custom may be the only way to preserve another. A favourable scenario unfolds if the former (the banning of inter-caste marriages in our example) is a harmful practice while the latter (universal marriage) is not.

Another illustration is directly relevant to our main argument here. The expansion of outside opportunities for women can increase their bargaining strength only if they are allowed to participate in the labour market, which requires that norms or customs limiting women's economic or physical mobility (such as women's seclusion rules in parts of India and the Muslim world) go away. In other words, the impact of new outside opportunities on some customs (say, patriarchal rules ensuring submission of wife to husband in a series of matters) is conditional on the relaxing of a particular norm. As the historical experience of Europe attests, norms compelling women to stay home seem to have persisted in the southern and eastern parts of the contin-ent (but not in the northwestern part) in spite of the rise of new economic opportunities (see Guirkinger and Platteau 2016). In India, seclusion norms persist in high castes and high income classes for which female (wage) labour is not needed for the household livelihood and is therefore regarded as a sign of low social status (Cassan and Vandewalle 2016).

The second remark is rather straightforward. In the discussion of this section, we have assumed that expansion of outside opportunities for women is an exogenous force, say because it results from the natural evolution of the wider economy. However, these opportunities may well be promoted by public agencies and voluntary organizations in a deliberate and purposeful manner that targets special categories of people. The expected effects will thus be quite different from those produced by a general, indiscriminate growth process that unfolds in a completely free way. And to the extent that public action tackles harmful norms in a roundabout manner rather than directly, such as when job opportunities for women are promoted, it avoids confronting customary ways of living head-on and, therefore, the perverse effects or backlash, which may be caused by legal reforms and information or sensitization campaigns, do not arise or are mitigated. We now turn our attention to the mechanism liable to yield negative unintended effects of policies generally associated with the social engineering approach, the legal approach in particular.

7. The Role of Culture

7.1. *Theoretical Considerations*

In all the foregoing sections, the role of culture has been overlooked: in the social norm approach, the focus is on people's desire to conform while in the bargaining and the magnet effect approaches it is placed on the determinants of women's bargaining strength, including the statutory law and outside economic opportunities. This ignores the fact that social norms and customs are typically embedded in a local culture from which they derive their symbolic meaning. They are part of a community-centred rather than an individual-centred system of values, and that accounts for the deep link between custom-following behaviour and expression of identity. Violating the custom might therefore have wider consequences than a purely rational view stressing conventional cost-benefit calculus would suggest. These effects can nevertheless be predicted in the light of the approaches presented in Sections 3 to 5.

In the social norm approach, a natural way to think about the identity effect consists of representing communities where traditional identity is strong as sets of individuals clustering around low values of θ. People deeply attached to their traditions have a low aversion toward harmful customs which are seen as an ingredient of their culture. Therefore, they are little inclined to depart from them. A related implication is that strong feelings of cultural identity tend to homogenize preferences inside the reference community, making the common component of the preferences more salient than the idiosyncratic component.

In the bargaining and magnet effect approaches, on the other hand, the cost of appealing to the modern court system is explicit. Since it includes non-material costs such as guilt feelings arising from going against the will of one's community, stronger community ties tend to make the cost of appealing large and, hence, to discourage the questioning of customary norms. The same consequence arises if severe punishment against norm-breaking (equally modelled in the magnet effect approach) also results from strong community ties. In the theory presented in subsection 4.2, the interests of the victims of harmful customs are better protected as the gap $a - f$ increases and as the gap $C_2 - C_1$ decreases. What we argue now is that cultural considerations empha-sizing tradition (with regard to division of gender roles, for example) has the effect of raising the value of C_2 relative to C_1, so that the empowerment of the victimized group is made more difficult. A few illustrations will help to better grasp the relevance of this argument.

7.2. Empirical Evidence

The example of FGC again seems appropriate. In Senegal, particularly in the Senegal river valley where Fulani or Toucouleur communities have powerful identity feelings based on their traditional culture, attempts to change cus-toms, such as that of cutting girls, are strongly resented. Negative reactions are pervaded by the fear of Westernization of the local cultures (O'Neill 2011: chapter 7). FGC is thus regarded as a cultural trait, or as a symbolic aspect of a traditional culture that stands on its own in the face of outside influences and pressures. It is identity-defining, and circumcision is seen as part of the initi-ation process that leads girls into genuine and moral womanhood (Gruenbaum 2001; O'Neill 2011). When this happens, outside attempts to eradicate the practice are perceived as an act of cultural aggression. Thus, laws banning FGC are seen as imposed by the Western world and arouse cultural resistance. It is therefore not rare to hear statements such as 'They want us to be like them', or 'We will not let our culture be destroyed' (Shell-Duncan et al. 2013: 830).

In Egypt, where FGC is overwhelmingly dominant, there has been an intense debate about the introduction of a law criminalizing FGC. The gov-ernment was trapped between international pressure and popular support for the practice (Boyle Heger et al. 2001), usually justified in terms of tradition, control over women's sexual desire, and cleanness (Assaad 1980). More generally, clashing interpretations regarding the meaning of FGC can lead practising communities to strongly resent attempts to eradicate the custom. The Western description of FGC as a mutilation which ensures patriarchal control over women's bodies and sexuality contrasts with the widespread perception among these communities that FGC does not affect marital sexual life (Fahmy et al. 2010; Shell-Duncan and Hernlund 2000). The custom is sometimes justified on the ground that, since men's libido is weaker that women's, a proper balance needs to be restored between the sexual desires of the two sexes. Whichever the justification, the criminalization of FGC is easily seen as a manifestation of blunt Western imperialism and, to that extent, it produces the perverse effect of radicalizing attitudes vis-à-vis harmful customs, the opposite of the intended effect.

In the light of the above, it is not surprising that NGOs which are heavily involved in sensitization work strive to persuade villagers that the harmful practice is separable from their cultural makeup. Entry into strongly traditional communities is nevertheless quite hard for external agencies and may even prove to be infeasible, as we (Platteau and Camilotti) personally experienced (in October 2012) in the Fulani communities around the southern Senegalese town of Medinha-Gounas. Ruled by a puritan Islamist brotherhood (the Tijane) under the leadership of a powerful maraboutic family, these communities denied access to the area to Tostan and other NGOs on the ground that they were trying to destroy or subvert their local culture. A word of caution is required here: behind the screen of cultural resistance arguments, may lie a strong determination of the local (religious) elite to maintain their political and patriarchal power. In other words, reference to culture and cultural identity may be tightly intertwined with the game of local politics. If this is the case, changing customary norms associated with culture is a still more daunting task as it requires some sort of political revolution.

8. Conclusion

How to fight against harmful customs is a complex issue that has attracted renewed interest during the last decades, particularly when the so-called human rights approach came to centre stage. Unlike what a common view suggests, there is little empirical evidence supporting a social norm story based on coordination incentives. The most naïve underlying assumption is the idea that all the people dislike the custom and follow it only because they hold pessimistic expectations about others' behaviour.

Much more realistic is the alternative assumption that people have different preferences regarding the desirability of the custom. Allowing for preference heterogeneity complicates the problem quite a bit: the impact of the law now depends critically on the distribution of individual preferences, even if we restrict our attention to its 'expressive' function. If the distribution is bimodal with many people strongly averse to the custom and many people strongly supporting it, or if the distribution is uniform, just enacting a pro-women law will be of no avail since the (stable) equilibrium is unique. By contrast, when many people have a moderate aversion to the custom, the law can possibly act as a new focal point with the effect of destroying the harmful custom.

Therefore, to eradicate harmful social norms, interventions aimed at modifying individual preferences or payoffs are often required. Modifying preferences typically requires identity-recasting and confidence-building actions that make people aware that they are the victims of a discriminatory treatment and that they are entitled to be in a better situation. Given the difficulty of converting the most ardent supporters of the custom, it is reasonable to bank on its partial rather than complete abandonment.

Changing payoffs can be achieved either through legal mechanisms or through well-targeted public policies. In the former case, violation of legal prescriptions must trigger sufficiently severe sanctions, which implies not only that punishment is sufficiently severe and actually meted out, but also that the detecting of violations is sufficiently effective. Or, alternatively, quasi-legal means may be used, such as when public agencies create a 'shaming' environment that increases the cost of following the custom. The impact of these interventions may be the total or the partial disappearance of the custom, or it may be nil depending upon the initial distribution of the preferences.

Payoffs can also be modified as a result of deliberate economic policies, or endogenous economic processes that have the effect of expanding economic opportunities for the victimized sections of the population, or of changing the costs of following the custom. A great advantage of this approach, compared to the legal approach, lies in the fact that, being indirect, it avoids a head-on confrontation with the tradition and the identity-defining culture in which it is embedded. Changes appear to be imposed by abstract forces that are beyond the control of customary authorities, and they better allow for face-saving among the upholders of tradition. The opposite happens when pro-women lawmaking is clearly inspired, or influenced, by the universalistic norms and values originated in the Western world.

Instead of examining the role of outside economic opportunities within a social norm (and coordination) framework, we can use the lens of a bargaining setup in which men and women have antagonistic preferences. Outside economic opportunities then appear as conferring enhanced bargaining strength upon women. Legal reforms can be analysed as another way to increase their negotiating power: in fact, the effect of pro-women laws on harmful customs is formally analogous to that of new economic opportunities available to women. The idea is that in both cases women can threaten to exit from the traditional judicial domain and escape the rule of the associated customary authority: they either appeal directly to the formal court system, or they seize economic opportunities outside their home and in this way hopefully place themselves under the purview of the new legal system.

In a bargaining framework, legal reforms and the development of outside economic opportunities should not be considered exclusive: both strategies can actually aggregate their effects. However, the fact that they are not complements means that one can be used in preference to the other if circumstances make either strategy relatively difficult to implement. Two main limitations jeopardize the success of legal reforms. First, if the law needs to yield a deterrent effect, and not only an expressive effect, it must be credible, implying that the court system works impartially and effectively. Second, as mentioned above, it involves a head-on confrontation with traditional culture.

On the other hand, the major limitation of the economic approach is that, in order to work, women must be able to move, or threaten to move, to locations outside their home where new economic opportunities are available. Since seclusion norms can prevent that outcome, one social norm may inhibit a change in other anti-women norms (say, norms associated with patriarchal control). Traditional social norms are thus better seen as interlinked inside a customary system and, when this is done, different situations can arise.

In particular, economic (or demographic) changes can break the complementarity between various parts of the customary system by significantly increasing the cost of following some norms while leaving unchanged the cost-benefit structure pertaining to the other norms. The best scenario unfolds when anti-women norms are those under attack, and the worst scenario corresponds to the opposite case. It is under this second scenario that the law should lend a helping hand to economic processes and strategies. Unfortunately, the same noxious custom that withstands the pressure of economic change may also put up strong resistance against law-induced change. This is probably the situation that most evidently calls for a combined effort on the three fronts of a broadly conceived social engineering approach: economic policies, legal reforms, and preference change. The third instrument, which together with legal reforms forms the basis of the human rights approach, is often achieved through community-based projects. These are based on a deep understanding of the local context and on long-term relationships with the victims, a setting that better enables them to transform the victims' perception of themselves.

The role of awareness- and confidence-building campaigns, and of identity-recasting interventions, is also justified when economic forces or strategies take a rather long time to produce their effects. When women's empowerment is slow to materialize, the struggle to achieve gender parity must be supported by reforms and institutional interventions directly addressing the problem (Duflo 2012).

References

Abdalla, R. H. D. (1982). *Sisters in Affliction: Circumcision and Infibulation of Women in Africa*. London UK: Zed Press.

Acemoglu, D., and M. O. Jackson (2015). 'History, Expectations, and Leadership in the Evolution of Social Norms'. *The Review of Economic Studies*, 82(2), 423–56.

Akerlof, G. (1976). 'The Economics of Caste and of the Rat Race and Other Woeful Tales'. *The Quarterly Journal of Economics*, 90(4), 599–617.

Akerlof, G. A. (1980). 'A Theory of Social Custom, of which Unemployment May Be One Consequence'. *The Quarterly Journal of Economics*, 94(4), 749–75.

Aldashev, G., I. Chaara, J.-P. Platteau, and Z. Wahhaj (2012a). 'Formal Law as a Magnet to Reform Custom'. *Economic Development and Cultural Change*, 60(4), 795–828.

Aldashev, G., I. Chaara, J.-P. Platteau, and Z. Wahhaj (2012b). 'Using the Law to Change the Custom'. *Journal of Development Economics*, 97(2), 182–200.

Ali, D. A., K. Deininger, and M. Goldstein (2014). 'Environmental and Gender Impacts of Land Tenure Regularization in Africa: Pilot Evidence from Rwanda'. *Journal of Development Economics*, 110, 262–75.

Ambec, S. (2008). 'Voting over Informal Risk–Sharing Rules'. *Journal of African Economies*, 17(4), 635–59.

Anderson, S., and G. Genicot (2015). 'Suicide and Property Rights in India'. *Journal of Development Economics*, 114, 64–78.

Appadurai, A. (2004). 'The Capacity to Aspire'. In R. Vijayendra and M. Walton (eds), *Culture and Public Action*, Chapter 3, 59–84. Palo Alto, CA: Stanford University Press.

Assaad, M. B. (1980). 'Female Circumcision in Egypt: Social Implications, Current Research, and Prospects for Change'. *Studies in Family Planning*, 11 (1), 3–16.

Auriol, E., and M. Benaim (2000). 'Standardization in Decentralized Economies'. *American Economic Review*, 90(3), 550–70.

Auriol, E., and J.-P. Platteau (2017). 'Religious Seduction in Autocracy: A Theory Inspired by History'. *Journal of Development Economics*, 127, 395–412.

Basu, K. (2015). 'The Republic of Beliefs'. World Bank Policy Research Working Paper.

Bauer, P., and B. S. Yamey (1957). *The Economics of Under-Developed Countries*. Cambridge: Cambridge University Press.

Bellemare, M. F., L. Novak, and T. Steinmetz (2015). 'All in the Family: Explaining the Persistence of Female Genital Cutting in West Africa'. *Journal of Development Economics*, 116, 252–65.

Benabou, R. and J. Tirole (2011). 'Laws and Norms'. NBER Working Paper Series, National Bureau of Economic Research.

Bidner, C. and P. Francois (2013). 'The Emergence of Political Accountability'. *The Quarterly Journal of Economics*, 128(3), 1397–448.

Bossen, L., W. Xurui, M. J. Brown, and H. Gates (2011). 'Feet and Fabrication: Footbinding and Early Twentieth Century Rural Women's Labor in Shaanxi'. *Modern China*, 37(4), 347–83.

Boyle Heger, E., F. Songora, and G. Foss (2001). 'International Discourse and Local Politics: Anti-Female-Genital-Cutting Laws in Egypt, Tanzania, and the United States'. *Social Problems*, 48(1), 524–44.

Brown, M. J., L. Bossen, H. Gates, and D. Satterthwaite-Phillips (2012). 'Marriage Mobility and Footbinding in pre-1949 Rural China: A Reconsideration of Gender, Economics, and Meaning in Social Causation'. *The Journal of Asian Studies*, 71(4), 1035–67.

Camilotti, G. (2015). 'Changing Female Genital Cutting: Evidence from Senegal'. Mimeo, University of Namur.

Camilotti, G. (2016). 'Interventions to Stop Female Genital Cutting and the Evolution of the Custom. Evidence on Age at Cutting in Senegal'. *Journal of African Economies*, 1(1), 133–58.

Cassan, G. and L. Vandewalle (2016). 'The Social Cost of Social Norms: Gender Quotas Meet Gender Norms'. Mimeo, Centre for Research in Economic Development (CRED), University of Namur.

Chesnokova, T. and R. Vaithianathan (2010). 'The Economics of Female Genital Cutting'. *The BE Journal of Economic Analysis & Policy*, 10(1).

Cooter, R. D. (2000). 'Three Effects of Social Norms on Law: Expression, Deterrence, and Internalization'. Berkeley Law Scholarship Repository, *Oregon Law Review*,. 79, 1.

Corno, L., N. Hildebrandt, and A. Voena (2016). 'Weather Shocks, Age at Marriage, and the Direction of Marriage Payments'. Mimeo, Università Cattolica del Sacro Cuore, Dipartimenti e Istituti di Scienze Economiche (DISCE).

Dasgupta, P. (1993). *A Inquiry into Well-Being and Destitution*. New York: Oxford University Press.

Diabate, I., and S. Mesple-Somps (2014). 'Female Genital Mutilation and Migration in Mali. Do Migrants Transfer Social Norms?' Document de Travail UMR DIAL.

Duflo, E. (2012). 'Women Empowerment and Economic Development'. *Journal of Economic Literature*, 50(4), 1051–79.

Easley, D., and J. Kleinberg (2010). *Networks, Crowds, and Markets: Reasoning about a Highly Connected World*. Cambridge: Cambridge University Press.

Economist (2015). 'Bare Branches, Redundant Males. The Marriage Squeeze in India and China'. (18 April).

Efferson, C., S. Vogt, A. Elhadi, H. E. F. Ahmed, and F. Ernst (2015). 'Female Genital Cutting is not a Social Coordination Norm'. *Science*, 349, 1446–7.

Fahmy, A., M. T. El-Mouelhy, and A. R. Ragab (2010). 'Female Genital Mutilation/ Cutting and Issues of Sexuality in Egypt'. *Reproductive Health Matters*, 18(36), 181–90.

Fan, X., and L. Wu (2016). 'The Economic Motives for Foot-Binding'. Department of Economics, University of California, Los Angeles. Mimeo.

Fudenberg, D., and D. K. Levine (1998). *The Theory of Learning in Games*, Volume 2. Cambridge, MA MIT Press.

Galbiati, R., and P. Vertova (2014). 'How Laws Affect Behavior: Obligations, Incentives and Cooperative Behavior'. *International Review of Law and Economics*, 38, 48–57.

Gates, H. (2001). 'Footloose in Fujian: Economic Correlates of Footbinding'. *Comparative Studies in Society and History*, 43(1), 130–48.

Goyal, S. (2012). *Connections: An Introduction to the Economics of Networks*. Princeton: Princeton University Press.

Granovetter, M. (1978). Threshold Models of Collective Behavior. *American Journal of Sociology*, 83(6), 1420–43.

Gruenbaum, E. (2001). *The Female Circumcision Controversy: an Anthropological Perspective*. Philadelphia: University of Pennsylvania Press.

Guirkinger, C., and J.-P. Platteau (2016). The Dynamics of Family Systems: Lessons from Past and Present Time. Forthcoming in: J.M. Baland, F. Bourguignon, J.P. Platteau, and T. Verdier (eds), *Economic Development and Institutions: Surveys of Frontier Issues*.

Harsanyi, J. C., and R. Selten (1988). *A General Theory of Equilibrium Selection in Games*. Cambridge MA: MIT Press.

Hartman, M. S. (2004). *The Household and the Making of History: A Subversive View of the Western Past*. Cambridge: Cambridge University Press.

Hirschman, A. (1958). *The Strategy of Economic Development*. New Haven and London: Yale University Press.

Hoogeveen, J., B. Van der Klaauw, and A. G. C. Van Lomwel (2003). 'On the Timing of Marriage, Cattle and Weather Shocks in Rural Zimbabwe'. World Bank Policy Research Working Paper N° 3112.

Jackson, M. O. (2008). *Social and Economic Networks*, Volume 3. Princeton: Princeton University Press.

Jensen, R., and E. Oster (2009). 'The Power of TV: Cable Television and Women's Status in India'. *The Quarterly Journal of Economics*, 124(3), 1057–94.

Kahan, D. M. (1997). 'Social Influence, Social Meaning, and Deterrence'. *Virginia Law Review*, 83(2), 349–95.

Kahan, D.M. (2000). 'Gentle Nudges vs. Hard Shoves: Solving the Sticky Norm Problem', *University of Chicago Law Review*, 67, 607–45.

Kandori, M., G. J. Mailath, and R. Rob (1993). 'Learning, Mutation, and Long Run Equilibria in Games'. *Econometrica*, 61(1), 29–56.

Kuran, T. (1987). 'Preference Falsification, Policy Continuity and Collective Conservatism'. *The Economic Journal*, 97(387), 642–65.

Kuran, T. (1988). 'The Tenacious Past: Theories of Personal and Collective Conservatism'. *Journal of Economic Behavior & Organization*, 10(2), 143–71.

Kuran, T. (1997). *Private Truths, Public Lies: The Social Consequences of Preference Falsification*. Cambridge, MA & London: Harvard University Press.

Lewis, A. W. (1955). *The Theory of Economic Growth*. London: George Allen & Unwin.

Mackie, G. (1996). 'Ending Footbinding and Infibulation: A Convention Account'. *American Sociological Review*, 61(6), 999–1017.

Mackie, G. (2000). 'Female Genital Cutting: the Beginning of the End'. In B. Shell-Duncan and Y. Hernlund (eds), *Female Circumcision in Africa: Culture, Controversy, and Change*, pp. 253–82. London: Lynne Rienner Publishers.

Mackie, G., and J. LeJeune (2009). 'Social Dynamics of Abandonment of Harmful Practices: a New Look at the Theory'. Special Series on Social Norms and Harmful Practices, Innocenti Working Paper.

Mbiti, I. M. (2008). Monsoon Wedding?: The Effect of Female Labor Demand on Marriage Markets in India. Mimeo, Southern Methodist University.

McAdams, R. H. (2000). 'A Focal Point Theory of Expressive Law'. *Virginia Law Review*, 86(8), 1649–729.

Meier, G. M., and R. E. Baldwin (1957). *Economic Development*. New York: John Wiley & Sons.

Merry, S. E. (2003). Human Rights Law and the Demonization of Culture (and Anthropology Along the Way). *Polar: Political and Legal Anthropology Review*, 26(1), 55–76.

Merry, S. E. (2009). *Human Rights and Gender Violence: Translating International Law into Local Justice*. Chicago: University of Chicago Press.

Munshi, K., and J. Myaux, (2006). 'Social Norms and the Fertility Transition'. *Journal of Development Economics*, 80, 1–38.

Novak, L. (2016). 'Persistent Norms and Tipping Points: Female Genital Cutting in Burkina Faso'. Mimeo, University of Minnesota.

Nussbaum, M. C. (2000). *Women and Human Development: The Capabilities Approach*. New York: Cambridge University Press.

OHCHR (1995). 'Harmful Traditional Practices Affecting the Health of Women and Children'. August, Fact Sheet No. 23.

O'Neill, S. (2011). 'Defying the Law, Negotiating the Change. The Futanke's Opposition to the National Ban on FGM in Senegal'. PhD thesis, Goldsmiths, University of London.

Platteau, J.-P. (2000). *Institutions, Social Norms, and Economic Development*, Volume 1. London: Routledge.

Platteau, J.-P., and R. Peccoud (eds) (2010). *Culture, Institutions, and Development: New Insights into an Old Debate*. New York: Routledge.

Platteau, J.-P. and Z. Wahhaj (2014). 'Strategic Interactions between Modern Law and Custom'. In V. A. Ginsburgh and D. Throsby (eds), *Handbook of the Economics of Art and Culture Vol. 2*, Chap. 22, pp. 633–78, Amsterdam, London and New York: Elsevier and North-Holland.

Roy, S. (2015). 'Empowering Women? Inheritance Rights, Female Education and Dowry Payments in India'. *Journal of Development Economics*, 114, 233–51.

Sanyal, P., V. Rao, and S. Majumdar (2015). 'Recasting Culture to Undo Gender: A Sociological Analysis of Jeevika in Rural Bihar, India'. World Bank Policy Research Working Paper N° 7411.

Schelling, T. C. (1960). *The Strategy of Conflict*. Cambridge, MA: Harvard University Press.

Shell-Duncan, B., and Y. Hernlund (2000). Female Circumcision in Africa: Dimensions of the Practice and Debates. In B. Shell-Duncan and Y. Hernlund (eds), *Female 'Circumcision' in Africa: Culture, Controversy, and Change*, pp. 1–40. London: Lynne Rienner.

Shell-Duncan, B., K. Wander, Y. Hernlund, and A. Moreau (2013). 'Legislating Change? Responses to Criminalizing Female Genital Cutting in Senegal'. *Law & Society Review*, 47(4), 803–35.

United Nations (1979). *Convention on the Elimination of All Forms of Discrimination against Women*, New York: United Nations.

Vogt, S., N. A. M. Zaid, H. E. F. Ahmed, E. Fehr, and C. Efferson (2016). 'Changing Cultural Attitudes Towards Female Genital Cutting'. *Nature*, 538, 506–9.

Voigtländer, N. and H.-J. Voth (2013). 'How the West "Invented" Fertility Restriction'. *The American Economic Review*, 103(6), 2227–64.

World Bank (2012). *World Development Report 2012: Gender Equality and Development*. Washington: The World Bank.

Young, H. P. (1993). 'The Evolution of Conventions'. *Econometrica*, 61(1), 57–84.

16

Are Caste Categories Misleading? The Relationship Between Gender and Jati in Three Indian States

Shareen Joshi, Nishtha Kochhar, and Vijayendra Rao[1]

1. Introduction

Indian society is highly stratified and hierarchical. Caste, class, and gender all contribute to an individual's status. A large body of literature explores the importance of each of these. The complex and dynamic interplay between these elements, however, receives less attention even though across India it drives significant regional and temporal variations in social structures (Drèze and Sen 2002).

This chapter examines the relationship between two of these categories: caste and gender. Numerous studies have argued that there is a paradoxical inverse relationship between caste and gender in Indian society. Stringent patriarchal codes designed to subordinate women have been observed to be restricted to high-status caste groups; women from low-status castes display higher labour force participation rates, fewer patriarchal restrictions on mobility and greater decision making autonomy (Boserup 1970; Mencher 1988; Chen 1995; Kapadia 1995; Eswaran et al. 2013). A related argument is that

[1] The authors are grateful to an anonymous referee and participants in the Economic Growth and Development Conference in ISI, Delhi, and in the WIDER workshop, *Towards Gender Equity in Development*, in Namur for very valuable comments on an earlier draft. They are indebted to the World Bank's South Asia Food and Nutrition Security Initiative, funded by the EU and DfID, and UNU-WIDER for financial support. This chapter reflects the individual views of the authors and does not in any way represent the official position of the World Bank or its member countries. A longer version of this chapter that provides results in more detail, and discusses the effects of caste on targeting of anti-poverty programmes, is available in the WIDER working paper series, Joshi et al. (2017).

increases in wealth and income among low-ranked castes can have a negative impact on the status of women: as these castes emulate the customs, practices, and patriarchal codes of higher-ranked castes, women become disempowered (Srinivas 1977).

However, some recent evidence from large-sample surveys challenges this idea of a negative relationship between caste and the status of women. Deshpande (2002) for example, argues that women from lower castes may be in a trap of material deprivation, low education, low opportunity, and chronic insecurity.

A rigorous examination of the relationship between caste and gender has been constrained by methodological challenges. First is the challenge of defining caste. There is no universally accepted definition of the term.[2] In Hindu texts, caste is equated with *varna*, the ancient organization of society into four vertical categories: priests (brahmins), kings and warriors (kshatriya), farmers and merchants (vaishyas), labourers (shudras), and a fifth group of 'untouchables' excluded from the system altogether.[3] The government of India defines broad categories, including Scheduled Caste (SC), Scheduled Tribe (ST), Backward Caste (BC), Extremely Backward Caste (EBC), and Other Backward Caste (OBC).

Aside from the government's categories, caste is lived, experienced, and practised in everyday life as *jāti* (henceforth, jati) (Srinivas 1976; Beteille 1996; Bayly 2001; Dirks 2011).[4] Jatis are hereditarily formed endogamous groups whose identities are manifested in a variety of ways: occupational status, property ownership, diets, gender norms, social practices, religious practices emphasizing purity and pollution, and systems of self-governance. Though jatis are usually regarded as sub-castes, placing them within the *varna* classification can be complicated (Dumont 1980). Each region of India has several hundred jatis and there is no pan-Indian system of ranking them (Srinivas 1976; Bayly 2001; Rao and Ban 2007; Dirks 2011). Anthropologists have documented numerous *local* criteria for ranking jatis, as well as significant regional differences in rank orderings, frequent conflicts over rank order, and numerous strategies and circumstances that can change rank order (Srinivas 1962, 1977, 1996).

Much evidence highlights the importance of jatis in everyday life in India.[5] Members of a given jati have strong social ties, even across villages (Srinivas 1976; Gupta 2000). Endogamous marriage within these groups creates an extensive finance and insurance network (Desai and Dubey 2012; Munshi and Rosenzweig 2006; Mazzocco 2012). Thus, jati-based networks shape an

---

[2] The very word 'caste' is a European term that comes from sixteenth-century Portuguese travellers who applied their word for clan, *casta*, to describe the visibly segregated groups they observed as outsiders.

[3] *Varna* is the Sanskrit word for type, order, colour, or class.

[4] The word *jāti* literally translates to 'birth'.

[5] Munshi (2016) provides a broad overview of this literature.

individual's prospects of marriage, employment, and out-migration (Munshi and Rosenzweig 2006; Munshi 2016). Jati identity is often endogenously determined—shifting to respond to incentives from the state or via the influence of social movements (Rao and Ban 2007; Cassan 2015). Recent work has also found large differences in the allocation of benefits within Scheduled Castes by jati (Kumar and Somanathan 2017), and evidence that jati-level population proportions have significant implications for electoral outcomes (Huber and Suryanarayan 2016).

Despite understanding the importance of jatis in everyday life, the Indian census and most large national surveys do not have jati-level identifiers. Caste, therefore, continues to be measured and generally understood only in broad terms, with the emphasis on categories such as SC, ST, OBC, and 'Forward Castes' (FC) (a term that includes any jati that is not included in one of the officially defined categories because they are considered more privileged).

A second methodological challenge to understanding the relationship between caste, class, and gender is the paucity of data with detailed information on economic indicators and women's status. Anthropologists and ethnographers have gathered in-depth qualitative information on these issues but their work has typically focused on small samples in a few villages or communities (examples include Chen 1995; Kapadia 1995; Srinivas 1979; and others). Enormous variations within India however, have limited the generalizability of the findings.

This chapter examines data with extensive information on caste and gender status from three states—Bihar, Odisha, and Tamil Nadu. Our data is unique in having broad geographic coverage and also detailed information on jati, consumption expenditure, and indicators of women's status. Conducted between 2011 and 2013, these surveys served as a baseline for the evaluation of state-sponsored livelihoods programmes that targeted rural women. The sampling strategy ensured that they were representative of vulnerable populations in rural areas who are currently eligible for a variety of poverty-alleviation programmes. As a result, the data are not representative of states, but rather, of poor rural populations within these states. The limitations of the data confer an advantage: we can better understand the relationships between caste and gender in poor rural communities.

We find that in our study areas, the relationship between caste and the status of women is more nuanced than suggested by the literature. We examine three sets of indicators for the status of women in all three states: employment, decision-making authority on key household decisions, and physical mobility. We use a simple reduced-form regression model to explore the role of caste in determining these outcomes. We analyse the data with broad caste categories as well as narrower jati-level definitions of caste and find considerable differences. Location and the exact definitions of caste matter.

The rest of the chapter is organized as follows: Section 2 discusses the literature on caste, empowerment, and inequality; Section 3 describes our sample and data; and Section 4 presents the main findings on inequality between castes including variations of female empowerment within castes and the role of economic advancement in female autonomy.

2. Background: Caste and Gender in India

It is often argued that India's patriarchal kinship system is typical of settled agricultural societies (Boserup 1970; Alesina et al. 2013). Private property rights and the use of agricultural technology created a storable agricultural surplus, which may have enabled social stratification. Patrilineal inheritance, patrilocal exogamy and a rigid sexual division of labour may have emerged to assure uncontested bloodlines that preserved the social, economic, and political status of families. In such settings, women's labour force participation, mobility, and decision making autonomy arguably falls in response to increased economic status. Goldin (1994) argues that the relationship is more complicated. Women's labour force participation (and, more broadly, their status) may follow a non-linear U-shape during the process of economic development.

In India, the status of women is also affected by the caste system. Ancient texts describe unequal gender relations. Documented observations of ruling and martial castes from the colonial period highlight the practices of *sati, purdah* (total female seclusion), female infanticide, dowry and polygyny among upper castes (Joshi 1995; Mani 1998). These sources however, may not be a valid lens for understanding contemporary gender relations. These texts can be biased in favour of certain groups. The practices they describe may be normative statements that are far removed from actual practices. Data from contemporary India provides some insight into this. We review two strands of the empirical literature below.

2.1. *Perspectives from Large Datasets*

Empirical work on caste and gender has frequently compared low-ranking castes with the rest of the population. The attempt to identify these groups began in the colonial period (Dirks 2011). The Government of India Act of 1935 created lists of castes and tribes entitled to affirmative action policies. Groups included in these lists were called 'Scheduled Castes (SC)' and 'Scheduled Tribes (ST)'. This practice continued in independent India. Groups who are eligible for inclusion in these groups have shifted over time. For example, in 1935, 429 castes were listed as SC by the colonial government at the time. In the most recent census of 2011, however, 1241 castes and 705 tribes had SC and ST status respectively (Census of India 2011). In recent years, affirmative action benefits have also been extended to additional groups who have faced similar disadvantages to SCs and STs, but were not previously eligible for compensatory programmes. The groups included in this category also vary across states and have changed over time.

Given these difficulties in making comparisons over time, many studies have relied on cross-sectional data to illustrate the inverse relationship between caste and female labour force participation. Boserup, for example, examines these broad categories to argue that most female agricultural labour is drawn from SC/ST groups, and they are largely employed on family farms belonging to wealthier men whose wives do not work (Boserup 1970: 69). More recently, Deshpande (2001) uses data from the NFHS survey and finds that 39 per cent of SC women, 51 per cent of ST women, and 30 per cent of 'Other' women report that they participate in the formal labour force.

But to what extent does greater employment translate into greater empowerment? Answering this question is quite difficult, because most large datasets lack information on female status. Deshpande (2001) uses data from the NFHS survey to show that SC and ST women have lower levels of education, fewer assets, and face greater insecurity. She also emphasizes that estimates of female labour force participation rates fail to adjust for the quality of working conditions and job security. Similar results are reported in Deshpande (2002) using NSS data.

Another perspective comes from the analysis of sex ratios. The value of female children, as measured by survival, has been shown to increase with the female labour force participation rate (Dasgupta 1987). Early literature noted female-male sex ratios were more favourable among SC/ST groups in the pre-independence period (Drèze and Sen 2002).[6] The decline in this ratio in the post-independence period has often been attributed to Sanskritization[7] of SC jatis, who have placed restrictions on women in an attempt to improve the group's status, particularly after benefiting from a variety of programmes for social upliftment.[8] Establishing the causal effect of Sanskritization, however, is quite difficult since there are many possible mechanisms linking changes in survival rates to caste status.

---

[6] Drèze and Sen (2002: 241–45) note that in pre-independence India, female-male sex ratios among SC/ST groups were significantly higher than the rest of the population, but by 1991, the sex ratio stood at 922 women per 1000 men, while the rest of the population was 927 per thousand men (Drèze and Sen 2002).

[7] The term Sanskritization was developed by M. N. Srinivas (1962) to be the process by which castes placed lower in the caste hierarchy seek upward mobility by emulating the rituals and practices of the upper or dominant castes.

[8] The decline in the sex ratio among SC/ST groups is largely driven by states with the highest concentration of SC/ST population such as Uttar Pradesh (UP). Drèze and Sen (2002: 242) note that the Chamar caste of UP, which is the largest SC caste in the state, had a female-male sex ratio of 986 in 1901, but by 1981 the SC/ST sex ratio had aligned with the rest of the population.

2.2. Perspectives from Field Studies

In recent years field studies have provided new insights into caste and gender. A series of ethnographies have largely confirmed that in most parts of rural India upper-caste women are more likely to practise *purdah* (female seclusion), are more likely to use the veil, and face significant restrictions on their mobility and labour force participation opportunities (Srinivas 1977, 1979; Chen 1995; Kapadia 1995; Jeffrey and Jeffrey 1996; Seymour 1999; and others). These studies have documented that increased caste status is associated with a greater subordination of women (Hutton 1946; Srinivas 1977).

Field studies have also provided insights into the rigid sexual division of labour by caste and class. Boserup (1970) for example, documents a rigid division of labour in agriculture. In her study of villages in India, Chen (1995) reports that villagers display high levels of preoccupation with ensuring status-appropriate work for women. Mencher (1988) conducted detailed analyses of female labour force participation in paddy cultivation in Tamil Nadu and highlights the reluctance of upper-caste women to enter the labour force, even when facing conditions of severe poverty that place them in a ranking of income below the SC and ST women in the village.

The sexual division of labour is also seen in non-agricultural occupations. Kapadia (1995), for example, finds that among the Pallar of Tamil Nadu—a highly impoverished, landless SC group—women form a major share of the local labour force and appear to enjoy considerable autonomy. In artisan jatis such as potters and weavers, men specialize in specific skills, while female household members are active participants in every other non-male stage of production (David and Kramer 2001).

In summary, large national sample surveys document a negative relationship between caste status and female employment, but this is difficult to interpret as empowerment. Field-studies provide in-depth information on this relationship, but the work has typically focused on small samples in a single community. These findings are difficult to generalize, even within a state.

3. Data

We use data from baseline surveys collected between 2011 and 2013 for the impact evaluations of State Rural Livelihoods Projects in three states in India: JEEViKA[9] in Bihar, TRIPTI[10] in Odisha, and PVP[11] in Tamil Nadu. There are strong differences between the three states (Table 16.1). Bihar is a

---

[9] Bihar Rural Livelihoods Project.
[10] Targeted Rural Initiatives for Poverty Termination and Infrastructure.
[11] Tamil Nadu Empowerment and Poverty Alleviation Project.

Table 16.1. State-level differences

	India	Bihar	Odisha	Tamil Nadu
GDP per-capita at current prices	Rs. 74,380	Rs. 33,199	Rs. 59,229	Rs. 128,366
GDP per-capita at 2004–2005 prices	Rs. 39,904	Rs. 16,801	Rs. 26,531	Rs. 66,635
GDP per capita in $ at current market exchange rates	$1,627	$682	$1,150	$2,464
Rank (among 33 states and union territories of India) for GDP	–	33	27	8
SC population	16.20%	8.20%	16.50%	20.00%
ST population	8.60%	1.30%	22.80%	1.10%
Literacy	74.04%	63.82%	73.45%	80.33%
Literacy among SCs	66.10%	48.65%	69.02%	73.26%
Urban Population	31.16%	11.30%	16.68%	48.45%
Sex-ratio	943	996	979	916
Female literacy	65.46%	53.33%	64.36%	73.86%

Source: GDP numbers are from the Ministry of Statistics and Programme Implementation (2015). Retrieved from http://statisticstimes.com/economy/gdp-of-indian-states.php (Nov 8, 2016). Demographic numbers are from the Census of India (2011).

predominantly rural state whose agrarian structure has a strong caste and class base (Rodgers and Rodgers 2001). Odisha is a coastal state with one of the highest populations of Scheduled Tribes (STs) in the country. STs account for 22.8 per cent of the total population of the state and 9.7 per cent of the tribal population of India (Census of India 2011[12]). Both Bihar and Odisha are considerably poorer than Tamil Nadu, which is the eighth wealthiest state in India and has made great strides in education as well as urbanization.

Our surveys include 9,000 households from seven districts in Bihar surveyed in 2011, 3,000 households from ten districts in Odisha also surveyed in 2011, and 3,900 households from nine districts surveyed in Tamil Nadu in the first half of 2013.[13] The survey populations are concentrated in the poorer regions of the three states; SC and ST households are oversampled because they were the intended targets of the project. For the purpose of this study, we restrict the sample to those households for which we have both household and woman-specific information. This yields a sample of 8,969, 2,470, and 3,384 households from Bihar, Odisha, and Tamil Nadu respectively.

Table 16.2, panel (a) summarizes the caste distribution for our data in the three states. Due to the oversampling of Scheduled Castes, almost 70 per cent of the sample in Bihar, 27 per cent in Odisha, and 32 per cent in Tamil Nadu are comprised of SCs. The BCs comprise the largest caste group in Tamil Nadu followed by SCs and Most Backward Castes (MBCs). Odisha is the only state

---

[12] See http://www.censusindia.gov.in/2011census/PCA/PCA_Highlights/pca_highlights_file/Odisha/Executive_Summary.pdf.

[13] We report districts in panel 1 of Table 2 in Joshi et al. (2017).

Table 16.2. Summary statistics: castes and jatis in our sample

Bihar		Odisha		Tamil Nadu	
	Sample %		Sample %		Sample %
SC	69.9	SC	26.7	SC	31.6
ST	1.1	ST	7.2	ST	1.8
EBC	4.7	OBC	33.8	MBC	24.7
OBC	16.88	Muslim	1.7	BC	41.9
Muslim	3.8	FC	30.3		
FC	3.6				
(iii) Jati Composition					
EBC/MBC: Others	4.7	BC/OBC: Others	13.0	Kallar	4.8
Brahmin	1.3	Brahmin	5.5	Naidu	1.3
Rajput	1.5	Karan	2.7	Parkavakulam	4.0
General: Others	0.8	Khandayat	18.7	Thevar	1.9
Muslim: Others	3.8	General: Others	3.5	Vellalar	10.1
Dhanuk	1.2	Muslim: Others	1.7	Yadava	2.1
Kurmi	1.3	Chasa	9.0	EBC/MBC: Others	6.0
Yadav	6.6	Goala	4.5	Adi Dravidar	22.3
OBC:Others	7.8	Guria	2.2	Pallar	4.2
Chamar	20.5	Tanti	2.5	SC: Others	3.5
Dobha/Dobh	2.5	Teli	2.5	ST: Others	1.8
Dushad	16.7	Barui	3.1	Ambalakarar	3.4
Musahar	25.9	Dobha	2.6	Muthuraja	1.9
Sardar	2.1	Keuta	2.5	Vanniyar	13.3
SC: Others	2.3	Kondara	3.9	Chettiar	1.6
ST: Others	1.1	Pana	7.5	Nadar	1.2
		SC: Others	7.4	Reddiyar	1.4
		ST: Others	7.2	Chakkaliyan	1.6
				Vishwakrma	1.3
				BC: Others	12.2

Panel (b): Household characteristics

	Bihar	Odisha	TN
Sample size	8969	2462	3384
Per capita household monthly consumption expenditure (average in rupees)	610.1	1176.9	2150.3
Land holding (average in acres)	0.5	0.6	1.96
Female household head	16.3	5.9	16.7
Number of members in the household (average)	5.9	5.2	4.4
Distance to nearest town (average in kilometers)	22.5	54.4	18.8
Employed adults females	68.2	17.5	62.1
Education profile of the household head			
Never went to school	56.6	20.5	31.3
Primary	18.2	33.2	10.1
Above primary but below or equal to senior secondary	22.5	20.1	54.7
Above senior secondary	2.6	26.2	3.9

Panel (c): Characteristics of female respondents (means)

	Bihar	Odisha	TN
Age	34.1	42.3	39.8
Age at the time of marriage	17.9	18.9	19.3
Employment	80.3	24.1	76.9

Marital status:			
Married	96.3	93.1	90.0
Unmarried	1.3	0.9	0.7
Widowed/Separated/Not cohabiting	2.4	5.9	9.3
Education profile of female respondents			
Never went to school	78.1	37.6	40
Primary	11.0	29.4	9.1
Above primary but below or equal to senior secondary	10.3	17.7	48.5
Above senior secondary	0.6	15.3	2.4
Intra-household decision making: Does respondent provide any input into the following decisions made in the household?			
Purchase of household durables	91.7	82.9	86.3
Children's education	84.1	63.0	84.8
Own livelihood activity	79.5	64.2	77.4
Politics (like who to vote for)	78.6	41.6	87.3
Mobility:			
Bank	20.1	21.1	76.0
Store	75.1	45.3	–
Health centre	93.1	94.1	–
Friend/neighbour/relative	97.4	96.0	–
Taluk Office	–	–	30.0
Police Station	–	–	5.5

Source: Authors' calculations based on data collected by Social Observatory, World Bank, and state Government of Bihar, Odisha, and Tamil Nadu, respectively.

with a significant sample of households from 'general' or 'forward' castes, which form the third largest caste category after OBCs and SCs. Odisha also has the highest share of ST households in our sample. Table 16.2 also contains the jati distributions considered for our analysis, arranged by state. In order to avoid unduly small cells, we focus on the major jati groups in the state and gather the smaller jatis into an 'Others' category for each broad caste group.

4. Results

Using these data, we examine the relationship between caste and female empowerment. We measure empowerment with variables that are consistent with the literature described earlier and include three categories of indicators:

Measures of intra-household decision making: women were asked who was the primary decision maker in the household on (i) purchases of household durables, (ii) children's education/tuition, (iii) their own livelihood activity, and (iv) voting behaviour. For each of these indicators, we examine two measures, whether a woman respondent provides any input into the decision, or whether she makes the decision entirely by herself.

- Measures of female mobility: Women were asked if they can go—without seeking permission—to the general store, health centre, bank, and to visit their friends, neighbours, and relatives.[14]
- Labour force participation: We use a dummy variable that takes a value of 1 if a woman works for income (in cash or in kind) outside the home in at least one season, and 0 otherwise.

One hypothesis, based on the literature described earlier, is that SC and ST women should have greater mobility, autonomy, and the highest levels of labour force participation rates. We test the hypothesis using a linear probability model, using a set of dummy variables for caste with the poorest group in each population (SCs in Bihar and Tamil Nadu, and STs in Odisha) treated as the omitted category.

We first regress empowerment indicators on official caste categories and then on jati identifiers. We report three sets of regressions. First, to ensure consistency with the existing literature, we use official (broad) caste categories (all defined as dummy variables). Next, we perform comparisons between jatis. We do this in two steps. First, we regress outcome variables on dummy indicators for all non-SC jatis, with SC jatis as the excluded group. Next, we regress our outcome variables on dummy variables for all SC jatis, with all non-SC castes omitted. We include a set of control variables and conduct an analysis for each state in our sample separately. Controls include household level variables: per capita monthly consumption expenditure; wealth (land-holding); number of members in the household; education and gender of the household head; female headship; and a set of individual controls that includes education level, age, age squared, and age at marriage of the woman respondent. To control for locational factors, we also include panchayat-specific fixed effects.

4.1. *Empowerment across Broad Caste Categories*

The results of our main specification for caste-level differences are reported in Table 16.3 and Figure 16.1 (panels (a)–(c) correspond to each of the three states). In each of these regressions, the omitted category is SC. In Bihar (Table 16.3, panel (a) or Figure 16.1(a)), OBCs and FCs (who are the wealthier groups), have significantly lower female employment relative to the SCs (9.2 and 27 percentage points respectively). This is also true of women's decision making authority on issues of their own livelihoods (9.4 and 18.5 percentage

---

[14] For Tamil Nadu, we use available indicators of female mobility, including whether a woman can go to the bank, the Taluk office (Block office), and the police station.

Table 16.3. Empowerment regressions with government-defined caste categories

Panel (a): Bihar

	(1)	(2)	(3)	(4)	(5)	(6)	(7)	(8)	(9)
			Input				Mobility		
	Employed	Durables	Tuition	Livelihoods	Politics	Store	Health Centre	Friend	Bank
ST	−0.0342	−0.0491	−0.0434	−0.0317	−0.105*	0.0252	−0.0753	0.00463	0.0460
	(−0.88)	(−1.37)	(−1.08)	(−0.80)	(−2.37)	(0.55)	(−1.92)	(0.24)	(0.98)
OBC	−0.0917***	0.00301	0.0226*	−0.0942***	−0.00350	−0.117***	−0.0239**	0.00192	−0.00377
	(−8.32)	(0.35)	(2.10)	(−7.09)	(−0.28)	(−8.44)	(−2.78)	(0.42)	(−0.28)
EBC	−0.0808***	−0.00748	0.0167	−0.0916***	0.0148	−0.0409*	−0.00227	−0.00809	0.0210
	(−4.67)	(−0.58)	(1.05)	(−4.43)	(0.77)	(−2.09)	(−0.20)	(−0.97)	(0.97)
Muslim	−0.191***	−0.000158	−0.00925	−0.134***	−0.0332	−0.118***	−0.000230	−0.0129	−0.0220
	(−8.72)	(−0.01)	(−0.44)	(−4.97)	(−1.38)	(−4.73)	(−0.02)	(−1.10)	(−0.91)
General	−0.271***	−0.0113	−0.00355	−0.185***	−0.0192	−0.271***	0.00219	−0.0210	−0.0501
	(−12.01)	(−0.80)	(−0.18)	(−6.59)	(−0.86)	(−9.52)	(0.16)	(−1.82)	(−1.85)
Some Schooling	−0.0936***	0.0198*	0.0364***	−0.0035	0.0256*	−0.0598***	0.0052	0.0084	0.115***
	(−8.62)	(2.38)	(3.49)	(−0.27)	(2.13)	(−4.49)	(0.67)	(1.79)	(8.85)
Female headed household	0.0507***	0.0193*	0.0338*	0.0596***	0.0272*	0.0462***	−0.0145	−0.0084	0.0158
	(4.98)	(2.34)	(3.03)	(5.13)	(2.21)	(3.85)	(−1.77)	(−1.51)	(1.26)
Per capita expenditure	−0.156**	−0.0684	0.0299	−0.106	0.122*	−0.0328	−0.0151	0.0335	0.225***
	(−3.00)	(−1.77)	(0.54)	(−1.70)	(2.00)	(−0.53)	(−0.42)	(1.31)	(3.34)
Per capita expenditure squared	0.0237	0.0223	−0.0440	0.0417	−0.0697*	−0.0343	0.00265	−0.0170	−0.0573
	(0.82)	(1.14)	(−1.45)	(1.24)	(−2.11)	(−1.04)	(0.15)	(−1.32)	(−1.51)
Land	−0.0112***	0.0007	0.004*	−0.005	0.001	−0.0163***	−0.0022	0.0023*	0.01**
	(−4.84)	(0.38)	(1.98)	(−1.45)	(0.38)	(−4.41)	(−0.91)	(2.45)	(2.93)
Observations	12584	8637	8637	8637	8637	8637	8637	8637	8637
Adjusted R-squared	0.302	0.087	0.122	0.118	0.135	0.205	0.090	0.024	0.086

Notes: (1) Source: Author's calculations based on data collected by Social Observatory, World Bank, and Government of Bihar. (2) SC is the omitted caste group. (3) Each column represents a separate regression wherein an 'empowerment indicator' is regressed on reported variables and additional controls, as reported in the text. The female employment regression is run for all female adults in the sample (individual level). (4) We report robust standard errors in the brackets. (5) We report the level of significance: * p value < 0.05, ** p value < 0.01 and *** p value < 0.001.

(continued)

Table 16.3. Continued

Panel (b): Odisha	(1)	(2)	(3)	(4)	(5)	(6)	(7)	(8)	(9)
		Input				Mobility			
	Employed	Durables	Tuition	Livelihoods	Politics	Store	Health Centre	Friend	Bank
ST	0.187***	-0.0166	-0.0354	-0.0610	-0.0613	0.0493	0.0256	0.0165	-0.0453
	(4.81)	(-0.45)	(-0.67)	(-1.19)	(-1.24)	(0.97)	(1.16)	(1.03)	(-1.03)
OBC	-0.0511***	-0.0899***	0.0017	-0.0864***	0.0460	-0.0346	-0.006	0.0078	0.0277
	(-3.31)	(-4.15)	(0.06)	(-3.34)	(1.66)	(-1.28)	(-0.41)	(0.60)	(1.18)
Muslim	0.101	0.119	0.148	-0.0703	0.0135	-0.00933	0.00558	0.0164	-0.0318
	(1.69)	(1.58)	(1.61)	(-0.77)	(0.14)	(-0.10)	(0.11)	(1.30)	(-0.47)
FC	-0.0859***	-0.0364	0.0173	-0.0572*	0.0335	-0.0521	0.0135	0.0110	0.0403
	(-5.63)	(-1.59)	(0.61)	(-2.10)	(1.16)	(-1.87)	(0.98)	(0.81)	(1.60)
Some Schooling	-0.0726***	0.0630**	0.0629**	0.0237	0.00656	-0.0751**	0.00636	0.0023	0.117***
	(-4.57)	(3.24)	(2.69)	(1.02)	(0.27)	(-3.17)	(0.51)	(0.23)	(6.06)
Female headed household	0.0767**	0.0206	-0.0164	-0.0616	0.188**	0.105	0.0270	0.0193	-0.0534
	(2.67)	(0.37)	(-0.26)	(-0.96)	(2.75)	(1.58)	(0.88)	(0.56)	(-1.00)
Per capita expenditure	-0.0087	-0.0007	0.0065	0.0147	-0.0067	-0.008	0.0046	0.0031	-0.0031
	(-1.77)	(-0.09)	(0.80)	(1.76)	(-0.86)	(-0.94)	(1.04)	(1.46)	(-0.38)
Per capita expenditure squared	0.0004*	0.0001	-0.0001	-0.0005	0.0003	0.0005	-0.00009	-0.0000	0.0003
	(2.10)	(0.20)	(-0.44)	(-1.50)	(0.91)	(1.35)	(-0.63)	(-0.14)	(0.90)
Land	-0.0087*	0.0088	0.0034	-0.0141	0.0033	-0.0328***	0.0029	0.0054*	-0.0090
	(-2.09)	(1.64)	(0.40)	(-1.76)	(0.39)	(-3.88)	(0.93)	(2.29)	(-1.36)
Observations	4077	2246	2246	2246	2246	2246	2246	2246	2246
Adjusted R-squared	0.212	0.141	0.188	0.199	0.201	0.244	0.075	0.063	0.088

Notes: (1) Source: Author's calculations based on data collected by Social Observatory, World Bank, and Government of Odisha. Notes (2)–(5) of Table 3(a) apply.

Panel (c): Tamil Nadu

	(1)	(2)	(3)	(4)	(5)	(6)	(7)	(8)
			Input:			Mobility:		
	Employed	Durables	Tuition	Livelihood	Politics	Bank	Taluk Office	Police Station
ST	0.0867	-0.0609	-0.111*	-0.0884	-0.0986	-0.0304	0.0165	-0.00567
	(1.78)	(-1.16)	(-2.07)	(-1.35)	(-1.73)	(-0.44)	(0.24)	(-0.16)
MBC	-0.00889	-0.0305	-0.0437*	-0.0201	-0.0454**	0.00678	-0.0584**	-0.00910
	(-0.52)	(-1.73)	(-2.55)	(-1.00)	(-2.67)	(0.32)	(-2.64)	(-0.78)
BC	-0.0486***	0.0101	-0.0143	0.00286	-0.0107	0.0411*	-0.0334	-0.0259**
	(-3.31)	(0.72)	(-0.93)	(0.16)	(-0.76)	(2.27)	(-1.76)	(-2.62)
Some schooling	0.0395**	0.00402	0.0000371	0.0347*	0.0118	0.0478**	0.0454*	0.00979
	(2.99)	(0.29)	(0.00)	(2.08)	(0.89)	(2.92)	(2.46)	(1.04)
Female-headed household	0.0601***	0.0703***	0.0842***	0.0151	0.0710***	0.0711**	0.0208	0.006
	(3.37)	(3.60)	(4.17)	(0.61)	(3.89)	(2.94)	(0.81)	(0.40)
Per-capita expenditure	-0.0196***	0.00143	0.00436	0.0110*	0.00678	0.0351***	0.0470***	0.0107**
	(-3.53)	(0.28)	(0.85)	(1.97)	(1.46)	(5.95)	(5.25)	(2.60)
Per-capita expenditure squared	0.0001***	-0.00001	-0.0003	-0.0001*	-0.0000	-0.0002***	-0.0003***	-0.0001**
	(3.94)	(-0.25)	(-0.87)	(-2.20)	(-1.25)	(-5.74)	(-5.61)	(-2.80)
Land	0.0001	-0.0011**	0.0003	-0.0012**	0.0004	0.0002	0.0004	-0.0002
	(0.25)	(-2.66)	(0.80)	(-2.59)	(1.95)	(0.43)	(0.66)	(-1.05)
Observations	5190	3284	3280	3283	3279	3299	3299	3299
Adjusted R-squared	0.276	0.119	0.119	0.150	0.077	0.135	0.149	0.051

Notes: (1) Source: Author's calculations based on data collected by Social Observatory, World Bank, and Government of Tamil Nadu. Notes (2)–(5) of Table 3(a) apply.

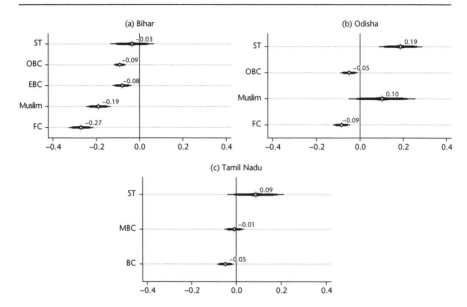

Figure 16.1. Coefficients on caste from employment regression

Note:

1) SC is the omitted caste group

2) 99%, 95%, and 90% confidence intervals included.

Source: Authors' illustration based on data used in column 1 of Table 3, panels (a), (b), and (c), respectively.

points), and their mobility in terms of accessing the local store (11.7 and 27 percentage points).

The patterns of caste variation that emerge in Odisha (Table 16.3, panel (b) or Figure 16.1(b)) are similar to those in Bihar. We observe that women in the Forward Caste category are 8.6 percentage points less likely to work than SCs, and 6 percentage points less likely to visit the store on their own when compared to their SC counterparts. OBC women are 5 percentage points less likely to work, 9 percentage points less likely to make decisions about durables, and 9 percentage points less likely to make decisions on their livelihood activities compared to SC women. ST women, on the other hand, are 18 percentage points more likely to be employed than SCs.

Tamil Nadu has less variation at the caste level than the other two states (Table 16.3, panel (c) or Figure 16.1(c)). ST women are 11 percentage points less likely to make decisions on their children's education. MBC women are less likely to make decisions related to their children's education or their own livelihood activity (by 5 percentage points each) and have less mobility in terms of accessing the block office. Women in the BC group are 5 percentage points less likely than SC women to participate in the labour market. However, they are 4 percentage points more likely to visit a bank.

4.2. *Empowerment across Jati Categories*

Next, we examine jati-level regressions. The results are in Tables 16.4, 16.5, and 16.6 and Figures 16.2, 16.3, and 16.4. For each state, we present two sets of regression results. In the top panel, we present estimation results for regressions with the jati-level categories for SC groups only (with all other castes treated as the excluded category), and in the bottom panel we present estimation results from regressions with the jati-level categories for other groups, excluding the SC groups. For reasons of brevity, in all these tables we only present jati coefficients. We do not report the effects of the control variables, which are not very different in their magnitude and significance from the results from the broad caste categories.

The level of variation within and across the three states is quite striking. In Table 16.4 and Figure 16.2(a), for example, we see in Bihar, Musahars have significantly higher female employment than any other SC jati. They are 17 percentage points more likely to work than the OBCs, FCs, and Muslims and are at least twice as likely to work as the Dobhas, Chamars, and 'Other' SC jatis. This is consistent with anthropological studies that have noted that this jati is one of the most politically, economically, and socially marginalized groups in India (Mukul 1999).[15]

In the lower panel of Table 16.4 and Figure 16.2(b) we see that relative to the SC and ST groups, female employment is 7–8 percentage points lower among the Yadavs, Kurmis, EBCs, and other jatis, who are also classified as backward castes.[16] Note that women from the highest ranked castes, Brahmins and Rajputs, are 33 and 22 per cent less likely to be employed compared to SCs. The lower labour force participation rates of women in the higher-ranked jatis is consistent with our hypothesis, as well as with the large body of literature described earlier.

We see similar patterns for women's input into livelihood decisions, as well as for patterns of mobility. In the top panel in Table 16.4, we see that Musahar women have the highest level of input in family decisions related to livelihoods and they have greatest freedom of mobility for going to a store. They appear to have lower input into children's tuition funds, though this may be

[15] Both the Musahars and Chamars are traditionally outcastes (i.e., they are outside of the caste system and regarded as untouchables (Hasan, Rizvi and Das 2005)). Traditionally rat-catchers, the Musahars are now largely agricultural labourers. Musahar men have increasingly migrated out of the state with women joining the labour force (Mukul 1999). The Chamar jati, on the other hand, though also classified as SC, is found throughout India and consists of many different sub-jatis that vary significantly in status. In many states such as Uttar Pradesh and Punjab, they have been successful in mobilizing themselves politically.

[16] Yadavs are traditionally a group of jatis whose main occupations were related to dairy farming and pastoral agriculture in the Bihar and Uttar Pradesh region (Hutton 1946). The group now includes a wide range of pastoral agriculturalists in numerous states of India. Since the late nineteenth and early twentieth centuries, it has mobilized itself to improve its social standing (Jaffrelot 2003).

Table 16.4. Empowerment regressions with jati identifiers, Bihar

| | | Input: | | | | | | | |
	Employed	Durables	Tuition	Livelihood	Politics	Store	Health centre	Friend	Bank
Panel (a): SC-ST Jatis									
SC: Chamar	0.125***	-0.00461	-0.00392	0.102***	0.0221	0.126***	0.00781	0.00661	0.00429
	(10.79)	(-0.52)	(-0.34)	(7.52)	(1.69)	(9.26)	(0.97)	(1.27)	(0.31)
SC: Dobha	0.0673**	-0.0264	0.0164	0.0667*	-0.0563	-0.00181	0.0291*	-0.00699	0.0154
	(2.70)	(-1.35)	(0.70)	(2.25)	(-1.89)	(-0.06)	(2.20)	(-0.57)	(0.53)
SC: Dushad	0.0872***	0.0152	-0.00129	0.0975***	0.00896	0.0979***	0.0159	0.00948	0.0467**
	(7.05)	(1.74)	(-0.11)	(6.75)	(0.67)	(6.84)	(1.84)	(1.87)	(3.19)
SC: Musahar	0.172***	-0.00449	-0.0312**	0.123***	-0.0102	0.156***	0.0189*	0.00109	-0.0219
	(15.93)	(-0.47)	(-2.68)	(9.61)	(-0.78)	(11.56)	(2.14)	(0.19)	(-1.67)
SC: Sardar	0.0366	0.0112	-0.0160	0.141***	0.0944*	0.0180	0.00144	0.000129	0.0251
	(0.93)	(0.31)	(-0.38)	(3.40)	(2.15)	(0.35)	(0.05)	(0.00)	(0.50)
SC: Others	0.0757**	0.0152	-0.0747***	0.143***	0.00961	0.0710*	-0.00892	-0.00359	-0.0389
	(2.87)	(0.85)	(-2.64)	(5.29)	(0.32)	(2.37)	(-0.45)	(-0.28)	(-1.40)
ST	0.0976*	-0.0492	-0.0634	0.0830*	-0.0977*	0.149**	-0.0603	0.00741	0.0455
	(2.47)	(-1.35)	(-1.55)	(2.05)	(-2.17)	(3.16)	(-1.52)	(0.39)	(0.96)
Observations	12584	8637	8637	8637	8637	8637	8637	8637	8637
Adjusted R-squared	0.300	0.087	0.123	0.117	0.136	0.204	0.090	0.023	0.088
Panel (b): Non–SC Jatis									
OBC: Dhanuk	-0.0424	0.0244	0.0159	-0.0558	0.00743	-0.0872	-0.0922**	-0.00324	-0.0292
	(-1.30)	(0.78)	(0.47)	(-1.43)	(0.18)	(-1.94)	(-2.62)	(-0.21)	(-0.76)
OBC: Kurmi	-0.0910**	0.0285	0.0571	-0.0394	0.00484	-0.0584	0.0179	0.00726	0.00790
	(-2.84)	(1.29)	(1.89)	(-0.94)	(0.12)	(-1.50)	(0.85)	(0.72)	(0.19)
OBC: Yadav	-0.0877***	0.00336	0.0184	-0.0936***	0.0284	-0.157***	-0.00916	0.00732	-0.0104
	(-5.36)	(0.26)	(1.20)	(-4.57)	(1.63)	(-7.20)	(-0.75)	(1.19)	(-0.54)
OBC: Other	-0.101***	-0.00327	0.0227	-0.109***	-0.0277	-0.104***	-0.0285*	-0.00269	0.00182
	(-6.69)	(-0.29)	(1.55)	(-6.07)	(-1.64)	(-5.53)	(-2.38)	(-0.41)	(0.10)

	(1)	(2)	(3)	(4)	(5)	(6)	(7)	(8)	(9)
EBC	−0.0801***	−0.00666	0.0173	−0.0913***	0.0165	−0.0423*	−0.000900	−0.00815	0.0202
	(−4.63)	(−0.52)	(1.09)	(−4.41)	(0.86)	(−2.16)	(−0.08)	(−0.98)	(0.93)
FC: Brahmin	−0.336***	−0.00521	−0.0136	−0.238***	−0.0166	−0.255***	0.0253	−0.0184	−0.0906*
	(−10.10)	(−0.25)	(−0.45)	(−5.34)	(−0.48)	(−5.60)	(1.41)	(−1.03)	(−2.28)
FC: Rajput	−0.218***	−0.00985	0.00279	−0.165***	−0.0491	−0.383***	0.00328	−0.0279	−0.0186
	(−6.21)	(−0.47)	(0.10)	(−3.90)	(−1.37)	(−9.30)	(0.15)	(−1.55)	(−0.44)
FC: Others	−0.242***	−0.0195	0.00648	−0.120*	0.0510	−0.106*	−0.0264	−0.0113	−0.0421
	(−5.51)	(−0.65)	(0.16)	(−2.22)	(1.33)	(−1.98)	(−0.92)	(−0.55)	(−0.79)
Muslims	−0.190***	0.000654	−0.00842	−0.133***	−0.0325	−0.118***	0.000623	−0.0130	−0.0223
	(−8.69)	(0.04)	(−0.40)	(−4.94)	(−1.36)	(−4.73)	(0.04)	(−1.12)	(−0.93)
Observations	12584	8637	8637	8637	8637	8637	8637	8637	8637
Adjusted R-squared	0.302	0.086	0.122	0.118	0.135	0.208	0.090	0.023	0.086

Notes: (1) Source: Authors' calculations based on data collected by Social Observatory, World Bank, and Government of Bihar. (2) In panel (a), Non-SC jatis are the excluded group while in Panel (b), SCs are the excluded group. (3) Each column represents a separate regression wherein an `empowerment indicator' is regressed on variables that are reported as well as additional controls. The female employment is run for all female adults in the sample (individual level). (4) We report robust standard errors in the brackets. (5) We report the level of significance: * p value < 0.05, ** p value < 0.01 and *** p value < 0.01.

Table 16.5. Empowerment regressions with jati identifiers, Odisha

	Input:						Mobility:		
	Employed	Durables	Tuition	Livelihood	Politics	Store	Health centre	Friend	Bank
Panel (a): SC-ST Jatis									
SC: Barui	0.179***	0.0695	-0.0483	0.00416	0.0719	0.183**	-0.0356	0.0173	-0.0190
	(4.53)	(1.22)	(-0.77)	(0.07)	(1.16)	(2.94)	(-1.07)	(0.70)	(-0.40)
SC: Dobha	0.0501	0.106*	0.0676	0.172**	-0.0123	0.0612	0.0210	-0.00333	0.00376
	(1.63)	(1.98)	(1.01)	(3.21)	(-0.17)	(0.87)	(1.94)	(-0.09)	(0.07)
SC: Keuta	0.0706	0.0980***	-0.0206	0.0957	-0.151*	0.0213	0.00288	0.0239*	-0.0653
	(1.82)	(3.53)	(-0.35)	(1.65)	(-2.40)	(0.34)	(0.09)	(1.99)	(-1.12)
SC: Kondara	-0.00784	0.126**	0.00819	0.0975*	-0.0259	-0.0184	0.0355*	0.0300	-0.0448
	(-0.29)	(2.96)	(0.17)	(2.00)	(-0.52)	(-0.39)	(2.24)	(1.53)	(-1.04)
SC: Pana	0.0152	-0.0105	-0.0186	0.0981*	-0.00120	0.0136	-0.0228	-0.0475	0.0167
	(0.63)	(-0.30)	(-0.42)	(2.27)	(-0.03)	(0.32)	(-0.88)	(-1.92)	(0.46)
SC: Others	0.111***	0.0452	-0.0423	0.00767	-0.114*	0.0449	-0.00315	-0.0248	-0.0827*
	(4.02)	(1.48)	(-1.02)	(0.20)	(-2.45)	(1.04)	(-0.13)	(-1.13)	(-2.29)
ST	0.250***	0.0492	-0.0468	0.0139	-0.105*	0.0889	0.0237	0.00590	-0.0762
	(6.77)	(1.45)	(-0.94)	(0.29)	(-2.27)	(1.86)	(1.22)	(0.47)	(-1.87)
Observations	4077	2246	2246	2246	2246	2246	2246	2246	2246
Adjusted R-squared	0.214	0.138	0.187	0.200	0.204	0.246	0.075	0.067	0.088
Panel (b): Other Jatis									
OBC: Chasa	-0.0533*	-0.122***	0.0117	-0.0604	0.115**	-0.0531	-0.00199	-0.00522	0.105**
	(-2.12)	(-3.86)	(0.29)	(-1.42)	(3.11)	(-1.24)	(-0.13)	(-0.31)	(2.79)
OBC: Goala	-0.124***	-0.131**	-0.00955	-0.0717	-0.0239	-0.0658	-0.00921	0.0246	0.00334
	(-4.48)	(-3.14)	(-0.19)	(-1.51)	(-0.48)	(-1.36)	(-0.42)	(1.19)	(0.08)
OBC: Guria	-0.114**	-0.0342	0.0762	0.00820	0.122	0.104	-0.0293	-0.0640	-0.0307
	(-2.99)	(-0.51)	(1.03)	(0.13)	(1.65)	(1.25)	(-0.72)	(-1.35)	(-0.45)
OBC: Tanti	-0.106**	0.0188	0.0700	-0.102	-0.00954	-0.0199	0.000958	0.00808	0.0851
	(-2.85)	(0.32)	(1.10)	(-1.54)	(-0.14)	(-0.27)	(0.02)	(0.24)	(1.43)

	(1)	(2)	(3)	(4)	(5)	(6)	(7)	(8)	(9)
OBC: Teli	-0.0382	-0.0311	0.0602	-0.0988	0.0210	-0.126	0.00476	0.0378	0.0249
	(-1.13)	(-0.63)	(0.88)	(-1.60)	(0.29)	(-1.96)	(0.16)	(1.56)	(0.41)
OBC: Others	-0.0893***	-0.0880***	-0.0195	-0.0979**	0.0561	-0.0436	-0.0174	0.00873	0.00812
	(-4.75)	(-3.36)	(-0.58)	(-2.99)	(1.60)	(-1.31)	(-0.85)	(0.58)	(0.27)
FC: Brahmin	-0.173***	0.0430	0.0492	-0.0384	0.0543	-0.0592	0.0457*	0.0200	0.0383
	(-7.64)	(1.15)	(1.00)	(-0.81)	(1.04)	(-1.21)	(2.24)	(0.89)	(0.83)
FC: Karan	-0.0940**	-0.0730	0.0220	-0.205**	-0.00969	-0.0698	0.0186	0.00570	0.0624
	(-2.96)	(-1.32)	(0.35)	(-3.05)	(-0.14)	(-1.19)	(0.52)	(0.23)	(0.94)
FC: Khandayat	-0.105***	-0.0569*	0.00384	-0.0496	0.0167	-0.0765*	-0.00327	0.00821	0.0334
	(-6.56)	(-2.20)	(0.12)	(-1.70)	(0.53)	(-2.44)	(-0.22)	(0.56)	(1.20)
FC: Others	-0.0995**	0.0101	0.0722	0.0190	0.146**	0.0206	0.0172	-0.000242	0.0879
	(-2.96)	(0.24)	(1.25)	(0.34)	(2.89)	(0.43)	(0.65)	(-0.01)	(1.74)
Muslims	0.0814	0.124	0.157	-0.0576	0.0192	-0.00512	0.00275	0.0106	-0.0339
	(1.34)	(1.65)	(1.70)	(-0.63)	(0.20)	(-0.06)	(0.05)	(0.79)	(-0.50)
Observations	4077	2246	2246	2246	2246	2246	2246	2246	2246
Adjusted R-squared	0.206	0.145	0.188	0.199	0.203	0.245	0.073	0.064	0.089

Notes: (1) Source: Authors' calculations based on data collected by Social Observatory, World Bank, and Government of Odisha. Notes (2)–(5) of Table 5 apply.

Table 16.6. Empowerment regressions with jati identifiers, Tamil Nadu

	Input:					Mobility:		
	Employed	Durables	Tuition	Livelihood	Politics	Bank	Taluk Office	Police Station
Panel (a): SC-ST Jatis								
SC: Adidravidar	0.0394**	0.0136	0.0400**	0.0222	0.0254	-0.0176	0.0599**	0.0208*
	(2.72)	(0.96)	(2.70)	(1.27)	(1.79)	(-0.96)	(3.05)	(1.99)
SC: Chakkaliyan	0.0454	-0.0276	0.0226	-0.0798	-0.0560	0.0126	-0.0342	0.0436
	(0.87)	(-0.46)	(0.41)	(-1.28)	(-0.96)	(0.20)	(-0.47)	(1.01)
SC: Pallar	0.0365	-0.0109	-0.0237	-0.00954	0.0541	-0.0160	0.0191	-0.00603
	(1.10)	(-0.34)	(-0.68)	(-0.25)	(1.83)	(-0.39)	(0.45)	(-0.32)
SC: Others	-0.0200	-0.0208	-0.0135	-0.0555	0.00477	-0.143**	-0.0167	0.0352
	(-0.51)	(-0.58)	(-0.36)	(-1.31)	(0.13)	(-3.03)	(-0.39)	(1.21)
ST	0.116*	-0.0497	-0.0784	-0.0792	-0.0730	-0.0565	0.0637	0.0139
	(2.36)	(-0.94)	(-1.46)	(-1.21)	(-1.28)	(-0.81)	(0.92)	(0.40)
Observations	5190	3284	3280	3283	3279	3299	3299	3299
Adjusted R-squared	0.276	0.117	0.119	0.151	0.076	0.136	0.149	0.050
Panel (b): Non-SC Jatis								
MBC: Ambalakarar	0.0463	-0.0110	-0.0867	0.00655	-0.0636	-0.0640	-0.141**	0.00288
	(1.25)	(-0.24)	(-1.95)	(0.14)	(-1.64)	(-1.36)	(-3.18)	(0.10)
MBC: Muthuraja	0.0383	-0.0558	0.0171	0.00438	-0.0263	-0.00620	-0.0146	-0.0165
	(0.77)	(-0.95)	(0.35)	(0.07)	(-0.59)	(-0.11)	(-0.24)	(-0.57)
MBC: Vanniyar	-0.00369	-0.0143	-0.0261	-0.0203	-0.0124	0.0388	-0.0440	-0.0154
	(-0.17)	(-0.68)	(-1.23)	(-0.79)	(-0.57)	(1.35)	(-1.40)	(-1.02)
MBC: Others	-0.0745**	-0.0492	-0.0485	-0.0299	-0.0729*	0.00309	-0.0549	-0.00608
	(-2.65)	(-1.61)	(-1.65)	(-0.89)	(-2.51)	(0.10)	(-1.62)	(-0.33)
BC: Chettiar	-0.0327	-0.0101	-0.00425	-0.0505	-0.0364	0.0261	-0.0150	0.0362
	(-0.57)	(-0.18)	(-0.08)	(-0.73)	(-0.60)	(0.40)	(-0.21)	(0.91)
BC: Kallar	-0.00500	0.0276	-0.00618	0.0739	-0.0458	0.00543	0.0194	-0.0103
	(-0.15)	(0.81)	(-0.17)	(1.78)	(-1.32)	(0.13)	(0.44)	(-0.38)

BC: Nadar	-0.0761	-0.0258	-0.0564	-0.0439	-0.0408	0.0539	0.00706	-0.0481**
	(-1.16)	(-0.45)	(-0.87)	(-0.66)	(-0.72)	(0.90)	(0.08)	(-2.62)
BC: Naidu	-0.155*	0.0730	-0.0141	-0.0149	0.0607	0.0948*	-0.0340	-0.0370
	(-2.14)	(1.39)	(-0.21)	(-0.20)	(1.39)	(2.11)	(-0.51)	(-1.06)
BC: Parkavakulam	0.0434	0.0354	0.00918	-0.0390	0.0129	0.0879*	-0.0472	0.00936
	(1.16)	(1.18)	(0.25)	(-0.80)	(0.46)	(2.08)	(-0.94)	(0.34)
BC: Reddiyar	-0.147*	-0.0949	-0.104	-0.0691	-0.123	-0.0652	-0.00880	-0.0601*
	(-2.52)	(-1.44)	(-1.54)	(-0.98)	(-1.82)	(-0.89)	(-0.13)	(-2.45)
BC: Thevar	0.0522	0.0191	-0.0178	0.0625	0.0224	0.0559	0.0616	0.00206
	(1.03)	(0.53)	(-0.43)	(1.87)	(0.56)	(0.95)	(1.02)	(0.06)
BC: Vellalar	-0.0669**	0.0177	-0.00181	0.0224	0.00684	0.00447	-0.0605*	-0.0404**
	(-2.74)	(0.73)	(-0.07)	(0.79)	(0.28)	(0.15)	(-2.08)	(-2.58)
BC: Vishwakrma	-0.0127	-0.0426	0.0312	0.0342	0.0414	0.0446	-0.0930	-0.0329
	(-0.25)	(-0.76)	(0.59)	(0.52)	(0.84)	(0.80)	(-1.34)	(-0.97)
BC: Yadava	-0.0692	-0.00205	-0.0310	-0.0200	-0.0276	0.171***	0.0448	-0.0363
	(-1.46)	(-0.04)	(-0.65)	(-0.35)	(-0.61)	(3.38)	(0.72)	(-1.18)
BC: Others	-0.0806***	0.00856	-0.0187	-0.00469	-0.0139	0.0506	-0.0572*	-0.0328*
	(-3.70)	(0.41)	(-0.82)	(-0.18)	(-0.64)	(1.89)	(-2.09)	(-2.39)
Observations	5190	3284	3280	3283	3279	3299	3299	3299
Adjusted R-squared	0.279	0.117	0.117	0.149	0.077	0.136	0.149	0.050

Notes: (1) Source: Authors' calculations based on data collected by Social Observatory, World Bank, and Government of Tamil Nadu. Notes (2)–(5) of Table 5 apply.

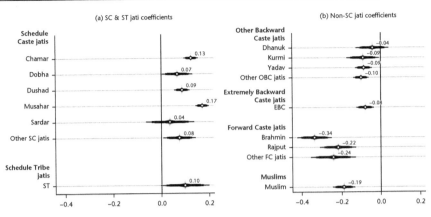

Figure 16.2. Coefficients on jati from employment regression, Bihar

Note:
1) OBC, EBC, FC, and Muslim jatis form the omitted group in panel (a), and SC and ST jatis are the omitted group in panel (b).

2) 99%, 95%, and 90% confidence intervals included.

Source: Authors' illustration based on data used in column 1, Table 16.4.

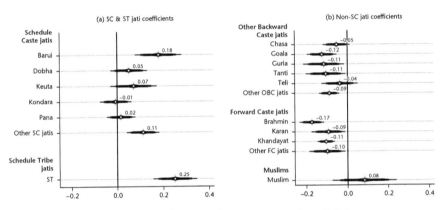

Figure 16.3. Coefficients on jati from employment regression, Odisha

Note:
1) OBC, FC, and Muslim jatis form the omitted group in panel (a), and SC and ST jatis are the omitted group in panel (b).

2) 99%, 95%, and 90% confidence intervals included.

Source: Authors' illustration based on data used in column 1, Table 16.5.

due to the lower levels of schooling in this group. In the bottom panel, we see again that Brahmin and Rajput women have significantly lower levels of empowerment on all indicators (employment, decision making autonomy, and mobility), but Brahmin women have even lower levels of labour force participation than Rajputs. We also note that Muslim women's employment is 19 percentage points lower than the SCs in Bihar.

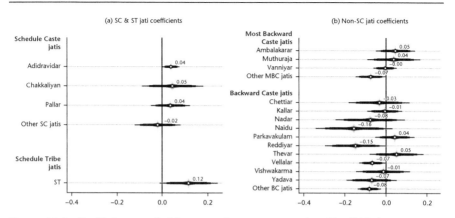

Figure 16.4. Coefficients on jati from employment regression, Tamil Nadu

Note: 1) OBC, EBC, FC, and Muslim jatis form the omitted group in panel (a), and SC and ST jatis are the omitted group in panel (b).

2) 99%, 95%, and 90% confidence intervals included.

Source: Authors' illustration based on data used in column 1, Table 16.6.

Similar mixed patterns are evident for Odisha. In the top panel of Table 16.5 and Figure 16.3(a), we see that in Odisha, ST women and SC women from the Barui caste are 21 percentage points more likely to be employed than the higher-ranked castes. In the bottom panel and Figure 16.3(b), we see that women from the highest ranked Brahmin, Karan, and Khandayat castes have 9–17 percentage points lower labour force participation rates compared to SC/ST groups. Chasa, Goala, and Tanti women of the OBC group are 5–12 percentage points less likely to work than SC/ST women. Higher-caste women from the Chasa, Goala, and Khandayat jatis are also less likely to make decisions on buying household durables. However, we do not see much evidence of jati-level variation for mobility indicators in this state. In the case of Odisha, it is plausible that location and issues specific to the tribal culture in the poorest regions could matter more than caste.

Finally, in Tamil Nadu (Table 16.6 and Figure 16.4), we find in the top panel and Figure 16.4(a) that Adi Dravidars exhibit higher employment among the SCs relative to higher castes.[17] The other SC castes—Chakkalians, Pallars, and others—do not appear to be statistically distinguishable from their upper-caste counterparts, possibly because these castes have mobilized themselves very successfully in the state.[18] The lower panel of Table 16.6 and Figure 16.4(b)

---

[17] Adi-Dravida or Adi-Dravidars are also known as Pariyars or Pareiyas. They have historically served higher castes and/or colonial officers (Bergunder et al. 2010). Today they are classified as a Scheduled Caste and are the largest SC group in Tamil Nadu.

[18] The Pallars of Tamil Nadu are also an SC jati. Largely concentrated in the southern area of the state, this jati has mainly consisted of agricultural labourers. The Pallars have been very effective in mobilizing and they created Tamil Nadu's first all-Dalit party (Mosse 2012).

show differences within the BC and MBC groups. Naidu, Gounder, and Reddiyar women of the BC caste are less likely to work than SC/ST women by 14.7, 7, and 15.5 percentage points respectively. These results stand in contrast to our findings when we used broad indicators of caste.

The caste and mobility relationships in Tamil Nadu are difficult to compare to the other states because we lack comparable indicators on mobility. Here we only measure whether women have the freedom to visit a bank, Taluk office, and police station without permission. In the top panel, we see that Adi Dravidar women visit the Taluk office 6 percentage points more often than the higher-ranked BC and MBC groups. They are also 2 percentage points more likely to visit a police station than their counterparts in these groups. In the lower panel of Table 16.5, we again see considerable within-caste variation. Yadava, Parkavakulam, and Naidu women in the BC group show higher mobility for trips to banks. Some other BC jatis show less mobility for trips to the Taluk office and police station. Moreover, MBC Ambalakarar women and Gounder women are 14 and 6 percentage points less likely to go to the Taluk Office than SC/ST groups.

We perform a test for pairwise equality of coefficients between SC/ST jatis, and between Non-SC/ST jatis. In Table 16.7, we combine the indicators of decision making autonomy and the indicators of mobility and report the percentage of pairwise coefficient differences. These results are consistent with the above analysis. In Bihar, there is substantial variation within SC/ST jatis and within Non-SC jatis. In Odisha, the differences between jatis are present for labour force participation but are less dramatic for decision making autonomy and mobility. We see very little difference, if any, between jatis in Tamil Nadu, except some evidence of variation in employment between BC and MBC jatis.

Overall, we find evidence in support of an inverse relationship between caste status and female employment, but there is considerable variation across

Table 16.7. Percentage of pairwise differences that are significantly different

		Employment	Input in intra-household decision making	Mobility
Bihar	SC-ST	47.6	28.6	25.0
	Others	66.7	45.8	58.3
Odisha	SC-ST	61.9	14.3	19.0
	Others	38.2	16.8	9.5
TN	SC-ST	10.0	15.0	13.3
	Others	31.4	7.6	9.8

Source: Authors' calculations based on data collected by Social Observatory, World Bank, and state Government of Bihar, Odisha, and Tamil Nadu, respectively.

jatis. There are also regional variations: the negative relationship is stronger in Bihar and Odisha than Tamil Nadu, and the effect is driven by a few jatis. Moreover, we see a negative relationship between caste and female intra-household bargaining authority only when we group households by jati. Broad caste categories conceal this pattern because they compute averages over heterogeneous groups.

5. Conclusion

This chapter has examined the relationship between caste and gender inequality in three states of India: Bihar, Odisha, and Tamil Nadu. We use detailed data on caste to understand its effects on three measures of female status: labour force participation, decision making autonomy, and mobility.

When we group households using conventional, government-defined categories of caste, we find overall patterns that are consistent with the literature on India. Lower-caste women are more likely to participate in the labour market, have greater decision making autonomy within their households and have greater freedom of movement. There are however, some regional variations.

When we group households by the narrower categories of jati, however, we find more variability. In all three states, the overall relationship between caste and female employment is driven by specific jatis. Evidence of a negative relationship between caste and female intra-household bargaining authority emerges only when we group households at the jati level. In conclusion, these results suggest that focusing on broad caste categories such as 'Scheduled Castes' and 'Scheduled Tribes' can be misleading because they mask important differences at the jati level.

References

Alesina, A., P. Giuliano, and N. Nunn (2013). 'On the Origins of Gender Roles: Women and the Plough'. *The Quarterly Journal of Economics*, 128(2): 469–530.

Bayly, S. (2001). *Caste, Society and Politics in India from the Eighteenth Century to the Modern Age*. Cambridge: Cambridge University Press.

Bergunder, M., H. Frese, and U. Schröder (2010). *Ritual, Caste, and Religion in Colonial South India* (Vol. 9). Wiesbaden: Otto Harrassowitz Verlag.

Beteille, A. (1996). *Caste in Contemporary India*. New Delhi: Oxford University Press.

Boserup, E. (1970). *Woman's Role in Economic Development*. Abingdon, UK: Earthscan Publications.

Cassan, G. (2015). 'Identity-based Policies and Identity Manipulation: Evidence from Colonial Punjab'. *American Economic Journal: Economic Policy*, 7(4): 103–31.

Census of India (2011). Primary Census Abstract for Total population, Scheduled Castes and Scheduled Tribes. Office of the Registrar General & Census Commissioner, Government of India.

Chen, M. (1995). 'A Matter of Survival: Women's Right to Employment in India and Bangladesh'. In M. Nussbaum and J. Glover (eds), *Women, Culture and Development*. Oxford: Clarendon Press.

Dasgupta, M. (1987). 'Selective Discrimination against Female Children in Rural Punjab, India'. *Population and Development Review*, 13(1): 77–100.

David, N., and C. Kramer (2001). *Ethnoarchaeology in Action*. Cambridge: Cambridge University Press.

Desai, S., and A. Dubey (2012). 'Caste in 21st-century India: Competing Narratives'. *Economic and Political Weekly*, 46(11): 40.

Deshpande, A. (2001). 'Caste at Birth? Redefining Disparity in India'. *Review of Development Economics*, 5(1): 130–44.

Deshpande, A. (2002). 'Assets versus Autonomy? The Changing Face of the Gender–Caste Overlap in India'. *Feminist Economics*, 8(2): 19–35.

Dirks, N.B. (2011). *Castes of Mind: Colonialism and the Making of Modern India*. Princeton, NJ: Princeton University Press.

Drèze, J., and A.K. Sen (2002). *India: Development and Participation*. New Delhi: Oxford University Press.

Dumont, L. (1980). *Homo Hierarchicus: The Caste System and Its Implications*. Chicago: University of Chicago Press.

Eswaran, M., B. Ramaswami, and W. Wadhwa (2013). 'Status, Caste, and the Time Allocation of Women in Rural India'. *Economic Development and Cultural Change*, 61(2): 311–33.

Goldin, C. (1994). 'The U-shaped Female Labor Force Function in Economic Development and Economic History'. Working Paper w4707. Cambridge, MA: National Bureau of Economic Research.

Gupta, D. (2000). *Interrogating Caste: Understanding Hierarchy and Difference in Indian Society*. New Delhi: Penguin Books India.

Hasan, A., B.R. Rizvi, and J.K. Das (2005). 'People of India: Uttar Pradesh'. In *Anthropological Survey of India*, Volume 42, Part 2. New Delhi: Vedams.

Huber, J.D., and P. Suryanarayan (2016). 'Ethnic Inequality and the Ethnification of Political Parties: Evidence from India'. *World Politics*, 68(1): 149–88.

Hutton, J.H. (1946). *Caste in India: Its Nature, Function and Origin*. London: Oxford University Press.

Jaffrelot, C. (2003). *India's Silent Revolution: The Rise of the Lower Castes in North India*. New York: Columbia University Press.

Jeffrey, P., and R. Jeffrey (1996). *Don't Marry Me to a Plowman! Women's Everyday Lives in Rural North India*. Boulder, CO: Westview Press.

Joshi, S., N. Kochhar, and V. Rao (2017). 'Are Caste Categories Misleading?: The Relationship Between Gender and Jati in Three Indian States'. WIDER Working Paper 2017/132. Helsinki: UNU-WIDER.

Joshi, V. (1995). *Polygamy and Purdah: Women and Society among Rajputs*. Jaipur: Rawat Publications.

Kapadia, K. (1995). *Siva and Her Sisters: Gender, Caste, and Class in Rural South India*. Boulder, San Francisco/Oxford: Westview Press.

Kumar, H., and R. Somanathan (2017). 'Caste Connections and Government Transfers: The Mahadalits of Bihar'. Working Paper 270. Delhi: Centre for Development Economics.

Mani, L. (1998). *Contentious Traditions: The Debate on Sati in Colonial India*. Orlando: University of California Press.

Mazzocco, M. (2012). 'Testing Efficient Risk Sharing with Heterogeneous Risk Preferences'. *The American Economic Review*, 102(1): 428–68.

Mencher, J.P. (1988). 'Women's Work and Poverty: Women's Contribution to Household Maintenance in South India'. In D. Dwyer and J. Bruce (eds), *A Home Divided*. Stanford, CA: Stanford University Press.

Ministry of Statistics and Programme Implementation (2015), 'Indian States by GDP', Available at: http://statisticstimes.com/economy/gdp-of-indian-states.php (Retrieved on 20 April 2017).

Mosse, D. (2012). *The Saint in the Banyan Tree: Christianity and Caste Society in India* (Vol. 14). Orlando: University of California Press.

Mukul, S. (1999). 'The Untouchable Present: Everyday Life of Musahars in North Bihar'. *Economic and Political Weekly*, 34(49): 3465–70.

Munshi, K. (2016). 'Caste Networks in the Modern Indian Economy'. In S.M. Dev and P.G. Babu (eds), *Development in India*. New Delhi: Springer India, pp. 13–37.

Munshi, K., and M.R. Rosenzweig (2006). 'Traditional Institutions Meet the Modern World: Caste, Gender and Schooling Choice in a Globalizing Economy'. *The American Economic Review*, 96(4): 1225–52.

Rao, V., and R. Ban (2007). *The Political Construction of Caste in South India*. Washington, DC: World Bank.

Rodgers, G., and J. Rodgers (2001). 'A Leap Across Time: When Semi-feudalism Met the Market in Rural Purnia'. *Economic and Political Weekly*, 36: 1976–83.

Seymour, S.C. (1999). *Women, Family, and Child Care in India: A World in Transition*. Cambridge: Cambridge University Press.

Srinivas, M.N. (1962). 'Caste in Modern India and Other Essays'. World Bank Policy Research Working Paper 7411, 40(10). Available at: https://ssrn.com/abstract= 2661137 (accessed 1 June 2017).

Srinivas, M.N. (1976). *The Remembered Village*. Orlando: University of California Press.

Srinivas, M.N. (1977). 'The Changing Position of Indian Women'. *Man*, 12(2): 221–38.

Srinivas, M.N. (1979). 'Future of Indian Caste'. *Economic and Political Weekly*, 14(7/8): 237–42.

Srinivas, M.N. (1996). *Caste: Its Twentieth-century Avatar*. New Delhi: Penguin Books.

17

Excess Female Mortality in Africa

Siwan Anderson and Debraj Ray

1. Introduction

Building on and extending the detailed work of demographers on sex ratios, Amartya Sen (1990, 1992) coined the phrase 'missing women'. In parts of the developing world—notably in India and China—the ratio of women to men is low. From ratios to numbers is an arithmetically trivial but nonetheless hugely significant step. Sen showed how skewed sex ratios can be translated into absolute numbers of missing women by calculating the number of extra women who would be alive (in China or India) if these countries had the same ratio of women to men as developed countries. These latter countries therefore embody a counterfactual: presumably, the sex ratios in these countries reflect a situation in which men and women 'receive similar care'. Sen measured missing women by the departures from this baseline sex ratio for developed countries today.

The resulting estimates suggest that more than 200 million women are demographically 'missing' worldwide, presumably due to inequality and neglect leading to excess female mortality. But the numbers suggest more than an alarming aggregate; they also point to a geographical distribution. Sen's calculations pointed to missing women as a predominantly Asian and North African phenomenon. In contrast, sub-Saharan Africa, with a low male-to-female sex ratio, appeared to do remarkably well. In the words of Sen (1990), this region, 'ravaged as it is by extreme poverty, hunger, and famine, has a substantial excess rather than deficit of women'. He conjectured that high female participation in sub-Saharan Africa's labour force plays a role in 'linking women's gainful employment and survival prospects'. Subsequent research aiming to comprehend the missing women phenomenon focused almost exclusively on excess female mortality in Asia.

The Sen approach, comparing as it does the overall ratios across populations, computes the stock of missing women. Suppose, however, that we wanted to understand the distribution of missing women across different age categories, such as birth, youth, or old age. We would then need to study the 'flow' of missing women in each age category, by comparing age- and gender-specific death rates in the regions of interest with their counterparts in developing countries.

This is exactly the approach taken in Anderson and Ray (2010), where we explicitly examine how missing women are distributed across different age groups and developing regions. Our methodology essentially applies a variant of the Sen counterfactual to every age group and region. Briefly, we suppose (for each age group after birth) that the relative death rates of females to males are 'free of bias' in developed countries. So for each age group, we posit a 'reference' death rate for females, one that would obtain if the death rate of males in that state were to be rescaled by the relative death rates for males and females (in the same age group) in developed countries. We subtract this reference rate from the actual death rate for females, and then multiply by the population of females in that category. We describe the resulting distribution, as well as the aggregate numbers. This exercise enables us to address which age groups and developing regions account for the missing women that were first identified overall by Sen.

This disaggregated approach yields a remarkable finding. In sharp contrast to the earlier literature, disaggregation shows that the annual flow of missing women is actually largest in sub-Saharan Africa, despite the fact that their overall male-to-female ratio is less than unity. Expressed as a fraction of the female population, the sub-Saharan numbers are significantly higher than their Chinese and Indian counterparts.

How can these numbers be reconciled with the overall absence of missing women in sub-Saharan Africa? To understand this, we focus on one particular comparison in these age-specific calculations, which is the computation of missing females at birth. It is well known that more boys are born than girls. (Subsequently, males have higher age-specific death rates, with the overall sex ratio averaging out to around one over the population as a whole.) In developed countries, the sex ratio at birth is around 1.06. A higher number is prima facie cause for suspicion that girls may have been deliberately removed at birth. The reason for that suspicion is simple: there is absolutely no evidence that sex ratios of 1.08 or more are somehow 'natural' for, say, Indian populations. So if we see those numbers, it is reasonable to conclude that there are missing girls in the region of interest.

But what if the number is lower? This is indeed the case for sub-Saharan Africa, where the ratio at birth is as low as 1.03. What we must suspect now is whether there are missing *boys* instead. Once again, the answer necessarily depends on whether there is evidence that the lower sex ratio is somehow 'natural' for certain populations. But here we have a more assured answer: indeed, there do appear to be genetic differences that determine this ratio. For instance, the sex ratio at birth for whites in the United States is around 1.06 whereas for blacks it is 1.03, just as in sub-Saharan Africa. The available data for births to sub-Saharan parents in the United States suggests similar numbers as well. While there are variations within Africa (see e.g. Garenne 2004), the average of 1.03 appears to be well known and its 'natural' difference from non-African populations generally accepted. If we accept it as well, then no missing boys can be 'debited' from the corresponding age-specific category (birth). But given that on the whole sub-Saharan Africa has sex ratios comparable with the developed world, that must point to missing females in the other age categories. That explains the discrepancy.

In this chapter, we explore how the phenomenon of missing females is distributed across Africa. We consider two age groups: zero to 14 years old, and 15 to 59 years old. With such high overall mortality rates in Africa, these two age groups comprise almost all of the excess female deaths on the continent. Overall, there are more than 1.7 million excess female deaths each year in Africa. Expressed as a fraction of the female population, the African numbers are significantly higher than their Chinese or Indian counterparts. Roughly 425,000 of these excess female deaths in Africa are in the younger age category (zero to 14 years old), while the remaining 1.3 million are in the older age category (15 to 59 years old). There is substantial regional variation in excess female mortality across the continent. In both age groupings, the largest numbers are in West Africa. In the younger age group, there are almost 200,000 excess female deaths in a given year in that region, and more than 450,000 in the older age category. East Africa is next, with close to 100,000 excess female deaths at the younger ages each year, and almost 400,000 in the older age category. By comparison, North Africa has the lowest excess female mortality, with roughly 100,000 excess deaths each year across the two age categories. Although excess female mortality is extremely high in Southern Africa in the older age group, by contrast there is virtually no excess female mortality in this region for the younger age category. Likewise, relative to other regions, excess female mortality is lower in the younger age category compared with the older in East Africa.

Our methodology also allows us to explore which diseases are primarily responsible for this extreme excess female mortality across Africa. In the younger age category, almost all of these excess deaths are from infectious and parasitic diseases and respiratory infections. A primary cause of excess young female deaths is malaria, with roughly 110,000 excess female deaths from this cause alone each year. The secondary major cause is respiratory infections, with around 95,000 excess female deaths each year; then diarrhoeal diseases, with approximately 77,000 excess young female deaths each year. In the older age category, HIV is the primary killer. There are close to 800,000 excess female deaths from HIV each year across Africa, with the largest proportions found in Southern and East Africa. Maternal mortality is also a major cause, particularly in East and West Africa. There are close to 400,000 excess female deaths from this cause each year.

The significant regional variation in excess female mortality across the continent makes it difficult to provide a one-dimensional explanation for the phenomenon. Further research is needed to specifically identify the different pathways that explain these numbers. What the estimates make clear, though, is that excess female mortality is a vastly overlooked problem across Africa.

2. Estimates of Excess Female Mortality

2.1. *Excess Female Deaths by Age*

Our estimation of missing women across different age groups and countries in Africa employs the methodology developed in our previous work (Anderson and Ray 2010). We use data from the Global Burden of Disease (GBD) study, initiated in 1992, which is a major collaborative effort between the Harvard School of Public Health, the World Health Organization (WHO), and the World Bank. The GBD study used numerous data sources and epidemiological models to estimate the first comprehensive worldwide cause-of-death patterns in fourteen age-sex groups for over 130 important diseases. The estimates reflect all of the information currently available to the WHO. We rely on the most recent data for the different countries in Africa, which is for the year 2011.[1]

Table 17.1 lists the total number of excess female deaths (in thousands) in the year 2011 for the different regions of Africa according to the UN classification. Overall, there are more than 1.7 million excess female deaths each year in Africa. The top panel considers the younger age group, zero to 14, and the lower panel the older age group, 15 to 59. We see from Table 17.1 that there is substantial regional variation across the continent. In both age groupings, in terms of the total number of excess female deaths, the largest numbers are in West Africa. In the younger age group, there are almost 200,000 excess female deaths in a given year in that region, and more than 450,000 in the older age category. East Africa is next, with close to 100,000 excess female deaths at the

---

[1] 'The Global Burden of Disease Study (GBD) is the most comprehensive worldwide observational epidemiological study to date. It describes mortality and morbidity from major disease, injuries, and risk factors to health at global, national, and regional levels. Examining trends from 1990 to present and making comparisons across populations enables understanding of the changing health challenges facing people across the world in the 21st century' (*The Lancet* 2017).

Table 17.1. Excess female mortality by UN subregion and age group: 000s

Region	Age group	Excess female deaths	% female population
East Africa	0–14	94	0.14
West Africa	0–14	196	0.32
North Africa	0–14	38	0.12
Southern Africa	0–14	0	0.00
Central Africa	0–14	98	0.35
East Africa	15–59	397	0.49
West Africa	15–59	452	0.59
North Africa	15–59	71	0.11
Southern Africa	15–59	207	1.18
Central Africa	15–59	191	0.61
Total		1742	

Source: Authors' computation using on data from GBD (2011).

younger ages each year, and almost 400,000 in the older age category. By comparison, North Africa has the lowest excess female mortality, with roughly 100,000 excess deaths each year across the two age categories. To an extent this regional variation reflects variations in population numbers across the continent. The last column of Table 17.1 demonstrates that as a proportion of the female population (for the respective age groups), excess female mortality is actually highest in Central Africa for the younger age group, and in Southern Africa for the older age group.

There are also some intriguing patterns across the age groups. Although excess female mortality is extremely high in Southern Africa in the older age group, by contrast there is virtually no excess female mortality in this region for the younger age category. Likewise, relative to other regions, excess female mortality is lower in the younger age category compared with the older ages in East Africa.

2.2. *Excess Female Deaths by Disease*

To understand these numbers further, we now take a closer look by accounting for excess female deaths over age and disease groups. The WHO divides the causes of death into three categories: (1) communicable, maternal, perinatal, and nutritional diseases; (2) non-communicable diseases; and (3) injuries. Infectious disease, as well as nutritional and reproductive ailments—the Group 1 diseases—predominate in higher-mortality populations. These are replaced in low-mortality populations by chronic and degenerative diseases (Group 2), such as cardiovascular ailments or cancer. This change in mortality patterns, with chronic and degenerative diseases replacing acute infectious and deficiency diseases as the leading causes of death, is referred to as the epidemiological transition (Omran 1971).

We begin with the younger age group in Table 17.2. We see that almost all of these excess deaths are from infectious and parasitic diseases, respiratory infections, perinatal conditions, and malnutrition. A primary cause of excess female deaths among children is malaria: there are roughly 109,000 excess female deaths from this cause alone each year. The secondary major cause is respiratory infections, with around 94,000 excess female deaths each year; then diarrhoeal diseases, with approximately 77,000 excess young female deaths each year.

We turn to the older age category in Table 17.3. Group 1 diseases, primarily infectious diseases and maternal complications, also form the majority of excess female adult deaths. HIV is the primary killer. There are close to 800,000 excess

Table 17.2. Excess female deaths (aged 0–14) by UN subregion and disease: 000s

Disease	East	West	North	Southern	Central
(1) Communicable	113	205	38	4	104
(A) Infectious/parasitic	76	123	18	4	65
HIV	22	11	0	4	4
Diarrhoeal	18	32	8	0	19
Childhood cluster	1	3	1	0	2
Meningitis	9	13	1	0	8
Malaria	23	55	3	0	28
(B) Respiratory	22	39	10	0	23
(C) Perinatal	5	30	7	0	7
(D) Malnutrition	5	7	2	0	5
(2) Non-communicable	0	0	0	0	0
(3) Injuries	3	4	1	0	2

Source: Authors' computation using data from GBD (2011).

Table 17.3. Excess female deaths (aged 15–59) by UN subregion and disease: 000s

Disease	East	West	North	Southern	Central
(1) Communicable	424	341	28	206	141
Tuberculosis	18	22	3	0	13
HIV/AIDS	328	194	5	199	67
Malaria	7	3	1	0	3
Respiratory	10	11	0	6	2
Maternal	132	161	25	8	70
(2) Non-communicable	70	127	31	9	68
Malignant	32	44	11	1	11
Diabetes	10	12	4	2	6
Cardio	61	73	28	8	38
Digestive	6	12	4	1	8
(3) Injuries	0	0	0	0	0

Source: Authors' computation using data from GBD (2011).

female deaths from HIV each year across Africa. Maternal mortality is also a major cause, particularly in East and West Africa. There are close to 400,000 excess female deaths from this cause each year.

2.3. Excess Deaths by Country

We now consider excess female mortality by country within each region of Africa. What becomes clear is that there is an enormous variation across countries.

We begin with the countries of East Africa in Table 17.4. Recall from Table 17.1 that East Africa has close to 500,000 excess female deaths each year. For the younger age category, we see from Table 17.4 (in the first column) that a significant proportion of the excess female deaths come from four countries: Ethiopia, Mozambique, Somalia, and Tanzania. The second column reports the number of excess female childhood deaths as a proportion of the female population of the corresponding age group. In terms of these magnitudes, Somalia, Mozambique, and Tanzania have the greatest excess female mortality in the younger age group. Countries such as Burundi and Malawi are next. We see from the fourth column that as a proportion of the female population, excess female mortality is significantly higher in the older age group. In this age group, extremely high excess female mortality countries include Burundi, Ethiopia, Mozambique, Zambia, and Zimbabwe. By contrast, the lowest excess adult female mortality countries in East Africa are Eritrea, Madagascar, Mauritius, and Tanzania.

Table 17.4. Excess female deaths—East Africa: 000s

Country	Age 0–14	% female population	Age 15–59	% female population
Burundi	2.5	0.08	21.1	0.46
Comoros	0.04	0.02	0.5	0.14
Djibouti	0.0	0.00	1.0	0.21
Eritrea	0.0	0.00	2.1	0.09
Ethiopia	19.0	0.05	124.5	0.30
Kenya	1.9	0.01	44.0	0.21
Madagascar	4.2	0.05	8.1	0.08
Malawi	5.4	0.08	19.0	0.26
Mauritius	0.0	0.00	0.0	0.0
Mozambique	19.6	0.20	40.6	0.36
Rwanda	0.8	0.02	11.2	0.21
Somalia	16.0	0.40	13.2	0.29
Tanzania	33.2	0.17	32.1	0.08
Uganda	0.0	0.00	11.7	0.15
Zambia	0.0	0.00	21.4	0.35
Zimbabwe	3.3	0.06	46.0	0.68

Source: Authors' computation using data from GBD (2011).

Table 17.5 considers the countries of West Africa, where there are close to 700,000 excess female deaths each year. We see from the first and third columns in the table that the single biggest contributor to these excess female deaths is Nigeria. This is partly driven by the very high population numbers there. But we also see from the second and fourth columns that excess female mortality is also very high as a proportion of the female population in Nigeria. For the younger age group, other big contributors are Côte d'Ivoire, Mali, and Niger. As a proportion of the female population, Burkina Faso also has high childhood excess female mortality. For the older age group, Nigeria again is the single biggest contributor, followed by Côte d'Ivoire, Sierra Leone, Guinea Bissau, Liberia, Togo, and Niger also have high adult excess female mortality as a proportion of the female population.

Recall from Table 17.1 that excess female mortality is very low in North Africa. We see from Table 17.6 that almost all excess female deaths in childhood

Table 17.5. Excess female deaths—West Africa: 000s

Country	Age 0–14	% female population	Age 15–59	% female population
Benin	5.0	0.13	2.5	0.06
Burkina Faso	0.4	0.25	2.6	0.03
Cape Verde	0.0	0.0	0.0	0.0
Côte d'Ivoire	10.0	0.12	43.0	0.39
Gambia	0.3	0.04	1.6	0.18
Ghana	0.0	0.0	9.0	0.07
Guinea	2.0	0.05	8.1	0.16
Guinea Bissau	0.0	0.0	2.8	0.34
Liberia	2.0	0.11	5.8	0.29
Mali	9.4	0.17	3.7	0.06
Mauritania	1.1	0.09	3.4	0.19
Niger	19.3	0.26	13.9	0.20
Nigeria	127.0	0.20	328.2	0.41
Senegal	1.9	0.03	9.0	0.14
Sierra Leone	3.6	0.15	10.4	0.35
Togo	0.0	0.0	7.9	0.22

Source: Authors' computation using data from GBD (2011).

Table 17.6. Excess female deaths—North Africa: 000s

Country	Age 0–14	% female population	Age 15–59	% female population
Algeria	0.0	0.00	11.2	0.05
Egypt	0.0	0.00	2.5	0.005
Libya	0.5	0.02	0.0	0.00
Morocco	0.0	0.00	4.3	0.02
Sudan	46.0	0.28	54.1	0.24
Tunisia	0.0	0.00	0.0	0.00

Source: Authors' computation using data from GBD (2011).

Table 17.7. Excess female deaths—Southern Africa: 000s

Country	Age 0–14	% female population	Age 15–59	% female population
Botswana	0.4	0.06	4.6	0.39
Lesotho	0.3	0.04	7.5	0.68
Namibia	0.0	0.00	2.0	0.16
South Africa	0.0	0.00	190.7	0.62
Swaziland	0.4	0.08	3.9	0.62

Source: Authors' computation using data from GBD (2011).

Table 17.8. Excess female deaths—Central Africa: 000s

Country	Age 0–14	% female population	Age 15–59	% female population
Angola	9.0	0.12	34.2	0.37
Cameroon	12.0	0.15	48.7	0.48
CAR	5.7	0.32	14.9	0.64
Chad	15.0	0.31	23.4	0.43
Congo	1.0	0.10	4.3	0.22
DRC	54.0	0.18	62.7	0.20
Equatorial Guinea	0.4	0.16	1.4	0.38
Gabon	0.0	0.00	1.7	0.20
Sao Tome & Principe	0.0	0.05	0.0	0.02

Source: Authors' computation using data from GBD (2011).

take place in Sudan. Likewise, the main excess adult female deaths are in this country as well. There is some adult excess female mortality in Algeria.

The countries of Southern Africa have very low excess female mortality in the childhood ages. By contrast, this region has the highest excess female mortality in the older age group. We see from the third column of Table 17.7 that South Africa is the single largest contributor to these excess deaths. From the fourth column, we see that as a proportion of the female population, there is also significant excess female mortality in all of the countries except Namibia.

Table 17.8 considers the countries of Central Africa. In this region, the majority of excess female deaths are in the Democratic Republic of the Congo (DRC) for both age categories. Other countries with high excess female mortality in both age groups are Angola, Cameroon, the Central African Republic (CAR), and Chad.

3. Southern Africa as a Benchmark

There is always the possibility that the use of developed countries as a reference group may be 'inappropriate' for poor countries in Africa. Elsewhere (Anderson and Ray 2010) we have discussed this issue in some detail, and

Table 17.9. Excess female deaths (aged 0–14) by UN subregion and disease: 000s—
Southern Africa as a benchmark

Disease	East	West	North	Southern	Central
All causes	137	243	45	0	126
(1) Communicable	134	228	41	0	119
HIV	7	4	0	0	1
Diarrhoeal	43	55	11	0	35
Childhood cluster	11	18	2	0	9
Meningitis	0	0	0	0	1
Malaria	26	62	3	0	32
Respiratory	34	52	12	0	32
Perinatal	72	97	21	0	42
Malnutrition	9	9	3	0	7

Source: Authors' computation using data from GBD (2011).

there is little we can add here at a conceptual level. Instead, for the younger age group, we can redo our computations using the countries in Southern Africa as a benchmark. This is the region in Africa with the lowest excess young female mortality.

We see from Table 17.9 that our estimates of excess young female mortality increase somewhat using this alternative benchmark. This is because relative to the developed-country reference group, the relative death rate of young males is actually higher in the countries of Southern Africa. The overall estimates of excess female mortality using this alternative benchmark increase by roughly 25 per cent. Moreover, the estimates for some diseases increase more than others. Comparing Tables 17.2 and 17.9, we see that excess female deaths from perinatal conditions increase more than threefold using Southern African countries as a benchmark. Estimates of excess deaths from diarrhoeal diseases also increase significantly, by about 50 per cent. The number of observations we have to derive our reference death rates for perinatal conditions as cause of death are roughly similar for the Southern African countries and the developed countries, so it does not seem to be a question of data reliability for these two different estimates.[2] For diarrhoeal diseases as cause of death, the number of observations is significantly higher in Southern African countries compared with developed countries. Thus, we might assume that, if anything, the estimates provided in Table 17.9 are the more reliable. All in all, using an alternative benchmark demonstrates that the earlier estimates are a lower bound on excess young female mortality in Africa.

[2] Moreover, of all the sub-Saharan African countries, South Africa collects the most reliable vital statistics at the national level.

4. Mechanisms

The above sections have demonstrated significant variation in excess female mortality across the continent. If we aim to explain this variation, a first consideration is poverty. We can examine the correlation at the country level between gross domestic product (GDP) per capita and adult female excess deaths as a proportion of the adult female population. Perhaps surprisingly, there is not a significant negative correlation between these two variables; if anything, the relationship is positive.

However, if we look to the very poorest countries in Africa (i.e. those with less than US$1,000 per capita), we do see that adult excess female mortality is lower among the better-off of that poor sample. Although very crude, these findings are suggestive that poverty alone cannot explain the striking number of excess female deaths in Africa.

We also consider the correlation between overall adult mortality rates at the country level and adult female excess deaths as a proportion of the adult female population. In this case, there is a very noticeable positive relationship: higher overall adult mortality rates (i.e. for both men and women) are positively correlated with excess female mortality.

Although there is clearly a significant positive correlation between excess female mortality and overall mortality rates, it is also evident that certain diseases seem to be associated with higher rates of excess female mortality. For example, high incidences of malaria and diarrhoeal disease are strongly correlated with excess female mortality in the younger ages. However, despite this strong correlation for both of these diseases, the earlier estimates demonstrate that there are far more excess deaths from malaria than from the other childhood diseases. From Table 17.1 we observed that young excess female mortality was highest in Central and West Africa, which are regions plagued by high death rates from diarrhoeal diseases and malaria in this younger age category. But these regions also suffer from high death rates from respiratory infections and perinatal conditions. In both Central and West Africa, the overall death rates from all four of these main causes of death are quite comparable within each region. However, excess female mortality is highest from malaria, which accounts for roughly 25 per cent of young premature female deaths in these regions. The next largest cause is respiratory infections, accounting for roughly 19 per cent. That is to say, even though the overall death rates in these two regions from malaria and respiratory infections are comparable to those from perinatal conditions, they lead to significantly more excess female mortality. This is the primary reason why we observe very little excess female mortality at the younger ages in Southern and North Africa, as in these two regions the primary cause of death in the younger age category is perinatal conditions.

It is also the case that a given disease can have more of an impact in some regions compared with others. For example, overall mortality rates from diarrhoeal disease are significantly higher in Central compared with Eastern Africa. However, the number of excess young female deaths from this disease is comparable across the two regions. In the older age category, HIV is responsible for roughly 45 per cent of the excess female mortality observed—roughly 800,000 excess deaths each year. There is correspondingly a strong correlation between HIV prevalence and excess female deaths in the older age category at the country level.

HIV explains almost all of the excess female mortality in the countries of Southern Africa, where death rates from other diseases are relatively low. In other parts of the continent, particularly in West and Central Africa, maternal mortality is responsible for significant excess female mortality, amounting to approximately 400,000 excess deaths each year. As in the younger age category, certain diseases can have more of an impact in some regions compared with others. For example, tuberculosis seems to have more of an impact in Central Africa for adult females, while respiratory diseases have a lower impact on excess female mortality in this region compared with elsewhere.

To better understand excess female mortality in Africa, it therefore seems necessary to further explore why certain diseases lead to much higher rates of excess death than do other diseases. Moreover, we need to understand why certain diseases have a larger impact on excess female mortality in certain regions compared with others.

There is likely a host of factors—biological, social, environmental, behavioural, or economic—that explain this variation in excess female mortality across Africa. Consider for example the extreme excess female mortality as a result of the HIV/AIDS epidemic in all regions except North Africa. These extra deaths mainly occur at the reproductive ages, 15–45. The death rate from HIV/AIDS for women aged 15–29 is 2.3 times that of males of the corresponding age. The overall female death rate from the virus is 1.2 times that of males. Elsewhere in the world, by contrast, the death rate from HIV/AIDS for males is higher at all ages. The ratio is as high as four to one in high-income countries.

There is little doubt that poverty, under-nutrition, and poor health care play their part in the overall transmission of HIV. But our interest lies not in the overall rate of transmission, but in its reversal of male-female incidence. It is therefore hard to escape arguments such as those made by the WHO, which emphasize the role of unequal power and violence. It seems evident that the multiplicity of female sexual partners among males, the prevalence of transactional sex, the existence of violent or forced sex, and the relative inability of women to negotiate safer sex practices have much to do with this extraordinary discrepancy.

There could be other reasons for greater heterosexual transmission that have nothing explicitly to do with discrimination against women. For example, it is possible that certain aspects of poverty can create 'unintended' gender biases relative to the developed-country benchmark. The accounting methodology that we follow is entirely silent on matters of interpretation. The case for (or against) lack of similar care has to be made separately.

Among younger women, malaria plays an important role in explaining their premature deaths. In Africa, insecticide-treated mosquito nets and indoor residual spraying commonly prevent this disease. It is conceivable that resource-constrained households might provide young boys with mosquito nets before girls. Alternatively, it is also possible that females have less protective immune responses to the disease. In many countries, progress in malaria control is threatened by the rapid development and spread of antimalarial drug resistance, and there may be a gender bias component to this resistance. It is well beyond the scope of this chapter to identify the key mechanisms behind these differences, but our estimates strongly suggest that it is crucial to better understand possible gender biases in the epidemiology of malaria-attributed illness and death. The magnitude and age distribution of malaria-attributable morbidity and mortality vary with the intensity of transmission (Leenstra et al. 2003). In areas with intense, stable malaria transmission, the risk of morbidity declines rapidly within the first years of life. Where transmission is less intense, clinical immunity develops at a slower pace, and children remain at risk of severe disease and death for a longer time. Under conditions of stable transmission, adolescents are at a markedly reduced risk of severe malaria morbidity and mortality compared with preschool children. Despite this reduced risk, adolescents continue to suffer from frequent asymptomatic infections and periodic clinical illness and death. The extent to which adolescent girls are also pregnant in Africa could be very relevant—there is already significant evidence that malaria infection during pregnancy carries substantial risks for the mother (Desai et al. 2007). Approximately 12 per cent of girls in sub-Saharan Africa are married before the age of fifteen (UNICEF 2016). Rates of child marriage are exceptionally high (between 28 and 29 per cent) in CAR, Chad, and Niger. These countries are also amongst those with the highest rates of excess female mortality from malaria for girls aged zero to fourteen. The first panel of Figure 17.1 demonstrates this positive relationship between the incidence of early marriage (i.e. the percentage of girls who are married between fifteen and nineteen years of age) and excess female mortality in the younger age category.

Acute respiratory infections, particularly lower respiratory tract infections, are also a leading cause of death among children under five years of age in East, West, and Central Africa, and cause significant excess female mortality in these regions. In developed countries, there is some suggestive evidence of sex differences in the incidence and severity of respiratory infections. In particular, the course of most respiratory tract infections is more severe in males that in females (Falagasa et al. 2007). Relative to these differences, our estimates suggest that in parts of Africa mortality from these infections is higher for young females. However, before we draw any strong conclusions, it is clear that the epidemiology and pathogenesis of such infections, particularly in Africa, must be further studied.

Diarrhoeal disease is also a leading cause of death in children under five years old throughout the developing world. Infection is spread through contaminated food or drinking water, or from person to person as a result of poor hygiene. Interventions to prevent diarrhoea, including safe drinking water, use of improved sanitation, and hand-washing with soap, can reduce disease risk. Diarrhoea can be treated with a solution of clean water, sugar, and salt, and with zinc tablets. Most people who die from diarrhoea actually die from severe dehydration and fluid loss. Children who are malnourished or have impaired immunity are most at risk of life-threatening diarrhoea. Our estimates of excess female mortality from this cause again evoke the importance of possible sex differences in susceptibility to and treatment of these diseases.

There is evidence that low levels of exclusive breastfeeding further contribute to morbidity and mortality among children in parts of Africa. For example, in East and Southern Africa only 40 per cent of babies are exclusively breastfed during the first six months, despite the fact that breast milk is the best form of nutrition for infants and significantly reduces the risk of diarrhoea, acute respiratory infection, and other child killers. A woman may fail to breastfeed exclusively due to inadequate support from her partner or family, or because of labour burdens. It is conceivable that mothers are more likely to breastfeed young sons compared with daughters.[3]

Some research points to gender inequality as an important underlying cause of female under-nutrition, which is further exacerbated by poverty and lack of access to resources. Because of gender norms, women often also have limited access to and control over resources, and may therefore be excluded from household decision making. For example, Thomas (1994) finds that a mother's education has a bigger effect on her daughter's height, whereas a father's education has a bigger impact on his son's height. Apparently, there are differences in the allocation of household resources depending on the gender of the child, and these differences vary with the gender of the parent.

Legislation that discriminates against women curtails the relative bargaining power of mothers in the household, and can then impede the well-being of their daughters. The second to fourth panels of Figure 17.1 demonstrate

---

[3] See Jayachandran and Kuziemko (2011) for evidence of this in India.

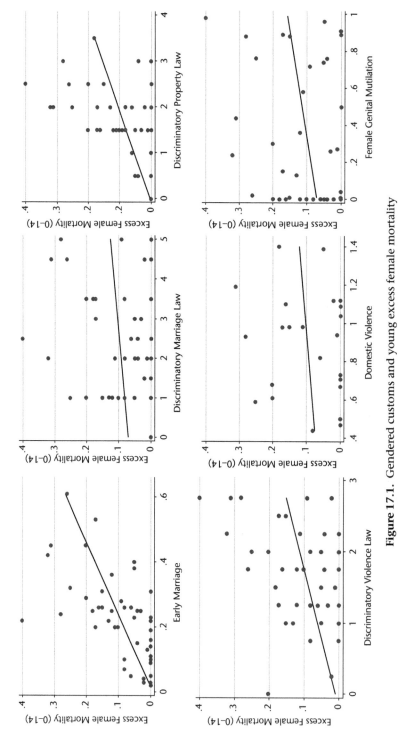

Figure 17.1. Gendered customs and young excess female mortality
Source: Authors' computation using data from GBD (2011) and OECD (2014).

how discriminatory laws against women in terms of marital and property rights as well as protection from violence against women are positively related to young excess female mortality.

In the second panel of Figure 17.1, discriminatory marriage law reflects an index that captures whether women and men have the same rights with regard to legal guardianship of a child during marriage or after divorce; inheritance from deceased parents or a spouse; and initiation of divorce proceedings. The index 'discriminatory marriage law' is higher when women do not have the same rights as men in these dimensions. In the third panel of Figure 17.1, discriminatory property law reflects an index that captures whether women and men have the same rights with regard to access, control, and ownership of land and non-land assets; access to formal financial institutions; and freedom of movement and access to public spaces. The index 'discriminatory property law' is higher when women do not have the same rights as men along these dimensions. In the fourth panel of Figure 17.1, discriminatory violence law reflects an index that captures whether the legal framework in a given country offers women legal protection from domestic violence, rape, and sexual harassment. This index increases as it becomes less likely for such legislation to be in place, and is positively correlated with young excess female mortality at the country level. From the fifth panel of Figure 17.1, we see that young excess female mortality is also positively correlated with the prevalence of physical or sexual violence from an intimate partner. The variable 'domestic violence' reflects the percentage of women in a given country who have experienced physical and/or sexual violence from an intimate partner at some time in their lives.

There may also be several cultural factors at play. Among the traditional religions within Africa, the archetypal institution is patrilineage, where at least one surviving son is highly desired, and as a result women can have inferior status (Paulme 1960). Now non-indigenous religions are very predominant across the continent. Islam is a strong presence in several parts of Africa. There is some evidence that in other non-African countries where Islam is the dominant or only religion, child female mortality exceeds that of males (Caldwell and Caldwell 1987; Svedberg 1990). In some Islamic cultural settings in Africa, boys and men traditionally eat first, and girls and women eat the leftovers. When food is short, this can mean females have very little or nothing at all to eat.

The sixth panel of Figure 17.1 demonstrates how one cultural trait, the prevalence of female genital mutilation (at the country level), is positively correlated with young excess female mortality.

5. Conclusion

The significant variation in the number of excess female deaths across the regions of Africa, as well as across the countries by region, makes it very difficult to pinpoint a single explanation for such excessively high excess female mortality within the continent. Part of the explanation lies in the prominence of particular diseases. But these patterns then beg the question why the relative female-to-male death rates from these diseases are so high. Is it the case that there is an inherent biological gender bias in these diseases, or is it instead the case that males are more likely to receive medical attention than females in case of illness? The estimated total number of excess female deaths across the continent is alarming, and makes very clear that further research focusing on this issue is crucial.

References

Anderson, S., and D. Ray (2010). 'Missing Women: Age and Disease'. *Review of Economic Studies*, 77: 1262–300.

Caldwell, P., and J. Caldwell (1987). 'Where There is a Narrower Gap Between Female and Male Situations'. Unpublished paper. Canberra: Australian National University.

Desai, M., F.O. ter Kuile, F. Nosten, R. McGready, K. Asamoa, B. Brabin, and R.D. Newman (2007). 'Epidemiology and Burden of Malaria in Pregnancy'. *The Lancet Infectious Diseases*, 7(2): 93–104.

Falagasa, M.E., E.G. Mourtzoukoua, and K.Z. Vardakasa (2007). 'Sex Differences in the Incidence and Severity of Respiratory Tract Infections'. *Respiratory Medicine*, 101: 1845–63.

Garenne, M. (2003). 'Sex Differences in Health Indicators Among Children in African DHS Surveys'. *Journal of Biosocial Science*, 35: 601–14.

Garenne, M. (2004). 'Sex Ratios at Birth in Populations of Eastern and Southern Africa'. *South African Journal of Demography*, 9: 91–6.

GBD (2011). 'Global Burden of Disease Study'. Available at: www.healthdata.org/gbd (accessed 2 May 2017).

Jayachandran, S., and I. Kuziemko (2011). 'Why Do Mothers Breastfeed Girls Less Than Boys? Evidence and Implications for Child Health in India'. *Quarterly Journal of Economics*, 126(3): 1485–538.

The Lancet (2017). 'Global Burden of Disease: Executive Summary'. Available at: the-lancet.com/gbd (accessed 19 April 2017).

Leenstra, T., F.O. ter Kuile, S.K. Kariuki, C.P. Nixon, A.J. Oloo, P.A. Kager, and J.D. Kurtis (2003). 'Dehydroepiandrosterone Sulfate Levels Associated with Decreased Malaria Parasite Density and Increased Hemoglobin Concentration in Pubertal Girls from Western Kenya'. *Journal of Infectious Diseases*, 188(2): 297–304.

OECD (2014). 'Gender, Institutions and Development Database 2014 (GID-DB)'. Available at: stats.oecd.org/Index.aspx?DataSetCode=GIDDB2014 (accessed 19 April 2017).

Omran, A. (1971). 'The Epidemiological Transition: A Theory of the Epidemiology of Population Change'. *Milbank Quarterly*, 49: 509–37.

Paulme, D. (1960). *Women of Tropical Africa*. Berkeley: University of California Press.

Sen, A. (1990). 'More Than 100 Million Women Are Missing'. *The New York Review of Books*, 20 December. Available at: www.nybooks.com/articles/1990/12/20/more-than-100-million-women-are-missing/ (accessed 18 April 2017).

Sen, A. (1992). 'Missing Women'. *British Medical Journal*, 304: 587–8.

Svedberg, P. (1990). 'Undernutrition in Sub-Saharan Africa: Is There a Gender Bias?' *Journal of Development Studies*, 26(3): 469–86.

Thomas, D. (1994). 'Like Father Like Son, Like Mother Like Daughter: Parental Resources and Child Height'. *Journal of Human Resources*, 29(4): 950–88.

UNICEF (2016). 'Percentage of Women Aged 20 to 24 Years Who were First Married or in Union Before Ages 15 and 18'. Available at: data.unicef.org/topic/child-protection/child-marriage/ (accessed 2 May 2017).

World Bank (2011). 'World Development Indicators'. Available at: data.worldbank.org/data-catalog/world-development-indicators (accessed 2 May 2017).

Index

An italic *f* or *t* following a page number denotes a figure or table.